I0462197

Photoshop® Elements 2: The Complete Reference

Ken Milburn
Gene Hirsh

McGraw-Hill/Osborne

New York   Chicago   San Francisco
Lisbon   London   Madrid   Mexico City
Milan   New Delhi   San Juan
Seoul   Singapore   Sydney   Toronto

The **McGraw·Hill** Companies

McGraw-Hill/Osborne
2600 Tenth Street
Berkeley, California 94710
U.S.A.

To arrange bulk purchase discounts for sales promotions, premiums, or fund-raisers, please contact **McGraw-Hill/Osborne** at the above address. For information on translations or book distributors outside the U.S.A., please see the International Contact Information page immediately following the index of this book.

Photoshop® Elements 2: The Complete Reference

Copyright © 2002 by The McGraw-Hill Companies. All rights reserved. Printed in the United States of America. Except as permitted under the Copyright Act of 1976, no part of this publication may be reproduced or distributed in any form or by any means, or stored in a database or retrieval system, without the prior written permission of publisher, with the exception that the program listings may be entered, stored, and executed in a computer system, but they may not be reproduced for publication.

1234567890 CUS CUS 0198765432

ISBN 0-07-222475-4

Publisher
  Brandon A. Nordin

Vice President & Associate Publisher
  Scott Rogers

Acquisitions Editor
  Megg Bonar

Project Editors
  Pamela Woolf, Laura Stone

Acquisitions Coordinator
  Tana Allen

Technical Editors
  Bryan O'Neil Hughes, Bill Bruns

Copy Editors
  Laura Ryan, Lisa Theobald

Proofreaders
  Linda Medoff, Paul Medoff

Indexer
  Valerie Perry

Computer Designers
  Carie Abrew, Michelle Galicia

Illustrator
  Michael Mueller, Lyssa Wald

Series Design
  Peter F. Hancik

This book was composed with Corel VENTURA™ Publisher.

Information has been obtained by **McGraw-Hill**/Osborne from sources believed to be reliable. However, because of the possibility of human or mechanical error by our sources, **McGraw-Hill**/Osborne, or others, **McGraw-Hill**/Osborne does not guarantee the accuracy, adequacy, or completeness of any information and is not responsible for any errors or omissions or the results obtained from the use of such information.

I'd like to dedicate this book to Nancy Miller, Janine Warner, Jane Lindsey, Bob Cowart, Markus Baue, Margot Maley, and all the other wonderful people who consistently let it be known that I can count on their support and honesty.

—Ken Milburn

I want to dedicate this book to my wonderful wife, Liane, and thank her for her unwavering support in this endeavor.

—Gene Hirsh

About the Authors

Ken Milburn has been taking photographs since the age of eleven and has worked as a professional photographer since he was seventeen. He has done editorial photography for numerous newspapers and magazines, including TV Guide and the Los Angeles Times Sunday magazine. Commercial accounts have included Universal Pictures, Capitol Records, Southern California Gas, and the Fluer Corporation. As an author, he has written nearly 300 articles and columns for national computer magazines and 17 technical books on the subjects of photography and graphics, including *Digital Photography: 99 Easy Tips to Make You Look Like a Pro!*, *Photoshop 7 Virtual Classroom*, and *Digital Photography Bible*.

Gene Hirsh grew up in New Jersey and came to California in 1978 to complete his formal education in art and environmental design. Hirsh now resides in a small town called Benicia on the banks of the Sacramento River, where he works in his digital art studio. He received a BFA from California College of Arts and Crafts. He also studied at University of Arizona, George Washington University, and Catholic University of America. Gene Hirsh, a classically trained painter and illustrator, became involved with digital art in 1985 while working as a layout artist when he discovered that desktop computers could actually interactively make pictures. That started his love affair with the art and computers. Hirsh has worked as a graphic designer, layout artist, architect, illustrator, multimedia artist, computer gaming artist, art director, web designer, animator, and fine artist, and has most recently taken up writing in an effort to share his many years of experience. Hirsh is an award-winning artist, exhibiting his digital art in galleries and exhibitions around the world and on the Web. He is presently showing in a number of galleries in California. His art has been featured in *Digital Fine Art Magazine* and *Digital Output Magazine*.

Contents

Part III

The Special Effects Workflow

Part IV

Preparing Your Photos for the Web, Print, and Presentation

Acknowledgments

We would like to thank all the wonderful people at McGraw Hill/Osborne for being so supportive in the writing and production of this substantial book. Our special thanks go to Acquisitions Editor, Megg Morin, for her strong direction and patience, which helped immensely in keeping this project on course and pulling it all together. Thanks to Acquisitions Coordinator, Tana Allen, for keeping us on track. Also a big thanks to the production department and Project Editors Laura Stone and Pamela Woolf for their dedication, support, and excellent work in making this a reality. We want to let Lyssa Wald know we appreciate her work on the color insert, and big thumbs up go to Copy Editors Lisa Theobald and Laura Ryan. Thanks to the Technical Editors, Bryan O'Neil Hughes and Bill Bruns, for helping us sort through the many-faceted technical aspects of this software.

Thanks to all the people at Adobe Systems for their excellent work in producing a superior product so rich in content that we were hard pressed to fit it all within this confines of this book. Our hope is that we have done justice to the depth of their work, so all who read this book will appreciate extent of their accomplishment. Thanks to Nikon, Olympus, and Epson for providing digital cameras and printers used in creating many of the exercises and suggestions used in the book.

Finally, a warm debt of gratitude to family and friends who have not seen us in months, for the patience they have shown and the support and love they have given.

Introduction

This book is all about the world's second-most-powerful image-editing program, Photoshop Elements 2. We have tried to cram as much information about the program as you can fit into 800 pages. There's so much information in this book that it makes a pretty good investment for learning some of the most commonly used Photoshop routines, as well.

It is a common misconception that Photoshop Elements is nothing more than a simple program for beginners who don't want to take the time to learn to control the subtleties of photo-editing. This misconception arises for several reasons:

- **Photoshop Elements' list price, which is never more than $99.50.** That is one-fifth the price of its parent product, Adobe Photoshop 7. However, unless you are preparing photos for offset printing or must do a very high volume of photo-editing, there is little that you can't do in Photoshop Elements—provided you have the guidance to know how.

- **It inherits the reputation of Photoshop LE, which it replaces.** That would be logical, if it weren't for the fact that Photoshop Elements adds many more (and more up-to-date) Photoshop capabilities and a myriad of tools that make it dead simple and nearly automatic to do some very sophisticated photo-editing tasks and image management. Three cases in point are automated panorama stitching, automated portfolio web pages, and a highly visual, interactive File Browser that allows for automated renaming of image files so that they can easily be grouped according to subject matter and given sequential numbers within a category.

- **It is a perfect platform for learning image editing.** The vast majority (who knows how one would establish an exact percentage) of the interface, location of interface elements, and the names and purposes of commands are exactly the same as for Photoshop. So is the code that performs most of the image-editing procedures. Thus, if you do decide you have a need to move up to Photoshop 7, you will already know how to use most of the program.

Who This Book Is For

This book is well organized for both linear and reference readers. It's also friendly enough to give both basic program information and routines to rank beginners, as well as detailed enough to be useful (hopefully even invaluable) to serious hobbyists. On top of that, *Photoshop Elements 2: The Complete Reference* is an outstanding value for the hordes of folks who are being introduced to digital cameras. That is because Photoshop Elements itself is best suited to those who want to manipulate photos (rather than to those who want to design layouts or create complex animations), and because it has features that are specially suited to digital cameras (such as panorama stitching and portfolio making).

This book is also good for

- Anyone who wants to learn more about image editing—even if they already own Photoshop.

- Any beginner who wants an easy-to-read-and-follow complete reference on how to accomplish more advanced techniques than the majority of Photoshop Elements books are willing to teach.

- Anyone who needs a complete reference to the program's components, commands, and interface. This comprises the first part of the book, which is meant to make it easy for you to look up details on what a component is used for, where to find that component, and the basics of using that component.

- Anyone who has Photoshop Elements (or Photoshop) and needs to know how to accomplish specific and practical tasks that involve image editing. The majority of the book (all but the first five chapters) is divided into task categories and to teaching easy ways to solve even complex and advanced problems. Don't worry, the basics are there, too.

How to Use This Book

Some people learn from books by reading them in sequence, from front to back. Others learn better by doing—reading only when they encounter a problem they don't have a solution for. We hope that we've made this book work for both groups of readers. For the front-to-back reader, the organization of the book is meant to follow the most efficient and logical image-editing workflow. For the reference reader, we've divided subjects into functional categories on a chapter-by-chapter basis, added cross-references wherever necessary, and made sure that the indexing makes it easy to find what you're looking for.

Because the Photoshop Elements landscape is so highly populated with tools, menus, commands, and dialogs boxes, we've carefully designed some conventions that we hope will make it easier for you to stay oriented as to where to find things.

We also wanted to make it easy for users of both Macintosh and Windows versions of Photoshop Elements to understand which keys to press in order to execute a given command. Because there is no significant difference between the way the program is used on either a Macintosh or Windows machine, the command for both platforms is given in the same word group. The Macintosh key is given first, and then the equivalent Windows key—with a slash separating the two. If the name of the key is the same on both kinds of machines, that key is only given once (SHIFT, TAB, and the function keys are the most common examples). Keys that are not abbreviated on the actual keyboards (such as DELETE/BACKSPACE and RETURN/ENTER) are spelled out. Thus, if you see CONTROL spelled out, you know that this is the Macintosh CONTROL key—which is *not* equivalent to the Windows CTRL key (CMD is the Mac equivalent of CTRL). Plus signs separate keystrokes that must be pressed at the same time. Here's an example of how you will see such a command written in the book: "To invert the selection, press CMD/ CTRL+SHIFT+I."

In Photoshop Elements, Photoshop, and most other graphics programs, *selecting* something refers to isolating that something so that only it will be affected by a command or by the use of a tool. Therefore, if you are picking a command, tool, or an item in a palette or dialog box, you will be told to *choose* it—not to *select* it. The word *choose* will always be followed by the location of the place where you will find the thing you are going to choose—unless what you are going to choose is a command that is located on the main menus. So if the sentence reads, "To place the selection on the program's clipboard, choose File | Copy or press CMD/CTRL+C," you know to drop down the File menu and choose (click on the name of the last command in the hierarchy) Copy from that menu list. The pipe (straight vertical line that separates commands) lets you know that a further command appears on a pop-up or fly-out submenu.

If you are told to choose from an interface component that is not accessed directly from the menu bar, you will first be told where to go before choosing. For example: "From the Toolbox, choose the Paintbrush. From the Options bar (choosing a tool always brings up its Options bar), in the Size field, enter the pixel diameter of the brush." In addition, there are number of interface components in Photoshop Elements that contain commands or tools that are not accessed from the menu bar: the Toolbox, options bars, dialog boxes, palettes, and in-context menus.

We hope you don't find the sheer size of this book intimidating. The size gives us room to make it a rich source of reference material, as well as to have some patience and clarity in explaining some very cool and useful routines. If you just relax and have fun with it, we hope you'll learn to value it more and more over time. To learn more about us or to view some of our work, check out the following web sites:

- **Ken Milburn's Site (www.kenmilburn.com)**   This is the site of one of this book's authors. It includes not only a much more extensive gallery of his work than can be shown in the color sections of individual books, but also tips and tricks that went into the making of many of these photos.

- **Digital Arts Group (www.digitalartsgroup.com)**   In an effort to promote digital painting and exhibit the work of high-quality digital art, Gene Hirsh founded the Digital Arts Group at www.digitalartsgroup.com. This non-profit organization is dedicated to the advancement of digital painting and is a good place to get a look at some of the best digital painters in the world.

The Complete Reference

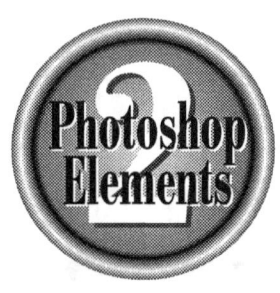

Part I

Photoshop Elements Orientation

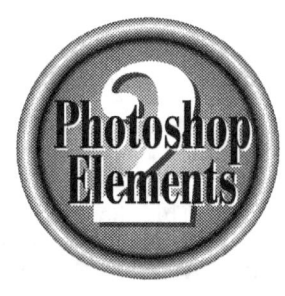

Chapter 1

Installing Elements for Peak Performance

This chapter shows you how to install Photoshop Elements for both Windows XP and Mac OS X, but doesn't stop there. It moves well beyond the standard installation and gives you insights into how you can optimize Elements to give you peak performance best suited for the way you work.

This chapter helps you through the tricky and sometimes confusing task of adjusting the application to your individual needs. Sometimes the installation instructions don't explain all the subtle aspects of installation in a way that is easy to decipher, with information scattered about in various sections of the user manual or help system, and if you don't know what you're looking for, you might never find the many things you can adjust to make life easier.

This chapter presents information in a consolidated form and gives you many ways to fine-tune your application and get the best possible results. It gives you the basic setup information first and then builds on that as you move to more professional levels of setup. Use what you need for the level you are at now. The demands on the system, application, and you will grow as your goals advance.

Elements Installation

Elements will not run directly from the application CD; it must be installed on the hard drive using the automated installation program that comes on the CD. The CD is equipped with an AutoOpen program that will, in most cases, start the installation program automatically after you insert the CD in the CD drive. If for some reason the AutoRun program does not run, you can also begin the installation by displaying the contents of the CD and then running the Setup program in the Adobe Photoshop Elements folder.

Whether the installation started automatically or you selected it by hand, the next thing you will see is the opening window of the installation program. This is a wizard type of installation. That means it will walk you through the steps you need to take, giving you options as you go along. You can step back in this process, so if you make an error or just want to change something, you can go back and do a step over until you get to the Install button.

Macintosh Installation

Here you will walk through the installation process for the Mac:

1. The first choice you are presented with is language. This determines what language will be displayed for the installation.

2. Read through the license agreement.

3. When you are through, click Continue.

4. Read the Adobe Photoshop Readme file. This file contains important information not contained in the other documentation, including last-minute changes to the

program, information about known bugs, and any other special issues you should know before you install. It is not a good idea to skip this the first time you install. If you don't understand all the information in this file, which is sometimes the case because programmers prepare them, call the customer support line and get them to explain. The support numbers are typically found on a card packed with your application or on the Adobe web site.

5. When you are finished reading, click Continue.

6. Next you are presented with a window that gives the installation types:

   ■ **Easy install**   This install the most typical components automatically. This is the best choice for first-time users. As you get more familiar with the program and you understand the different components, you might want to customize your installation for more efficiency.

   ■ **Custom install**   This brings up a list of components that you can select to install. Click the I button next to each component to get a better description.

7. The installation program usually chooses a default location on your hard disk. If you want to change that location, choose Select Folder from the menu and then enter the location you want.

8. Click Install.

9. The next window asks you for personal or business information and the serial number of the product. The serial number is on the registration card that came in your package or on the application CD cover. Write the serial number on the inside flap of your user manual; this is a good place for the technical support number, too.

10. Click Next.

11. Click Install Now and follow the remaining steps to complete the installation.

12. The program takes few moments to copy files from the CD to the hard drive.

13. After the files are copied, you see a window prompting you to install Adobe SVG Viewer. If you are planning to do much work with Web content, you might want to take a look at this plug-in. If not, you might want to save some hard-drive space. Click either the Yes button to install SVG or the No button to cancel SVG installation.

Windows Installation

Follow these steps for installation process on a Windows platform:

1. The first choice you are presented with is language. This determines what language will be displayed for the installation.

2. Read through the license agreement.

3. When you are finished reading, click Continue.

4. Next you see a window that gives the installation types:

   ■ **Typical install**   This installs the most typical components automatically. This is best choice for first-time users. As you get more familiar with the program and you understand the different components, you might want to customize your installation for more efficiency.

   ■ **Compact install**   This installs only the minimum amount of components required to run Elements. This option is very quick and requires less disk space, but includes no Photoshop bells or whistles.

   ■ **Custom install**   This brings up a list of components that you can select to install. If you click on a component, a description displays. The installation program usually chooses a default location on your hard disk. If you want to change that location, choose Select Folder and then enter the location you want or select the Browse button and locate the directory to select.

5. Click Next.

6. Specify file type associations and click Next.

7. This window displays options for setting the file associations. This allows you to choose which image file types launch Elements and load the file if you double-click them from a file list. Let's say you want JPEG files always to open in Photoshop Elements. You would select the PS (Photoshop) next to that file type. If you have associated any of these file types with another application and you do not want that to change, make sure Do Not Change is selected.

8. The next window asks you for personal or business information and the serial number of the product. The serial number is on the registration card that came in your package or on the application CD cover. Write the serial number on the inside flap of your user manual; this is a good place for the technical support number, too.

9. Click Next.

10. Confirm that the information is correct. Click Next.

11. Follow the remaining steps to complete the installation.

12. The program will take a few moments to copy files from the CD to the hard drive.

13. After the files are copied, you see a window prompting you to install Adobe SVG Viewer. If you are planning to do much work with Web content, you might want to take a look at this plug-in. If not, you might want to save some hard-drive space. Click either the Yes button to install SVG or the No button to cancel SVG installation.

14. Read the Adobe Photoshop Readme file. This file contains important information not contained in the other documentation, including last-minute changes to the

program, information about known bugs, and any other special issues you should know before you install. It is not a good idea to skip this the first time you install. If you don't understand all the information in this file, which is sometimes the case since programmers sometimes prepare them, call you the customer support line and get them to explain.

Now that you have you have the application loaded, it is time to fine-tune it so it runs like a race car, that is, unless you are planning to take only weekend drives. In that case, maybe all you need is a well-tuned sedan. Whatever your goals are, here are some pointers on how to get the most out of your system.

Setting Up the Maximum Fidelity Display

Your window on the world for Photoshop Elements is your monitor. This is a very important piece of equipment for any computer user, but paramount for those who work in digital imaging. It is the canvas. The accuracy of what you see there is critical to the final outcome. If the monitor does not give you an accurate representation of color, size, and spatial relationships, then you are working blind—or at least with a bad pair of glasses.

Choose a monitor that is big enough; 17 inches is considered to be the minimum for a comfortable working area. This allows you to work with all the windows you have open and still see enough of the image you're working on without having to move windows around all the time. Even with a 17-inch monitor, it can get pretty crowded. A 19- or 20-inch model is a welcome relief, and at today's prices, it's not out of reach. Your monitor can never be too big. Some artists use dual monitor systems, moving all their menus to one monitor so they can see their image unobstructed on the other.

Screen and color resolution are also important considerations when setting up your system. One way to get some more real estate on the screen is to increase the screen resolution so you can display more information in the same area. This is similar to zooming out on an online map so you can see more territory. At a minimum, resolution should be 1024×768; otherwise you won't have enough room. Your graphics board determines how high you can set your resolution. The goal is to get your resolution as high as you can yet still be able to read your text on the screen menus. On larger monitors you can go higher without losing the text, which is another advantage of big monitors. You will want to do a certain amount of your image editing at 100 percent magnification—meaning that the actually pixel resolution is shown in full detail on the screen—so your screen needs to be large enough to allow you to see each and every pixel. This means that if your screen is displaying at 1024×768, you can display an image of the same size or less at 100 percent magnification. An image larger than the screen resolution would be cropped at 100 percent magnification, and you would only see a portion of the image displayed. You would then need to zoom out to see the whole image, and some of the visual detail displayed would be compromised.

Another, often overlooked issue is the Windows theme colors. Because you are working with color imaging, it is important to keep the color theme scheme neutral in color and intensity. The best choice is midtone grays. You might be surprised at how much the color theme of your desktop can effect your perception of color relative to the images you are editing in Elements. You don't want it to compete or clash with your work, for example, a red theme misleading you into thinking all your pictures are a bit too red.

To change the color theme for Windows, follow these steps:

1. Right-click anywhere on your desktop. An in-context menu appears.

2. Choose Properties.

3. To change all the components at one time, select the Themes tab as shown here:

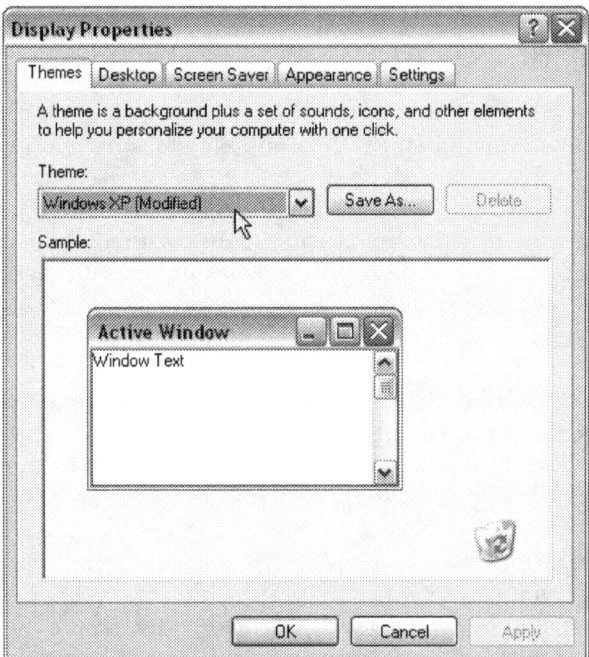

4. To adjust individual components separately, select the Appearances tab and click the Advanced button.

To change screen resolution Windows, follow these steps:

1. Right-click anywhere on your desktop. An in-context menu appears.

2. Choose Properties. The Display Properties dialog box appears.

3. Choose the Settings tab.

4. To increase or decrease the screen resolution, click and drag the Screen Resolution slider. When you see the resolution you want above the slider, release your mouse button.

5. In the Color Quality menu, choose 24-bit color as a minimum (shown here). This displays true color (16 million colors), which gives you very accurate color. Lesser color modes alter the appearance of images so you are not getting a true representation of what is there. For nongraphical applications this is okay, but not for art or especially photography. Click OK.

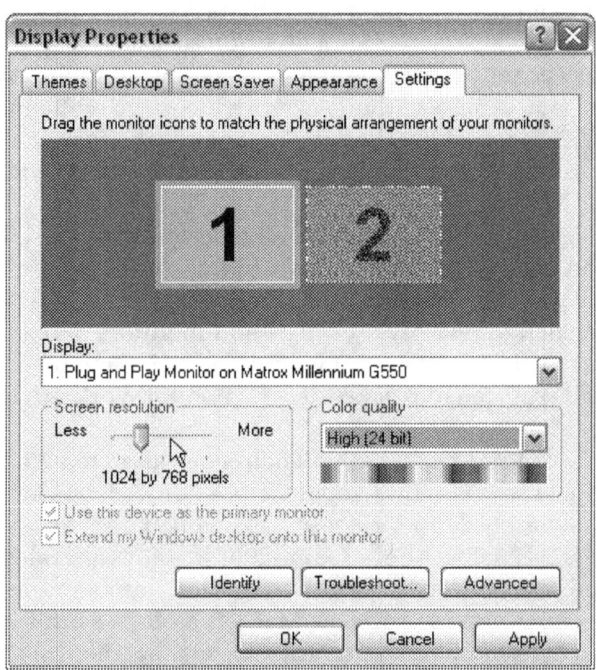

A window appears asking if you want to make the change permanent. Select No if you do not. If you make no selection, Windows assumes you want to make the change permanent and your screen resolution changes automatically. As we move into color calibration and management, keep in mind that color management gives even professionals headaches on occasion. All the aspects of controlling color on computer systems, applications, and peripherals can be overwhelming, so we'll stick to the basics here. If you just get your color monitor calibrated, that alone will put you ahead of many users. Most third-party software produced for advanced color management has good information to walk you through the necessary steps. Also, if you are planning on working with an outside printer, you can confer with them on how to optimize your system to work with theirs.

The next thing to accomplish is to calibrate the monitor on your system to give you the most accurate picture. Calibration makes it compatible with other input and output devices such as printers and scanners and assures that the color on all your devices matches.

The first thing to realize is that not all monitors are created equal, even if they're the same brand and model. The most generally respected technology for constructing color tubes is from Sony and is called Trinitron. Because Trinitron (and some Mitsubishi) tubes use a single electron gun rather than separate ones for each primary color, there is less chance that the gun will come out of alignment over time. Also, Trinitrons mask the horizontal borders of pixels so that neighboring pixels can't "bleed" their color into one another. These are important considerations when you need to preview color critically. Even though other monitors might look perfectly fine to the untrained eye, Trinitrons and Mitsubishis have become the workhorses of professional digital artists, publishers, and the like for many years. Sony sometimes sells Trinitron tubes to other monitor manufacturers, who sometimes use their own private name on them. If the proprietary name ends in "tron," it's a good bet that you're looking at a tube that uses Trinitron technology. If you're serious about your digital art career, a Trinitron monitor would be a good investment.

If you don't want to invest in a Trinitron, all is certainly not lost. If the picture looks sharp and displays a portrait photograph with accurate colors, it is probably good enough for everyday use. The range of monitor sizes, styles, and types is wide and can be confusing. Try to stick to mid-level or high-end monitors and avoid the bargain-basement types. Just remember that you want good adjustment controls so you can tune the monitor well. You can make any decent monitor work for you by calibrating it correctly.

There are a number of products that will help you calibrate your monitor. Let's begin with the one that comes with Elements. This is the Adobe Gamma calibration utility, which does a decent job, and it doesn't cost you extra. Furthermore, if you are using Windows Me or XP, using Adobe Gamma now color-calibrates system-wide. That is, color will be just as accurately calibrated for (for example) Macromedia Freehand or Flash as for Adobe's products. Mac OS X offers a built-in updated version of ColorSync, an excellent industry-standard color-management system. If you are serious about calibration on a more professional level, then you may wish to invest in some third-party calibration systems that do an excellent job, which we cover in more detail in the "Calibrating Your Monitor" section.

Note   *You should work in a room that has consistent light levels. If it has outside windows, install light-controlling curtains or blinds. If that is not possible, at least do your serious Photoshop work when the light is consistent. This is because the calibration of the monitor depends on a constant light level. If you don't control the light level, your perception of color will change as the light levels do. To avoid that, you will need to do a separate monitor calibration profile for every significant change in the light levels—and that's a major hassle.*

Calibrating Your Monitor

One of the most common issues that people face when beginning to use a more sophisticated image-editing application is, "How do I get what I see on the screen to resemble what comes out of a printer or is displayed on the Web?" The answer is revealed in a closer look at color-management systems and techniques. Color management is at the heart of the professional world of computer graphics, and understanding it is an important stepping stone to the next level. After all, the reason you purchased this software was to produce visuals, so it makes sense first to understand how best to get those visuals input, displayed, and output properly. The result will be that what you see will be acceptably close (for most of us) to what you get.

The next thing to get under control is your monitor and how it displays color. We've already covered how to adjust color and screen resolution, which controls the amount of displayable area and the possible number of colors that can be displayed; however, we have not discussed the nature of the color itself and how to determine the accuracy of the color displayed. Understanding this is not a trivial matter because it is the bridge from the virtual world to the real world. If you see green on the monitor and the printer prints blue, then you're out in left field. Let's learn how to hit home runs!

Color control in the computer environment is accomplished by color management systems that use both hardware and software to adjust the monitor to display to a standard so it can be matched with other monitors and peripheral devices such as printers and scanners. You probably have noticed that the pictures on the display TVs in electronics stores—even if they're the same brand and showing the same program—can differ dramatically. Usually the really dramatic differences result from the fact that customers and sales people adjust individual monitors to their own satisfaction and then walk away. The same problem exists with your computer display. Color-management systems provide a way to calibrate all those displays to show nearly identical pictures. In this section, we look at a simple solution. In subsequent sections, we move on to more professional-level systems.

Monitor Calibration the Simple Way: Adobe Gamma

If you are approaching Elements from the hobbyist direction, then there is no need to spend $300 or more on sophisticated calibration systems. Adobe includes its own calibration software called Adobe Gamma, and it does a decent job of getting your monitor calibrated. In the course of calibrating your monitor, you need to adjust the video controls of your monitor. Familiarize yourself with the controls on your model before you start. Be sure to read your monitor manual and that you've adjusted your monitor so that there's no barrel or pincushion distortion (that is, so that all four edges are straight) and so that there is as little black space around the picture as possible (none at all if your monitor is an LCD flat-panel display). Also make sure that all the edges of the picture are equidistant from the edges of the monitor.

Once you have adjusted your monitor, here is how you can find Adobe Gamma:

1. Go to Start | Control Panel and double-click Adobe Gamma.

2. When the window comes up, you have the option of going to the control panel or running the wizard (shown here). Unless you have experience in color management, we recommend you run the wizard.

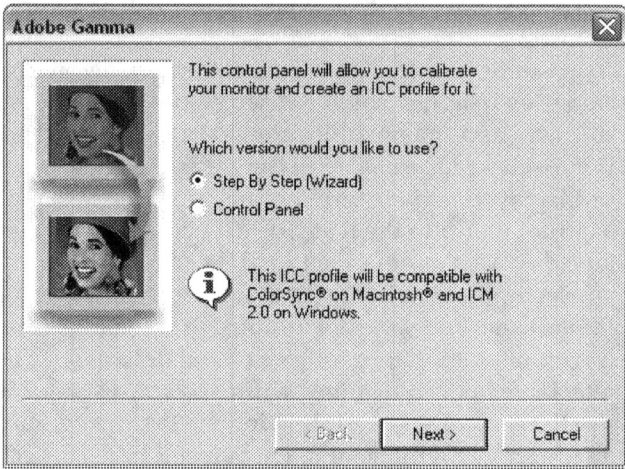

3. Follow the easy instructions that run you through a series of tests that calibrate your monitor. Here is an example of the Adobe Gamma Wizard:

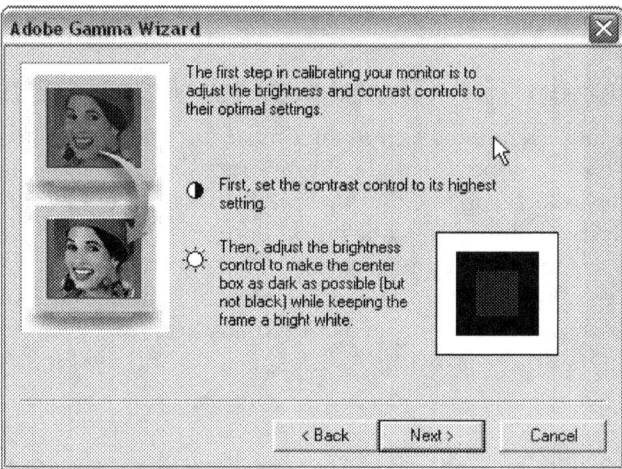

Monitor calibration changes over time. The phosphors (the light-activated elements inside the picture tube) weaken and change the display characteristics. If you are using your monitor a fair amount, it's a good idea to recalibrate it every few months.

What About Laptop and LCD Flat-Panel Monitors?

Wonderful as they are, very few LCD monitors can be adjusted and properly calibrated. The most notable exception is Apple's newest generation of studio displays and laptops. If you are serious about calibration, purchase the latest generation of ProveIt or another instrumented calibration system that specifically claims to be able to calibrate LCD monitors.

Instrument Calibration of a Monitor

If you are using Elements at a company that makes a point of calibrating all its art department monitors, have them calibrate your monitor as well.

For the ultimate in color accuracy and capability you need to acquire an instrumented calibration system. Some of the systems that are good are Monaco EZ-color, Colorblind-Prove it, Pantone/Colorvision's combination of Spyder and either Optical or Photocal. These systems use varying methods for calibrating, but all of them give good results. They all use hardware devices that attach themselves to a "target" that the software projects onto your monitor surface to give precise color, brightness, and contrast feedback from the monitor to the software, making it very accurate. The software associated with these devices can then make the proper monitor adjustments. All these systems are easy to use and provide detailed instruction on how to calibrate your system. The methods vary from one package to another, so we won't go into the details here, but if your time is valuable and you need have the color right the first time, these are essential tools to have.

Some monitor-calibrating programs are also equipped to profile other devices on your system that contribute to how the color, contrast, and brightness of images are judged on your system. These devices include flatbed scanners, film scanners, digital cameras, printers, and other output devices.

Using Color Profiles for Input and Output Devices

It is important to understand the basic concept of color management and how it can make your life much easier if you want accurate color when you output your images to various devices. You want the reassurance that what you have on your screen matches what prints. You also want the scanned image to match the source image. Input, output, and display devices all use different methods for producing color. To have visual control over all these sources and destinations, the monitor must become the gauge to determine what is real. Color-management systems attempt to fix the calibration of the monitor, profile all the devices, and then coordinate that with what you see on your monitor so you have a basis for comparison and control.

So far we have strictly talked about the monitor calibration, not about the other devices that produce color such as printers and scanners. Some color-management systems can help with these devices also. Standards have been developed to help coordinate the production of color across platforms and devices. These gives each device a means to measure the accuracy of its color relative to a standard color set. The standard that has been accepted at this time is the International Color Consortium (ICC). By using a consistent ICC profile of an image across many devices, it helps mitigate the color fluctuations. If you are displaying an image on a properly calibrated monitor using an ICC profile, when you send that image to the printer with the ICC profile attached, the printer understands how to adjust the color to match your screen, measuring the image against the standard. Another way to look at it is that you are seeing what the printer sees when you use the profile for display. There are many color-management system products that provide easy ways to develop ICC profiles for input, output, and display devices. Without this kind of control, you are left to trial and error, taking your best guess and rescanning and reprinting until you get close. This is frustrating and wastes time and money. With the cost of ink and paper, an investment in better color management can pay for itself rather quickly. Although many of these profiling systems are quite pricey, Monaco EZ-Color is one product that is notable for its comparatively low price.

You can also purchase premade color profiles for your printer. Companies such as Inkjet Mall have produced preset ICC profiles that cover a wide range of printers, papers, and inks. This is a good alternative to getting into a full-fledged color-management system. We go into more detail about how to use color management profiles for printing in Chapter 19.

Tweak for the Peak in Performance

Remember that race car we mentioned earlier? It takes a careful fine-tuning to make that car run to peak performance. The same is true of computer systems that run graphic software. There are hardware configurations and software settings that can give you better performance as you work with your images in Elements. In this section, we point out some of the options you have to adjust and improve your system performance for your needs. When the system is tuned well, it will enhance the flow of your work, making it a more rewarding experience.

Hardware Considerations

There are a number of factors that determine the overall performance of Photoshop Elements on your system. The first thing to understand is that the minimum configuration requirements are just that. Running at that level is like using regular gasoline in a formula one race car, so don't do it. You want Elements to perform in a manner that doesn't get in your way when you are concentrating on what counts: the artwork. So you decide what is important to you. Do you want to be waiting for the system while you watch that infernal hourglass, or do you want to get some work done? Here are some suggestions on how you can tune up your operating system to help Photoshop Elements perform better.

The first rule is more memory is good, very good, no let's say outstanding. The more active memory (RAM) the system has, the better the performance of graphic applications in general. The reason for this is that digital image files tend to be big and when you do a global operation on them, it takes a lot of memory to do all that work and still remember all the undos, clipboards, and *history states* (stored application settings that allow you to move to a previous point in workflow timeline) it's holding onto. The general rule is that for each file open, you need three to six times its size in memory. This might seem a bit extreme, but nevertheless it's practical. If the program runs out of active memory, it uses virtual memory (the hard drive) to compensate. When the system has to use the hard drive to substitute for volatile RAM, the system grinds to a slow crawl. This is when you might see computer artists really start to act strange, gesturing and talking to their computers in aggressive ways. You want to avoid that if you possibly can. 500 megabytes of RAM is a good start, and many professionals keep at least a gigabyte of internal memory handy. Memory is cheap and can make a very, very big difference—not an area to skimp on.

Another hardware consideration is the central processing unit (CPU). Once again, faster is better. Graphic applications tend to be on the cutting edge of technology and always starved for horsepower, so if you stay current with the latest versions, you can be sure they are going to want processing speeds in line with the latest computer models. If you computer is more than two or three years old, it is probably not going to run your newer graphic applications at optimal levels (although Elements will run on less powerful and well-equipped computers than its bigger cousin, Photoshop 7). The CPU can never be too fast, and Photoshop Elements, regardless of version, will make good use of every ounce of power it has.

The next factor that contributes to system performance is the operating system. With Windows, the major point of consideration is whether to stick with older versions such as Windows 95, 98, and ME or move up to operating systems based on Windows NT, rather than the ancient DOS. Photoshop Elements is currently supporting Windows 98, 98SE, 2000, ME, NT4SP6, and XP (Home and Pro), and Mac OS9 and OSX. It is not supporting Windows 95, Mac OS8, or older systems. If you have an older operating system, the simple answer is to upgrade, especially with contemporary software that makes the best use of the new features in the latest operating systems. The newer generation OSs are full 32-bit systems, which translates into much faster processing and better memory management so graphic applications are much more efficient in these environments.

Next let's take a look at the graphics board. This is an often-overlooked part of the system in terms of its importance to performance and display accuracy. Graphics boards are divided into a number of types according to the kind of graphics environment they support. The environments are 2-D, 3-D modeling, games, and video/multimedia. Elements is a 2-D (two-dimensional) environment, so you want a graphics board that is optimized for that kind of operation. If you are planning to do a lot of multimedia, you can get 2-D boards with those capabilities. 3-D and gaming boards tend to be optimized for virtual gaming and usually are not as good for graphics. If you're a gaming fanatic, it is still possible to find boards that do both pretty well, but you will get peak performance only from graphics boards that are dedicated to one type of operation. Professionals often have multiple systems configured for different types of applications. This speeds up certain types of transform operations such as rotations, transformations, screen refreshing, and resizing. They can do this because there are built-in routines in the graphics board's chips to augment the program. Graphics boards also come with varying memory configurations. Get as much memory as you can. This can reduce the demand on the computer's RAM. Stick with quality graphics boards because they are critical in the quality of the color displayed. It doesn't make sense to buy a $900 monitor and then use a cheap graphics board to drive it. Also, the better graphics boards often come with many utilities to help manage your desktop and color controls.

Another area of the hardware that can effect the total performance is data transfer rates to and from various input and output devices you will be using on a regular basis such as your printer, scanner, digital camera, and data storage devices. You need a fast hard drive so your files load and save quickly, and if your system does need to go to virtual memory, a faster hard drive will improve performance. A CD burner drive is an essential item for any graphics system. Make sure you get the fastest model available so you can do backups, create archives, and transfer files to other systems quickly. Connecting your printer, scanner, and digital camera or card reader to your system via a USB connection can increase the speed of operation significantly. It is all time, and it all adds up.

The formatting of your hard drive can make a difference in performance on both the Windows and Mac platforms. You can make sure you performance is at its peak by seeing that your drives are formatted correctly. For Windows, you should be using FAT 32 format, which is standard for Windows OSs after 95. On the Mac, use the HFS+ format, which is standard after OS 8. Photoshop Elements does not supporting the use of UFS format in Mac OS X . Partitions were designed to save space only on database systems, which have many small files. Larger partitions tend to work better on graphics systems because of the large file sizes, so do not split the drive into many smaller partitions.

Software Considerations

Now let's turn to the software for the next round of performance adjustments. You will see just why we are focusing on memory as the big issue. All the following tweaks have to do with memory or lack of it. As you move through these options, keep in mind that optimization is a movable feast. Changing settings to let you work more efficiently usually has both an up side and a down side. You have to measure the trade-offs when you change settings.

When you are working in Elements, the application keeps track of what you do by saving successive actions in memory as history states and displays them in the History palette up to a maximum amount that is preset in preferences. You can set the total number of these saves that are held in memory at any given time. Every action takes more memory, and depending on what type of action you take, the amount of memory can be quite substantial. You can reduce the total number of history states to reduce the demand on memory, but the trade-off is that you might not have the security of backtracking to a previous state. As the RAM fills up with history states, it reduces the memory available for graphic processing, so actions you take might slow down. You have some flexibility here. You can reduce the history states, or purchase more physical memory and not worry about it. The choice is yours. In the meantime, here is how you reduce the history states:

1. Choose Edit | Preferences | General and enter a number for History States in the box (shown in the following illustration). The default number is 20, and the maximum is 100. Adjust this amount lower if you experience performance slowdowns due to running out of RAM (because your system starts using virtual memory more often than usual). Raise it if your memory can handle it and you want to be able to take more steps back on an important job. The more system memory you have, the more likely that you can afford to keep more history states in memory. On the other hand, if you need to process a file that is significantly larger than your routine files, you might want to eliminate saving more than one or two history steps. You can always save different versions of the file to disk.

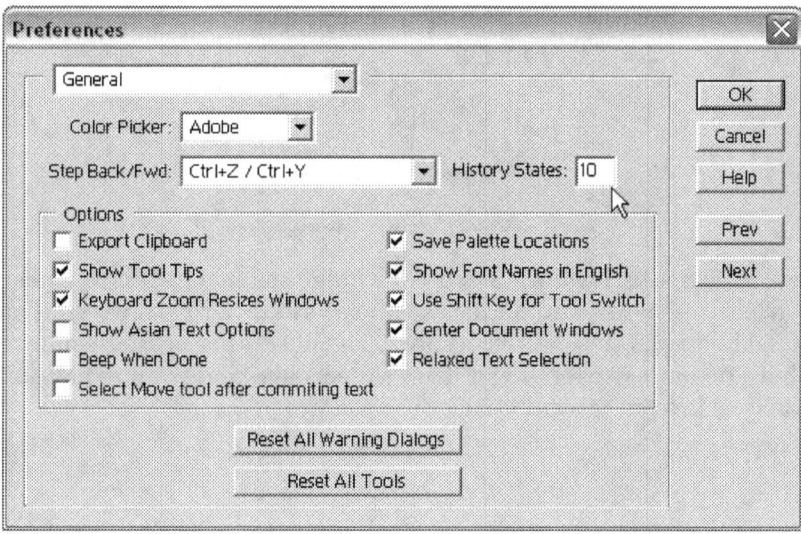

2. After you have entered an amount, click OK. If you lowered the history amount, you might want to stick a note on your monitor or keep the History palette open so you can see the current states because it is easy to assume that you have that buffer when you are working away—only to find you don't.

This next option might seem to be a small thing, but when you back it up against the memory wall, every little bit helps. The first time you have to sit through a large transformation that went to virtual memory processing, you will want to have every trick at hand. Everything Elements displays costs some memory. One thing you can reduce or turn off is the thumbnail displays on the Layers palette.

To reduce their size or turn them off completely, follow these steps:

1. Open the Layers palette.
2. Click and drag on the small arrow within the circle on the upper right. This opens the Layers palette menu.
3. Select Palette Options.
4. Make your selection of three different sizes (shown here) or None. For the most savings, choose None.

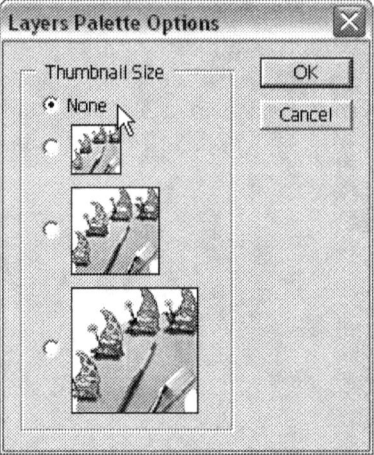

Another way to free up memory is to use the Purge command. This separately removes all history states, clipboards, and undos as you're working. You can even remove all history states, clipboards, and undoes at once. The idea is to free up memory quickly when you have no more use for any of these saved states and want to have all the memory possible directed toward image processing.

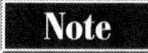

Always duplicate your file and save it under another name before you issue a Purge command. That way, you can always pick up where you left off. You can't save history steps, however, because your files would simply grow too large.

Follow these steps to perform a purge:

1. Choose Edit | Purge. A fly-out menu appears.

2. From the submenu, choose Undo | Clipboard | Histories, or All. Make sure you want to do this because a purge cannot be recovered.

Tuning Your OS

Sometimes the application knows better how to manage its function than the OS. When you are working on very large files, you can run out of RAM, so the system has to use virtual memory (hard-drive space) to augment the memory operation. When this occurs, you want Elements to manage the memory swapping because it does it more efficiently. You can force the issue by not giving the application much of the system's virtual memory. Then Elements is forced create its own virtual memory. To do this, you need to reset the attributes on the OS's virtual memory.

To set virtual memory to a minimum on the Mac, use these steps:

1. Choose Apple | Control Panels | Memory. The Memory dialog box appears. There are three sets of radio buttons. Click the Off buttons under Virtual Memory and RAM Disk.

2. Click the Close button on the upper left to hide the window.

3. Restart your Mac.

To set virtual memory to a minimum in Windows systems other than XP, follow these steps:

1. Right-click the My Computer icon on your desktop.

2. From the type/Name menu, choose Properties | Advanced | Performance Settings | Virtual Memory Change. The System Properties dialog box appears.

3. Under Virtual Memory click the Change button. The Virtual Memory dialog box will appear (see Figure 1-1).

4. Click the Custom Size radio button.

5. Enter the minimum and maximum fields to equal exactly the amount of RAM installed on your computer. This will force Elements to manage the virtual memory required when you demand goes over the amount of RAM available.

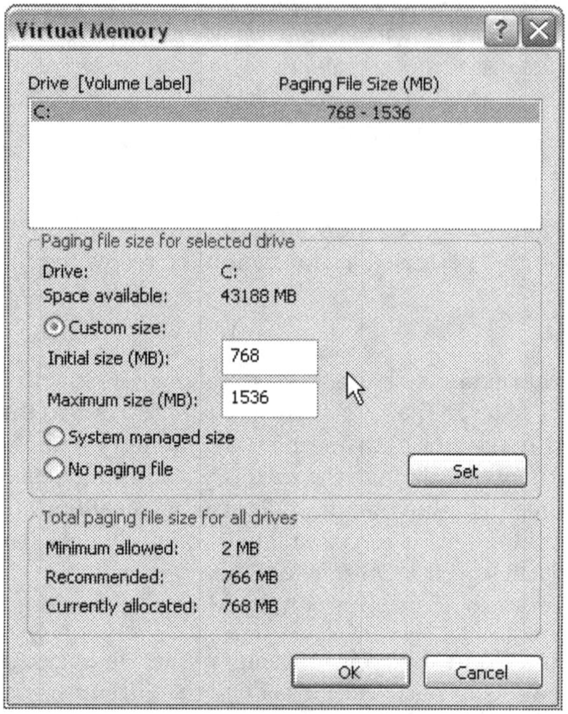

Figure 1-1.   *Windows Virtual Memory dialog box*

A word of caution with setting up virtual memory this way. This works with Elements because the program has a built-in cache technology that manages the need for virtual memory. Other programs you are using may not have this capability, so you will be limiting their use of virtual memory with these settings. You can always reset your virtual memory to optimize for other applications.

To set virtual memory to a minimum in Windows XP, follow these steps:

1. Choose Start | Control Panel | System and click the Advanced tab. The System Properties dialog box appears.

2. Under the Performance section click the Settings button, and the Performance Options dialog box will appear.

3. Click the Advanced tab and, under the Virtual Memory section, click the Change button; the Virtual Memory dialog box appears.

4. Choose the disk with the virtual memory file you want to change.

5. Click the Custom Size radio button.

6. Enter the minimum and maximum fields to equal the amount of RAM installed on your computer. This will force Elements to manage the virtual memory required when your demand goes over the amount of RAM available.

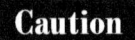

Caution *A word of caution with setting up virtual memory this way. This works with Elements because the program has a built-in cache technology that manages the need for virtual memory. Other programs you are using may not have this capability, so you will be limiting their use of virtual memory with these settings. You can always reset your operating system's virtual memory to optimize for other applications.*

More on Tuning Photoshop in Preferences

Now let's take a look at what you can do to from within Elements to give your performance another kick. The are a number of settings that can be modified to take some of the load off the system and let Elements manage some tasks more efficiently:

1. Choose Edit | Preferences | General. The General Preferences dialog box appears, as shown here:

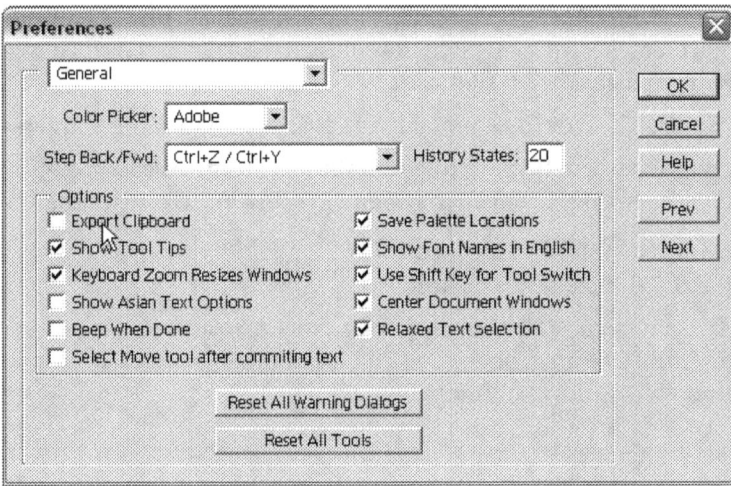

2. Click the Export Clipboard box so it is unchecked. This will not affect cut/paste operations within the application, but does turn off the ability to cut a selection to another application. You just need to recheck the Export Clipboard option if you need that function.

3. Choose Edit | Preferences | Saving Files to open the Saving Files preference dialog box, as shown here:

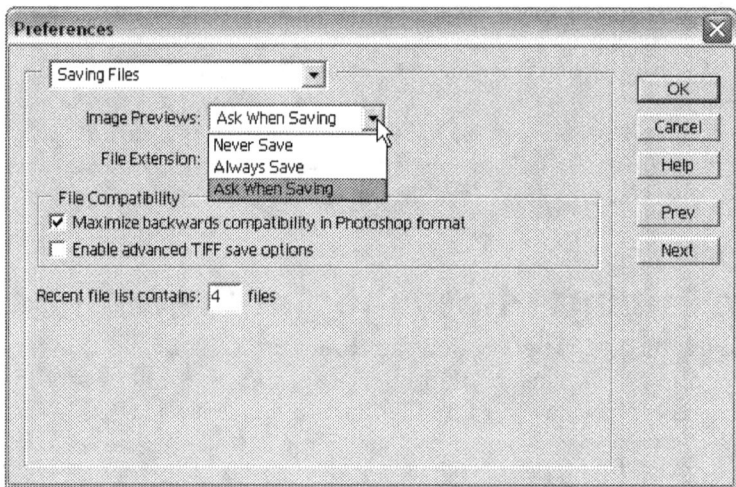

4. On the Mac, choose Always from the Append File Extension menu. On Windows, choose Ask When Saving from Image Preview menu. This will prompt you before Elements creates a preview, which will increase the file size. This can affect the load performance of Web files.

5. Check the Use Lower Case box. Lower-case extensions are universally accepted.

6. Check the Maximize Backward compatibility in the File Compatibility box. If you move files around to other systems, you want to ensure that your files load.

7. Choose Edit | Preferences | Displays & Cursors.

8. Click the Brush Size radio button.

9. In the Display area of the Display & Cursors dialog box, as shown in the following illustration. Check the Pixel Doubling box. This uses a faster display algorithm for previews in filter dialog boxes.

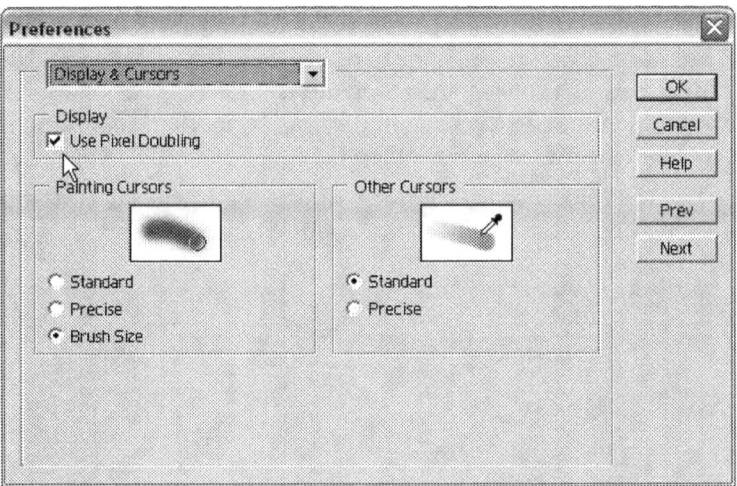

10. Choose Edit | Preferences | Plug-Ins & Scratch Disks. The Plug-Ins & Scratch Disk preferences dialog box will appear, as shown here:

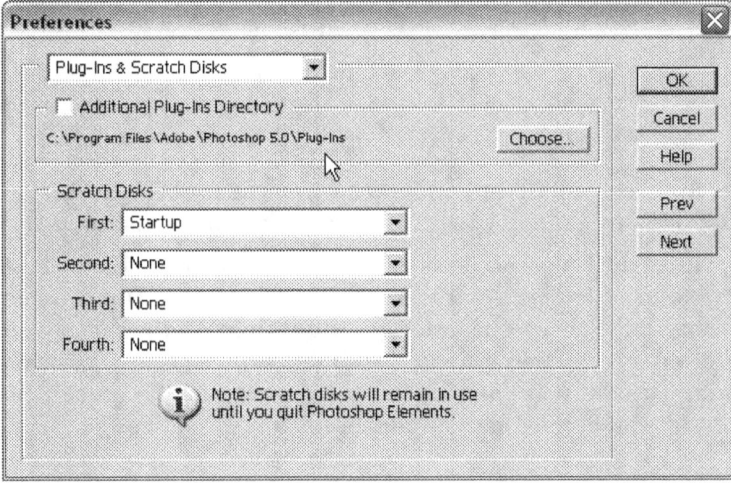

11. From the Scratch Disk pull-down menu, select the drives you are allocating. You can list up to four. Start with your fastest and add others in descending order of speed. Ideally, Elements wants to have a second drive for a scratch

disk. With today's giant disk sizes, it is not as much of an issue as it was in the past. If you do happen to have more than one drive, make the fastest one your scratch disk Be sure it has at least 2 gigabytes of free space all the time. It is important that you keep the scratch disk defragmented for efficiency. Elements wants to create contiguous files when it can.

12. Choose Edit | Preferences | Memory and Image Cache. The Memory and Image Cache dialog box will appear, as shown here:

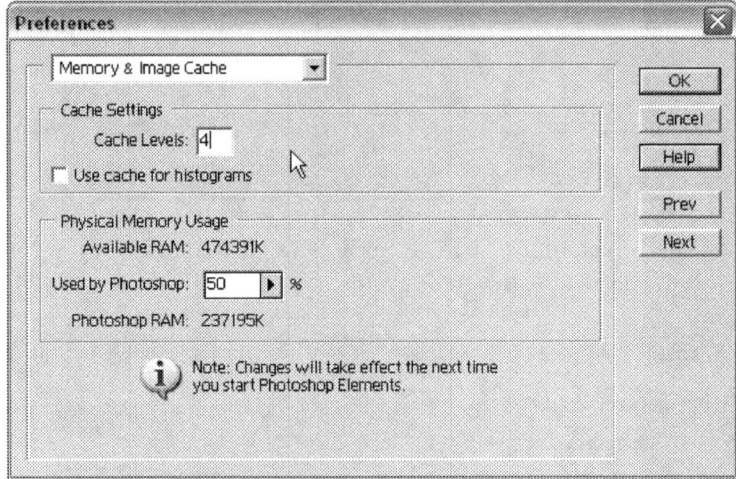

13. Change the cache setting to **1** and uncheck Cache for Histograms. Lowering the cache reduces the amount of saved states for keystroke zooming and histograms.

14. You can raise the Physical Memory usage, which allows Elements to grab more memory to use exclusively at startup. It calculates what it can use by what is available at the time you start your application, so if you have a lot of other applications open when you start Elements, then it uses less memory by percentage. If you want ensure that Elements gets the greater portion of memory, open it before other applications.

Installing Third-Party Plug-Ins

Plug-ins made to install separately from the main application are a most wonderful part of the Photoshop Toolbox, and Photoshop Elements is no exception. You can use any Photoshop compatible plug-in. Most plug-ins come with installation programs, and install the files in the proper directory with the use of a setup program. There are many plug-ins that are produced by creative programmers and distributed on the Web that require you to place the file(s) in the directories. The default plug-in directory for Elements is Adobe/Photoshop Elements/Plug Ins. Where you locate your Adobe folder depends on where you installed it originally. You can also choose to install them in an alternative directory that you set up in preferences.

If you are going to use other programs that accept Photoshop-compatible programs, install all your third-party plug-ins into a top-level folder on your most capacious hard drive. Then you can tell each program to use that folder as the alternative folder for plug-ins. Now you have to install the plug-ins only once, regardless of whether you add or subtract Photoshop plug-in-compatible applications on your computer(s).

You can also allocate a separate folder for storing plug-ins by following these steps:

1. Choose Edit | Preferences | Plug-Ins & Scratch Disk. The Plug-In & Scratch Disk dialog box appears, as shown here:

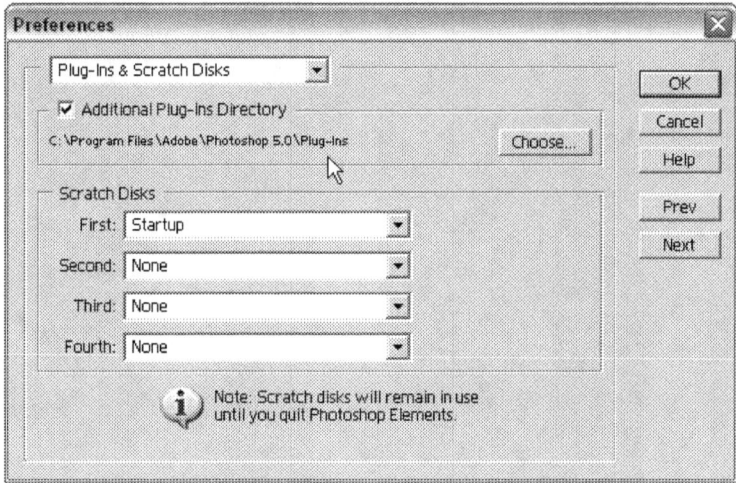

2. Check Additional Plug In Directory and click Choose.

3. Select or create a directory.

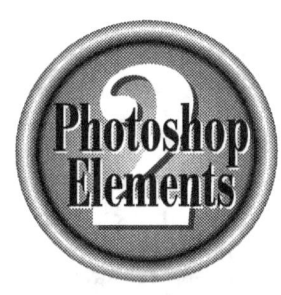

The Complete Reference

Chapter 2

What Elements Does Best

Although Photoshop Elements doesn't provide you with the ability to create your own automated multiprocess commands (aka *actions*), it does provide a whole library of point-and-click shortcuts that let the inexperienced user work like a professional digital darkroom technician. These shortcuts are accessed by either clicking a button or using a "wizard"-type interface with an onscreen guide that shows each step of the way. Don't be afraid to jump around looking only for exactly what you need.

This chapter not only explains how to use these features, but also explains how to use them in conjunction with one another. It also helps you make good decisions by informing you of situations for which another series of more conventional Photoshop Elements processes are likely to do a more professional-looking job.

Perfectly Suited for the Busy Business Pro

Don't think for a second that the easy tricks that have been prepackaged for you in Photoshop Elements are beneath the dignity of a professional user. At least from a strictly scientific standpoint, these commands will do a technically expert job of guessing at what you need and then providing it for you—as long as the promise has been made. If you're a business person whose primary goal is to get the image to look technically good enough to print in a business document or post to a web site, you'll find that Photoshop Elements 2.0 will do a great job for you far more often than not.

There is one thing that no program can do for you, though. It can't read your mind. If the program produces a print that sets a happy mood and looks as though it were shot in perfect conditions when what you wanted was the feeling of a romantic, dark, winter afternoon, you're going to have to learn to take over control yourself. Just take comfort in the fact that Photoshop Elements won't let you down. There's more raw power in this "everyperson's" version of Photoshop than there was (with a few specialized exceptions) in the first five professional versions of Photoshop.

Recipes for Navigating Complex Tasks

Recipes are nothing more than sets of instructions for performing a specific task, pretty much like what you find throughout this book. However, the built-in Photoshop Elements recipes are full of clickable instructions that say "Do this step for me." So if you don't have time to figure out the *how* or the *why* when it comes to performing a particular part of the task, you don't have to worry about it to get the job done. Just click "Do this step for me" and let the program do the rest. You can always come back after you've had a little more time to learn the subtleties, rationales, and alternatives.

For a closer look at the How-To palette, which is the interface for recipes, see Chapter 4. In Chapter 6, we go into more depth about each recipe and give you a detailed conceptual and contextual overview of each recipe so you have a better idea of how to make the task work for you. Illustrations are included, where appropriate, to show you what the final effect should look like.

Chapter 2: What Elements Does Best **29**

PHOTOSHOP ELEMENTS ORIENTATION

Quick Fixes

Quick Fixes are "near instant" results that you can obtain from a single dialog box in Photoshop Elements called the Quick Fix dialog box. You can see an example of the interface in the next illustration.

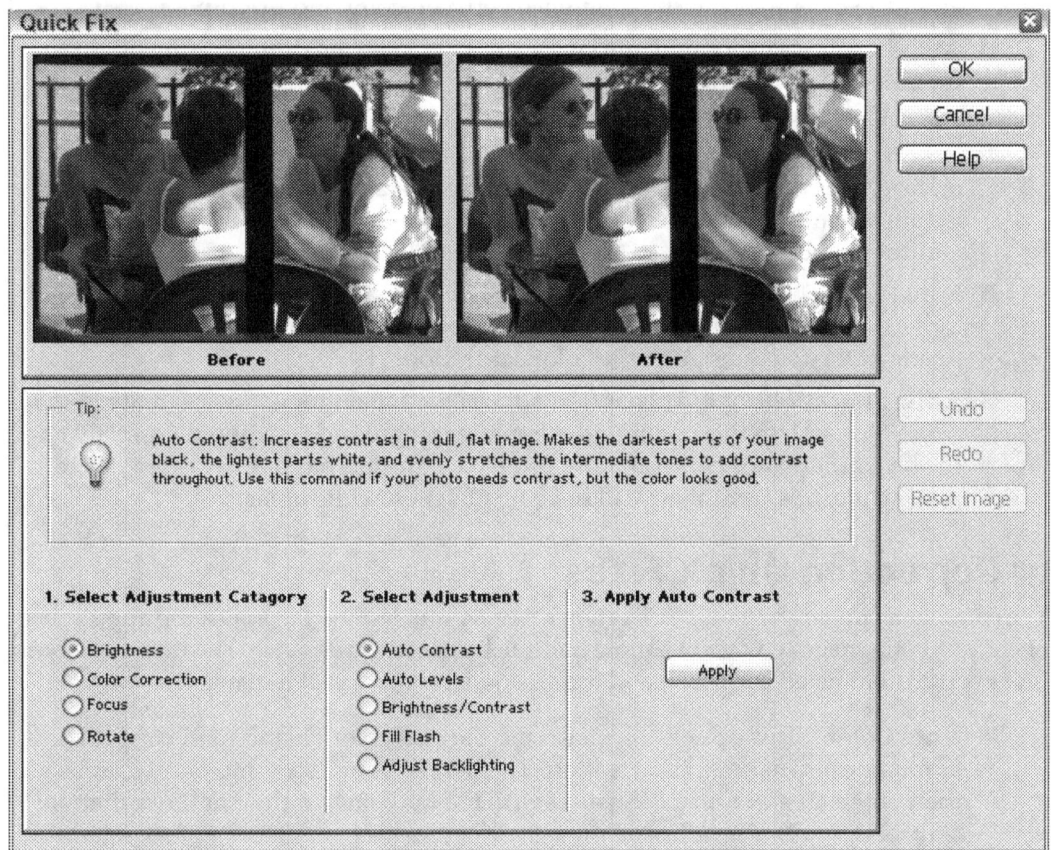

Actually, the contents of this dialog box change every time you choose a radio button in either of the first two columns. The radio button you choose in the first category (Select Adjustment Category) determines the contents of the second column (Select Adjustment). When you choose a radio button in the Select Adjustment column, you will either see an Apply button or a set of options and/or sliders for the option you have selected. Any time you click the Apply button or choose an adjustment option, the result is added to any other adjustments you've made while the Quick Fix dialog box is open. When you click OK, the cumulative effective of all the adjustments you've made is applied to your image.

Brightness Quick Fixes

These are all the permutations of the Quick Fix dialog box when Brightness is the chosen Adjustment Category:

■ **Auto Contrast** This option automatically calculates the optimal contrast in an image by enhancing the difference between color and brightness.

■ **Auto Levels** This option automatically calculates the optimal adjustment to the color, contrast, and brightness levels by evenly redistributing the tonal range using the lightest and darkest pixels in the image as reference.

■ **Brightness/Contrast** This option provides manual adjustment capabilities on brightness and contrast. The brightness will raise the color and luminance values toward white. The contrast will enhance the differences between color and luminance.

■ **Fill Flash** This option simulates the function of a fill flash and works to lighten dark shadows or lighten the photograph in general. Move the sliders to adjust the tonal range or the color saturation.

■ **Adjust Backlighting** This option adjusts the tonal range in areas that appear overexposed. Use this command when the foreground is exposed correctly and the background appears too light. If the background has been washed out to pure white, this command will have no effect on white areas.

Color Correction Quick Fixes

The commands under the Color Correction category are designed to adjust the appearance of color in your image so you get a more natural, balanced appearance. The first command gives you an automated correction and the second lets you correct it manually:

■ **Auto Color** This option calculates the optimal color balance and contrast and automatically makes the correction. This works better on some photographs than others. If you are not satisfied with the outcome, undo it and use manual controls to make the adjustment.

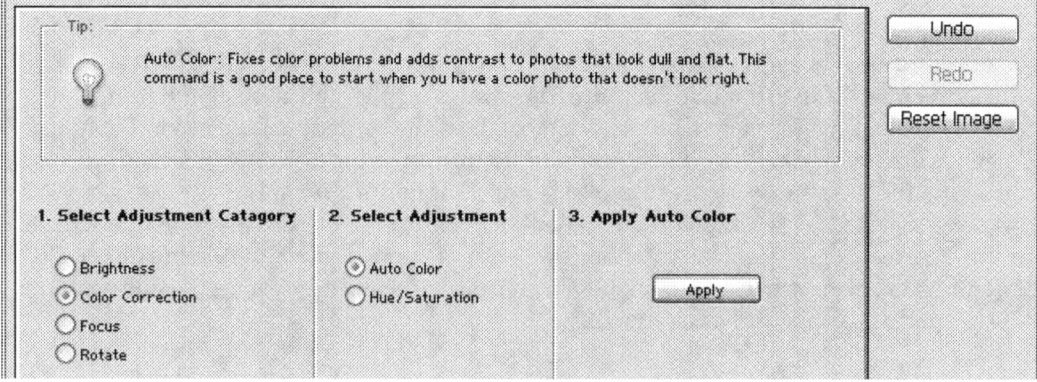

■ **Hue/Saturation** The Hue/Saturation option will bring up three sliders that allow you to adjust hue (pure color), saturation (color intensity), or lightness (the lightness or darkness of the image). The Hue slider shifts the colors through the spectrum as you move it. The Saturation slider will raise intensity as you slide it to the right and remove color as you slide it to the left, to the point of reducing the image to grayscale at the extreme left.

Focus Quick Fixes

These commands are designed to automatically adjust the sharpness or softness of an image. They can be applied to the whole layer or selected areas of the image.

■ The Auto Focus command, shown in the following illustration, sharpens the image by a fixed preset increment.

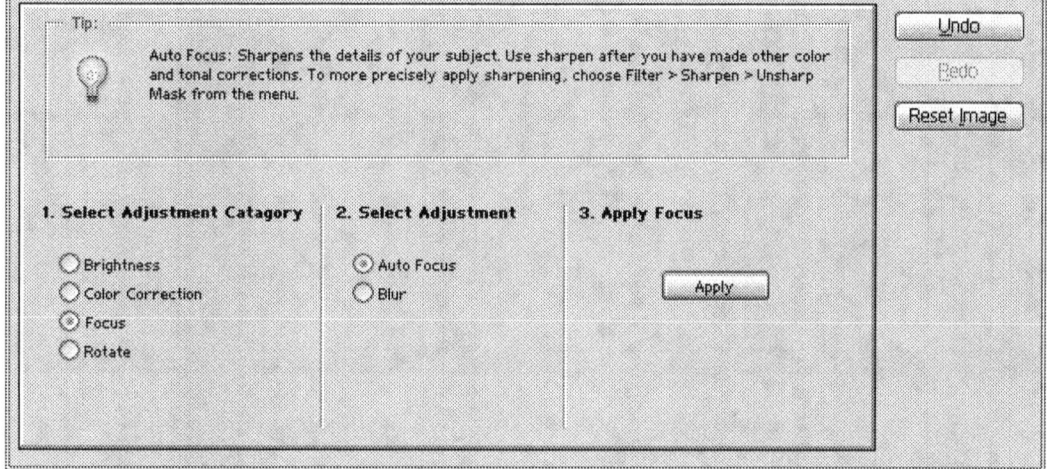

■ The Sharpness command creates higher contrast along edges while preserving the softer areas. You can do this sharpening manually by using Filter | Sharpen | Unsharp Mask. For all of these commands, you can increase the effect by running the command again.

■ The Blur command softens the whole layer or selected parts of the image. This is useful when you want to make sharper parts of an image stand out against a background, such as for a portrait shot.

Rotate Quick Fixes

The Rotate command enables you to reorient your image with a number of rotation options:

- One of the most common orientation issues comes from photographs shot with the camera turned 90 degrees to orient the image in the vertical (longer) dimension to enable better framing for some subjects. Most people turn the camera counter-clockwise to do this, so you need to reorient the image 90 degrees clockwise to correct for this. You can see the interface for a 90-degree clockwise rotation in the next illustration.

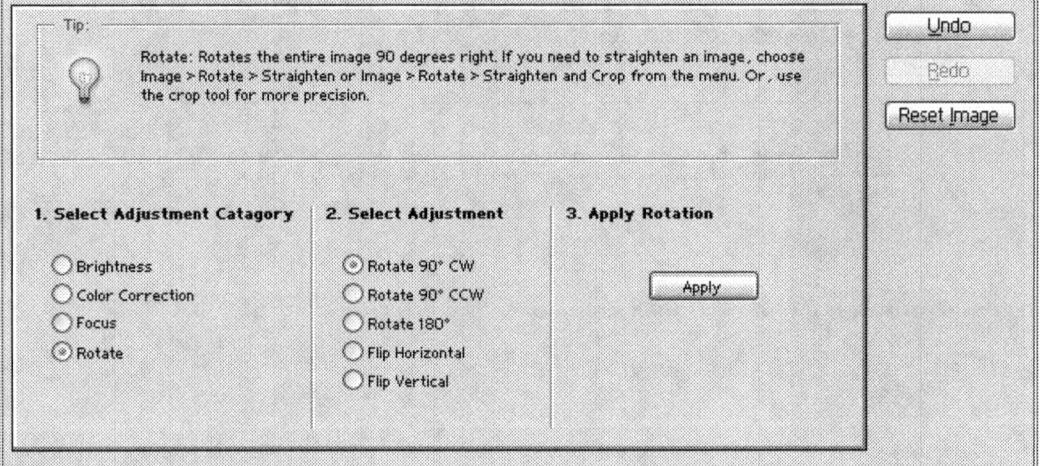

- For those of you who like to rotate the camera in the other direction, you can also rotate counter-clockwise.
- Rotating the image 180 degrees turns the image upside down.
- Flipping the image horizontally produces an image that looks like a reflection of the original off a vertical surface.
- Flipping the image vertically produces a reflected image off of a horizontal surface; left-right orientation is maintained.

One-Click Tricks

The one-click tricks we will be referring to here can all be found in the Image and Enhance menus. We will organize them in that way because they have related functions in their respective categories. One-click tricks sounds pretty snappy, and it is. Some of the commands you'll need most often are just a single click away in Photoshop

Elements—namely, automatic image straightening and cropping, compensation for the over-bright highlights that occur when the light is behind your subject and you expose for your subject's face, and automatic compensation for the overly dark shadows when you (properly) expose for the highlights but forget to turn on your camera's fill flash or use a reflector to bounce light back into the shadows. These are just some of the issues addressed by the automated tools available to you in Photoshop Elements.

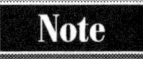 *Just in case you didn't notice, most of these commands are also found in the Quick Fix dialog box—where they do exactly the same thing.*

Automatic Enhancements

The automatic enhancement commands include Auto Levels, Auto Contrast, Auto Color Correction, Adjust Backlighting, and Fill Flash, all of which can be found in the Enhancement menu. These commands adjust exposure, contrast, brightness, and color balance. They are all based on algorithms that take their best calculated guess at what the proper adjustments should be. Just realize that the automatic corrections cannot anticipate every situation, and it may be necessary to use manual controls to do the final adjustments. For every automated command, there is an equivalent manual way of accomplish the same task.

Auto Levels

The Auto Levels command automatically places the black-and-white points at the extreme ends (where the histogram goes to zero) of the brightness range and then proportionately distributes the brightness range of all the pixels in between. To make this a bit easier to visualize, Figure 2-1 shows a Levels histogram before and after the Auto Levels command is executed. The Levels dialog box on the left shows the original distribution of pixels (indicated by the histogram) varying along the brightness range

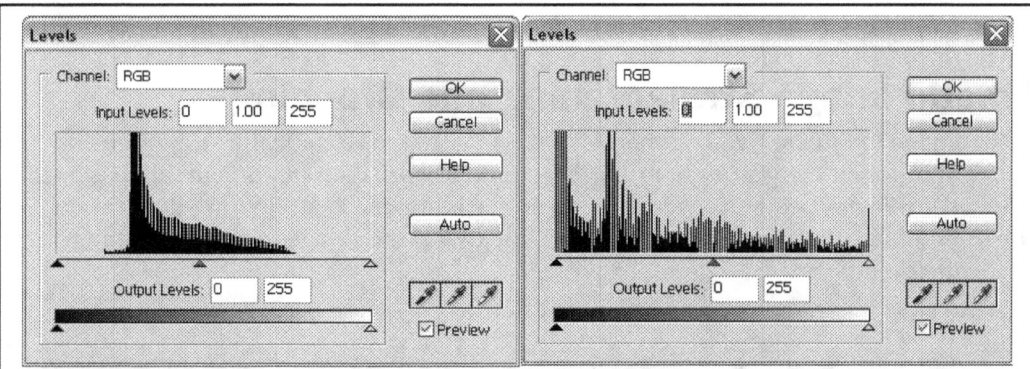

Figure 2-1. *The Levels dialog box on the left shows the original histogram of an image; the Levels dialog box on the right shows a histogram of the same image after Auto Levels.*

from black to white (indicated by the bar along the bottom). On the right, you see the histogram for the same image after Auto Levels—with the pixels redistributed to cover the whole brightness range. To choose the Auto Levels command, choose Enhance | Auto Levels (or press OPT/SHIFT+CMD/CTRL+L).

You can also choose Enhance | Adjust Brightness/Contrast | Levels (or press CMD/CTRL+L) to bring up the Levels dialog box (shown twice in Figure 2-1). When the dialog box appears, just click the Auto button, and you'll get exactly the same result, but you can now adjust the midtone by dragging the midtone (gray arrow) slider. We get into the use of the Levels command in depth in Chapter 12.

Auto Contrast Correction

The Auto Contrast command differs from the Auto Levels command in that it never redistributes the brightness of the pixels on the basis of individual color channels. This makes it a safer path to automatic exposure correction if you like the color balance of the original image and/or don't want the program second-guessing you as to how you'd like to use color balance to set a mood in the image. To choose the Auto Contrast command, choose Enhance | Auto Contrast (or press OPT/ALT+SHIFT+CMD/CTRL+L).

Auto Color Correction

We're going in menu order, so we're saving the best for last: the Auto Color Correction command. This is a new command in version 2.0 of Photoshop Elements and it combines the job of both the Auto Levels and Auto Contrast commands to provide a one-click exposure and color-balancing experience that works most of the time. To use the Auto Color Correction command, choose Enhance | Auto Color Correction (or press OPT/SHIFT+CMD/CTRL+B).

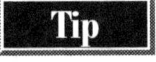 *A quick way to preview the "correction potential" for an image is to click the Auto Color Correction command (SHIFT+CMD/CTRL+B). Then, if you know you want to have manual control of the job, press CMD/CTRL+Z to Undo the Auto Color Correction command and use the controls described in Chapter 12.*

Automatic Image Straightening and Cropping

In the Image menu are two commands that will either automatically straighten an image or automatically straighten and crop (in one operation) an image that has been scanned while not being properly aligned in the scanner. The following illustration shows an image that needs straightening, along with the Image menu commands needed to do this.

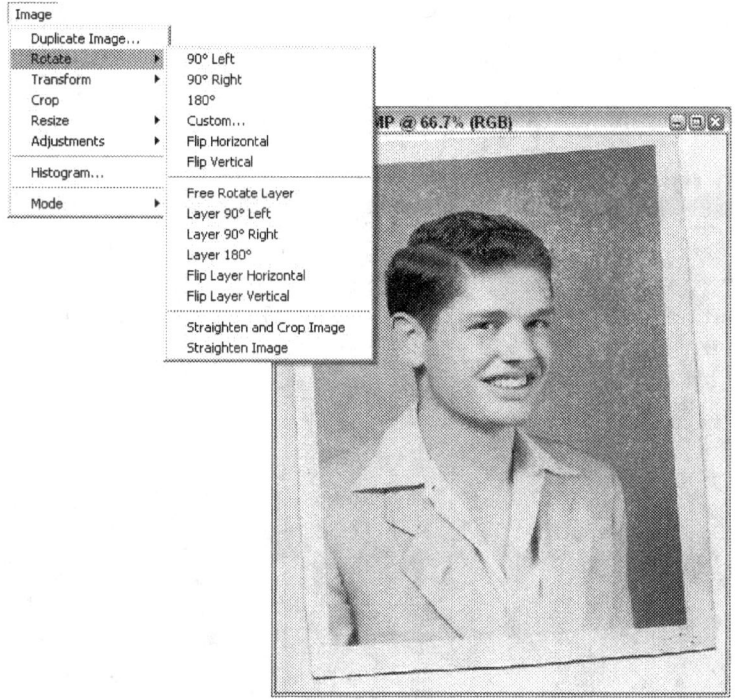

Straighten And Crop Image

If you want to automatically straighten and crop an image in one operation, choose Image | Rotate | Straighten And Crop Image. In most cases, this can be accomplished in one pass. If the image has more then one set of edges, as shown in the following example, you straighten in several steps by repeatedly running the Straighten And Crop Image command. This will first straighten the outer edges and crop them away, and then, in the next pass, focus on the next set of edges, making sure that the edge of the photograph itself is aligned properly.

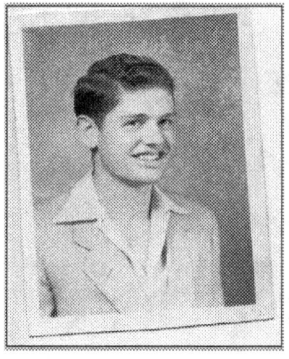 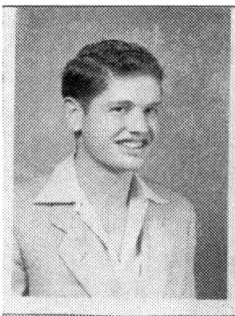 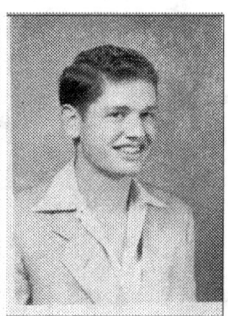

This command is useful in aligning images that have been mounted crooked, making them very difficult to align in a scanner properly. However, photos that are trimmed in a shape other than a rectangle will confuse the Straighten command. In such cases, the program will attempt to align the longest edge.

Straighten Image

Choosing Image | Rotate | Straighten Image will set the image upright, but it doesn't crop it. If you want more cropping precision, use this command in conjunction with the Crop tool. First, do the straightening, and then choose the Crop tool to drag a marquee around the portion of the image you want to keep. Use the handles on the crop box to fine-tune the size and position of the crop. When you are satisfied, click the Commit button in the Crop tool's Options bar. You can see the result of straightening and then cropping in this illustration:

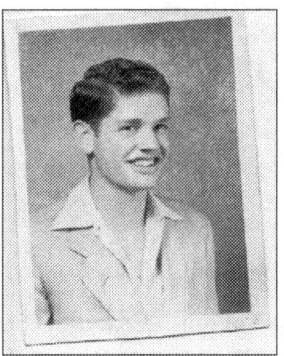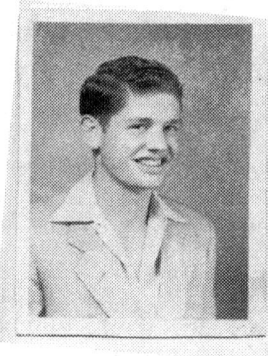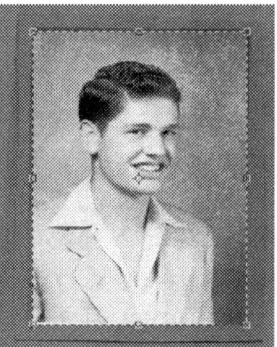

Specialized Tools and Commands

There is another set of tools and commands that don't exactly qualify as one-click tricks because they require some additional user interaction, but they still entail an aspect of automation. They are discussed here because of their unique methods on specific tasks and their emphasis on quick solutions. Adjust Backlighting and Fill Flash can be found in the Image menu, and the Red Eye brush is in the Tools category. In this section, we look at how these tools provide easy solutions to some common problems.

Adjust Backlighting

Ordinarily, one of the toughest problems to fix is the washed-out highlights that result from having metered for the detail in the shadows. It takes a lot of time to burn in individual highlights. The Enhance menu's Backlight Compensation command does a much quicker, more believable, and more seamless job.

Choose Enhance | Adjust Lighting | Adjust Backlighting. The Adjust Backlighting dialog box appears, as shown next.

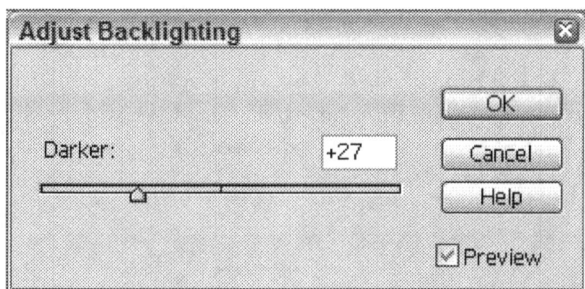

All you have to do is watch your image so that you can preview the effect as you drag the slider to the right. The highlight areas will darken while the midtones and shadows stay relatively unaffected. You can see the results of the Adjust Backlighting command performed on an image in the illustration that follows.

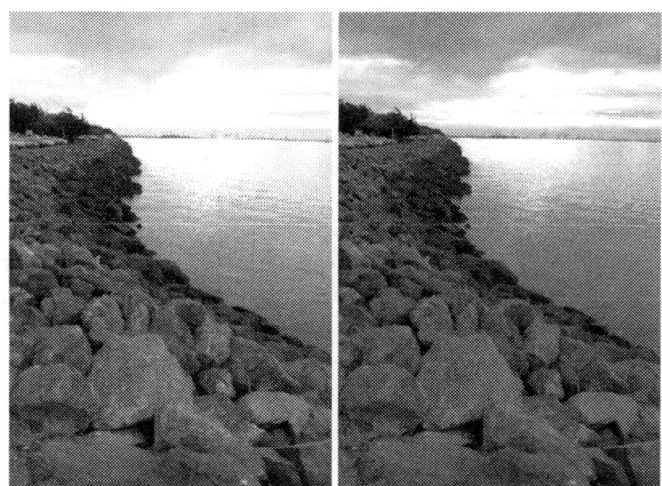

Fill Flash

The Fill Flash command is just the opposite of the Adjust Backlight command. It is especially handy if you're a digital camera photographer because digital images tend to block up in the highlights more easily than film images. The conventional advice to digital photographers is to expose for the highlights. Of course, this often leaves shadows that are a bit too dark to show all the detail that we'd like to see. The cure is to use the camera's built-in fill flash—except that if you're not careful, you'll get a harsh shadow line around a subject's nose.

The Fill Flash command does a good job of fixing such problems by filling in shadow detail. Here's all there is to it: Choose Enhance | Adjust Lighting | Fill Flash. The Adjust Fill Flash dialog box appears, as shown in the next illustration. To adjust the shadows, use the two sliders in the dialog box. The Lighter slider will adjust the density of the shadow areas. The Saturation slider will control the intensity of the color in the same areas.

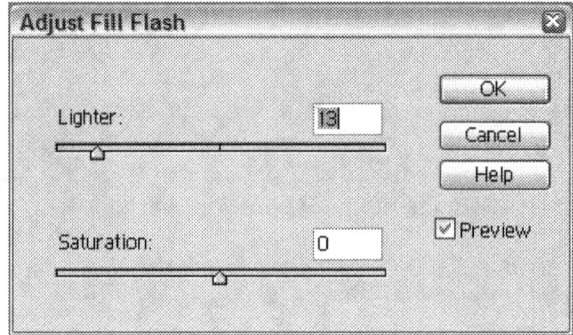

Removing Red Eye

Photoshop Elements endeavors to make your life easier by including as many automated tools as possible so you can get results quickly. The removal of small defects is one area where it excels in providing some quick-and-easy tools to clean up your photos.

Red eye happens when a flash is fired that is so close to the lens (as is usually the case with built-in flashes) that the bright light enters the iris of the eye and is reflected from the back of the eyeball. Because the eyeball is filled with blood, a bright red light emanates from the subject's irises. Here's how to fix red eye:

1. Choose the Magnifier tool and zoom in on the subject's eyes.

2. Choose the Red Eye brush from the toolbox (a brush with a small eye icon at the upper left).

3. Make sure the menu choices in the Options bar are the same as those shown here:

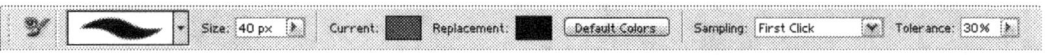

4. In the Red Eye brush's Options bar, choose a slightly feathered brush that is about the same size as the subject's pupil. Once you've chosen a brush shape and size, you can make small variations by pressing the] key to enlarge the brush and the [key to make it smaller. Each click of the square bracket keys enlarges or reduces the brush by 1 pixel in diameter.

5. Place the center of the brush cursor over the red in the eye's iris and click. Notice that in the Options bar, the Current color becomes red. When you drag, the red will be replaced by the Replacement color (usually black or dark brown).

Removing Dust and Scratches

No mater how well you clean your camera lens or scanner, or how carefully you handle your negatives and prints, it is inevitable that you will need to clean up some dirt and defects in your images. The Dust & Scratches filter, found in Filter | Noise, was born for this task. It works by spreading highlights or shadows past a certain threshold. This has the effect of blurring or softening the image somewhat, though the threshold adjustment will keep the edges sharper than they would have been if one had simply blurred the image. If you're working with the Dust & Scratches filter, it's a good idea to eliminate the dust and scratches from skies, walls, and other large areas of relatively flat color first. Because blurring shows up very little in these areas, you can remove a large amount of dust and scratches before blurring becomes objectionable.

When you get into removing small flaws from subject areas where sharpness counts, try using the Clone Stamp tool to retouch small areas. That way, sharp edges are affected as little as possible.

To remove dust and scratches from flat areas of the picture:

1. Choose the Freehand Lasso tool and press the OPT/ALT key while making a series of small selections that isolate small areas where dust and scratches are prominent.

2. Choose Filter | Noise | Dust & Scratches. The Dust & Scratches dialog box will appear, as shown here:

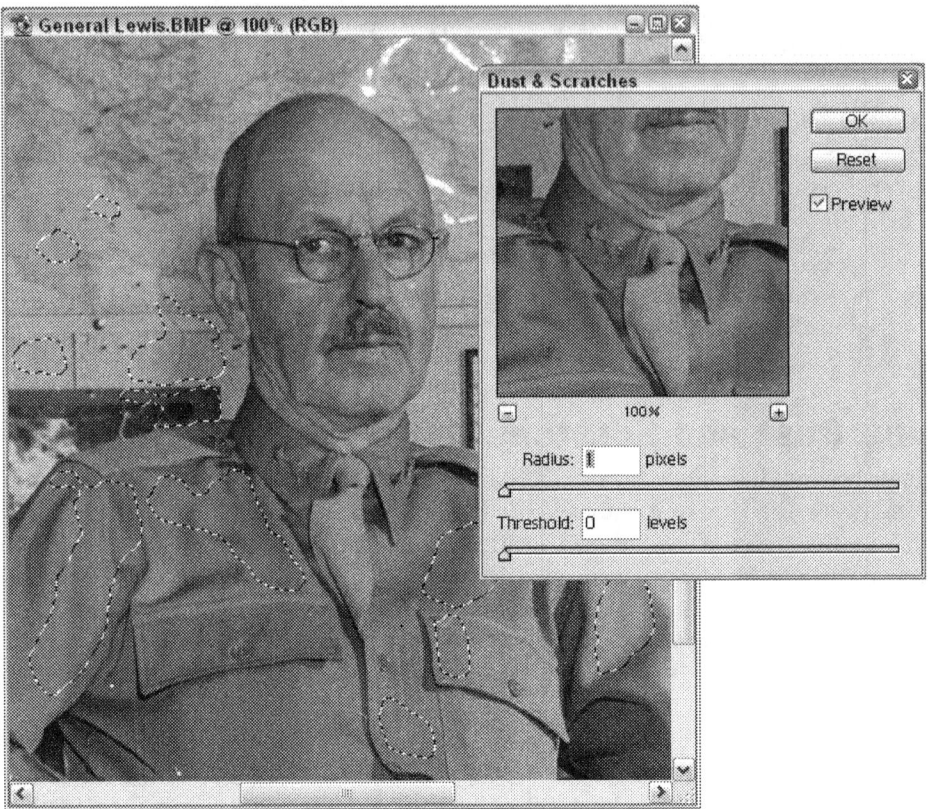

3. Drag the Radius slider slowly to the right until the dust, scratches, and other small defects disappear.

4. Drag the Threshold slider to the right until edges sharpen as much as possible without restoring the dust and scratches. When you are satisfied, click OK.

Note   *You may want to adjust the sliders so that only smaller specks are eliminated to avoid too much blurring. You can eliminate the larger defects with the Clone Stamp tool.*

5. Press CMD/CTRL+D to drop the selection marquees.

6. Choose the Clone Stamp tool to eliminate the remaining dust and scratches so that you don't also remove the sharpness in such areas as the subject's face.

Multi-Level Undo

Photoshop Elements automatically keeps track of up to the last 100 image edits. In this context, an image edit is as minor as a brush stroke or as major as the application of an elaborate special-effects filter—in other words, whatever happens when you click or drag. All these actions are recorded in a palette called the Undo History palette, which records each command or stroke by name. If you are familiar with the Undo History palette that has been around in Photoshop since version 5.5, you are already familiar with the basics of Photoshop Elements' Undo History palette. However, you should note a very important difference: you can't take snapshots, which are a Photoshop capability that allows you to back up to any point in time that has been saved. Photoshop Elements automatically records history states up to the number of history states designated in the preferences. You can get around this limitation by saving your files with unique filenames at key points in development.

The maximum number of steps that Photoshop Elements allows to be recorded is 100, and the default is 20. Just remember that the program has to use enough storage space for each step it's tracking to hold all the data that has changed since the previous step. So, if you run a filter on an entire layer, that step will require as much memory storage as an entire layer of the image you are working on—which is to say, as much memory as your original image required. If you don't have a gigabyte or so of RAM installed in your machine and you tell the History palette to store more than 20 steps, you are going to find that your computer will frequently slow down so that it can store those excess steps on your hard drive. The Undo History palette is shown in Figure 5-2.

You can back up directly to any step you've previously taken by clicking its Name bar. If you then add a new step, all the subsequent steps in the History palette will disappear.

If you want to clear all the steps after a certain step, click the Name bar of the step that follows the last step you want to keep, and click the Clear History Step icon. A dialog box will ask if you are sure you want to delete the remaining steps. Click OK to delete them.

One thing you can do in Photoshop Elements that you can't do in Photoshop 7.0 with the History brush is use keystrokes to step forward and backward one step at a time each time you click a key combination. You can set your own step forward/backward keystrokes (for instance, some find it faster to use a single function key for stepping backward and another for stepping forward). To set special keys for stepping forward and backward:

1. Choose Edit | Preferences | General.

2. Choose from one of three choices in the Step Back/Fwd menu. The defaults are CMD/CTRL+Z to step backward and CMD/CTRL+Y to step forward.

3. When you have made your choice, click OK.

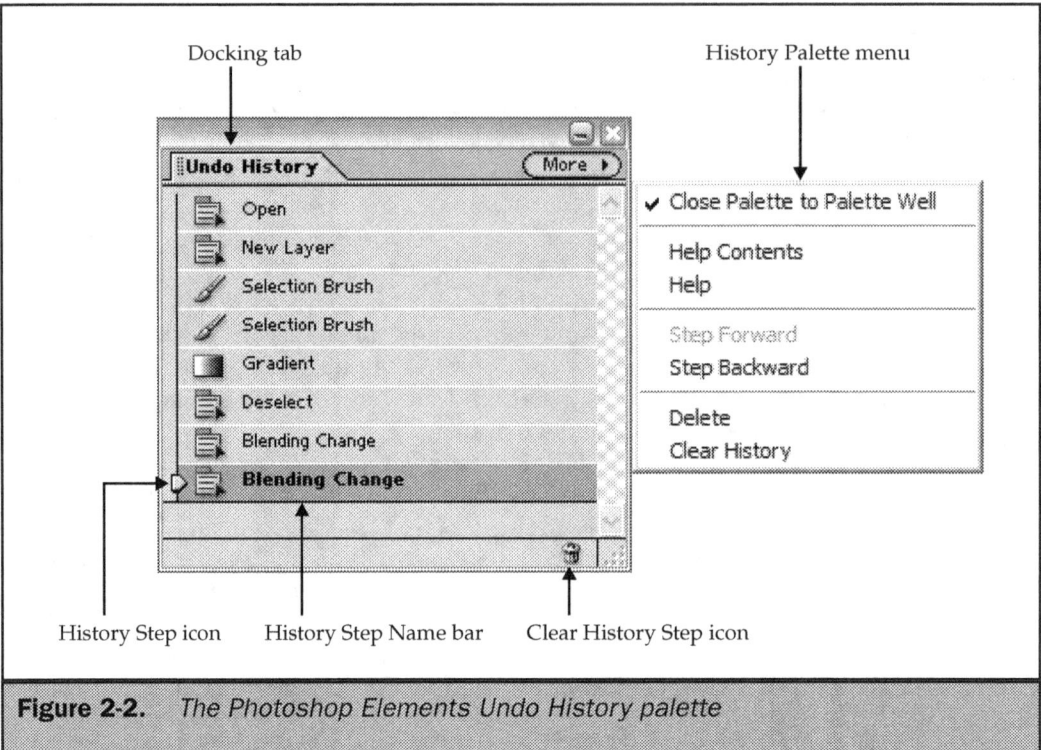

Docking tab   History Palette menu

History Step icon   History Step Name bar   Clear History Step icon

Figure 2-2. *The Photoshop Elements Undo History palette*

Hints: Online Help for Just About Everything

The Hints palette's primary job is to explain each of the tools. If you're just getting to know the program, drag the Hints palette out of the Palette dock and place it next to the Toolbox. Each time you choose a different tool, the illustration in the Hints palette (shown in Figure 5-3) will change to show you what that tool does. At the same time, you'll see a paragraph of clear explanatory text.

The Hints palette also provides yet another way (in addition to choosing Help | Photoshop Elements Help, or pressing F1) to bring up the standard online help for Photoshop Elements. The online help is quite comprehensive.

Tip   *One of the fastest ways to get information on just about any topic related to Photoshop Elements is to press F1 and then click the Search button when the online Help screen appears. Then simply type the keyword related to your question and press RETURN.*

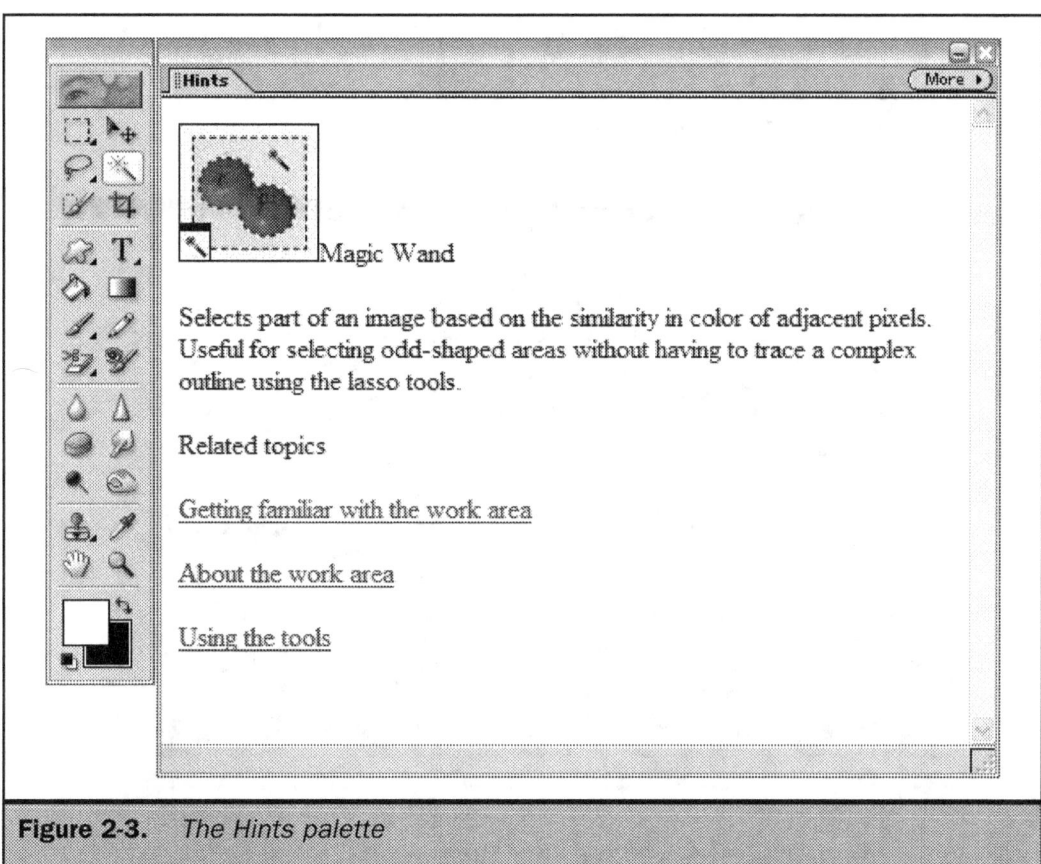

Figure 2-3. *The Hints palette*

Instant Effects

The Effects palette lets you automatically apply a complex special effect by clicking an icon that is a picture of the special effect. Notice we said that these are "complex" special effects. In other words, you couldn't re-create them by executing a simple command in Photoshop Elements. These effects are the result of a combination of commands that produces an often-needed result on the chosen image or layer. Effects are divided into four categories:

- Frames
- Textures
- Text effects
- Image effects

There's also a category called All that lets the Effects palette display all the effects available in your current version of Photoshop Elements. To use the Effects palette, either drag it from its default location in the Palette Docking well (see the next illustration) or choose Window | Effects.

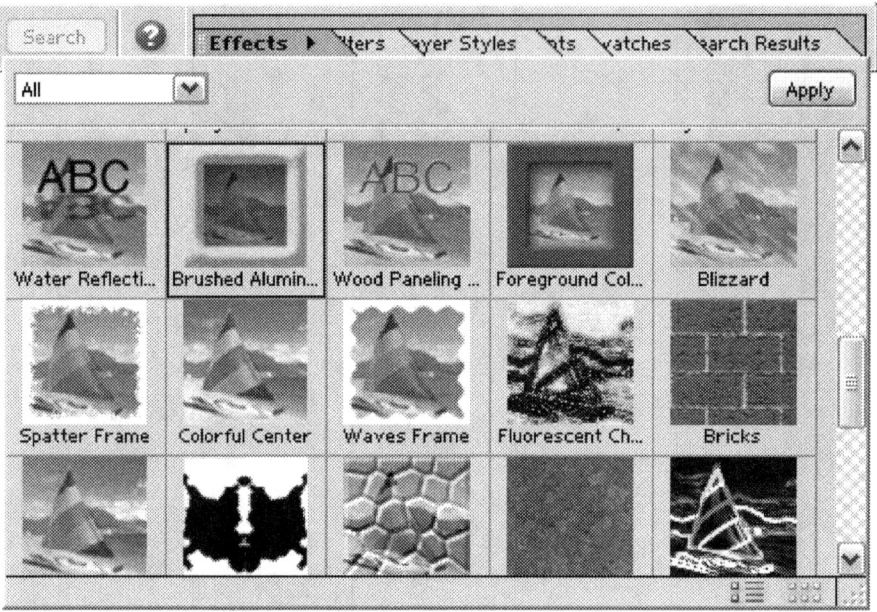

To apply any of these effects, follow these steps

1. Choose Window | Layers or drag the Layers palette out of the dock. Remember that any effect you choose will be applied to the currently active layer. So before you apply the effect, be sure you have chosen the intended layer by clicking its Layer Name bar in the Layer's palette.

2. Locate the effect in the palette that you want to apply and click its icon, or drag the icon onto the currently active image window.

That's all there is to it. Wait a moment, and the effect will be automatically applied to the layer you've chosen. In the following sections, you'll see examples of effects from each category.

Frame Effects

Frames are applied to a whole layer or (if parts of several layers are visible) to a whole image. If multiple layers are present, the program will ask whether you want to collapse the layers. You will have to click OK for the Frame effect to work. You can see the aluminum frame automatically surround the image, as shown next.

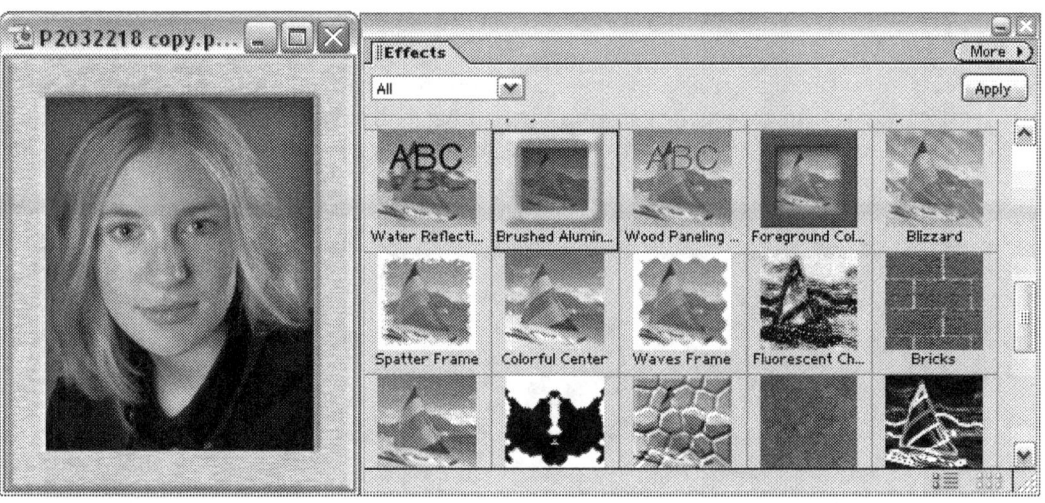

Texture Effects

The Texture effects create a new layer as the top layer in the image. This new layer is actually a picture of the texture. Once you've double-clicked the icon of the texture you want to apply, open the Layers palette, select the texture layer's Name bar, and then cycle through the Blend modes until you see the effect you want to create. Here's an Asphalt Texture effect applied to an island.

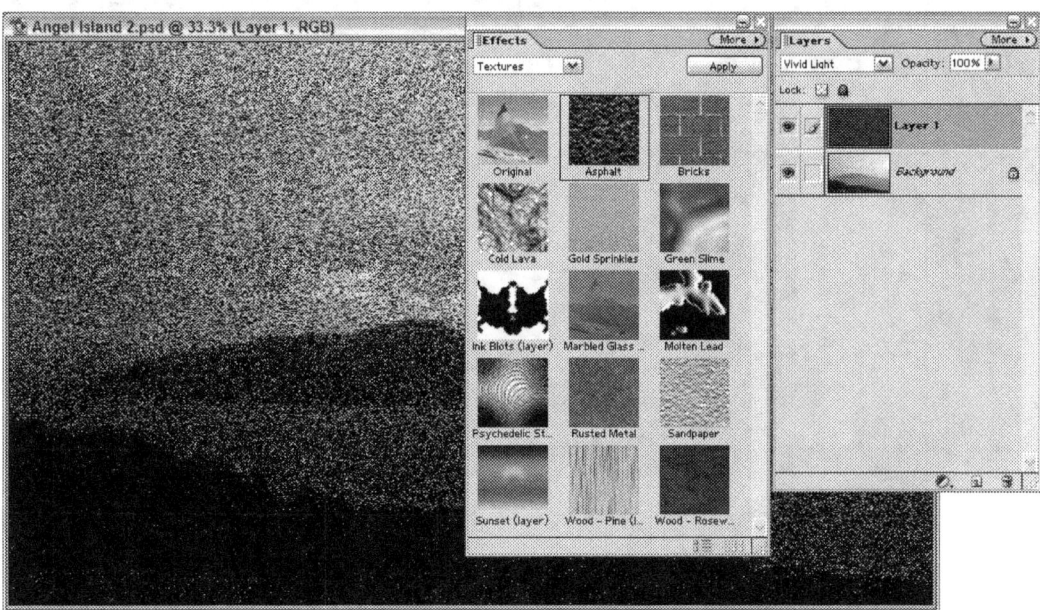

Text Effects

Text effects are typically applied to a text layer, but they can be applied to shapes with equal effectiveness (in case you want to make some really cool buttons for your web site or PowerPoint presentation). This illustration shows a soft dropped shadow effect:

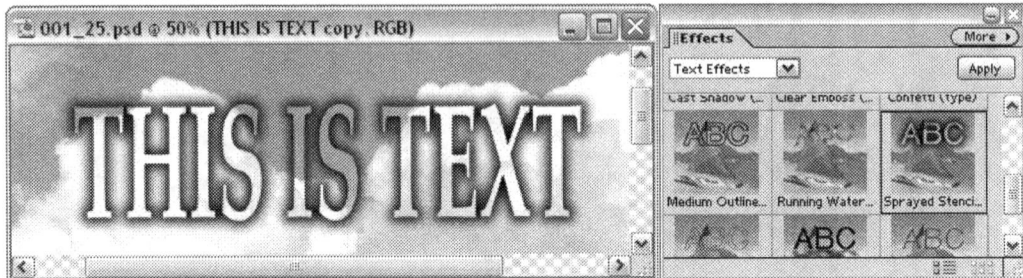

Image Effects

Image effects are applied only to the current layer. Be sure that you have chosen the layer to which you wish to apply the effect before clicking the Apply button, dragging the thumbnail onto the image, or double-clicking the thumbnail. This illustration shows how the effect of falling snow affects the entire image when the Blizzard effect is applied.

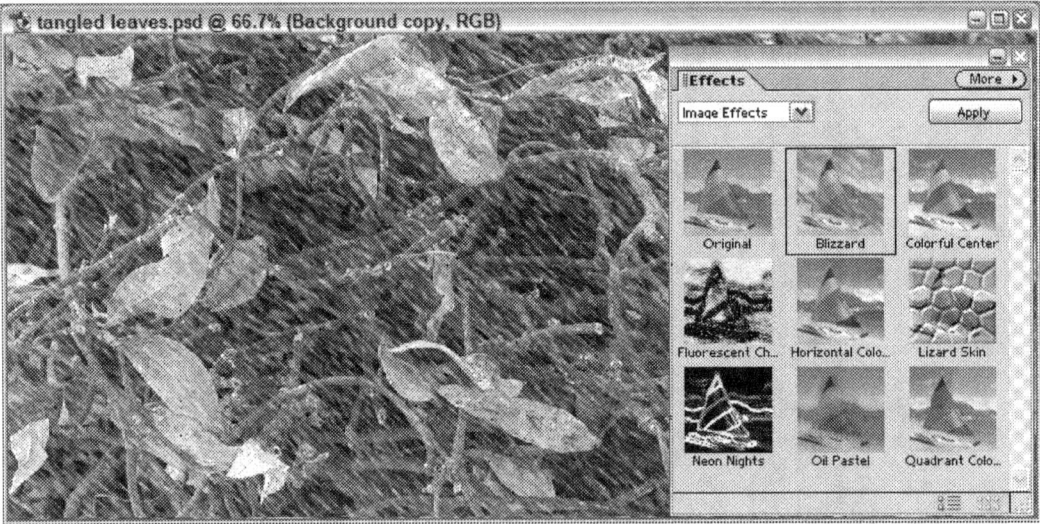

Built-In Panorama Building

Have you ever been frustrated because you couldn't fit enough of that gorgeous scene into one photograph because the lens didn't give you a wide enough view? With Photoshop Elements' Photomerge, you can take a series of panoramic shots and "stitch" them together into a seamless panorama. The result is an image that can be a full 360-degrees wide—or anything in between. Using Photomerge, much of the work is automatically done for you in true Photoshop Elements style.

You can photograph panoramas using any kind of camera. You'll get the best results if you use a tripod, and if the camera can be set in a manual exposure mode so that the exposure of each frame in the sequence can be forced to be identical to all the others.

Do *not* shoot in automatic mode. If the camera is set in automatic mode, it will lower the exposure when the camera is pointed toward the sun and raise the exposure when the camera is pointed into an area of shadow. The result will be streaking in the stitched image—especially in areas where two overlapped images differ in exposure.

Ideally, the camera should be mounted on a tripod head that is made especially for shooting panoramas so that the camera always rotates about its optical axis. This is especially important if the camera is to be mounted vertically. In that case, you want to mount the camera on a bracket that will place the camera's optical axis directly over the tripod thread. The camera's optical axis is generally at the center of the lens and about halfway between the front element of the lens and the film (or digital image sensor) surface. If you can't mount the camera precisely enough to center it over its optical axis, make sure there are no objects in the picture that are closer than the primary focus distance. Otherwise, those objects will appear to shift position as the camera is rotated.

If you take the pictures on film, you will need to scan the film frames before turning them into a panorama. Make sure that each frame is scanned at the same size, resolution, exposure, and color settings. Unfortunately, not all scanners make this an easy thing to accomplish. A much simpler choice is to use a digital camera that has manual settings. Digital cameras also automatically number the sequence of their frames, so it is easy to tell in what order each frame should be placed.

Assuming you have photographed your sequence and downloaded it to your computer, here's how to use Photoshop Elements to stitch together a horizontal panorama for you. You should end up with an effect similar to the following image.

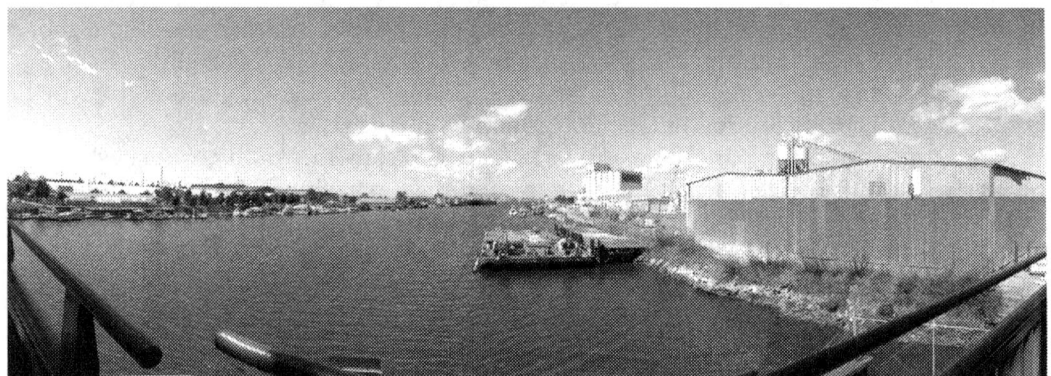

Assuming you've followed our instructions for taking the photos for your panorama, assembling it is quite easy:

1. Make sure all the photos for your panorama are numbered in the sequence in which they were shot, from left to right.

2. Place all the photos into the same folder.

3. Choose File | Create Photomerge. The Photomerge dialog box will open, as shown next.

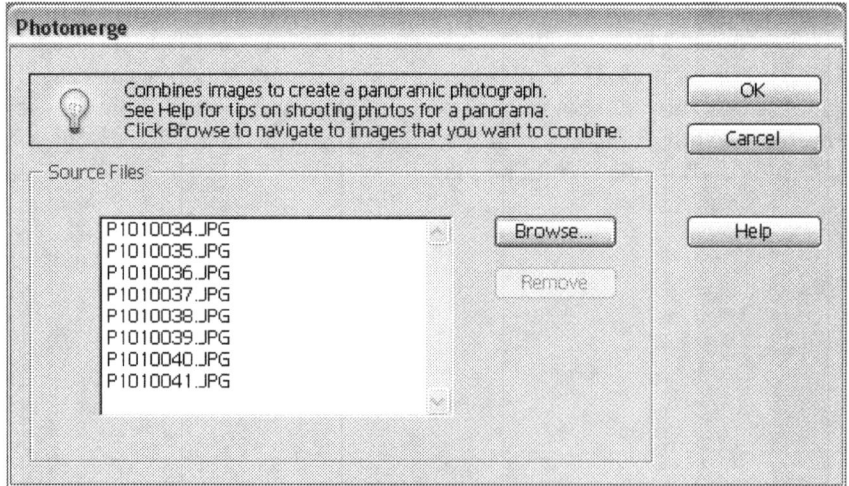

4. Click the Browse button and navigate to the folder where you stored your images. Open all the images in the Source Files list in the Photomerge dialog box. Click OK.

5. You will see each of the shots open in sequence in Photoshop Elements. Then there will be a pause while the Photomerge interface opens, and you will see a rough version of the panorama in the Photomerge window.

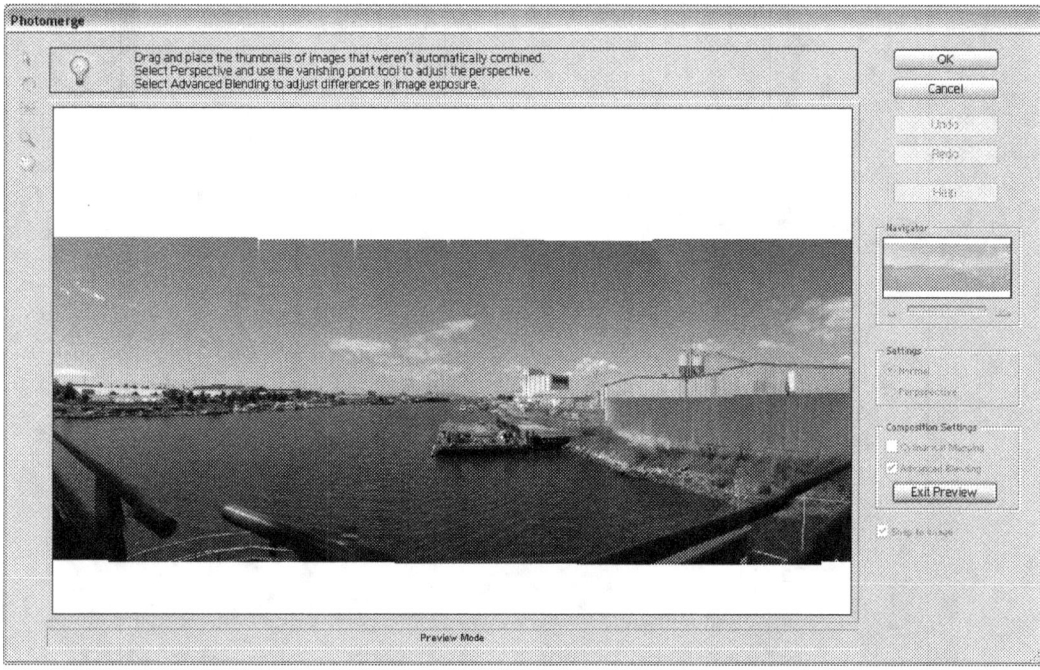

6. You can also drag photos into different positions to see if they merge more smoothly.

The
Complete
Reference

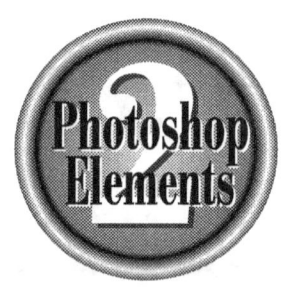
Photoshop
Elements
2

Chapter 3

Touring Elements' Functional Components

51

This chapter, and the next two, synopsize the benefit and purpose of each of the interface components in Photoshop Elements in the left-to-right, top-to-bottom order that one would find them. If you've encountered something you're unsure about in the course of working in Photoshop Elements, this is the place to look for it. It's also where you'll find a few task-related, command-based exercises for operations that don't quite fit anywhere else in the book.

Note	*Photoshop Elements has a few features that aren't easily categorized to fit the subjects in other chapters in this book. However, you will probably consider some of these features the most valuable in the entire program—so we can't very well leave them out of this book. The how-to exercises for most of these orphans are found in this chapter. (If you think of a better place to put them, give us a call.)*

If you are already an experienced Photoshop user, you might think you can skip much of this chapter. Before you do, though, you should know that Photoshop Elements goes about its business in many new and innovative ways that demand a serious look. Following are some important new features in Photoshop Elements that make it much easier to perform routine jobs in a hurry:

- Auto-commands that perform an image repair such as color balance or exposure correction in one or a few keystrokes

- Effects that you can accomplish by dragging an icon that's graphically representative of that effect onto the workspace (Document window)

- Wizard-type hints that amount to a whole manual of online in-context help

- Recipes that let you perform task-oriented, complex (but often needed) jobs by following online instructions

Those who have either been using other (probably less capable) image-processing programs and those who are new to image processing will find this chapter an invaluable map to any Photoshop Elements function and its purpose. It not only points out the physical location of each of the program's functional components, but it tells the reader when each of those components is likely to appear, encapsulates what problems are most likely to be solved by a component, and provides some general hints about how best to use those components. Each description is followed by a sidebar that tells you which of this book's task-oriented chapters covers specific ways in which you can use each tool and component. Come to think of it, even if you are an experienced image editor, you'll probably learn lots of things you weren't aware of before. We certainly did in writing it.

The Splash Screen

Splash screens are hardly mentioned in most computer how-to books. That's a shame because you can find lots of valuable information on a splash screen, and you can get to it any time the program is running. Of course, the splash screen is the first thing you see after you click the Photoshop Elements desktop icon or use any of your operating system's other devices for starting up a program. Figure 3-1 shows what a splash screen looks like.

You can find out a lot about Photoshop Elements by examining the splash screen, such as to whom the program is registered (if you see a name other than the person who's computer you're using, you know that the program has probably been illegally copied), the exact version number, the product serial number with the last four digits hidden for privacy, all the copyright information, and the names of the people who were primarily responsible for developing the product.

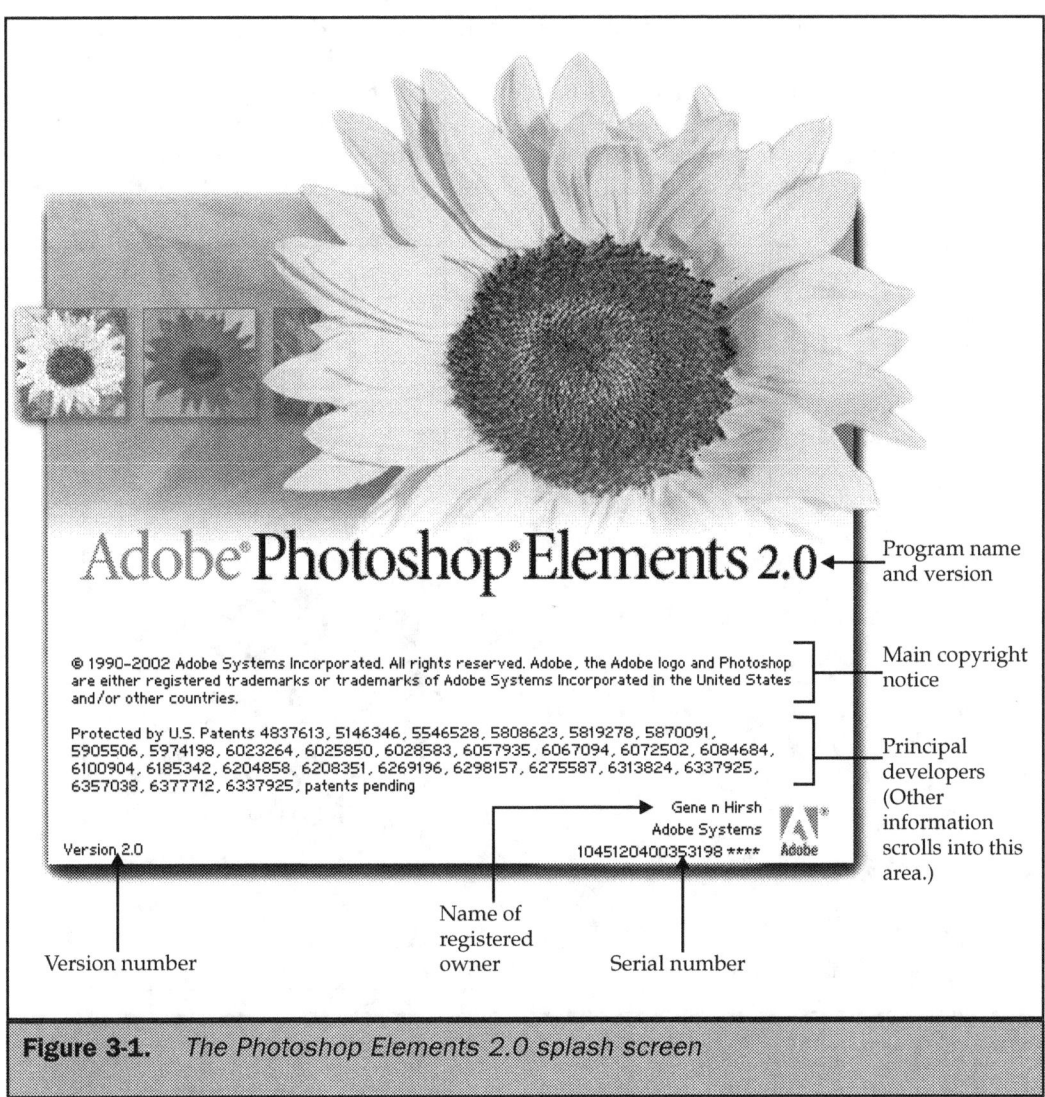

Figure 3-1. *The Photoshop Elements 2.0 splash screen*

You can find out even more by calling up the splash screen after you've already opened Photoshop Elements by choosing Help | About Photoshop Elements. If you wait a few moments, the information in small type below the Elements logo will begin to scroll. It will list all the patents associated with the product and all the patented programs and technologies that have been licensed from other companies. Eventually, the splash screen will also reveal the name of practically everyone who's ever been associated with the program—even the development team in India.

The Welcome Screen

After you have started the program and the splash screen has done its thing, Photoshop Elements 2.0 presents a redesigned Welcome screen, shown in Figure 3-2. If you tire of the Welcome screen or find it an annoying interruption after you've learned the program well, just click the Show This Screen At Startup check box to toggle it off (deselect it). If you or another user of your computer wants it to appear later, choose Window | Welcome and the Welcome screen will appear. Select the check box at the bottom of the

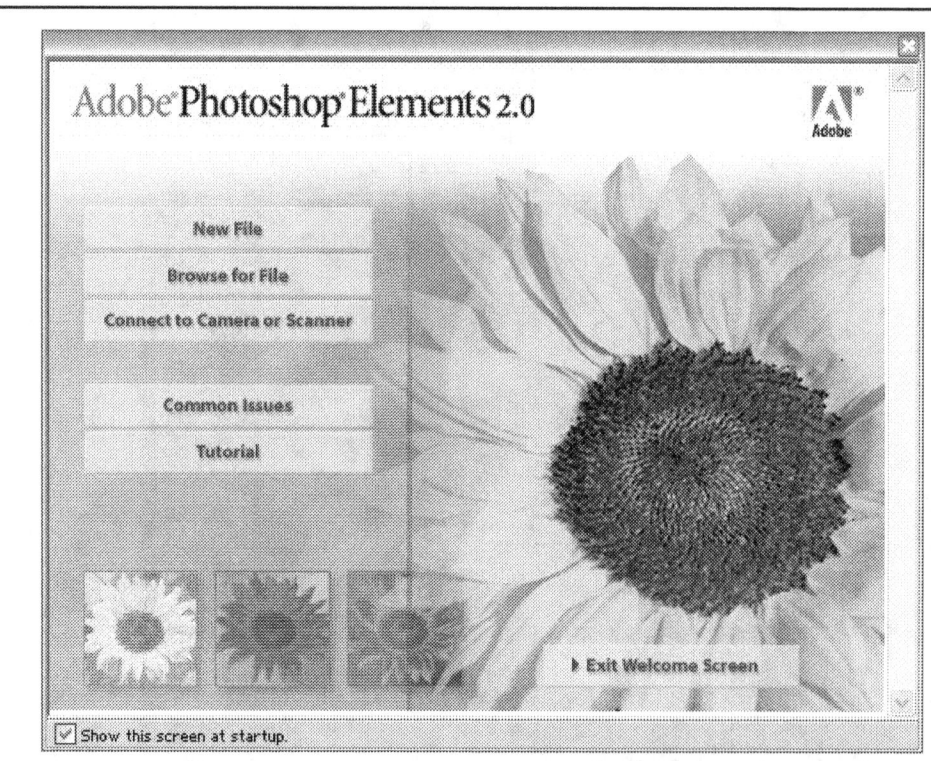

Figure 3-2. *The Welcome screen*

screen that says "Show this screen at startup." The screen will once again appear automatically on program startup.

Note   *If you use your operating system directly to open a specific file or files in Photoshop Elements, Photoshop Elements will skip the Welcome screen when it opens. Once you've gotten past the Splash screen and its program loading messages, you'll see the Photoshop Elements interface with the Document window(s) for the files you want opened and the files loaded.*

New File

Clicking the New File button opens the New file dialog box, shown in Figure 3-3. Enter the name of your new file in the Name field. You can choose from any of a number of preset document sizes from the Preset Sizes drop-down menu, or choose Custom and enter size dimensions of your choice. If you have already copied a document to the clipboard, that document's size will appear by default. You can choose any of Photoshop Elements' supported Color modes from the Mode drop-down menu (don't confuse these with blending modes, which perform an entirely unrelated function that you can read about in Chapter 9).

When you open the new file, it won't yet contain an image. You can click one of the radio buttons in the Contents section to designate whether you want the Document window to be white, whatever the current background color happens to be, or transparent.

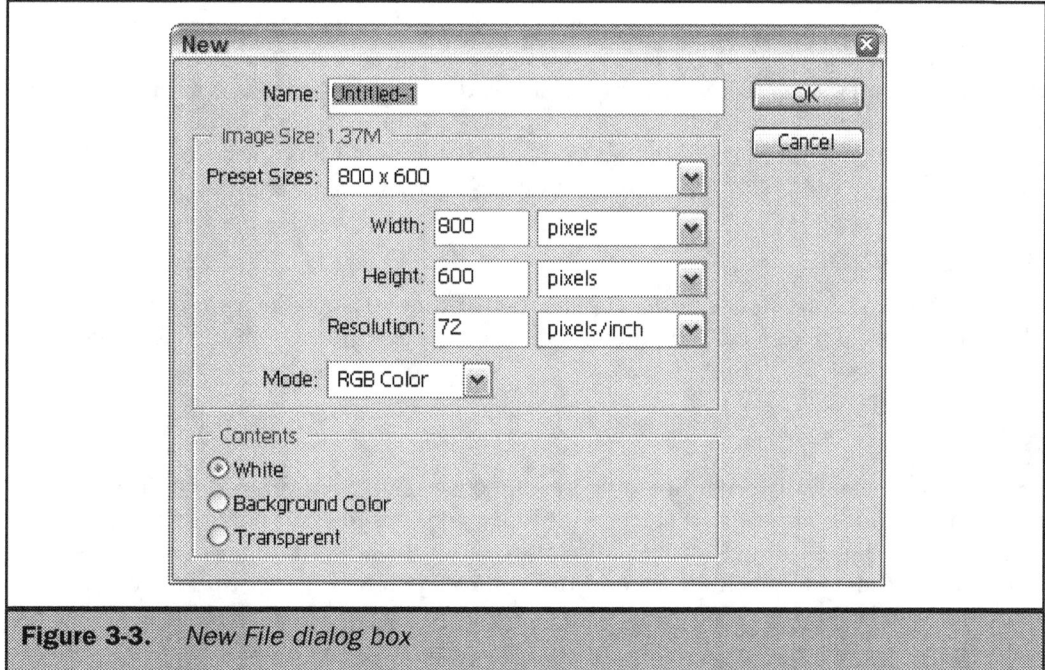

Figure 3-3.   *New File dialog box*

If you choose Transparent, no Background Layer (see Chapter 8 for more on the Background Layer), the first layer will be automatically numbered 0. When you have chosen or entered the options you want, click OK. A new Document window will appear just as you've specified it.

If, at that point, you have an image in the clipboard that you've copied from another document (possibly in another application) and you want to place it in your new file, choose Edit | Paste and that image will appear on its own layer. If you haven't specified another document size in the New dialog box, the image will precisely fill the canvas and be automatically centered in it. If you have specified a different size, your pasted document will still be centered in the Document window but will either extend past its boundaries or will only partially fill them, depending on its own native size and resolution in relationship to the size and resolution of the new document.

Browse for File

Clicking the Browse For File button will open Photoshop Elements' File Browser. The File Browser allows you to search for a photo visually, rather than having to depend on its name or a tiny icon. You can discover much more about the File Browser in Chapter 4 and Chapter 10, which is all about collecting, cataloging, and managing photos—not only through Photoshop Elements 2.0's much enhanced File Browser, but also in the context of whatever operating system you use.

Connect to Camera or Scanner

To connect to a digital camera or scanner you will need to install a Twain-compatible driver. When it is properly installed, you will see the device listed in the menu that opens when you choose File | Import. Click the device and the interface for that device will appear. See the instructions for your camera or scanner for operating information. If you have any doubts about whether your particular camera is supported, check your camera's documentation or check the Adobe web site (www.adobe.com, of course).

Common Issues

Clicking the Common Issues button opens the Common Issues Recipes found in the How To (Recipes In Version 1.0) palette. For a complete rundown on the How To palette, take a look at Chapter 4.

Tutorial

The Tutorial is basically an online help system organized according to the functional components of the program. It starts with Release Notes to keep you apprised of any last-minute changes or bugs, moves into giving you a basic system map (an abbreviated version of what's in this chapter), and then shows you how to set up Photoshop

Elements. From there, it moves on to providing the functional category lessons on such topics as fixing photos; using layers; understanding the use of the new painting tools; and applying filters, layer styles, and other special effects. Of course, this is only a partial list of its contents—which include 21 "chapters," plus a glossary and lists of shortcuts for Mac and PC. (By the way, shortcuts later in this chapter show you the equivalent keys for Mac/PC according to the much-less-crowded and isolationist convention used by this book; for example, the shortcut for lift selection contents to new layer is CMD/CTRL+J.)

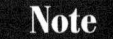 *It is a good idea to read the release notes, especially before you run the program for the first time. These notes often include important information that did not make it into the standard documentation, and some of this information may be necessary for the proper operation of Elements and to avoid unnecessary calls to Customer Support.*

Exit Welcome Screen

Clicking this button exits the Welcome screen, not Photoshop Elements. You'll find yourself in the regular Photoshop Elements user interface with no document or window open. You can, of course, open any image file from any standard source, such as a camera, or start a new document.

Show This Screen at Startup

Once you get used to working in Photoshop Elements, you might start to find the Welcome screen more annoying than helpful. Major kudos go to Adobe for having the courtesy to place this check box conveniently so that you can deselect it. When you do, the Welcome screen will stop appearing automatically. Choose Window | Welcome to reload the Welcome screen.

The Menu Bar

The Menu bar is the part of the interface that Photoshop Elements shares with every other application made for either Windows or Mac, as well as most any other operating system that uses a graphical user interface (often called the GUI— a "point-and-click" interface that doesn't require that you type commands at the command prompt on a blank screen). It is this part of the interface that contains the title for each category of program commands. It is also here that you access all those Photoshop Elements operations that start with a command (as opposed to starting with the use of a tool, or commands that appear in a palette or dialog box menu as a result of opening that palette or dialog box).

In Photoshop Elements' Menu bar are ten items. Below each of these items is a definition of the application for each command on that menu.

File Menu

All the commands required for transferring, saving, importing, managing, automating, batch processing, and printing files are located in the File menu. It even includes a command that will create a panorama from a sequence of files. Each of these commands is individually described in the sections that follow, along with any keyboard shortcuts that can be employed.

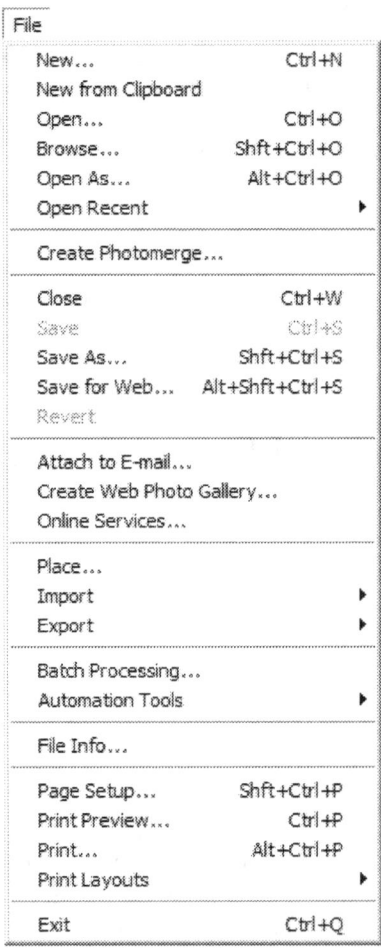

New

Choosing New or pressing CMD/CTRL+N opens a dialog box (shown back in Figure 3-3) for opening a new file that contains no image. You can specify the size of the file, choose the size from a menu of often-used formats, specify the resolution of the file, and choose the background color, as discussed earlier in the chapter.

New From Clipboard

This command opens the contents of the clipboard as a Photoshop bitmap. If the image is a vector file created in an illustration or drawing program (such as Illustrator, Freehand, Flash, or CorelDRAW), it will be *rasterized* (converted to a bitmap) and can no longer be scaled to any size or proportion without loosing image fidelity.

Open

Choosing Open or pressing CMD/CTRL+O allows you to open a Photoshop-compatible (and PhotoDeluxe, or .pdd, –compatible) file from any type of storage device that your operating system recognizes as being attached to your computer or to your computer's network. The Open command utilizes a typical Open dialog box for this operation that can perform tasks similar to those of your operating system's file browser. This dialog box is shown in Figure 3-4.

Note   *All Photoshop-compatible files are also Photoshop Elements compatible.*

The following sections discuss the options in the Open dialog box.

Look In Menu   This command lists the folders in which you can look for your files and lets you navigate through them.

Navigation Icons   These let you navigate to the main organizational resources for locating files on your computer or network.

Image Thumbnails (or Other Methods of Viewing)   Lists all files in the folder if you have chosen All Types from the Files Of Type menu, or only files of a specific file type (such as JPEG or Photoshop PSD) if you have chosen a specific file type from the same menu.

If you place your cursor over a file folder in this area, a Help balloon shows you the folder size and a brief glimpse of the listed contents in that folder. If you place your cursor over a filename in this area, a Help balloon shows you the file type, date last modified, and size of that file.

File Name Field and Menu   You can enter any filename by typing it directly into the File Name field, or you can click the adjacent down arrow to choose from any of the last 25 files you've opened from this computer, regardless of their location. This is handy if you have a network and a horde of external drives.

Files Of Type Drop-Down Menu   As mentioned, the Files Of Type drop-down menu lets you choose whether you want to see a listing of all types of files that can be opened in Photoshop Elements or just those of a particular Photoshop-compatible file type. Photoshop Elements is compatible with Photoshop-compatible files , but it doesn't open those that are in color modes that aren't supported by Photoshop Elements, such as CMYK or Lab, until you've answered Yes to a dialog box that asks whether you want to convert the file to RGB mode.

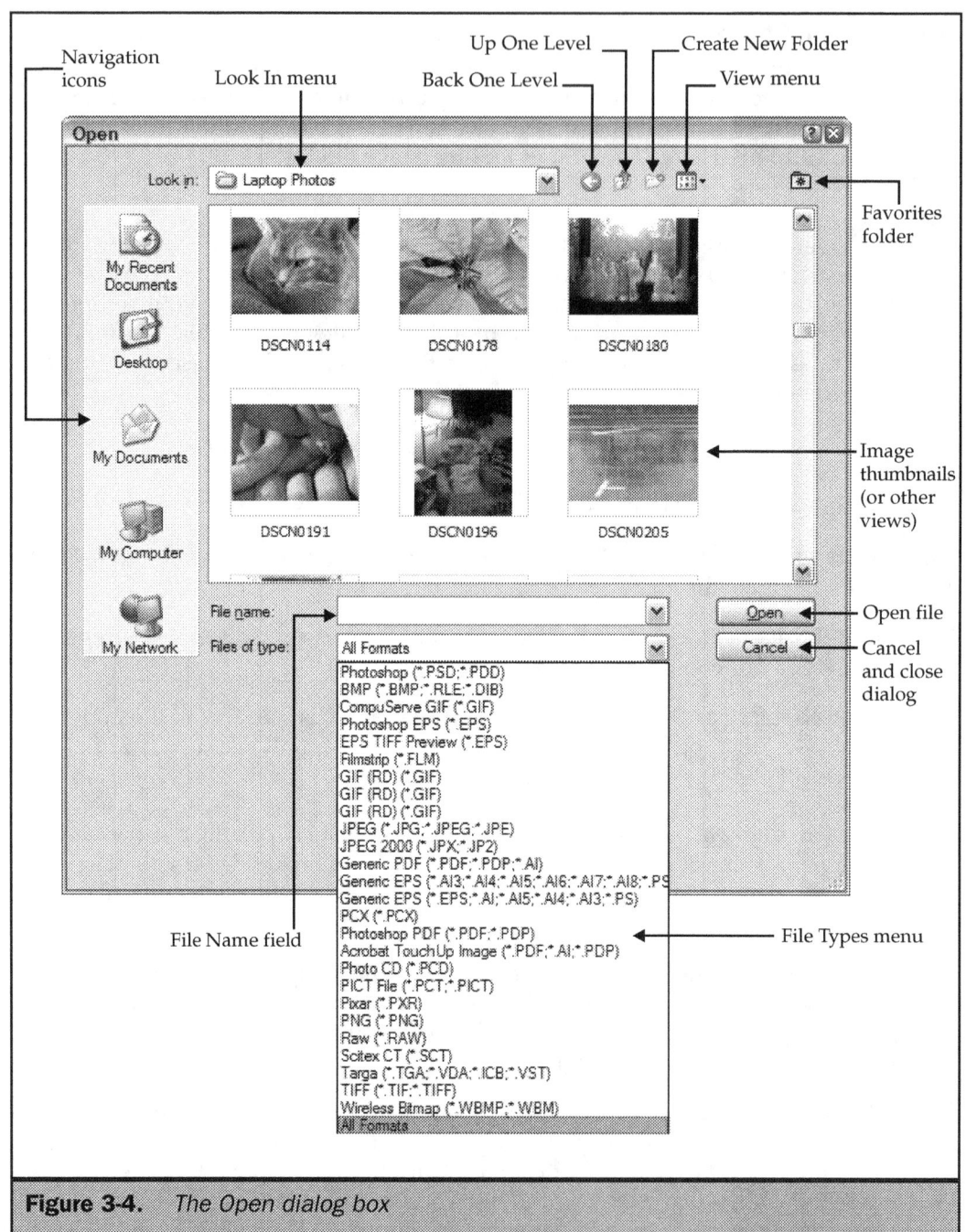

Figure 3-4. *The Open dialog box*

Back   Clicking the Back button moves you back to the directory structure level that preceded the one to which you've presently navigated. If you haven't proceeded through other directories, the Back button will be *inactive*.

Up One Level   Clicking this button moves you up one level in the hierarchical structure of folder organization. If you are already at the top level, the Up One Level button is inactive.

Create New Folder   This button creates a new folder within the directory in which you are presently located. When you click the Create New Folder button, an empty folder appears in the directory window and the title "New Folder" automatically appears highlighted in the name field, so all you have to do is type in a new name. You can double-click the filename to highlight it and rename it. If you want to change just a part of the name, highlight only the letters you want to change and retype them.

View Menu   Here you can choose how you want your files listed. The following illustrations show how the files are presented for each menu command. As you can see, you have considerable flexibility in trading off visual information for the ability to see more filenames at once.

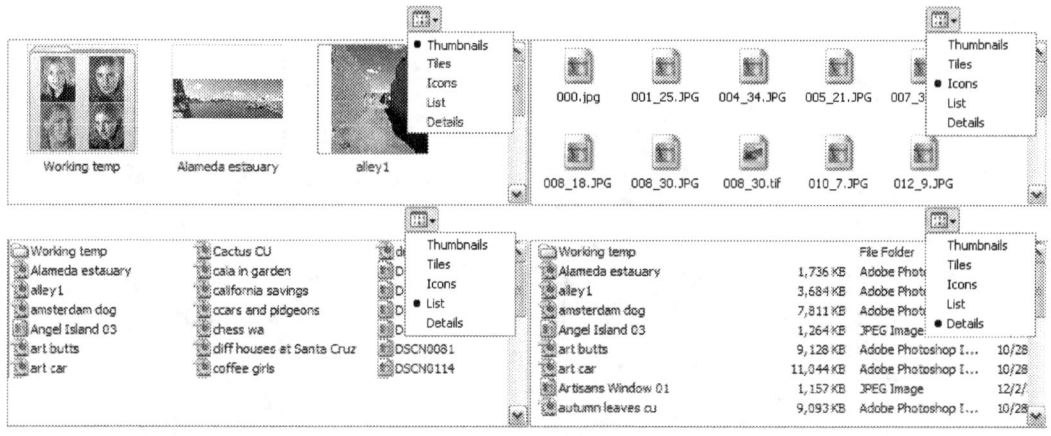

Note   *When you're in a hurry to see all the files in a crowded folder, viewing as List or Details will show the files much faster than any of the visual modes—especially Thumbnails. On the other hand, Thumbnails are handy when you need to distinguish files whose content is visually similar—especially when it's difficult to provide unique and descriptive names to such files.*

Favorites   You can add a currently selected file to the list of files in the Favorites menu by choosing Add Favorite. To delete a file from the favorites list, choose Delete Favorite.

Open   Clicking the Open button loads the file whose name currently occupies the File Name field. Alternatively, you can open any file in the list by selecting it (clicking to highlight its name) and pressing RETURN/ENTER, or by double-clicking its name.

Cancel   Clicking this button closes the Open dialog box without loading any file.

Browse

Pressing SHIFT+CMD/CTRL+O opens the brand-new version of the Elements File Browser, which shows you thumbnails that are large enough to distinguish images by small details. When you open the Browser menu or glance at the Status bar under the window, you realize that this browser is much more versatile than the browser in version 1.0. (For more information on the File Browser, see Chapters 4 and 10.)

Choose Thumbnail Sizes   You can also now choose any of three thumbnail sizes (S, M, L, of course). The view in the smallest thumbnail size is similar to the icon-size view in Windows XP Explorer. It also provides more information about the file. In the following illustration, small thumbnails are at the left, medium are in the middle, and large are at the right.

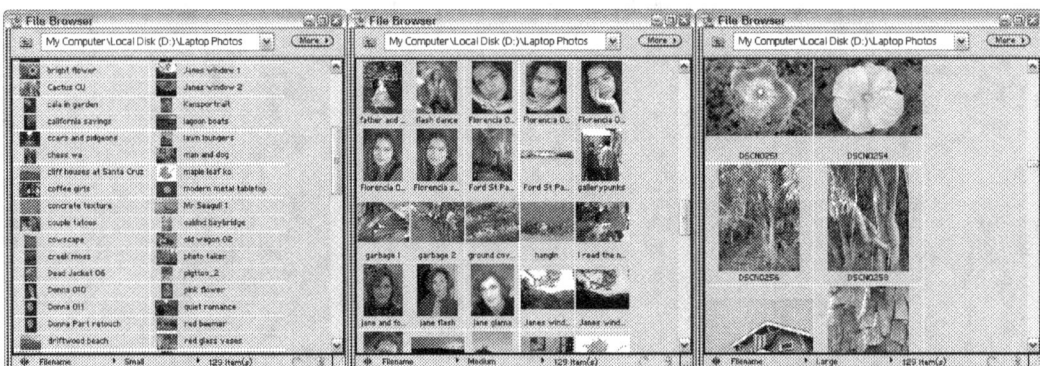

Being able to view smaller thumbnails has two advantages:

- The thumbnails generate quickly, so there's less waiting time if you have a slow computer or folders that contain more than one camera card full of images.
- It's faster to locate a specific group or category of files when you can see more files at once.

Expand or Contract the View   You can expand or contract the view, which turns on and off the column that holds the hierarchy directory. You can find out much more about the File Browser in Chapter 10.

Batch Rename Files   This command is especially useful. You can rename an entire directory while copying files to another directory, if you like. You can also highlight different files in the same directory, followed by a sequential number of any number of digits up to four, serial letters in either caps or lowercase, or the filename extension. However, you cannot place more than two of these components in the filename. The Browser's method of batch renaming may not sound nearly as handy as it is until you see an example of it, so take a look at the following illustration.

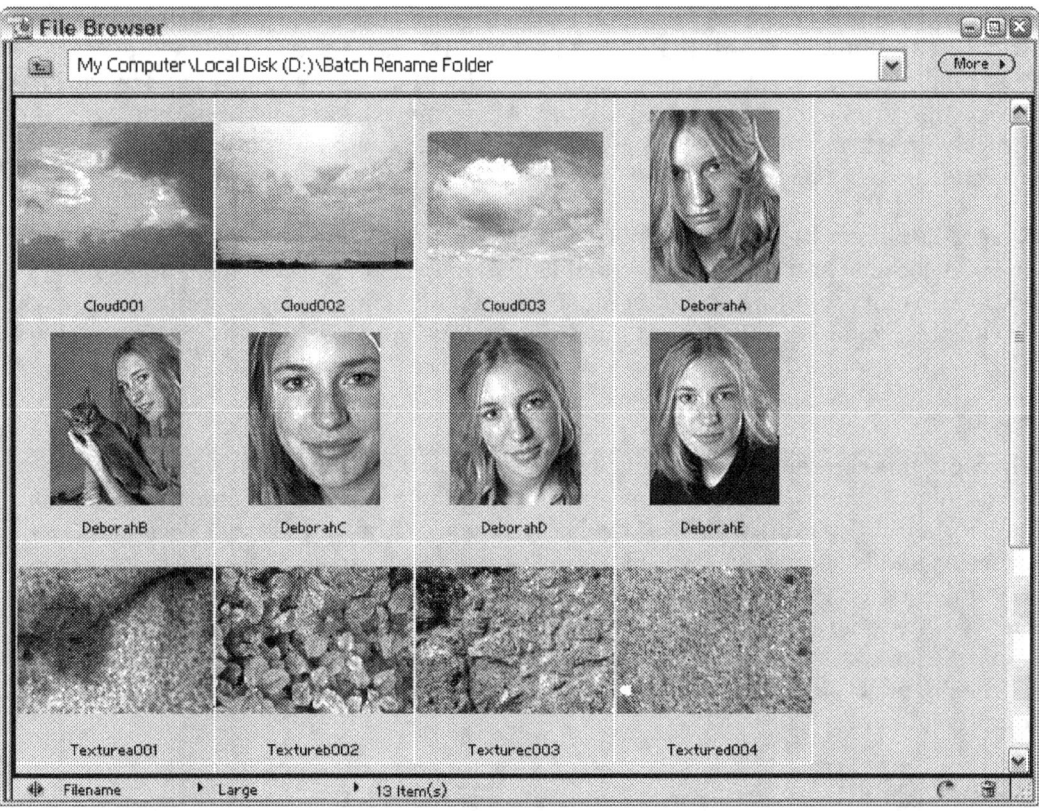

You'll notice that by giving each file in the group a filename that starts with a category name, the browser will automatically group together all the pictures in a category. This is a great way to keep your images organized. Because many cameras use the same naming sequence for each session, the batch renaming capability of the File Browser comes in handy for renaming digital photographs so they are nonrepetitive, and therefore can reside in the same folder.

Note	*You can create a group of category file names by adding a unique name to the first field and a sequence in the second field that will create a list of category file names (for example, Nature01, Nature02, and so on). Then, if you want to add still more information to the filename, you can run Batch Rename again. Use Document Name for the first field, which will use the names you just created, and choose something else, such as a date, for the second field. When the files are renamed, the date will be added on the filename. The names will appear as Nature01021202, Nature02021202, and so on. You can keep this up and add more information to the name as many times as you like—until you use up the 35 spaces that are legal in the latest version of most operating systems.*

Rotate Thumbnails Without Resampling the Image   You can rotate the image thumbnails 90 degrees clockwise or counterclockwise (press OPT/ALT+click) by clicking the rotation icon in the Browser's status bar. Alternatively, you can use the choices in the Browser Palette menu: Rotate 180, Rotate 90 CW (clockwise or right), or Rotate 90 CCW (counterclockwise or left).

Reveal Location In Finder/Explorer   Choosing this option actually takes you to the directory location of the file you have highlighted in the File Browser, opens an Explorer/ Finder directory window, and then highlights the file name, icon, or thumbnail for you. Of course, if you look at the top of the Browser window, you will also see the directory path nicely displayed.

Open As

Choosing this command or pressing OPT/ALT+CMD/CTRL+O opens the Open As dialog box, shown in Figure 3-5, which permits the opening of files in a format specified from the drop-down menu. This is useful when you want to open a file that does not have an extension and you know what the file format should be. It can also be a way to investigate the format of a file you are unsure of by trying to open it in different formats until you find the one that will open it. If the file in question will not open in any listed formats, it may be a file of an unsupported format or a corrupt file. If you open a file with no extension, make sure you add an extension when you resave it so you will be able to identify it later.

Open Recent

Choosing Open Recent pops up a submenu of the files you've opened most recently. The number of files in this list is limited to the number you entered in the Preferences dialog box. The default is 10.

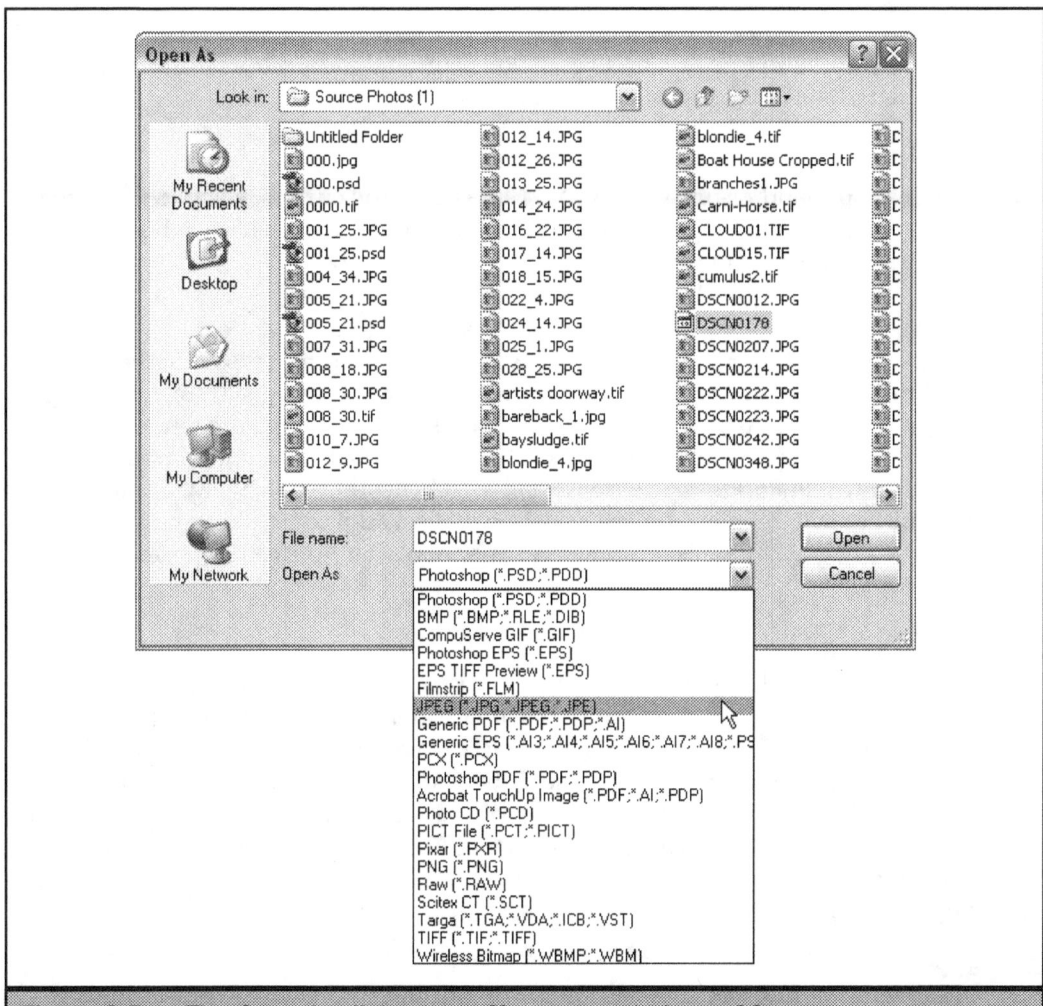

Figure 3-5. *The Open As dialog box offers many choices of formats.*

Create Photomerge

This command activates the Photomerge program that allows you to "stitch" together a series of digitized photographs that were shot in a panoramic method into a seamless panoramic photograph. See Chapter 2 for a detailed description on using Photomerge.

Close

Choosing this command or pressing CMD/CTRL+W immediately closes the currently active (selected) open file. This command does not close the program.

Save

Choosing this command or pressing CMD/CTRL+S saves the currently active file to the same file format and name as it was opened from. Any changes that have been made in the meantime will be kept in the end result.

Save As

Choosing this command or pressing SHIFT+CMD/CTRL+S operates in exactly the same way that it does in any other program that runs on your operating system. Choosing Save As opens the Save As dialog box, which allows you to change the name of the file, the file format, and the directory location of the file. This is the command to use when you need to protect the original file from change (which should be always—otherwise, you'll never be able to retrieve the original data when you find better ways of enhancing the image...which is guaranteed to happen after you've read some or all of this book).

Save For Web

Choosing this command or pressing OPT/ALT+SHIFT+CMD/CTRL+S opens a nearly full-screen dialog box designed to make it easier to choose those options that will ensure that JPEG, GIF, and PNG files are *optimized* (saved with the best compromises for a given image size and purpose to ensure the fastest download speed consistent with acceptable image quality). The Save For Web dialog box also makes it possible to create animated GIFs automatically by converting Photoshop Elements layers into sequential animation frames. The considerations for these options are complex enough to be the subject of several books and are discussed in depth in Chapter 18.

Revert

Choosing this option closes the current active window and reopens the last-saved version of the file. This is an excellent way to go back more steps than you've been able to save with the Undo History (or Step Backward) command. Be sure the first thing you do with an original file is issue the Image | Duplicate Image command, and then save the duplicated image. The duplicated image is automatically renamed. Then remember to save each time you think you might want to go back to that state at a later time. Photoshop Elements doesn't allow Snapshots in the Undo History palette, so there's no other way to go back further than the maximum number of History States you've set in the Edit | Preferences | General dialog box.

Attach to E-mail

One of the biggest problems with sending photos along with your e-mails is remembering where you put the pictures you want to send. Now you can send images at the instant you finish working on them. You won't have time to forget the location of the folder in which you buried them. As soon as the picture is ready (or any other time you come across a picture you want to send), just choose the Attach To E-mail command. Unless you've already resized it for the Web, converted it to JPEG, and optimized it, you'll get a warning dialog box, shown next, that tells you that you need to either do all these things or let Photoshop Elements do them automatically. If you click the Auto Convert button, you'll see Photoshop Elements resize and optimize the file in JPEG format, and your web browser's dialog box for creating a new e-mail will open. The file that was originally in the active document window will already appear in the attachment field. All you have to do is fill in the other fields as necessary, write a letter (if you like), and press the Send button.

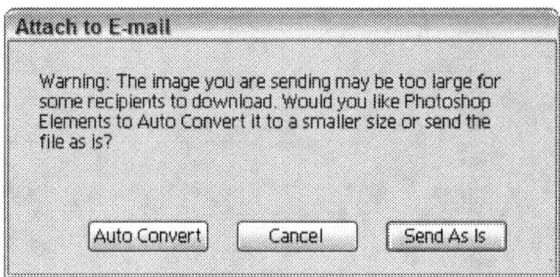

In the warning dialog box, if you click the Send As Is button, you will attach the file in its current form and size with no compression. Because most ISPs limit the size of e-mail attachments to as little as 1 megabyte in some cases, it is possible that the send may be refused if the file is too large. The size will also affect the download rate. Large files will increase upload and download times and cause the recipient to wait while a large file transfers. Unless you have a specific reason for sending high-resolution images, click the Auto Convert button in the dialog box.

Create Web Photo Gallery

If you take a lot of pictures and have always wanted to put them on a web site but just don't have the time, an angel called Adobe has been listening to your wishes. Although this isn't a new feature, quite a few new (and better-styled) templates are available in Photoshop Elements 2.0.

You'll find all the gritty details about using the Create web Photo Gallery command in Chapter 18. For now, know that it lets you create a photographer's web portfolio in a matter of minutes. It will even do a decent job of making this portfolio look professional. If you have even a cursory knowledge of HTML, you can easily change the code it automatically writes to tweak it in any direction you like.

Here's the short story about how it works: Place all the images you want to add to this particular portfolio into one directory folder, and give the files names that will also make good captions. There is no need to resize, convert, or optimize the images. All that will be done for you. Just choose Create Web Photo Gallery and the Web Photo

Gallery dialog box appears. In that dialog box, you'll find options that let you perform a pretty complete customization. Once again, check out Chapter 18 for complete details.

Online Services

You must be connected to the Internet to take advantage of this command. If you are connected, the Online Services Wizard appears.

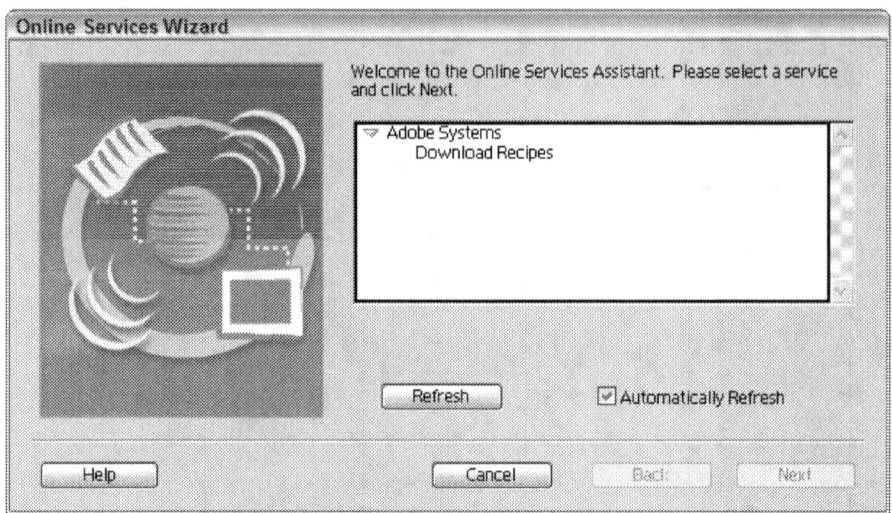

A list of services, including additional Photoshop Elements templates, recipes, and so forth, will appear. This list is "live," and Adobe promises that it will keep growing as time goes by. You can download any of these additions and tutorials by clicking the name of a service in the list, clicking the Next button, and then continuing to follow the instructions that appear.

Place

Choosing this command lets you import vector files from PDF (Acrobat), Adobe Illustrator, and EPS files to an open and active Photoshop Elements bitmap document, automatically *rasterizing* (converts vector to pixel matrix bitmaps) them in the process. Vector art is created out of lines, curves, and filled areas that are defined with mathematical formulas. This means the image is created on-the-fly at any resolution, making them resolution independent. When you rasterize vector art, you freeze it at a set resolution and convert it to a matrix of pixels that can be resized only with interpolation algorithms. If the vector artwork is larger than the Photoshop file, it is automatically proportionally resized to fit. In any case, this is accompanied by a bounding box that lets you resize, transform (with all the standard Photoshop Elements Transform options), and place the artwork before *rendering* it (converting it to bitmap). Rendering occurs when you click the OK (check mark) button in the Options bar. If you decide you want to cancel the operation, click the Cancel button (NO sign) in the Options bar.

Import

The Import command differs from the Place command in that it is used exclusively to import images from specialized or special-purpose formats and from devices whose drivers write a routine that places their name on this menu. This includes many digital film card readers, digital cameras, scanners, and so forth.

Export

The Export command remains inactive unless you have special plug-in modules that are designed to save in formats not covered with the Save As command.

Batch Processing

Batch Processing works by performing one or more operations on all the files that reside in a folder designated in the Batch dialog box. The Photoshop Elements Batch Processing command can't execute macros (Photoshop actions) on a whole series of files, so it is much less versatile than its Photoshop counterpart. In fact, it can automate only three types of operations:

- **File type** Converts all the files in the folder to a single file type.
- **Image size** Forces all the target folders images into a given height or width and a specified resolution. There's also the option to force resizing to both a given height *and* width by toggling off the Constrain Proportions check box.
- **File renaming** The options are the same as for the Batch Rename Files command on the Browser Palette menu. The difference is that here you can do the renaming while performing either or both of the preceding two operations and that you have to rename an entire folder of images rather than being able to batch-rename a selected group of specific files.

When you execute the Batch Processing command, the Batch dialog box appears, shown in Figure 3-6.

Here's how you go about batch processing an entire folder of images:

1. Choose File | Batch Processing. The Batch dialog box appears.

2. In the Batch dialog box, from the Files To Convert drop-down menu, choose among the open files, imported files from a PDF file, or a source folder.

   - If you choose Folder, click the Source button. A Finder/Explorer-type window opens and lets you navigate to the folder that contains the images you want to batch-process. If you also want to include files in the folder's subfolders, click to select the Include All Subfolders check box.

   - If you choose Import, the program will prompt you for the location of the PDF file when the batch runs.

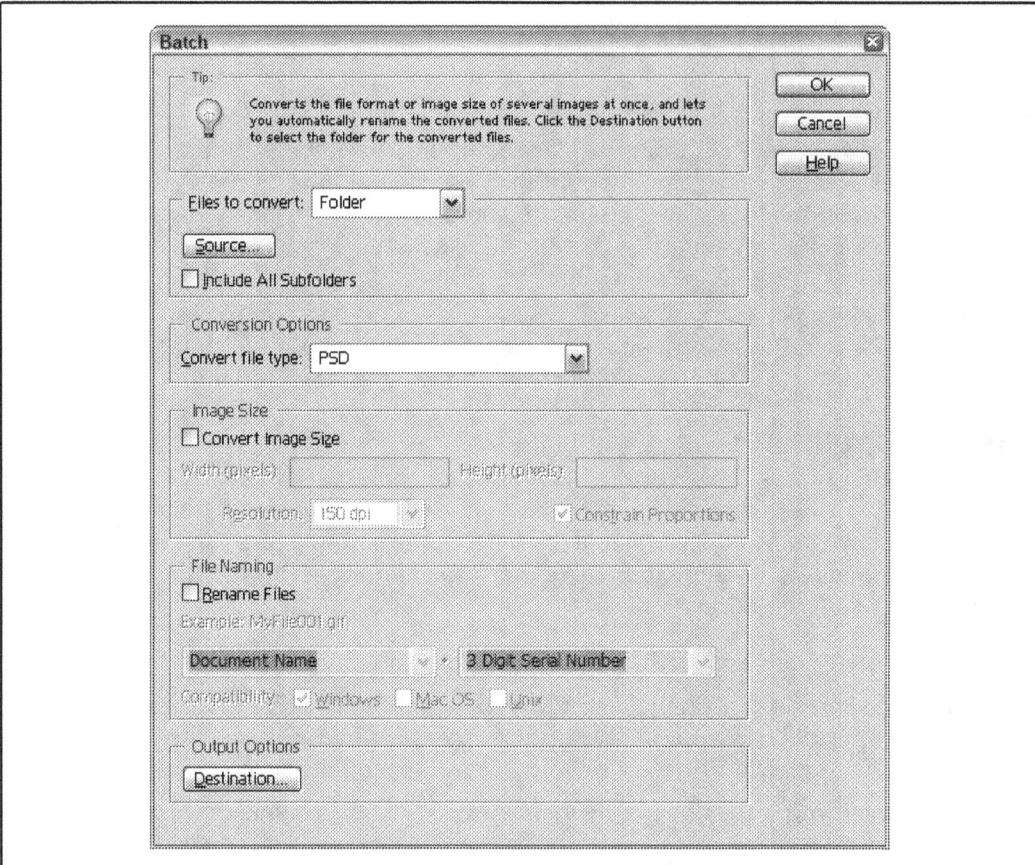

Figure 3-6. *The Batch dialog box provides options to batch-process all of the files in a folder you specify*

3. To convert files from their existing type to a uniform specific type, choose the target file type from the Convert File Type drop-down menu. Note that no check box is here to allow you to ignore converting all the files to one specific type, so your files will be converted to the chosen type in any case. Therefore, you'd better make sure you've chosen a type that you like (of course, you can always do the conversion over again).

4. To convert the existing files to be or fit within a specific target image size, select the Convert Image Size check box. If you want to make sure the images fit within a specific height or width, select the Constrain Proportions check box, and then enter the height or width you want the image to fit within into the appropriately labeled field.

5. To change both the height and width of all files to the same target dimension, deselect the Convert Image Size check box. Enter the appropriate dimensions into both the Height and Width fields.

6. To rename files according to a specified scheme, select the Rename Files check box. If you want the filenames to start with a particular name, enter that name into the text box on the left. If you want the current filename to be used, choose any of the capitalization variations called Document Name from the drop-down menu on the left. To add a serial number, serial letter, date, or file extension to the name, choose the variation you want from the drop-down menu on the right.

7. To make sure that your converted files don't overwrite the originals, choose a different destination folder from the one that contains the files from which you are converting. Click the Destination button. A file browsing dialog box will appear, and you can navigate to or create a different folder.

Note   *If you want to lengthen the filename by adding any of the other choices, simply run the Batch command again on the files in the target folder (the one in which the converted files have been placed). Be sure to set the file type conversion to the same type to which the files have already been converted and leave the Image Size check box unselect. Document Name should also appear in the left field so that all of the existing filenames will be retained. Add to the filename by choosing any of the options in the menu on the right.*

Automation Tools

One assumes that other automation tools will be added to this menu as time (and new versions) of Photoshop Elements goes by. However, at the moment, only two automation tools are available: PDF Slideshow and Multi-Page PDF to PSD. PDF stands for Portable Document File, the native format for Adobe Acrobat, which makes it possible to design a document on one computer and have it look the same on any other computer (exclusive of color limitations) or output device—as long as that device has a driver or plug-in installed that can read PDF files.

PDF Slideshow   You could own Photoshop Elements for years and not even realize that this (universally) handy command is available. It creates a slideshow that will run on your computer, or anyone else's computer that has a PDF (Acrobat) reader, or on any web site that can display PDF files. If you're running the slideshow on a computer (maybe from one of those cool little mini-CDs which some people use to print their business cards), each picture is automatically sized to fill the screen.

Here's all it takes to make a PDF slideshow:

1. Choose File | Automation Tools | PDF Slideshow. The PDF Slideshow dialog box appears, as shown in Figure 3-7.

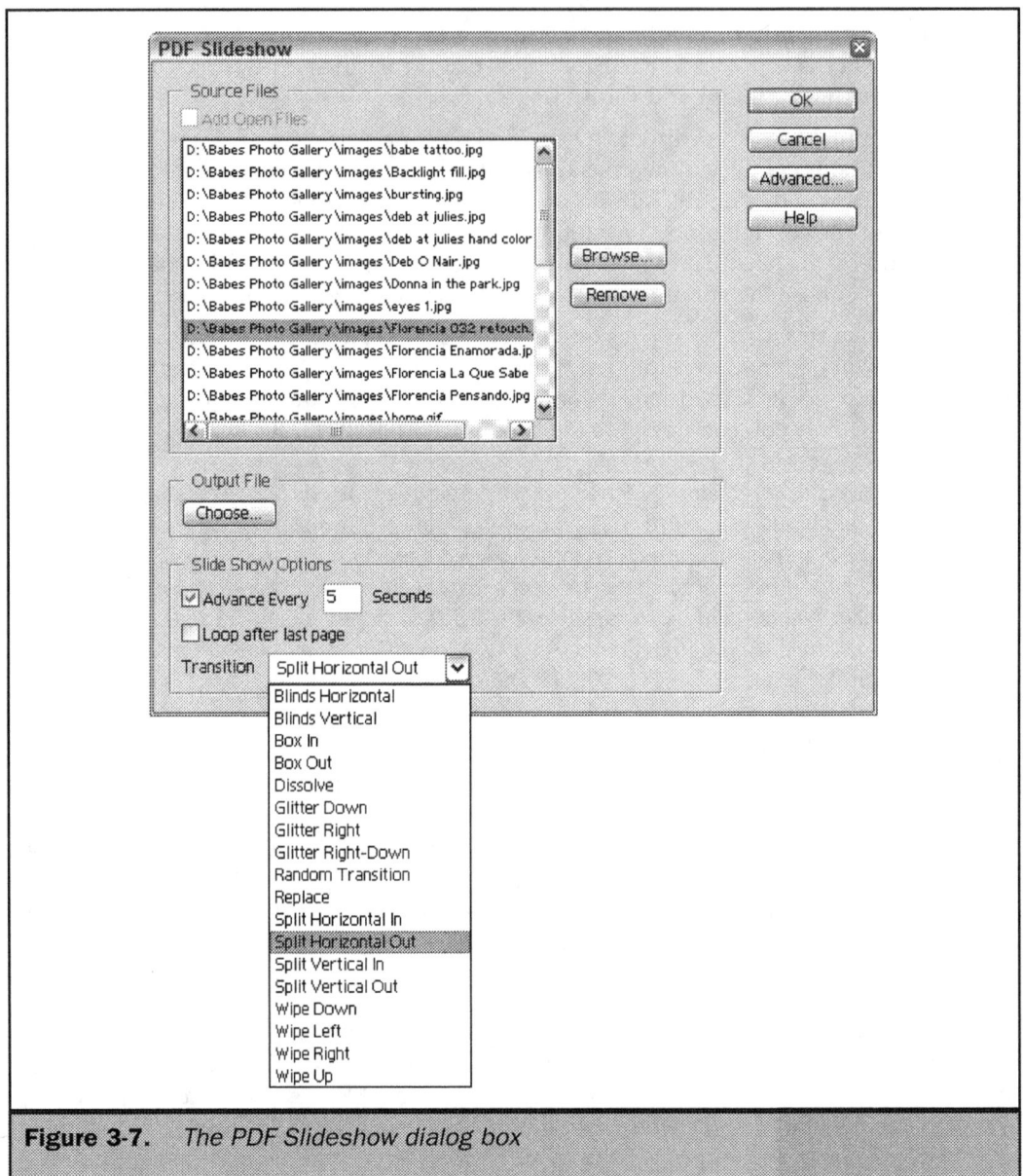

Figure 3-7. *The PDF Slideshow dialog box*

2. To choose which images will be included in the slideshow, do one of the following:

■ Select the Add Open Files check box. All the files that are currently open in Photoshop Elements will be included in the slideshow.

■ Click the Browse button to open the Photoshop Elements Browser. You can then visually choose the images you want to include/exclude from the slideshow.

3. Click the Choose button so that you can use a file browsing window to navigate to and name the file to which you'd like to add your slideshow.

Note

If you want to be able to show a portfolio at a moment's notice, place it on your computer's desktop. Then, all you have to do is double-click its icon and it starts playing. You might even want to download one of the shareware icon-making utilities from the Web and use it to convert a photograph to the icon for the slideshow. (www.download.com will present you with several choices to try.)

4. Set the optional variables for your slideshow in the Slide Show Options area: If you want the slides to advance automatically, select the Advance Every __ Seconds check box. You should enter a number of seconds in the Seconds field, although the default 5 seconds seems to be just about right. If you want the slideshow to repeat after the last slide, click to add a check mark to the Loop After Last Page check box. Finally, you can choose from a long list of transitions to use between slides (but it will be the same transition of the same length for every slide).

5. Click OK to create the slideshow. Photoshop Elements does all the work for you. To play the slideshow, double-click its icon.

Note

If you are going to create a slideshow that will play on unknown computers and (especially) display systems, be sure to preprocess your images so that they will look their best on any screen. It's best if you calibrate for a screen gamma of 2.0, so you'll get the best display gamma to compromise between the standard Mac gamma of 1.8 and the standard Windows gamma of 2.2. You might also want to make a slide that instructs the viewer to adjust his or her monitor with Adobe Gamma or a screen calibration program, and that LCD screens (especially those on most laptops) should be viewed so that the viewer's eyes are absolutely parallel and perpendicular to the screen.

Multi-Page PDF to PSD   We're not sure why you'd want to rasterize (turn into a bitmap) a PDF file that consists of multiple pages of type, but nevertheless you *can* do this with hardly any effort. It could be a nice way to get a spec sheet onto a Web page or into a presentation. Here's how you'd want to do it:

1. Choose File | Automation Tools | Multi-Page PDF To PSD. The Convert Multi-Page PDF To PSD dialog box appears, shown in Figure 3-8.

2. To locate the PDF file you want to rasterize, click the Choose button. A file navigation dialog box will appear. Locate the file you want to rasterize, highlight that file, and click OK. The name and location of the file will appear below the Choose button.

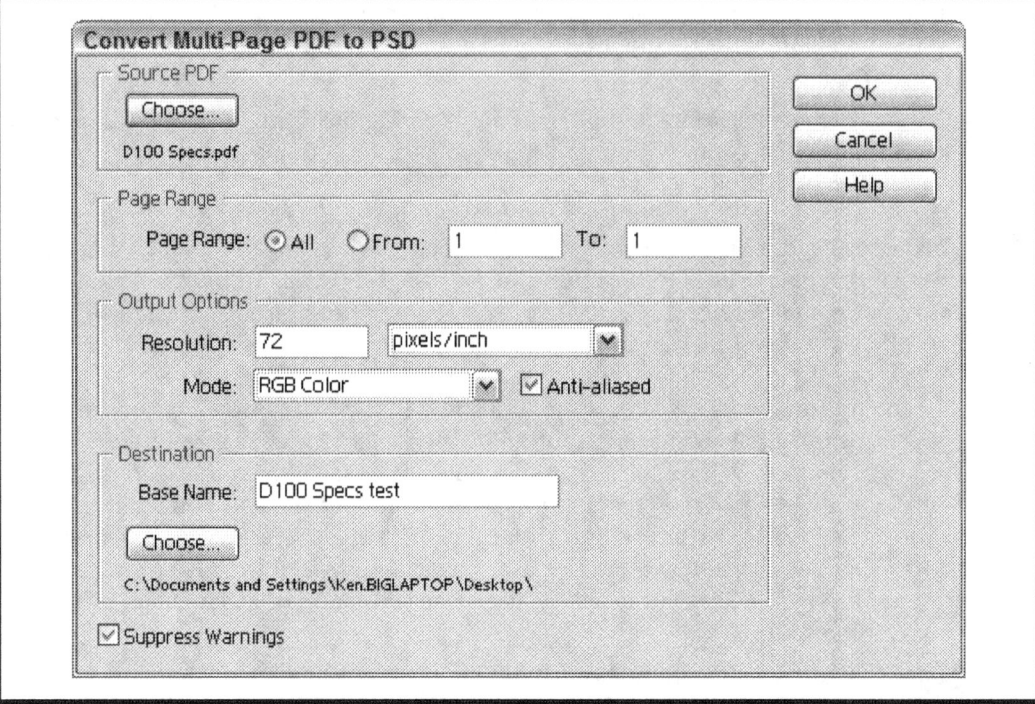

Figure 3-8.   *If you want to turn a PDF into a bitmap, use the Convert Multi-Page PDF To PSD dialog box.*

3. Just as you would in a printer dialog box, click the All radio button if you want to rasterize the whole document (each page will appear in its own file), or click the From radio button (only one radio button in a group can be on at the same time) and enter the first page in the range in the From field and the last in the To field.

4. To determine the size of the file (and the readability of small type), enter the resolution of the file in the Resolution field and choose from pixels per inch or pixels per centimeter (cm) from the Resolution drop-down menu.

5. Choose between RGB color and Grayscale from the Mode drop-down menu.

6. If you want the edges of type and curves to appear as smooth as possible, select the Anti-aliased check box.

7. In the Destination area, you can enter a new name for the file—or just keep the old name, which will already appear. There's no danger of overwriting the original because you are creating a different file type.

8. Decide where you want to store the new file, and click the Choose button to bring up a file navigation window that will let you navigate to that desired location. When you've found it, place the name of the file in the Base Name field and click OK.

9. To render your file as a bitmap, click OK.

File Info

Choose this command when you want to know all about the currently active document (image). Choose File | Info, and the File Info dialog box appears.

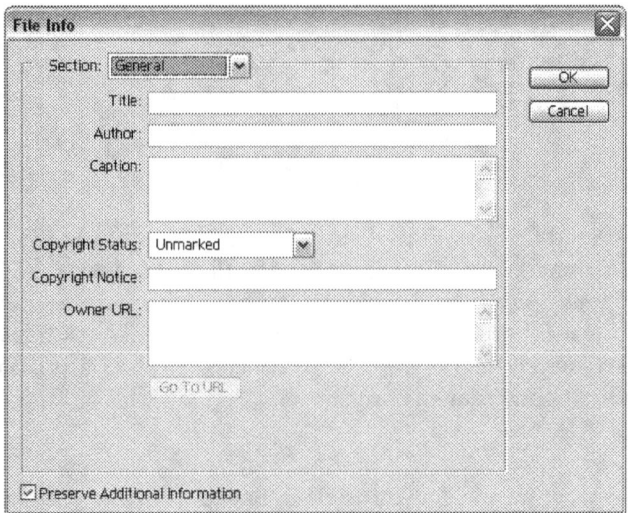

Two functions are served in this dialog box:

■ You can enter your own information about the file, as shown in the preceding illustration (and the entries in some of these fields can be made to appear automatically when you create a web portfolio).

■ You can view all the EXIF (Exchangeable Image File) information about the file, as shown next. This format is designed to allow compliant devices to attach and read extended information to image files.

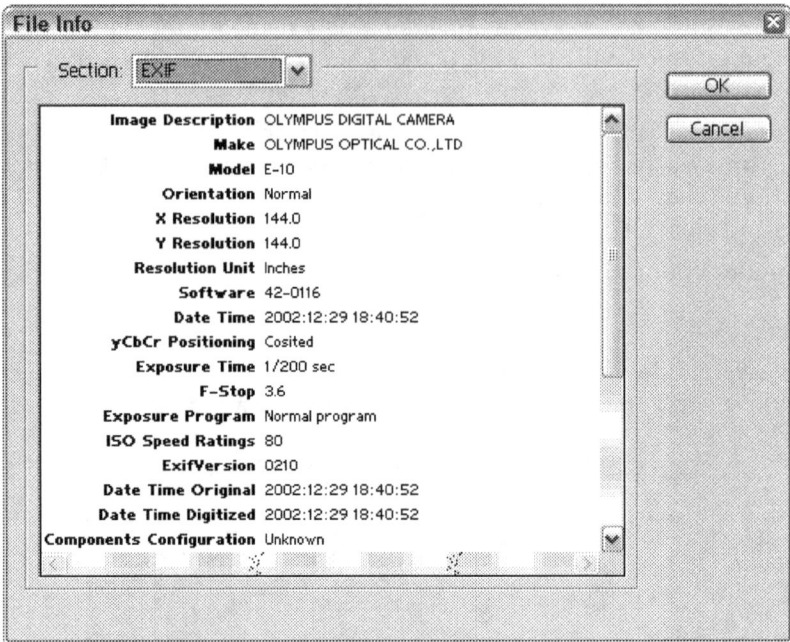

After you've entered information, it stays in the header of the file, even if you save the file to another format. We haven't tested them all, but for sure the File Info header stays with PSD, TIF, and JPG files. Thereafter, anyone who sees the file can find out most anything you want them to know about it. If they then click the Go To URL button, they will be taken to the Owner URL web site. (Too bad this information doesn't stay with the file when you create a slideshow.)

Page Setup

When you choose this command and the Page Setup dialog box opens, choose a preset paper size from the drop-down menu and choose a paper feed source and a paper orientation (Portrait or Landscape). Click the Printer button at the bottom of the dialog box to access the setup options for your particular printer. Click OK when you have finished.

Print Preview

Choosing this command causes the Print Preview dialog box, shown in Figure 3-9, to appear. When the dialog box opens, you see a large preview window that shows how the size and resolution choices you've made in the Image | Resize | Image Size dialog box will affect the size, quality, and positioning of your image when it's printed on the currently chosen printer, and the settings that have been currently chosen for that printer. This is useful because you can instantly see how large the border is going to be, get an idea of how using lower- or higher-than-recommended resolution will affect the quality of

PHOTOSHOP ELEMENTS ORIENTATION

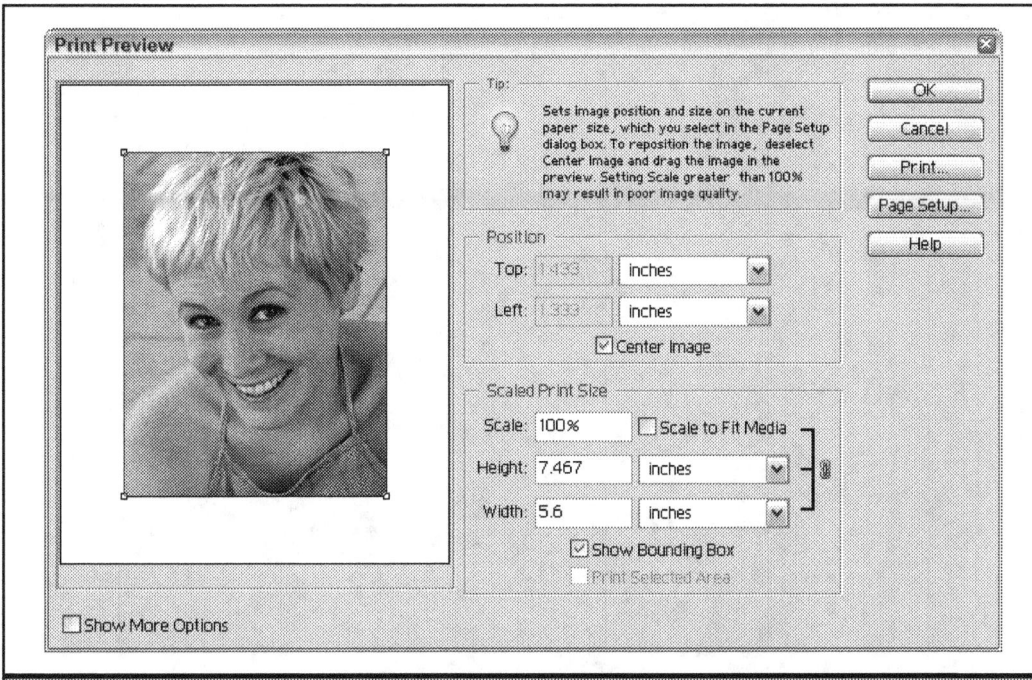

Figure 3-9. *The Print Preview dialog box gives you an advance view of how your image is going to look on the printed page.*

the image, and see the position of the image on the currently chosen size of paper in that printer.

If the Show Bounding Box option is checked, you can drag a corner handle to proportionately rescale the image, or you can reposition the image by clicking the Center Image check box to toggle it off and dragging inside the bounding box. You can scale the image to an exact percentage of its ideal size by typing a positive or negative percentage into the Scale field. Finally, you can force the image to fill the paper by simply clicking the Scale To Fit Media check box.

But there are still more options. To get to them, check the Show More Options check box at the bottom of the dialog box. You can choose either Output or Color Management as the category of extra options from the More Options menu.

If you choose Output, you can choose a background color for the area outside the picture (the Color Picker appears when you click the Border button), place a black border up to 10 points wide around the image (you can specify the width in inches or millimeters, but the max width is still approximately the same), and choose to include the caption you've previously placed into the File Info dialog box; caption text always appears as 9-point Helvetica. Finally, you can choose to place crop marks at the corners of the picture. You can see these choices in the following illustration.

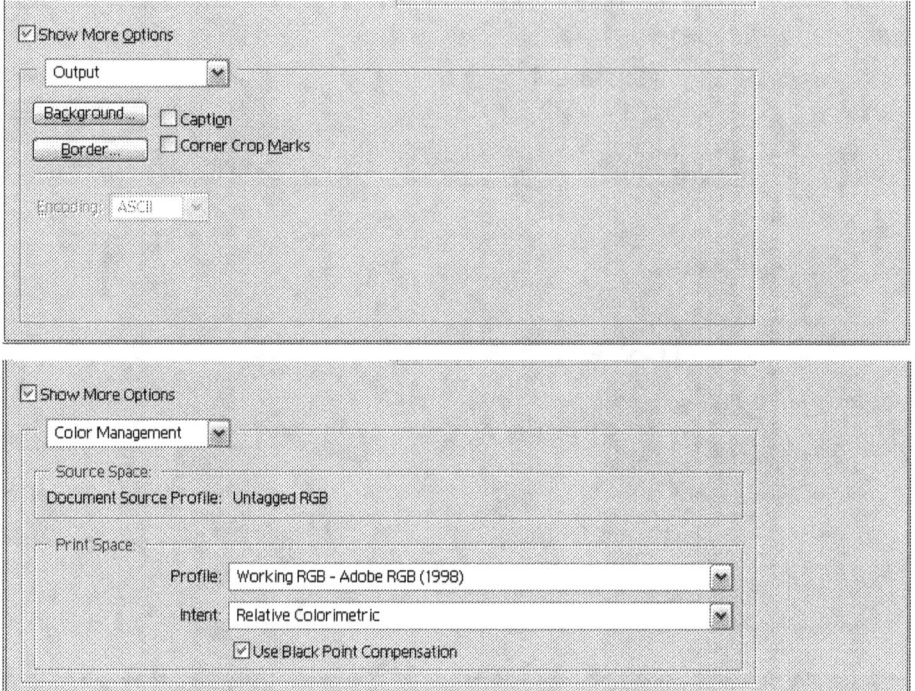

The Encoding field has to do with how the printer "reads" a pixel. You can choose between ASCII, Binary, and JPEG encoding. In brief, here are the differences: ASCII assigns 2 bytes per image pixel, so the files are twice as large as binary files. Their advantage is that they can be recognized by the widest variety of printers. Binary files are half the size of ASCII files because they assign only 1 byte of information per pixel. This makes the files print more quickly in theory, but the smaller amount of data causes some printers to have to spend more time "guessing" at the proper printer protocols. The last choice, JPEG, creates the smallest files because they compress the data sent to the printer. The result can be a lower-quality printout. Furthermore, first-generation and less-expensive PostScript printers that use Level 1 protocols can't make use of JPEG files.

When you choose Color Management from the Show More Options drop-down menu (see the preceding illustration), you can choose the predefined device profiles that you set up in Chapter 1 for monitor calibration. All the color profiles that came with Elements and those that you have downloaded, transferred, or created and stored on your system will appear in the Profile menu. You simply select the one that pertains to the particular devices that will be used to output this particular print. Some profiles, such as many of those created for Epson printers, also modify the profile with an *intent* (optional adjustment that maximizes the profile for viewing the result when the image is intended to meet certain interpretative criteria).

The most commonly seen and used intents are as follows:

- **Perceptual**   Usually most appropriate to photographs because the exact colors used are chosen on the basis of how adjacent colors influence human perception of those colors.

- **Saturation**   Best suited for graphics, logos, and presentations. In those applications, the brightest and most "sockit to 'em" colors are the most effective and the precise definition of colors is less important.

- **Absolute Colorimetric**   Colors are interpreted strictly according to the way the device profiles say they should be interpreted, taking into account the color and brightness of the paper on which they are being printed. Best used when you want the interpretation to match your expectations regardless of the paper type being used (but, of course, you must have a profile loaded for that type of paper).

- **Relative Colorimetric**   Prints the colors exactly as dictated by the input and output profiles, regardless of the *substrate* (paper, canvas, and so on) on which they are being printed.

Print

Choosing this File menu option lets you send your image to any type of printer that is configured for and attached to your computer. The printer that is set in your computer's operating system will appear first, but you can also choose any other printer that has been recognized by your computer. Of course, Elements is most likely to work best with a full-color printer that's capable of printing photographic-quality images. You can find much more information about choosing, calibrating, and getting great results from printers and printing presses in Chapter 19, which also discusses the considerations for choosing various printing options, printers, inks, and papers.

Print Layouts

Choosing Print Layouts opens a submenu that lets you choose between printing contact sheets or picture packages.

Contact Sheets   A *contact sheet,* in photographer's language, is a proof print that's made by sandwiching negatives in tight face-to-face contact with printing paper. The result is positive prints that are the same size as the original negative. The benefit is that you can choose pictures from a whole roll of film at a time. However, if you want somewhat larger prints so you can more easily choose between subtle differences in shots, contact sheets just won't cut it. That's where Photoshop Elements' Contact Sheets provide a distinct advantage. You can tell the command's dialog box how many rows and columns you want to use and whether you want the images labeled with their filenames, and the program will size the files accordingly. The Contact Sheet dialog box is shown in Figure 3-10.

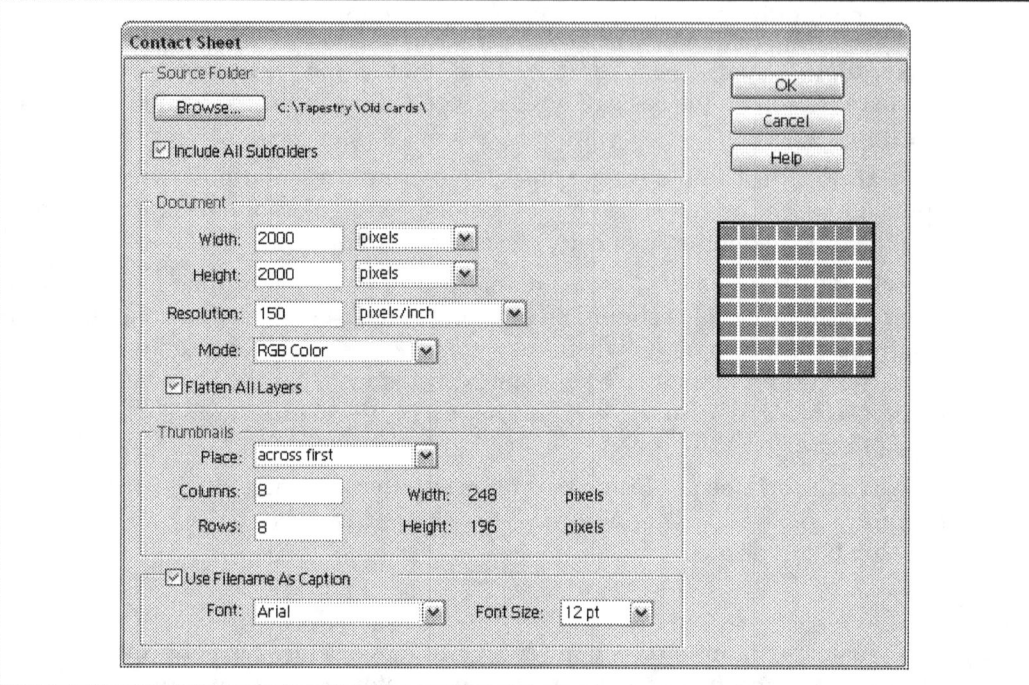

Figure 3-10. *The Contact Sheet dialog box provides more choices than the classic photographer's contact sheet.*

Here's how you create a set of contact sheets:

1. Choose File | Print Projects | Contact Sheets. The Contact Sheet dialog box appears.

2. Click the Browse button. The Browse For Folder dialog box will appear (much less capable that the Photoshop Elements Browser). This browser behaves similarly to your computer's Finder/Explorer. Navigate to the folder in which the images you want to print reside, and click OK. The path to the folder will appear in the Contact Sheet dialog box, immediately under the Browse button.

3. If you like, you can also choose to include images from all the subfolders in this group of contact sheets. (Photoshop Elements will print as many sheets as required by the number of images contained in the chosen folder, given the number of individual files you've chosen to proof on a single page.)

4. The size of your printing paper will also determine the size of individual proofs. Enter the number of units in the paper size (minus the margin) you want to print on in the Width and Height fields. For each of these fields, you can choose whether the measurements you entered will be in inches, centimeters, or millimeters from the adjacent pull-down menu.

5. You can choose whether these proofs will be color or monochrome by choosing RGB Color or Grayscale from the Mode menu.

6. You can tell the dialog box to arrange the proofs from left to right and then top to bottom (across first), or top to bottom and then left to right (down first), by making the choice from the Place menu.

7. Enter the number of Columns and Rows you want to use. This will be one of the factors that determine the size of individual proofs. You can see a preview diagram of the layout that results from the chosen number of rows and columns in the right margin of the dialog box.

8. Finally, you can decide whether to use the individual filenames as captions. Doing so will make the proofs smaller, but toggling off this checkbox will make it much more difficult to identify which file belongs to which proof. It is a good idea to choose the smallest font size you can manage because Photoshop Elements will reduce image size to accommodate both the height and the length of filenames.

9. Click OK when you're ready to create the contact sheet. Photoshop Elements will then open each image in the folder, duplicate it, and resize and position the duplicate to fit the specifications you've entered in this dialog box. When it has done this to all the files, a finished contact sheet appears, as in the following example.

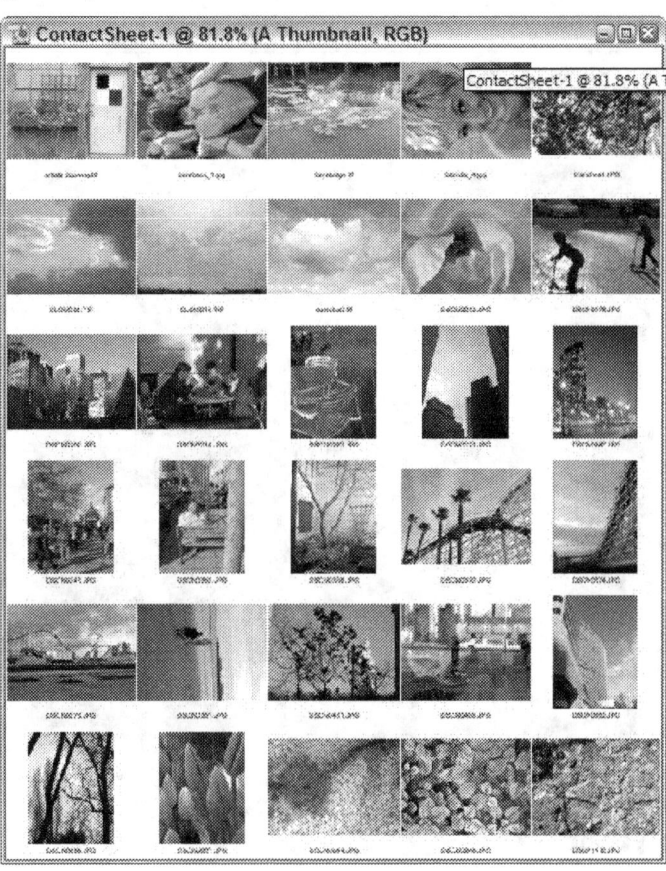

Picture Package   *Picture package* is a term used by professional portrait, wedding, and event photographers to describe a type of print they often sell at an especially attractive price because all the prints are made at the same time on the same piece of photographic paper. Furthermore, it is usually up to the client to cut the pictures apart, thus resulting in a labor cost savings. For you, making picture packages results in a savings of printer paper and of your time loading and waiting for individual sheets of paper to print. Picture Packages are also a nice way to send scrapbook and wallet-sized prints to friends.

Here's how you make a picture package:

1. Choose File | Print Projects | Picture Package. The Picture Package dialog box appears, as shown in Figure 3-11.

2. From the Use menu, choose File, Folder, or Use Frontmost Photo. These choices are merely for your convenience. No matter which you choose, you will be able to place any photo on any drive attached to your computer into any of the spaces. If necessary, photos will automatically rotate to fit the proportions of the image. Therefore, if you want the photos to face in a consistent direction, you will have to choose those of the right proportions or precrop the images to fit those proportions.

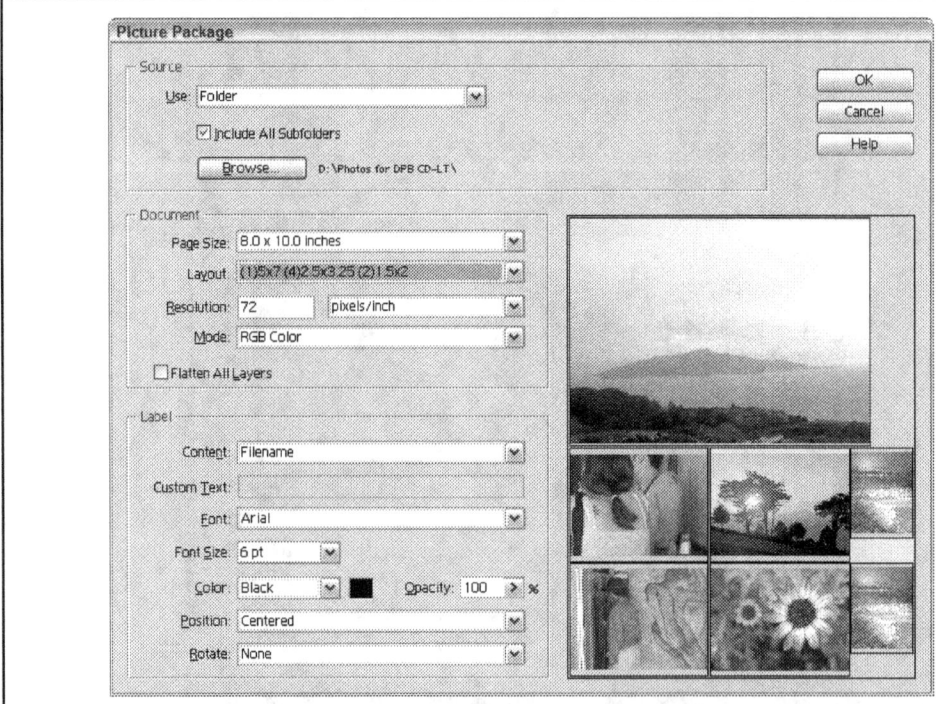

Figure 3-11.   *The Picture Package dialog box helps you print multiple photos on a page to save paper.*

3. If you choose Folder in step 2, click the Browse button and navigate to the folder from which you want to choose the first picture. The first picture in the folder will appear in all the image spaces. Later we'll replace some instances to show you that you can place any photo you want into any of the spaces.

4. Choose the size of the paper you want to print on from the Page Size menu. You can choose between 10×16, 8×10, and 11×17 inches. Don't choose a size that is larger than your printer can print.

5. From the Layout menu, make the choice that lets you make the mixture of sizes and the number of prints per page that you want.

6. In the Resolution field, enter the image file resolution you want to use and choose whether you want this resolution at pixels per inch or centimeters.

7. The Label area of the dialog box is pretty self-explanatory. Choose the options that will label your individual prints as you like them. Labels are overprinted on the images, so be sure to choose a color, size, and opacity that work best with the mixture of pictures that you have chosen.

Exit   Choosing this command ends the operation of Photoshop Elements—quits the program. Elements will prompt you to save files if any files have not been saved before closing.

Edit Menu

The Edit menu contains (mostly) those commands that affect the whole document, selection, or currently active layer. It also contains commands that affect options for how Photoshop Elements will handle all image documents. The primary commands on the Edit menu are shown here.

Edit	
Undo State Change	Alt+Ctrl+Z
Step Forward	Ctrl+Y
Step Backward	Ctrl+Z
Cut	Ctrl+X
Copy	Ctrl+C
Copy Merged	Shft+Ctrl+C
Paste	Ctrl+V
Paste Into	Shft+Ctrl+V
Clear	
Fill...	
Stroke...	
Define Brush...	
Define Pattern...	
Purge	▶
Color Settings...	Shft+Ctrl+K
File Association...	
Preset Manager...	
Preferences	▶

Undo

Choosing this command or pressing OPT/ALT+CMD/CTRL+Z reverses the effect of the last command, tool, or action you executed. Remember that if you're making brush strokes or using any other tool that affects only a small portion of the image, issuing the Undo command will affect only that small change in the image.

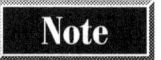 *Because you can Undo only as many steps as you've chosen to allow to be recorded in the Undo History palette, you may want to insert a higher number of recordable Undo steps in the Preferences dialog box (see the "Preferences" section, later in this chapter).*

Step Forward

Choosing this command or pressing CMD/CTRL+Y moves one step forward (down) in the Undo History palette. Of course, you can move forward or backward by choosing a specific Step Name bar in the History palette; but when you want to move only a few steps forward or backward, or flip between states to preview the result of a change, it is usually faster to use this command (and even faster if you use the keyboard shortcut).

Step Backward

The inverse of the Step Forward command, choosing this command or pressing CMD/CTRL+Z moves one step up in the Undo History palette.

Cut

Choosing this command or pressing CMD/CTRL+X deletes the contents of the current image, layer, or selection and places them on the operating system's clipboard.

Copy

Choosing this command or pressing CMD/CTRL+C copies the contents of the current image, layer, or selection, and places them on the operating system's clipboard but does not move or delete the original information.

Copy Merged

Choosing this command or pressing CMD/CTRL+SHIFT+C copies to the clipboard all the visible content from all layers in the image, regardless of which layer is selected. If you have made a selection, only image information from inside that selection will be copied—but you still get all the visible information within that selection, regardless of how many layers that information resides on.

Paste

Choosing this command or pressing CMD/CTRL+V places the clipboard image onto a new layer and positions it dead center in the canvas (workspace). You can then reposition the item by choosing the Move tool from the toolbox and dragging the contents of the pasted layer to any position.

Paste Into

Choose this command or press SHIFT+CMD/CTRL+V if you want to paste the clipboard contents into an irregular shape or into a specific position within the overall image. First, make a selection, and then use the Paste Into command. The center of the contents of the clipboard will be pasted as close to the center of the selection as the canvas will allow. If the selection is smaller and/or shaped differently than the clipboard contents, the selection will mask the layer onto which the clipboard contents were pasted. The result is a cropped or reshaped pasted selection. As is the case with the Paste command, you can use the Move tool to drag the contents of the layer mask to any position you like.

In the following illustration, the contents of two identically sized images have been combined using the Paste Into command. You can see how the position and shape of the selection have trimmed and repositioned the contents of the clipboard (pasted-in) image.

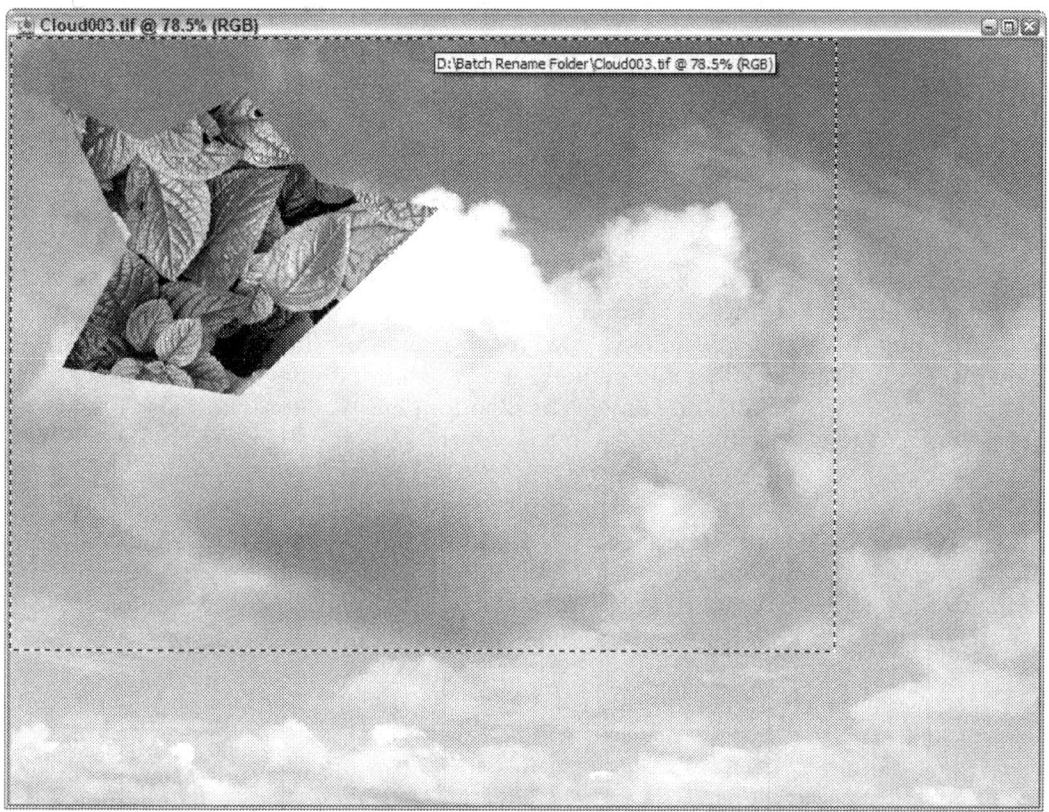

Clear

Choosing this command deletes the image (if the only layer is the Background layer), currently selected layer, or the contents of a selection. The deleted image is *not* placed into the clipboard—so if you make a mistake, you must use Undo or use the Undo History palette to recover.

Fill

Choosing this command lets you fill the current image, selected layer, or current selection according to the options you choose in the Fill dialog box, which appears as soon as you issue the command. The Fill dialog box is shown here:

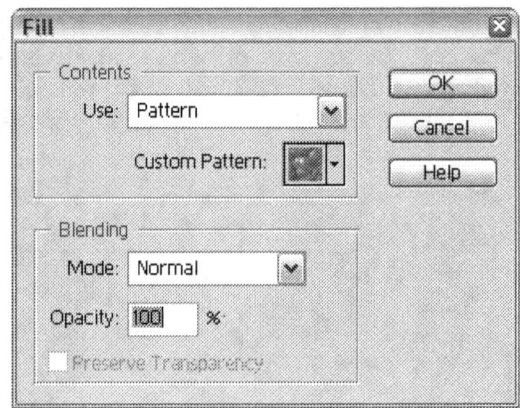

You can fill with the foreground color, background color (see Chapter 5 for information about choosing a background color with the Color Picker), Black, White, 50% Gray, and (here's the most interesting part) any of Photoshop Elements' custom patterns—including those that you've designed yourself with the Define Pattern command. You can also fill using any of the Blend modes that apply to brushes and at any percentage of opacity.

Stroke

This command lets you paint perfectly smooth brush strokes along any selection. Unfortunately, you are limited to a hard-edged stroke, but you can specify the width of the stroke and its color; whether to stroke along the inside, outside, or center of the selection; what Blend mode to use; and the percentage of opacity in the stroke.

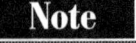

Strokes must be made along closed paths. If you want to stroke an open shape, first create a new, transparent layer while your selection is active. Then, while the new layer is selected (its name bar in the Layers palette will be highlighted if this is the case), use the Selection tools (see Chapters 5 and 7) to draw a closed path that, except for the line that closes the stop and start points, is your open path. Then execute the stroke command with your chosen options. Because the stroked path is on a transparent layer, you can use the Eraser tool to remove any part of that path.

Define Brush

The Define Brush command records the contents of an existing and active selection as the shape and shading of a new brush.

Here's how you define a brush:

1. Either use Photoshop Elements' existing brushes to originate a new pattern, or load a bitmap image that contains an object or pattern you want to turn into a black-and-white version of your brush shape.

2. If necessary, resize your photo or scale a portion of it so that the contents of a selection that you're defining as a brush will be as small as you want the brush to be. The quickest and easiest way to do this is to choose Image | Resize | Scale. If your image is a single background layer, you'll be asked whether you want to change it to layer 0. Click Yes. A bounding box will appear around the image. Press SHIFT and drag a corner handle to keep scaling proportionate to the original; drag diagonally toward the center until the area you want to define is the size you want it to be when you're zoomed to 100 percent. Then click the OK check mark at the right side of the Scale Options bar.

3. Make a selection whose shape is what you want the outside shape of the brush to be, as shown next. (Adobe says that ideally the background should be white, but you can do the same thing by making a Lasso selection.)

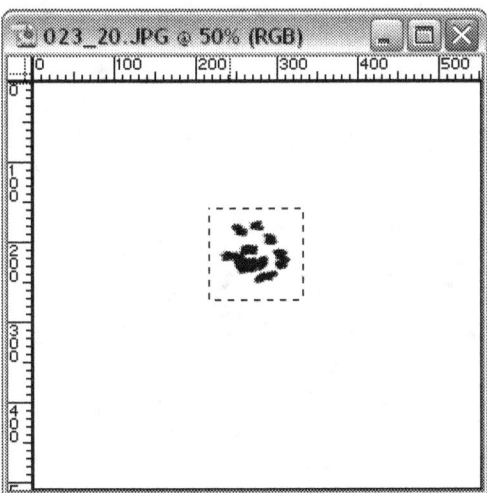

4. Choose Edit | Define Brush. The Brush Name dialog box appears. Notice that your brush is a monochrome version of the image inside your selection.

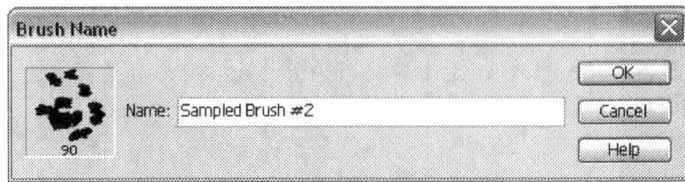

5. Enter a name for this brush and click OK.

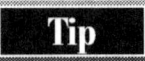

You can close the file you used to define the brush or choose File | Revert so that you don't accidentally save the file with a portion of the image scaled.

To use the brush you just defined, choose the Brush from the toolbox. In the Options bar, scroll down the Brush menu to your newly defined brush, as shown in Figure 3-12. Change any other settings in the Options bar (as appropriate to your use) and paint away.

Define Pattern

The difference between defining a pattern and defining a brush lies mostly in the end result. Patterns are used for fills and repeat themselves. In the next illustration, you can see the image we defined as a brush redefined as a pattern and used to fill a new file. You can also fill the current document, currently chosen layer, or any selection with a pattern once you've defined it. Like a brush, a pattern can be any portion of a bitmapped image. However, in the case of a pattern, the selection must be rectangular.

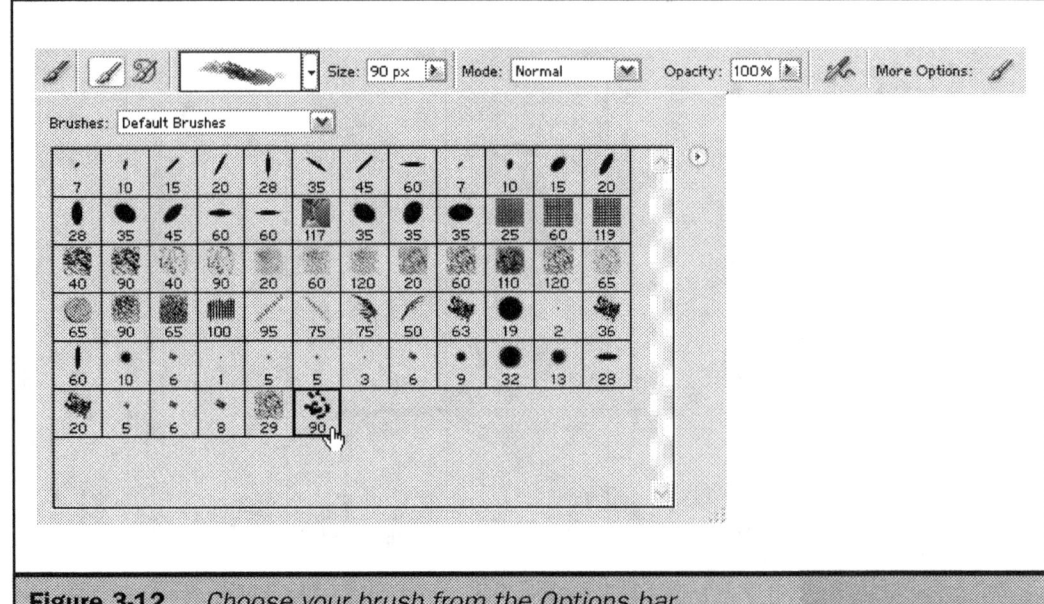

Figure 3-12. *Choose your brush from the Options bar.*

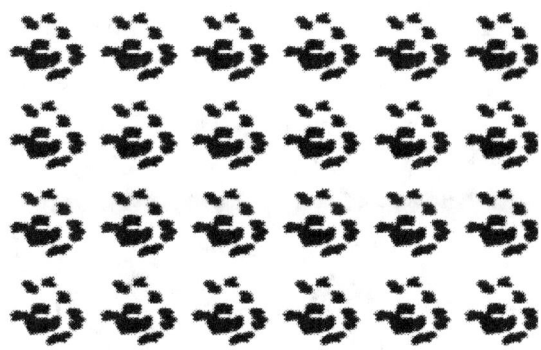

Note   *When you define a pattern, it is automatically saved with the pattern set with which it was defined. If you want to create a set of new patterns, first delete all the patterns in the current set, and then save the patterns under a new name, create new patterns, and use the save patterns commands. These commands are all found in the Patterns palette. Detailed instructions are in Chapter 4.*

To define a pattern, follow these steps:

1. Either use Photoshop Elements' existing brushes to paint a new pattern, or load a bitmap image that contains an object or pattern you want to turn into a black-and-white version of your brush shape.

2. If necessary, resize your photo or scale a portion of it so that the contents of a selection that you're defining as a brush will be as small as you want the brush to be. The quickest and easiest way to do this is to choose Image | Resize | Scale. If your image is a single background layer, you'll be asked whether you want to change it to layer 0. Click Yes. A bounding box will appear around the image. Press SHIFT and drag a corner handle to keep scaling proportionate to the original; drag diagonally toward the center until the area you want to define is the size you want it to be when you're zoomed to 100 percent. Then click the OK check mark at the right side of the Scale Options bar.

3. From the Toolbox, choose the Rectangular Marquee and drag a marquee around the portion of the image you want to turn into a pattern. (If you've scaled a whole layer and it's still selected, you can just press CMD/CTRL+A to Select All.)

4. Choose Edit | Define Pattern. The Pattern Name dialog box appears. You will see a small preview of your pattern to the left of the Name field. In the Name field, enter a name for your pattern and click OK.

Here's how to fill with a pattern

1. Choose Edit | Fill. The Fill dialog box appears.

2. From the Use menu, choose Pattern.

3. From the Custom Pattern palette, choose the pattern you defined (or any other you might want to use), and then click OK.

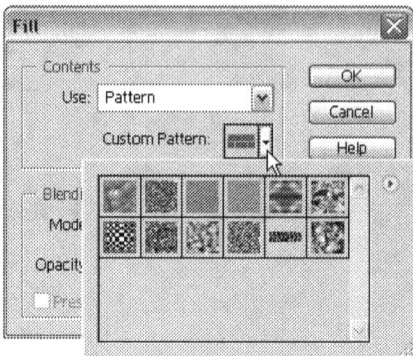

The rules for saving and loading patterns are the same as for saving and loading brushes. You will find much more detail about using and creating patterns in Chapters 15 and 16.

Purge

When you find Photoshop Elements slowing down, chances are memory is being used by too many applications. The Purge command lets you get rid of some or all of the other memory hogs (or nibblers, as the case may be). Purge affects all open documents, whether active or not. In Photoshop Elements, the Undo command can be used to completely dump the following:

- **Undo** Removes all the image states that have been preserved in memory. You get a warning that this cannot be undone, but the fact is that you can still use the states in the Undo History palette unless you've chosen to Purge All.

- **Clipboard** You may have forgotten that you made a large selection and then issued the Cut or Delete command, thus possibly placing many megabytes of data in memory that is then protected from use. Thus, this is often the safest and most beneficial item to purge.

- **History** All the History states in the Undo History palette are erased. The Undo History palette in the active document (or in any other open document once it's been activated) will immediately begin recording states thereafter. If you want the Undo History palette to stop recording or to record fewer states before it purges the least recent step, change the number of History States permitted in the General Preferences dialog box (choose Image | Preferences | General).

- **All** Purges all three of the preceding at once.

Color Settings Choosing this command or pressing SHIFT+CMD/CTRL+K sets the "state" of Photoshop's Color Management to none, limited, or full-color management.

This command has nothing to do with setting up the way various device profiles are installed or determined, only with how or whether they will be used.

File Association   Choosing this command brings up the File Association Manager dialog box, shown here.

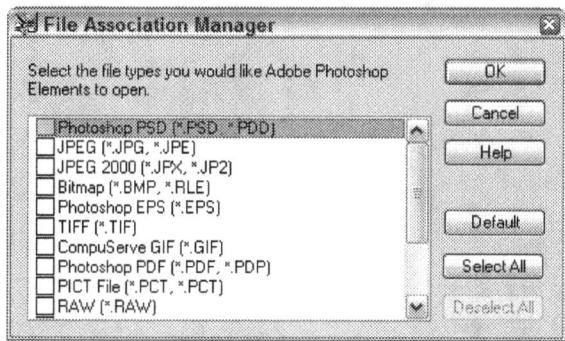

Click to toggle any of the check boxes on/off if you want that file type to open automatically in Photoshop Elements when you double-click a filename in the Finder/ Explorer. This is a useful tool if you often install other programs that set your operating system to open image files automatically in the most recently loaded application. That can be annoying if Photoshop Elements is the image-editing application you're most likely to want to open those files in most of the time. At least the File Association command gives you a handy way to reset your image file opening preferences to be your preferences rather than the selfish preferences of a software publisher.

Preset Manager

The Preset Manager is a palette that lets you change the sets of presets (previously chosen settings) that are available in the Preset palette (visual menu) for Brushes, Swatches, Gradients, and Patterns. This dialog box is discussed in more detail in Chapter 4, which is all about Photoshop Elements' Palettes.

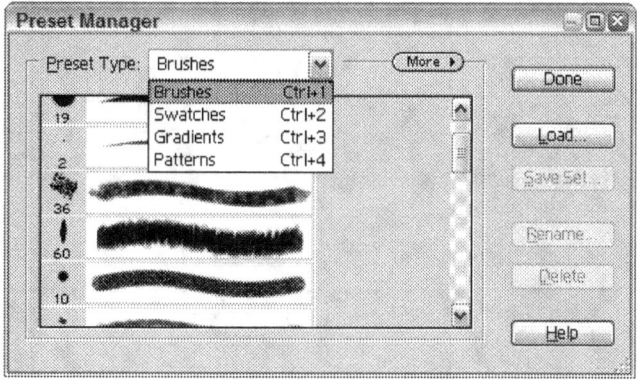

Preferences

Setting Preferences determines what conventions Photoshop Elements will use in determining how it operates in regard to many aspects of the program. Choosing Edit | Preferences brings up a submenu that lists preference dialog boxes for the following categories:

- General
- Saving Files
- Display & Cursors
- Transparency
- Units & Rulers
- Grid
- Plug-Ins & Scratch Disks
- Memory & Image Cache
- Adobe Online

A different dialog box appears for each of these submenu choices. Each is shown and discussed in the following.

General   The General preferences, shown in Figure 3-13, really should be called miscellaneous preferences. These settings don't really belong in any specific category.

The topmost field lists the name of this particular dialog box. You can choose to go to any of the other Preferences dialog boxes from this menu without having to rechoose them from the Edit menu.

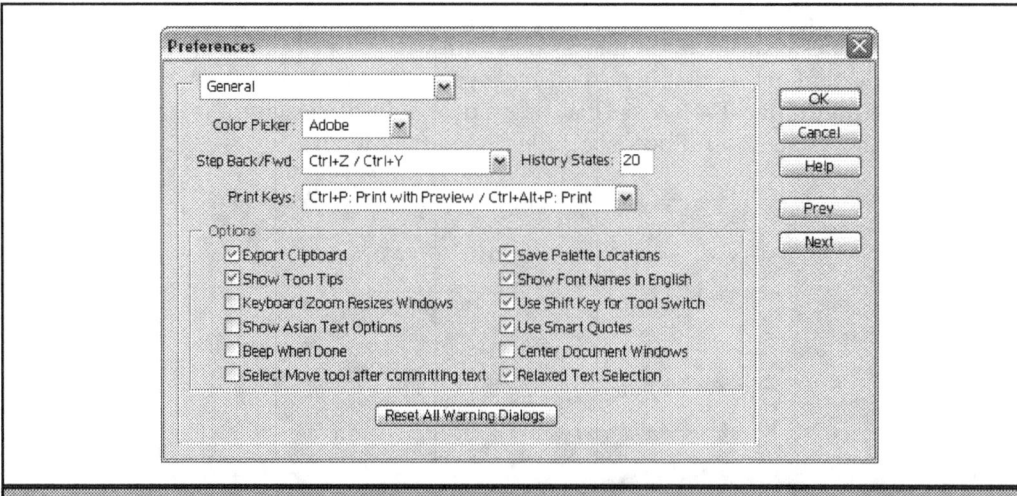

Figure 3-13.   *The General Preferences dialog box*

The Color Picker menu lets you choose which color picker you prefer to use for picking the colors in the Foreground and Background Swatches at the bottom of the Toolbox. You can choose between the Mac/Windows color picker and the Adobe color picker. The Adobe color picker is used by nearly every major graphics program, so we recommend that you stick with it for consistency between programs and applications. If your personal habits dictate otherwise, so be it.

The Step Back/Fwd menu gives you a choice between several keyboard shortcuts so that you can avoid conflicts that might exist in installed third-party plug-ins or in keyboard shortcuts for your operating system. These keyboard shortcuts let you move up and down the Undo History states without having to call up a particular palette. It's tantamount to having unlimited Undo capability, but how many steps you can Undo/ Redo are actually limited by the number of steps you enter into the History States field just to the right of the Step Back/Fwd menu.

The Print Keys menu lets you choose whether CMD/CTRL+P will open the Print With Preview dialog box, and CMD/CTRL+OPT/ALT+P will open the Print dialog box, or vice versa. CMD/CTRL+P is easy to remember, so you might want to use it for the Print With Preview dialog box, which lets you accurately preview the way your image will look in print and how it will be positioned on the paper before you commit your image to print. It's a good idea because truly photo- or fine-art quality substrates (papers and other materials to which the ink can be applied) and archival inks can be expensive—as can be the time it takes to make the print itself.

The Options section of the Preferences dialog box is populated by 12 check boxes that toggle on/off when clicked. The effect of each of these options is described next.

- **Export Clipboard**   The default in most applications, it allows information to be cut from one application and pasted into another. However, it is considerate of Adobe to let you automatically dump the clipboard when you exit the program, in case the clipboard might use so much of your system's memory that you can't run another program.

- **Show Tool Tips**   This displays a tip balloon showing the name of a Tool, Options Bar option, or palette icon when the cursor is paused over it.

- **Keyboard Zoom Resizes Windows**   This causes the document window to automatically resize itself when you press CMD/CTRL+– to zoom out or CMD/CTRL++ to zoom in. Choosing this option has no effect on window resizing when using any of the other methods (such as clicking or dragging with the Zoom tool) for changing the view magnification.

Tip   *This is a great way to arrange windows when working with several open files. If this option is turned on, you can quickly shrink the windows that are "on standby" and enlarge those in which you need to do some editing.*

- **Show Asian Text Options**   Bet you didn't even know you *had* Asian text options. If this box is checked and you choose the Text tool, you will see options that are particular to the use of Asian fonts when you have Asian fonts loaded into your system and have chosen one of these fonts for entry.

- **Beep When Done**   This makes the computer emit a short beep when any lengthy task completes. Leaving this choice on is handy if you're rendering a large and complex image (such as a Liquify mesh on an 80MB file) or a batch operation on hundreds of files. Otherwise, it could go off often enough to make you and your colleagues a little batty.

- **Select Move Tool After Committing Text**   This does just what it says. When you click the OK button in the Text Options bar, the Move tool is automatically selected so that you can manually position the text in the document.

> **Tip**   *It is handy to turn on the Select Move Tool After Committing Text option when you're designing a web page or layout in which you want to be able to reposition text interactively in nonstandard ways to achieve a fresh design look.*

- **Save Palette Locations**   This keeps all palettes where they were positioned when you last closed the program. This option can be handy if you're working on an extensive project and you have to close the program or turn off the computer between sessions.

- **Show Font Names In English**   English fonts are always shown in English. If this box is unchecked, however, the names of Asian fonts will be shown in their native language and characters.

- **Use Shift Key For Tool Switch**   If checked, pressing the SHIFT key will rotate the choice of tools that are in the same position in the Toolbox. Such tools are those that display a small arrow at the lower-right side of their icons. So, for instance, if this box is checked and you press SHIFT+M more than once, you will alternate between the Rectangular marquee and the Elliptical marquee.

- **Use Smart Quotes**   If this box is checked and you are entering text with the Text tool, quotation marks will curl in toward the quoted text at either end of the quotation.

- **Center Document Windows**   If you check this box, all your document windows will immediately hide behind one another. Of course, this could be a good thing if you want to show a client different versions of an image or different choices for a photograph that could be used for the same purpose. You could then choose the visible image from the Window | Images submenu.

- **Relaxed Text Selection**   Lets you select text in a Text layer by clicking near it—instead of having to click directly inside a layer.

Saving Files   The Saving Files Preferences dialog box, shown in Figure 3-14, lets you decide whether you want Photoshop Elements to ask you before saving a space-consuming image preview; choose whether or not to add a file extension automatically and whether or not it should be in caps; whether or not you want TIFF files (the most universally cross-platform and cross-application file format for true-color, high-resolution files) to offer the latest options (such as layers and layer transparency); and, finally, how many files will appear on the Most Recent Files list in the File menu.

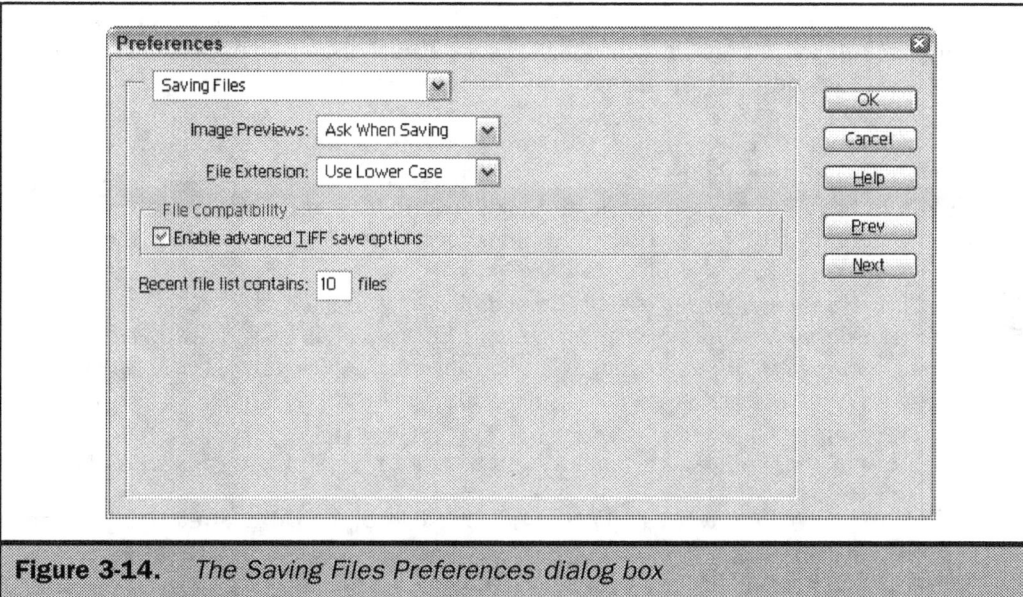

Figure 3-14.   *The Saving Files Preferences dialog box*

Here's how to use the Save Files dialog box:

1. Choose Edit | Preferences | Save Files; or, if you're already in another Preferences dialog box, choose Save Files from the Preferences pull-down menu.

2. Pull down the Image Previews menu and choose Ask When Saving, Never Save, or Always Save. The best all-around choice is Ask When Saving because you don't want to save a preview accidentally for files that will only be used in a presentation, slideshow, or web page—doing so serves no purposes and slows performance when files load. If you are creating a large project with a series of images that doesn't require previews, go back to Preferences and choose Never Save Until You're Done With The Project. If you are almost always creating and storing files that you want to see as thumbnails, choose Always Save.

3. Pull down the File Extension menu and choose Use Lower Case. Lowercase file extensions are recognized by all operating systems, web servers, and browsers. You should always use extensions with your filenames. They don't take up any additional room and immediately identify whether the file has been saved with lossy compression and should not be resaved (.jpg), whether it has been saved in an editable format with layers (.psd), or whether it has been saved in a lossless format for sending to clients or print shops (.tif).

Note   *Mac owners especially should pay attention to the advice in step 3.*

4. Click the Enable Advanced TIFF Save Options check box to toggle on the check mark. You will still have a choice about whether to save layers and so on when you save to the TIFF format and the TIFF Options dialog box appears.

Display & Cursors The Display & Cursors Preferences dialog box, shown in Figure 3-15, used to be mandatory for Photoshop and Photoshop Elements users because it's just silly not to have your brush shape and size outlined for you at its present size. Now it's the default. However, you might have special requirements from time to time.

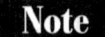 *For future reference, the Photoshop Elements Brush tools are Eraser, Pencil, Airbrush, Paintbrush, Impressionist Brush, Background Eraser, Magic Eraser, Red Eye Brush, Clone Stamp, Pattern Stamp, Smudge, Blur, Sharpen, Dodge, Burn, and Sponge tools. (Although some of these tools may not sound like brushes, they all use the Brush presets.)*

Here's how to change the settings that will be used for displaying Brush tools:

1. Choose Edit | Preferences | Display & Cursors; or, if you're already in another Preferences dialog box, choose Display & Cursors from the Preferences pull-down menu.

2. Decide which is most important to you: workspeed or 1:1 pixel previewing accuracy. If speed (especially when working with large files and large brushes) takes precedence, click to toggle on the Use Pixel Doubling check box. The preview will then show 2 pixels for every 1 in the image. You can rest assured that the fidelity of the actual file won't be affected—only the speed of the preview.

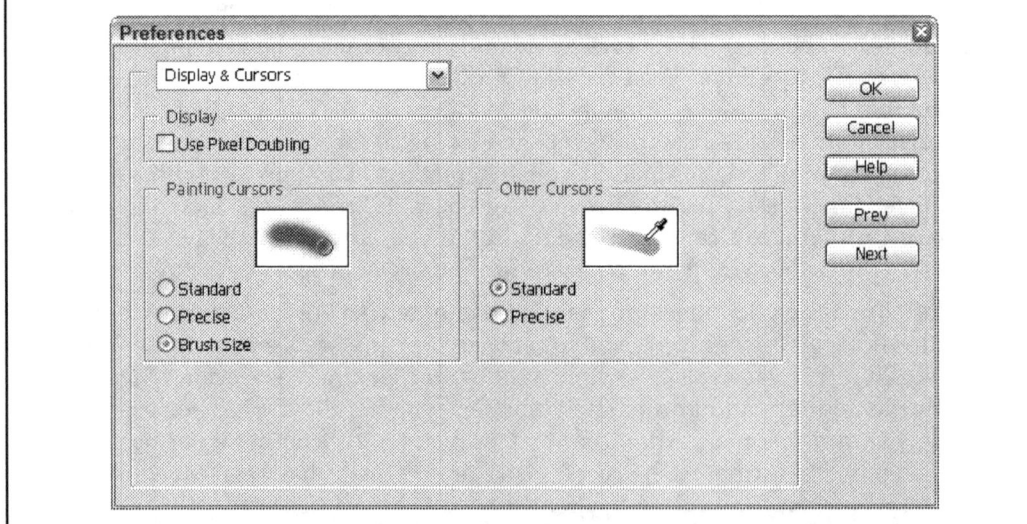

Figure 3-15. *The Display & Cursors Preferences dialog box*

3. You can show the brush cursor in one of three ways, which you can choose by clicking the radio buttons associated with Standard, Precise, or Brush Size. The last shows the exact diameter of any brush you are currently using. Clicking this button will save you from wasting a lot of time and from swearing in public because you didn't anticipate how much area the stroke might cover. Choosing Standard displays the icon for the currently active brush tool. Choosing Precise displays a cross hair to make it easy to know exactly where the center of the brush will be.

4. You set the appearance for all other cursors by choosing between Standard and Precise—because brush size isn't pertinent to their application. Choosing Standard makes it easier to know which tool is in effect. Precise is handier when you need to place a marquee accurately.

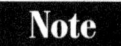

You can switch between Standard and Precise or Brush Size and Precise by pressing the CAPS LOCK key, but it's awfully easy to press CAPS LOCK accidentally, and it doesn't work for every tool cursor.

Transparency   The Transparency preferences allow you to decide how you want the program to show the transparent areas of a layer. The default is a gray-and-white checkerboard of small squares. Most of the time, this is the most useful choice because the pattern makes it fairly easy to identify which areas are transparent, and the gray color won't mislead your color perceptions when you're making adjustments to the image. However, at times this can be a drawback:

■ The default grid can make it difficult to see delicate areas of partial transparency—especially gradual borders that occur after using the Extract filter to create a *transitional knockout* (the image is removed from its background in such a way that complex edges will blend naturally into any new background).

■ There is too little contrast between the light gray of the transparency checkerboard and the subject to distinguish readily between foreground and transparent areas.

Options for showing the transparent areas of a layer are found in the Transparency Preferences dialog box, shown in Figure 3-16.

Here's how to change the options for the display of transparent areas of a layer:

1. Choose Edit | Preferences | Transparency; or, if you're already in another Preferences dialog box, choose Transparency from the Preferences pull-down menu.

2. Choose your preferred grid size from one of the three named in the Grid Size pull-down menu: Small, Medium, or Large.

3. If you want to change the colors of your grid squares, two choices are available:

■ From the Grid Colors menu, choose one of the eight preconfigured options.

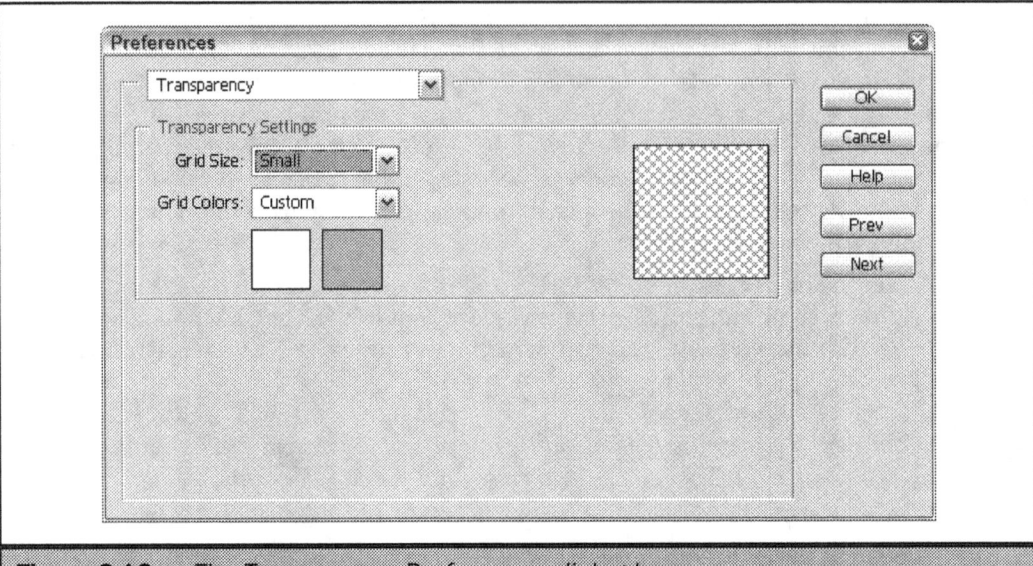

Figure 3-16.   *The Transparency Preferences dialog box*

■ Click the color swatches to choose any color from the Color Picker that you've chosen from the General Preferences dialog box.

4. The results of your choices will immediately be shown in the preview box at the right of the dialog box. When you're happy with your choices, click OK.

Units & Rulers   The Units & Rulers preferences set what unit types (such as inches, centimeters, points, or pixels) and image resolution will be used to determine how Rulers, Grids, Type, and anything in the program that is measured (such as the page size or the canvas size) will be shown. The Units & Rulers Preferences dialog box is shown in Figure 3-17.

1. Here's how to choose the sizing options that you prefer as defaults: Choose Edit | Preferences | Units & Rulers; or, if you're already in another Preferences dialog box, choose Units & Rulers from the Preferences pull-down menu.

2. From the Rulers menu, choose pixels, inches, cm, mm, points, picas, or percent. The first three choices are common to most rulers. Points and picas are used mostly for page layout purposes—especially when lots of type is involved. The most intriguing choice is percentage, which is a good choice when you're trying to place items in a composition according to such compositional rules as the "Rule of Thirds."

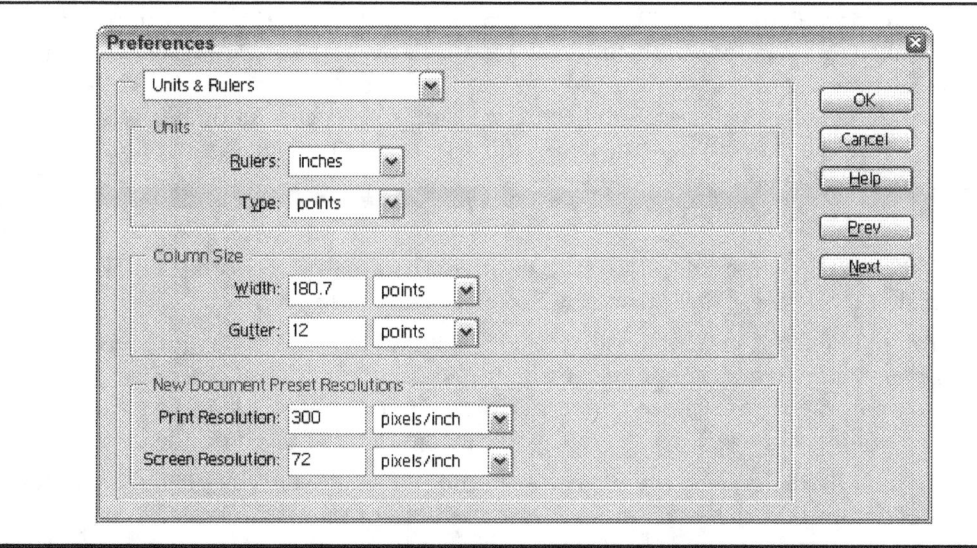

Figure 3-17.   *The Units & Rulers Preferences dialog box*

Note   *When you choose to display rulers (View | Rulers or CMD/CTRL+R), the cursor's position coordinates are indicated by a dashed line in both the horizontal and vertical rulers.*

3. To determine how type will be measured, from the Type menu, choose pixels, points, or mm (millimeters). If you want the type to be the same size as when typeset, choose points. If you care about the size of the type in terms of its height in proportion to the resolution of the image, choose pixels. If you want the type to reflect its size relationship to the size of the paper on which it will be printed (assuming that you don't change it at printing time), choose mm.

4. You can also choose settings for column size and gutter size. This allows the user to size images to the columns in a newspaper or magazine, for example. From here, you create a new image with a set number of columns.

5. Finally, you can preset the resolution of any new document for both print and screen. This is a good idea because then you more easily create your files in a dimension that will transfer to print (or to your desktop printer). Choose the units and unit types that suit the requirements for your highest resolution output—you can always make an image smaller with much less loss of apparent detail than if you have to make it larger.

Grid Photoshop Elements will let you display a nonprinting grid above your photo that lets you snap the cursor to the intersection of the grid points. This makes it quick and easy to draw geometric shapes and selections and to position selections at specific mathematical distances from one another. The Grid Preferences dialog box lets you set the distances between grid lines, the color of the grid, and the number of subdivisions between grid intersections. The Grid Preferences dialog box is shown in Figure 3-18.

Here's how to choose grid options:

1. Choose Edit | Preferences | Grid; or, if you're already in another Preferences dialog box, choose Grid from the Preferences pull-down menu.

2. You may want to choose a color for the grid lines that contrasts more with the image you're working on. If so, from the Color menu, choose one of the nine predefined colors or choose Custom Color. If you choose Custom Color, the Color Picker dialog box will appear and you can choose any color your heart desires.

3. By default, the grid is drawn with solid lines. If you want the grid to be a little less obvious, from the Style menu, choose either Dashed Lines or Dots.

4. Set the spacing between lines by entering the number of lines per unit in the Gridline Every field and then choosing the unit type from the associated pull-down menu. Unit choices are pixels, inches, cm, mm, points, picas, and percent. You will usually want to make your choices for grid spacing the same as for ruler markings, but you don't have to.

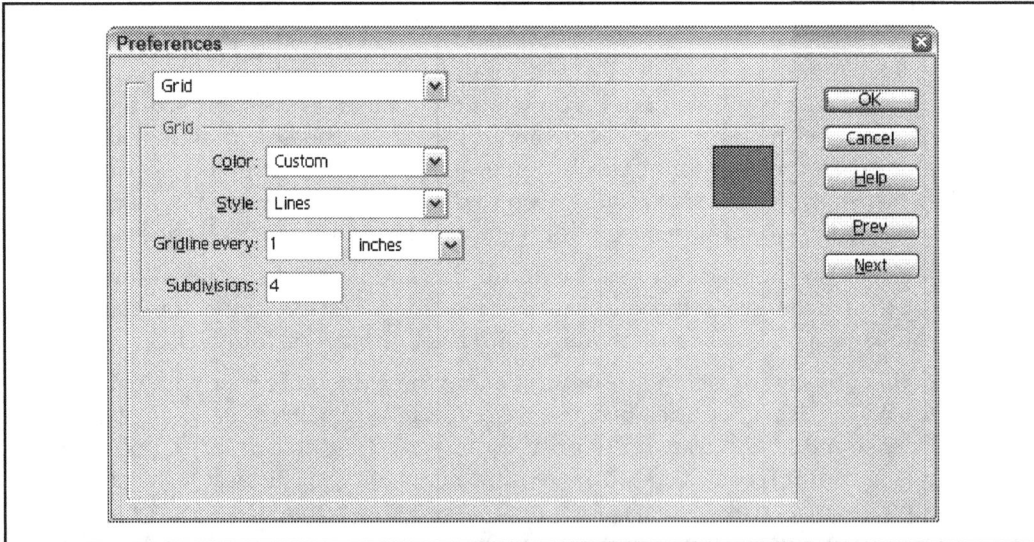

Figure 3-18. *Grid Preferences dialog box*

Note *If you want to change to a custom color quickly, you can click the color swatch that appears on the right of the Grid Preferences dialog box. The Color Picker dialog box will appear, and you can choose any color you want.*

Plug-Ins & Scratch Disks Here's where you get to designate which directory will store your third-party plug-ins and which disk drives will be used to store your clipboard and other temporary data when the program is out of RAM space (this can happen pretty frequently, actually).

When it comes to creating a directory for your third-party plug-ins, we recommend that you put them in the root directory of one of your more capacious drives (not a portable drive because, being a removable, the drive may be not be connected when Photoshop Elements goes looking for it). The main reasons for *not* storing these plug-ins in the same folder as the native Photoshop Elements plug-ins are because it complicates how you tell other compatible programs where to find them and because you may run out of space on the drive that normally holds your applications. (Remember that you can collect hundreds of free third-party plug-ins.) Refer to Figure 3-19 for the Plug-Ins & Scratch Disks Preferences dialog box.

Note *You should always put each set of third-party plug-ins (such as KPT 5) into its own folder. Photoshop Elements and other Photoshop plug-in–compatible programs will always find the plug-ins if they are stored in any subfolder inside the folder you've designated as the Additional Plug-Ins Directory.*

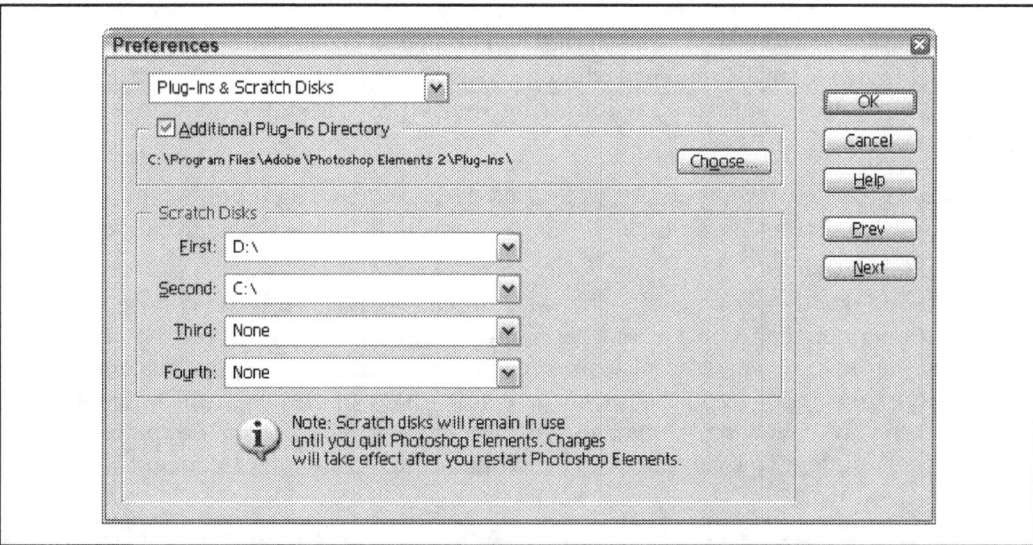

Figure 3-19. *The Plug-Ins & Scratch Disks Preferences dialog box*

Here's how to change the locations for plug-ins and scratch disks.

1. Choose Edit | Preferences | Plug-Ins & Scratch Disks; or, if you're already in another Preferences dialog box, choose Plug-Ins & Scratch Disks from the Preferences pull-down menu.

2. If you want to create a directory for additional third-party plug-ins (and if you're going to install them, you should), click the Additional Plug-Ins Directory check box to toggle it on. When you do, a Finder/Explorer-type dialog box appears. Navigate to (or create) the folder you want to use, and click OK to return to the Plug-Ins & Scratch Disks Preferences dialog box.

3. You can designate up to four disks as scratch disks. When you install Photoshop Elements, you should make sure that none of these is the same drive that the program resides on (unless you have only one drive, of course). Also, choose as many other drives as you have attached to your machine—you're simply ensuring a smaller likelihood that you'll run out of scratch disk space when you start working on that really big project. Pulling down any of the Scratch Disk menus will show all the attached drives, so all you need to do is pick one.

Note *If you change scratch disk assignments during a Photoshop Elements session, the change won't take place until you quit the program and restart it.*

Memory & Image Cache   This Preferences dialog box lets you designate the number of cache levels that Photoshop Elements will use and whether you'll cache histograms. It also tells you how much RAM is available to Photoshop Elements and lets you choose the maximum amount of RAM available to Photoshop Elements. The Memory & Image Cache Preferences dialog box is shown in Figure 3-20.

We tell you in the context of the following steps how each of the items in this dialog box are used.

1. Choose Edit | Preferences | Memory & Image Cache; or, if you're already in another Preferences dialog box, choose Memory & Image Cache from the Preferences pull-down menu.

2. Decide whether you need to change your cache levels. You can choose a number between 1 and 8, and Photoshop Elements will resample the image in that number of smaller image sizes (each half as small as the previous one). The more resamplings you do, the faster whole image operations can be regenerated when you're viewing them at a small size. In short, you'll get a nice performance boost—unless you run out of RAM. The resampled images are meant to be

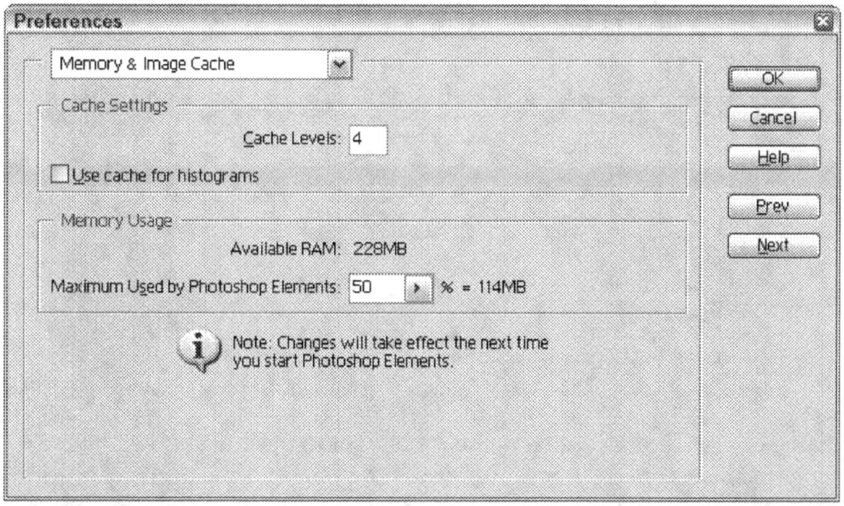

Figure 3-20.   *Memory & Image Cache Preferences dialog box*

stored in RAM, and, if you run out, they must be stored on much slower hard-disk temporary files. That will cost you the speed advantage you gained from choosing more cache levels. Another consideration is that the fewer cache levels you choose, the more accurate your histograms will be after you've made an image adjustment.

3. Click to toggle on (or off) the Use Cache For Histograms check box. If it is checked, performance will suffer slightly, but you'll get smoother looking histograms. Those vertical bars that you see in the Levels histogram after making adjustments aren't usually the result of your having lost any data, but they result from the fact that data is being temporarily held in a cache level(s) other than Level 1.

4. In the Memory Usage area, enter a number (representing the percentage of memory that should be used) in the Maximum Used By Photoshop Elements field. The default is 50%. If you have more than 256MB of RAM, you'll want to up that percentage. Make sure you don't crowd out your operating system's required memory or that of any program you want to run concurrently with Photoshop.

Adobe Online   This command appears only if your computer is currently online. When you choose it, the Adobe Online Preferences dialog box appears.

```
┌─────────────────────────────────────────────────────────────┐
│ Adobe Online Preferences                                  ✕  │
│ ┌─Update Options─────────────────────────────────────────┐   │
│ │                                                          │   │
│ │   Check for updates:  ┌──────────────────────┬───┐      │   │
│ │                       │ Once a Day           │ ▼ │      │   │
│ │                       └──────────────────────┴───┘      │   │
│ │                                                          │   │
│ └──────────────────────────────────────────────────────────┘ │
│   Please use the Internet Control Panel to specify your network settings. │
│                                                               │
│  ┌──────────────────┐ ┌──────────┐    ┌──────────┐ ┌──────┐  │
│  │ About Adobe Online...│ │ Updates... │    │  Cancel  │ │  OK  │  │
│  └──────────────────┘ └──────────┘    └──────────┘ └──────┘  │
└─────────────────────────────────────────────────────────────┘
```

This dialog box lets you decide whether you want to update your Photoshop Elements automatically to any recent changes and, if so, how often you want the program to check for updates. The one thing you should remember is that having the system check too often can interrupt your workflow and drive you crazy.

Here's how to set up updates.

1. Choose Edit | Preferences | Save Files; or, if you're already in another preferences dialog box, choose Save Files from the Preferences pull-down menu. The Adobe Online dialog box appears.

2. From the Check For Updates pull-down menu, choose the frequency with which you want the system to check for updates.

3. If you want the program to perform the checking, click the Updates button and answer Yes to the question you're asked. Otherwise, Adobe will not update your system without your permission.

Image Menu

The Image menu contains mostly commands that affect the entire image, although some can affect only the currently selected layer if the image has more than one layer.

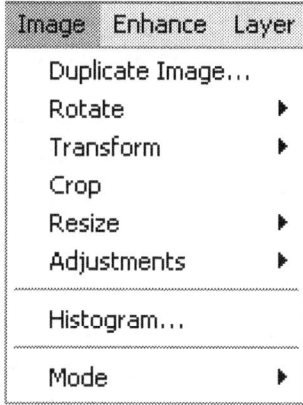

Duplicate Image

This command makes an instant copy of the image, and it should be one of the first commands you use in your Photoshop Elements workflow—immediately following the opening of any original file (even more so if that file is a lossy JPEG image). Working on duplicates will ensure that your original maintains its integrity. Many times, you'll simply be opening and duplicating the original so part of that image can be used in another image. In this case, you don't want to perform any changes to the original image itself.

As soon as you issue this command, the Duplicate Image dialog box appears. Either click OK to accept the original file's name with the word *Copy* attached, or enter a new filename.

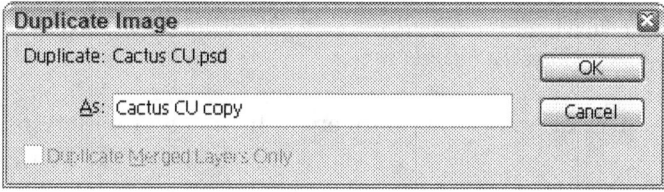

Rotate

The Rotate command's submenus let you turn the image (or layer) either in 90-degree increments or to any angle by either dragging or entering an exact numeric value between 1 and 360 (degrees). You can enter numeric values either in the Transformation Options Bar that appears when you choose Free Rotate, or in the Custom Rotation dialog box when you choose Custom.

90° Left   Choosing this option flips the image on its left side. Ninety-degree Left and Right rotations are the first actions you want to take when you open an image that will be viewed in portrait orientation (the image is taller than it is wide). Typically, to capture such shots, the camera must be rotated, as most cameras shoot in the horizontal, or landscape, orientation. In Photoshop, these photos often need to be flipped after they've been scanned or downloaded.

90° Right   Choosing this option flips the image on its right side. Otherwise, it's the same as the preceding.

180°   Choosing this option flips the image upside down, which is useful if your digital camera has one of those swiveling LCDs that lets you see what you're getting if you turn the camera upside down and hold it over your head to avoid the obstacles directly in front of you (or just to get a higher angle).

Custom   This brings up the Rotate Canvas dialog box, shown next. In the Angle field, enter a number between 1 and 360. Next, click the °Left (negative angle) or °Right (positive angle) button to dictate the direction of rotation, and then click OK to execute. The Rotate Custom command will rotate the entire image, including all layers, at once.

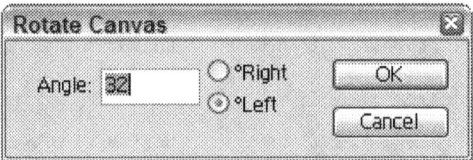

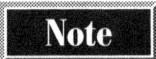   *You can work around the entire-image-rotation limitation by using the Free Rotate Layer command and entering precise positive or negative numbers in the Set Rotation field (marked by a degree symbol on the right).*

Flip Horizontal   Choosing this option reverses the image from left to right producing a mirror image.

Flip Vertical   Choosing this option flips the image upside down. These flips are mirror images. They differ from 180-degree rotated images in that whatever's on the left side of the image will stay on the left side of the image, and vice versa.

Free Rotate Layer   Choosing this option places a transformation box around the layer. This makes it possible for you to rotate the layer by placing the cursor just outside one of the transformation box's handles until the cursor turns into a curved-shaft, double-headed arrow. Once that happens, dragging to the left will rotate the image to the left and dragging to the right will rotate it to the right.

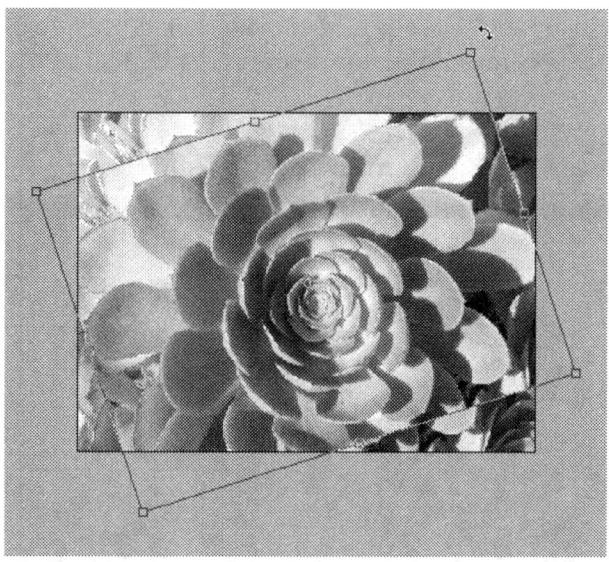

If you want to move the entire layer while the Transform marquee is still active, you can drag the center symbol. However, Photoshop Elements won't let you move the center of the symbol within the current location of the layer so that you could rotate around a different center point.

Layer °90 Left   Choosing this option turns only the currently selected or linked layers on their left sides.

Layer °90 Right   Choosing this option turns only the currently selected or linked layers on their left sides.

Layer °180   Choosing this option turns only the currently selected or linked layers upside down (by rotating, not flipping).

Flip Layer Horizontal   Choosing this option reverses, from left to right, the image on the selected layer or linked layers only. Whatever was at the top and bottom stays at the same relative distance from the top and bottom edges of the image.

Flip Layer Vertical   Choosing this option reverses, from top to bottom, the image on the selected layer or linked layers only. Whatever was at the left and right sides of the image stays at the same relative distance from the left and right edges of the image.

Straighten And Crop Image   This command and the next are meant for straightening images with perpendicular edges that have been skewed by partial rotation. The most common cause of this is crooked placement of an image on a flatbed scanner bed.

If you choose the Straighten And Crop command, the image is straightened and then cropped to its edges. You can see the before and after here:

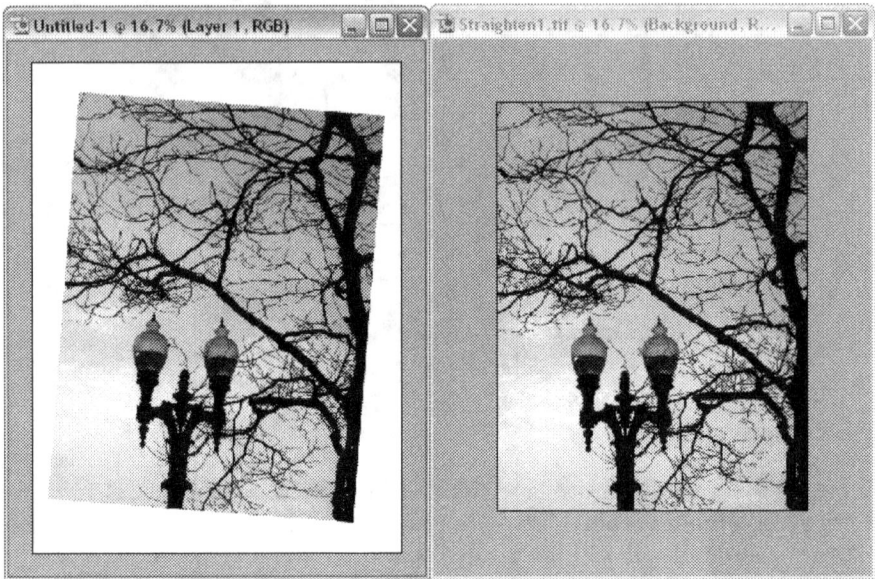

Note   *Sometimes extra area remains on one or two sides of the image. Issuing the Straighten And Crop Image command a second time may cure the problem, but that's a bit unpredictable. The best course is to switch to the Straighten Image command, and then trim the border with the Crop tool.*

Straighten Image   Use this option to straighten a parallel image while enlarging the canvas to accommodate the rotation. If you want the background color of the canvas to be white, be sure to press D to change the Color Swatches in the Toolbox to their default black foreground and white background before proceeding. Otherwise, the background of the rotation will be a different color from that in the original tilted image. Here's an image that has been Straightened with a different color background.

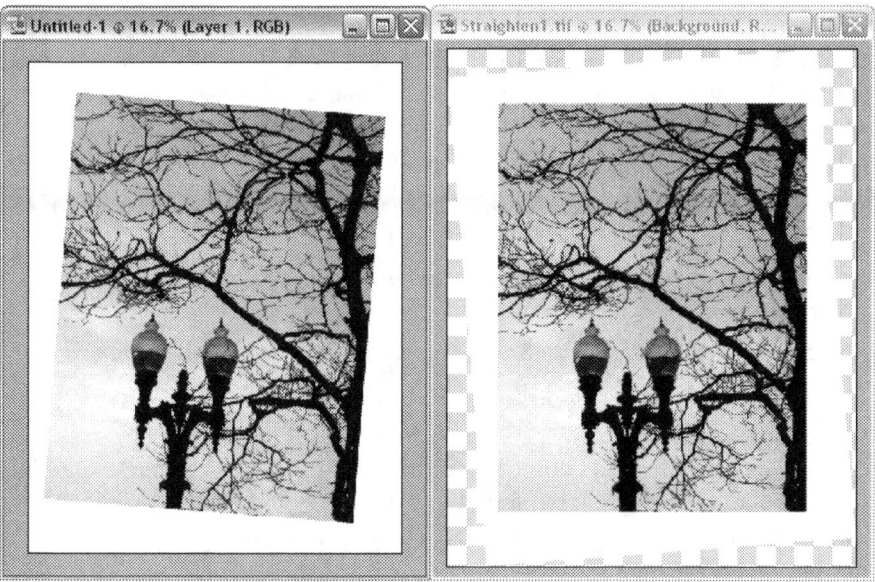

Transform

Transform is the general label Photoshop Elements applies to anything that will change in size, orientation, or distortion. Various transformation commands allow you to scale, skew, distort, perspective distort, rotate, or stretch (horizontally or vertically). During a *transformation,* the program recalculates the position that each pixel occupied before the transformation, places the pixels in a new location for the transformation, and mathematically figures out what to do about creating new pixels to fill spaces created when these pixels are moved around. The general name for this process is called *rendering,* a name that makes graphic artists shudder because they know that rendering takes time. Fortunately, today's computers are so fast that most transformations will render in little time—unless you are working on images that are too large to fit comfortably in your system's RAM.

The following sections describe the function of each of the Transform commands in Photoshop Elements.

Free Transform   Choosing this command or pressing CMD/CTRL+T lets you perform several kinds of transformations interactively *before* rendering. Because the computer has to render only once, significantly less loss of image data occurs.

When you issue the Free Transform command, an Options bar appears that lets you input precise mathematical figures for each type of transformation. You can also transform by dragging the transform handles or by dragging them in conjunction with a modifier key. The following tasks can be performed interactively:

- **Scale**   Drag any of the corner handles until the image is the size and shape you desire.
- **Scale proportionately**   Press SHIFT and drag any corner handle.
- **Stretch**   Drag a center handle.
- **Distort**   Press CMD/CTRL and drag a corner handle. Remember that you can do this as many times as you like before rendering, so you can use a distort transformation to correct perspective from any viewpoint.
- **Skew**   Press CMD/CTRL and drag one of the side handles.
- **Skew in two directions**   Press CMD/CTRL+OPT/ALT and drag one of the side handles. The opposite side handle will move at the same distance from the center of the image and in the opposite direction.
- **Rotate**   Place the cursor outside any of the control handles and drag. The layer will rotate from the center.

To transform numerically while the Free Transform command is in effect, use these tasks:

- **Scale**   Enter numeric values in the Options bar's Width (W) and Height (H) fields. The default unit is percentage of the current size, but you can also type in the abbreviations for units if you like: in = inches, px = pixels, cm = centimeters, mm = millimeters, and pt = points.
- **Scale proportionately**   Click the Link (chain) icon between the two scale fields. Any number you enter in one of the fields will enter the proportional measurement for the other dimension in the other field.
- **Stretch**   Just make sure the Maintain Aspect Ratio link is unlocked (grayed) and enter disproportionate scaling dimensions.

When you have finished making your free transformations, click the Commit (large check mark) button to render.

Skew   Choosing the Skew command lets you skew the image by dragging the size handles or distort the image by dragging the corner handles (no need to press CMD/CTRL to distort while the Skew command is active).

The Skew Options bar also lets you scale and rotate by entering numeric values. Click the Commit button to render.

Distort   Only the corner handles are active. However, you can rotate, scale, and skew by clicking the appropriate buttons or entering the appropriate fields in the Options bar.

Perspective   Dragging any of the corner handles moves a corner in any direction, and the opposite corner moves equidistantly in the opposite direction to produce a symmetric keystone distortion. Pressing CMD/CTRL while dragging a corner handle permits you to distort from only one corner at a time.

Crop

This is the command to use when you want to crop an image automatically to the maximum dimensions of a selection or when you want to use the rectangular marquee to designate an area you want to crop. Using the rectangular marquee is the best rectangular cropping method to use when you don't want the cropping area to snap to the edge of the image automatically.

The Crop command works only if you have already made a selection. Otherwise, choosing it affects nothing. The Crop command executes automatically, meaning that no resulting options, palettes, dialog boxes, or submenus are involved.

Resize

The Resize command changes the overall size of the image, either by making the image itself a different size or by changing the size of the canvas (the area in which you can edit—the workspace).

Whenever you change the size of the image, the number and location of the pixels must be recalculated. You will usually want the result to look as faithful to the original as possible. The extent to which that will be true is determined by two factors: how drastic the resizing is and which *interpolation* method you use.

When you resize, you need to remember that Photoshop Elements can't invent detail. The more you change the size of the original (or, more especially, the larger you make the image), the more important it becomes to use the most sophisticated interpolation method so that Photoshop Elements can at least keep the edges as sharp as possible. That would mean choosing Bicubic interpolation, but that also results in the slowest rendering times. On the other hand, if you want to enlarge the pixels themselves so that they become bigger and more jagged-looking squares, you can choose the least sophisticated Nearest Neighbor interpolation. Bipolar interpolation produces a result somewhere in between.

Note   *Keep in mind that you're probably going to be dissatisfied with the result of enlarging an image too much more than twice its original size unless you pay extra for a program that uses more sophisticated resampling technology that can redraw sharp edges and re-create some textures. Check our Lizard Tech's Altamira Print Shop Pro program and S-spline Photoshop–compatible plug-ins.*

Four choices are offered on the Resize command's fly-out submenu. Each of these is explained here.

Image Size   Whenever you want to reduce the overall size of your image for use on a web page or enlarge it for printing as an exhibit print, this is the command to choose. This command also tells your printer what image resolution will be used when printing the image at the size indicated in the Document Size area of the Image Size dialog box. Here's how to use the command:

1. Choose Image | Resize | Image Size. The Image Size dialog box appears, shown in Figure 3-21.

2. Optional: You can use the Pixel Dimensions area of the dialog box to change the overall dimensions of the image by entering numbers in the Width and Height fields, either as pixels or as a percentage of the original image size. Choose Pixels or Percentage from the Width or Height menu to determine which method of calculation will be used. If you are changing the image size but want to maintain the current aspect (height to width) ratio, be sure the Constrain Proportions check box is checked. If it is checked, you need to enter dimensions in only one field. They will automatically change in all other fields.

3. Optional: If you want to specify the exact size the image will print on your printer, keep the Constrain Proportions check box checked and enter one of the dimensions in the Document Size area's Width or Height field. If one of the dimensions doesn't fit, you can "cheat" by unchecking the Constrain Proportions check box and then entering the exact Height or Width you need to make up; the opposite dimension won't change at all.

4. To specify the resolution at which the image will print, uncheck the Resample Image check box and enter the resolution at which you want to print. The

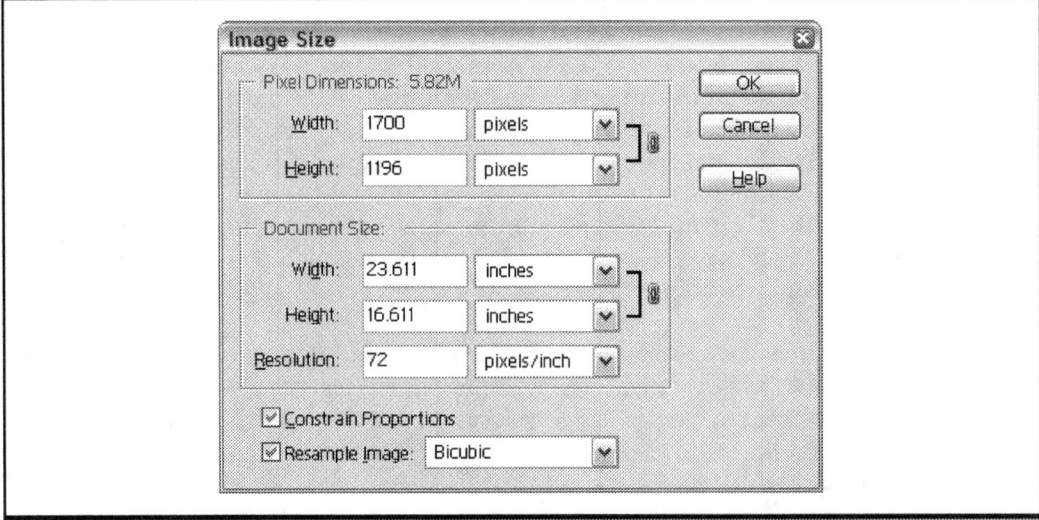

Figure 3-21.   *The Image Size dialog box enables you to adjust the size of your image.*

dimensions will change automatically to show the size at which you can print the image without resampling. If you want to change the dimensions but are willing to resample the image to keep the needed resolution, click to select the Resample Image check box and then enter new Document Size Height and Width dimensions.

Note *Usually, you will not want to resize the image with the Constrain Proportions box unchecked because it results in distorting the image in one direction. If you can't make the image the exact size you want for printing, enter the exact width you want in one direction and let the other dimension take care of itself. You can then use the Rectangular Marquee or Crop tool to trim the image to the exact size needed (see Chapter 5).*

Canvas Size Use this command if you want to change the size of your canvas without changing the size of the image itself. For instance, you might want room to add a border or frame around an image. Or you might want to make one dimension slightly taller or wider and then use the Clone Stamp tool to clone parts of an existing image to fill the empty edge or edges. This is also a handy command for making the canvas large enough to hold a set of several pictures inside a panel. (That's how we created most of our "before and after" illustrations for this book.)

Here's how to use the Canvas Size command:

1. Choose Image | Resize | Canvas Size. The Canvas Size dialog box appears, shown in Figure 3-22.

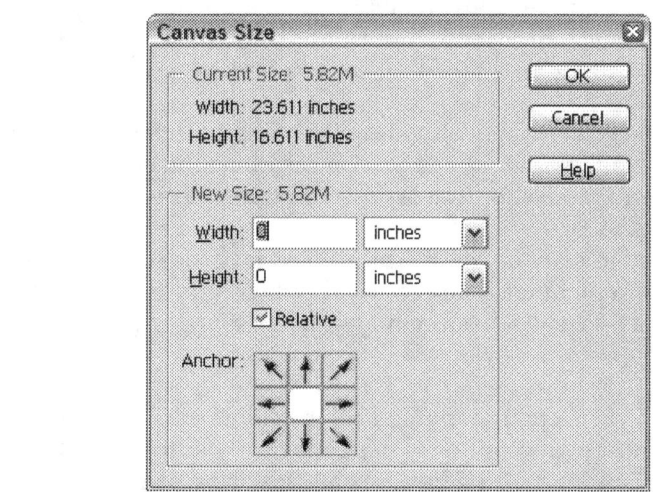

Figure 3-22. *The Canvas Size dialog box enables you to change the size of the canvas you're working on without changing the actual image.*

2. Enter the new size for the Canvas in both the Width and Height fields (there is no automatic way to maintain aspect ratio). Also, choose the units to be used from the Width and Height menus. You can choose inches, percent, pixels, cm, mm, points, and picas.

3. To position the image on the canvas, click one of the squares in the Anchor indicator. The square you choose will determine whether the image is centered on the canvas or aligned with one of the corners or sides of the image.

4. When you've completed these steps, click OK to render.

Reveal All   The Reveal All command is designed to reveal information that was created in a Photoshop 7 PSD file format when part of the image was hidden with the Crop command. When you load a file that was saved with the hidden portion, the Reveal All command will expose the hidden portions. You cannot hide parts of an image with the Crop command in Photoshop Elements.

Scale   This command places transform handles on the active layer border so you can scale the active layer by dragging the handles. Use OPT/ALT while dragging to scale from the center of the layer. Use SHIFT to scale the layer proportionally from any corner handle. Use OPT/ALT + SHIFT to scale proportionately using the selected reference point on the Options bar.

Adjustments

Fewer Adjustments commands appear in Photoshop Elements' Image menu than in the same menu in Photoshop because many of the commands that are frequently used have been moved to the Enhance menu in Photoshop Elements. Those that remain, generally speaking, make the most extreme adjustments to the image or create some kind of special effect. Five commands appear on Photoshop Elements' Image | Adjustments menu, and the purpose and method for using each is described next.

Equalize   The Equalize command is often used to bring up detail in a layer that couldn't be clearly seen in the original image. You can clone the detailed areas from that layer or use the Blend modes for that layer to combine those details with other details in the underlying layer.

   This command automatically makes the brightness level of all colors in the image roughly equal. Because "a picture is worth a thousand words," Figure 3-23 shows an image before and after the Equalize command has been issued, with each showing its associated histogram.

Gradient Map   This bizarre command maps all the colors in the current image into those in the currently chosen gradient. This happens nearly automatically. You issue the command and the Gradient Map dialog box appears. If you've planned ahead, you can

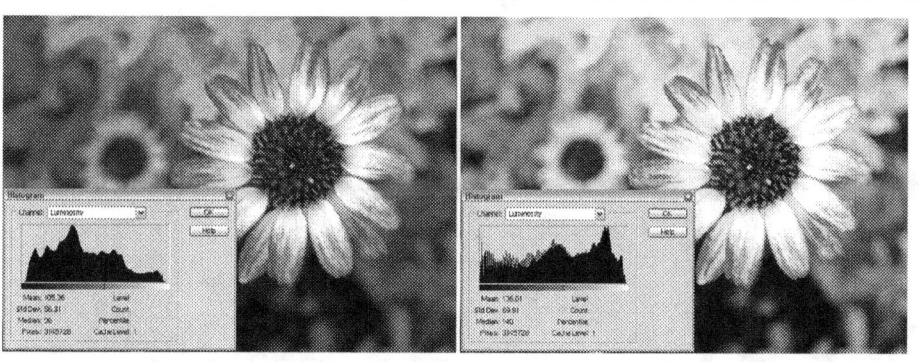

Figure 3-23.   *An image and its associated histogram before and after the Equalize command has been issued*

create a specific gradient, place it in the gradient presets, and then use it to remap an image into a duotone. Using this command is simply a matter of issuing it, toggling the appropriate check boxes, and then choosing a gradient from one of the gradient sets (see Chapter 5).

Invert   Choosing this command or pressing CMD/CTRL+I converts the image from positive to negative, or vice versa. Unfortunately, there's no option for getting rid of the orange mask that accompanies color negative film, but most film (and flatbed, for that matter) scanner software will do this for you.

Posterize   The Posterize command reduces the number of colors in the image to whatever you specify. When the Posterize dialog box appears, you type in the number of color levels to which you'd like to convert the image. This is a great way to make simplified, fast-loading web graphics that you can easily store in web-safe colors in GIF format. See Chapter 18.

Threshold   This command turns all the pixels in the image to either black or white. It can be handy for turning a Find Edges layer into an edge selection (see Chapter 7) or for making area selections. If you first turn the image into pure black and white, and then paint out the areas you don't want selected, you can easily select all the others with the Magic Wand tool.

When you choose Image | Adjustments | Threshold, the Threshold dialog box appears. If the Preview check box is checked, you will immediately see what turns pure black and what turns pure white in the image. Move the slider to change the threshold until you see what you want. Then click OK.

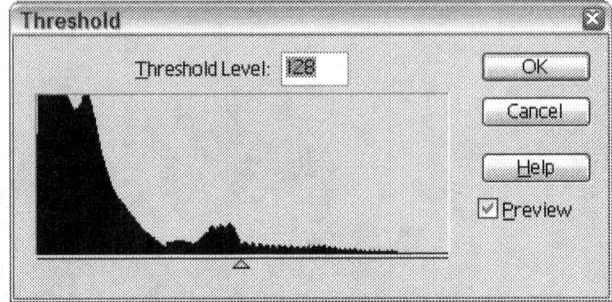

Histogram

The Image | Histogram command lets you check the density of pixels at each of the 256 levels of brightness in the image by *graphing* them. It's a quick way to get an idea of how and where you want to color-correct your image.

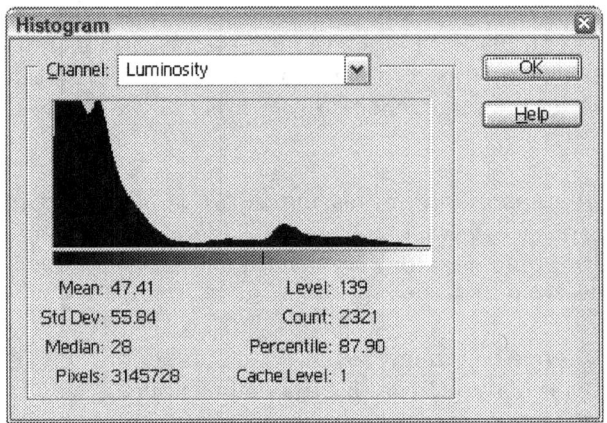

The same histogram is available when you choose the Levels command. However, choosing Histogram alone lets you discover much more information about the image. You can get the following information, the meaning of which is described in the paragraphs that follow.

- ■ **Mean**   The average value of the brightness intensities in the image.
- ■ **Std. Deviant**   The degree to which brightness intensities vary.
- ■ **Median**   The middle value of the brightness range in this image.
- ■ **Pixels**   The total number of pixels appearing in the image.
- ■ **Level**[*]   The brightness level of exactly that point in the histogram where the cursor is currently placed.

---

[*]   Information provided only when cursor is atop the histogram

- **Count**[*]   How many pixels are at the current cursor's exact location in the histogram.
- **Percentile**[*]   What percentage of the pixels are at the current brightness level.
- **Cache Level**   How many cache levels are being used to store the pixels shown in the histogram. If the cache level is higher than 1, the total number of pixels being shown is the number of total pixels in the image divided by the number of levels.

Mode

The commands on the Mode submenu determine whether the image can contain only black-and-white or grayscale, whether it will be limited to 256 colors, or whether it can display all the available colors. You can use a Mode command to convert an image to another mode with fewer colors, but it can't work the other way around. The two most popular conversions are from RGB color to Indexed Color to produce images that can be used on the Web as GIF files or to reduce images from full color to grayscale. Grayscale images are usually referred to as black-and-white images, although they actually display a full range of continuous tones of gray (the 256 gray tones that do display are actually more than our eyes can readily distinguish between adjacent tones). Images that are composed of only black and white are called *bitmaps* (even though all photos are bitmaps as opposed to vectors).

Bitmap   Bitmapped images in the context of this command have only one bit per pixel. This means the pixels can be either black or white. The Bitmap dialog box allows you to choose the resolution you want to use for the converted (output) image, and whether you want the image to simulate grayscale by converting the image to either a pattern or diffusion image that can create the illusion of being grayscale. Bitmapped images are commonly used in monotone printing and on monotone LCDs that are found on wireless communication devices. The Bitmap dialog box that appears when you choose this command is shown next.

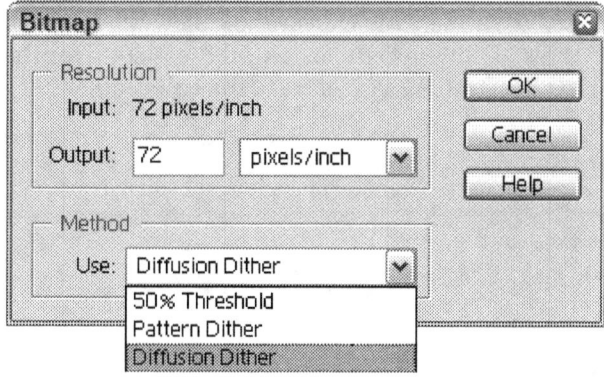

Grayscale   Grayscale images contain the full spectrum of 256 shades of gray. They represent what we are used to seeing as black-and-white photographs. When you choose this command, a dialog box appears that asks whether it's okay to discard color information. If you don't want the warning to appear, you can check the Don't Show Again check box. Otherwise, click OK and the conversion is done automatically with no further options or adjustments.

Indexed Color   Indexed color images are also referred to as *bitmapped* images because each pixel in the image is mapped (indexed) to one of the 256 colors that are possible in any image (out of a total palette of 256,000 colors). This means that when you change an instance of color, all pixels with that color indexed to them will change also. Because indexed images have to store much less color information, they are ideal for small, highly graphical web images that are meant to be displayed as GIF files. Indexing also allows for making a key color transparent. For much more on how indexed images are used on the Web, see Chapter 18.

RGB Color   RGB color is the full-spectrum color mode that makes all the Photoshop Elements commands available to you. For that reason, you should edit your images in this mode until you know that you've made all the edits and enhancements you need. Then duplicate the image and convert the duplicate to any color mode that might be needed for a special purpose. This method preserves an RGB color original that will give you the most flexibility in editing. Because this is the default color mode for Photoshop Elements, no dialog box exists. Your settings either are already there or can't get there from one of the other smaller spectrum modes. Be aware that when you change color modes away from RGB, you are going to reduce the color content to some extent. That doesn't mean that you can't open a grayscale, indexed color, or bitmapped image and then switch to RGB color mode. It just won't change any of the existing colors to a wider spectrum. It means that you can then add any color you want to the image.

Color Table   The Color Table is active only when the image is in Indexed color mode. An Indexed image is capable of displaying a maximum of 256 colors (out of a possible palette of 256,000). When you choose the Color Table command, an array of color swatches displays, telling you the extent of the palette for the current indexed color image. In the next illustration, you can see the color table that was created from the flower image.

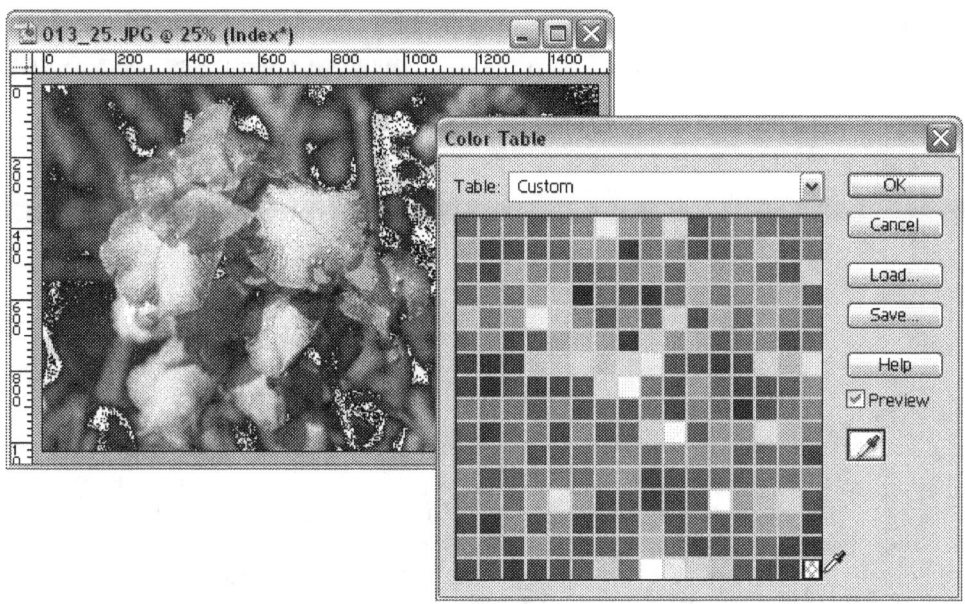

The Eyedropper tool can be used to select a transparent color by clicking in the image or selecting a color from the table. You will see the colors highlighted in the image and on the table, as you will see in the image after the color in the lower-right corner of the table is selected. You can save a color table to an ACT format file, and those files can be loaded and applied to other indexed images. You can also apply some preset palettes from the Table drop-down menu.

Note   _To remap a saved color table to an image, the image must be in RGB mode to start; then you must use the Indexed conversion command with Custom selected in the Forced menu so you can load a saved color table and get it to remap the image. If you load saved palettes from the color table, it will just replace the index without remapping it, which can give you nice psychedelic effects._

Enhance Menu

The Enhance menu specializes in the commands that are used to adjust image brightness, contrast, and color balance. You can get a more in-depth look at how to use the Enhance commands in Chapters 12 and 13. Most of these commands are used for exposure correction, rather than special effects—but always for one or the other. For that reason, all you'll find here is a short synopsis of what each command does. You'll find much more detail in the chapters that specifically cover image correction and special effects.

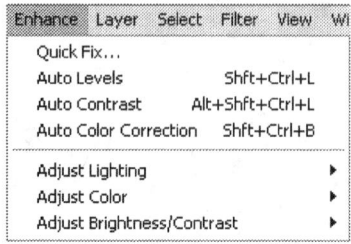

Quick Fix

The Quick Fix command provides you with a simple but effective interface for performing a whole range of image corrections, with each command being added to the overall correction before all are rendered to the final image by clicking the OK button. This is a great way to bring all but the most hopeless shots into at least presentable form. The Quick Fix dialog box is shown next, but be aware that the lower half of the dialog box changes each time you select one of the items in the leftmost column. You'll find explicit instruction on each of these categories and their subcommands in Chapter 2. In addition, all the Quick Fix commands are found individually as commands on the Enhance menu, so their functions are discussed in somewhat more detail in the following sections.

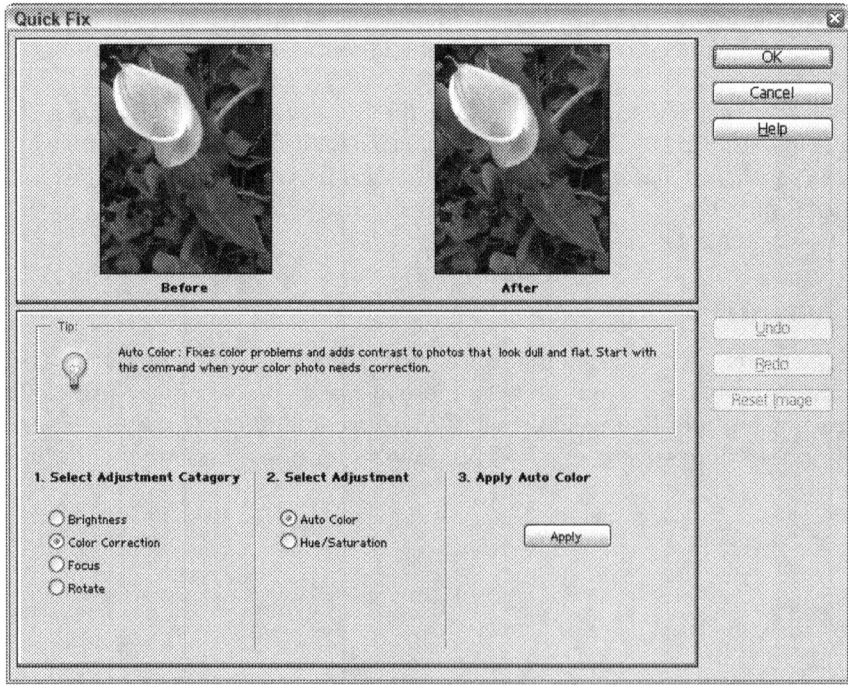

Auto Levels

Choosing this command or pressing SHIFT+CMD/CTRL+L automatically performs the method of operation we recommend for using the Levels command—except it does it in a single click. The only real advantage in doing this manually is that you can subjectively judge where to place the highlight and shadow sliders for each channel.

Auto Contrast

Choosing this command or pressing OPT/ALT+SHIFT+CMD/CTRL+L gets exactly the same results as using Auto Levels, except the highlight and shadow sliders are automatically placed at the lightest and darkest points of the composite channel's histogram, so it doesn't change or correct color balance.

Auto Color Correction

Choosing this command or pressing SHIFT+CMD/CTRL+B can be similar to the two preceding commands, except this command uses a more accurate method of determining gamma (brightness range) and color balance. Rather than using histograms, Auto Color Correction finds the actual lightest and darkest pixels and then distributes all brightness values between them. Then it balances color by finding the pixels that are closest to midtone brightness and also closest to being neutral. Then it adjusts the overall color balance according to what it will take to make that tone neutral.

Adjust Lighting

Choosing this command reveals a submenu with two items, Adjust Backlighting and Fill Flash. These controls are designed to help correct for poor lighting conditions in photographs by selectively adjusting tonal range in light and dark areas of the image.

Adjust Backlighting   Choose this command to darken the brightest pixels, and then redistribute the histogram to bring detail into highlights that become washed out when the subject is backlit and the photographer exposes for the subject's shaded side. Unfortunately, it can't create information where there was none, so it just turns an area of flat white to an area of flat gray. The dialog box has a single slider to control the intensity of the effect.

Fill Flash   Choose this command or press SHIFT+CMD/CTRL+F to turn on Fill Flash. This feature is so good that one can't help wondering why it isn't in Photoshop 7.0 (we'll show you another way to do the same thing in Chapter 12). A dialog box appears that has one slider. The further you drag the slider to the right, the more the deep shadows are lightened, but the darkest pixels stay black. Excellent for pictures when the Fill Flash you used wasn't powerful enough to reach subjects that were too far away or where the shadows cast by the Fill Flash were just too darn dark.

Adjust Color

The commands on this submenu are all related to color correction or color interpretation (tinging to create a mood or effect). One command can even be used to change the color of a specific object, such as a car in an auto ad or the color of an article of clothing.

Color Cast   The Color Cast command provides instant color correction. The Color Cast Correction dialog box presents you with an Eyedropper tool. Click any pixel that should be neutral (white, black, or gray), and the color balance of the image is automatically corrected. If you don't like the result, you can just keep clicking until you do.

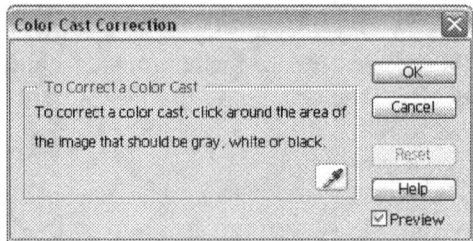

Hue/Saturation   Choosing this command or pressing CMD/CTRL+U provides three sliders that let you adjust overall color tint (hue), color intensity (saturation), and midrange brightness level. You can also colorize (tone) a grayscale version of the image by clicking the Colorize check box to toggle it on.

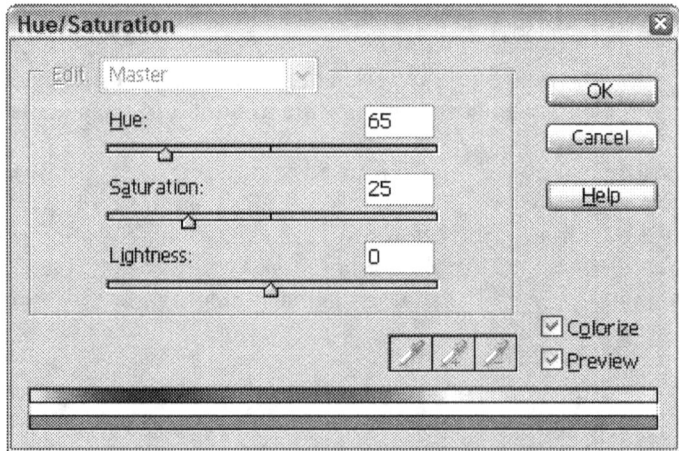

Remove Color   Choosing this command or pressing SHIFT+CMD/CTRL+U takes all the color out of the image and still leaves you with an RGB image. This command lets you convert any color picture to black and white in a single click while still allowing you to add colors after the fact, unlike a grayscale image. This is useful for creating a tinted look in a photo.

Replace Color   This dialog box, shown next, lets you select a color range with an Eyedropper. Add or subtract to the range by using the plus or minus Eyedroppers and then drag the Fuzziness slider to expand or contract the tolerances associated with your choice of colors. This will allow you to select the areas that you want to replace with the new color you create with the Transform sliders. The new color will be indicated in the color square. You can see the effect of the color change by checking it in the preview box.

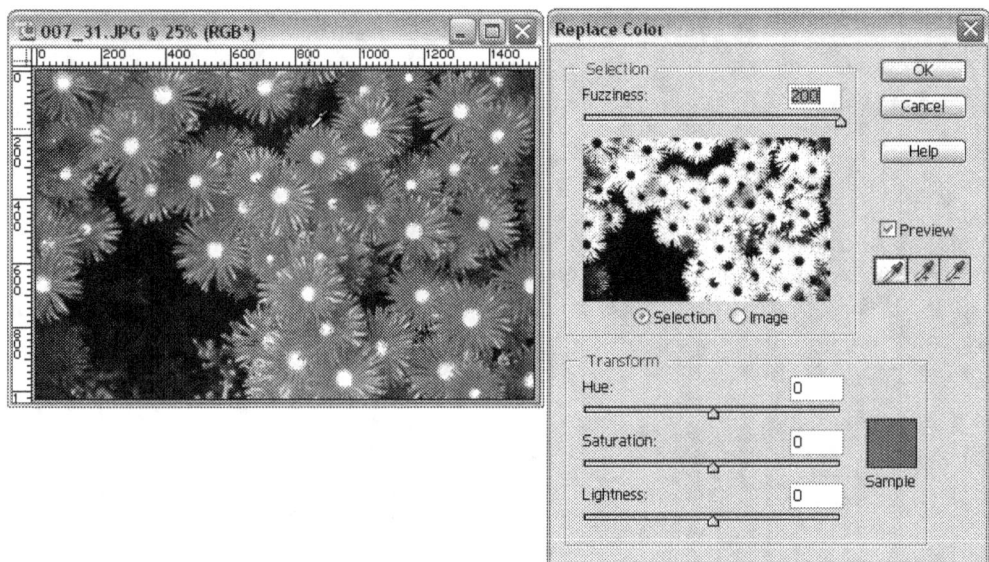

Color Variations   This command is a slightly simplified version of the Variations command found in Photoshop, but you're not likely to miss what's missing. The purpose of this command is to let you visually and simultaneously compare the result of the most likely image-enhancement choices by looking at a contact sheet in which each thumbnail image has already been color or brightness corrected. All you have to do to make a change is click the change you like. That change is automatically added to the last change you chose. You can keep making changes until what you see in the before and after thumbnails corresponds with the result you want. If you go overboard and don't like any of the results, you can reset the thumbnails and start all over.

Adjust Brightness/Contrast

Two subcommands appear under this menu choice, each offering a different way to correct overall image brightness and contrast.

Brightness/Contrast   This dialog box consists of a pair of sliders—one each for Brightness and Contrast. Drag the appropriate slider to make a change in either. If the Preview box is checked, you immediately see the result in your image. Changes affect only the midtones.

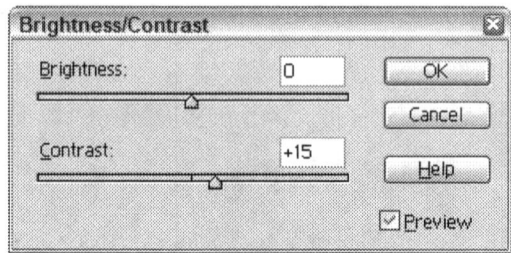

Levels   Choose this command or press CMD/CTRL+L to access Photoshop Elements' most accurate method for controlling brightness, contrast, and color balance. In Chapter 12, you see a high-precision routine for getting the most detail and information from your image while you also set it up in a way that will get you the most eye-pleasing color balance.

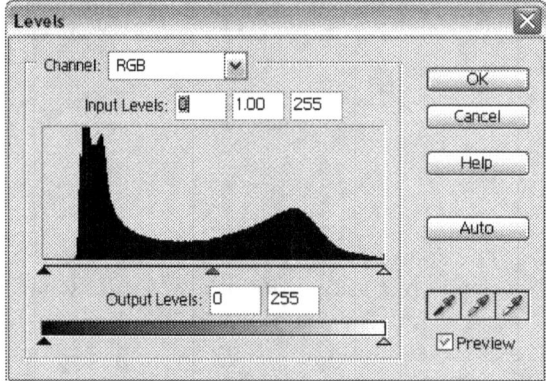

Layer Menu

The commands on the Layer menu have to do with managing and editing layers. See Chapter 8 for more information on using Layers.

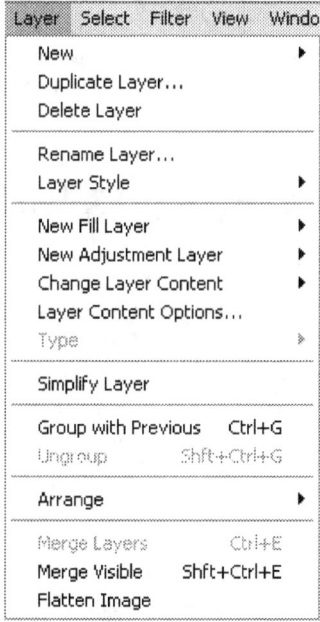

The following five layer types in Photoshop Elements 2.0 layers are essentially the same as those in Photoshop 7:

- Image
- Adjustment
- Text
- Style
- Fill

Image layers are the basis for layers. Think of a layer as a sheet of clear acetate; when no portion of an image appears on the layer, you can see through to underlying layers. Layers make it possible for you to isolate a portion or version of an image by duplicating all or a portion of the background image (the whole image as it was originally scanned or photographed) or by using any of the various means of importing additional content from other sources (imported content is always placed on its own layer). Any tool or command in Photoshop Elements 2.0 will normally affect only the currently active (selected in the Layer's palette) layer or whatever portion of that layer you've placed inside a marquee selection.

Adjustment layers don't contain images. Instead, they are used to apply commands in the Image and Enhance menus to all the visible portions of all the underlying layers.

Text layers are created as soon as you use the Text tool to enter text in the workspace. One reason for keeping text on its own layer is so that you can always go back and add more text or correct any mistakes you might have made without affecting anything else.

Style layers contain all the adjustments and other procedures needed to impose special effects on the currently active image or text layer. In Photoshop Elements, you create a style layer by double-clicking an icon in the Styles palette or by dragging its icon onto the image.

Fill layers can be filled with any of the options in the Fill dialog box: Foreground, Background, White, Black, Gray, Gradient, or Pattern.

Chapter 8 is devoted to the use of layers and goes into extensive detail about each facet of their use and all the practical ways that they can be used to solve problems. Here, for quick reference, is a brief synopsis of the commands on the Layers menu.

New

These commands let you create a new layer in one of five different ways: Layer, Layer From Background, Background From Layer, Layer Via Copy, or Layer Via Cut. In Chapter 8, you'll also learn of other ways to create layers.

Layer   Choosing this command or pressing SHIFT+CMD/CTRL+N creates a new, empty layer.

Layer From Background   Choosing this command turns the background layer (which can't be reordered, have transparency, or change its Blend mode) into a regular layer.

Background From Layer   Choosing this command converts the currently active layer into a background layer and renames it as such. This command isn't on the menu unless no background layer currently appears in the Layers palette. When this command is present, the Layer From Background command isn't available.

Layer Via Copy   Choosing this command copies the current selection or layer into a new layer. This is handy if you want to use a special effect filter on the current layer without modifying the current layer or if you want to preserve two states of the same layer.

Layer Via Cut   Choosing this command removes the contents of the current selection from the currently active layer and automatically places them on a new layer. It's useful when you want to isolate part of an image from its original surroundings or replace the background.

Duplicate Layer

Choosing this command from the Layer menu copies the entire currently active layer, regardless of whether a selection is active. In the Duplicate Layer dialog box, you can rename the document or send the layer to another document, as shown here.

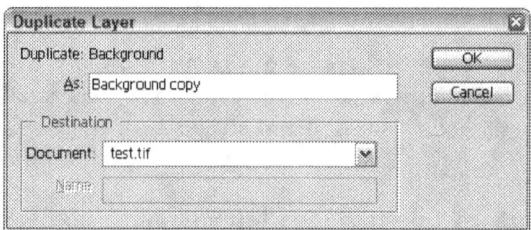

Delete Layer

Choosing this command deletes the currently active layer.

Rename Layer

Choosing this command causes the Layer Properties dialog box to appear so you can enter a new name in the Name field.

Layer Style

The Layer Style command is designed to provide an extra set of controls for style effects that were applied to layers from the Layers Styles palette. The commands will affect the current layer if it has an active style indicated by the *F* symbol in the layer name bar. Following are the subcommands you can choose from in the Layer Style command menu:

Style Settings   Choosing this command brings up a dialog box (shown next) that allows you to change the settings for any currently selected layer that has been styled. The contents of this dialog box vary, depending on the kinds of settings that are applicable to the particular style.

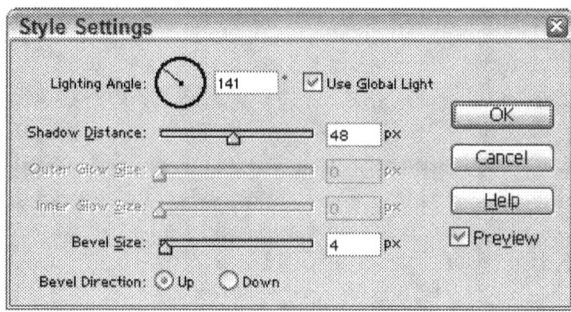

Copy Layer Style   Choosing this command copies all the current layer style settings to the clipboard. No dialog boxes or submenus appear with this command.

Paste Layer Style   This command is not available unless a layer style has been copied from another layer. It applies the Layer style to a layer other than the background layer.

Clear Layer Style   Choosing this command removes all style settings from the current layer. In other words, it lets you return the layer to normal. It is useful if you try a style and then decide that the styling is not suitable for the message you wanted to convey.

Hide/Show All Effects   Choosing this command hides *all* the effects applied to all layers with styles in the document. If all the effects are already hidden, the Hide All Effects command changes to Show All Effects, which will turn on all the effects that have been placed in the document previously.

Scale Effects   Choosing this command changes the measurements and intensities of the current effects settings by the percentage you enter in the dialog box shown next. Think of it as a master control to crank up or down all the attributes in the style settings. It affects only the currently active layer—not all layers to which effects have been assigned.

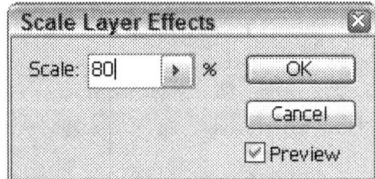

New Fill Layer

Choosing Layer | New Fill Layer creates a new fill layer. This differs from the procedure for creating a new layer and then choosing Edit | Fill because, using this command, you can easily change the settings later, just as you can change Style settings. In addition, each choice on the submenu lets you prechoose blend mode and transparency from a dialog box *before* creating the fill.

Solid Color   Choosing this command brings up the New Layer dialog box, shown next, and lets you choose the Blend mode and Opacity you'd like to use for the layer (you can change these settings after the fact in the Layers palette; see Chapter 8). When you click OK, the Color Picker dialog box you chose in Preferences (the default is the operating system's Color Picker) lets you choose any color in the rainbow. As soon as you choose the color, the new fill layer appears.

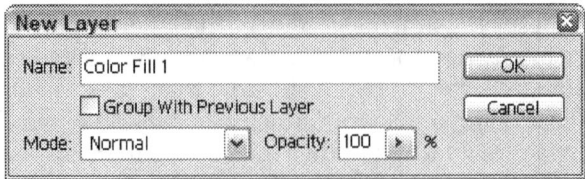

Gradient   Choosing this command creates a new, filled layer using any gradient that's currently loaded into your gradient presets. Once you've set the parameters in the New Layer dialog box (the same dialog box used for Solid Color) the Gradient Fill dialog box appears, as shown next. Here you choose gradient style, the angle of the gradient, its scale, whether the gradient will be in the same color order shown in the Gradient menu or reversed, and whether the fill will be aligned with the current layer.

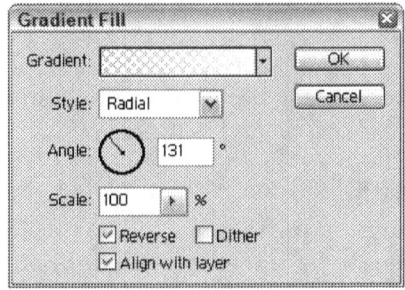

Pattern   Choose this command to create a new layer automatically filled with any pattern you choose from your current pattern presets, using the same procedure as for Solid Color and Gradient Fill layers, just described. When you click OK in the New Layer dialog box, the Pattern Fill dialog box appears (as shown here) and you can scale the pattern to the layers, click a button to snap the upper-left corner of the layer to the origin of the pattern, and toggle a check mark to link the pattern to the layer.

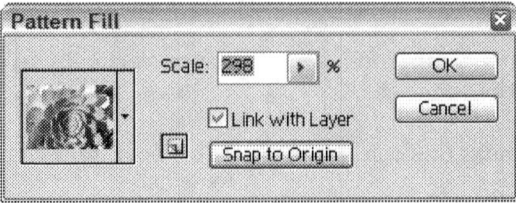

New Adjustment Layer

Adjustment layers let you perform all sorts of image adjustments (specifically, Levels, Brightness/Contrast, Hue/Saturation, Gradient Map, Invert, Threshold, and Posterize).

You choose which of these adjustments you want the layer to perform from one of the submenus listed in the following sections. The commands associated with any Adjustment layer work on everything visible on any layer below that Adjustment layer in the Layer's palette. Otherwise, these commands work exactly as they do when chosen from the main menu to which they're attached (either Image or Enhance)—however, the effects remain separate and editable all the time, which gives you ultimate flexibility. You can find a more detailed description for each of the commands for Adjustment layers in the "Enhance Menu" and "Image Menu" sections, earlier in this chapter. The Adjustment layers are Levels, Brightness/Contrast, Hue/Saturation, Gradient Map, Invert, Threshold, and Posterize.

Change Layer Content

This command lets you change the content of the currently active layer from one Fill or Adjustment layer type to another. Choosing any of the following commands from the submenu will change the type and open the appropriate dialog boxes. Refer to the "Image Menu" and "Enhance Menu" sections, earlier in this chapter, to read more about what you can do in these dialog boxes. The submenu commands correspond to the complete list of adjustment and fill layers types.

Layer Content Options

Choosing this command brings up the Options dialog box for whatever the current Content layer content happens to be and allows you to change those options.

Type

Choosing this command lets you choose and adjust exactly the same options for Type as you can choose from the Type Options bar. The only difference is that using the commands from this location gives you easier access for a type layer that has already been created—perhaps several editing stages previous to the one you currently find yourself in. Be sure to first open the Layers palette and select the layer you want to affect.

Horizontal Choosing this command orients the type horizontally.

Vertical Choosing this command orients the type vertically in a stacked text method, not a 90-degree rotated baseline.

Anti-Alias Off Choosing this command produces text with sharp, jagged edges with no softening.

Anti-Alias On Choosing this command softens the text edges by blending the edges into the background colors.

Warp Text Choosing this command brings up the Warp Text dialog box, which presents a number of options from the pull-down menu for bending and distorting the text.

Simplify Layer

Choosing the Layer | Simplify Layer command converts the content of certain layer types to raster image format. To put it another way, the command rasterizes the current layer. Because image layers are raster graphics (that is, they're pixel based rather than vector based), this command is unavailable if the currently active layer is an image layer. Layer types that are candidates are type, shape, all three types of fill layers, and imported layer sets.

Group With Previous

Choosing this command or pressing CMD/CTRL+G lets the shape of one layer act as a clipping path for the contents and blending modes created with another layer (or layers) that are grouped with it. The command lets the transparent parts of the base layer act as a mask for the layers above that are grouped with this command. For detailed information on using this command, see Chapter 8.

Ungroup

Choosing this command or pressing SHIFT+CMD/CTRL+G ungroups the currently selected layer from the rest of the group. If layers are linked, all layers will be ungrouped.

Arrange

This command lets you change the stacking order of layers. You can do this more easily by dragging the layers in the Layers palette, but Photoshop—even Photoshop Elements—has made its reputation by providing a seemingly infinite number of ways to perform any task. To move the currently active layer in the stacking order, make one of the choices here:

Bring To Front   Choose this command to place the currently selected layer at the front of the stack.

Bring Forward   Choose this command to move the currently active layer to the position immediately forward of that layer. In other words, the current layer trades places with the layer currently above it.

Send Backward   Choose this command and the current layer trades places with the layer immediately below it.

Send To Back   Choose this command and the current layer becomes the layer immediately above the background layer—not the bottom layer in the stack, unless there is no background layer.

Merge Linked

Choosing this command or pressing CMD/CTRL+E combines all linked layers into a single layer.

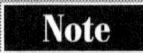 *Any hidden parts of layers are lost when layers are merged or flattened.*

Merge Visible

Choosing this command or pressing SHIFT+CMD/CTRL+E merges all the visible portions of layers into a single layer.

Flatten Image

Choosing this command combines all layers into one.

Select Menu

The Select menu, shown next, provides commands for globally selecting, deselecting, or inverting selections made with the selection tools. This menu also includes commands for modifying and saving selections made with the selection tools.

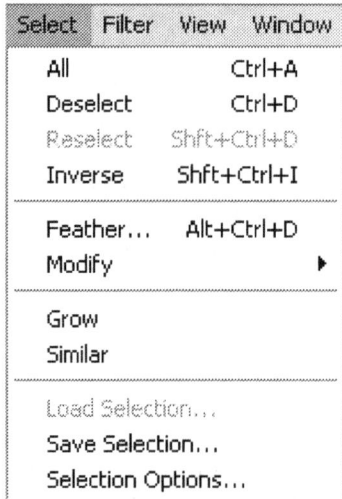

All

Choosing this command or pressing CMD/CTRL+A selects the complete contents of the active image file and places a "marching ants" border at the parameter of the image. This command supersedes any selections already active.

Deselect

Choosing this command or pressing CMD/CTRL+D deselects any active selection.

Reselect

Choosing this command or pressing SHIFT+CMD/CTRL+D reselects the last selection that was deselected.

Inverse

Choosing this command or pressing SHIFT+CMD/CTRL+I inverts the active selection. Inverting the selection is an efficient technique that is useful when you need to work on complimentary areas of an image, as shown next. This operation creates a new selection that includes every pixel that was excluded by the original selection. The command can be rechosen to return to the original selection.

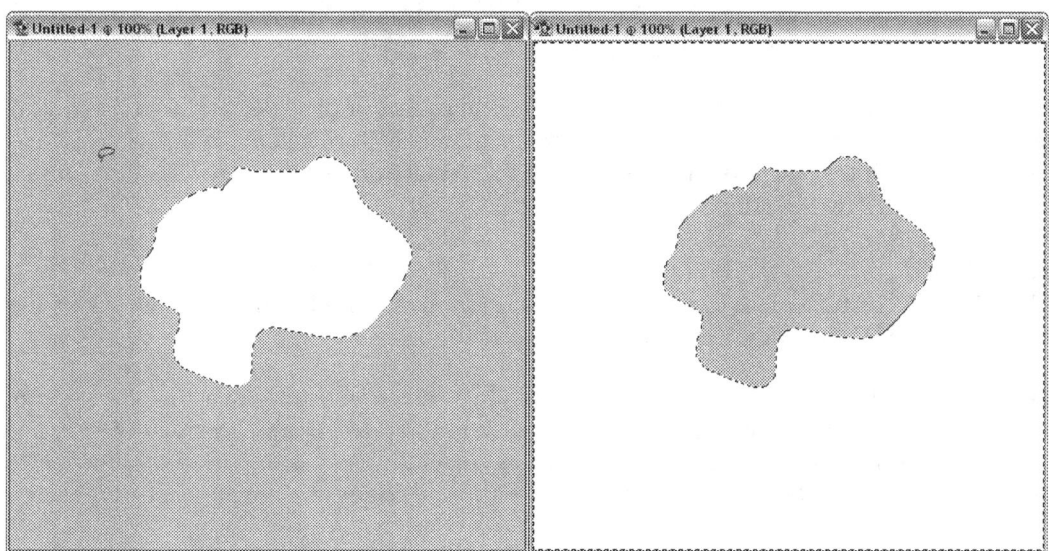

Feather

Choose this command or press OPT/ALT+CMD/CTRL+D to soften the transition at the borders of selections by blending the selection into the surrounding image area. You can use the Feather command on any active selection created with marquee, lasso, polygon lasso, magnetic lasso, magic wand, or selection brush. The effect of feathering will not become apparent until you move, cut, paste, copy, transform, or fill the selection. You may notice a smoothing of the selection border after applying the command. The edge of the selection affected by the Feather command is essentially composite with the background pixels.

   To activate the Feather command, choose Select | Feather. The Feather Selection dialog box, shown next, will appear. Enter the Feather Radius in the input field to set the distance in pixels that the effect will cover relative to the selection border. The distance is measured with the selection border as the centerline, so the command will affect pixels equally for both the inside and outside selection marquees. You will need to reset the Feather Radius every time you make a new selection unless you issue the Feather command on the Options bar for the selection tool you are using (see Chapter 5). You can apply the Feather command multiple times to the same selection and the effect accumulates. You cannot cancel or back off the command once you have initiated it, unless you use Undo.

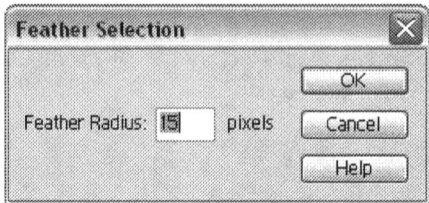

If you select a Feather Radius that exceeds the radius of the selection area itself, you will see a message that says, "No pixels are more than 50% selected." If this occurs, reduce the radius amount or choose OK to let the selection be faint. See Chapter 7 for more on feathering selections.

Modify

The Modify command provides four separate methods for modifying an active selection. These are Border, Smooth, Expand, and Contract.

Border   The Border command is used to create a selection border of a specified width around an active selection. This inverts the selection and then limits the area of effect for the new selection by the number of pixels you set in the Width field in the Border Selection dialog box (a value between 1 and 200). The edges of a border will always be anti-aliased.

The border is indicated by an inner and outer selection boundary. The area between the two selections can be filled, as shown here.

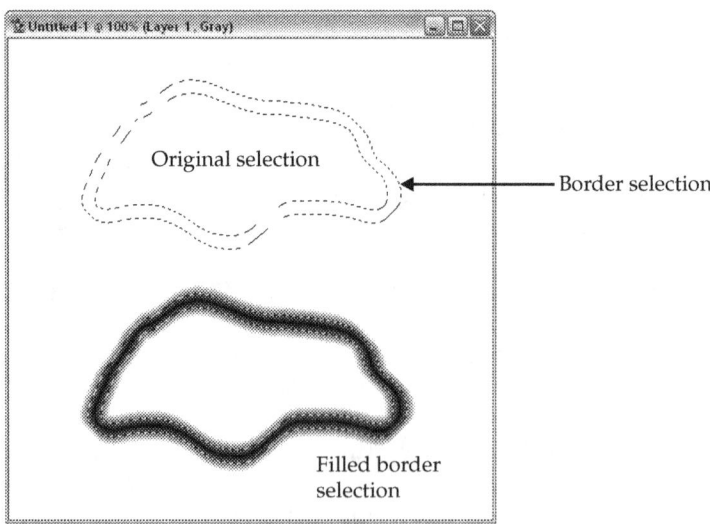

Smooth   The Smooth command is used to select or deselect stray pixels within the selection area. It does this by using a pixel range that you define. The program then checks to determine whether most of the pixels in that range are selected or deselected. If most are selected, it will remove any deselected pixels. If most are unselected, the program will remove any selected pixels. The value between 1 and 100 entered in the Smooth Selection dialog box's Sample Radius text box represents the pixel distance the program will search in all directions from any pixel that is selected. For example, entering 10 will cause the program to search in a 21×21-pixel square around the targeted pixel. This command can be helpful when using the Magic Wand selection tool, which often leaves stray pixels.

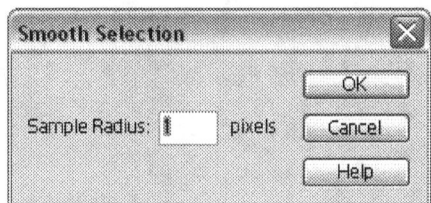

Expand   The Expand command enlarges the active selection by the pixel dimension entered in the Expand Selection dialog box. Enter a value between 1 and 100.

Contract   The Contract command shrinks the active selection by the pixel dimension entered in the Contract Selection dialog box. Enter a value between 1 and 100.

Grow
The Select | Grow command is used to extend an active selection by selecting pixels adjacent to an active selection that fall into the Magic Wand tolerance range found on the Magic Wand Options bar. (See Chapter 5 for more on the Magic Wand tool.) You can run the command successively to increase the area of effect. This command will not work on bitmapped images.

Similar
The Similar command is used to extend an active selection by selecting all pixels in the whole image that fall into the Magic Wand tolerance range found on the Magic Wand Options bar. (See Chapter 5 for more on the Magic Wand tool.) You can run the command successively to increase the area of effect. This command will not work on bitmapped images.

Load Selection
The Load Selection command loads any selection that was saved with the Save Selection command. In the Load Selection dialog box, shown next, choose a selection to load from the drop-down Selection menu. Click any of the radio buttons under Operation.

New Selection will replace the active selection with the saved selection. Add To Selection will add the saved selection to the active selection. Where the selections overlap, they will merge. Subtract From Selection will use the saved selection to subtract from any active selections where they overlap. Intersect With Selection will use the saved selection to create a new selection, which is delineated by the intersection of the saved and active selections. The intersect will have no effect if the selections do not overlap. Add a check mark to the Invert check box to invert the saved selection before it is placed. Saved selections remain in memory only while a document is loaded; they are not saved with the document. (See Chapter 7 for more on loading selections.)

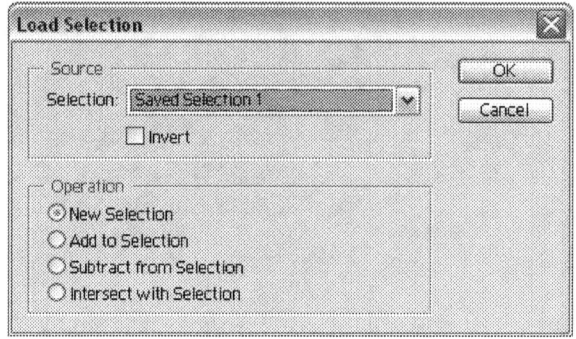

Save Selection

The Save Selection command saves the active selection so it can be retrieved later with the Load Selection command. In the Load Selection dialog box, choose New from the Selection drop-down menu. Type a name for the saved selection in the Name field. If you do not type in a name, the program will apply a default name and number. Click OK to save the selection.

To modify a saved selection with an active selection, choose the name of the saved selection from the drop-down Selection menu. Choose one of the four radio buttons under Operation. Replace Selection (this option only shows up when you select a previously saved selection to save over) will replace the saved selection with the active selection. Add To Selection will add the active selection to the saved selection and save the result. Where they overlap, they will merge. Subtract From Selection will subtract the active selection from the saved selection wherever they overlap and save the result. Intersect With Selection will use the active selection to create a new saved selection that is delineated by the intersection of the two selections. Saved selections remain in memory only while a document is loaded and are not saved with the document. (See Chapter 7 for more on saving selections.)

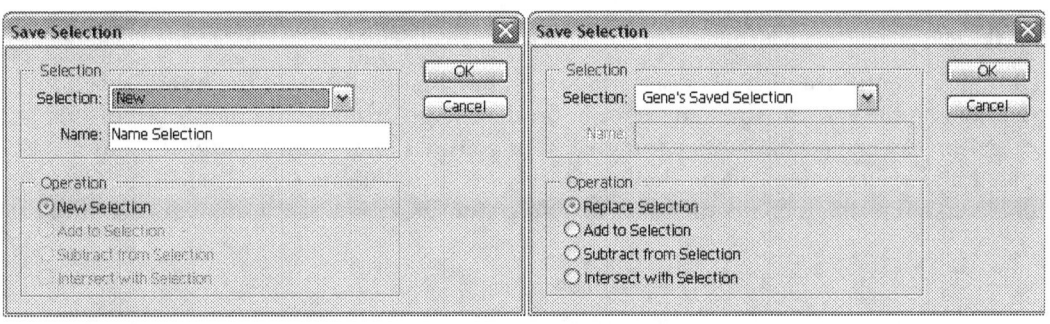

Filter Menu

The Filter menu commands offer a significant amount of imaging power. Adobe has packed this menu with 99 built-in filters that can transform your images in ways you probably haven't imagined. You can also combine and modify filter effects to extend the possibilities almost indefinitely. If you are familiar with Photoshop, you will recognize these filters. We suggest that you take some time to explore the long list of time-tested, built-in filters that Adobe has provided.

The filters are divided into 13 categories, as you can see in the following illustration. You can find a complete description of all the filters in each of these categories in Chapter 15.

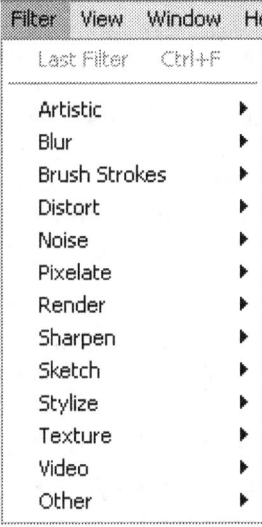

View Menu

The View menu provides a set of commands that change the way the image window displays on the screen. You can zoom in on the image or make the picture fit on the screen so you can see the entire image. Other commands let you hide or display selections, activate the grid and rulers, and show annotations. The Rulers and Grid tools make it possible to position and size selections, text, shapes, and layers accurately.

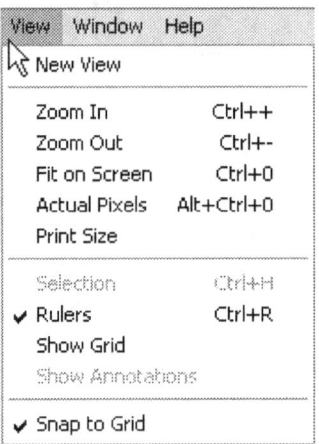

New View

Choose the New View command to open a new instance of the image window. You can open multiple instances, which provides you with multiple views of the same file. You can change the view in the new windows by zooming in on a detail in one while you perform an edit in the second window, or vice versa. Any changes you make, other than selecting View commands, will be reflected equally in all instances of the image window. This way of working makes it possible for you to visualize how a change will affect the whole work while you are making the change. The open windows will be listed in the Window menu.

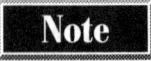
Because every instance of an image window will take extra memory, the amount of instances you can have open at any given time may be restricted.

Zoom, Fit To Screen, Actual Pixels, and Print Size

The Zoom In (CMD/CTRL++), Zoom Out (CMD/CTRL+–), Fit To Screen (CMD/CTRL+0), Actual Pixels (OPT/ALT+CMD/CTRL+0), and Print Size commands are also reflected in the Zoom tool found in the Toolbox palette. For detailed information on the functions of the Zoom tool, see Chapter 5. The Navigator palette also provides a visual interface for the Zoom function. You can get detailed information about the Navigator palette in Chapter 4.

Selection

Choosing this command or pressing CMD/CTRL+H allows you to toggle between hiding and showing the current selection outline. The command will be preceded by a check mark if the outline is visible. When the selection outline is invisible, the selection still remains active. This allows you to view changes to the selection without the visual interference from the outline.

Rulers

Choosing this command or pressing CMD/CTRL+R allows you to toggle between hiding and displaying the rulers, which appear along the top and left-hand edges of the image window. Rulers give you a guideline for sizing and positioning your work. As you move the cursor, you will see line markers on both the horizontal and vertical rulers that move with the cursor to give you a reference in the units of measure according to the rulers' settings. You can reset the zero point by clicking in the square where the two rulers intersect in the upper-left corner of the image window and then dragging in the image area. You will see a horizontal and vertical reference line extending from the ruler to the cross hair cursor. When you have positioned the new zero points where you want them, release the mouse and the rulers will reset. You can see the steps for resetting the zero point in the following illustration.

Click here and drag diagonally   Drag cross hair cursor to the new coordinates you want   The rulers and grid reset to the new zero points

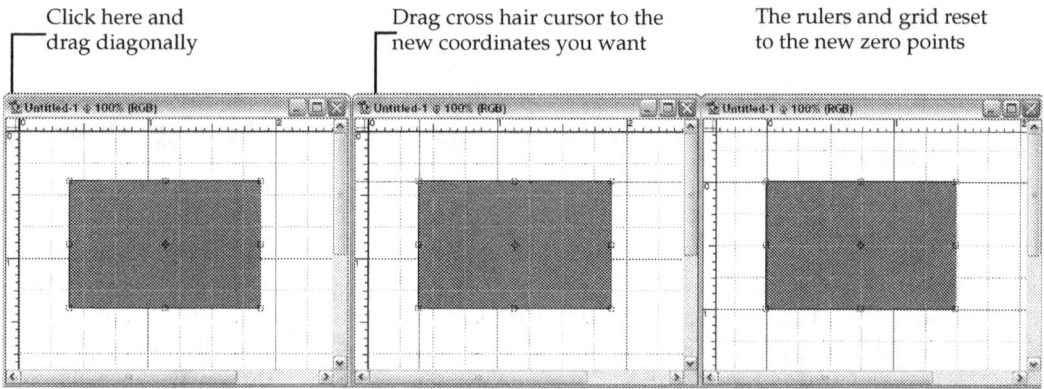

The rulers and the grid can use separate or the same units of measure; when the units of measure are synchronized, you can use them in conjunction with one another. Double-click anywhere on the rulers to open the Preferences dialog box, where you can set the units of measure. You can also click the Next button to open the Grid dialog box and enter the same units of measure. (See the sections "Edit Menu" and "Preferences," earlier in this chapter.) Coordinating the Rulers and the Grid will make aligning things much easier.

Show/Hide Grid

The Show or Hide Grid command allows you to toggle between hiding and displaying the grid. The grid is a horizontal and vertical mesh of evenly spaced guidelines that are superimposed over your image area to make it easier to align and size elements of your image. The units of measure, line style, grid color, and subdivisions can be set by choosing Edit | Preferences. See the "Edit Menu" section, earlier in this chapter, for more detailed information.

Show/Hide Annotations

The Show or Hide Annotations command lets you toggle the display of annotations that were created in Adobe Photoshop files, as well as Acrobat (PDF) annotations. Photoshop Elements does not have the ability to create annotations, but it can display annotations created in Photoshop 6 and 7.

Snap To Grid

The Snap To Grid command toggles on and off the snap feature of the grid. The snap feature assures the drawn elements gravitate to grid lines so you cannot draw in between grid lines. This feature makes it easier to assure that drawn elements always align precisely to the grid. You can refine the positioning ability by adding more subdivisions to the grid or use fewer subdivisions to simplify the choices. If you want to size an object independent of the grid, turn off Snap To Grid by toggling it from the View menu. When the command is active, a check mark precedes the menu command.

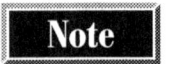

Snap can be annoying when you want to make a fine selection, so make sure it's turned off if the selection border is snapping to grid lines instead of precisely where you want to place it.

Window Menu

The Window menu allows you to control how the various interface components in Photoshop Elements are displayed and arranged. You can open and close the palettes, Status bar, Options bars, Toolbox, and the Welcome screen. You can also reset all the components to their default positions. A current list of the open documents makes it easy to sift through all the images you may have open at one time. Many of the palettes listed in the Window menu can also be opened from the Palette Well. For more information on the Palette Well, see Chapter 4.

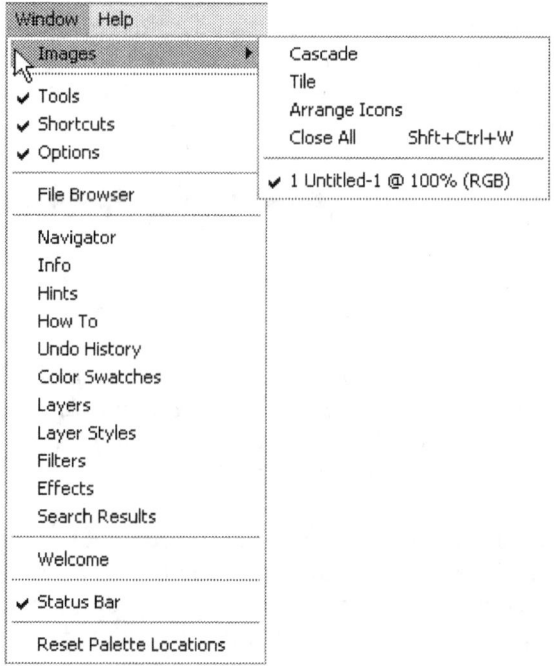

Images

The Images command allows you to arrange the order of open files on your screen with a series of subcommands that automatically rearrange and size the file windows. It also allows you to choose a new active file from a list of files that are open and on the Elements desktop.

Cascade   The Cascade command stacks any open windows slightly offset to the right and down (like a dealer spreads a deck of cards) so you can see the title bar for each one. If you have more windows open than the program can cascade in one pass, it will start cascading windows again at the top of the screen, covering the stack underneath.

Tile   The Tile command creates a view of all the files simultaneously by reducing the size of the window to fit into a column/row format. This is most commonly used for viewing files side by side for comparison. You may need to change the display magnification to get a full view of the image because the Tile command does not adjust for that. If you have too many windows open at one time, the image areas will not be easy to see.

Arrange Icons   When you minimize open files, Photoshop Elements creates an icon to indicate that the file is still open and minimized in the background. If the icons move to new locations on the screen, you can use the Arrange Icons command to stack them in order at the bottom of the Elements desktop.

Close All   Choosing this command or pressing SHIFT+CMD/CTRL+W closes all the open windows, including minimized and nonactive windows. This is handy when you have opened a large amount of windows, and it would be time consuming to close them one at a time. The program will stop the close of files that have been edited and not saved and will ask you whether you want to close without saving.

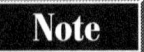   *One good use of the Close All command is when you drag all your digital camera images into the workspace to open them, and then save them with different names and formats. When you're done, the Close All command will close all the files you didn't want to bother with and any that you forgot to close.*

Open File List   You will find a list of names of the current files open at the base of the Images submenu. The active window will be preceded by a check mark. The filename will be followed by the zoom percentage and the color mode. Click the filename to make it active. The image window of the file you choose will come to the foreground.

Tools
The Tools command toggles the display of the Toolbox palette. The menu item will be preceded by a check mark when it is active.

Shortcuts
The Shortcuts command toggles the display of the Shortcuts bar. The menu item will appear with a check mark when it is active.

Options
The Options command toggles on and off the display of the Options bar. The menu item will appear with a check mark when it is active.

File Browser to Effects Commands
File Browser, Navigator, Info, Hints, How To, Undo History, Color Swatches, Layers, Layer Styles, Filters, and Effects are all palette windows that can also be accessed through the Palette well on the right side of the Shortcuts bar. These palette windows will be explained in detail in Chapter 4. The Filters commands are explained in detail in Chapter 14.

Search Results
The Search Results palette displays the information requested when you use the search field in the Shortcuts bar. Two types of search information can be returned: information

from Photoshop Elements' help files and/or information from the How To recipes. You can display that information combined or separately by choosing the appropriate command from the drop-down menu, as you can see in the following illustration. Click on any of the search results to bring up a Help or How To window that provides detailed information.

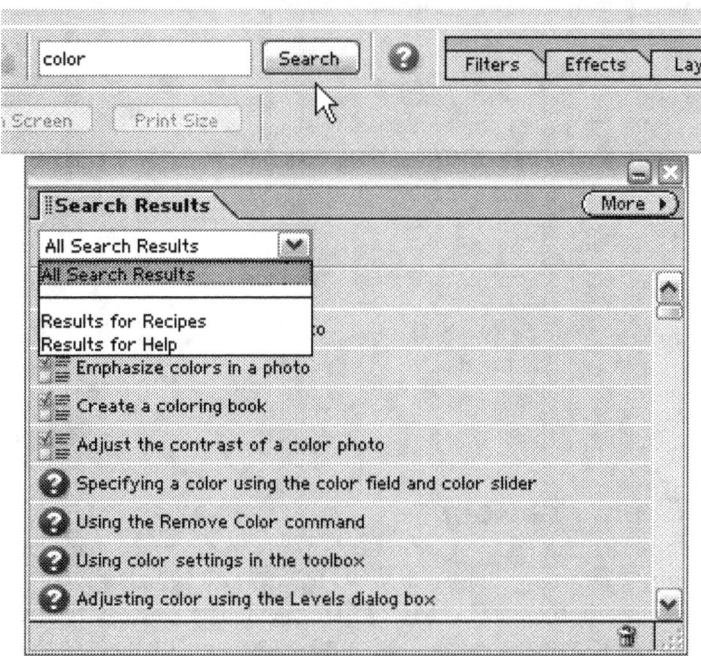

Welcome

The Welcome command opens the Welcome screen. For more details about the Welcome screen, see the section "The Welcome Screen" at the beginning of this chapter.

Status Bar

The Status Bar command toggles the display of the Status bar, which appears at the bottom of the application window. See the section "The Status Bar," later in this chapter.

Reset Palette Locations

You'll often find yourself rearranging the location of palettes to turn them off or to keep a palette close at hand for some repetitive operation. This handy command returns all open Palette windows to their default locations and sizes. This command is handy if you buried palette windows under others or have moved them off the screen.

Help Menu

The Help menu, shown next, provides a portal to an abundance of information about Elements functionality, copyrights and creators, version number, (partial) serial number, and owner. In addition, you can get creator information on all the plug-ins, augment your education with a glossary and tutorials, and get online support and updates through automated Internet connections.

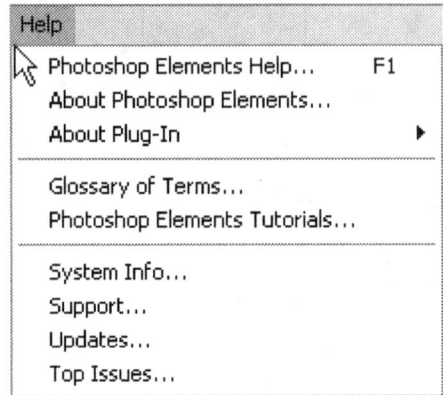

Photoshop Elements Help

This command activates the Help system and opens the introductory Help screen. The Help system in Photoshop Elements uses the default web browser to display help categories, so it is classified as an HTML help system. The information is displayed in two frames, as shown in Figure 3-24. The frame on the left provides information that allows you to navigate the help system. The frame on the right provides detailed information about the topics listed on the left.

A number of categories are always listed at the top of the navigation frame:

- **Using Help**   Includes a number of topics that will familiarize you with the various areas of the Help system.

- **Contents**   Click any category to get a more detailed list of topics that will appear in the topic frame.

- **Index**   Provides a complete alphabetized listing of all the information in the help system

- **Site Map**   Provides a complete list of all topic titles and index in one list.

- **Search**   Provides an input field to enter words or phrases to search for in the Help system. Searching will return the related topics in the navigation frame. You can also search the Help system from the Search box found on the Shortcuts bar.

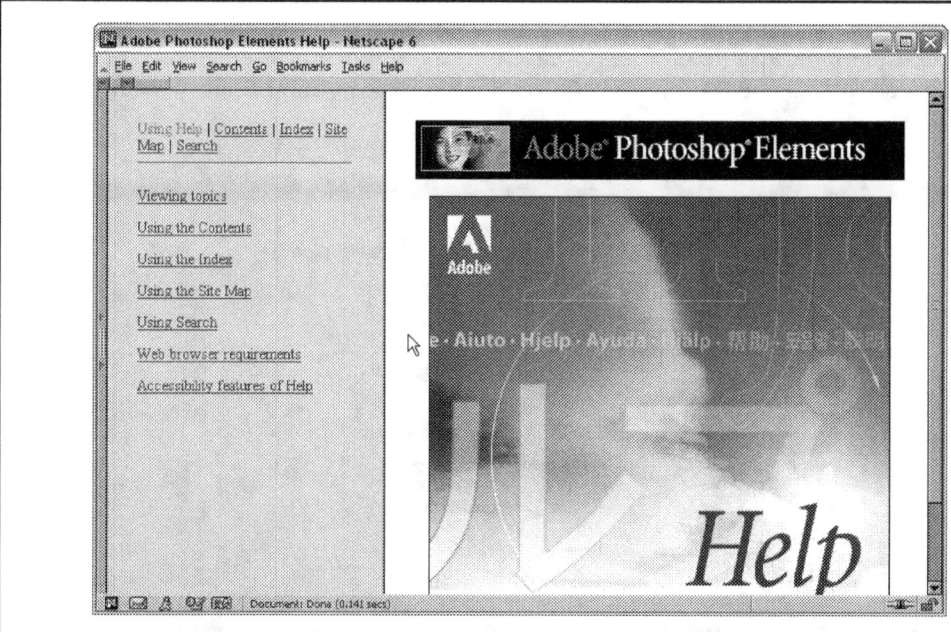

Figure 3-24.   *Navigate help topics in the frame to the left and read the results in the frame to the right.*

About Photoshop Elements

This command opens the Help system splash screen. After a few seconds, part of the screen will begin to scroll, providing a complete list of all the people involved with creating Photoshop Elements along with patent and trademark information. Click anywhere in the splash screen to close it.

About Plug-In

This command brings up a menu listing all the plug-ins that are currently loaded in your application. Click a plug-in name to make a screen appear that gives the creator information on that plug-in.

Glossary Of Terms

This command takes you to a glossary listing in the Help system, where you can see definitions and descriptions of terms used in Photoshop Elements.

Photoshop Elements Tutorials

This command takes you to a list of current tutorials in the Help system. The list of tutorials can be updated through online connections to Adobe Systems, Inc.

System Info

This command opens an information screen that lists all the pertinent settings for your application, as well as your computer's chip set, architecture, and memory configuration.

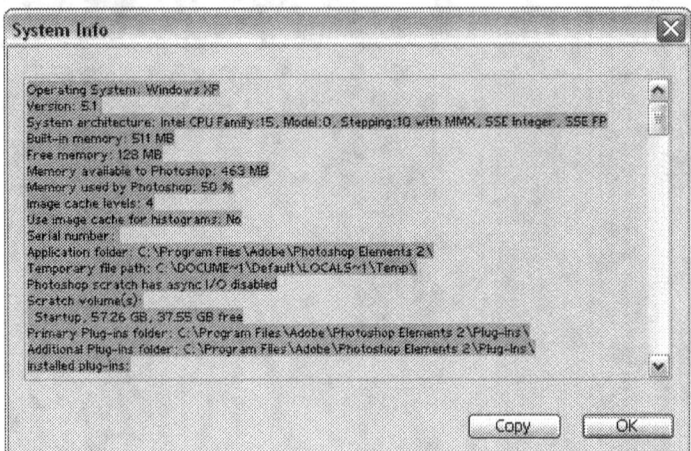

Support

This command will put you directly in touch with the Adobe Systems support group web site if you have an active Internet connection.

Updates

This command allows you to download updates to keep your application current with the latest versions, improvements, and bug fixes.

Top Issues

This command takes you to the Adobe web site if you're already online and connects you to a page that discusses all the post-release issues for Photoshop Elements 2.0 as they occur.

The Shortcuts Bar

Just under the Menu bar in the Photoshop Elements interface is a row of icon buttons that Adobe calls the Shortcuts bar, shown next. Everything you can do by clicking an icon in the Shortcuts bar can be done equally well by choosing a menu item from elsewhere in Photoshop Elements. The icons are placed on the Shortcuts bar purely for the purpose of keeping within immediate reach the commands typically used the most.

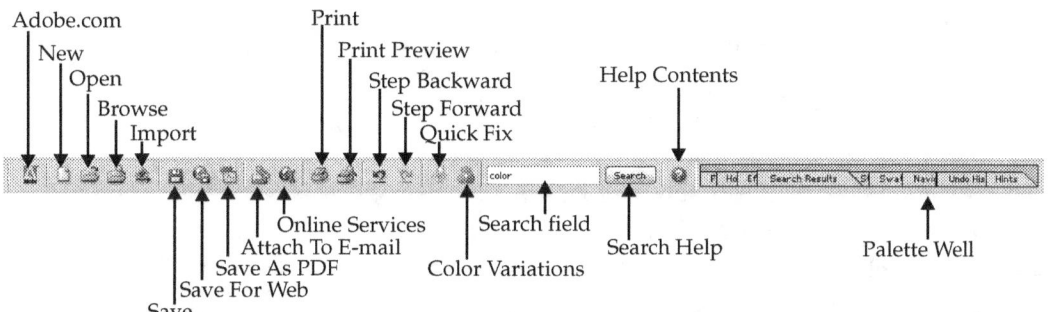

The commands that execute when you click one of the icons in the Shortcuts bar are as follows (the cross-references indicate where you will find a more elaborate description of the purpose and effect of each of the commands):

■ **Adobe.com**   Connects you to the Adobe web site

■ **New**   Opens a new file (File menu)

■ **Open**   Opens an existing file (File menu)

■ **Browse**   Opens the Photoshop Elements Browser (File menu)

■ **Import**   Lets you open a raster graphics file from an illustration program (File menu)

■ **Save**   Opens the Save dialog box (File menu)

■ **Save For Web**   Opens the interface for optimizing web images and saving them to web file formats (File menu)

■ **Save As PDF**   Saves the file in Photoshop PDF file format (File menu)

■ **Attach To E-mail**   Lets you directly attach your currently active file to an e-mail (File menu)

■ **Online Services**   Connects you, via the Internet, to online services at Adobe and affiliated sites. You can download recipes and plug-ins or upload images to photo services. More services may be added in time. (File menu)

■ **Print**   Brings up the Printer dialog box (File menu)

■ **Print Preview**   Brings up the Print Preview dialog box (File menu)

■ **Step Backward**   Takes you back one step in the Undo History palette (Edit menu)

■ **Step Forward**   Takes you forward one step in the Undo History palette (Edit menu)

- **Quick Fix**   Brings up the Quick Fix dialog box for one of the two handiest routes to image correction (Enhance menu)
- **Color Variations**   Brings up the Variations dialog box for the other of the two handiest routes to image correction (Enhance menu)
- **Search Field**   Lets you type in a word or phrase for something you wanted some Photoshop Help on (Help menu)
- **Search Help**   Activates the search for the word or phrase that you wanted help on (Help menu)
- **Help Contents**   Takes you to your browser and displays the help contents
- **Palette Well**   This section on the right side of the Shortcuts bar allows you to dock a series of palette windows in a tabbed menu. See the following section for more detailed information.

The Palette Well

The Palette Well, shown in Figure 3-25, is a recent addition in the Photoshop family interface and certainly a welcome one. It allows you to dock a series of palette windows in a tabbed menu on the right side of the Shortcuts bar so you can have quick and easy access without cluttering up the screen with multiple palette windows that you constantly need to move out of your visual field. The palettes that normally reside in the Palette Well are File Browser, Navigator, Info, Hints, How To, Undo History, Color Swatches, Layers, Layer Styles, Effects, Filter, and Search Results. For detailed information on these palettes, see Chapter 4. In addition to the palettes that normally reside in the Palette Well, you will find that the Dock To Palette Well command is the first choice on any palette's window—or you can simply drag the Palette name to the well and drop it in.

Click a Palette name tab in the Palette Well to open a Palette window. The window opens in place. Click the small arrow to the right of the tab name to bring up the Palette menu, which will present you with options for that particular palette. Click the tab again to close the Palette window (or just click in the workspace if the palette's tab is still docked in the Palette Well. If you right-click the Palette name tab, a pop-up menu will appear, presenting options for repositioning the tab to another part of the Palette Well; or you can drag the tab to another position. You detach the Palette window from the Palette Well by dragging the tab off the Palette Well into the application window, as shown in the following illustration. If you choose the Close Palette To Palette Well option from the Palette menu, the Palette window will return to is Palette well location when you close it. If the palette is not available on the Palette Well menu, you can access it through the Window menu.

PHOTOSHOP ELEMENTS
ORIENTATION

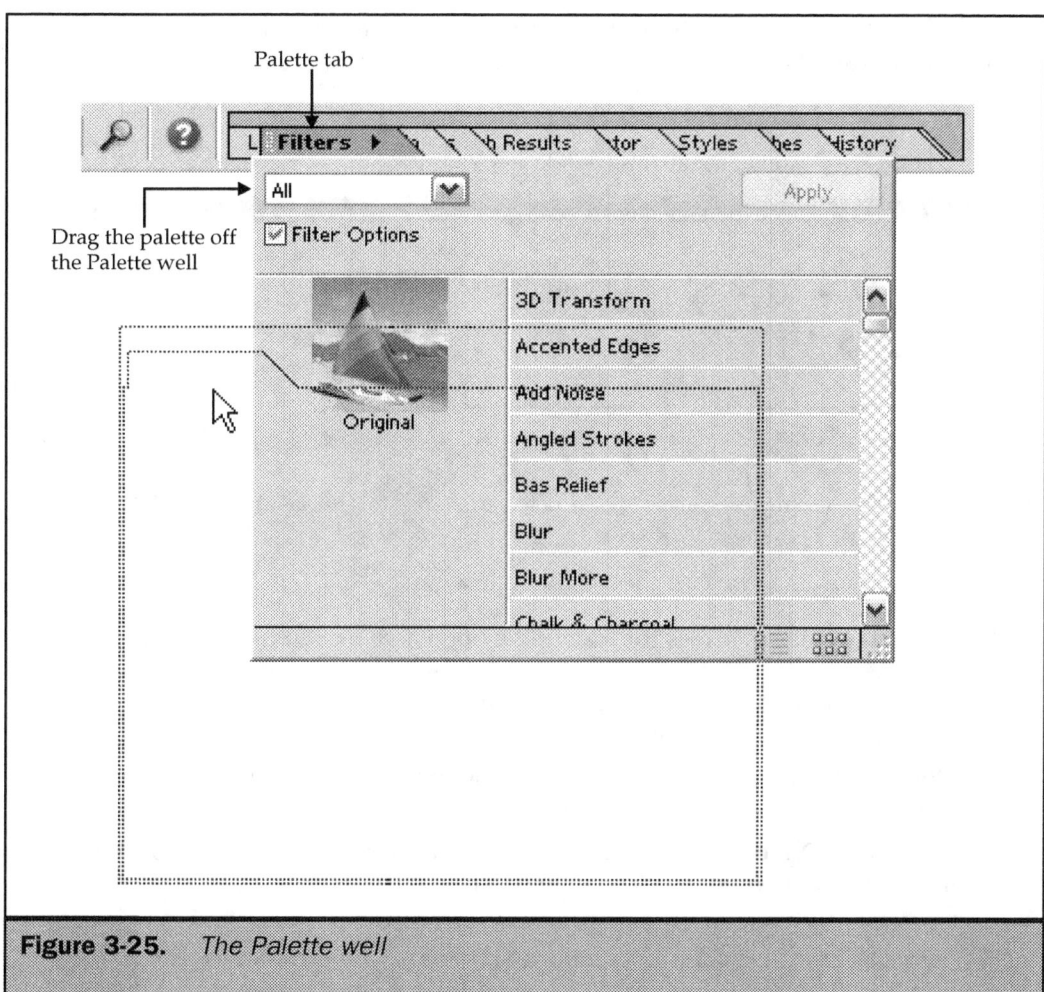

Palette tab

Drag the palette off
the Palette well

Figure 3-25. *The Palette well*

The Status Bar

The Status bar is designed to give you useful and current information about the active
open document. The Status bar is located in a thin strip at the bottom of the application
window. The information is separated into three sections. You can see the Status bar
layout in the following illustration. Starting from the left, the first section displays the
current zoom percentage of the active image window. The second window can display

a number of different types of information about the current file. The information type can be chosen from the pop-up menu just to the right of the second section.

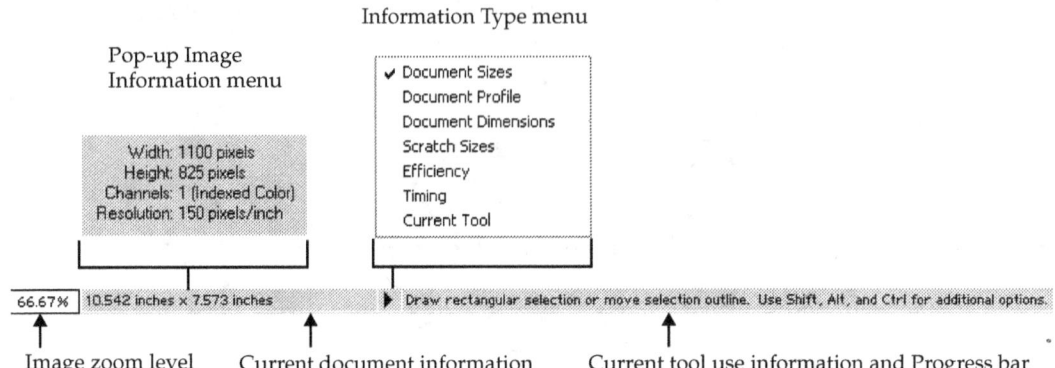

From the Status bar, you can choose the following:

- **Document Sizes** Gives the size of the open active document in megabytes. Two sizes are listed by numbers separated by a slash mark. The first number shows the flattened file size, and the number on the right indicates the size of the file if saved unflattened.

- **Document Profile** Lists the color profile the current document is using—for example, RGB, Grayscale, or Indexed.

- **Document Dimensions** Lists the horizontal and vertical dimensions of the current document in the units of measure currently selected in the Preferences area.

- **Scratch Sizes** Displays the amount of memory the program is using. The number on the left is the current RAM usage by all open images, and the number on the right is the amount of memory available for the program to use for processing.

- **Efficiency** Shows the percentage of time spent actually performing a task rather than writing to the scratch disk. If the file is using a lot of memory, the program will have to go to the scratch disk to perform an operation and it will run more slowly and lower the efficiency percentage.

- **Timing** Displays the amount of time it took to perform the last task.

- **Current Tool** Shows the current tool selected.

If you click and hold down the mouse button anywhere in the second bar section, an information box will appear, providing the Width, Height, Color Mode, and Print Resolution of the current image.

The last bar section on the right provides information on how to use the current tool. it also provides a Progress bar to present a visual queue for operations that take time, such as resizing or applying filters.

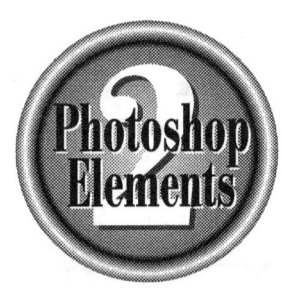

The
Complete
Reference

Chapter 4

The Palettes

P*alettes* are tabbed windows that can be used to monitor and change various aspects of working with windows. All palettes have a menu that is accessed by clicking the More button in the upper-right corner of the menu. Also, all palettes have an icon bar at the bottom of the palette that contains shortcuts to the palette's menu commands.

There are two ways to access palettes: Choose them from the Window menu or (if they're there) click their tabs in the Palette Well. You can also drag their tabs out of the Palette Well if you want to keep the palette open and accessible while you're working. Otherwise, the palette closes and returns to the Palette Well as soon as you click outside the palette.

Palette Well

The Palette Well is a recent addition in the Photoshop style interface and certainly a welcome one. It allows you to dock a series of palette windows in a tabbed menu on the right side of the Shortcuts bar so you can access them quickly and easily. You no longer need to juggle multiple palette windows around a crowded screen to clear your workspace. The palettes that can reside in the Palette Well are File Browser, Navigator, Info, Hints, How To, Undo History, Color Swatches, Layers, Layer Styles, Filter, Effects, and Search Results. The use and operation of each of these will be described later in this chapter.

Click a palette name tab in the Palette Well to open a palette. The palette opens in place. Click the More button to the right of the tab name to bring up the Palette menu, which gives you options for that particular palette. To close the Palette, click the tab again or click any where in the workspace except the palette itself. If you right-click the palette name tab, a pop-up menu appears with options for repositioning the tab to another part of the Palette Well, or you can drag the tab to another Palette Well location.

You can detach the Palette from the Palette Well by dragging the tab off the Palette well into an application window, as shown in Figure 4-1. If you choose the Close Palette to Palette Well option from the Palette menu, the Palette window returns to its Palette well location when you close it. If the palette is not available in the Palette Well, you can access it through the Window menu.

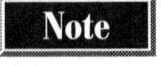

If you plan to use a palette for an extended period of time, it is a good idea to detach it from the Well because the attached palettes close automatically when you take another action.

Anatomy of a Palette

Palettes are designed to provide a flexible working interface to sets of options and tools that you use frequently. The term refers to how each provides a range of options that apply to a particular task, much like an artist's palette does with colors. All palettes have certain attributes in common and in other ways differ widely according to the task they pertain to. Palettes are designed to work alongside you as you create and edit

PHOTOSHOP ELEMENTS
ORIENTATION

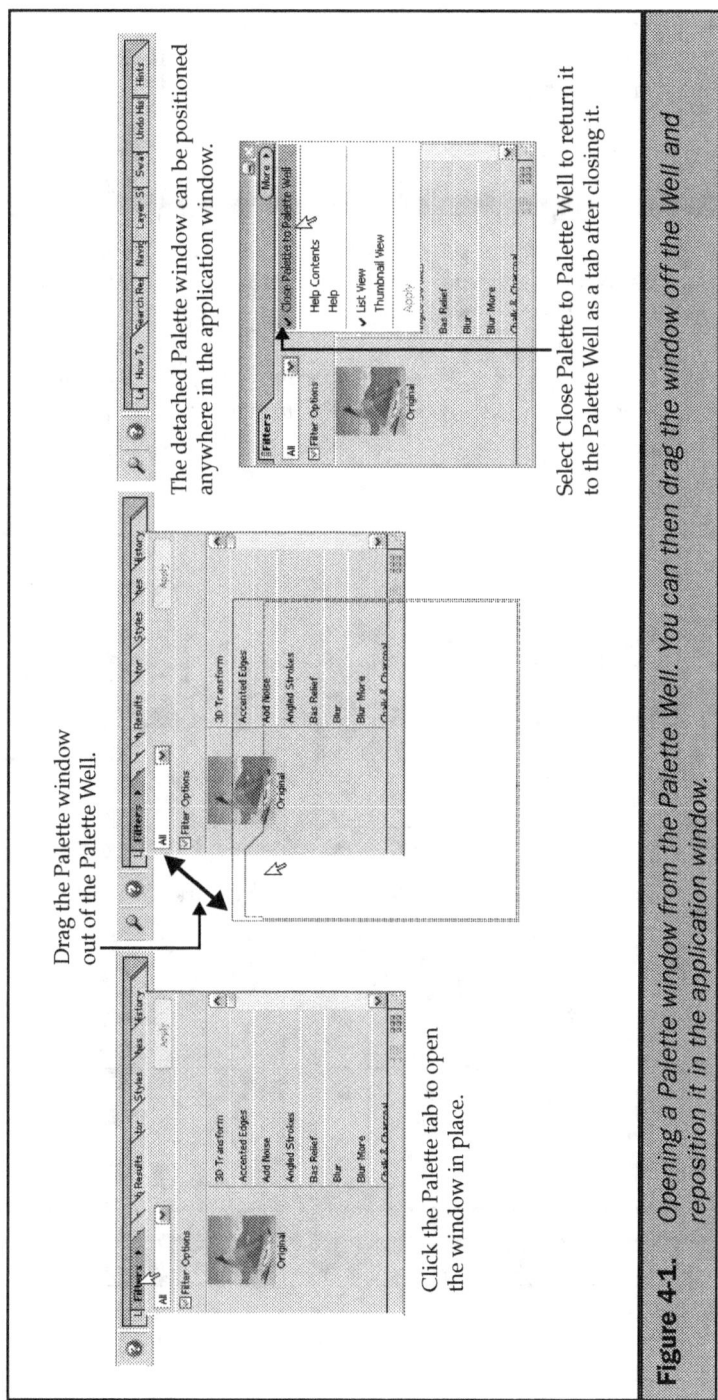

Drag the Palette window out of the Palette Well.

Click the Palette tab to open the window in place.

The detached Palette window can be positioned anywhere in the application window.

Select Close Palette to Palette Well to return it to the Palette Well as a tab after closing it.

Figure 4-1. Opening a Palette window from the Palette Well. You can then drag the window off the Well and reposition it in the application window.

your images. They can be floated, sized, moved, hidden, and docked to adapt to your particular needs as you work. Palettes can be accessed from the Window menu, Palette Well menus, and Options bars, and through floating palettes that have been detached from the Palette Well.

This first section looks at the basic features of the palette interface so you can familiarize yourself with how they work in general (see Figure 4-2). We then look at each one individually and discuss their unique features and functions. You can find out more about specific features in any palette by using the context-sensitive help system. If you want to know about a particular component, simply hold your cursor over it, and a descriptive text box appears next to your cursor

Note   *There are three kinds of palettes. First are tabbed palettes, which appear in the Palette Well. Second are pop-up palettes, which appear primarily in Options bars for various tools. Third are special palettes, which appear as menu items only—for example, the Preset Manager.*

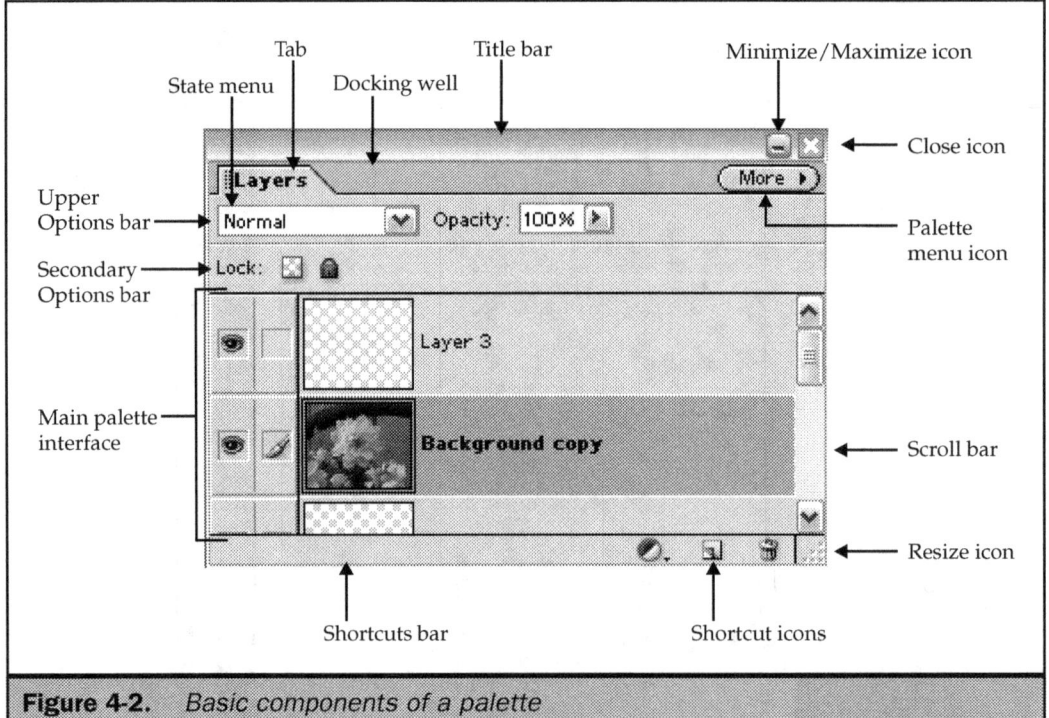

Figure 4-2.   *Basic components of a palette*

PHOTOSHOP ELEMENTS
ORIENTATION

Minimize/Maximize and Close

There are two icons on the right side of the Title bar. The X icon closes the palette. If the Close Palette to Palette Well option on the Palette menu is active, the X icon closes the palette and places a tab on the Palette Well, which you can then use to reopen the palette. You can also reopen the palette from the Window menu. The Dash icon to the immediate left of the Close icon minimizes the palette in place, collapsing the palette window to its smallest size. Clicking the Dash icon again expands the window to its default open size. If you are trying to see more of an image, minimizing palettes allows you to keep more palettes open without taking up too much of the screen.

Tab

The tab is the portion of the palette at the top left that looks like a standard file folder tab and contains the name of the palette. To open a palette, click on the tab in the Palette Well. You can also click and drag the tab to move the palette from the well to a floating position in the applications window. See the "Palette Well" section at the beginning of this chapter. You can also click and drag the tab over the Palette Well to dock it back in the well.

Docking Well

Like the Palette Well, each palette has its own docking well that can receive other palettes to form a subset of the Palette Well, as you can see in Figure 4-3. The docking well is the shaded bar that the Tab and Palette menu icons appear in.

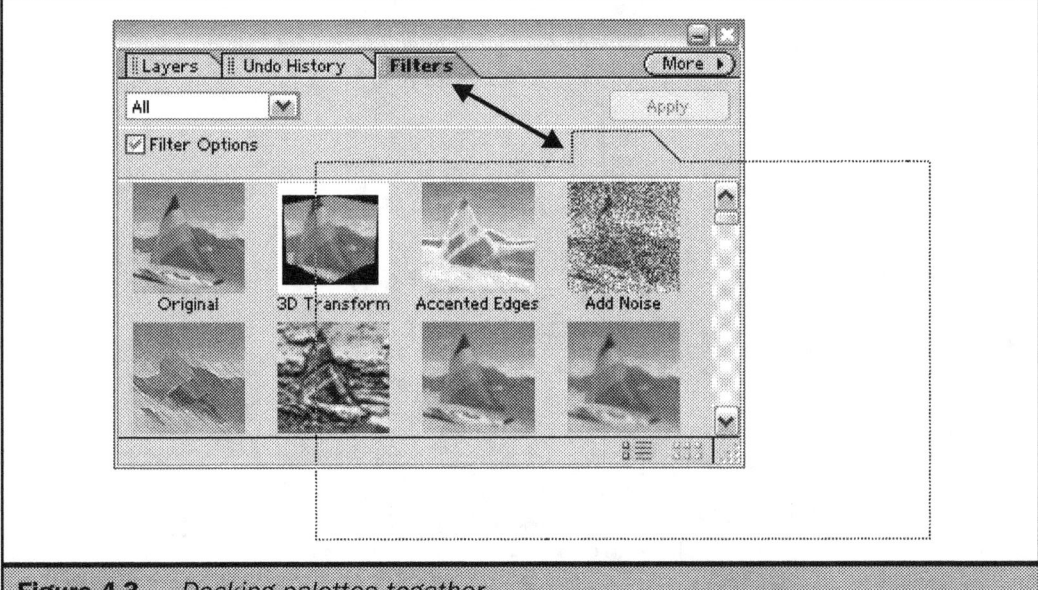

Figure 4-3. *Docking palettes together*

To dock a palette into another floating palette, click and drag the tab of the first palette over the Docking Well of the second. The Docking Well will appear highlighted. Release the mouse button, and the first palette minimizes to just a tab on the Docking Well of the second palette. You can add multiple palettes to form a group. Grouping the palettes you most commonly use together will increase your efficiency.

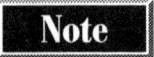

If you deselect the Close Palette to Palette Well option on the palettes you dock together, you can maintain them as a group after closing them. You then need to open them from the Window menu. If you open any palette in a group, all the palettes in the group will open and remain docked together. You can create a permanent palette group in this fashion.

Palette Menu

The Palette menu (see illustration) is accessed by clicking the More button that appears on the right side of the Docking well. This brings up a pop-up menu that lists the options available for the palette. Some menu items are toggle switches, which indicate their active state by a preceding check mark. Most of the palettes include an option at the top of the menu that provides the option of docking the palette in the Palette Well on closing. This option is Close Palette To Palette Well, which is active when preceded by a check mark. Activate it if you want that action every time you close the palette.

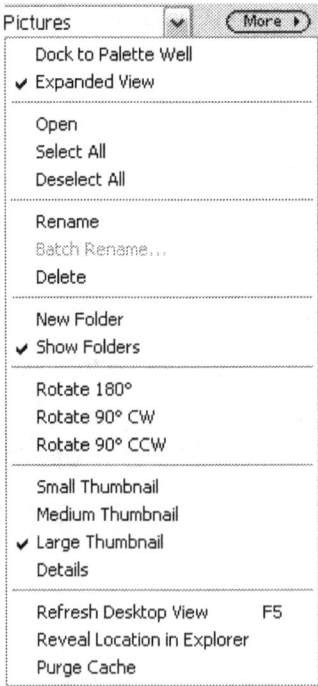

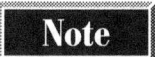   *At any time, you can instantly return the palettes to their default locations. When you want to do so, just choose Window | Reset Palette Locations.*

Upper Options Bar

The upper Options bar appears directly below the Palette tab and Docking well and contains some of the basic options common to many palette windows. These options usually incorporate state changes, which offer subsets of main palette interface icons and actuation icons. These options can take the form of drop-down menus, text fields, sliders, and icons. Not all palettes have an Options bar.

State Menu   The State menu is a drop-down menu on the left side of the upper Options bar. This menu provides a list of state and mode change options. Selecting these menu items changes the appearance and attributes of the main palette interface in the center of the palette window or one of the components of the main palette interface. You can see an illustration of the State menu here:

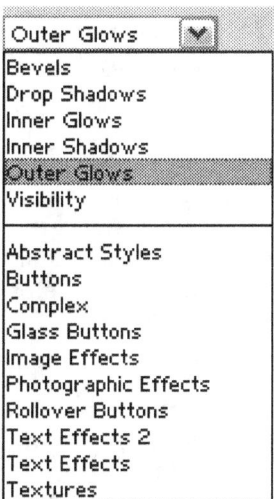

Option Icons and Controls   The upper Options bar contains controls that extend your ability to control components in the main palette interface. The Opacity control is a good example of this kind of feature. Not all palettes have an upper Options bar. Options bars appear as necessary in various palettes. You will also find a variety of icons on the right side of the upper Options bar that start, stop, or undo actions.

Secondary Options Bar

The secondary Options bar appears just below the upper Options bar. Not all palettes have a secondary Options bar. This bar holds a subset of options that take the form of check boxes or mode change icons. These options can affect individual components or the entire main palette interface.

Shortcuts Bar

The Shortcuts bar appears on the bottom of the palette window. This bar displays icons that represent shortcuts to options on the Palette menu. These icons are designed to provide you with an easy interface to access tasks that are typically used most often. A black arrow next to the icon indicates a drop-down menu. Occasionally there will be unique icons that do not reflect any categories on the Palette menu, such as the Create A New Fill Or Adjustment Layer icon on the Layers palette. It is good to familiarize yourself with the shortcuts in each palette because they can save you time.

Trash The Trash icon commonly appears and allows you to discard components found on the main palette interface, for example, a layer in the Layers palette or a color in the Swatches palette. Drag the component you want to discard over the Trash icon until it becomes highlighted, and then release it.

Resize Palette Icon The Resize Palette icon appears in the lower-right corner of the palette. Click and drag the icon vertically, horizontally, or diagonally to resize the palette window.

Scroll Bar

The vertical scroll bar appears on the right side of the palette window and allows you to move the main palette interface up and down vertically when the palette is sized so all the contents of the interface are not visible. Click and drag the slider, click on the arrows at the top and bottom, or click in the bar itself to move the interface.

File Browser

For years Photoshop users wanted a thumbnail interface for managing image files from within the Photoshop application. Finally Adobe has answered those requests with the addition of the File Browser in Photoshop Elements 1, which is probably more than anyone hoped for. In Version 2 of Photoshop Elements, Adobe has enhanced the File Browser and made it much more robust. The File Browser is a complete image- management application neatly packaged into the most complex palette to date (see Figure 4-4). The File Browser allows you to view in multiple thumbnail formats, sort in multiple categories, rotate, move, delete, view info, rename, batch rename, and preview any image or groups of images on your system or network—all from within the confines of Photoshop Elements. You never have to leave the application to accomplish all your image management and editing tasks, but if you do, the File Browser transports you directly to the folder you are working in, with no searching at all.

The File Browser falls into a unique palette category because it doesn't follow all the rules set down for the rest of the palettes. It is a palette in that it docks in the Palette

PHOTOSHOP ELEMENTS
ORIENTATION

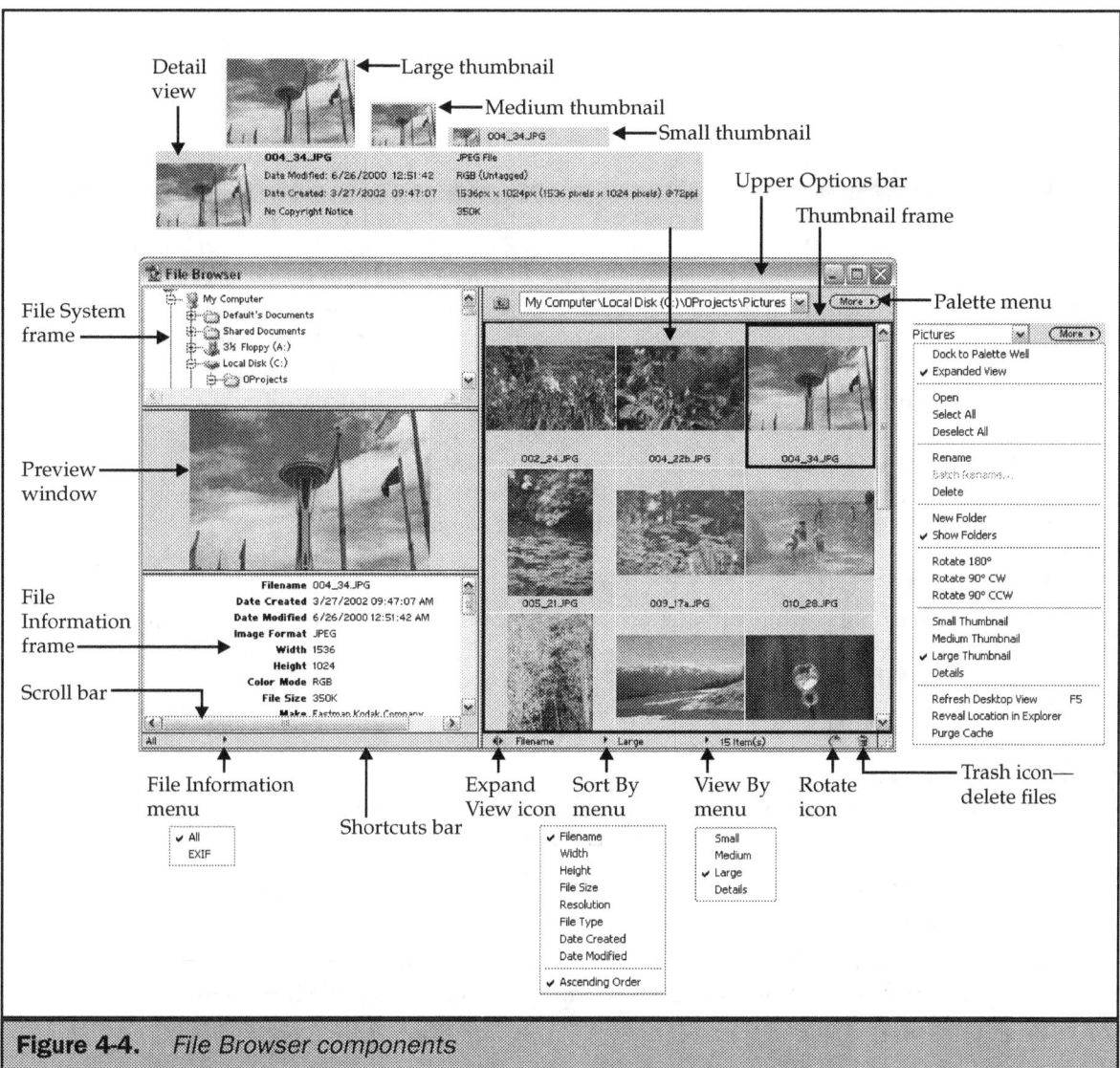

Figure 4-4.   *File Browser components*

well and can be detached and floated in the applications window. When it is detached, it does not maintain a Palette tab. It cannot be docked directly with other palettes. The File Browser can extend its view to include three extra windows on the left side of the palette. These windows allow you to interact directly with your computer's file system, preview the selected file, and view detailed textual information about your image file.

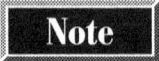 *You can use the File Browser instead of the regular File menu options for opening, renaming, copying, moving, and deleting files.*

Refer to Figure 4-4 for the following list of File Browser components.

File System Frame

The File System frame gives you direct access to the file system on your computer so you can locate the image files you want to work with using a hierarchical file menu. The disk drives, directories, and subdirectories are displayed in the Thumbnail frame as icons. When you click a folder in either the File System or Thumbnail frame that contains image files, they are displayed in the Thumbnail frame in thumbnail form. The File Browser gives you access to all the graphics files on your system in a visual display. The File System frame emulates the file system on your computer so it will be familiar.

You can move images from one folder to another by dragging the thumbnail onto the folder you want to transfer it to in the File System frame. If there are subdirectories in the Thumbnail frame you can drag over those icons also. If you want to copy it to another folder, hold down CMD/CTRL as you drag the file over.

Upper Options Bar

The upper Options bar contains the Directory Path icon. By clicking on the drop-down menu icon you can get a complete hierarchy of the directory path you are in. The small folder icon just to the left of the Directory Path takes you back one level with each click. To the far right is the Palette Menu icon.

Palette Menu

Clicking the icon on the far right of the upper Options bar accesses the Palette menu. The following are descriptions of the options on the Palette menu:

- **Dock To Palette Well**   Forces the File Browser to dock in the Palette Well on closing.
- **Expanded View**   Toggles the expansion of the palette window to the left and opens three new frames: File System, Image Preview, and File Information.
- **Palette Well Open**   Opens the selected file(s) in Photoshop Elements.
- **Select All/Deselect All**   Selects or deselects all the files in the current folder.
- **Rename**   Allows you to edit the file name of the selected file.
- **Batch Rename**   Allows you to rename a group of selected files (shown here).

PHOTOSHOP ELEMENTS
ORIENTATION

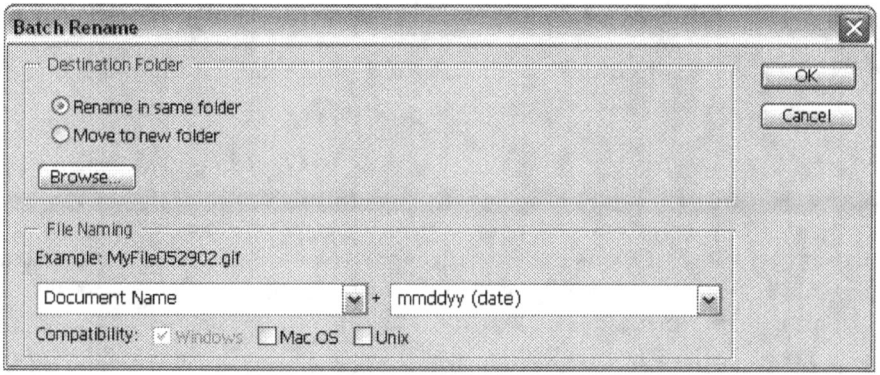

- **New Folder** Creates a new folder in the current folder.
- **Show Folder** Toggles the display of folder icons.
- **Rotate** Reorients thumbnails 180 degrees, 90 degrees clockwise, and 90 degrees counterclockwise. The file is reoriented when it is opened the first time after the thumbnail was rotated.
- **Small, Medium, Large, and Detail** Alters the size of the thumbnail displayed and the information that appears with it.
- **Refresh Desktop (F5)** Refreshes the contents of the Thumbnail frame.
- **Reveal Location** Opens a new window and displays the directory location of the selected file(s).
- **Purge Cache** Deletes the stored thumbnail file index.

Thumbnail Frame

The Thumbnail frame is the area of the palette that displays the contents of the File System selection. If you are in a folder with image files, the Thumbnail frame will display the files in thumbnail format. There are four thumbnail format types: detail, small, medium, and large.

- **Detail** Displays a stacked list of medium-sized thumbnail and list of detailed pertinent textual information about the file to the right
- **Small** Displays a stacked list of small thumbnails with the file titles to the right
- **Medium and large** Displays respective sized array of thumbnails with file titles just below each thumbnail

Scroll Bar

The Scroll bar allows you to move up and down through the Thumbnail frame so you can view all the file thumbnails.

Shortcuts Bar

The Shortcuts bar holds a number of icons that perform a variety of tasks:

- **Expanded View** Opens the extension portion of the File Browser, revealing the File System, Image Preview, and File Information frames, and a shortcut to open the File Information menu

- **File Information Menu** Allows you to choose between displaying all the file information or just EXIF information. A preceding check mark tells which is active.

- **Sort By Menu** Offers nine sorting criteria for the Thumbnails frame: Filename, Width, Height, File Size, Resolution, File Type, Date Created, Date Modified, and Ascending/Descending Order

- **View By Menu** Gives you four selections for displaying the thumbnails, Small, Medium, Large, and Details. See the "Palette Menu" section earlier in this chapter.

- **Rotate** Reorients the selected thumbnail by 90 degrees, clockwise only. The file is reoriented when it is opened the first time after the thumbnail was rotated.

File Information Frame

The File Information frame has two states. The first displays all information relating to the file from both the system and file header. The second state displays only the EXIF format information that was recorded when the image was created. This is usually information encoded by the camera or scanner that created the digital file. EXIF can give you detailed information of the settings that were used when the image was captured so you can re-create the same result later. The File Information frame provides pertinent information such as date created, date modified, pixel dimensions, size, color mode, make and model of the hardware and software that created it, orientation, color depth, and frame number. The amount and type of information varies with the device that created the image. We suggest you take a look at the EXIF information. You might be surprised at how much useful information you can glean.

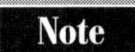 *The EXIF information is very useful for photographers because it provides a detailed, accurate record of your camera setting so you can track your results and then reproduce them.*

PHOTOSHOP ELEMENTS ORIENTATION

Image Preview Frame

The Image Preview frame gives you a blown-up view of the selected thumbnail. The frame can be resized by dragging the bars that separate the frames up or down. The image preview resizes itself to fit the frame size while maintaining its proportions. To get the largest image preview, maximize the browser and the Image Preview frame.

Navigator Palette

The Navigator palette (Figure 4-5) is designed to give you an easy interface for zooming and panning (moving side to side or up and down) your image. The view box (displayed as a solid colored rectangle) indicates the extent and position of the viewable area that you will see in the image window. You can click and drag the view box around in the Preview window to display a different portion of the image.

Preview Window

The preview window shows a thumbnail view of the current image display.

View Box   This is a solid color rectangle within the Preview window that shows the extent and position of the zoomed image.

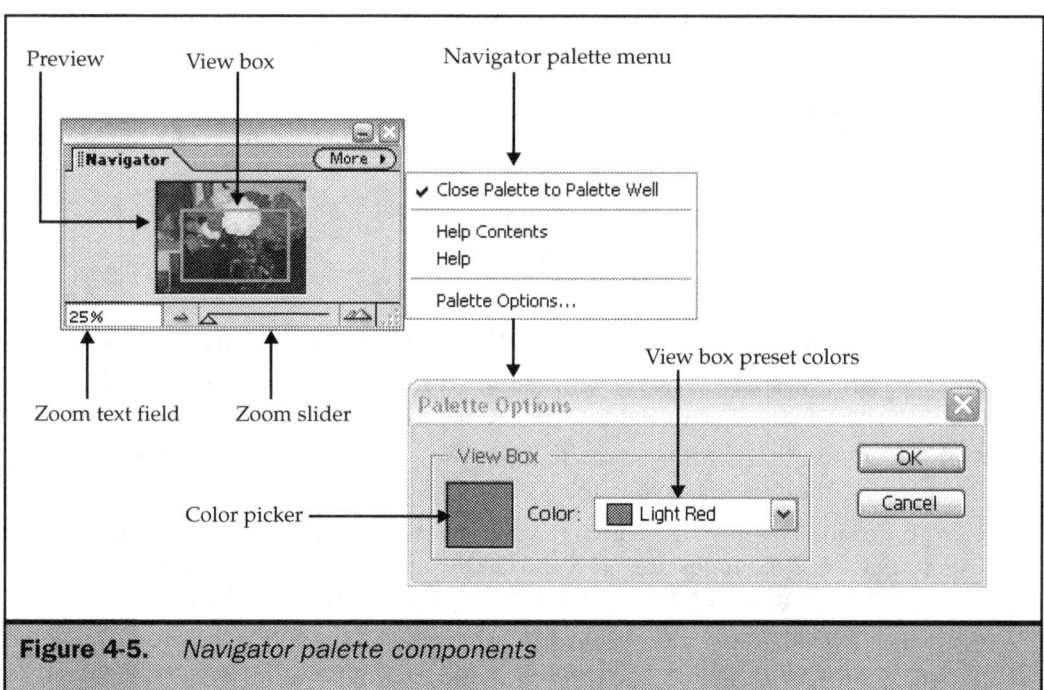

Figure 4-5.   *Navigator palette components*

Navigator Palette Menu You can choose the option to dock the palette to the Palette Well on closing. Palette options (refer to Figure 4-5) brings up a dialog box that gives you the option of changing the color of the view box with the color picker or from a list of preset colors on the Color drop-down menu.

Zoom Text Field This displays the current percentage of zoom. You can also enter the zoom percentage and press ENTER.

Zoom Slider The zoom slider allows you to change the zoom level by sliding the pointer left or right or clicking anywhere along the bar. You can also change the zoom level in increments by clicking on the mountain icons on either side of the zoom slider.

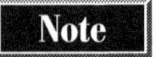 *Using the Navigator can make life much easier when you working in larger files, where it is hard to get the whole image on the screen at one time. The navigator can help you stay oriented.*

Info Palette

The Info palette is designed to give you informational feedback on the pixel mode, pixel position and the size of selections, layers, shapes, transformation angles, gradient angles, and line angles.

The Info palette is separated in to four areas (see Figure 4-6).

Upper-Left Area

This displays the color mode display. This can be set to display in five separate modes:

- **Actual Color** Sets the color mode to that of the current image.
- **Grayscale** Displayed with a K symbol; gives the percentage of luminance for the current cursor location from 0 to 100 percent.
- **RGB** Displays the three-color channels (red, green, and blue) of the current cursor position on a scale of 1 to 255, 255 being white.
- **Web Color** Displays the colors that can be properly display in the 216-color web palette. The values are expressed in hexadecimal format. If the image is in indexed format, it will display the palette position from 0 to 255.
- **HSB** Gives the hue, saturation, and brightness values. Hue is stated in degrees, the other two in percentages. Access the menus to change the color mode readout by clicking the dropper icon or choosing Palette Options from the Palette menu and then choosing the Mode menu.

PHOTOSHOP ELEMENTS
ORIENTATION

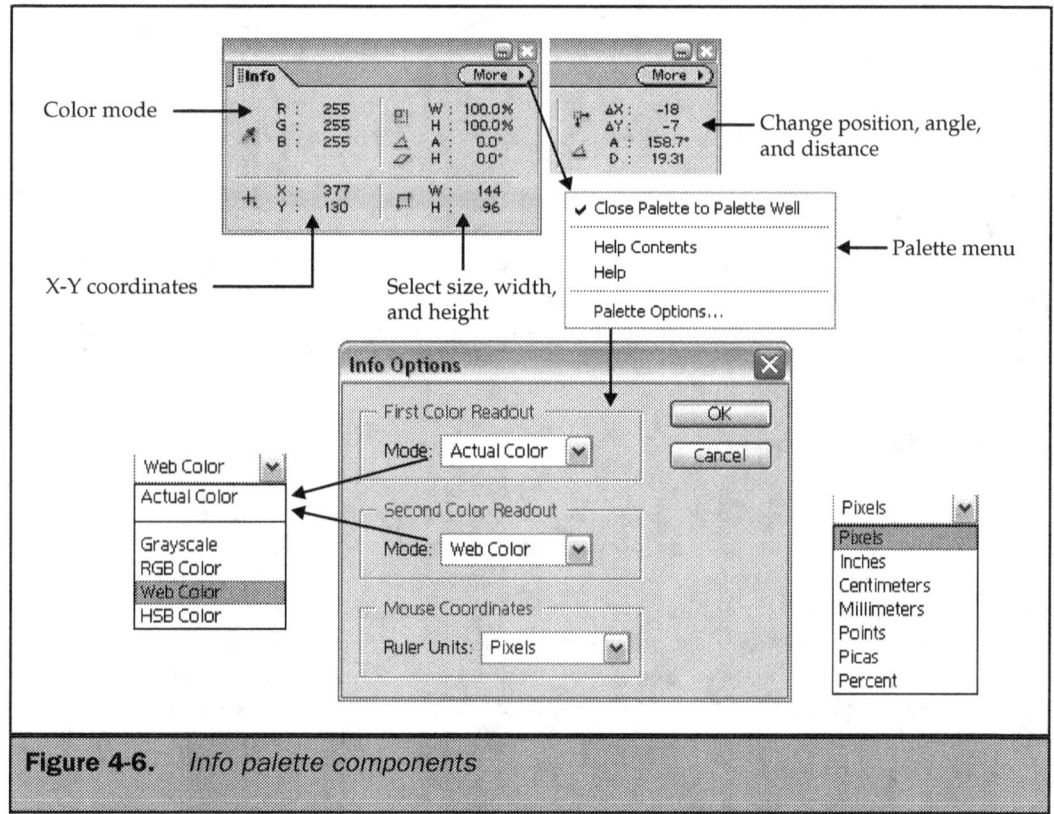

Color mode

Change position, angle, and distance

Palette menu

X-Y coordinates

Select size, width, and height

Figure 4-6. *Info palette components*

Upper-Right Area

This displays the freeform area of the Info palette. This area changes its display based on the type of tool or option you are using. It defaults to a second color mode readout, which can be set to an alternative color mode readout that is different than the primary readout. This gives you the ability to see the values for two different modes simultaneously. When you create a selection, shape, or transformation, this area displays symbols that relate to those operations. Here is a list of those readouts:

 ■ This icon indicates the relative change in position as you move a layer, shape, or selection, indicated by a delta sign and X-Y coordinates.

 ■ This icon indicates the change in the angle, indicated by A or D. A is the angle of a line or gradient, angle of movement in a shape, selection, layer, or angle of rotation. D is the change in the distance that a shape, selection, or layer has moved along the angled path.

■ This icon indicates the change in the percentage of scaling in the height and width.

 ■ This icon indicates the angle of any transformation handle realignment. H is the horizontal angle and V is the vertical.

Lower-Left Area

This displays the pixel position readout. This gives the X-Y coordinates of the cursor position displayed in the units you choose from the Ruler Units menu. To display the Ruler Units menu, click the Crosshair icon. You can also change the units of measure by accessing the Palette Options from the Palette menu.

Lower-Right Area

This displays the height and width of the current active selection or shape in the selected units of measurement. The values change as you drag the cursor when creating an object so you can size it on the fly.

It is a good idea to take note of the information in the Info palette if you want to be able to duplicate your creation, positioning, and transformation of selections and objects with fidelity. The color mode readouts can help you analyze the color values of individual pixels, which can help when making selections that require tolerance settings, setting a target for the Color Cast command, or setting color balance for example. You can never have too much information, and this palette gives you a few more pieces of the puzzle.

Hints Palette

The Hints palette (Figure 4-7) is basically a context-sensitive help system in the form of palette. It gives you concise information on the tools in the Toolbox and palettes in the Palette Well. To use the Hints palette:

1. Open and drag the Hints palette to a floating window.
2. Hold the cursor over any of the tool icons or palette tabs in the Palette Well. You will see the hint change to reflect the tool or palette you are over.

The Hints palette supplies a visual that gives some indication of what the filter does. In the case of tools, the picture shows the tool in operation, plus the toolbox icon. In the case of palettes, it shows a piece of the interface indicative of that palette inside a tabbed folder graphic, indicating it is a palette. The name of the tool will be just to the right of the picture. Just below the picture is a short description that tells you what the tool or palette is used for.

Hints Palette Menu

This menu contains some useful options. It gives you ability to access

- Search
- Keyboard shortcuts
- Tutorials
- Adobe web site

The Hints palette is handy when you are first learning Photoshop Elements. It provides a quick way to get the basic operation information on all the tools and palettes, which will help you become familiar with the interface much faster. Once you have mastered the tools and palettes, your need for this palette will diminish and you can save some space by removing it from the Palette Well by deselecting Close Palette To Palette Well from the Palette menu. As later versions of Elements add new tools and palettes, the Hints palette will be a good first stop to see what they are.

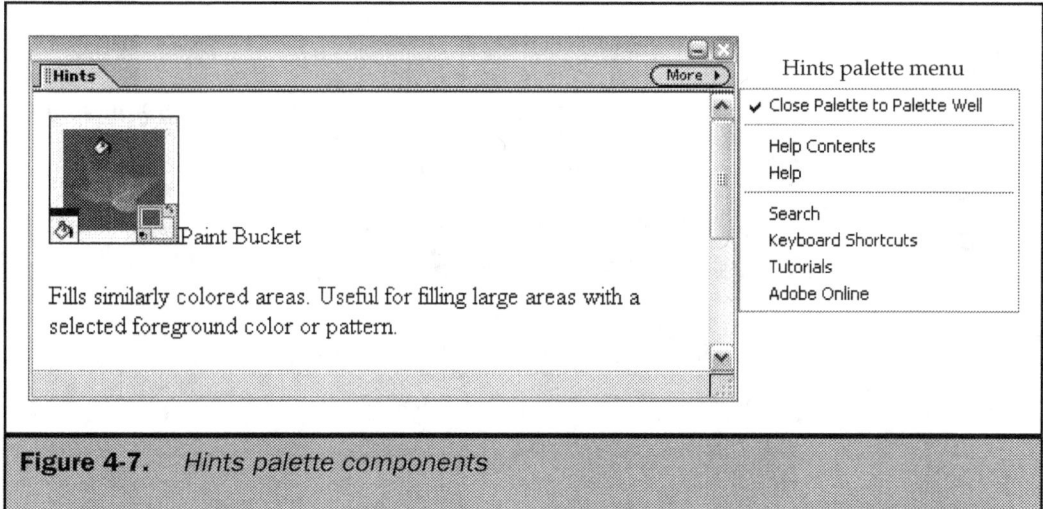

Figure 4-7. *Hints palette components*

How To Palette

The How To palette is the interface that gives you access to the recipes. Recipes are exercises that have been created to teach you about a particular task in Elements. Each recipe walks you through a series of numbered steps that walk you the task. The recipes are talked about in more detail in Chapter 6, but we will go over the palette components here.

State Menu

The menu acts as a table of contents for the How To palette (see Figure 4-8). Choose from these categories:

- Add Elements
- Color Correction
- Image Cleanup
- Layout and Sizing
- Photoshop Elements Features
- Techniques
- Tools
- Download New Adobe Recipes

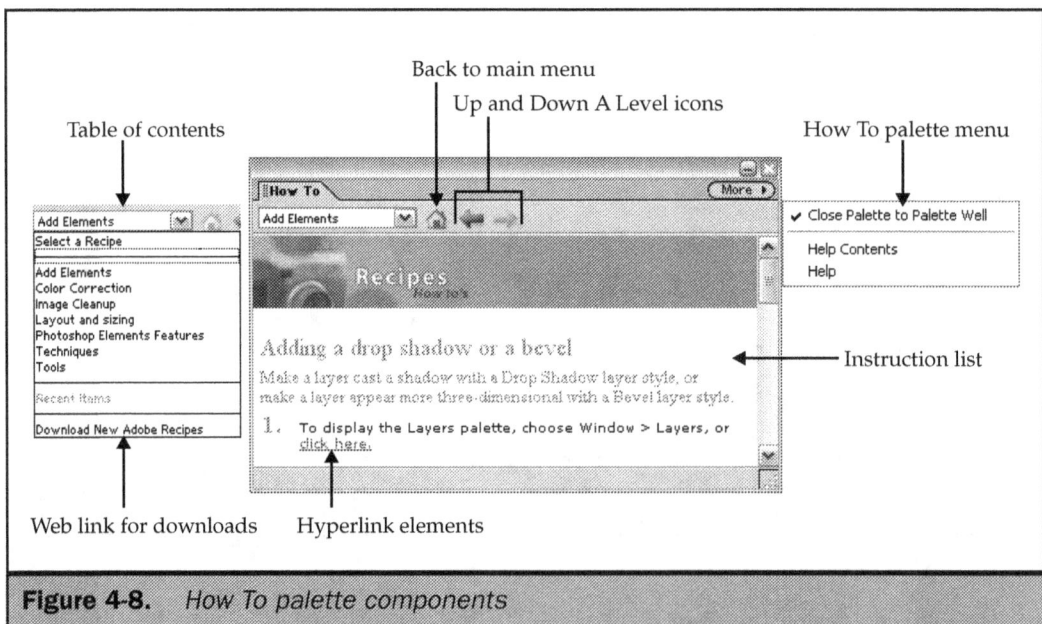

Figure 4-8.   *How To palette components*

Download New Adobe Recipes is the last item in the menu. This will connect you with Adobe online, where you can download new recipes to add to the library as they become available.

Home Icon Just to the right of the State menu is a small house icon. This is the Home icon, which takes you back to the starting screen for the category you are in.

Arrows Icon The arrows to the right of the Home icon take you up or down one level.

Recipe Screen When you get to a recipe you see the recipe logo, the title of the exercise, a brief description of what the exercise is intending to demonstrate, and a numbered list of instructions. Underlined hyperlinks within the instruction list shortcut the process as you move through the instructions by opening various tools, palettes, and options as you move through the exercise.

The How To palette starts you on your way learning more complex tasks that require the use of multiple tools, options, and palettes. The recipes provide a wide range of exercises that cover the more basic operations of Elements, giving you a good spring-board to more advanced subjects. See Chapter 6 for a more in-depth look at the recipes.

Undo History Palette

The Undo History palette is an extremely useful palette. It stores every action that you take in a sequential list, which is displayed in the palette (see Figure 4-9). You can, at any time, revert to a past history state by selecting that state from your palette list. You

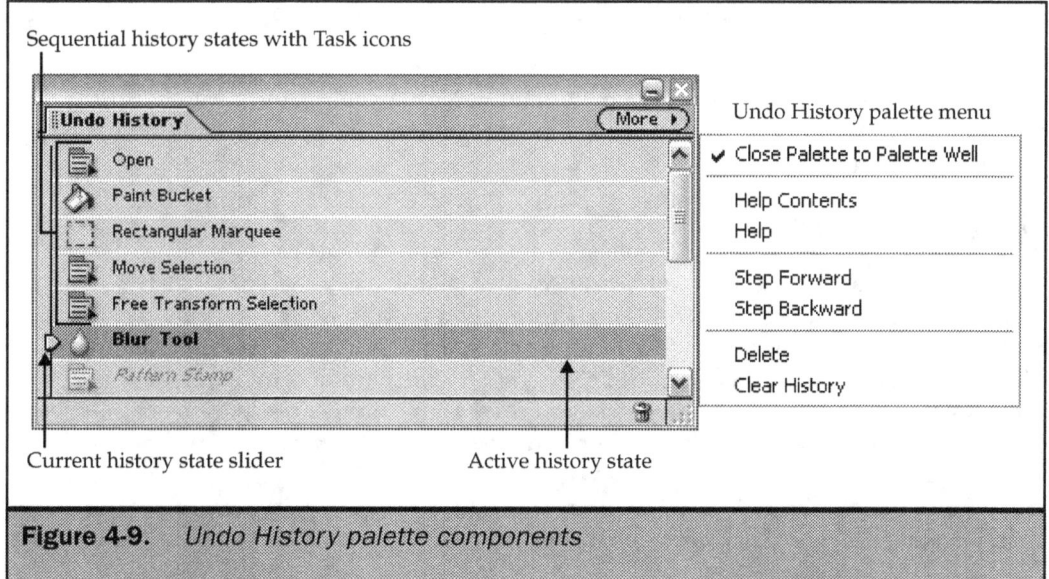

Figure 4-9. *Undo History palette components*

can also delete any history state in the sequence to undo all the actions from that point forward.

History State

Each history state occupies a row in the palette. The history state displays an icon, which indicates which tool was used in the step or if the step was a menu option. To the right of the icon is the name of the tool or option chosen, for example, Move, Cut, or Paint Bucket. The active state will be highlighted.

History State Slider   You can activate any history state by clicking on it or by moving the history state slider (just to the right of the list) up and down. The history states below the active state will gray out, showing that they are not included in the current image displayed. You can reactivate them by sliding the pointer back down or simply clicking in the state you want to become active.

Undo History Palette Menu   The following is a list of options on the Undo History Palette menu:

- **Step Forward/Backward**   Move up or down in the history state list by one each time you choose one.
- **Delete**   Deletes the active history state. You also can delete a history state by right-clicking on it or by clicking and dragging it to the Trash icon. Once you have deleted a state, all the states that came after are erased.
- **Clear History**   Erases the complete history list without changing the image. You also can clear history by right-clicking the active history state. To purge and free up memory used by the history list, choose this option while pressing ALT/OPT.

You can copy a history state to a new document by clicking and dragging the history state to the new document. This adds the new state to the bottom of the new document's history list.

Swatches Palette

The Swatches palette allows you to use preset or custom sets of color swatches to enable you to pick foreground and background colors from a predetermined set. The Swatches palette comes closest to what we commonly understand to be a palette, the kind that painters use. You can add, delete, modify, and move color swatches around in the display. The Swatches palette gives you presets of colors commonly used in web production which makes it much easier to develop graphics for the Web. Develop custom palettes that reflect the colors you are using in a project and save them so you can refer to them later and maintain your color theme. This is very handy when you are doing commercial graphics where color matching is critical. Color swatches give you means to group and store sets of colors for use later. See the "Preset Manager and Pop-Up Palettes" section later in this chapter.

Swatches

The swatches are small squares of solid color that have been grouped together in the main window of the palette (see Figure 4-10). As soon as you move the cursor over any swatch it changes to an eyedropper and displays the name of the swatch you are over in a small text box to the right. Click on the swatch to change the foreground color to the color of the swatch. Clicking while pressing CMD/CTRL changes the swatch to the background color.

The names of the swatches can be anything you want. You can change the names by double-clicking on any swatch. You will see the Color Swatch Name dialog box appear. Enter a new name on the Name field and click OK. Name the swatches with color values (23, 45, 78), the area of the image they appear in (skin tone 1, sky blue), or after artist colors (cadmium yellow, cobalt blue). This can put the color names in a form that is easiest for you to work with. The palette gives you one-click access to the colors instead of opening the color picker constantly.

Preset Menu

The Preset palettes menu is a drop-down menu that gives you a list of preset color swatch palettes that are commonly used for various applications. All the preset palettes that come with Photoshop Elements are designed to work with 8-bit color environments with 256-color palettes. They include standard Mac OS, Windows, and Web Safe palettes.

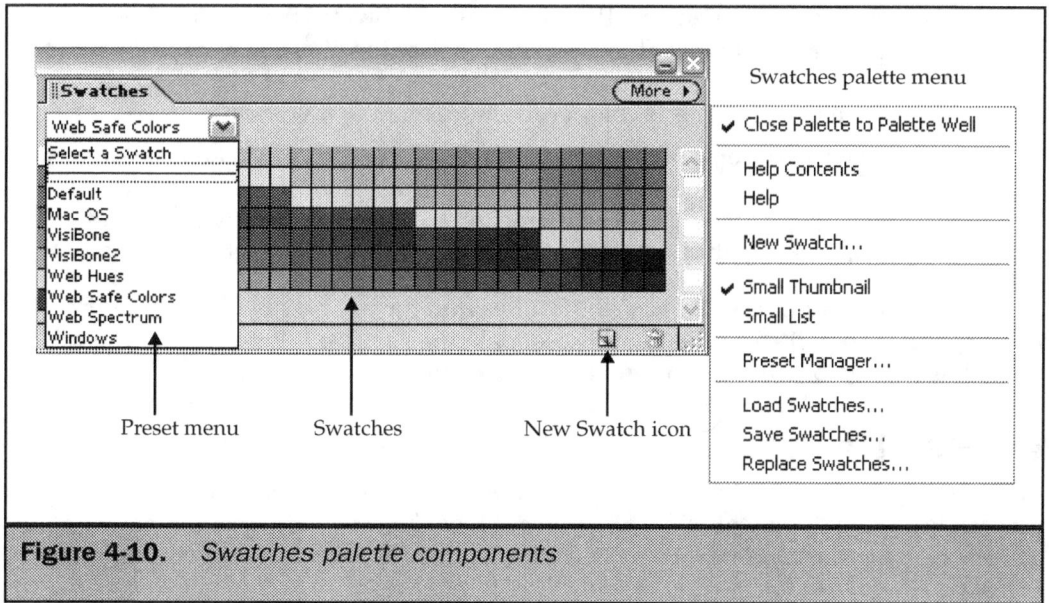

Figure 4-10.   *Swatches palette components*

This does not limit you. The palettes can be customized into any set you desire out of the 16 million available in 24-bit color. Choose a preset from the drop-down menu, and the main palette display will display the new palette colors swatches. The preset palettes all display the names of the swatches in hexadecimal, which is handy if you are editing web pages because some web editors require that format. The default palette uses common names.

New Swatch Icon

Click the New Swatch icon (see Figure 4-10), and a new color swatch will be added to the end of the palette, filled with the foreground color. You can also create new swatches to add to the current set by placing your cursor over the clear space at the end of the palette swatches. You will see the cursor change to a paint bucket. Click, and a new swatch will appear, filled with the foreground color.

Swatches Palette Menu

The Swatches Palette menu places a preset group of colors within easy reach so that you can quickly choose your most frequently needed colors without having to reuse the Color Picker for each change.

- ■ **New Swatch**   Adds a new swatch filled with the foreground color to the end of the current set

- ■ **Small Thumbnail and Small List**   Small Thumbnail displays an array of small color squares. Small List displays small color squares with the names to the right in columns.

- ■ **Preset Manager**   Opens the Preset Manager in Swatch mode. The Preset Manager is a palette that allows you to manage the libraries of color swatch sets that come as presets or that you customize. See the "Preset Manager Palette Menu" section later in this chapter for more on how it works.

- ■ **Load, Save, and Replace Swatches**   Use to load or save a custom set or replace a preset with a modified version. You can create a new preset by saving the existing color palette with a new name in the same directory where the other presets are stored. The new palette then appears on the Preset menu.

You can load multiple color swatch libraries into the main display by using the Load option. You will see subsequent preset palettes stack up in the display. You can then save this combination palette with a new name.

Layers Palette

The Layers palette (Figure 4-11) is probably the palette you will use more than any other in Photoshop Elements. The function of layers lies at the heart of the power of all Photoshop programs and will allow you to accomplish a wide range of editing tasks

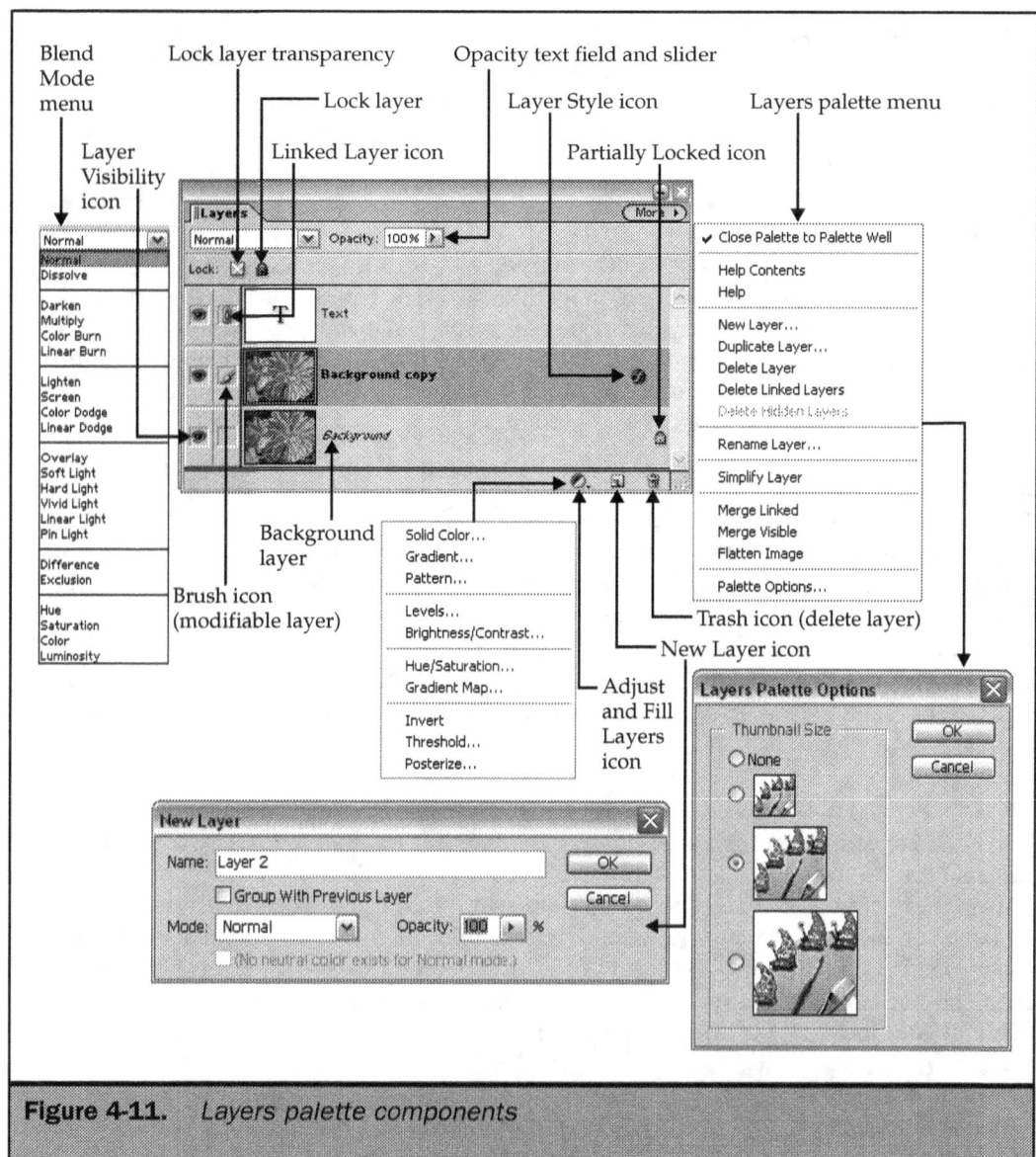

Figure 4-11. *Layers palette components*

that cannot be done any other way. We have devoted an entire chapter to do justice to the layers function so we can go into detail on how to master the art of using them. We will go over the palette interface here so you have a good working knowledge of how that works before we get into more advanced functions in Chapter 8.

Blend Modes Menu

The Blend Mode menu is a drop-down menu that gives you a list of all the blend modes available. You click on any Blend Mode to apply it to the active layer. For in-depth information on how to use blend modes and a description on what each one functions, see Chapter 9.

Opacity

You can change the transparency of the active layer by adjusting the Opacity control. The Opacity control has two aspects to its interface. The first is the text field, where you can enter a percentage value from 0 to 100. You can also access a slider control by clicking on the arrow just to the right of the text field. Move the slider pointer to the left or right to decrease or increase the opacity. You will see the underlying layer show through as you lower the opacity percentage.

Lock Transparency Icon

The Lock Transparency control preserves the transparent of any pixel that has any degree of transparency in the locked layer. This allows you to edit that layer and still preserve the original relationship of transparency in the pixels. This makes the locked transparency equivalent to a complex mask.

To lock the transparency of the active layer, click the Lock Transparency icon. You will see a light lock symbol appear on the right side of the layer listing. Click on the Lock Transparency icon again to unlock. Get more information on using transparency with layers in Chapters 8 and 17.

Lock Layer Icon

The Lock Layer control freezes all interactions with the active layer. Use this to protect information on the locked layer from being changed accidentally. When you have critical information on a layer that you don't want to loose inadvertently, lock it. To lock a layer, make the layer you want to lock active. Click on the Lock Layer icon in the upper Options bar, and a second Lock Layer icon will appear on the right side of the layer listing. Click the Layer icon on the upper Options bar again to unlock a layer. When it is unlocked, you can resume editing that layer.

Layers Palette Menu

Most of the options found in the Layers Palette menu are discussed in Chapter 3 in the "Layer Menu" section, so this section covers only the options in the Layers Palette menu that are not repeated in the Layers menu.

Delete Linked Layers   Link layers allows you act on them as a group. You can link a layer by clicking in the first control box to the left of the layer thumbnail. A small chain icon appears (see Figure 4-11). You can link as many layers as you want. The Delete Linked Layers option deletes all the layers that have the linked icon active.

Delete Hidden Layers   The eye icon in the second control box to the left of the layer thumbnail indicates that the layer is visible in the image window. Toggle the eye icon on and off to make the layer show or hide the layer. The Delete Hidden Layers option deletes all the layers that have been hidden by turning off the eye icon. This is a good way to get rid of all the extra layers that are really not going to be in the final work and are just taking up space.

Palette Options   The Palette Options command brings up a dialog box that gives the choice of three layer thumbnail sizes or to display no thumbnail at all. Select one and click OK.

Adjustment and Fill Layers Icon and Menu

Adjustment and fill layers are covered in Chapter 3 in the "Layer Menu" section. The Adjustment and Fills Layer icon brings up a pop-up menu that lists all the options for the types of adjustment and fill layers you can add. Click on a layer type, and it will add the layer just above the active layer. If the Layer type has a dialog box associated with it, it will open at the time you create the layer. You can adjust the controls for that layer and click OK to make the layer active. If there is no dialog box, it will just become active. Get more in-depth information on using adjustment and fill layers in Chapter 8.

New Layer Icon

The New Layer icon creates a new transparent layer above the active layer. It also represents the easiest way to duplicate a layer. You just drag an existing layer to the New Layer icon, and the layer is instantly copied to a new layer.

Background Layer

The background layer is the bottom-most layer and is created automatically anytime you create an image file that is opaque. The background layer is partially locked so it cannot be moved in the stack, accept transparency, or accept blend modes. If you want to edit the background image in those ways, you need to convert it to a regular layer. To change the background layer into a regular layer:

1. Double-click in the background and rename it when the dialog box appears.
2. Click OK, and the layer will convert. The lock icon will disappear.

To convert a layer to a background:

1. Make the layer you want to convert to a background active.
2. Choose Layer | New | Background from Layer, and the active layer will assume the position at the bottom of the stack and be called Background in a partially locked mode.
3. If there is transparency in the layer you convert, the transparent portions will be filled with the background color because backgrounds cannot have transparency.

Visibility Icon

The Visibility icon is the small eye that appears in the left-most column adjacent to each layer. It toggles the layer from visible to hidden. When the eye is visible, so is the layer. Click it to hide both the eye and the layer. Click in the same position again, and the layer and the eye become visible again. This allows you to control which layers display at any given time. Making a layer hidden will also make it hidden to effects from layers above.

Brush icon

The Brush icon tells you that the active layer can be modified.

Link Icon

When you click in the first column of any layer you can activate the Link icon that associates the layers that have the link icon showing with the active layer. You can also use the link mode to perform commands that will act on all linked layers, as mentioned in the "Layers Palette Menu" section earlier in this chapter and in the "Layer Menu" section in Chapter 3.

Layer Style Icon

The Layer Style icon indicates that a layer style has been applied to that layer. Double-click the Layer Style icon to bring up the Layer Style dialog box.

Layer Styles Palette

The Layers Styles palette, shown in Figure 4-12, allows you to add special effects to your image, shapes, and text by changing the fill, luminance, color, and edge characteristics. You click on or drag the thumbnail version of the effect you want over the image or object you want to apply it to. The effects can be applied in an additive manner, so you can build more complex effects by applying them in succession. The layer styles have their most profound effect when they are applied to objects or image areas that have transparent areas over another image layer. It is common for these styles to be used for stylizing text and shapes. You can learn much more about how to use the layer styles in Chapter 15.

Layers Style Palette Menu

This is one of the simplest of all the palette menus. The first three commands are common to all palette menus. In addition, you can set the view (Thumbnail or List) and the option Close Palette to Palette Well.

Layer Styles Categories Menu

This menu gives you access to the preset style sets that come standard with Photoshop Elements. The first six are basic, but there is wide variety of styles

PHOTOSHOP ELEMENTS
ORIENTATION

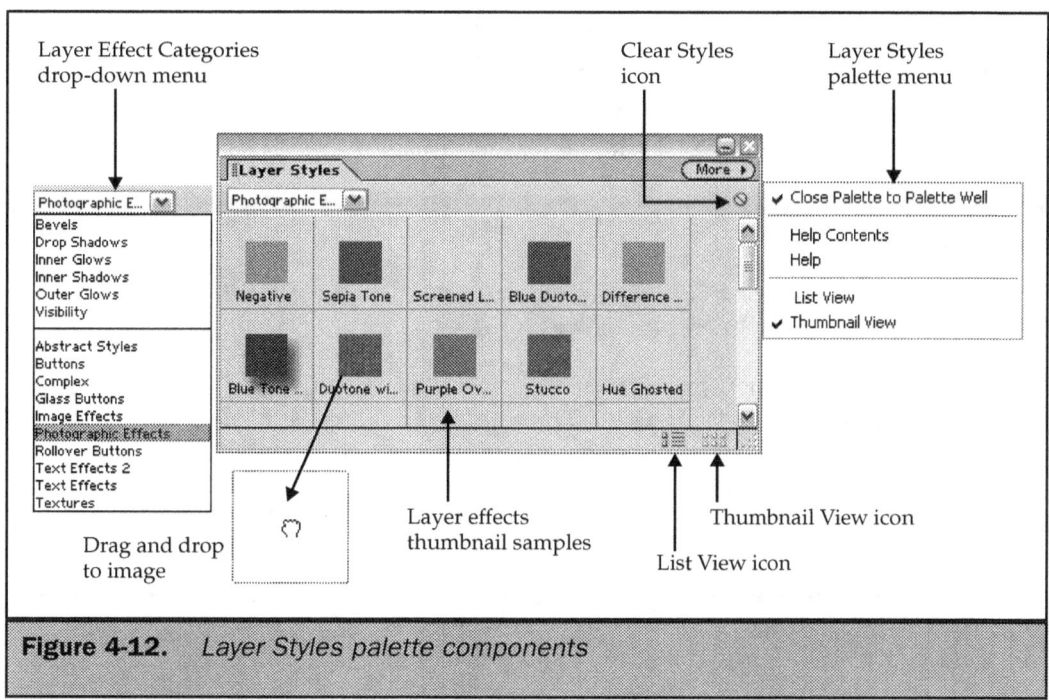

Layer Effect Categories
drop-down menu

Clear Styles
icon

Layer Styles
palette menu

Drag and drop
to image

Layer effects
thumbnail samples

List View icon

Thumbnail View icon

Figure 4-12.   *Layer Styles palette components*

that can be combined in thousands of ways to produce an endless stream of
styles to choose from. Experiment!

- **Bevels** Produces a slanted or chiseled edge effect
- **Drop Shadows** Produces the effect of the object casting a shadow on the
  background
- **Inner Glows** Produces the effect of glowing highlighted center
- **Inner Shadows** Produces a cutout effect with shadows
- **Outer Glows** Produces the effect of a glowing object with an aura
- **Visibility** Makes the object visible, hidden or ghosted (dimmed)
- **Abstract Styles, Complex, and Image Effects** A mixture of more radical styles
- **Buttons, Glass Buttons, Rollover Buttons** Styles designed to look good on
  buttons that you might use on web pages and other types of multimedia projects
- **Photographic Effects** Tinting styles and some textures designed to work with
  photo images
- **Text Effects** Styles designed to work well with text
- **Textures** A wide array of surface textures

- **Clear Styles icon**   Clears all the applied styles
- **List and Thumbnail View icons**   Shortcuts to setting the view of the filter to a List view or a Thumbnail view
- **Layer Effects samples**   Thumbnail representation of each style effect. Click on the thumbnail or drag it to the image to activate the style.

Filter Palette

For a complete description of all the filter effects and their uses, see Chapter 14. We will describe the palette components here (see Figure 4-13).

Filters Selection Menu   Presents a list of filter categories. Click to see the subcategories displayed as thumbnails. Select All to see all the subcategories displayed at one time.

Apply Button   Clicking this button applies the selected Filter to the current layer.

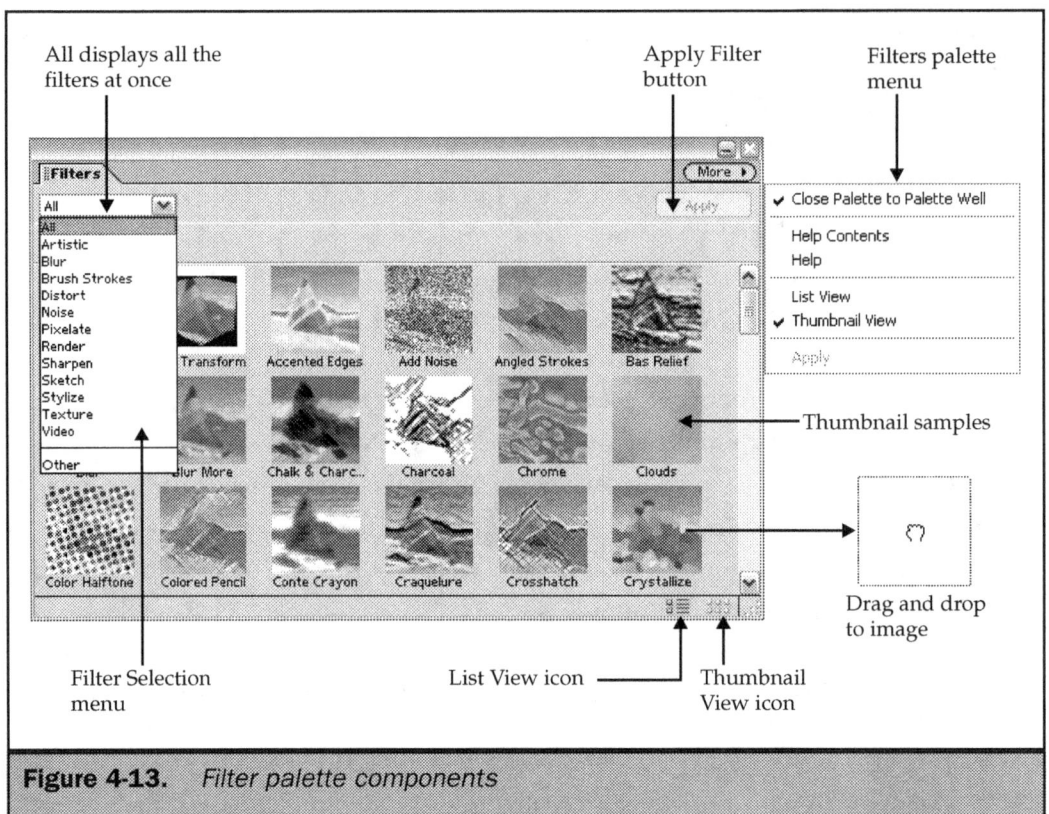

Figure 4-13.   *Filter palette components*

Filters Palette Menu   You can set the view (Thumbnail or List) and the option Close Palette to Palette Well.

List and Thumbnail View Icons   Shortcuts to setting the view of the filter to a List view or a Thumbnail view. These options also appear on the Palette menu.

Filter Options Check Box   When the box is checked the dialog box for the filter, if the filter has one, will appear when you select it. This allows you to set the options before applying the filter to the image.

Effects Palette

The Effects palette (Figure 4-14) is designed to give you a wide range of automated special effects, which can affect various elements in the image. Effects can change the whole image, a selection, or text. The palette accomplishes its special effects by combining multiple filters, styles, and other program elements to achieve unique looks. You cannot change any options on effects in the Effects palette. They are preset. Some effects might require that the image be flattened, while other might create new layers in the process. The effects are employing a batch command mode, so the program is going through a series of operations to accomplish the effect. You might notice that the layers are being created and the Status bar is displaying various commands as it proceeds. See Chapter 15 for more detailed information on the creative application of effects.

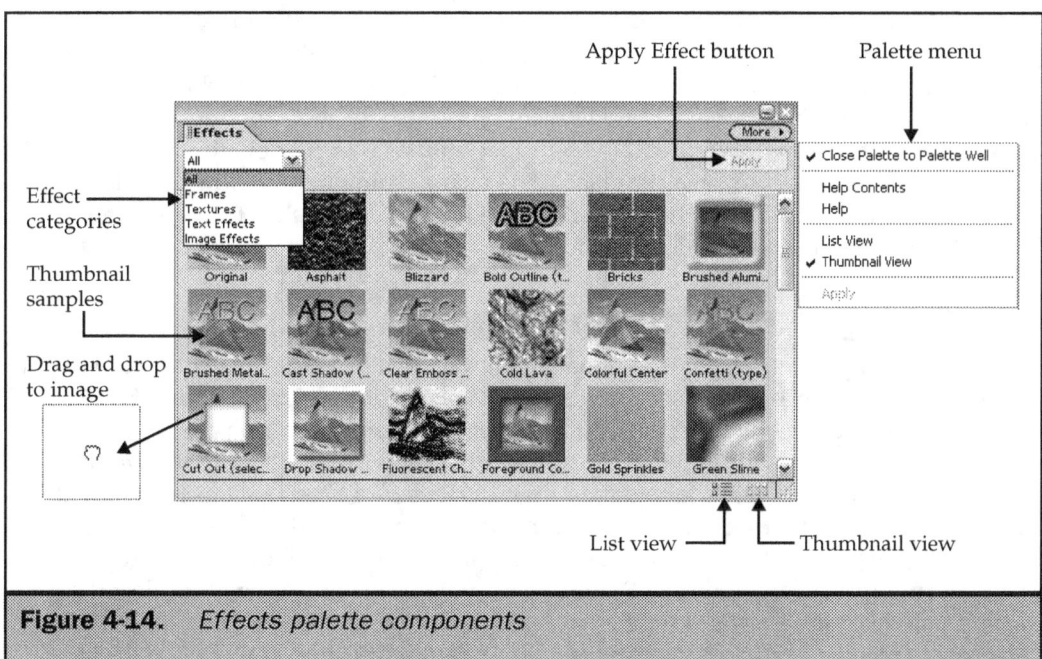

Figure 4-14.   *Effects palette components*

To apply a special effect click and drag the thumbnail, double-click the thumbnail, or click the Apply Effect button.

Effects Category Menu

This menu lists the four categories of effects that are supplied with Photoshop Elements:

- **Frames** Produces a border effect around the image
- **Textures** Applies a texture to a selection or the whole image in a new layer. It can sometimes include fill layers.
- **Text Effects** Designed specifically to alter the look of text
- **Image Effects** Provides a wide range of effects that affect the whole image

Thumbnails

Displays small illustrations that give you some indication of the visual impact of applying the effect.

List View and Thumbnail View

Shortcuts to setting the view of the filter to a List view or a Thumbnail view. These options also appear on the Palette menu.

Search Results

The Search Results palette (Figure 4-15) returns a list of subjects found when you initiate a search from the Shortcuts bar. See Chapter 3 for more on the Shortcuts bar. The Search Results palette will locate two types of information, Recipes and General Help topics. You can isolate each help type or display them all at once by choosing the appropriate category from the drop-down menu in the upper options bar. To view the details on the subjects listed, double-click on any subject. The recipes bring up the How To palette, and the Help subjects activate the browser-based help system. Select the Close Palette to Palette Well option from the Palette menu to keep it in the Palette well.

Preset Manager and Pop-Up Palettes

The Preset Manager palette helps you manage libraries of brushes, swatches, patterns, and gradients. Figure 4-16 shows the Preset Manager palette in Brush mode. You access the Preset Manager palette from the Edit Menu or from select pop-up palette menus.

The pop-up palettes allow you to interface directly with the Preset Manager or a modified form of the Preset Manager through various tool bars, options bars, palette menus, and palette shortcut menus. Anytime you see a small thumbnail with a small down facing arrow next to it, that is a pop-up palette. See the following illustration of a pattern pop-up palette on the Pattern Stamp Options bar. When you select the pop-up palette or the Preset Manager from a palette menu, it will show you the currently loaded preset palette for the element type. Every time you use a pop-up palette, you are essentially using the Preset Manager minus a few options. The only

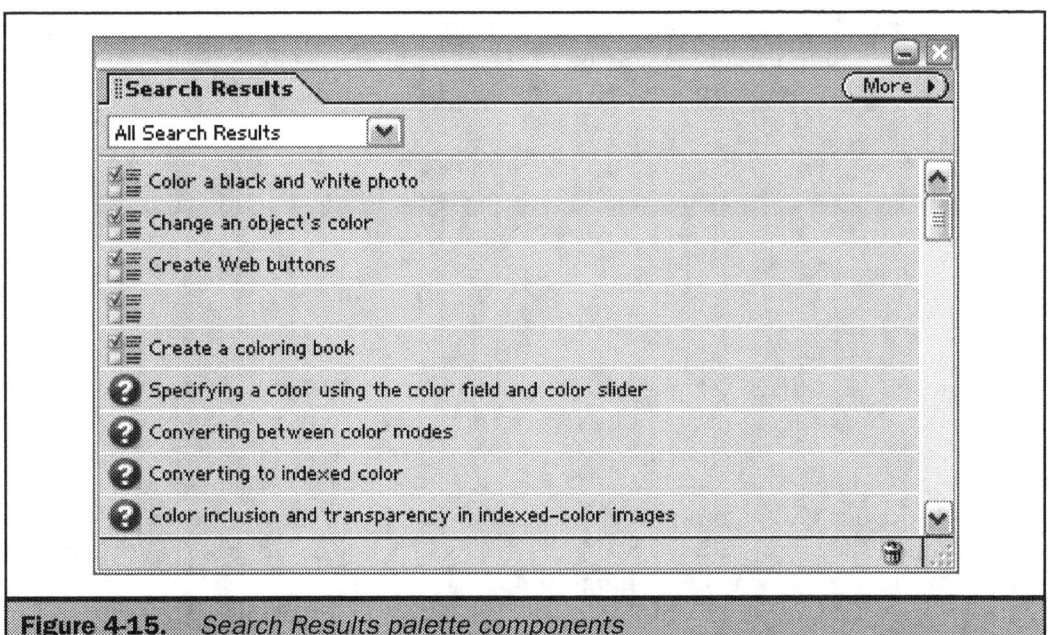

Figure 4-15. *Search Results palette components*

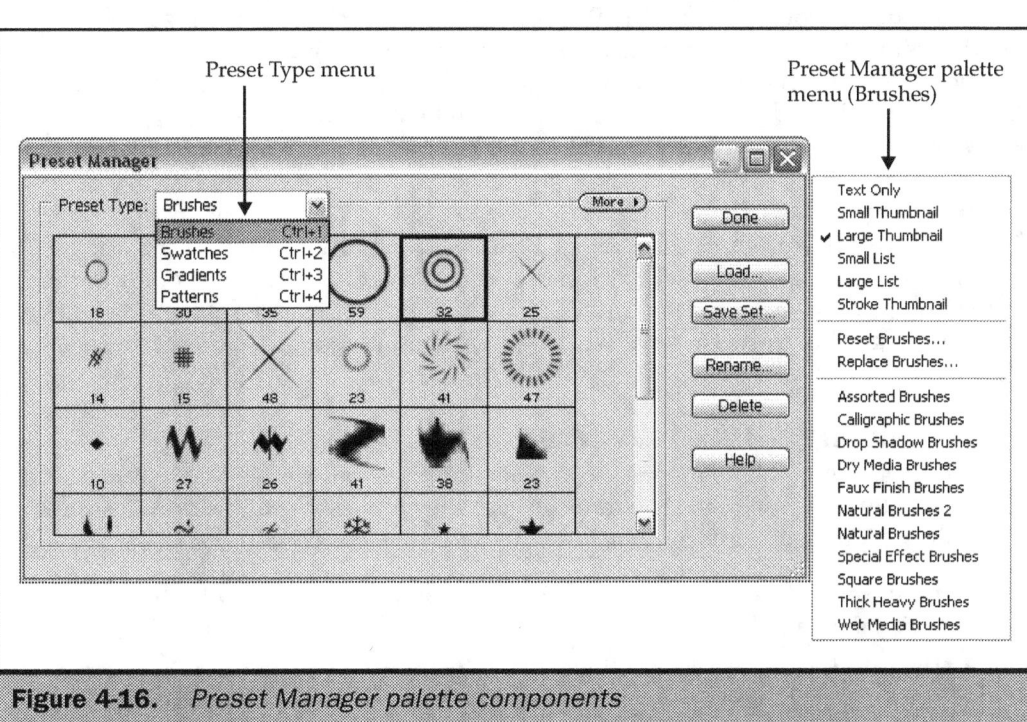

Figure 4-16. *Preset Manager palette components*

real difference between the Preset Manager palette and the pop-up palette is that the Preset Manager allows you to save selected sets of elements to a new library and some of the palette options are displayed as buttons instead of menu options.

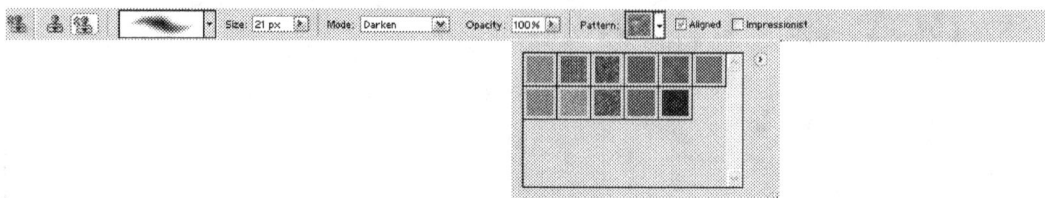

When you create a new element (brush, pattern, and the like) it is reflected as a new thumbnail in the current preset library for that type. The newly created library element is stored in the current preset temporarily until you load a new preset library or reset the current preset library to its default. If you do either, it will erase any new elements you have added. To keep your new elements from being erased, you must save them to an existing or a new library. It is a good idea to create a new library to preserve the preset libraries that came with the program.

As you work more with Elements, you will probably start customizing things. As you start modifying or creating new gradients, swatches, brushes, and patterns you will want to save them so you can use them later. It is also likely that you will develop some favorites as you progress. The Preset Manager can help you organize your favorite elements into custom libraries and save them with unique names.

The Preset Libraries are stored in the Elements program folder in a folder called Preset. The Preset folder contains folders for each Preset type. When you want to load or save preset libraries, you need to access these folders

Preset Type Menu

You can choose one of four preset types: Brushes, Gradients, Patterns, or Swatches. Each type displays a unique set of thumbnails and offers a different set of libraries on the Preset Manager Palette menu. First, we will cover the general features of the Preset Manager Interface; then we will go over the unique features for each Preset Manager type.

Preset Manager Palette Menu

The Preset Manager palette menus are arranged in three parts. The palette menus on pop-up palettes are essentially the same, except they have some of the options found on the Preset Manager's interface included in their palette menu instead.

- The upper part of the Palette menu gives you options on how to display the thumbnails.

- The middle part has two options. Reset Current Preset Type sets the current library to its default settings. Replace Current Preset Type loads a library to replace the one displayed, otherwise loading a new library appends the current one.

■ The bottom part of the palette menu lists the standard preset libraries for that preset type.

Load Button

Loads a preset library or custom library and appends its elements to the current preset library. The Load option is on the Palette menu in pop-up palettes.

Save Set Button

Saves a subset of the current elements to a new library. Appending the current library is a way to reorganize the elements between different preset libraries. When you have loaded all the libraries you want to work with, hold SHIFT while clicking on the elements you want to place into a new library. This will select multiple elements that can be saved as a set to a new library by clicking the Save Set button. The Save Set option is unique to the Preset Manager.

Rename Button

This option allows you to change the name of the active element. It brings up the name dialog box. You can enter a new name in the text field and click OK. The Rename option is on the Palette menu in pop-up palettes.

Delete Button

This option will delete the active element from the palette. It does not delete the element from the library unless you save over the library file. Choose the Reset option to restore the default library if necessary. The Delete option is on the Palette menu in pop-up palettes.

The
Complete
Reference

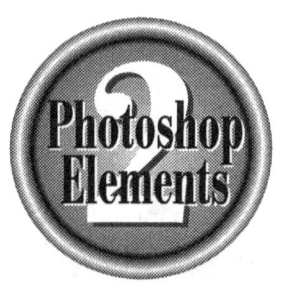

Chapter 5

Tools and the Toolbox

The Photoshop Elements Toolbox is the home of all the tools that are used to isolate specific areas of the image, paint, locally adjust image quality, create shapes, enter text, and choose colors. These are the tools that you apply by clicking and dragging with your mouse or pressure-sensitive pen. The Toolbox also provides access to changing foreground and background colors.

In this chapter, we'll describe the purpose and options of each of the Toolbox tools. Whenever it seems pertinent, we'll also let you know when a particular tool is likely to be the key to solving specific problems that face digital photographers, artists, and designers who work with Photoshop Elements 2.

The Toolbox

The default position for the Toolbox, shown in Figure 5-1, is in the upper-left corner of the Photoshop Elements workspace.

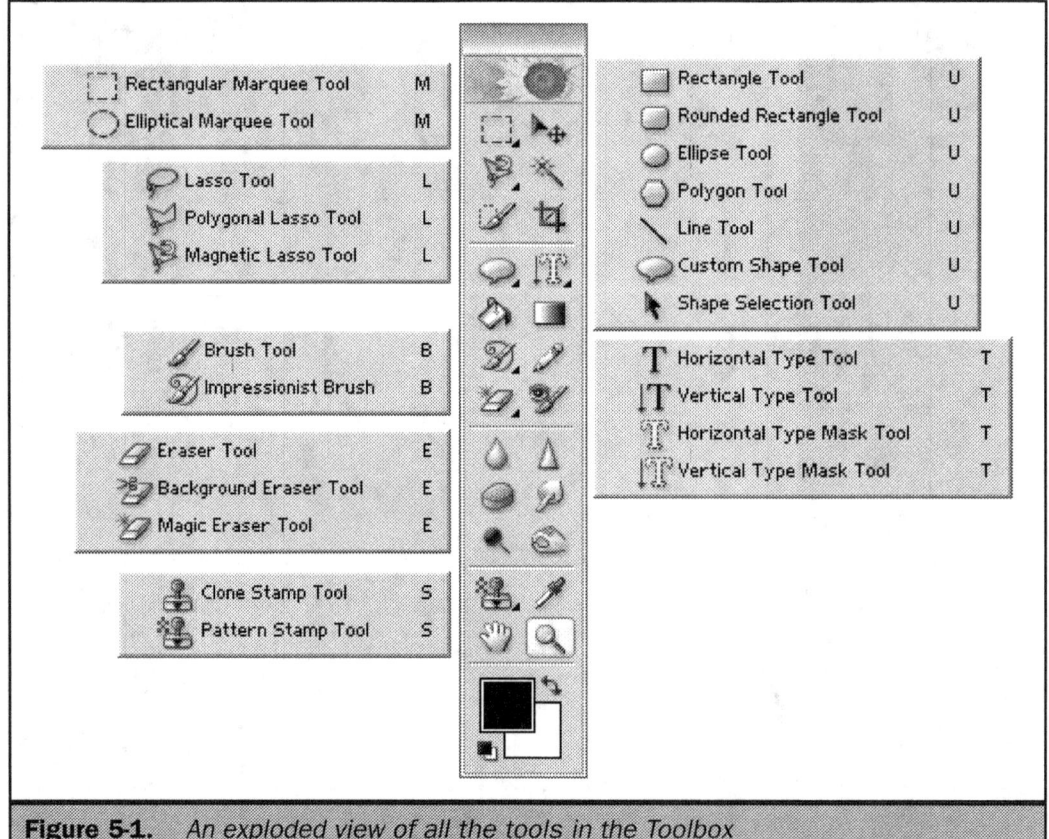

Figure 5-1. *An exploded view of all the tools in the Toolbox*

In a sense, however, the Toolbox is a floating palette, except that you can't hide it by dragging it to the Palette Well. You can, however, drag the Toolbox anywhere within the workspace—even to a second monitor if you're using a two-monitor setup.

Note   *The workspace can get a little crowded with the Toolbox and palettes, especially if you're trying to preview and work on a large area of the image. You can temporarily hide the Toolbox, the Shortcuts bar, the Options bar, and any palettes that have been placed in the workspace, by pressing the TAB key. Then you can make a sweeping stroke or show your colleague an image without all those obstacles in the way. To bring those items back to the workspace, press the TAB key again.*

The Tools

You will notice that each of the tool names in this chapter is followed by a letter in parentheses. The letter indicates the keyboard shortcut to all the tools that occupy the same button slot in the Toolbox. (You can also see shortcuts by holding the cursor over a tool.) If you spend considerable time working in Photoshop Elements, these shortcuts will help you work more quickly.

If only one tool is available in a particular slot, pressing the keyboard shortcut activates that tool—it will be highlighted in the Toolbox. Often, several tools occupy the same slot. You can tell that a slot has multiple tools options when you see a small, down-facing arrow to the lower right of the tool icon. If you press the appropriate key or click the particular tool in that slot, it will become active. You can choose a currently invisible tool that occupies the same slot as a visible tool in two ways:

- Press SHIFT and then press the letter for that tool slot as many times as it takes to cycle through the tools in that slot. When you highlight the tool you want to use, simply stop pressing the letter, and that tool will be activated and its icon will appear in the Toolbox.

- Place the cursor over the slot in which the tool resides and hold the left mouse button. A drop-down menu appears that pictures each of the tools in that slot. Drag to highlight the tool you want and then release the button.

Each of the following sections describes a tool in detail, along with its Options bar. Each option for each tool is also described in detail.

The Go To Adobe Online Button

 When you click the flower logo at the top of the Toolbox palette, a dialog box will appear offering two options: to load updates and to set preferences for Adobe Online. Adobe Online provides quick and easy Internet access to current updates and additions to your program. Preferences can be set to look for updates automatically once a day, once a week, once a month, or never.

If you choose Updates, the program will search the Adobe site for update files and download them to your system. If program additions are available, another dialog box shows a list and description of the updates. These are optional downloads.

Click the Go Online button to jump directly to the Photoshop Elements 2 page on the Adobe web site.

Rectangular Marquee (M)

The Rectangular Marquee tool lets you make either square or rectangular selections. To ensure that the selection is a perfect square, hold the SHIFT key as you drag to establish the size of the selection; or choose Style | Fixed Aspect Ratio and enter **1** into both the Height and Width fields.

The Rectangular Marquee tool serves two basic functions: to make square and rectangular selections, and to serve as a Crop tool if the user chooses Edit | Crop while a selection is active. The following Options bar appears immediately above the Toolbox as soon as the Rectangular Marquee tool is chosen.

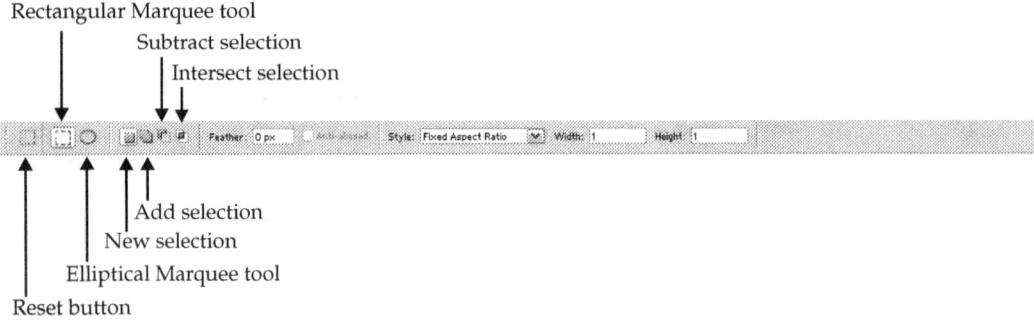

Reset Button   Click and drag to choose between resetting the options for the current tool and resetting options for all the tools in the Toolbox. The Reset button resets all the options to their defaults. Otherwise, the last options chosen stay in effect until you deliberately make a change. (If you don't remember this, you're likely to get unexpected feathering. See "Feather Field," a little later in this section.)

Rectangular Marquee Tool   Selects the Rectangular Marquee tool. See the information at the beginning of this section.

Elliptical Marquee Tool   Selects the Elliptical Marquee tool. See the information at the beginning of the upcoming section, "Elliptical Marquee."

New Selection   If this is chosen, each time you click and drag, any existing selection will be automatically dropped and you will make a new selection.

Add Selection   Adds each selection you make to any selections that have already been made.

Subtract Selection   Subtracts the overlapping portion of any new selection from the shape of any selections that have already been made.

Intersect Selection   Leaves only the overlapping portions of sequentially selected areas as a selection.

Feather Field   If you want the selection to fade from fully transparent to fully opaque, enter the distance in pixels over which you would like to see the fade occur. If you enter feathering here, it will stay in effect for the current group of selection tools, even after closing and reopening the program, until you reset the tools or change the number in the Feather field. If you want to feather the selection temporarily to a different degree, choose Select | Feather and enter a feathering dimension that is greater than the currently chosen setting for feathering.

Anti-aliased Check Box   If checked, the edge of any selection will be anti-aliased (smoothed) to eliminate the appearance of pixelization (jagged edges).

Style Drop-Down Menu   This menu gives you three options for controlling how your marquee operates: Normal, Fixed Aspect Ratio, or Fixed Size. Normal gives you free access to size the vertical and horizontal dimensions at will as you drag the marquee. Fixed Aspect Ratio uses the proportion of the numbers entered in the Width and Height fields to determine the proportional shape of the selection. Fixed Size uses the absolute pixel values entered into the Width and Height fields to constrain the size of the selection.

Width Field   Enter a pixel value that determines the pixel size or proportion of the width of the marquee.

Height Field   Enter a pixel value that determines the pixel size or proportion of the height of the marquee.

Elliptical Marquee (M)

The Elliptical Marquee tool makes either circular or oval-shaped selections. To ensure that the selection is a perfect circle, hold the SHIFT key as you drag to establish the size of the selection; or choose Style | Fixed Aspect Ratio and enter **1** into both the Height and Width fields.

The Elliptical Marquee tool's Options bar is identical to the Rectangular Marquee tool's Options bar in the preceding section. So to save us ink and paper and you from tedium, we won't picture it again here.

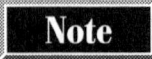 *The Elliptical Marquee tool is useful for creating a number of effects, such as oval picture frames or old-fashioned oval vignettes portraits, quickly darkening or lightening the corners of pictures, and creating the effect of spots of light hitting the background or a wall.*

Move (V)

 The Move tool is used to adjust the position of layers, selections, shapes, or text—whichever happens to be active at the time the Move tool is chosen or active (highlighted) in the Toolbox. The Move tool's Options bar has only two options.

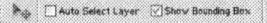

Auto Select Layer Check Box   Click to toggle the check box on or off. If toggled on, a check mark appears in the box, and clicking the visible portion of any layer will automatically select that layer in the Layers palette.

Show Bounding Box Check Box   If this box is checked, a transformation bounding box appears around the selection. You can then use any of the Free Transform moves to transform the selection (see Chapter 11).

Move Tool Operations

Although the Move tool has only two options, it can perform many operations that are crucial in image editing. The following sections describe the Move tool functions. These functions are applicable to all types of selections.

Move the Contents of a Selection   Place the Move tool cursor inside the selection and drag to select it. This will cut and move the contents of the selection along with the Selection marquee.

Copy and Move the Contents of a Selection   Place the Move tool cursor inside the selection. Hold down the OPT/ALT button as you drag. This will leave the selected area in place while creating a floating copy that is free to move above the original. The copied selection can be moved freely until you deselect it; then it merges wherever it is positioned with the active layer. If you want to move the selection to a new layer, choose the Rectangle Marquee tool, right-click within the selection, and choose the Layer Via Cut command.

Transform Selections and Layers   Select the Show Bounding Box check box in the Move tool's Options bar. This will allow you to perform transformation commands such as rotate, scale, skew, distort, and perspective on a layer or selection by manipulating the bounding box handles (see Chapter 11).

PHOTOSHOP ELEMENTS ORIENTATION

Move a Layer Place the cursor outside any existing selection and drag the layer with the Move tool. If the layer is a Background layer, it cannot be moved. When you attempt to move the background layer, a dialog box will automatically appear to apprise you of that fact.

Copy a Layer Hold down OPT/ALT while you drag anywhere in the active layer to make a copy of the active layer on a new layer and move the copied layer simultaneously. This maintains the selection as movable and editable. If you want to keep the copy of the layer as a floating selection in the same layer, choose Select | Select All first, and then hold down OPT/ALT while you drag anywhere in the active layer to make a copy that you can move around on the same layer. The floating layer selection will merge with the active layer when you deselect it.

Lasso (L)

The Lasso tool is Photoshop Elements' way of letting you make free-form selections. To make a Lasso selection, you simply drag to trace the selection shape. If you release the mouse button before you reach the point where the selection started, it will close the selection automatically with a straight line between the start and end points.

The Options bar is the same for both the Lasso and Polygonal Lasso tools, so it will be shown only once here:

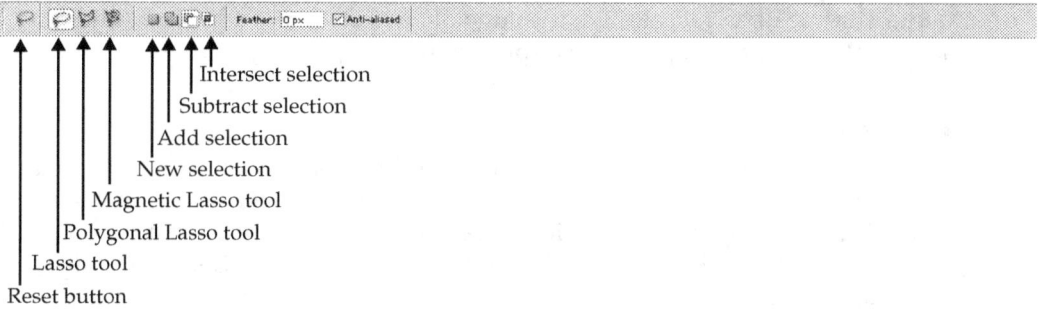

Reset Button Resets all the options to their defaults.

Lasso Tool Drag to trace the selection shape. Clicking any of the three Lasso icons lets you switch tools from the Options bar. All the other chosen options stay in effect for all three tools.

Polygonal Lasso Tool Selects the Polygonal Lasso tool. See the information at the beginning of the upcoming "Polygonal Lasso" section.

Magnetic Lasso Tool   Selects the Magnetic Lasso tool. See the information at the beginning of the upcoming "Magnetic Lasso" section.

New Selection   If this icon is chosen, each time you click and drag, any existing selection will be automatically dropped and you will make a new selection.

Add Selection   Adds each selection you make to any selections that have already been made.

Subtract Selection   Subtracts the overlapping portion of any new selection from the shape of any selections that have already been made.

Intersect Selection   Leaves only the overlapping portions of sequentially selected areas as a selection.

Feather Field   If you want the selection to fade from fully transparent to fully opaque, enter the distance in pixels over which you would like to see the fading occur. If you enter feathering here, it will stay in effect for the current group of selection tools, even after you close and reopen the program, until you reset the tools or change the number in the Feather field. If you want to feather the selection to a different degree temporarily, choose Select | Feather and enter a feathering dimension that is greater than the currently chosen setting for feathering.

Anti-aliased Check Box   If selected, the edge of any selection will be anti-aliased (smoothed) to eliminate the appearance of pixelization (jagged edges).

Polygonal Lasso (L)

The Polygonal Lasso tool can create selections in the shape of polygons with defined vertices and connected straight lines. This is accomplished by clicking to set a vertex and then moving the cursor to a new point and clicking again. When you are through placing vertices, double-click to complete the selection. This tool is useful for making selections around areas that have straight-line edges

The Polygonal Lasso tool uses the same options as the Lasso tool, so refer to the Lasso tool illustration in the preceding section for the Options bar information.

Magnetic Lasso (L)

This tool is pure redemption when you have to select complex edges that often twist, turn, and change direction. The Magnetic Lasso tool looks for contrasting pixels that depict edges in a bitmapped image and attaches a selection marquee to those edges automatically. Anchor points are automatically inserted at intervals (see the Options bar illustration, coming up) to anchor the selection so that it doesn't start "wandering" unpredictably. Any time you click, insertion of an anchor point is forced. You should insert an anchor point at any edge corner that forces a change in direction.

The Magnetic Lasso tool can be a lifesaver, but it can also seem quite temperamental. You'll find more advice on how to deal with this tool in Chapter 5.

Except for the items discussed in the following sections, the items in the Magnetic Lasso tool's Options bar are the same as those for the Lasso and Polygonal Lasso tools.

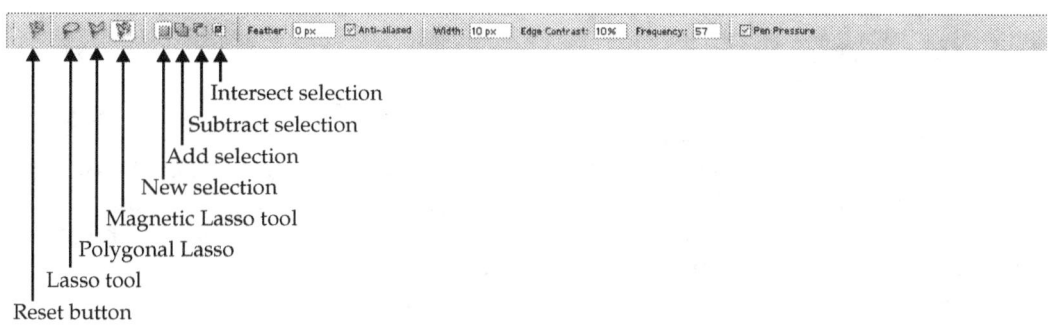

Reset Button Resets all the options to their defaults.

Lasso Tool Drag to trace the selection shape. Clicking any of the three Lasso icons lets you switch tools from the Options bar. All the other chosen options stay in effect for all three tools.

Polygonal Lasso Tool Selects the Polygonal Lasso tool. See the information at the beginning of the earlier "Polygonal Lasso" section.

Magnetic Lasso Tool Selects the Magnetic Lasso tool. See the information at the beginning of this section.

New Selection If this icon is chosen, each time you click and drag, any existing selection will be automatically dropped and you will make a new selection.

Add Selection Adds each selection you make to any selections that have already been made.

Subtract Selection Subtracts the overlapping portion of any new selection from the shape of any selections that have already been made.

Intersect Selection Leaves only the overlapping portions of sequentially selected areas as a selection.

Width Field Enter the number of pixels on either side of the cursor that you want the "magnet" to search for a contrasting edge to which to attach the marquee.

Edge Contrast Field Enter the percentage of difference in contrast between pixels that you'd like to have the magnet consider enough of a contrast to be an edge.

Frequency Field   Enter the number of pixels between automatically inserted anchor points.

Pen Pressure Check Box   If checked, pen pressure will determine width and edge contrast.

Magic Wand (W)

The Magic Wand is the tool to use when you have to select rambling edges set against areas of fairly uniform color—for example, you can select the horizon line between land and sky by clicking the sky with the Magic Wand tool. The Magic Wand tool lets you select areas that are within the range of colors that you specify in its Options bar. You can also select only integral areas of color or any noncontiguous areas of the color range that happen to occur anywhere in the image.

The following options can be chosen from the Magic Wand's Options bar, shown here:

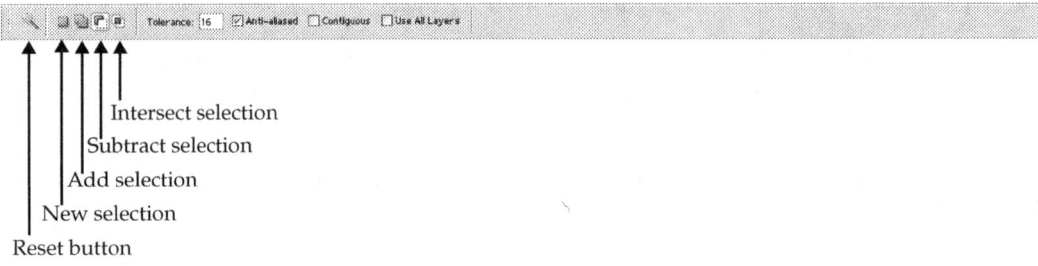

Intersect selection
Subtract selection
Add selection
New selection
Reset button

Reset   Resets all options for this tool to defaults.

New Selection   If this icon is chosen, each time you click and drag, any existing selection will be dropped and you will make a new selection.

Add Selection   Adds each selection you make to any selections that have already been made.

Subtract Selection   Subtracts the overlapping portion of any new selection from the shape of any selections that have already been made.

Intersect Selection   Leaves only the overlapping portions of sequentially selected areas as a selection.

Tolerance Field   Enter any number between 1 and 255 to indicate the brightness range over which similar colors will be considered as part of the selection. Experience and experimentation will train you to select the right tolerance.

Anti-aliased Check Box   If checked, the edge of any selection will be anti-aliased to eliminate the appearance of pixelization (jagged edges).

Contiguous Check Box   If checked, only a contiguous (connected) range of colors will be selected.

Use All Layers Check Box   If checked, all visible portions of layers that contain colors that fall within the range specified in the Tolerance field will be selected.

Selection Brush (A)

If you're familiar with Photoshop Professional, we can flatten the learning curve for the Selection Brush tool for you: it is Quick Mask mode in disguise. In the Photoshop Elements 2 version, the difference is that you use this specific brush, rather than the Paintbrush, to paint the selection, and the selection's outer limits look like a freehand Lasso selection, but with smoother-looking edges. The brush can be any brush you choose, and it can have any of the characteristics of any of the brushes in the default Brush Library. However, you can't load libraries from the Selection Brush tool Options bar, nor are options available for changing brush dynamics.

The Selection Brush has two modes: Selection and Mask. The only real difference is that if you choose Mask mode, the brush stroke is in the Mask color (which defaults to Rubylith orange—just like Quick Mask mode in Photoshop). The command for inverting a selection (making what's protected the reverse of what was originally protected) is the same as it is for any other selection.

You can also save selections in Photoshop Elements 2, but you'll learn all about that in Chapter 7. The Selection Brush tool's Options bar comes in two variations, depending on whether you're in Selection or Mask mode.

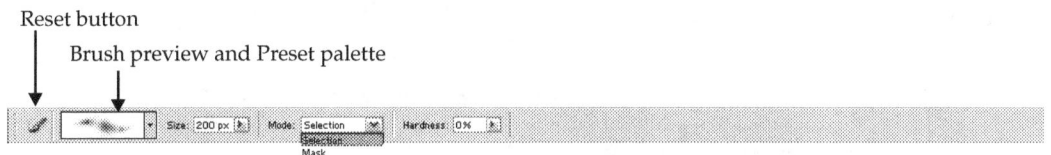

Reset Button   Resets the brush to its default options settings.

Brush Preview and Preset Palette   Lets you choose from any of the Brush preset styles in the current menu.

Size Field and Slider   Either enter a number of pixels for the diameter of the brush or click the slider button and drag the slider that drops down.

Mode Menu   Click the button to choose between Selection and Mask mode.

Hardness Menu and Slider   Enter a number of pixels to feather the brush, or click the slider button and drag the slider that drops down.

Crop (C)

The Crop tool is obviously made to crop an image, but it offers several advantages over using the Rectangular Marquee tool:

- Using the Crop tool, you can get a much more accurate preview of the area to be cropped because as soon as you drag to delineate the bounding box, the area outside the bounding box darkens.

- You can keep dragging the handles until the image is cropped exactly as you'd like.

- If you need to crop an image so that it will fit a specific-sized frame, you can enter that size in the Height and Width fields and then enter the resolution at which you want to print. Photoshop Elements will then not only crop to form an image of exactly that size, but also resample to the correct printing or display resolution for that size. It's a real time-saver if you're doing production printing to fit a group of images to a particular size for framing, or to fit a particular position in a layout, or to fit a particular size on a web page.

- You can rotate the cropping marquee and Photoshop Elements will resample and straighten the image automatically when you click the Commit button.

The Crop tool has two Options bars. The first sets the options for how the Crop tool will behave, and the second lets you toggle the shield (darker color outside the cropping marquee) on and off and lets you choose the color and opacity of the shield. The second Options bar appears as soon as you place the crop marquee. This is also your first encounter with the Cancel and Commit buttons (see the Crop tool's second Options bar illustration) that are used on many Options bars. The first of these two Options bars is shown here:

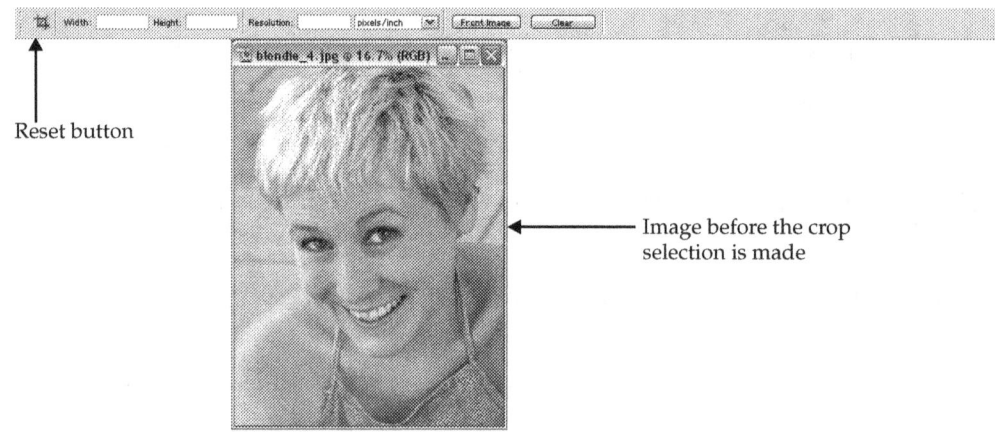

Reset   Resets the brush to its default options settings.

Width Field   If you want to crop to a specified final size, enter the width and units here.

Height Field   If you want to crop to a specified final size, enter the height and units here.

Resolution Field   Enter the resolution to which you want Photoshop Elements to resample the image after cropping to the size specified in the Width and Height fields.

Units Menu   Lets you choose between pixels per inch or per cm (centimeter).

Front Image Button   Lets you apply the sizing and resampling values set for the Crop tool in the Front Image to all of the other open images so that they can all be cropped to the same size.

Clear Button   Clears all the settings in the Options bar and lets you size the marquee to any proportion.

The second Options bar is shown here:

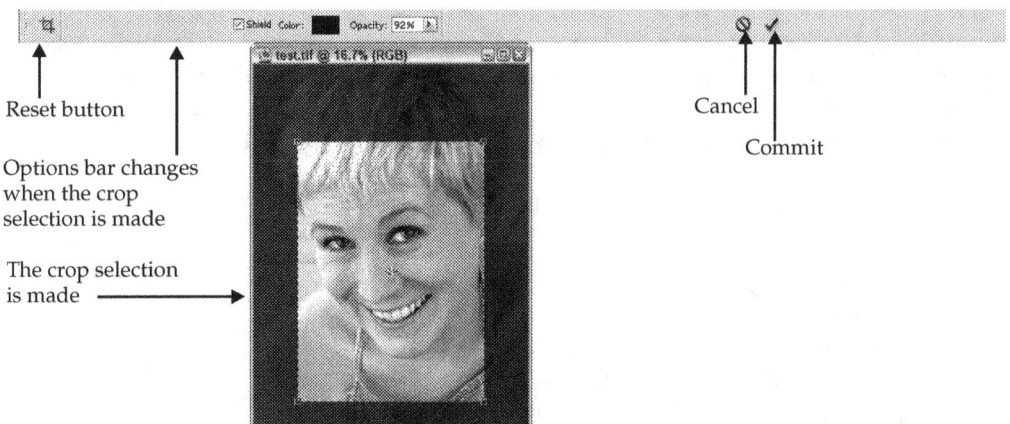

Shield Check Box   Click to toggle the dark frame outside the Crop marquee. When the check mark is in the box, the Shield is toggled on.

Shield Color Swatch   Click to bring up the Color Picker. You can then choose any color as the color for the shield. Although it's sometimes helpful to be able to choose a color that contrasts strongly with the image, remember that non-neutral colors can misguide your mind's eye when it comes to judging color in the picture.

Opacity Field   Lets you control the transparency of the shield. Either enter a percentage of opacity or choose a percentage from the drop-down menu.

Cancel Button   Cancels the cropping operation and leaves the image as it was.

Commit Button   Renders the crop.

Rectangle (U)

The Rectangle tool is the first in the set of shape tools that occupy this slot, which includes Shape Selection, Rounded Rectangle, Ellipse, Polygon, Line, and Custom Shape tools.

You can draw a shape in Photoshop Elements just by dragging diagonally until the shape has the desired dimensions and proportions. Shapes are great for creating graphical elements, such as buttons and picture frames that will be used on Web pages. Shapes in Photoshop Elements are drawn with vectors, so they can transform in any way without loosing their clarity and definition.

Shapes are always drawn on their own layer automatically. You can use the Free Transform command to transform any shape by CTRL-right-clicking the shape. A context menu appears that lets you make a selection from the shape, simplify the layer, or transform the shape.

The rectangle created by the Rectangle tool is a square-cornered, parallel-sided rectangle. Pressing SHIFT while you draw the shape restricts the rectangle to a square shape. The Shape options for the Rectangle are shown in the Options bar that follows. The Rectangle tool's Options bar contains all of the same options as the Shape tool Options bars, except for the Shape Selection Options bar. In the first illustration, all the standard elements on the Shape tools' Options bar are identified; thereafter, we'll identify only the options that are specific to the particular shape tool.

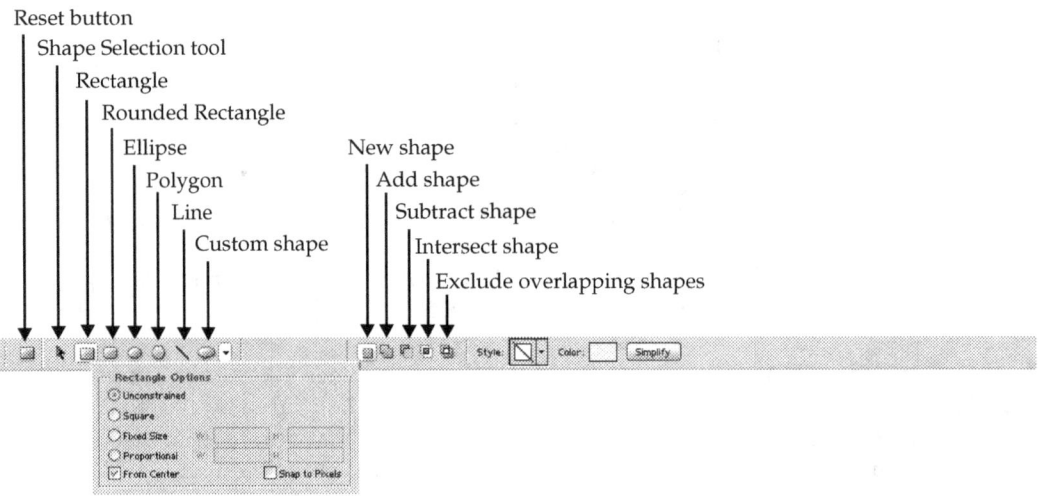

Reset Button   Resets all the Shape tool options to their defaults.

Shape Selection   Selects the Shape Selection tool and Options bar.

Rectangle   Selects the Rectangle tool and Options bar.

Rounded Rectangle   Selects the Rounded Rectangle tool and Options bar.

Ellipse   Selects the Ellipse tool and Options bar.

Polygon   Selects the Polygon tool and Options bar.

Line   Selects the Line tool and Options bar.

Custom Shape   Selects the Custom Shapes tool and Options bar.

Rectangle Options Pop-Up Palette   Allows you to set the Rectangle options on the pop-up menu palette to Unconstrained, Square Only, Fixed Size, Proportional, From Center, and Snap To Pixels. The Fixed and Proportional options require you to enter width and height in pixel dimensions in the text fields to the right.

New Shape Layer   Creates a new shape that has the characteristics of the other chosen options.

Add Shape Layers   Joins two shape layers into one.

Subtract Shape Layers   Leaves a cutout in the first shape that is made by the edge of the overlapping shape. You can use this option to make various shaped holes in shapes.

Intersect Overlapping Shapes   Leaves the shape carved out by the two overlapping shapes.

Exclude Overlapping Shapes   The overlapping portions of the shapes are excluded, leaving a sort of "hole" between the two.

Style Menu   Choose a layer style from this iconic menu and the style is immediately applied to the shape. To apply multiple styles to a shape, use the Layer Styles palette.

Color Swatch   Click this swatch to open the Color Picker, where you can choose the interior color of the shape.

Simplify Button   Renders the currently active shape layer as a bitmap.

Rounded Rectangle (U)

This tool creates a rectangle with rounded corners. You determine the radius of the corners by entering them in the Radius field that appears in the Options bar when this shape is chosen. You can also choose other options from the Rounded Rectangle Options pop-up palette:

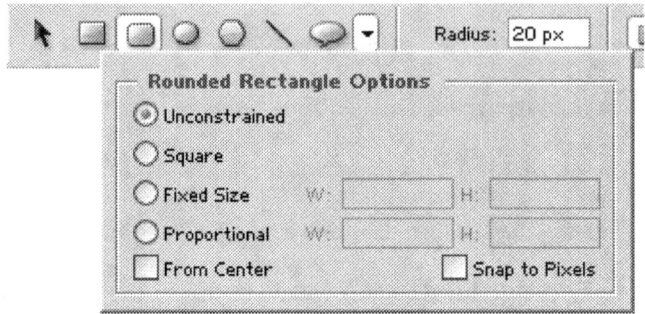

Rounded Rectangle Options Pop-Up Palette   Allows you to set the Rounded Rectangle options to Unconstrained, Square, Fixed Size, Proportional, From Center, and Snap To Pixels. The Fixed and Proportional options require you to enter width and height in pixel dimensions in the text fields to the right.

Radius   Sets the radius, in pixels, that is used to determine the quarter round arch at each corner of the rectangle.

Ellipse (U)

The Ellipse tool can be used to draw circles or ellipses, unconstrained, from the center, proportional, or of fixed dimensions. Press SHIFT to restrict the shape to a circle as you drag the marquee, or press OPT/ALT as you drag to draw the ellipse centered from the point at which you first clicked. You can choose a number of constraint options from the pop-up palette on the Ellipse options bar:

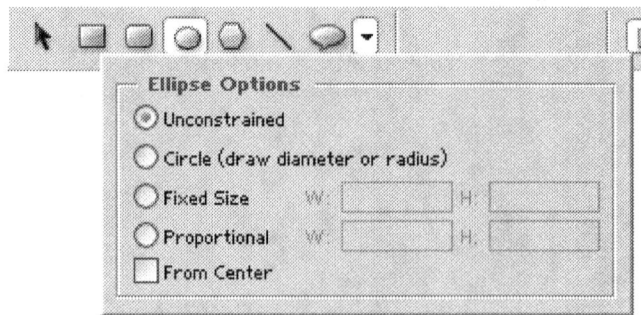

PHOTOSHOP ELEMENTS ORIENTATION

Ellipse Options Pop-Up Palette   Allows you to set the Ellipse options on the pop-up palette to Unconstrained, Circle, Fixed Size, Proportional, and From Center. Fixed and Proportional options require you to enter width and height in pixels in the text fields to the right.

Polygon (U)

 You use this tool to create regular polygons. Enter the number of sides in the Sides field that appears in the Options bar when the Polygon shape is chosen. The Options bar for the Polygon tool is shown here.

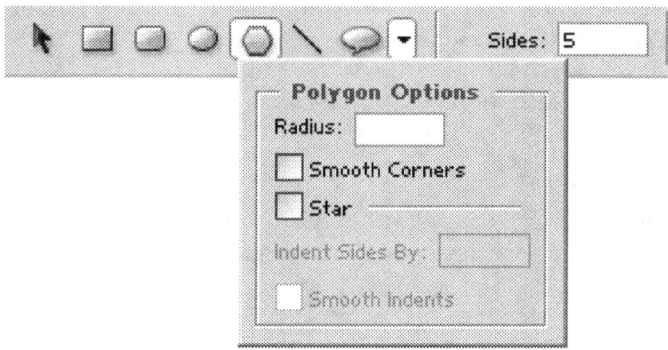

Polygon Options Pop-Up Palette   Allows you to set the Polygon options to a particular radius, with Smooth Corners, or as a Star (alternating inside and outside vertices). You can also set the amount of star indent in percentage of radius, and you can set Smooth Indents (smoothes inside corners of the star).

Sides   Sets the number of sides of the regular polygon.

Line (U)

 Simply Use the Line tool to draw a vector-based line. A Weight field appears in the Options bar when the Line tool is chosen, and you can enter a width in any of the types of units supported by Elements, such as points, pixels, inches, or millimeters. To specify a unit type, enter its two-letter abbreviation immediately after the number: for example, 2 px (2 pixels). Note that the line can have arrowheads at either or both ends and the arrowhead is specified as a percentage of line width and length. The arrowheads can also be specified to have concave sides.

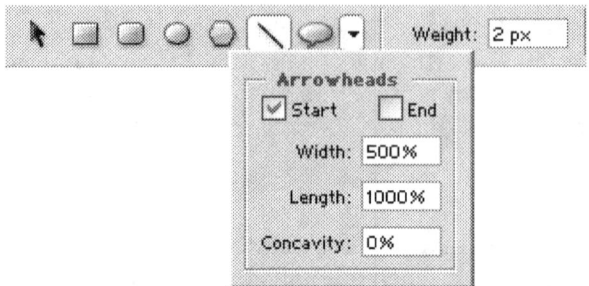

Arrowheads Pop-Up Palette Allows you to set the line options for arrowheads. The arrowheads can be created at the start or end of the line as it is drawn. The proportions of the arrowheads' width and length are set by percentages of the line thickness in respective fields. The Concavity setting determines whether the sides of the arrowheads have an arched appearance.

Weight Sets the line width in pixels, points, inches, or millimeters.

Custom Shape (U)

  The Custom Shape tool is one of a library of 352 iconic and symbolic shapes that ships with Photoshop Elements. The Butterfly shape is shown here.

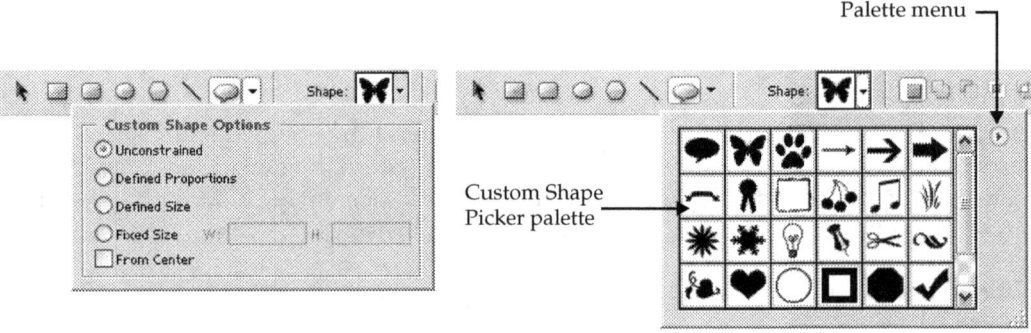

Palette menu

Custom Shape Picker palette

Custom Shape Options Pop-Up Palette Allows you to set the Custom Shape options to Unconstrained, Defined Proportions, Defined Size, Fixed Size, and From Center. The Fixed and Proportional options require you to enter width and height in pixel dimensions in the text fields to the right.

Custom Shape Picker This pop-up palette provides you with a menu of preset custom shapes. You can change the display and access other preset libraries through the Palette menu.

Shape Selection (U)

The Shape Selection tool lets you select the layer that a given shape is on. A number of special operations give you increased capabilities when creating shapes that apply to all of the shape types discussed here because they have some relation to the Shape Selection tool functions. If the shape layer has been simplified, this tool is not functional.

Pressing SHIFT while drawing a number of shapes will constrain all the shapes to one layer. With multiple shapes on a single layer, you can use the Shape Selection tool to SHIFT-click on shapes to select a number of shapes. Their bounding boxes will appear when they are selected. You can then click the Combine button on the Shape Selection tool's Options bar to combine them into a single shape. This lets you create more complex shapes.

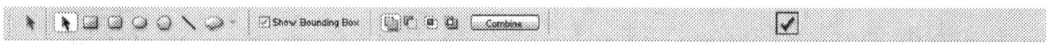

Show Bounding Box   This option toggles the display of the bounding box when you select a shape.

Combine Button   Combines selected shapes on the same layer into one shape.

Type (T)

The Type tool slot contains four tools: Type, Vertical Type, Horizontal Type Mask, and Vertical Type Mask. Like Shapes, Type is automatically entered on its own layer and is drawn from vector curves so that it can be infinitely transformed without losing definition and grace. If you enter type by simply clicking in the image area, all the type stays in one line. If the line of type is too long to fit within the image, it simply keeps going outside the frame.

Chapter 15 covers text operations in detail, as well as all the options. However, for reference purposes, the Text Options bar is shown here. It is essentially the same for all four text tools.

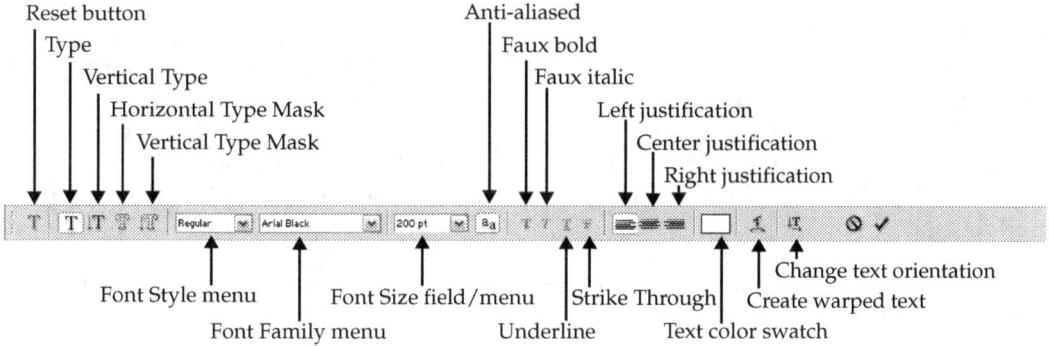

Reset Button   Resets the Text tools to their default options.

Type   Selects the normal Type tool and Options bar.

Vertical Type   Selects the Vertical Type tool and Options bar.

Horizontal Type Mask   Selects the Horizontal Type Mask tool and Options bar.

Vertical Type Mask   Selects the Vertical Type Mask tool and Options bar.

Font Style Menu   Lets you choose between whatever variations are available for your currently chosen font. Variations are such characteristics as bold, italics, and underline.

Font Family Menu   Lets you choose from any font that is currently loaded onto your system.

Font Size Field/Menu   You can either choose the size of the font from a number of preset sizes from 6 to 72 points, or enter any custom size you like in this field, up to 1291 pixels.

Anti-aliased   The pixels on the edge of a letter "blend" from black to white in about four intervals. This avoids the jagged look that results when a letter that is not anti-aliased is simplified (rendered). It's generally preferable to turn off anti-aliasing when creating text for the Web because the additional colors result in significantly larger and slower-loading files.

Faux Styles   The text shape is recalculated to emulate the look of a boldface and italic style font when no such style font exists in your computer's font library.

Underline   Underlines selected text

Strike Through   Places a line through the middle of selected text

Justification Buttons   Causes the lines in a paragraph of text to be aligned left, center alighted, or right aligned. If, for instance, text is *aligned left*, the first letter of each line of text starts at the left margin (not including lines that are indented). If the line is center aligned, the letter in the center of the line is aligned with all the letters in the centers of all the lines. If the line is *right aligned*, all of the lines will end at the right margin. When the text is in Vertical mode, the justification buttons will align text top, middle, and bottom.

Text Color Swatch   Click to bring up the Color Picker so that you can choose the color of your text.

Create Warped Text   Lets you choose from a menu of 15 different styles for warping text. Once you choose a style, the Warp Text dialog box appears and allows you several levels of control over how the text is warped. The Warped Text dialog box lets you choose between horizontal or vertical warping. You can use three field/sliders to vary the degree of blend and the horizontal and vertical distortion. You'll find more detail and photos in Chapter 15.

Change Text Orientation   Toggle this button to change text orientation from horizontal to vertical.

Cancel   Drops the text layer and returns you to image editing mode.

Commit   Click to end your text editing session.

Vertical Type (T)

The Vertical Type tool places letters one under the other. This tool does not achieve the same results as rotating the type 90 degrees. The Options bar is identical to the Type tool Options bar with the exception of the type alignment icons, which will change to indicate vertical type.

Horizontal Type Mask (T)

This tool makes a selection in the shape of the text that you enter. You can fill the text with a color, paste a photograph into it from the clipboard, copy the contents to another layer, or do anything else that you can do with a selection. The difference is that in this case, the selection is perfectly shaped to form the letters you typed.

Vertical Type Mask (Y)

This tool is the same as the Horizontal Type Mask except that the text is stacked vertically, from top to bottom.

Paint Bucket (K)

The Paint Bucket is a fill tool that works much in the same manner as the Magic Wand because it uses the tolerance range to determine what areas get filled. You can fill with either the current Foreground color or with any pattern in the currently chosen Pattern Presets Library.

    The Paint Bucket's Options bar is shown here:

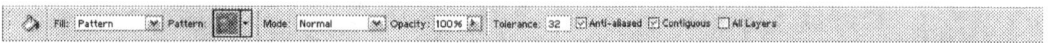

Reset Button   Resets all options for this tool to defaults.

Fill Menu   Lets you choose between filling with the current Foreground color or any pattern in the currently loaded Pattern Presets Library.

Pattern Presets   Lets you choose the fill pattern from an icon library of presets. You can learn all about patterns and how to use them for best effect in Chapter 16.

Mode Menu   Lets you choose from any of the blending modes available for painting. (See Chapters 9 and 16.)

Opacity Field/Slider   Before executing the fill, enter a percentage of opacity or drag the slider to indicate that percentage. You cannot change the percentage of opacity once the fill has been made.

Tolerance Field   Enter any number between 1 and 255 to indicate the brightness range over which similar colors will be considered as part of the fill. Experience and experimentation will train you to select the right tolerance.

Anti-aliased Check Box   If checked, the edge of any fill will be anti-aliased to eliminate the appearance of pixelization (jagged edges).

Contiguous Check Box   If checked, only a contiguous (connected) range of colors will be filled.

All Layers Check Box   If checked, all visible portions of layers that contain colors that fall within the range specified in the Tolerance field will be filled.

Gradient (G)

Gradients are colors that blend smoothly from one to the other, forming a sort of rainbow effect. Photoshop Elements ships with several preset libraries of gradients. You can also make your own gradients and save them to a library. The Gradient tool fills either the currently active layer or a selection with any gradient in the currently chosen library of gradient presets.

You fill with a gradient by placing the cursor to indicate a start point and then dragging to indicate the fill direction and end point. If the area to be filled is larger than the length of the line you drag, the areas on opposite ends of the line will be filled with the starting and ending colors in the gradient.

Five different types of gradient fills are available: Linear, Radial, Angle, Mirror, and Diamond. Each of these is illustrated in the same order in the next illustration.

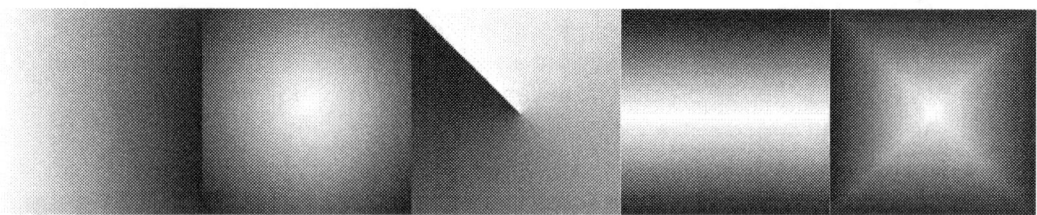

When specifying the starting point of Radial, Angle, Mirror, and Diamond gradient fill types, start dragging the line at the center of the fill, so that the gradient radiates out from that point.

To make a new gradient:

1. Select the Gradient tool. In the Options bar, click the Gradient Sample or the Edit button. The Gradient Editor dialog box appears (see Figure 5-2).

2. More than two colors may be selected. If so, to get rid of colors you don't want, drag the color stop away from the Gradient bar until it vanishes. At that point, the color will vanish as well.

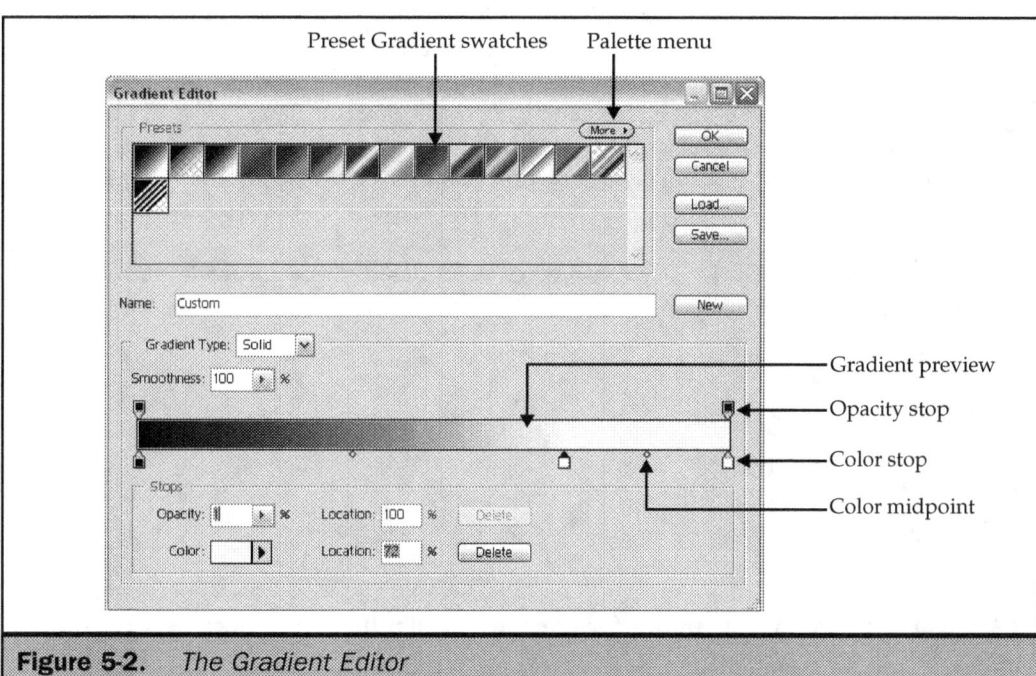

Figure 5-2. *The Gradient Editor*

3. To add a new color, click at any point immediately under the gradient bar. When a balloon tells you to click to add a color, do so. A new color stop will appear at the point you click. You can then drag the color stop to any point in the gradient bar.

4. To change the color represented by the color stop, click inside the color stop box. The Color Picker will appear. Choose a new color in the Color Picker. (See the "Color Picker" section at the end of this chapter.) Choose a color and it will appear in both the gradient bar and the color stop.

5. To adjust the spread of colors in the gradient bar, drag the small diamonds (color midpoint) on either side of the color point. You can add new colors and change the midpoints to your heart's content.

6. To change the opacity of a point in the gradient, click the desired point at the top of the gradient bar. An opacity stop will appear. You can add as many opacity stops as you want with this method. To change the opacity of an opacity stop, click it, and then, in the Opacity field, click the arrow to bring up the slider and drag until you see the opacity you like in the gradient bar.

7. To save the gradient you just created to the current preset library, click the New button. Your new gradient will appear in the Gradient Presets Library. Click the Save button to save the presets in the current library.

Note *If you want to create a whole new library of presets, you can either delete all the presets in the current library or edit any that you'd like to change. Then click the Save button. When the Save dialog box appears, enter the name for your new library in the File Name field and click Save. Make sure the directory you're saving to is the Gradients folder.*

The Gradient tool's Options bar also gives you considerable control over the ways you make gradients look:

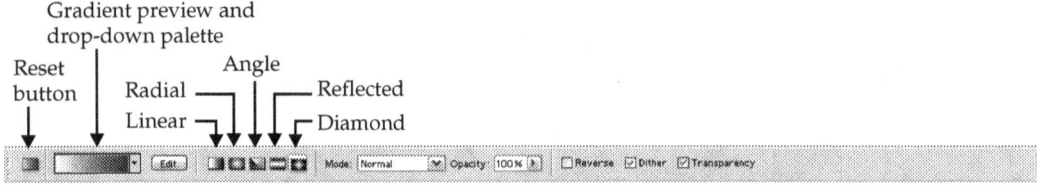

Reset Button   Resets all options for this tool to defaults.

Gradient Preview and Preset Palette   Lets you visually choose gradients in the currently chosen gradient preset library. This bar also shows a preview of the currently selected gradient.

Edit Button   Opens the Gradient Editor (refer back to Figure 5-2) so that you can either modify the characteristics of the current gradient or create an entirely new one.

Gradient Types   Click to change the type of gradient that will be made from your currently chosen gradient preset: Linear, Radial, Angle, Reflected, or Diamond.

Mode Menu   You can choose the blending mode, and the gradient fill will interact with the image just as if it were blended with another layer. To find out all about blending modes, see Chapter 9.

Opacity Field/Slider   Sets the overall percentage of opacity for the gradient fill. If transparencies are part of the gradient, making the overall gradient partially transparent will increase the effective transparency of the transparent portion of the gradient. In other words, the opacity value will have an additive effect on the transparency built into the gradient with the Gradient Editor.

Reverse Check Box   Like all check boxes, this toggles on/off when you click it. If a check mark appears, the gradient's color sequence is reversed.

Dither Check Box   If checked, creates a smoother blend. Especially useful if you have to work in indexed color.

Transparency Check Box   If toggled on, allows the gradient's transparency settings to take effect. Otherwise, the entire gradient will be opaque.

Brush (B)

The Brush tool is part of a set of tools in this Toolbox slot, which also includes the Impressionist Brush tool. The Brush tool in Photoshop Elements 2 makes available a significantly wider range of adjustments than were available either in version 1 or in Photoshop versions previous to the current version 7. You can see the Brush Options bar in the following illustration.

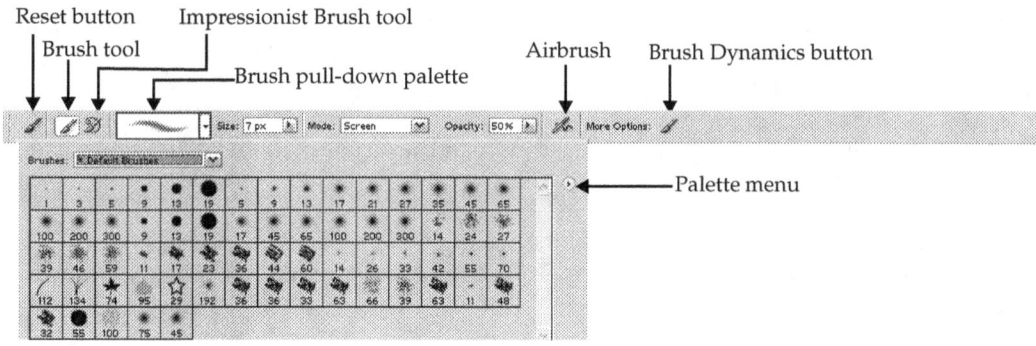

Reset Button   Resets all options for this tool to defaults.

Brush   Selects the Paintbrush tool.

Impressionist Brush   Selects the Impressionist Brush tool. Allows over painting of the image with a variety of impressionistic brush strokes. (See the following section, "Impressionist Brush.")

Brush Preview and Preset Palette   Click to reveal the Brushes drop-down palette. You can choose from any of the currently loaded brush presets from this palette.

Size Field/Slider   Determines the diameter of the brush.

Mode Menu   You can choose the blending mode the brush will use to interact with the image just as if it were blended with another layer. To find out all about blending modes, see Chapter 9.

Opacity Field/Slider   Sets the overall percentage of opacity for the brush. This will allow you to build up the brush strokes gradually.

Airbrush Button   Enables airbrush characteristics so that paint gets more opaque the longer you hold the cursor in one place, and strokes become darker as you paint over them.

More Options

In the More Options area, you will find the Brush Dynamics button (see Figure 5-3), which gives you a broad range of controls described in the remainder of this section.

Spacing   Dictates how far apart, as a factor of a percentage of the brush diameter, each brush shape will be spaced. Spacing that is less than 100 percent will make brush strokes seem to flow. Spacing that's more than 100 percent will cause strokes to appear as a scattered pattern—perfect for painting stars, a field of flowers, or raindrops.

Fade   Determines how long the stroke will be before it fades in both size and opacity, so that the stroke appears to trail off. A stroke that never fades is indicated by moving the slider all the way to the left. A stroke that fades within a single brush diameter is indicated by moving the slider all the way to the right.

Color Jitter   Indicates the frequency with which the stroke will switch between the Foreground and Background colors.

Hardness   Indicates the percentage of feathering of the radius of the brush shape. If the slider is at the extreme left, the brush is 100-percent feathered; if at the extreme right, the brush has a perfectly hard edge.

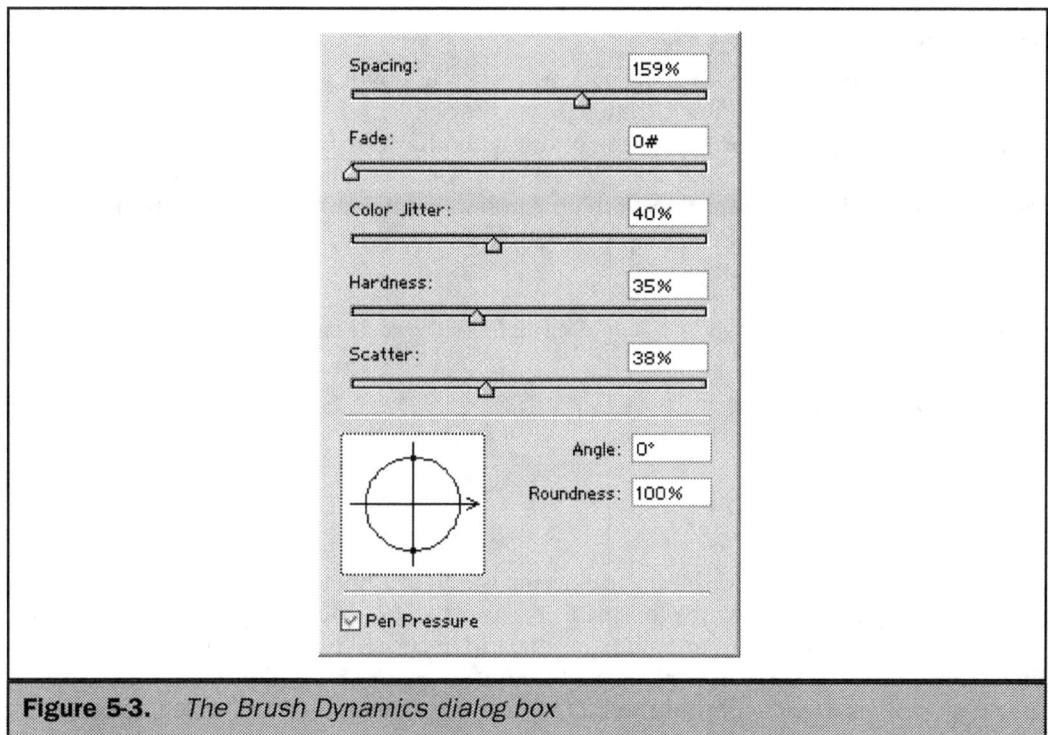

Figure 5-3.   *The Brush Dynamics dialog box*

Scatter   Indicates the distance over which the brush strokes are allowed to "spatter." Instead of following the brush in a smooth stroke, the brush stroke is dappled over the indicated percentage of the brush's width. A small percentage will seem merely to thicken the brush stroke.

Angle   If the brush shape is made to be an ellipse instead of a circle, you can choose the angle at which the brush "bristles" will be held.

Roundness   Determines whether the brush will be circular or elliptical and to what degree.

Pen Pressure Check Box   Toggles whether pen pressure will have an effect on the intensity of the preceding settings.

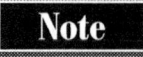   *If you have had your pressure-sensitive stylus for more than a few months, check the maker's web site for a driver update and download and install it. Some older drivers do not enable 100 percent of pressure sensitivity when being used with Photoshop Elements 2.*

Impressionist Brush (B)

This brush tool lets you create bizarre blobs and swirls over your underlying image. I've never seen anything done with this brush that looked like a keeper, but you may find a use for it if you experiment long enough and hard enough.

The Options bar settings for the Impressionist Brush tool are the same as those of the Brush tool, with the exception of the Impressionist Brush Dynamics button in the More Options area, which brings up this drop-down palette:

Impressionist Brush Dynamics button

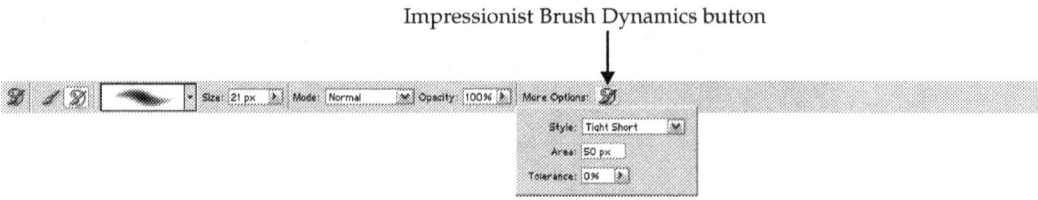

If you have encountered the Impressionist Brush in Photoshop Elements 1 or the similar History Brush in Photoshop prior to Photoshop 7, you'll be pleasantly surprised at the added versatility that you get from the added brush dynamics in Photoshop Elements 2. Because you can control scatter and color jitter and other factors that give the brush strokes a more natural-media feel, the range of "looks" that you can get with this brush is much greater.

To use the Impressionist Brush tool, choose the brush preset that you think will work best, and then set the brush's options just as you would for the Brush tool. Finally, click the Impressionist Brush Dynamics button in the More Options area to get the Impressionist Brush Dynamics drop-down palette. Choose the brush style that seems best suited to what you're after. Ten different styles are available, and you can experiment with them to see what they do. The Impressionist Brush works from the pixels on the currently active layer, so the results you get will depend greatly on the size of the area you've chosen and on the tolerance you've chosen. In the Area field, add the size of the area you want the strokes to fill; this value is independent of the size of the brush as designated in the Options bar. Tolerance is adjusted low when you want the brush to paint almost anywhere and high when you want the brush to paint only within a limited range of the colors that your first strokes covered. This may sound backward, but a low tolerance means the Impressionist Brush will paint almost anywhere; a high tolerance means you can paint only very limited areas.

Pencil (P)

The Pencil tool is designed to simulate the hard-edged drawing of a real pencil, no matter which brush you use. You can choose any of the brush preset libraries, many of which have soft-edged brushes designed for painting. While using the Pencil tool, the shape of the brushes will be maintained, but the soft edge attributes will not be in effect. You cannot use pen pressure to vary line thickness, and Brush Dynamics is not available. However, if pen pressure, scatter, and other brush dynamics have been built into a brush's preset, which is the case with many brush presets, the dynamics will be active when you use that preset with the Pencil tool.

The Options bar for the Pencil tool, shown next, is virtually the same as for the Brush tool, except no Airbrush button or More Options area appears. The Pencil tool's Options bar also includes a feature that is unique to the Pencil tool Options bar—the Auto Erase option.

Reset button

Pencil preview and Preset palette

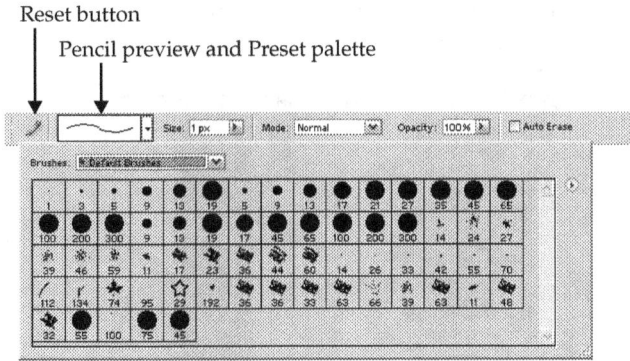

Reset Button   Resets all options for this tool to defaults.

Size Field/Slider   The Size field/slider determines the diameter of the brush.

Mode Menu   You can choose the blending mode the brush will use to interact with the image, just as if it were blended with another layer. To find out all about blending modes, see Chapter 9.

Opacity Field/Slider   The Opacity field/slider sets the overall percentage of opacity for the brush. This enables you to build up the brush strokes gradually.

Auto Erase   When this option is checked, you can use the Pencil tool to paint with the background color, as long as your pencil stroke begins in an area of the image that has the foreground color.

Eraser (E)

The Eraser tool removes pixels from a layer, leaving a transparent area. It has three different modes. These are not blending modes, but brush "behaviors": Brush, Pencil, and Block. If you're working in Brush mode, the Eraser tool will act just like the Brush tool would act given the current choice of brush presets—except that instead of laying down color, it removes color.

- Use Brush mode if you want to feather the edge of an erasure or if you want it to be textured and to have pressure-sensitive settings for size, opacity, and so forth.

- Pencil mode works just like a pencil. You can choose any brush, but the stroke edges are always hard-edged and not anti-aliased.

- Use Block mode when you want to clean out large areas absolutely and you want to be sure you haven't left even the most nearly transparent of pixels. Block mode is a white square. You can't change its size, but it stays the same size regardless of the zoom level. If you want to erase individual pixels, simply zoom in until the block is the same size as a pixel.

The Eraser tool's Options bar, shown next, offers few options we haven't already seen, other than the Eraser mode choices

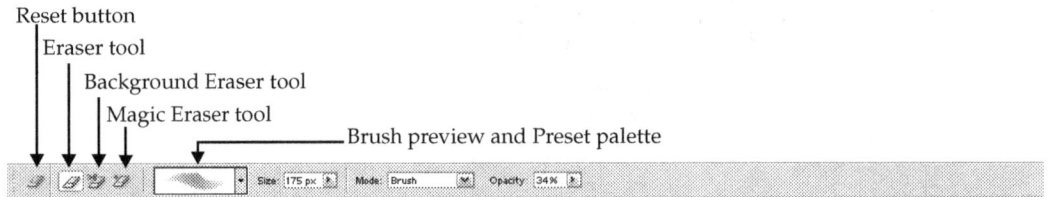

Reset Button   Resets all options for this tool to defaults.

Brush Preview and Preset Palette   Click to reveal the Brushes drop-down palette. You can choose from any of the currently loaded brush presets from this palette.

Size Field/Slider   Determines the diameter of the Eraser tool brush.

Mode Menu   Choose among Brush, Pencil, or Block eraser modes.

Opacity Field/Slider   Sets the overall percentage of opacity for the brush. This will allow you to build up the brush strokes gradually.

Background Eraser (E)

The Background Eraser tool lets you remove the background pixels that surround virtually any object edge, but its forte is removing the pixels around complex edges, such as the leaves of trees or a person's flying hair. You'll find a complete exercise on using the Background Eraser tool in Chapter 17.

The Background Eraser tool's Options bar has only a couple of unique options that differ from the Eraser Options bar.

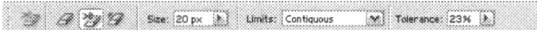

Limits Menu The choices on this menu are Contiguous and Discontiguous. If you choose Contiguous, the Background Eraser tool will erase any pixels under the brush as long as they are within the tolerance range and adjacent. If you choose Discontiguous, it will erase any pixels under the brush as long as they are within the tolerance range, regardless of whether they are adjacent or not. This is useful for cleaning up random stray pixels and noisy edges.

Tolerance Field/Slider This setting is similar to the one used by the Magic Wand tool. Its purpose is to limit the range of colors insofar as how different they can be from the original before they are ineligible for erasure. You'll adjust this control when you're deciding how sensitive the eraser is and how much it erases. Trial and error will help you learn how to set this parameter.

Magic Eraser (E)

The Magic Eraser tool works exactly like the Magic Wand tool—the only difference being that the areas the former selects get erased automatically. (You can do exactly the same task with the Magic Wand tool with an extra keypress: after the selection is made, press DELETE/BACKSPACE.)

The Magic Eraser tool's first four options are identical to the Eraser tool's options. The rest are listed next.

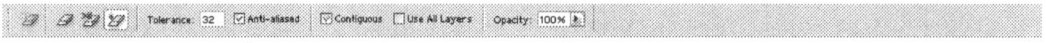

Tolerance Field Enter any number between 1 and 255 to indicate the brightness range over which similar colors will be considered as part of the selection. Experience and experimentation will help you select the right tolerance.

Anti-aliased Check Box If checked, the edge of any selection will be anti-aliased to eliminate the appearance of pixelization (jagged edges).

Contiguous Check Box If checked, only a contiguous (connected) range of colors will be selected.

Use All Layers Check Box If checked, all visible portions of layers that contain colors that fall within the range specified in the Tolerance field will be selected.

Opacity Field/Slider   Sets the overall percentage of opacity for the brush. This will allow you to build up the brush strokes gradually.

Red Eye Brush (Y)

The Red Eye Brush tool is a great retouching tool that can be handy for more than just fixing red eye. It replaces the color you click first with a replacement color. You make one click and then paint to replace the color. It's a great way to get rid of moles, pimples, and any kind of discoloration or blemish. The beauty of it is that it doesn't change the texture or tonal value of what's being recolored. You'll find an exercise on using the Red Eye Brush tool in Chapter 13.

The Red Eye Brush tool's Options bar is shown here:

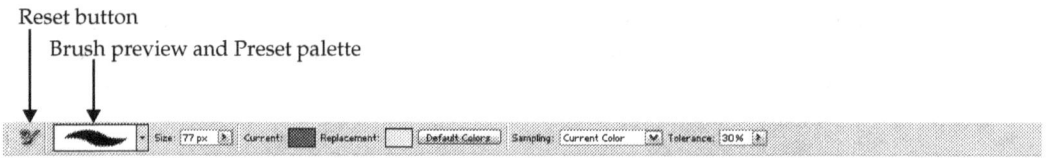

Reset   Resets all options for this tool to defaults.

Brush Preview and Preset Palette   Click to reveal the Brush Preset palette. You can choose from any of the currently loaded brush presets from this palette.

Size Field   Determines the diameter of the Red Eye brush.

Current Color Swatch   This displays the current color being used as a reference for replacement. This would most commonly be red if you are correcting red eye. You can choose other colors for replacement by clicking the color swatch to open the Color Picker.

Replacement Color Swatch   This color will be used to replace the referenced pixels of the current color. It can be any color, but is most often black if you are fixing red eye. To change the color, click the color swatch to open the Color Picker.

Default Colors Button   Click this button to replace the current and replacement colors with the system default red and black, respectively.

Sampling Menu   This drop-down menu gives you two options. The First Click option will take the current color for the first place you click in the image. You will see the color you selected reflected in the current color swatch on the Options bar. The second option,

Current Color, will use only the color you select by clicking the current color swatch on the Options bar and choosing a color from the Color Picker.

Tolerance Field   Enter any number between 1 and 255 to indicate the brightness range over which similar colors will be considered part of the colors to be replaced.

Blur (R)

The Blur tool lets you soften the focus on specific areas of the image. You might, for instance, want to take the moiré pattern out of the scanned portion of an image or soften certain fine wrinkles in a person's portrait. The Blur tool works just like a paintbrush, and its size and intensity can be controlled by a pressure-sensitive pen. You'll find more information on Blur and Sharpen in Chapter 13.

The Blur tool's Options bar is shown here:

Reset button

Brush preview and Preset palette

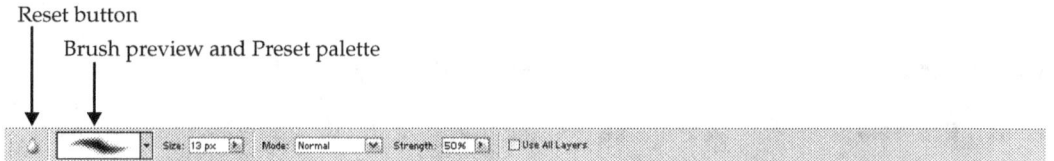

Reset Button   Resets all options for this tool to defaults.

Brush Preview and Preset Palette   Click to reveal the Brushes Preset palette. You can choose from any of the currently loaded brush presets from this palette.

Size Field/Slider   Determines the diameter of the Blur tool.

Mode Menu   This menu contains a limited library of blending modes applicable to this tool.

Strength Field/Slider   Enter a number between 1 and 100 percent to indicate how extensive you want the blurring to be.

Use All Layers Check Box   If this box is toggled on (checked), the blurring would affect all visible pixels, regardless of their layer of residence.

Sharpen (P)

The Sharpen tool is virtually the same as the Blur tool, but it works in reverse. It's an excellent little gadget for sharpening eyelashes, eyebrows, and other fine details that you want to feature in an image. Just be careful not to overdo it, or you'll end up with jagged or "haloed" edges. The Options bar features for the Sharpen tool are the same as those for the Blur tool.

Sponge (Q)

The Sponge tool is a brush type that increases or decreases color saturation in the brushed area. It can also be useful in a grayscale photo as a way to increase or decrease contrast in an area. The Sponge tool's Options bar is shown here:

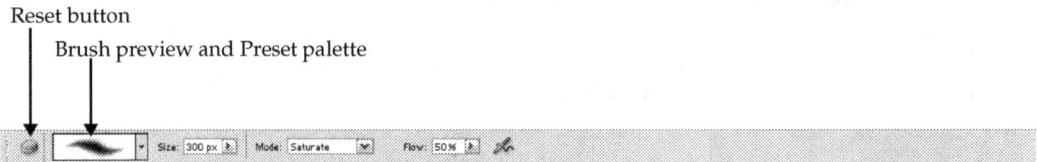

Reset Button   Resets all options for this tool to defaults.

Brush Preview and Preset Palette   Click to reveal the Brush Preset palette. You can choose from any of the currently loaded brush presets from this palette.

Size Field/Slider   Determines the diameter of the Red Eye brush

Mode Menu   Choose between the two choices on this menu: Saturate and Desaturate.

Flow Field/Slider   This control sets the rate of change in the saturation or desaturation in a single stroke. Set the value lower to build up the effect gradually with multiple brush strokes.

Smudge (F)

The Smudge tool pushes pixels around ahead of the brush, so it could be called the finger-painting tool. Its icon even looks like finger-painting. You can get some nice painterly distortions using nothing but this brush. It is also used in retouching to perform such effects as pushing in the bridge of a nose or giving a slight arch to an eyebrow. However, the Liquify filter is much better at that sort of thing. Here's the Options bar:

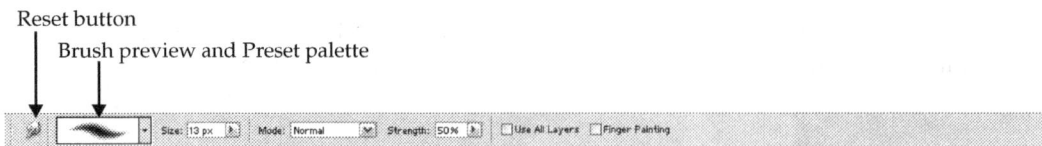

Reset Button   Resets all options for this tool to defaults.

Brush Preview and Preset Palette   Click to reveal the Brushes Preset palette. You can choose from any of the currently loaded brush presets from this palette.

Size Field/Slider   Determines the diameter of the Smudge tool.

Mode Menu   Limited to Darken, Lighten, Hue, Saturation, Color, and Luminosity. Each of these produces a different effect when pushing one color into another.

Strength Field/Slider   Enter a number between 1 and 100 percent to indicate how blurry you want the smudge to be.

Use All Layers Check Box   If this box is toggled on (checked) the smudging affects all visible pixels, regardless of their layer of residence.

Finger Painting Check Box   If checked, the Foreground color is pushed into the pixels ahead of the brush.

Dodge (O)

The Dodge tool is used to lighten in an area the size of the brush. You usually use this tool to lighten small but odd-shaped areas that are larger than the brush by "scrubbing" with it. Scrubbing is an artist's term that means making multiple brush strokes back and forth over the same area. Scrubbing allows you to blend as you lighten, so that the end result looks natural.

The Dodge tool is really a brush that lightens, so you can choose any of the brush presets for the shape of the Dodge tool. However, a round shape with semi-soft edges usually works best.

Here's the Dodge tool's Options bar:

Reset button
Brush preview and Preset palette

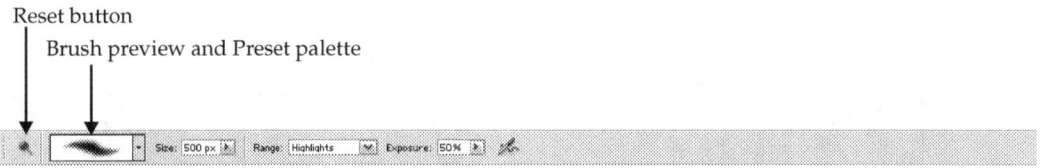

Reset Button   Resets all options for this tool to defaults.

Brush Preview and Preset Palette   Click to reveal the Brushes Preset palette. You can choose from any of the currently loaded brush presets from this palette.

Size Field/Slider   Determines the diameter of the Dodge tool.

Range Menu   Determines whether the highlights, midtones, or shadows will be most affected.

Exposure Field/Slider   Controls how much of a change in brightness will occur. It is usually best to set this at a fairly low setting (such as 15%) and then build up the change by scrubbing to blend the overall effect.

Burn (J)

The Burn tool darkens an area, rather than lightening it. Otherwise, the methods for using it and the options on its Options bar are identical to the Dodge tool.

Clone Stamp (S)

The Clone Stamp tool is part of a set for this Toolbox slot that includes the Pattern Stamp tool. The Clone Stamp tool copies a brush-sized portion of the image from one image, layer, or area to another image, layer, or area. Although this tool is generally used for retouching (for instance, to copy a smooth section of skin over a blemish), it can also be used in image compositing or to blend portions of one image (such as a better-exposed detail) into another image.

To use the Clone Stamp tool after choosing it from the Toolbox, place the cursor cross hairs over the portion of the image from which you want to clone, press the OPT/ALT key to let the program know that you are choosing a sample point, and click. You can then move the cursor to any other area of the photo and "paint in" the part of the image that was under the sample point. You'll find a detailed demonstration of how to use the Clone Stamp in Chapter 13.

The Clone Stamp tool's Options bar is shown here:

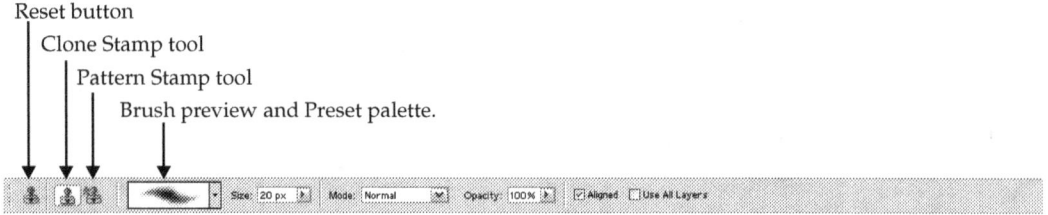

Reset Button   Resets all options for this tool to defaults.

Clone Stamp   Switches from the Pattern Stamp tool to the Clone Stamp tool and Options bar.

Pattern Stamp   Switches from the Clone Stamp tool to the Pattern Stamp tool and Options bar.

Brush Preview and Preset Palette   Click to reveal the Brushes Preset palette. You can choose from any of the currently loaded brush presets from this palette.

Size Field/Slider   Determines the diameter of the Clone Stamp tool.

Mode Menu   Select from the complete list of blending modes that will allow the Clone Stamp tool to blend the source image into the painted area in a variety of ways.

Opacity Field/Slider   Sets the overall percentage of opacity for the brush. This enables you to build up the brush strokes gradually.

Aligned Check Box   If this box is checked, the sample point stays in parallel with the brush. So you will be able to paint in the whole image that's under the sample tool, offset by the distance between the sample point and the first click. If the Aligned check box is toggled off, each click and drag will repeat painting the image from the sample point until you release the mouse button.

Use All Layers Check Box   If this box is toggled on (checked), the cloning affects all visible pixels, regardless of their layer of residence.

Pattern Stamp (S)

The Pattern Stamp tool is nothing more or less than a way to paint with patterns. You can paint with any of the pattern presets by choosing one from the Pattern Picker drop-down palette, or by selecting any part of an image and then choosing Edit | Define Pattern. This tool is useful if you want to hand-paint texture onto almost any smooth surface or you want to add the appearance of more definition by painting a texture pattern into an otherwise flat area of a photograph.

The Mode menu for the Pattern Stamp tool offers the full set of blending modes, so you can have quite a range of effects as you paint from the patterns. You can also give the patterns a more abstract look by first choosing the Impressionist Brush and then selecting its options for painting in a particular style. Then switch to the Pattern Stamp tool and click the Impressionist check box to turn it on. The Pattern Stamp tool will use the last-chosen Impressionist Brush options to paint from the currently chosen pattern.

The Options bar for the Pattern Stamp tool is identical to the Clone Stamp Options bar except for the addition of a few items listed next.

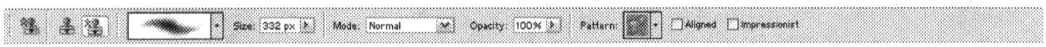

Pattern Preset Drop-Down Palette   Lets you choose from any of the patterns in the currently loaded library or any new patterns that you've defined and saved since the current library was opened. You can switch patterns at any time.

Aligned Check Box   Click to check if you want to make sure the pattern tiles stay aligned on all four sides, no matter where you paint. If you want to "mix up" the texture, click to toggle the check mark off and paint with multiple independent strokes.

Impressionist Check Box   Paints the currently chosen pattern with the settings last chosen for the Impressionist Brush.

Eyedropper (I)

 The Eyedropper tool is used to pick up the color of the pixel you click as the Foreground color. It is extremely useful when you want to match the color in one area of the picture in another area of the picture and don't want to have to set specific colors in the Color Picker to achieve that match.

Reset Button   Resets all options for this tool to defaults.

Sample Size   You can select the average color within either a 3- or 5-pixel radius of the click point. This is especially useful for matching the apparent color of an area that has been dithered to simulate colors or when colors have been dithered to create a gradient.

Hand (H or Spacebar)

 The Hand tool is used to pan in any direction across an image that is being shown at too large a zoom level to allow it to fit the current window or computer screen. It is indispensable when working on retouching at 100-percent zoom (which is how you *should* do retouching). You can temporarily access the Hand tool without deselecting your current brush tool by holding down the SPACEBAR. The Hand appears as the cursor, and you can drag the image in any direction until you release the SPACEBAR.

Double-clicking the Hand tool in the Toolbox automatically sizes the window to the largest size that it can be without overlapping any palettes, given the proportion of the image. After all, if you have to zoom out to get an overall view, you might as well at least be able to see the image as large as possible.

The Options bar, shown next, has only four buttons.

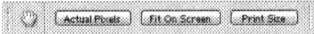

Reset Button   Resets all options for this tool to defaults.

Actual Pixels Button   Click to instantly zoom to 100 percent.

Fit On Screen Button   Click to make the image as large as possible on the current screen.

Print Size Button   Click to show what the definition of the image will be at actual print size.

Zoom (Z)

The Zoom tool is one of many ways that Photoshop Elements provides for magnifying or demagnifying the image within its window. Once the tool is chosen, clicking in the workspace window doubles the current magnification and centers the view at the point where you clicked it. Pressing ALT before clicking toggles to a Zoom Out tool.

If you double-click the Zoom tool in the Toolbox, the image will zoom to 100 percent (actual pixels). If you want to zoom in to a specific area and the percentage of magnification isn't as important as being able to focus on that area at the highest possible magnification, drag the Zoom tool diagonally until a marquee surrounds the area you want to see. That area will then fill the current window—so what you actually see will be all of the area you chose, plus whatever else fits within the proportions of the window.

Finally, the Options bar offers some interesting choices:

Reset button
Zoom In
Zoom Out

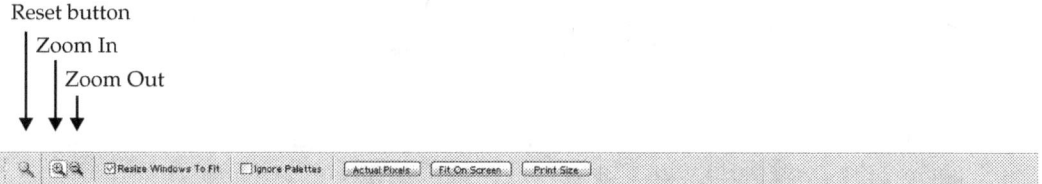

Reset   Resets all options for this tool to defaults.

Zoom In   Click to increase the image size on the screen display by preset increments. Click this tool if you know you are going to want to zoom out several times in a row and you don't want to press the OPT/ALT key each time.

Zoom Out   Click to reduce the image size on the screen display by preset increments. Click this tool if you know you are going to want to zoom in several times in a row and don't want to have to press the OPT/ALT key each time.

Resize Window To Fit Check Box   Click to check this option if you want the window to resize itself automatically to fit the image. This is handy when you want to compare several image windows side by side.

Ignore Palettes Check Box   If this box is checked, palettes will be ignored when you click the Fit On Screen button.

Zoom Buttons   This is a set of buttons that will automatically resize the image to the actual pixels dimension, to fit on screen, or to the designated size for print output set with the Image Size command.

Color Control Area

In the Color Control area of the Toolbox, you can access, change, and manipulate your foreground and background colors You can see the four function control icons in the illustration that follows.

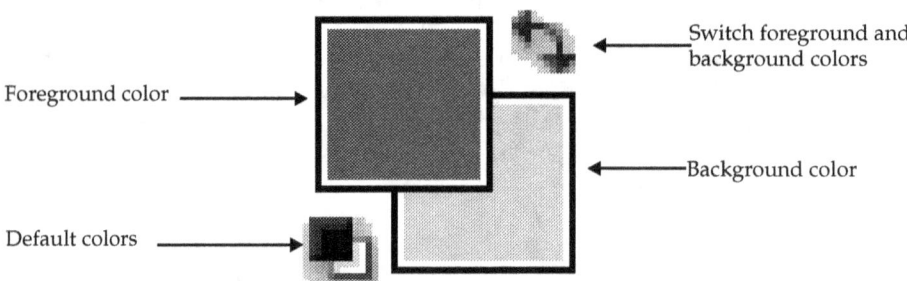

Foreground Color   This swatch represents the current Foreground color—the color you'll get any time you paint with a brush or choose Foreground Color from the Fill dialog box after choosing Edit | Fill. You can change the Foreground color in three ways:

- Click any color in the image with the Eyedropper tool.
- Pick a color from the Swatches palette.
- Click the Foreground color swatch to bring up the Color Picker, and then choose a color (see "Color Picker," the next section).

Background Color   The Background color is the color you get when you erase from the Background layer. The Background color is also the last color used when you make a default fill with the Fill tool. When you fill, you can also specify the Background color as the Fill color.

Switch Foreground and Background (X)   Click the double-headed arrow to make the Foreground color the Background color, and vice versa. The Foreground color is also the first color used when you make a default fill with the Fill tool. When you fill, you can also specify the Foreground color as the Fill color.

Default Colors (D)   When you want the default pure white Foreground color and solid black Background color, click the small icon that looks like miniature overlapping black/white swatches. You can do the same thing by simply pressing D.

Color Picker

The Color Picker is the dialog box that Photoshop Elements uses to let you choose a color no matter where you are working in the image. You can choose a color in the Color Picker dialog box in several ways. The most often employed way is to slide the slider on either side of the Color bar until the Color Shade window shows colors in the general range of shades that you are looking for. Then click the exact shade that you want in the Color Shade window.

The Color Picker dialog box is shown in Figure 5-4.

Target Name Tells you for what you are selecting the color.

Color Field Click at the point in this box where the color shade is what you want it to be as the chosen color.

Only Web Colors Check Box Click to toggle the check mark on if you want to be able to choose only web colors from the web-safe palette. Only those colors will appear in the Color Shade window.

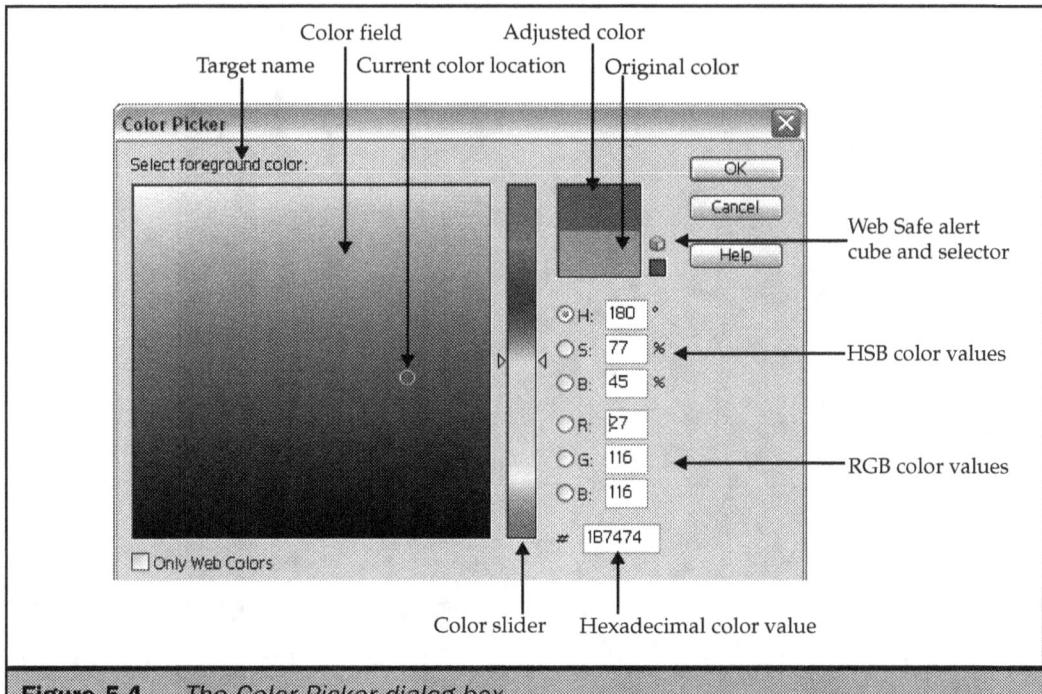

Figure 5-4. *The Color Picker dialog box*

Color Slider   Drag either of the sliders to choose the Hue (or Saturation, Brilliance, Red, and so on) you want to show in the Color Shade window.

Adjusted Color   This is the color you have currently selected.

Original Color   This was the chosen color when you opened the Color Picker.

HSB (Hue, Saturation, Brightness) and RGB Color Values   Click the radio button that corresponds to the type of display you want to see in the Color Shade window.

Hexadecimal Color Value   If you know the hexadecimal code for the color you want to choose, you can enter it here. All the colors in this dialog box will change accordingly. Otherwise, the code for the color you choose is automatically displayed here.

Web Safe   If this icon is visible, the color you've chosen is not a web-safe color.

Web Safe Alert Cube and Selector   The cube will appear when the adjusted color is outside of web-safe parameters. If you click in this box, the Color Picker will automatically choose the closest web-safe color.

The
Complete
Reference

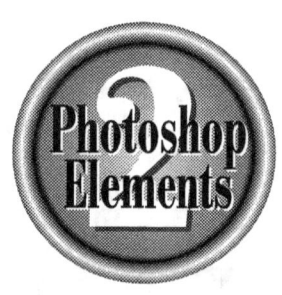

Photoshop
Elements
2

Chapter 6

A Deeper Look
at Recipes

Recipes are concise sets of instructions that tell you how to perform common tasks in Photoshop Elements 2.0. These are designed as a convenient reference to support you as you learn and work with Photoshop Elements 2.0. The How To palette is filled with recipes—38 of them, to be exact. You can access recipes through the How To palette by selecting or dragging it from the Palette well or choosing it from the Window menu. Recipes are an excellent aid for beginners and a handy reference for those tasks that you might need a bit of a refresher on. You can see the How To palette interface in Figure 6-1.

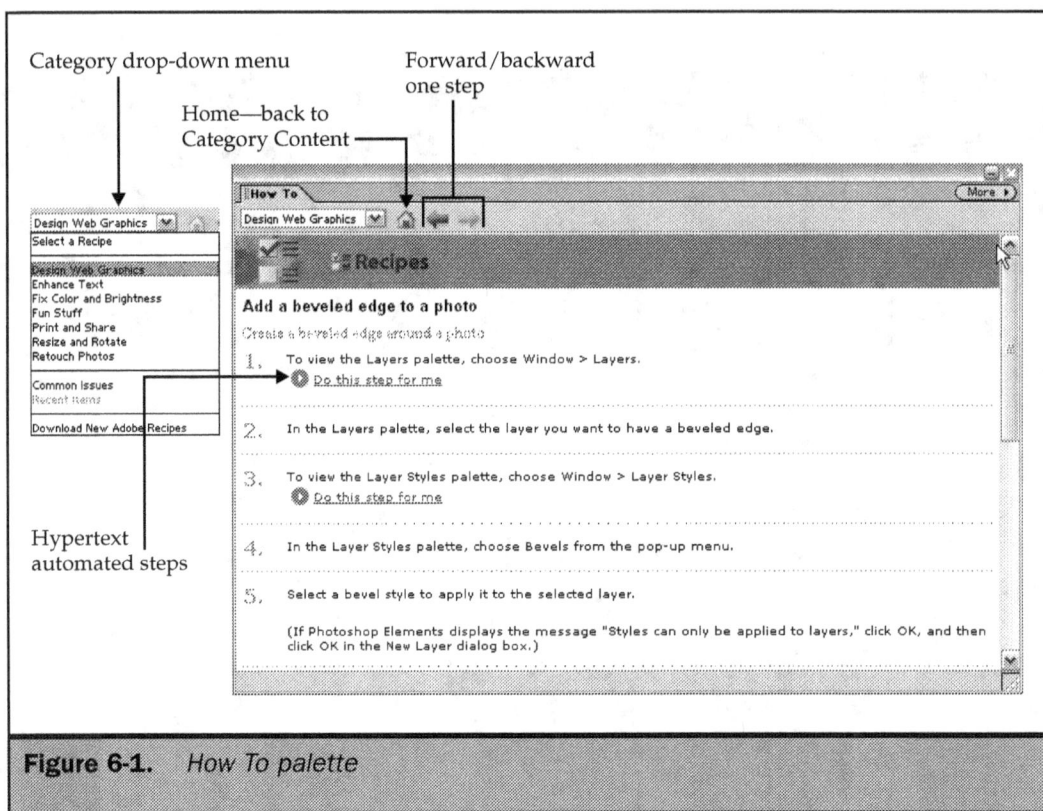

Figure 6-1. *How To palette*

Using Recipes

The recipes are accessed by category from the How To drop-down menu. The recipes are nicely arranged in the following categories:

- **Design Web Graphics**   Routines to help you develop optimized web graphics
- **Enhance Text**   Routines designed to do creative things with text
- **Fix Color and Brightness**   Adjustments for digital images
- **Fun Stuff**   A look at some of the fun extras in Photoshop Elements 2.0
- **Print and Share**   Routines to help you print and distribute your images
- **Resize and Rotate**   Routines to change the size and orientation of your image
- **Retouch Photos**   Fix common flaws

Adobe will add more categories and recipes to their download web site as they become available. You can connect directly to that site by choosing Palette | Download New Adobe Recipes.

To open and use a recipe, follow these steps:

1. In the Palette well or the Window menu, drag the How To tab into the workspace. This keeps the Recipes palette from disappearing back into the Palette well each time you do something in the workspace.

2. Select a recipe category for the task you want to perform from the Name drop-down menu. A submenu of recipes appears with a brief description of what each does. A more detailed description of each recipe is given in the next section. You can also choose from a list of Recent Items, which are the recipes that the program discovers over time that you are in the habit of using most often.

3. From time to time, Adobe posts new recipes to its web site. These are free for the downloading. While your computer is logged onto the Web, all you have to do is choose Download New Adobe Recipes.

4. Once you have chosen a recipe, simply follow its instructions step by step. You will often see an arrow with colored underlined text in the instructions that says "Do this step for me." If you click on this text, the program performs the necessary action for that step in the instructions, for instance, selecting a tool or opening a dialog box. This is a nice way of simplifying the process for you, a characteristic Photoshop Elements has a reputation for.

Recipes by Category

Adobe has divided the Recipes into functional categories, each of which, along with the recipes that fall into each of the categories, are discussed in detail in the sections that follow.

Design Web Graphics

This set of recipes gives you instructions on a number of common tasks associated with creating graphics for the Web. They can't really teach you to be a designer, but they can be a great help in getting a specified task done easily.

Add a Beveled Edge to a Photo

Beveling the edge of the photo gives a dimensional quality and makes it stand out from the background. This recipe takes you through the steps to add a beveled edge to a photo, as in the following illustration. There are 10 bevel styles to choose from in the Layer Styles palette. Use the Style Setting dialog box to adjust the width, the lighting angle, and whether the effect looks indented or raised.

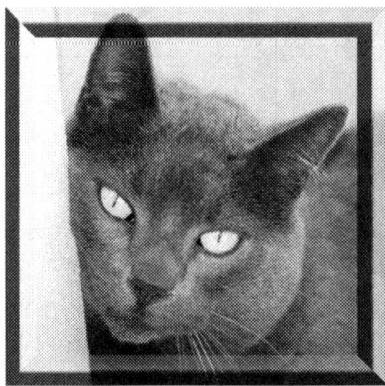

Add a Drop Shadow to a Photo

Drop shadows are a good way to apply images over background and keep them visually in the foreground without the use of a border. Drop shadows add dimensionality and can point out order by varying the depth of the effect from one photo to another. The more pronounced the shadow offset, the closer the photo appears to the viewer. Keep in mind that there must be enough area around the photo for the drop-shadow offset to show. If you try to add a drop shadow to a photo that is all the way to the borders of the image, the effect appears outside the visible area. You must make the photo float above whatever background you want and then leave some transparent area (20 percent of the image dimension is good) around the photo so there is room for the drop-shadow effect to show.

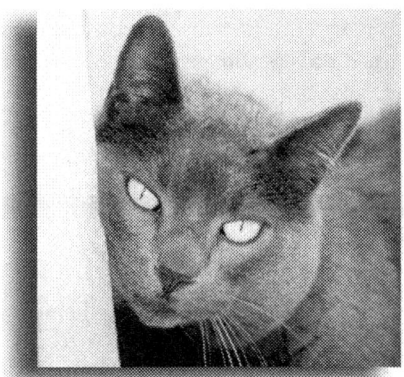

Add a Glow to a Photo

This recipe gives objects the appearance of outer-glowing light, as though they were a light source, as you can see in the following example. As with the drop-shadow effect on images, to accomplish the glow effect, you need to create some transparent space around the image and place it on a layer above the background. You have 11 Outer Glow styles to choose from.

You can also choose Inner Glow instead and make an object appear to have an internal light source or to have light reflecting off the interior surface. As with other styles, you can combine other styles with these. Use the glow styles to make image objects stand out from the background and other surrounding objects. It also works well when you want to accentuate dramatic lighting.

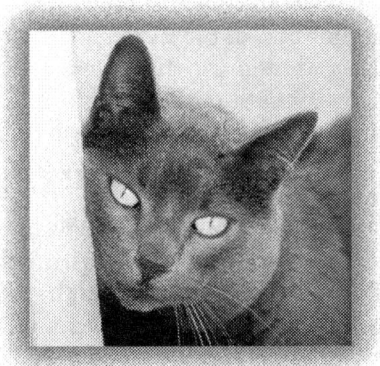

Create Web Buttons

Creating a button requires a number of steps. The basic steps are creating the shape, adding some text, and then optimizing the button graphic for the Web. You can add a step to create a more sculpted button effect, as we did on the following illustration.

This entailed applying a button style to the shape from Layer Styles | Glass Buttons. A button shape can have any number of styles applied to it. If you are using a solid-colored background on your web site, you can even add drop-shadow and glow effects. Just make the background color the same as the web page background when you create the button and the matte color in the Save for Web dialog box. The button then blends seamlessly into the background. You can also apply styles to the button text so it looks raised, reflective, glowing, floating, recessed, and so on. We go into more about how you can create special effects for the Web in Chapter 18.

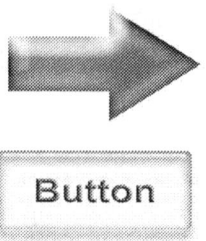

Create a Web Animation

GIF animation is commonly used in banner ads to attract attention to key areas of a site or just to provide some comic relief. They are also used for demonstration purposes, when words are not enough to get the point across. You can find out more about producing Web animation on Chapter 18.

This recipe takes you through the steps in creating a simple GIF animation using the layers in Photoshop Elements as cells. Each layer is a cell or frame in the animation, and the order of appearance goes from bottom to top. You can use a photo sequence, hand-drawn images, or a combination of the two to make the frames of the animation. Select any sequence of images, and then use the Save for Web command to optimize and convert the frames to a GIF animation by setting the parameters in the Save for Web dialog box. Remember that GIF files contain only a maximum of 256 colors, so if your images are in full-color RGB, continuous tones might flatten and become banded when the program converts them to GIF.

You might want to test the effect by converting your image with the Image | Mode command before you start so that you can make adjustments if you need to. You can make background colors in the frames transparent so the animation can float over the web-page background. GIF animations are generally small in size, so they load quickly and run smoothly.

Once you've created your GIF animation in Photoshop Elements, all you have to do to see it operate in a web browser is drag the file into an open browser window. The result will look something like this.

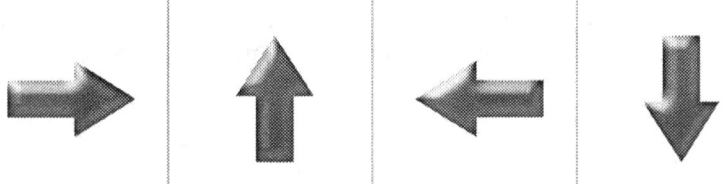

Create a Web Banner

Web banners are the billboards of the Internet. Web sites sell space to businesses and organizations to advertise their products and services. Clicking on the banners takes you to the web site that placed the ad. If you do much web surfing, you have probably seen entirely too many of them, but if not, you can see one in the following illustration.

Banners have certain size and memory requirements, and this recipe takes you through the proper steps to make sure your banner meets those requirements. You can add graphics, text, styles, and animation to your banner to make it attractive to the audience you want to reach.

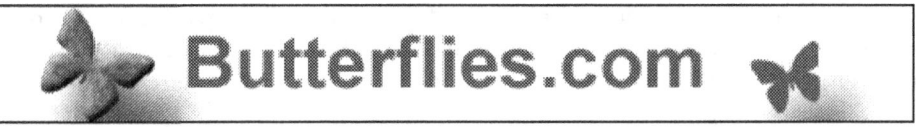

Enhance Text

This set of recipes gives you instructions on how to accentuate you text with a number of techniques.

Add Beveled Edges to Type

Bevels add a dimensional aspect to text, as you can see from the following example. This recipe guides you in adding any of the 10 bevel layer styles to the text or shape layer. You can get a sense of the bevel styles from the thumbnails in the Layer Styles palette. Simply choose the layer with the text or shape and then select from Layer Styles | Bevels, and the effect is automatically applied to the shape or text. You can fine-tune the bevel style within the Layer Styles Setting dialog box, allowing you to get many looks from one style. Experiment with the setting to get a sense of the range the style has. The color and brightness of the text can also have an effect on the outcome. Options allowing you to change the direction of the light to match a background can help blend the elements together. Having a number of objects with different settings can give a sense of chaos and tension. You can combine layer styles, for instance, you can put a drop shadow on the beveled text. The ability to combine layer styles gives you almost a limitless number of styles to choose from.

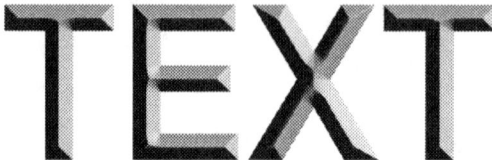

Add a Drop Shadow to Type

Drop shadows are a good way to make text or shapes stand out from the background or to add a sense of depth and light source. Drop shadows give the object the appearance of floating above the background and casting a shadow based on a selected light-source direction, as you can see in the following illustration. This recipe guides you through the steps for putting a drop shadow on a text or shape layer. You can choose from eight drop-shadow styles found in the Layer Styles palette. You can even control the floating illusion by choosing the distance of the shadow offset. Choose Inner Shadow to make it look as though there is a hole punched through the object, casting a shadow to the surface below. There are also other styles in many of the preset libraries that include droop shadows. In addition, you can combine styles to make you own unique styles.

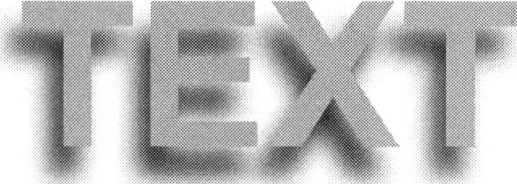

Apply a Layer Style to Type

This recipe goes through the steps to apply layer styles to your text and shapes. There are many layer styles to choose from on the drop-down menu on the Layer Styles palette. In addition to bevel, drop shadow, and glows, categories include complex, glass button, image effects, patterns, photographic effects, wow chrome, wow neon, and wow plastic.

You can mix and match many of these styles in combinations that run into the thousands, giving you an almost limitless supply of unique looks. You can see some stylized text in the following examples. Layer styles give you text a more exciting and dynamic appearance, which can be good for illustrations, brochures, web pages, and greeting cards, to name a few. See Chapter 7 for how to covert text and shapes into selections, which allows you to create you own fill-in effects. See Chapter 15 for more on using layer styles for special effects.

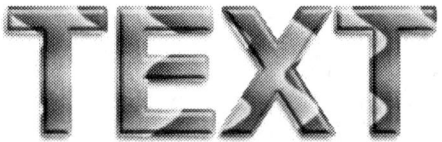

Create a Highlighted Panel for Type

This recipe walks you through the steps to place a shaded panel behind your text
to make the text stand out. Text sometimes doesn't stand out properly from the background it is on. One way to mitigate that problem is to create a new field for the text
to reside over so it contrasts the text and makes it easy to read. Placing a neutral panel
behind the text is one way to accomplish this. The brightness, color, size, and shape of
the panel depends on the style, size, and color of the type. The panel can blend with the
background somewhat to tone the panel down while still providing good separation
for type, or the panel can contrast with the background strongly. One good trick is to
make the panel semitransparent so some of the background shows though, but is toned
down. You can also use blend modes, gradients, and patterns to affect the panel's
appearance. Here's an example of a text panel.

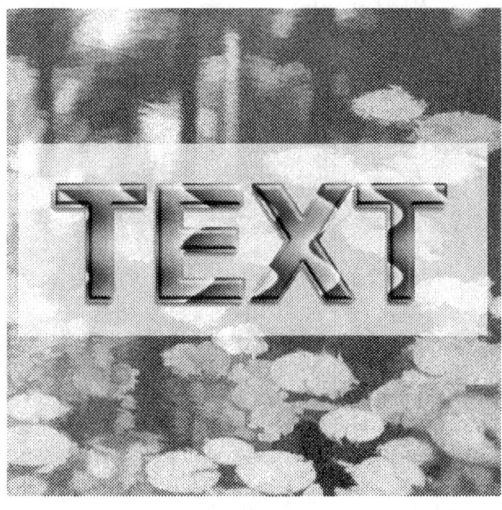

Fill Type with Gradient

Gradients blend adjacent colors smoothly—a sort of "rainbow" effect. Gradients can give the text a spectral or reflective effect or even cause to look as if it is fading away. The fade effect is accomplished by allowing the color at one end of the gradient to be the same as the background. This recipe uses the Layers | Group with Previous command to use the type as a mask, which lets only the gradient in the layer above show where the type is. You can use a number of types of gradients: linear, radial, angled, reflected, and diamond.

With this technique, you can make the type appear as though each letter is changing color by properly spacing the color transitions in the Gradient dialog box. Gradients are often used as effective templates for applying blend modes, which allows the text to combine in unique ways with the background it is on. See Chapter 9 for more on blending modes.

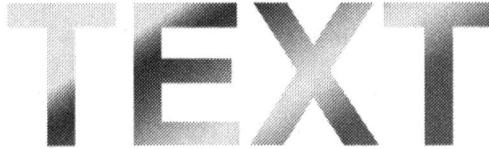

Fill Type with an Image

This recipe uses the same technique as filling type with a gradient (see previous recipe). The difference is the layer above contains an image instead of a gradient. The Group With Previous command forces the image to be revealed through the text mask. You can use the Move tool to position the image relative to the text, as was done with the stars and stripes in the next illustration.

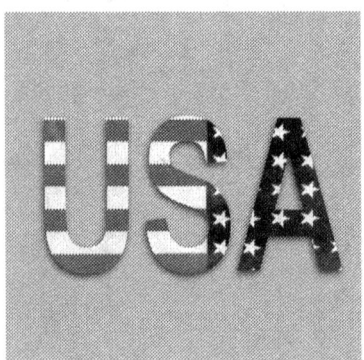

It is also possible to create a number of layers and group all of them and align them so each letter or group of letters gets a separate image, as you can see in this illustration. Notice the three layers above the text layer. This is a very versatile technique that opens the door to many possibilities.

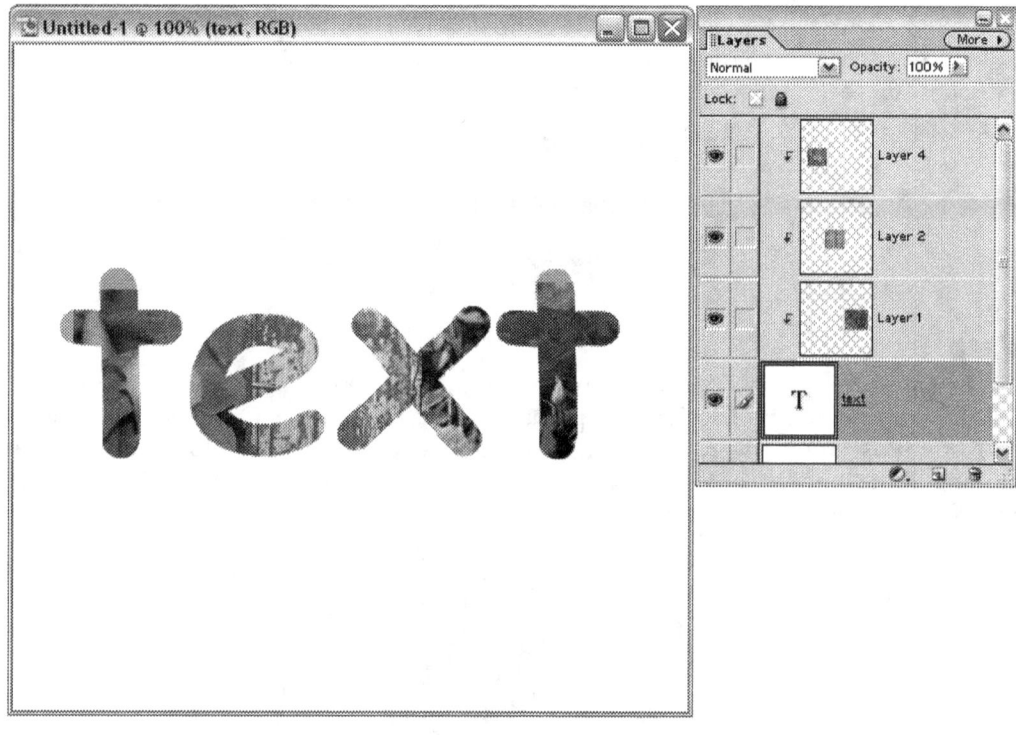

Fill Type with Fire

This recipe demonstrates how combining multiple filters and effects can build more complex effects. A gradient, Ripple filter, and Motion Blur were all combined to create the effect of fire inside the text, as you can see in this illustration. You could also do this with a photograph or painting of fire, using the image-in-text effect described in the previous recipe. If you are feeling really ambitious, try doing a number of versions of the fire in text with different settings and then animate them using the layer technique and Save To Web command, so it looks like the fire is flickering.

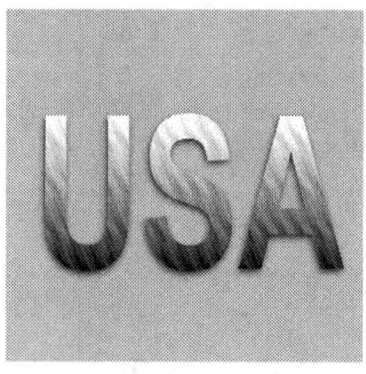

To change the effect to ice instead, use the Render | Glass filter and then the Inner Glow layer style, as seen here. Experiment with different combinations of style and filters to achieve a wide range of effects.

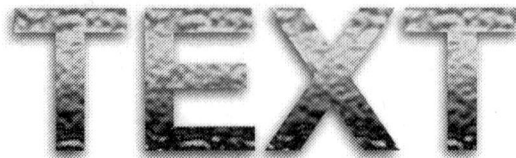

Warp Text

This recipe shows you how to bend text into many different shapes using the text tool's built-in warp capability. The Text Warp option is on the Text tool Options bar. In the following illustration, the stars-and-stripes text was warped to make look as if it were flapping in the breeze. There is a long list of warp routines you can choose from the Text Warp Options pull-down menu.

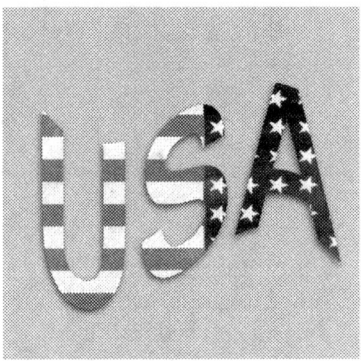

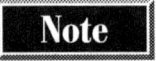 *The Liquify filter lets you warp text with a great deal more control over which specific portions of the text get warped and in what style and to what extent. The drawback is that text must be simplified before it can be liquefied.*

Fix Color and Brightness

This set of recipes gives you instructions on how to correct the appearance of your images. The recipes in this category cover some of the basic ways to color-balance and correct the exposure of you images. For more information on adjusting your photos, see Chapter 12.

Adjust Contrast of a Color Photo

This recipe teaches you how to use the contrast and brightness command found in the Enhance menu. Moving the contrast slider increases or decreases the contrast between light and dark areas of the image, producing a more intense image with less subtlety in tonal gradations. When the image is too washed out, adjust the contrast up to add more punch. Adjust the contrast down when you want to lower the contrast between different areas of the image. Reducing contrast can be used to create a foggy or misty effect.

The brightness slider increases or decreases the overall luminance range and lightens or darks the image. You can see the effect of contrast and brightness adjustments on the image of the cat. The left half is the before image. You will most likely use these commands time and time again, so it is good to familiarize yourself with the way they function.

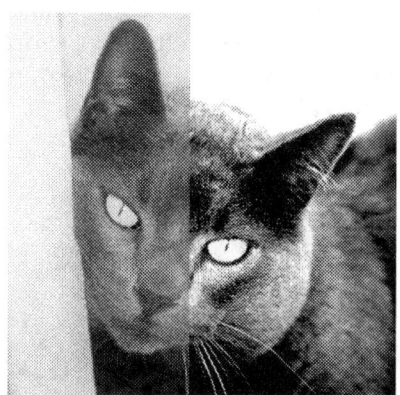

Emphasize Colors in a Photo

This recipe teaches you how to adjust the color levels in your photo. You accomplish this by adjusting the Hue/Saturation control found in the Enhance menu. The colors in a photograph might not always turn out as bright and rich as you might have imagined when you took the photo. This is partly because our eyes interpret and compensate for color, enhancing what we see with our minds.

Cameras are much more literal than we are, and record color as they "see" it. The intensity, color, and dispersion of light can all affect the color that ends up being recorded, and it is often washed out by too much reflected or atmospheric light. The saturation control adds intensity to the color by making it less gray and more of a pure hue. This can add new life to drab photos, and sometimes take them a bit into the surreal range, where color becomes extraordinary. You can control the effect to higher degree by selecting areas of the image to work on independently. Don't be afraid to use color boldly. It can add a lot of power to ordinary photos. On the other hand, too much saturation can cause digital images to become quite grainy and noisy, so be sure to view the image at 100% so you can judge the image quality before you commit to the final saturation adjustment.

Fix a Black-and-White Photo

This recipe allows you to readjust your photos to maximize the tonal range. It demonstrates how to control levels to adjust the overall tonal range of a black-and-white photo by using the Levels command found in the Enhance menu. A black-and-white photo is strictly made of black, white, and shades of gray. The most powerful black-and-white photos make use of the entire gray scale to render the greatest amount of detail.

The Levels dialog box shows you a histogram, which is a graph of the distribution of lights, darks, and midtones in the image, darks on the left, and lighter tones on the right. The height of the histogram bars indicates the number of pixels in the image that are in that tonal value range. This allows you to see the relationship of the tonal values in the image. You adjust the range by moving the sliders. To readjust the overall tonal range, move the outside black-and-white sliders into where the first graph lines begin. This has the effect of adjusting the contrast. Then move the middle (gray) slider to adjust the midtones to lighter or dark range. The Levels command gives you a wide range of control in adjusting exposure. You can see the effect of a simple level adjustment on the following image. For a much more detailed discussion on how to use all the features of the Levels command, see Chapter 12.

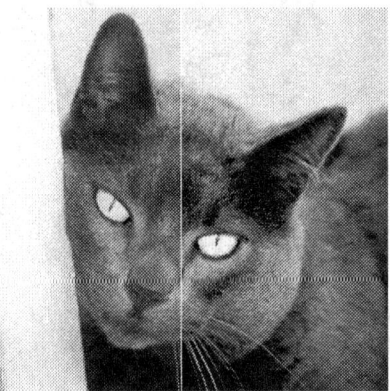

Fix the Exposure of a Photo

This recipe uses the Layers palette's Multiply or Screen Blend modes to improve the overall lightness or darkness of the image. The result of using these techniques, which we preach throughout this book, is a much broader range of tonality that would not result if you were to use only the Brightness/Contrast command to adjust exposure. You can see the before (left) and after (right) in this illustration.

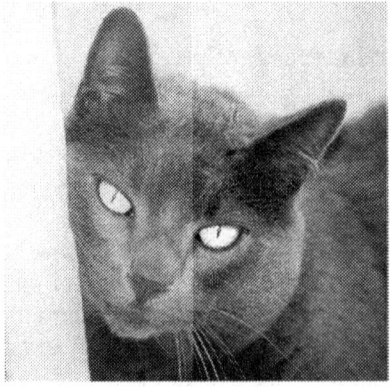

Lighten Dark Areas of a Photo

This recipe teaches you how to use the Fill Flash command to lighten areas of shadow that are bit too dark. The over-darkening of shadows in a photo usually happens as a result of very high-contrast lighting such as direct sunlight. The typical way to deal with this problem is to use the camera's built-in flash to artificially lighten the shadow areas. You can perform a similar function with the Fill Flash command in Photoshop Elements 2.0 by selectively lightening darker areas of the image more than lighter ones. Learn more about this command in Chapter 12. You can see the effect of the Fill Flash command in the following illustration.

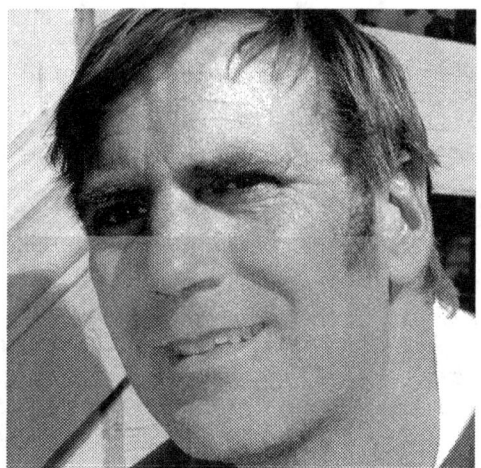

Remove a Color Cast

This recipe gives you a brief lesson in how to properly and quickly color-balance an image by using the Color Cast command. When you are taking photographs, the lighting is not always constant and might affect the overall ambient color of the scene. Fluorescent and incandescent light and various weather conditions can produce what is called a color cast. This means the photo might be shifted to blue or yellow and just looks off. Normally the white balance in the camera adjusts for these color shifts, but many times it cannot compensate for the lighting. The Color Cast command gives you a second chance to correct the white balance in the image by queuing the program to what should be pure white, pure black, or shades of gray. When you have done this, the program can adjust all the colors accordingly and produce a properly colored picture.

Fun Stuff

This set of recipes gives you instructions on a number of projects that you might find useful and entertaining.

Color a Black-and-White Photo

This is a retouching technique that goes back to the early days of photography before there were color photographs. The coloring was accomplished back then by laboriously painting over black-and-white photos with transparent color. Fortunately Photoshop Elements 2.0 makes hand-coloring your photos fun and easy. You can also use this technique to recolor any color photo.

Another way to color a black-and-white photo is this:

1. Duplicate the black-and-white photo layer.

2. Convert the image to RGB.

3. Put the duplicate layer in Multiply Blend mode

4. Create a new layer and place it just below the duplicate layer.

5. Make the new layer active and use the paintbrush with any colors in the new layer to tint the photo.

Create a Coloring Book

This is a great recipe if you have kids. You can take any photo, make it an outlined image, and then use the Multiply Blend mode technique to color it in. See the horse before (left) and after (right) outlining in the following image. You can print photos to make an old-fashioned coloring book to color with crayons or makers. Add text and shapes to spice it up, and use photos of your kid's favorite animals, toys, or people to make it personal. Put a story on one page and a picture to color on the facing page. This is a nice rainy-day project and a great way to get your kids interested in Photoshop Elements.

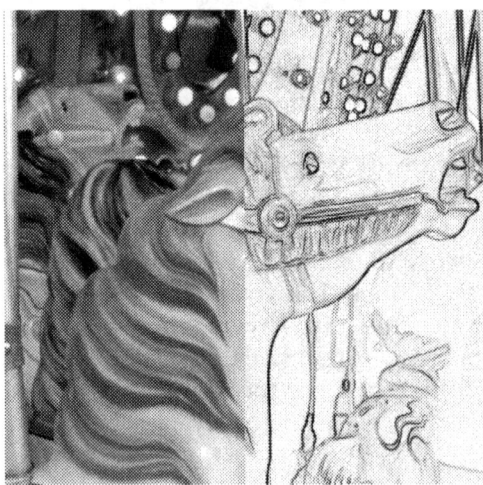

Create a Photo Collage

This recipe shows you how to use the Move tool to move multiple images onto the same canvas. This collage technique is useful in creating a digital scrapbook. You can include family photos and even scans of memorable items such as a diploma, birth certificate, or invitation. You can print the pages and bind them for a keepsake. Save the scrapbook with the layers intact in PSD or TIFF format so you can go back and edit it to keep it up to date.

The photo collage recipe instructs you to use various transformation tools to resize, rotate, and reshape image layers. You can further increase you ability to create interesting collages by using the Eraser and Selection tools to cut out parts of each layer so they fit together in a more creative manner. In the example that follows, the flowers were cut from their background using the Magnetic Lasso tool.

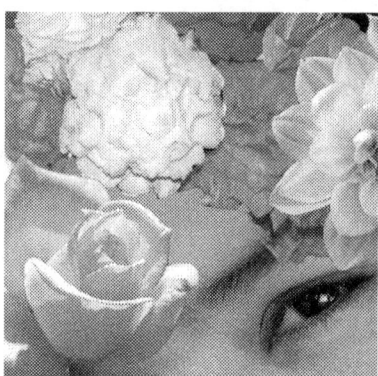

Create an Old-Fashioned Tinted Photo

This recipe lets you use the Color Variations dialog to sepia-tone the image and then add some grain and blur it slightly. This sepia tinting and graininess simulates what antique photos look like. If you are ambitious, you can scan a sheet of paper that has been creased and dirtied. Then by inverting it and using the Screen Blend mode, you can superimpose it on the tinted photograph to give it some blemishes to make it look more authentic.

Here are other ways to get the tinted effect.

1. Open the photo you want to tint.

2. Choose Enhance | Adjust Color | Hue/Saturation. The Name dialog box appears.

3. Check the Colorize box to change the whole image to a single hue.

4. Adjust the hue and saturation sliders until you get the look you want.

5. You add noise, as in the first color-variations recipe, to give it a vintage look.

Print and Share

This set of recipes gives you instructions on how to best manipulate and adjust your images to get the best possible prints. You will also discover how to distribute your images in a variety of ways.

Create a Web Photo Gallery

This recipe lets you automatically create a series of web pages suitable for showing a photographer's portfolio. You can use the same technique to create a product catalog. The recipe walks you through the steps to create a web photo gallery that is automatically formatted in HTML (hypertext markup language) and ready for display on the Web or locally in your web browser. A web photo gallery is a web page or pages with a menu of thumbnail images that you can click to see larger versions of those images. The Web Photo Gallery creator in Photoshop Elements 2.0 is basically a mini-application that takes a group of images placed in a single folder and creates web-ready pages according to style templates that you select from the Styles menu. The pages are automatically formatted with decorative graphics, titles, labels, thumbnails, navigation buttons, links, other pertinent information, and enlarged images. All you have to do is get them loaded on your web site. It is also possible to edit the pages with a web-editing application and customize them to your specifications. For a much more detailed description of web gallery creation, see Chapter 18. You can see an example of a typical style template in the following illustration.

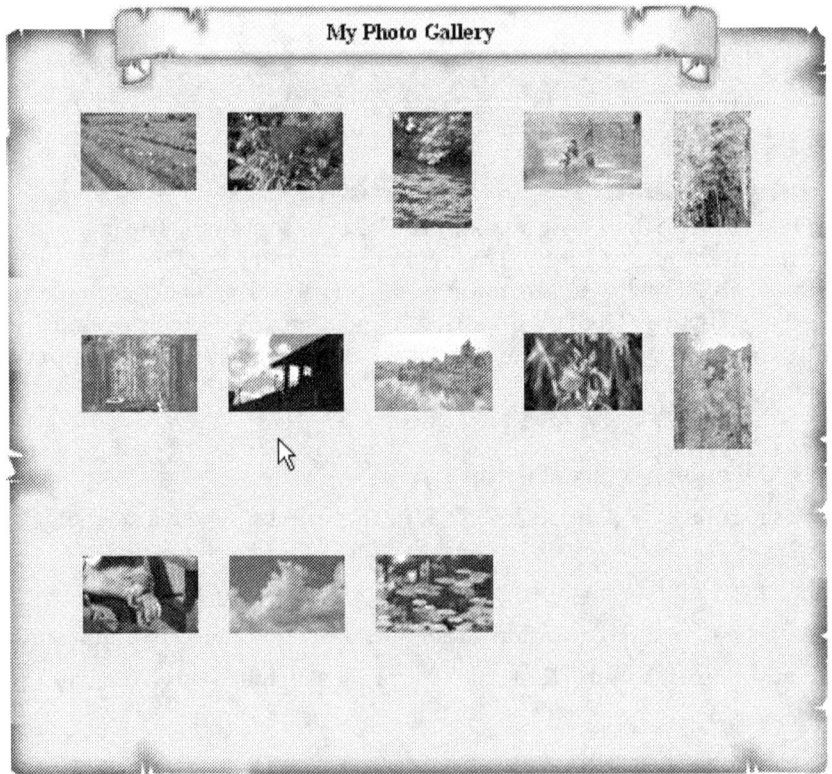

My Photo Gallery

7/3/2002

Create a Photo Caption

This recipe lays out the steps to make a caption for a photo using the Shapes and Text tools. This is really a very simple task. You can expand on this recipe by adding layer styles to the shapes and text, making them partially transparent, or applying blend modes. A nice trick is to use different levels of drop shadow to make the labels appear to float at different distances above the photo. The addition of arrows can be instructive. Another way to approach photo captioning is to create a solid-colored space off one of the edges where you can place some text. You can easily accomplish this by choosing Image | Resize | Canvas Size. See Chapter 11 for more on using this command. You can see an example of a comic-style caption in the illustration below.

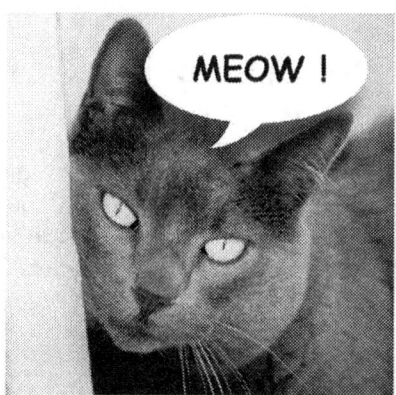

Create an Onscreen Slideshow

This recipe shows you how to create a portable slideshow by creating an Acrobat PDF (portable document format) file with any open images in Photoshop Elements 2.0 or images stored in folders. You can choose to have stylized transitions between slideshow images by setting that option from the Transition menu. PDF slideshows are a very good way to distribute your images because the Acrobat PDF format can be read on any platform with Acrobat or the free Acrobat Reader. The Acrobat program is designed to adapt to the system it is displaying on so the slideshow optimizes to the local environment. This takes the guesswork out of sending images to others. The slideshow runs automatically when the PDF file is loaded on the receiving system. If you press ESC, the slideshow stops and a normal PDF file is displayed. You can then look through the images at your discretion. You can also choose the Advanced options, which allow you to save the images in compressed format, making it more practical to send a slideshow by e-mail.

E-Mail a Photo

This recipe teaches you to instantly append the photo in the active workspace to an e-mail with the Attach to E-Mail command found in the File menu. This convenient feature lets you send an open image via e-mail directly from Photoshop Elements 2.0 by automatically bringing up your e-mail application when prompted. This is very handy in situations where you might receive an image via e-mail, make some changes to it in Photoshop Elements 2.0, and then send it right back again or send it to yourself so you can download it later from a remote location. The Attach to E-Mail command works with the default e-mail program you have loaded on your system. It assumes you have an e-mail account and are connected to the Internet.

The Attach to E-mail command offers you an alternative for larger image files. You can send them as is or have the program compress them so they are more efficient in transmission. Many e-mail services limit the size of e-mail attachments to anywhere from 1 to 4 megabytes per e-mail, so using compression can be a way of avoiding returned e-mail. To learn more about sending images via the Web, see Chapter 18.

Export an Image to a Palm OS or Pocket PC Device

This recipe shows you how to export your images to be displayed on a hand-held computer. It shows you how to prepare your images to be placed in an Acrobat PDF file and exported to the right format for a Palm OS or Pocket PC hand-held computer. This allows you to view files from your main system on your PDA. There are a number of considerations when preparing the images. You need to know the screen size and resolution so you can size the image properly for optimum display. Each brand and model can have different sizes and resolution, so you need to resize your images accordingly. The sizes for the most popular models are listed in the recipe. Check the specification for your device if it is not on the list.

Resize and Rotate

This next set of recipes demonstrates how to manipulate a photo to change its size and orientation.

Crop a Photo

This lesson shows you step by step how to use the Crop tool with the primary focus being to straighten an improperly aligned photo. Many photos are not framed exactly right at the time they are taken so you need to reframe them in the editing process. The Crop tool allows you to designate a new frame edge and then clip away the unwanted portions. You can also use the Rotate option when grabbing any of the corner handles on the crop bounding box to rotate the image to correct for any alignment problems.

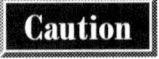 *Remember that cropping an image eliminates pixels and, as a result, the image might not have enough resolution to make as large a print as you had in mind.*

Resize a Large Photo for Printing

This exercise shows you how to resize an image for printing by changing the print resolution (pixels per inch) but not the overall size of the file. The Resampling check box must be unchecked for this to work. This method changes the relative size, which means it adjusts the number of pixels that are assigned to an inch of the actual print, therefore giving you a method for adjusting the size of the output to the printer. It is best understood with an example.

Let's say you have an image that has the overall pixel dimensions of 1800×1200 pixels, and the print resolution is set at 200 pixels per inch. By dividing 200 into the overall dimensions, you end up with an output of 9×6 inches. Now let's say that you wanted the final printed image to be smaller. Let's raise the print resolution to 300 and divide again. Now the final size will be 6×4 inches. If you have an exact size in mind, you can divide the critical print dimension into the pixel dimension of the same orientation to determine the print resolution. If you wanted the final print to be 10 inches high, you would divide 10 into 1200 (the vertical dimension) and get a print resolution of 120. By dividing 120 into 1800, you get the horizontal dimension of 15 inches. For more information on sizing prints, see Chapter 19.

Straighten a Photo

This recipe instructs you on how to automatically rotate an image that was aligned incorrectly when it was scanned using the Image | Rotate | Straighten Image command. For this command to work properly, there must be a clear and defined edge to the photo. The program uses math computations to find the edge of the photograph as it is contrasted to the background. It then calculates the angle of misalignment and rotates the image accordingly. Of course, if your camera was slightly rotated when you took the photo, you need to use manual methods to align it correctly. For more information on rotating images, see Chapter 11.

Retouch Photos

This set of recipes gives you instruction on how to fix common flaws that appear in scanned and photographed images.

Fix a Torn Photo

This recipe gives you instructions on how to repair a torn photo using the Clone Stamp tool. You can use the Clone Stamp tool in all sorts of retouching operations such as covering blemishes, eliminating spots, or removing unwanted details. The Clone Stamp tool accomplishes this by targeting detail in the image that is similar to the areas you want to repair or modify and using it as a paint source for your brush. By using a soft brush, you can blend in the detail so it appears seamless. You can also target detail from another layer or image. You can see the effect of using the Clone Stamp in the following illustration. If your repairs don't blend in as well as you like, adding a bit of grain or noise might help.

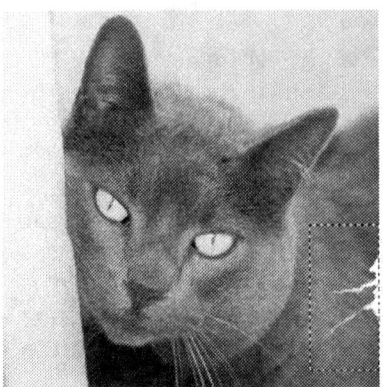 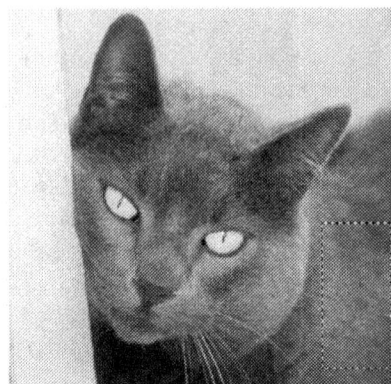

Remove Red Eye

Red eye occurs because the flash is so close to the lens that it bounces off the back of the eyeball and projects the blood color out through the iris of the eye, thus making your best friend look like a vampire. Some cameras (especially the digital variety) have built-in red-eye avoidance settings. The problem is that they work by firing a preflash that causes the subjects pupils to contract in advance of the flash, and in some cases, you end up capturing the subject closing their eyes after the initial flash. The Photoshop Elements 2.0 tools for eliminating red eye work a lot better because they don't cause your subject to blink and they don't wear out your camera batteries prematurely.

The Red Eye brush works by targeting the red hue in the pupil and replacing it with a selected hue (black is the default) based on a tolerance range around the selected pixel. The higher the tolerance, the greater the range of colors affected. You can use the Red Eye brush to change the hue in any part of a picture, so experiment to see what other uses you can find for it. It could be used just as easily to change the color of the iris, so blue eyes become green or brown. See Chapter 13 for more detailed information on using the Red Eye brush.

Remove Scratches and Specks

This recipe shows you how to remove unsightly dust and scratches automatically using the Dust & Scratches filter. The filter accomplishes this by using the settings in the radius and threshold sliders to blend areas of high contrast to smooth out imperfections. The trade-off is that the image is slightly softened. By adjusting the controls and previewing the results, you can determine the proper balance. Some more pronounced dirt and scratches might need to be repaired with the Clone Stamp tool described in the previous recipe. Using this filter is also a clever way to glamorize portraits of people whose skin you want to look velvety smooth. To learn more about retouching techniques, see Chapter 13.

Remove Spots and Blemishes

This recipe is the same as Fix a Torn Photo, only applied to many small areas rather than one larger repair. One difference is that you will probably have to reset you target more often as you move around the image to closely align the detail to the repair.

Restore a Faded Photo

This recipe uses the Multiply Blend mode to add in darker detail to a faded photo. Once you have set up the duplicate layer above the original and set it to Multiply Blend mode, you can use the opacity slider to adjust the intensity of the effect. You can see the results of three different opacity settings in the following example. You can also apply the inverse using the Screen Blend mode to lighten a dark photo. Using the Blend modes helps preserve detail better than if you just used the Contrast and Brighten commands. For more information on adjusting photos, see Chapter 12.

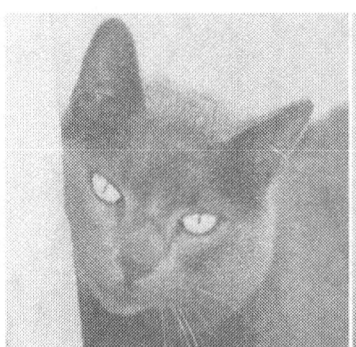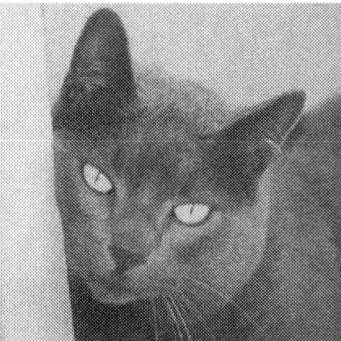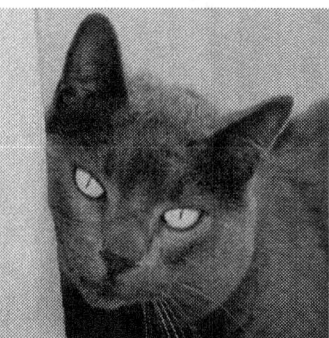

Sharpen Details in an Image

This recipe lays out the steps for using the Unsharp Mask filter to sharpen the details in a photo. The Unsharp Mask filter is unique in that it allows you to control the parameters by which edges are identified for sharpening. This allows you to control which areas remain unsharpened and to focus the sharpening effects on the important details. You can also use the other filters such as Sharpen and Sharpen Edges, but they do not have the range of control that Unsharp Mask does. You can see an example of the Unsharp Mask effect in the following illustration. For more information on the Unsharp Mask filter, see Chapter 14.

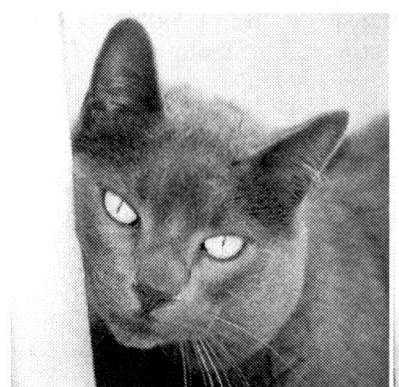 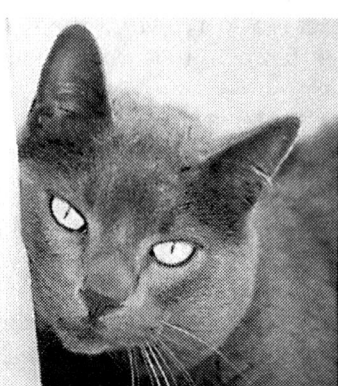

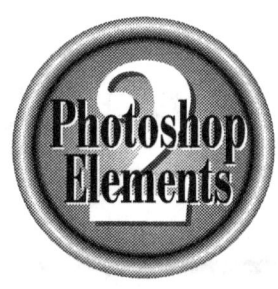
Chapter 7

The Art of Selections

Photoshop Elements provides many tools and effects to change your images in many ways. Selections allow you to control the editing process more precisely, and therefore give you many more creative possibilities. Selections make it possible for any tool, option, or effect in Photoshop Elements to be restricted to the selected area inside a "marching ants" marquee. This gives you the power to designate what you want to happen to any specified area that you define with selection tools. This sounds simple enough, but the truth is, working with selections is subtle, and it takes practice and a good understanding of all the interactions to make the changes blend seamlessly and produce a cohesive result. Developing the talent to work with selections helps advance your proficiency with Photoshop Elements in significant ways.

No single selection technique works with all subject matter or in all situations. The selection process is thoughtful and creative—after all, it is about making selections, and you are the one who ultimately makes them. Making selections is really an art because there are so many possibilities at every juncture and there is rarely just one way to approach any situation. This is one of your chances to get creative.

This chapter will make you an expert at isolating part of a subject from its surroundings, transforming that subject in many ways, and putting pieces together in a new composition. We explore how combining the versatility of selections with the power of layers gives you the ultimate control over how you build and fit the pieces for your final image. Just remember that none of these techniques is exclusive to the subject it is demonstrated with. Also, remember that a technique that is usually best suited to certain subjects or situations might well be just the thing for an entirely different type of subject in a different photograph. Now let's learn how to put Photoshop Elements' selection tools in high gear.

The Purpose of Making Selections

There are many processes in Photoshop Elements that can have a global effect on the image; for example, you can change the color, brightness, or size of the image. All these options, and many more, affect the entire image at one time; however, it quickly becomes apparent that these are not enough, and that to accomplish more sophisticated and subtle alterations of the image requires a way to isolate portions of the image to process individually. You might want to put in a new sky, change the color of one flower, or seamlessly combine elements from separate photographs. For this reason, the selection process was incorporated into image-editing programs. The selection tools in Photoshop Elements are some of the best, having been fashioned after those in Photoshop, and give you a great degree of choices on how to accomplish your editing tasks.

By being able to select and designate an area of the image with a definable boundary, it becomes possible to act on that area as though it were a separate image. Because Photoshop Elements sees the selected area as a separate image, it can be modified in almost every way any image can. Just for starters, a selection can be resized, transformed, recolored, blended, filtered, moved, cut, copied, pasted, and erased. While contained by the marquee, the pixels within the selection boundary are allowed to change independent of the unselected parts of the image. You can take selections and place them on separate layers where you can alter them and blend them in complex ways. By keeping the individual selections separated on layers, you gain total control over the editing process. Selections also allow you to move portions of one image to another so that they can be recombined into something new. Think of every selection as a personally designed puzzle piece that you create and put in place to eventually realize the total picture. The puzzle is composed of a set of pieces as big as all the digital images you can gather. The game of controlling all these pieces and finding how to cut them up, alter them, and then finally make them fit back together correctly is what selections are all about.

Lifting Selections to New Highs

First, you need to select a portion of the image and separate it from the rest. There are a number of ways to accomplish both these tasks. As soon as you make a selection, Photoshop Elements creates a special invisible and temporary layer where the selection can float above the image. What the program has done is to cut the selection out of the image and let it float just above it in the exact location. If you move a selection made on a background layer, for example, you will see that the background color shows through the hole that is left behind. If the selection was made on an ordinary layer, moving the selection leaves a transparent hole.

What if you don't want to see a gaping hole in the original image? Here's how to get a floating selection and leave the original image intact:

1. Make a new selection.

2. Place you cursor inside the selection. While pressing ALT/OPT, drag the selection. You will see that the selection content moves and that there is no hole left behind (see Figure 7-1).

3. From the new position of the selection contents, release the mouse button and repeat the preceding step. You will see that a copy of the selection is left behind as you move it. You can repeat this as many times as you like, and this operation will drop a copy in each new location. If you just want to move the selection around without copying it, use the Move tool.

Copying a Selection to a New Layer

Placing the selected portion of the image in a new layer is the ideal way to manage selections. Here is a method to do that:

1. Make a new selection using any of the selection tools.

2. You can also press CMD/CTRL+C or choose Edit | Copy to copy the selection, or press CMD/CTRL+X or choose Edit | Cut to cut the selection to the clipboard.

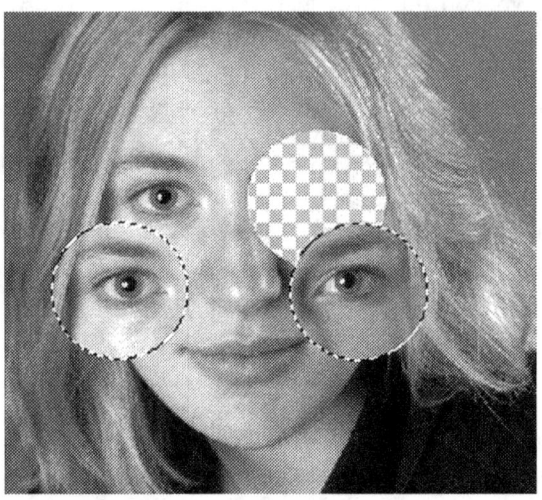

Figure 7-1.   *The difference between just moving a selection (right) versus copying and moving it (left)*

3. Press CMD/CTRL+P or choose Edit | Paste to paste the selection to a new layer. The layer is created automatically when you paste.

4. Choose Layer | New Layer | Layer Via Copy (or right-click and choose Layer Via Copy).

Instant Selection Lifting

Here is a method for lifting a selection directly to a new layer in one quick command:

1. Use the Marquee tool to make a new selection.

2. Right-click the selection and choose Layer Via Copy from the pop-up menu.

3. If the Layers palette is open (as it's recommended that it always be), you see that there is a new layer.

This is a convenient way to select various portions of the image and quickly put them into separate layers where they can be edited separately later.

Moving the Contents of a Selection from One Image to Another

One very popular operation that you will probably get into at one point or another is using elements from one digital image to modify a second. The selection process can make this task much easier. Here's a simple method for moving any portion of an image into another image as a layer:

1. Open two images of similar size (the images can actually be any size, it's just easier to demonstrate this way). Arrange the images on the screen so they are both visible.

2. In the first image, make a selection using any of the selection tools. If you want to copy the entire image, press CMD/CTRL+A. or choose Select | All.

3. Place your cursor inside the selection and, while pressing CMD/CTRL, drag the selection over the second image window. When you see a small plus sign next to the cursor as you bring it over the second image, you can drop in the image (see Figure 7-2). You will then see the selection appear over the second image on a separate layer. You can repeat this operation as many times as necessary, and each new selection will create a new layer.

Tuning a Selection's Edges and Position

Now that you understand more about how to create, move, and save a selection, it is time to move on to how to control and manipulate them to a higher degree. This section covers methods used to transform, size, and reshape a selection.

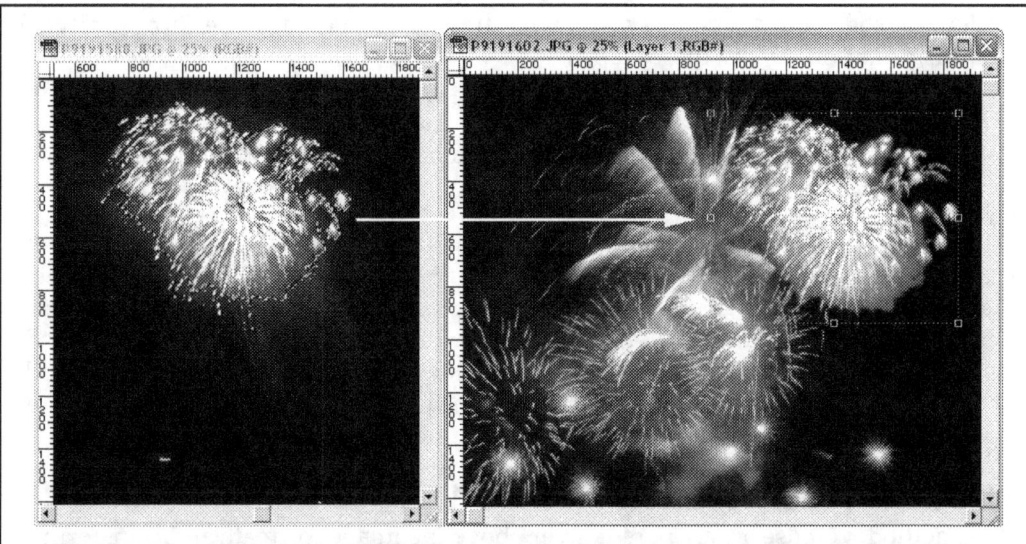

Figure 7-2. *Moving a selection from one image to another is as easy as select and drag.*

Transforming a Selection

A transformation is an operation that changes the size, orientation, and shape of the selection as a whole. Transformations are a powerful feature of computer imaging. The fact that digital images have a uniform pixel structure makes it possible to apply all kinds of mathematical algorithms to them, which can transform the image in countless ways. Any defined block of pixels can be transformed, including a selection.

Once you have made a selection, you can then transform it by using a number of commands found in the Image menu. These commands are separated into three categories: Rotate, Resize, and Transform. Under Rotate, you can change the orientation by rotating in 90-degree increments or flip the selection horizontally or vertically. Under Resize, you can choose Scale to make the image larger or smaller. Under Transform, you can choose Free Transform, Skew, Perspective, and Distort. Choosing any of these commands brings up the Transformation Options bar, shown here, which allows you to choose quickly between most of the transformation commands in the Image menu and enter numbers to change size and rotation.

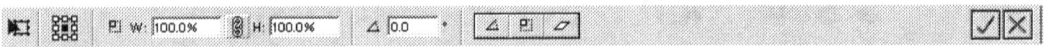

It is important to point out the difference between the two types of transformation categories that can be performed on selections. The first is performed on the image area the selection has defined within the marquee. We will refer to this type as *selected-area* transformation. This means that when you change the shape, size, or orientation of the selection, the shape inside changes along with the transformation. To perform a selected-area transformation, follow these steps:

1. Make a selection.
2. Choose Tools | Move. The Free Transform handles appear. You can now transform the selection and the pixels contained by it.

The second type of transformation, which we will refer to as *selection* transformation (because that's what Photoshop calls it), changes the selection marquee independent of the image it contains so that the image area pixels defined within the marquee remain unchanged as you transform the selection. Unlike Photoshop, Photoshop Elements does not provide tools to do selection transformation directly, but there are two methods that work, shown in Figure 7-3 and described in the next sections. Each method requires preprocessing the selection itself before acting on the underlying pixels.

Selection Transformation Method 1

In this method, you use a transparent layer above the image to create and transform a selection and then drop it as a floating selection on the image layer.

1. Load the image you want to work on.

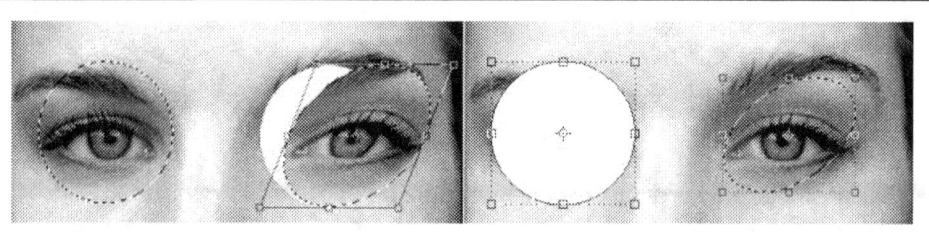

Figure 7-3.   *Two ways to perform a selection: moving the selection and its contents (the image within the marquee, left), and transforming just the selection marquee itself (right)*

2. Make a new layer with opacity set at 50 percent and fill it with any solid color. For Photoshop Elements to make a selection in that layer, the area must be filled. Reducing the opacity to 50 percent makes it much easier to see the image you're selecting on the layer below.

3. In the new layer, create your selection using the image layer as a reference.

4. Right-click the selection and choose Free Transform. You will see the handles appear with the bounding box. You can now perform any transformation on the selection without affecting the image in the layer below.

5. When you have adjusted the selection the way that you want, click the Layer Name bar of the image layer to activate the selection. The selection you just created is now active on the image layer and can be manipulated as a normal section.

Selection Transformation Method 2

In this method, you use the Shapes command to create a shape, transform it, convert it to a selection, and drop it onto the image layer. This method allows you to use any of the preset shapes available on the Shapes Options bar, including the custom shapes. If you need freeform shapes that are created with the Lasso tool, then you need to use Method 1.

Here's how to use Selection Transformation Method 2:

1. Create a shape with the Shape tool in the Tools palette. This creates a new shape layer directly above the image.

2. Open the Layers palette and adjust the shape layer opacity to 50 percent so you can reference the image below. You can now position the shape with the Move tool. The Free Transform handles appear. You can now transform the shape using any of the transform commands.

3. When you have finished transforming the shape, use the Shape Selection tool to select the shape.

4. Right-click the shape and choose Make Selection. You will see the marquee outline appear.

5. Make the shape layer invisible and then activate the image layer. This makes the image active in the image layer.

6. Choose the Marquee tool, right-click inside the selection, and choose Layer Via Copy to place a copy of the selection on a layer above.

If you want further detailed information on the types of and methods for doing transformations, see Chapter 11.

Getting the Size Just Right

It is often important to get selections positioned and sized accurately. This is not always possible by manual manipulation, or at least it can be very time consuming. Photoshop Elements includes some handy tools to make this task painless.

Information Palette

You can monitor the size of your Marquee tool by opening the Information palette, shown next. The Information palette has a readout for width and height that changes as you drag the Marquee tool across the image, showing the exact size of your selection. The units of the readout reflect the type of units specified in the Units & Rulers preferences. If you want another type, go to Edit | Preferences | Units & Rulers and change the unit of measurement.

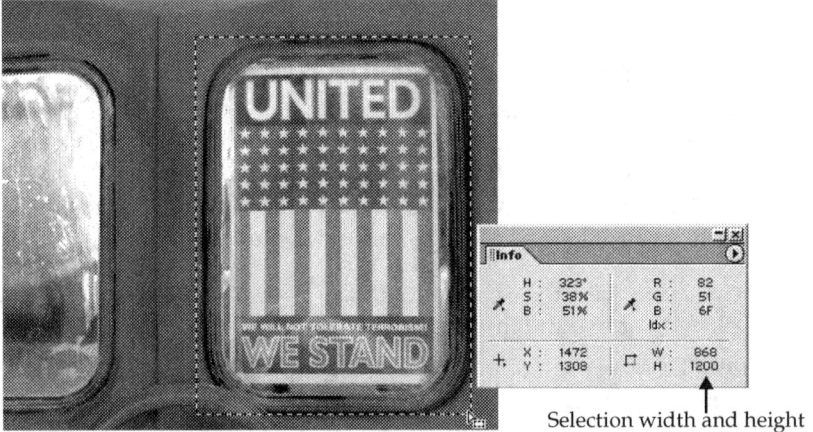

Selection width and height

Controlling Selection Sizing with Grid and Rulers

Another way to control selection sizing is to use the grid and rulers. These act as guidelines to accurately size and lay out your sections. There is also a Snap To Grid option that forces your cursor to stay on the grid lines. These are very useful tools, especially when you are laying out a sign or brochure and need to align and size everything precisely.

To use the built-in ruler and grid system to help size and align selections:

1. Choose View Menu | Show Grid.
2. Choose View Menu | Show Rulers.
3. You can change the size of the rulers and grid. Choose either Edit | Preferences | Grid, or Edit | Preferences | Units & Rulers. You can also change the grid and ruler origin point by moving the cursor over the intersection of the rulers in the upper-left region of the window, and dragging to the right and down over the image and to the new point that you select. The zero point for the rulers and the grid will be reset to the point you selected. Make sure the Snap To Grid option is deselected when you are adjusting the origin.

Tip   *For the best results in using the grid and rulers, make the rulers and grid unit of measure correspond in Preferences.*

4. When you are satisfied with your ruler and grid settings, choose View | Snap to turn on the Snap option. Now Marquee selections snap to the grid points, and you can monitor size by tracking the rulers.

Figure 7-4 shows the use of grids and rulers to size selections.

Note   *To turn off the grid, use the same steps as you used in the preceding exercise to turn it on. In other words, the command to use the grid "toggles" like a switch. Choose the command once to turn it on; choose it again to turn it off. Throughout this book, when you see a command in the form "Choose Menu Name | Option Name to toggle it on," then you know you can also do the same thing to toggle it off.*

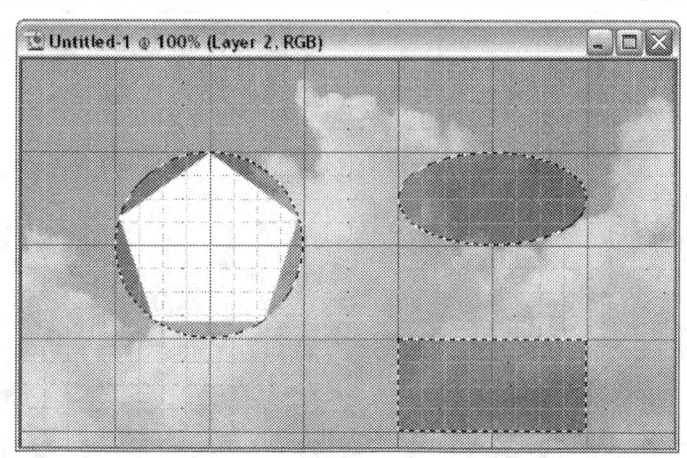

Figure 7-4.   *Using the grid and rulers to size selections*

Tweaking Your Selection Size with Expand and Contract

After you have created a selection, it might be necessary to make the selection slightly larger or smaller to get rid of unwanted pixels near the edge or to give a bit more room for feathering or blending (see the "Feathering Selections" section, later in this chapter). Modifying the edge of a selection by hand is a laborious task. Using the Expand and Contract commands can make this as quick as a few mouse clicks.

1. Make a selection with any of the Selection tools.

2. Choose Select | Modify | Expand or Contract. A dialog box appears.

3. Enter a value between 1 and 100 in the field that represents the number of pixels in distance you want the selection to grow or shrink.

If you eventually want to feather or add border to the selection, but you don't want the area of the original selection to be changed, then it is a good idea to expand the selection by the full amount of feather value and half the border value you plan to apply. Feather and border calculate the area of affect equally to either side of the section border.

The Expand and Contract options are also very good for producing multiple nested selections that get bigger or smaller by equal or progressive increments, as you can see in Figure 7-5. This can be accomplished by reducing or expanding the size of the selection by a set amount and, at each juncture, copying the current selection to a layer.

Note *Alternatively, you could save each selection so that you could instantly recall the selection of the size you wanted. Just choose Selection | Save Selection. The Save Selection dialog box appears. Be sure to enter a name for the selection that is descriptive of the selected object and the size of the selection so that you can recall the desired selection later by choosing Select | Load Selection.*

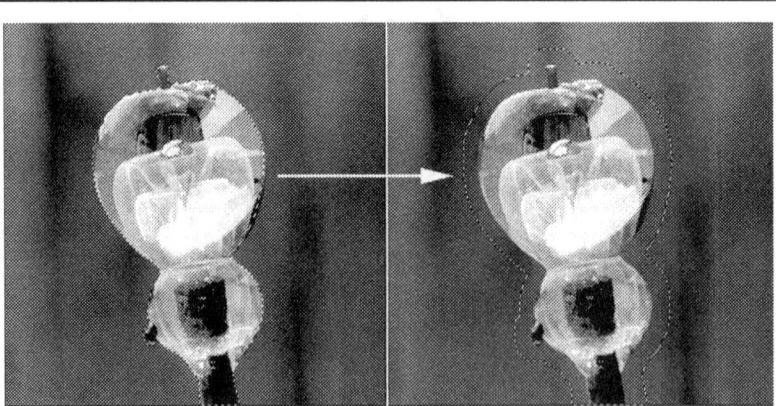

Figure 7-5. *Before and after using the Expand option on a selection*

You will end up with a series of layers with nested selections. With some effects, such as drop shadow, this can have a dramatic impact.

Making Several Selections the Same Size and Shape

The first line of defense is the Selection Options bar, which appears as soon as you select the Marquee tool. This is how you set the options to make Marquee tools draw the same-sized selection.

1. Select a Marquee tool.

2. From the Options bar, choose Style | Fixed Size.

3. Just to the right of the Style menu are two fields where you can enter a numeric value for the height and width in pixels, as you can see here.

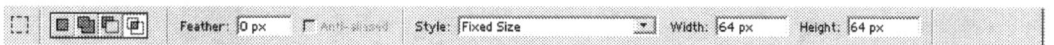

4. When you use the Marquee tool, it will draw a fixed-size box or ellipse.

You can also use the rulers and grid with the Snap To Grid option on to act as an exact reference guide to produce selections of identical size. Another option is to use the method for converting shapes to selections (as demonstrated in the section "Selection Transformation Method 2," earlier in this chapter). Set the Shape Options to Fixed Size, as shown in Figure 7-6, so you can produce identical shapes.

Giving All Selections the Same Proportions

Here's how to make sure that your selections maintain a given height to width ratio:

1. Select a Marquee tool.

2. From the Options bar, choose Style | Fixed Aspect Ratio.

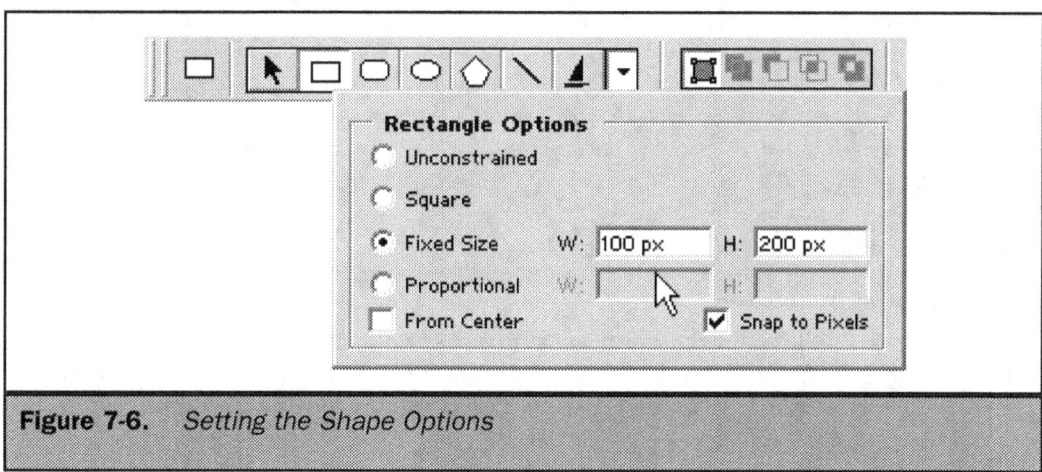

Figure 7-6.   *Setting the Shape Options*

3. Just to the right of the Style menu are two fields where you can enter a numeric value for the height and width in pixels. The proportion will be maintained for any set of numbers you enter. It doesn't matter whether you enter 2 for width and 3 for height or 10 for width and 15 for height; both sets of numbers produce a proportion of 2:3.

4. When you use the Marquee tool, it will draw a box or ellipse of any size, but with the exact height-to-width ratio you specified in the Options bar, which is pictured here.

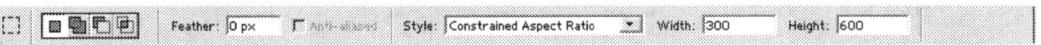

You can also use the method for converting shapes to selections (as demonstrated in the section "Selection Transformation Method 2," earlier in this chapter), but this time set the Shape Options to Proportional (refer back to Figure 7-6).

Reshaping a Selection

When you are using the Magic Wand or the Lasso tool to outline a selection, it is hard to get it perfect the first time. With the Magic Wand, color values in some areas might be too close, and you will need to finish the job by hand. It is hard to get perfect results with the Lasso tool the first time, and you don't want to go back and start over every time you slip up in following that edge. Photoshop Elements provides a very flexible set of tools for editing selections in a variety of ways. You can add, subtract, and select the intersection between two selections. You'll probably find that quickly outlining the selection the first time through and then going back and editing it down to a precise shape is more efficient than tediously trying to get it all right on the first try. Precision editing is essential for working with selections, so it is good to get familiar with adding, subtracting, and intersecting selection marquees.

Note   *Selection and selection editing tools can seem so slick and magical that we can be fooled into thinking that this, that, or the other selection tool will do a perfect job in an instant. To keep this book reasonably compact, we'll usually show you the most direct way to make the basic selection. In real life, you'll almost always have to edit that selection, soften the edges for better blending, or have to fully erase what you'd hoped would be completely transparent areas of the layer. So, if you come across these problems, don't be discouraged. It's just a normal part of the image editor's life.*

To add to a selection:

1. Make a selection.

2. Press and hold SHIFT. You will see a plus sign appear next to the cursor. Drag the cursor anywhere in the image to add to the selection or you can select the Add Selection icon from the Options bar (two dark boxes overlapping).

3. If you are using the Magic Wand, just click in the color area you want to add.

To subtract from a selection:

1. Make a selection.

2. Press and hold ALT/OPT. You will see a minus sign appear next to the cursor. Drag the cursor to any part of the current selection to subtract from that selection, or you can select the Subtract Selection icon from the Options bar (one dark and one light box overlapping).

3. If you are using the Magic Wand, just click in the color area you want to subtract.

To select the intersection between two selections:

1. Make a selection.

2. Press and hold ALT/OPT+SHIFT. You will see an X appear next to the cursor. Drag the cursor over the current selection to define the selection you want to leave, or select the Intersect With Selection icon from the Options bar (two light boxes with an overlapping dark area).

Note *There is a significant difference between using the modifier keys to add, subtract, and intersect selections and using the Options bar icons. The Options bar icons stay in effect until you choose a different icon, so if you start by making a rough selection, you can zoom in and modify all the areas where you need to subtract, and then switch icons and modify all the areas where you need to add. If you work this way when making selections with the Lasso selection tools (especially the Magnetic Lasso), you'll cut the time needed to make a precision selection by at least one-half to two-thirds. (Time is money, so you can send the money you save to us!)*

Cleaning Up Stray Pixels

The Smooth command helps you clean up extraneous pixels from noise in the selection. This causes the automated selection tools to include or exclude pixels here and there. It is a tedious task to remove them by hand. The Smooth command was designed to help with this.

To run the Smooth command, do this:

1. Choose Select | Modify | Smooth. A dialog box appears.

2. Enter a value between 1 and 100 in the Sample Radius field. Click OK.

Because there is no preview, it becomes a trial-and-error process, so you might need to undo and rerun it several times to get optimal results.

The radius value is used to set a range for the program to scan around each pixel in the selection to determine if random pixels should be included or excluded from the selection. If most of the pixels in the scan range are selected, then any unselected pixels within the specified radius will be included in the selection.

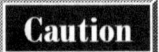 *Don't use the Smooth command when the object you're selecting has sharp corners or jagged edges that suddenly change direction. The Smooth command will round all those corners and you'll have to draw them back in by hand.*

Saving Your Selections

There are times when you want to be able to quickly repeat a selection exactly as you did earlier. It can take a lot of time to accomplish some selections, so it is not something you want to do over and over again. In addition, if you're making very complex selections, it's a good idea to save them as you move along. Then, if you accidentally drop the selection, you can retrieve what you've already created instead of spending another two hours getting back to where you left off. In Photoshop Elements, there is a method for saving selections and reusing them at any time.

1. Start making your selection. Pretend you need to go to lunch and come back later to pick up where you left off. Choose Select | Save Selection. The Save Selection dialog box appears.

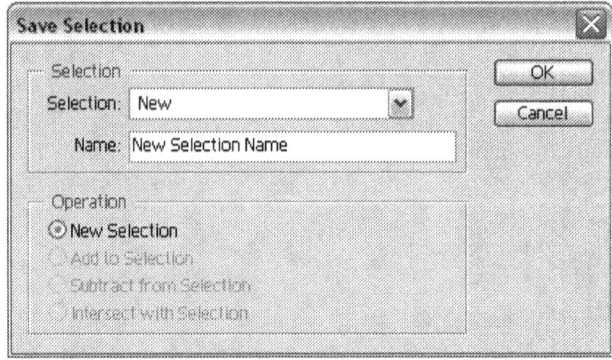

2. If this is the first time you've saved the selection, enter a name for your selection in the Name field.

3. If you have dropped the selection or have saved the file and want to come back to where you left off, be sure your file is open in Photoshop Elements and then choose Select | Load Selection. The Load Selection dialog box appears.

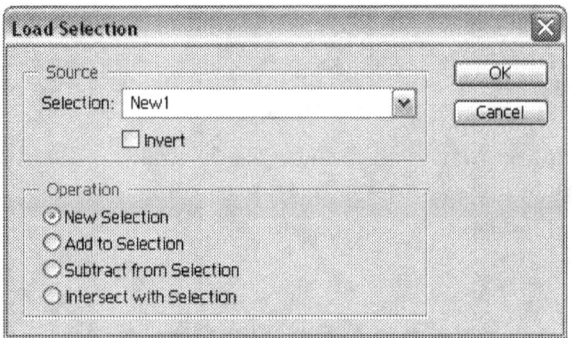

4. Click the New Selection radio button to toggle it on.

5. From the Selection menu, choose the name of the selection you saved earlier and click OK. The selection you saved before reappears.

6. Choose the tool you want to use to continue making the selection, click the Add To Selection icon in the Options bar, and continue adding to the selection you started earlier.

Note *When you load a selection, the dialog box lets you choose between New Selection or modifying the current selection by choosing among Add To Selection, Subtract From Selection, and Intersect With Selection. It doesn't matter which of these functions might be indicated in the Options bar; those options affect only what you might do with the selection tool you work with next.*

Quick Selections with Select Similar and Grow Commands

Here are two ways to expand selections in Photoshop Elements. They both use the tolerance setting in the Magic Wand Options bar to determine how much expansion happens with each execution. If the Tolerance setting is 30, the Grow and Similar commands increase the range by 30 each time. If you want the increments to be smaller, set the Tolerance lower. The basic difference between the Grow command and the Similar command is that Grow selection works on contiguous color and Similar selects similar color anywhere in the image.

To expand a selection to include areas with similar color:

1. Choose Select | Grow to include all adjacent pixels falling within the tolerance range specified in the Magic Wand options.
2. Choose Select | Similar to include pixels throughout the image, not just adjacent ones, falling within the tolerance range.
3. To increase the selection in increments, choose either command more than once.

Cool Tricks with the Magic Wand

The Magic Wand tool has been named very appropriately. It really does seem like magic, and the time it can save in making selections is miraculous. The Magic Wand can accomplish in seconds what it might take you hours to do with the lasso. For that reason alone, it becomes essential to learn every aspect of how to control it. In this section, we give you some insights into how to control this tool in Photoshop Elements so you get the most out of it.

Just the Right Touch

In the game Minesweeper, if you hit the wrong square, the whole game board blows up. Hitting the wrong pixel with the Magic Wand can have the same effect, so selecting the right starting-point reference pixel can be critical to the outcome of the Magic Wand selection. A stray pixel that is not representative of the general color in that area can change the result dramatically, as shown in Figure 7-7. In the image on the left, clicking a stray dark pixel in the background results in a selection that picks up portions of the cat rather than the background. On the right, clicking in a more typical portion of the background selects mostly the light-colored background.

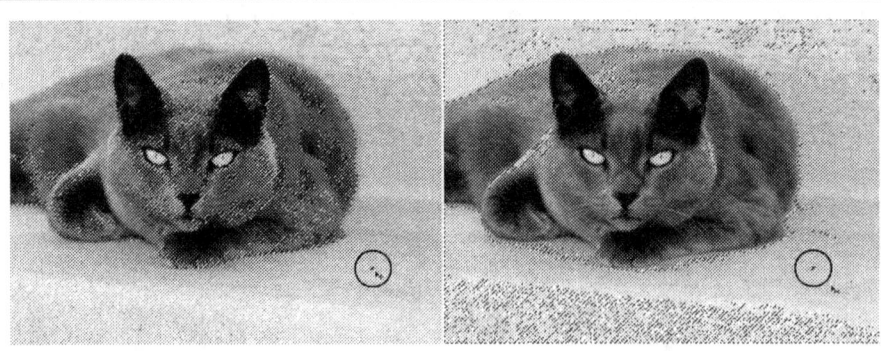

Figure 7-7.   *Hitting this stray pixel in the color area changes the outcome of the selection dramatically.*

Photographs have noise in them and can be subject to random fluctuations in color in what seems like a smooth-color area. Take a close look at a digital photo by zooming in, and you might be surprised at how much variation there can be in what looks to be a single color (see Figure 7-8). If you happen to hit on one of the noisy pixels, it will throw the whole value of your selection off. It is a good habit to zoom into the area and take a look at what is going on, and make your pixel selection in zoom mode so you can better judge which pixel you are targeting. This should make your Magic Wand selections more accurate. Try to pick a pixel that represents a good midrange value for the area that you are trying to select because the Magic Wand is looking at both sides of that pixel's value.

Tuning the Tolerance Value

The tolerance value is the governing factor in controlling the basic function of the Magic Wand. Once you select a color pixel as the start point reference, the Magic Wand function starts evaluating pixels in the entire image to see which pixels are a match based on the tolerance value and, in certain cases, proximity. The lower the value, the more closely it must match the original color selection in terms of luminance value and hue to become part of the selection. By moving the tolerance values up or down, you can fine-tune the range of the selection, as in Figure 7-9.

When tuning the tolerance value, try to pick the same reference pixel or at least a similar one every time. Keeping the pixel selection constant reduces the variables that affect the selection range.

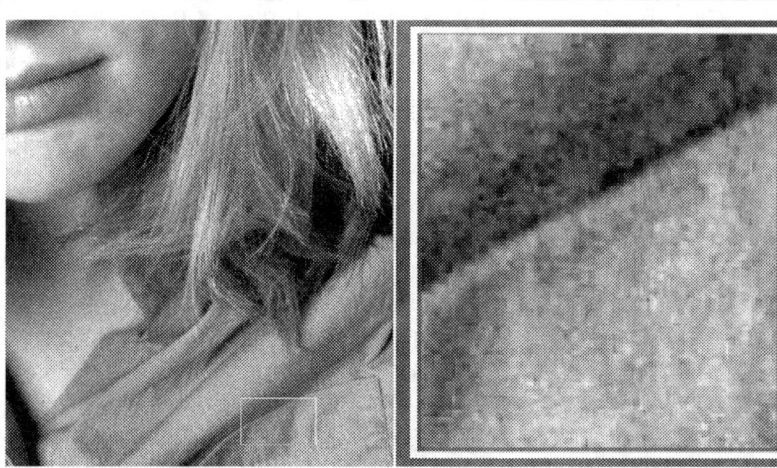

Figure 7-8. *Zooming in on the blouse enables you to see the fluctuations in color.*

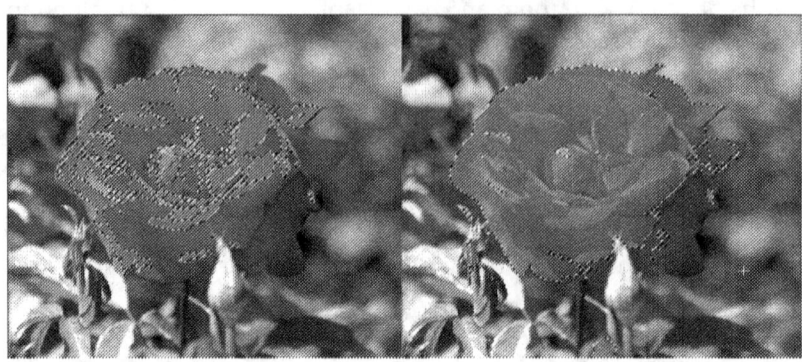

Figure 7-9.   *Tolerance set at 40 (left) and 80 (right)*

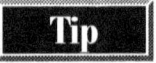 *A good way to set your pixel target is to use the grid and rulers to set the origin of the grid over the pixel you want to use for your target. This gives you a consistent reference point.*

Contiguous Versus Noncontiguous Selections

The Contiguous option for the Magic Wand is an extremely useful one. It allows you to choose between selecting only adjacent color values or values anywhere in the image. This option was not available in older versions of Photoshop. It is often the case that colors in one part of an image also appear in other unrelated parts. For example, if you want to select just the sky, you don't want the colors that happen to be similar in the flowers in the foreground selected also. If you use the Magic Wand with the Contiguous option (found in the Magic Wand Options bar) off, the sky and the flowers will be selected even though they are not anywhere near one another. The program is selecting by color value alone and makes no adjustment for proximity. When the Contiguous option is selected, the program searches for color value and proximity and selects only the sky-colored pixels that are adjacent, therefore not selecting the flowers.

Now let's look at this problem from another angle. Let's say that same sky had a branching tree that effectively cut the sky into hundreds of small areas, all separated from one another by branches. The Contiguous option will not work very well because the branches get in the way—so back to noncontiguous. Now here's how to deal with those pesky flowers. Make the selection with Contiguous off. This will select all the sky pieces and the flowers. Now switch Contiguous on again and also switch the Subtract option on. Now select the flower areas to eliminate them from the selection. Because the flower images are not adjacent to the sky, the second selection will not affect the sky areas.

Here's another quick method for getting rid of unwanted selections when the Contiguous check box is toggled off: Choose the Lasso tool and click the Subtract button in the Options bar to make it active. Now just drag a marquee around all the items outside the main selection that you don't want to keep selected. When you release the mouse button, the selection closes and all the extraneous selections disappear. This second method is more appropriate when the extraneous selections are limited to an area in the image that is mostly not selected by the Magic Wand because it eliminates the need to click each individual extraneous selection.

Limiting the Selection Area of the Magic Wand with the Other Selection Tools

Sometimes you want to use the Magic Wand in a noncontiguous manner, but you keep getting unwanted selections all over the image (and adjusting the tolerance doesn't solve this problem because it has to be set high enough to capture the area you are after). There is a remedy for this that greatly reduces the amount of cleanup you might have to do after making a selection. Here is how you do it:

1. From the Toolbox, choose the Lasso tool. Drag to place a marquee around the area in which you wish to keep your Magic Wand noncontiguous selections.

2. Choose the Magic Wand tool. In the Options bar, click the Subtract from Selection icon. Click within the bounds of the Lasso's selection marquee. The noncontiguous areas selected by the Magic Wand will be contained to just the area you specified.

Making Selections with the Threshold Command

In images that have a high degree of contrast between areas, the Threshold command can be very useful in making selections. The Threshold command turns the image into a high-contrast, black-and-white image. You can interactively set the dividing line luminance value that will determine which pixels go to white and which to black. This can be a good way to isolate certain areas of an image for selection if the areas fall into an easily defined luminance range. It doesn't necessarily work on all images, so you need to experiment to determine if it will work for the selection you want to make. You'll have the greatest degree of success with images that have well-defined edges. Here is how it works:

1. Open the Layers palette and click the Layer Name bar of the layer you want to make a selection from using the Threshold command.

2. From the Layers palette, choose Duplicate Layer. The new layer will become the template for the selection.

3. In the Layers palette, set the opacity of the threshold layer at 50 percent so you can see how well the edges of the threshold image match the edges of the original image.

4. Choose Image | Adjustments | Threshold. The Threshold dialog box appears. Make sure that Preview is checked.

5. Move the slider arrow left or right until the areas you want to select are either solid black or solid white (see Figure 7-10). Some images process better than others. You might also try adjusting the contrast and brightness of the threshold layer to enhance the effectiveness of using the Threshold command. When you are satisfied with the threshold, click OK.

6. Use the Magic Wand to select either the white or black areas.

7. Click to toggle the eye icon in the Visibility button to make the template layer invisible so the selection can be seen over the image layer.

8. Click the Layer Name bar of the image layer to make it active so you can use the selection on that layer.

Using Selection Inversion as a Tool

Selecting the opposite of what you really want to select can sometimes save you a lot of time. The ability to invert a selection can make selecting some areas much easier. Let's say that the area you want to select is a complex subject with all kinds of colors and patterns so it not easily defined in a color range. Fortunately, this subject has been photographed against a simple background that contrasts strongly with the subject. You could take the time to outline it with the Lasso tool—but you don't have a week

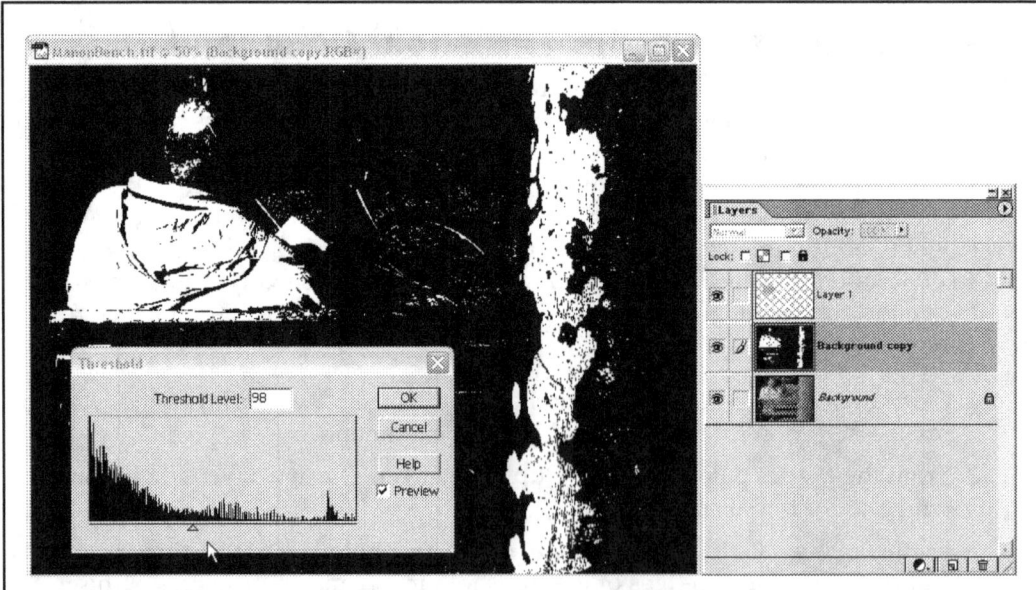

Figure 7-10.   *Using the Threshold dialog box to create a template layer over an image to define selection areas*

to do it. Here's the quick way to select an object that is surrounded by a contrasting background:

1. Open the file containing the object you want to select.

2. Choose the Magic Wand tool. From its Options bar, select the Contiguous checkbox.

3. Enter a high enough tolerance to get all of the background, but little or none of the object you eventually want to select. Every image varies, so you have to experiment to see what the exact number should be.

4. Click the background area you want to temporarily select. A selection marquee should appear around the background and around any holes in the foreground image where the background shows through.

5. If there are areas selected that should belong to the foreground object and not the background, choose the Lasso tool and click the Subtract From Selection icon in the Options bar. Then draw a selection around the area you want to remove.

6. Double-click the Zoom tool to get 100% magnification of the image. Use the Lasso tool and the Add, Subtract, and Intersect icons in the Options bar to edit the edges of the selection so that it fits exactly along the edges you want selected.

7. Choose Select | Inverse (SHIFT+CMD/CTRL+I) to invert the selection. Now only your foreground object should be selected. You can do any further editing, as required.

Refer to Figure 7-11 for an example of how this technique works. You can use this technique in conjunction with a preliminary selection to limit the area of effect (see the "Limiting the Selection Area of the Magic Wand with the Other Selection Tools" section, earlier in this chapter).

Automatically Selecting and Changing Large Areas of Color

The Replace Color command allows you to define areas of similar color and change them interactively. What is nice about this command is that it allows you to work quickly and experiment with a lot of possibilities for isolating areas of color. It uses a range evaluation method that is similar to the Magic Wand. This command does not produce a selection marquee. The selection area is active while the dialog box is open and is discarded as soon as you exit the command. It is a good idea to make a duplicate layer as a working layer.

To use the Replace Color command to alter color in selected areas, follow these steps:

1. Choose Enhance | Color | Replace Color. The Replace Color dialog box appears. The cursor changes to an eyedropper so you can sample the colors in the image that you want to replace. The display box should be set to Image

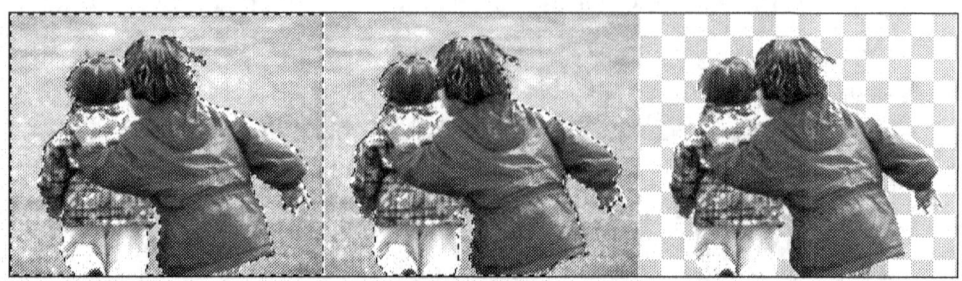

Figure 7-11.   *Selecting the negative space around an area (left) and then inverting the selection (center) allows you to separate that area from the background (right)*

mode at first so you can key the area that you want to use for sampling. Once you have set the reference point, switch to Selection mode so you can see the effect of the settings. The sample color shows in the color-swatch window on the lower right.

2. The area you sampled displays in white. If the fuzziness is set very low, the area in white you see might be very small. Raise the value of the Fuzziness slider to expand the area of effect. The white areas represent the portions of the image that are not masked and therefore will be affected by any color change.

3. You can also add and subtract from the mask with interactive eyedropper tools on the right. These can be used in the dialog box or the image itself.

4. Once you have the area of color isolated and masked, you can then use the color sliders to change the hue, saturation, and lightness of the unmasked areas. You can change the colors in one area, and then redefine your mask and change them again.

5. When you have finished, click OK.

The Magic Wand can also be used in this procedure. If you want to select just one color, then set the Tolerance value on the Options bar to 1. Photoshop Elements will look for the exact color value that you have sampled in the pixel you selected with the Magic Wand. The higher you raise the Tolerance value, the more variation from the original pick can be found.

Feathering Selections

Feathering selections into new backgrounds is a big part of the art that makes image compositing work. Feathering is used for a few different things—first of all, to separate an image from the background with a smooth transition effect. If you are making changes to the background, such as creating a soft focus, you need to transition the focus effect to the area of the image that will be in focus.

When you move selections from one image to another, you might need to blend the image into the new background. Feathering the edge will help merge the images together (see Figure 7-12).

Here are three ways to feather a selection edge:

■ Set any of the Lasso and Marquee tools for Feathering on the Options bar. When you set the Feathering option on the Options bar, it will be in effect for every selection you place.

■ Right-click an individual selection and, from the in-context menu, choose Feather. You will be prompted for a value. You can enter pixel values from 1 to 250.

■ Choose Selection | Feather.

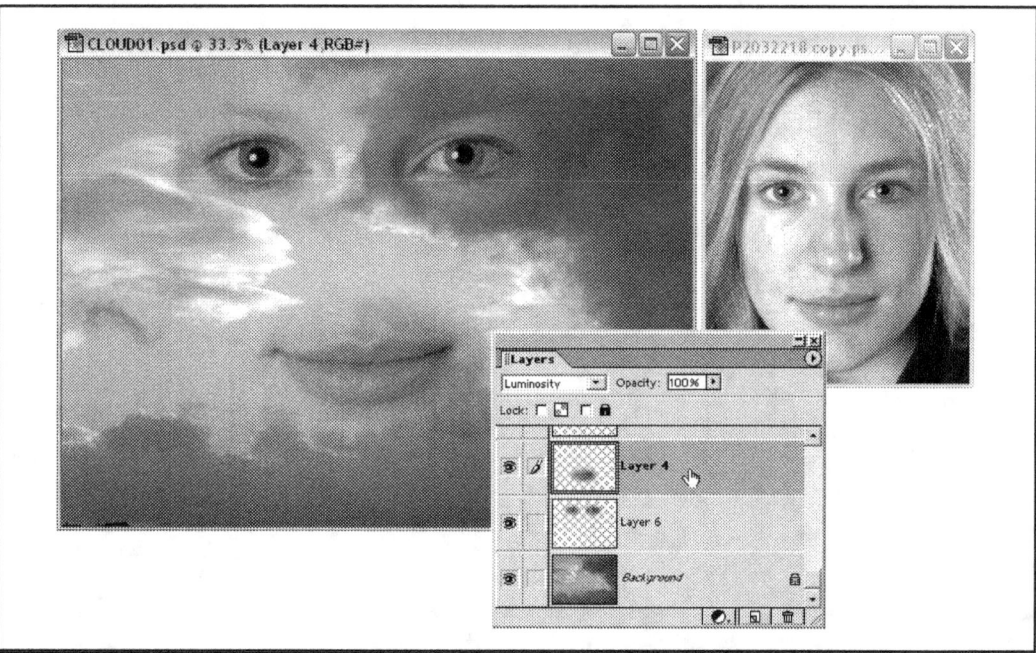

Figure 7-12.   *Feathering was used to blend the facial element selections into the background.*

The
Complete
Reference

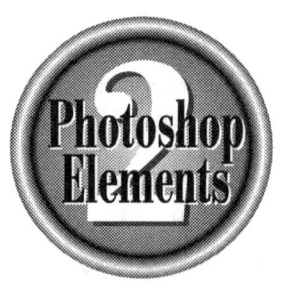

Chapter 8

Understanding Layers

If you've got Photoshop Elements 2.0, you've got the power. You'll never make full use of the power, though, until you get a solid grasp on what layers are and what they can do for you. The short answer to what layers can do for you is they make it possible to make changes to any specific part of an image without having to re-edit the entire image. However, that answer is way too short. This entire chapter is devoted to all the things

- You can do to affect a single layer (aside from blending modes and creating composites, which are covered in Chapter 9 and 17, respectively).

- A layer can do to affect other layers.

- You can do to affect groups of layers simultaneously.

Introducing Layers

Layers are no longer just image layers; now there are many specialized types. Each layer can be affected by dozens of commands, most of them accessible through your choice of the Menu bar, the Layers Palette menu, or in-context menus or by clicking an icon at the bottom of the Layers Palette. You can also right-click in various parts of the palette or the selection itself to bring up other options. Some of these commands are available through only one or two of these menus, others are available on all of them. However, the flexibility given to you by the presence of layers doesn't stop there. Each layer can be changed in many ways. Here is an overview of the major layer interactions:

- Layers can be added, deleted, renamed, or duplicated.

- Layers can be moved to new positions in the stack simply by dragging them.

- Any layer can be temporarily hidden.

- Overall layer transparency can be adjusted from 0 to 100 percent opacity.

- Portions of a layer can be erased and become transparent to layers below.

- Any transparency within a layer can be locked so it is not affected by any other editing.

- Any layer can be assigned a blending mode that can affect the layer below it (see Chapter 9).

- Each layer can be assigned a separate layer style that can affect the image, type, or shape on that layer.

- Adjustment and fill layer content and attributes can be changed at any time.

- Edit fill layer masks in order to change the area of the effect on layers below.

- Text, shape, fill, and adjustment layers can be simplified so they become image layers, allowing you to apply additional effects.

■ Layers can be merged with other layers so the contents of the layers are combined into one image.

■ All layers can be flattened, which merges all layers to produce a single image.

■ Layers can be transformed, which means they can be rotated, scaled, distorted, skewed, and moved.

■ A layer can be linked with another layer so that when it's moved, the other layer moves in alignment with it.

■ Layers can be grouped so the first, or base, layer in the group defines the boundary of all the other layers.

■ Individual layers can be fully or partially locked, placing limitations on the editing of that layer.

■ Layers can be moved to other documents or copied from other documents by simply dragging them.

■ Any portion of layer can be copied to another layer.

As you can see, the power of layers is the extent of the control you have over them with the many tools and commands at your disposal.

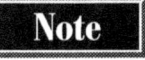

The default is for commands and tools to affect only the active layer. Grouping, linking, transparency, checking the All Layers box in a tool's Options bar, and using fill and adjustment layers all allow you to affect multiple layers at one time.

Now let's delve into what layers are and what they can do to help you create more than you ever thought possible.

What Is a Layer?

Think of a layer as a piece of clear plastic that's perfectly aligned above all the other layers in a stack. If the piece of transparent plastic has an image "painted" on it, anything other than that image remains transparent, so that you can see through to the layer(s) below. If there are images on the layers below, wherever those images overlap one another, the overlaying image hides the underlying image.

Okay, it's not quite that simple, but it gives you the basic concept. Now consider that you can change the order in which you stack these plastic sheets. In addition, you can change the transparency of the plastic layers in many ways. Whenever that's the case, you can see through the image to whatever extent its opacity allows. Now if you look down from above, you can see a composite image that is a combination of all the images on the shelves. This is what you see on the screen. Figure 8-1 shows how this works.

The layers really lie at the center of Photoshop Elements functionality. There are not many operations in Photoshop Elements that don't require you to interact with layers. Anytime you are changing the image in any way, you are always working on a layer,

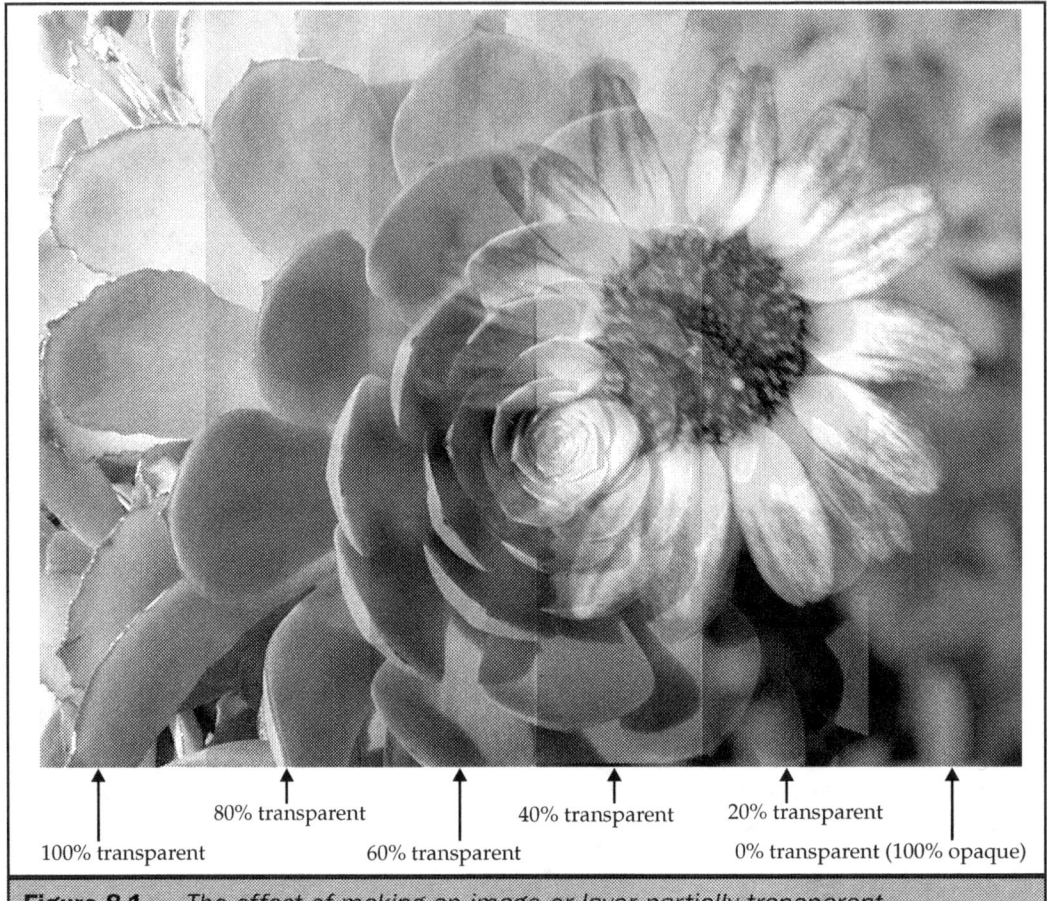

100% transparent   80% transparent   60% transparent   40% transparent   20% transparent   0% transparent (100% opaque)

Figure 8-1. *The effect of making an image or layer partially transparent*

even if it is only the background layer. Layers give you the ability to apply different modifications and effects to portions of an image while keeping all the parts separated for editing. This process gives you the ultimate control on how you edit and assemble all these pieces to create the final image, which is the combination of all the pieces.

There is one way of using layers that falls into a different category, and that is using layers to create an animation. We go into that in Chapter 18. This chapter focuses on using layers to create still images.

Background Layer

The background layer is a layer with special attributes and represents the start point layer for any image in Photoshop Elements. It always occupies the first position in the Layers Palette and is labeled Background (see Figure 8-1). If you've just started a painting or just imported a photo from a camera or scanner, the background layer *is* the image. The background layer is automatically partially locked, which is indicated by the light-colored lock symbol in the name bar. This means you cannot change the transparency or the stacking order of a background layer. If you try to erase, you'll merely paint in the current background color. You also can't change the Blend mode of a background layer.

Just in case all that makes it sound as though you can't do much of anything with a background layer, the truth is that you really *shouldn't* do anything to a background layer. By maintaining it as is, you can return to the original image in case you make a mistake at some point. All you have to do is drag the background layer to the New Layer icon at the bottom of the Layers Palette or right-click in the name bar and choose Duplicate Layer, and—bingo!—you've made a copy.

If you insist on making the background layer editable, double-click on the background layer name, and the Layer Properties dialog box appears. Click OK, and the background layer is renamed and unlocked as a normal image layer. To convert any layer back to a background layer, choose Layer | New | Background from Layer. This works only if there is currently no background layer. You can always make the background layer hidden if you don't want to see it. Just click the eye icon at the far left of the background layer's name bar, and the background layer is hidden. Click the Hide/Show button again, and the eye icon reappears (you can hide or show any layer in the same way).

Layers Palette

The Layers Palette—the control center for most of your interactions with layers—is the palette that you will have open more than any other. It represents the heart of how you work with images in Photoshop Elements. There's an in-depth map of the Layers Palette and a description of all its components and individual commands in Chapter 4. We won't redescribe every component here. In Figure 8-2, you see a screen shot of the Layers Palette and all its menus with callouts that name all the components. This chapter focuses on how all these commands work together to create new images.

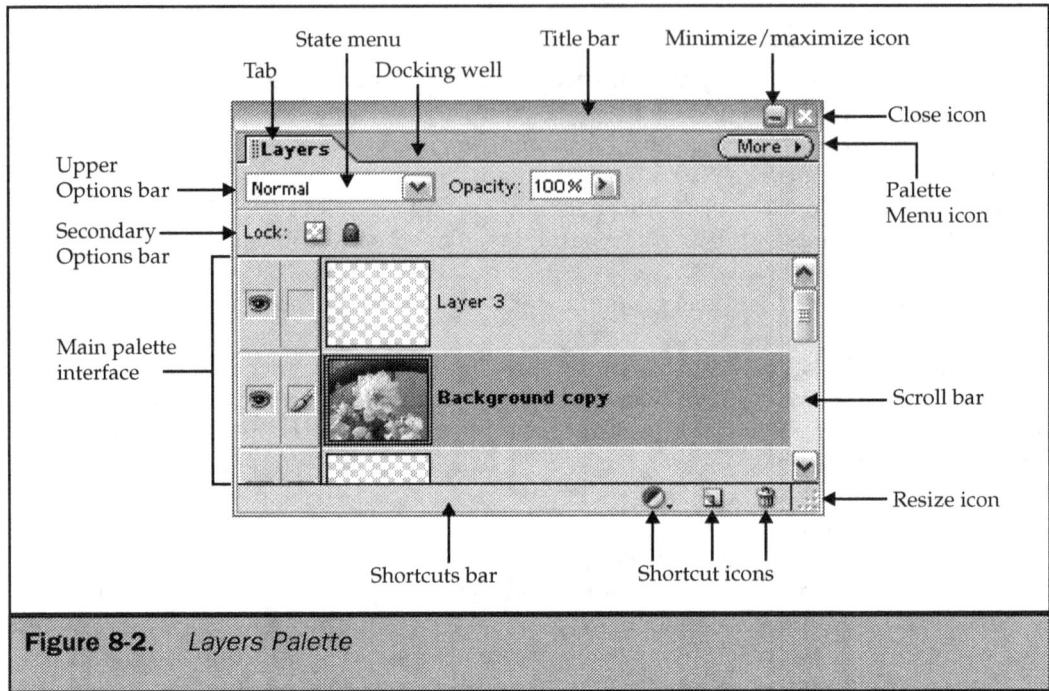

Figure 8-2.   *Layers Palette*

Basic Layer Manipulation

This section gives you a quick rundown of the basic features in manipulating layers in Photoshop Elements so you get a general understanding of how you can make layers work for you. The "Stacking Order and Layer Interaction" section, later in this chapter, goes into more advanced techniques.

Selection and Status of Layers

To select a layer, click anywhere on the name bar. The bar turns gray to indicate that it is active. You can have only one layer active at time, so when you click on the name bar of another layer, the current active layer deactivates automatically.

The Status button is blank if the layer it's associated with is inactive (not selected) unless you choose to link an inactive layer or layers to the currently active layer. When the layer is selected, an icon indicates what you can do in that layer. A brush icon appears if it's a straight image layer, indicating that you can paint directly into that layer or affect it by using Photoshop Elements tools or commands. If the selected layer is a fill or adjustment layer, a mask icon appears, indicating that you can create a mask in this layer, in which case the Blend mode or adjustment will affect only that portion of the image.

Adding and Deleting Layers

When you first open an image document and then open the Layers Palette, you can see that there is only one layer present. This is the background layer. As you work on your project, you will need to add layers as you perform various operations on the image and separate parts for individual attention. Adding a layer is as simple as clicking the Add Layer icon on the lower Options bar (see Figure 8-2) or choosing Add New Layer from the Layers or Palette menus. A new transparent layer appears above the active layer.

Deleting any layer is just as simple. Select the layer you want to delete, click the Trash icon on the lower Options bar, and the layer disappears. You can also drag the layer over the trash (see Figure 8-2) or choose Delete Layer from the Layer or Palette menus. Another option is to just hide the layer temporarily until you are sure you want to delete it.

Duplicating Layers

This is a very important basic feature and one that we hope you use often because it will save you from many frustrations and make your layer editing more foolproof. Duplicating a layer makes an identical copy of the active layer directly above the active layer. Select the layer you want to duplicate, right-click in the name bar, and choose Duplicate Layer or select Duplicate Layer from the Layer or Layers Palette menus. A dialog box appears that lets you enter a unique name for the new layer, or you can accept the default name.

The first layer you should duplicate is the Background layer so you can edit it if you so desire. Making duplicates gives you a safety net so you can experiment with different effects and still be able to go back to where you started. Think of it as creating you own history states (snapshots of the past operation).

Duplicating is also the way many composite (see Chapter 17) operations start out. Let's say you want to combine a number of special effects to an image. You would make several duplicates of the image, apply different effects and editing to each layer, and then recombine into a new image. There could be a face you want isolate, or a flower you want to move. Making a duplicate allows you to isolate each of these elements and cut them from the background, edit them, and then move them to new positions and composite them. You will use duplicate many times if you like to work with images this way.

Moving Layers

You can move a layer to a new position in the stack by clicking on the name bar and dragging it to a new location. This might have a radical effect on the image you see in the image window, depending on how you have your layers interacting. A more in-depth discussion on moving images to new positions in the stack and how that affects layer interaction is in the "Stacking Order and Layer Interaction" section later in this chapter. You can also move a layer one position up or down or to the very front or back by choosing Layer | Arrange and then selecting the appropriate option.

Repositioning Layers

Reposition sounds like moving, but it is something else entirely. This refers to moving the image horizontally or vertically in the layer frame. You can reposition the entire layer image by making the layer you want to reposition active. Choosing the Move tool, click in the image window and drag the layer image to a new location. The entire image remains intact, even if part of it moves out of the image frame.

Repositioning lets you move elements on separate layers around to align them to one another. Making the layer you are repositioning partially transparent can help with lining it up properly to layers under it. See Figure 8-11 in the "Erasing Portions of Layers" section later in this chapter.

Hiding and Showing Layers

Hiding layers is a nice convenience. As you make duplicates and edit each one, you can often end up with quite a few layers. You might not want to have them all visible at the same time so you can concentrate on the interactions of a few. The Hide option lets you remove the visual influence of a layer from the stack temporarily so you can concentrate on the visible layers. Click on the eye icon just to the left of the name bar, and the icon vanishes. When the eye icon is not present, the layer is hidden. Just click on the slot where the eye icon was, and it reappears, making the layer visible once more.

You will find the Hide/Show capability of layers invaluable when you want to try out various layer effects that influence other layers. You can set up a number of adjustment layers, for instance, and then hide and show them in different combinations to see the effect on the layer they influence. As you create various versions of layer images, you might want to copy them to separate layers, keep them hidden, and view them as you need to. This is good technique if you have a lot of source and reference layers that you want to have handy but do not want involved with your stack interaction. We go into stack interaction more in the "Stacking Order and Layer Interaction" section later in this chapter.

A common use for showing and hiding layers is to show a colleague or client alternative "looks" for an image by turning various layers on or off. When imaging a composite image that has various flying composite components, such as a dirigible, an airplane, and Superman, as well as a text headline, you could easily copy all these layers and place each copy in a different position. Then all you have to do to show the alternative positions is click layers on and off.

Locking Layers

You can partially or fully lock layers to further control how the locked layers are affected by the editing process. The partial lock locks only the transparency of a layer. If there is no transparency present, then it has no effect. When you lock the transparency, you cannot change any pixels in that layer that are fully transparent, and you can change partially transparent pixels only to the extent of their opacity.

Fully locked layers cannot be edited at all and are in a protected state. This is good to do to layers where you have performed some critical editing and you want to prevent any accidental alteration of that layer.

Transforming Layers

Layers can be treated as objects and transformed in the same manner as selections. You could say that the active layer is automatically selected. Before we go any further, though, it is important to understand how Photoshop Elements defines and selects layer objects. If an image is on a layer surrounded by transparency, transforming that layer will be contained to the area defined by the bounding box around that image object, not the whole layer. The transparency of a layer (referring to 100 percent transparent) is used to define the *bounding box* of the image objects on the layer. The bounding box is the minimal rectangular area that can contain the object. The extent of the object, which determines the dimensions of the bounding box, is determined to be where the pixels surrounding it become totally transparent or where it initially meets the edge of the layer. Therefore, if the image fills the entire layer with no transparency, the edges of the layer frame are the bounding box. The exceptions to that are type, shape objects, and selected image objects that have been moved outside the layer frame. This means that if type runs off the screen while you are entering it or a selected image object is moved so part of it is outside the frame, you can pull it back into the frame and it all will be there, unlike a paint stroke, which ends at the layer's, edge even if your hand keeps moving. You can reveal the portions of the image that lie outside the layer frame using the Image | Resize | Reveal All command. This will enlarge the image to the extent that the object lies outside the layer. If an object has a smooth or feathered edge, the bounding box might appear to be rather far from the object, as you can see in Figure 8-3, which shows the bounding box for a skew transformation on two objects in a single layer. The bounding box will be indicated by a dotted line with transformation handles on the corners and sides. Whenever you transform layer objects, you do so with its bounding box and its handles.

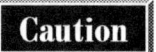

If you move objects outside the layer frame, it can increase the file size dramatically because the program holds on to the entire object, whether it is completely visible or not. You need to either flatten or crop the image to cut the object portions that lie outside the visible frame.

The following circumstances dictate how a bounding box is defined when you transform a layer:

- If the layer contains no transparency or partial transparency throughout the image, then it will be bounded on the layer frame.
- If the layer contains an image object that has transparency around it, then the bounding box will just contain the object and ignore the transparent portions.

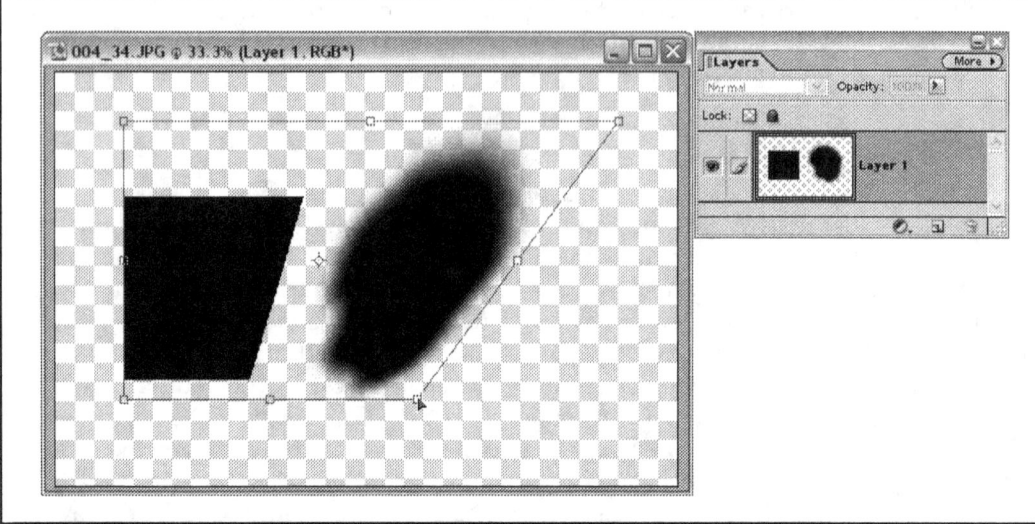

Figure 8-3.   *When the transformation is selected, the bounding box automatically appears at the extent of the objects with handles.*

- If the object is round or irregular in shape, a rectangular bounding box will be defined by the maximum of the object.
- If there is more than one image object on the layer, the bounding box will contain all the objects.
- If you extend the object out of the image frame, the extents will be maintained and can be moved back in again.

You can perform transformations in image, type, and shape layers. The type layers do not allow distort or perspective transformations but do allow warping. If you want to perform those types of transformations on text, you first need to simplify the layer to convert it pixels. For more information on how to manipulate transformations, see Chapter 11.

Layer transformations can be very useful when you are trying to make objects on separate layers match up in terms of size and orientation. You can scale the layer objects to be proportionate, or rotate them to line up correctly (see Figure 8-4). Distortions and skews push and bend images and shapes to create effects, such as italicized text, or to correct perspective distortion. If you need to use transformation on just a portion of layer that has other image areas in the same layer, you need to use selections to confine the area you want to transform; otherwise the program will look for all objects on the active layer.

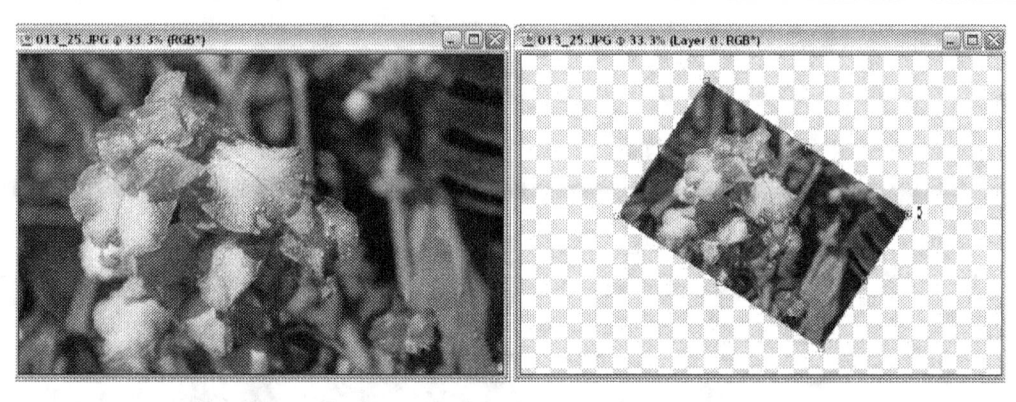

Figure 8-4.   *The layer image on the left was scaled and rotated to the new size and orientation on the right.*

Layer Types

Once upon a time, you could have any kind of a layer you wanted, as long as it was an image layer. Today, given the advances in modern technology from Adobe, you can have your choice of five layers: image, adjustment, fill, type, and shape. If you're going to make the most of layer power, you should familiarize yourself with what each can do for you and how to realize their potential. You can see an example of the layer types in Figure 8-5. The first icon changes with each fill and adjustment type to indicate what type it is. For example, the level adjustment shows the histogram.

Image Layers

An image layer is simply a layer with a raster (pixel-based) image on it. The image can be a drawing, painting, photograph—even type and vector shapes that have been rendered (simplified) from vectors to pixels. All background layers are image layers. Image layers have all the properties, options, and capabilities described earlier.

Image layers can be created in any way that you can create a raster image. You can create a new image layer by doing any of the following:

- *Copy an existing layer.* Choose Layers Palette | Duplicate Layer, or right-click on the layer name and choose Duplicate Image. To copy a layer to another document, have both documents open. Make the layer you want to copy active and then drag that layer over the document. A copy of the layer is placed on the new document.

- *Copy a selection from an existing layer.* Make a selection with any of the selection tools and then right-click inside the selection to bring up the context menu.

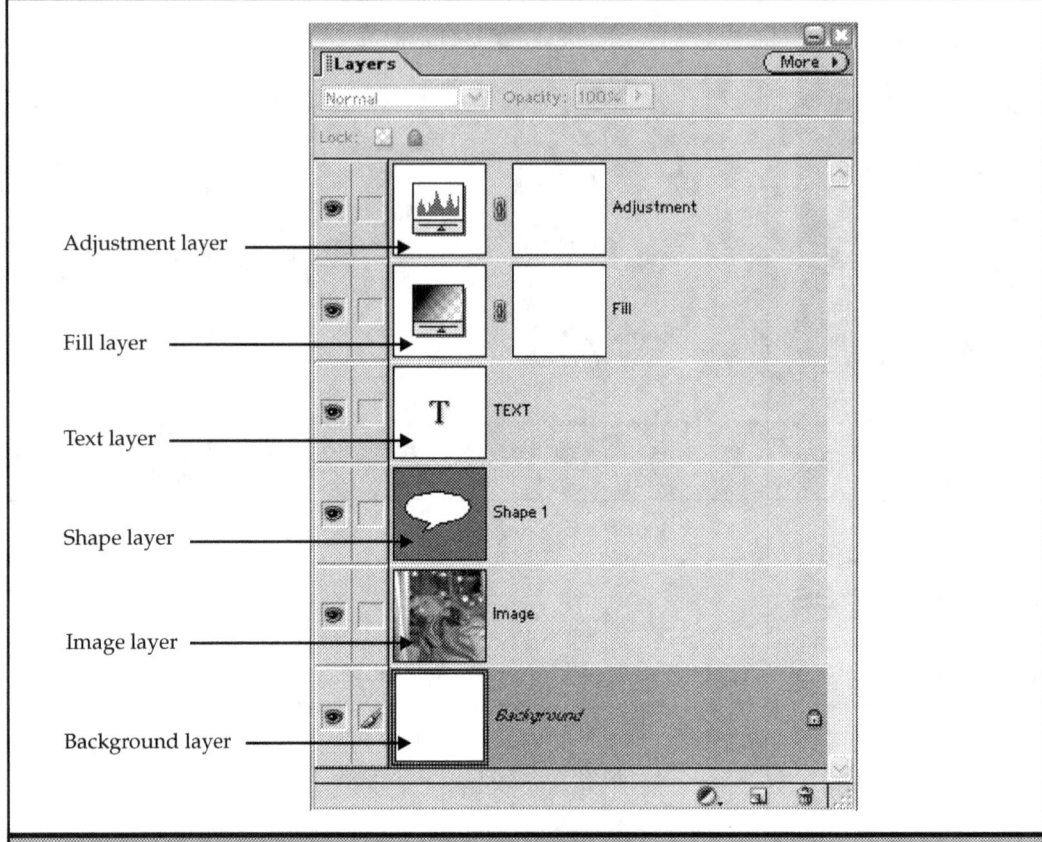

Figure 8-5.   *This is the typical look of each layer type.*

Choose Layer Via Copy. To cut the selection to a new layer, choose Cut Via Layer. A new layer with just the selection is created above the active layer.

- *Drag a layer out of another document window and drop it into your document.* To copy a layer to another document or vice versa, have both documents open. Make the layer you want to copy active, and then drag that layer over the other document. A copy of the layer is placed on the new document.

- *Paste in an image from any other application.* Open the image you want to copy. Choose Select | Select All (CMD/CTRL+A) to select the whole image and place it on the clipboard. Make the document you want to copy too active and choose Edit | Paste (CMD/CTRL+V) to paste the selected image to a new layer.

- *Draw or paint in a blank layer.* Create an empty (completely transparent) layer. Choose Layer | New | Layer, or press SHIFT+CMD/CTRL+N, or choose New

Layer from the Layer Palette menu, or (most easily and directly) click the New Layer icon at the bottom of the Layers Palette. Then use any of the paint or draw tools to create an image on this layer.

- *Create an image layer from text or shape objects.* When you first create text or shape layers, the type and shapes are created using vector methods so the objects remain resolution independent and editable. If you want to convert the vector art into raster art, you can use a command called Simplify to accomplish this. Choose the Simplify command from the Layers Palette menu, or right-click on the layer name and choose the same command from the pop-up menu. The big T icon vanishes, and the layer is converted to an ordinary image layer. The type or shape is no longer editable in the way it was as a vector object and now must be edited as an image.

- *Convert fill or adjustment layers.* When you simplify an adjustment or fill layer, it becomes an image layer. To simplify a fill or adjustment layer, make the layer active. Choose Layers Palette | Simplify or right-click on the layer name bar and choose the same command from the pop-up menu. The icons vanish, and the effect is left on an image layer.

- *Merge layers.* Merging text, shapes, fill, or an adjustment layer with each other or with an image layer results in a new, combined image layer. You can merge almost any combination or number of layers. To do this, make only the layers you want to merge visible by making the eye icon visible next to the layer. Once you have the layer you want to include visible and those you don't want to include invisible, choose Layers Palette | Merge Visible to combine them into an image layer.

Note *When you're working on an image that has layers, it's a good idea to keep the Layers Palette open and on screen by dragging its tab out of the Palette well. If you open it by just clicking the tab, the palette disappears as soon as you start work on the image. Keeping the Layers Palette open provides a constant reminder of which layer is active and which options are in force on that layer. It also makes it very convenient get to layer commands, options, and adjustments. If you prefer, you can uncheck the Close Palette to Palette Well option in the Layers Palette menu so it opens to the application workspace when you open it from the Window menu.*

Type Layers

As soon as you choose the Type tool, you can enter type directly over the image. As soon as you type the first letter, a new layer (marked with a big black T) is created. This type layer keeps the type you enter as a separate entity, which makes it possible to come back any time to edit the text. This means you can change the type color and characteristics and apply a layer style that allows you to give the type all sorts of edge effects, drop shadows, patterns, and other cool characteristics. You can also use transformations on type layers, with the exception of the Distort or Perspective commands. Simplifying the type once you have sized correctly allows you to then apply all the transformations, but the type does not remain editable as before. You can maintain the editable version by duplicating the layer and making the type layer invisible.

The specifics of using the Type tool such as the Options bar settings, choices and uses of fonts, text formatting, and text warping are discussed in detail in Chapter 15.

Shape Layers

Shape layers are just like type layers except that they're reserved for vector shapes that you create with the Shape tool. As soon as you start to draw a vector shape, the shape layer is created. You can then go back later and edit the shape characteristics. You can use all the transformation commands to modify the shape, and apply the same layer styles that you can apply to text. Check out Chapter 15 for more on creating, editing, and using shapes.

Adjustment Layers

Adjustment layers are the one way that you can make exposure adjustments, color corrections, and certain special effects that uniformly affect all visible portions of all the underlying image, type, and shape layers. Adjustment layers have been present in the Photoshop family for only a couple years. Before that, if you had 50 layers and you wanted to change the overall brightness of the image, you had two choices: You can either adjust each layer and make absolutely sure you'd made exactly the same sequence of adjustments on each of the layers, or you can flatten the image (merge all the layers) into a single background layer and then make a single adjustment. If you took the easy road and flattened the image, it was impossible to later make a change in what once was one of the layers. Adjustment layers have resolved that dilemma by allowing a single adjustment layer to affect the entire layer under it.

Note *Adjustment layers affect only those layers that are beneath the adjustment layer in the Layers Palette. If you create a new layer while the adjustment layer is active, the new layer is created above the adjustment layer. If you want that layer to be affected by the adjustment in the adjustment layer, be sure to drag it underneath the adjustment layer. Conversely, if you want one or more layers to not be affected by the adjustment layer, you can drag them above the adjustment layer.*

Adjustment layers are currently subdivided into seven subtypes, each of which corresponds to a command that is in either the Image or Enhance menu of Photoshop Elements 2. You'll find a really thorough discussion of these commands in Chapter 12. Each of these commands performs in exactly the same way when used as an adjustment layer as when used to independently adjust a single layer; the only exception is that adjustment layers can affect multiple layers, whereas the menu commands affect only the active layer.

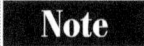 *Image adjustments are often used for affecting only the contents of a specific area in the image by preselecting that portion of the image with one of the marquee selection tools. Be reassured that you can still use exactly the same technique on an adjustment layer. To get a selection to work with an adjustment or fill layer, you need to have the selection active when you create the adjustment layer so the adjustment layer mask reflects the selection. If you want to add a selection later, you need to edit the layer mask, which we cover in the "Layer Masks" section later in this chapter. The adjustment affects only that portion of all layers beneath the adjustment layer that are both visible and enclosed within the marquee.*

 ■ **Levels**   This is the most powerful and versatile of the enhance commands. You can adjust brightness, color balance, contrast, and tonal range in a variety of ways.

 ■ **Brightness/Contrast**   Two sliders control the overall brightness and contrast of the image.

 ■ **Hue/Saturation**   Three sliders control overall hue, saturation (intensity of color), and brightness. You can also adjust the parameters by the color range you can choose from the Edit drop-down menu. You can change the color range by adjusting the range sliders on the color bars at the bottom of the dialog box. You can also colorize the image by checking that option.

 ■ **Gradient Map**   Using a gradient map adjustment layer creates a special effect by reassigning all the colors in the image to those of any gradient in the current gradient presets library. The gradient follows the tonal range of the image from darkest colors on the left to the lightest on the right. If you use a black-to-white linear gradient, it converts the image into a grayscale image. This adjustment layer can be used to colorize with some nice special effects. You can find out more about using gradient maps in Chapter 15.

 ■ **Invert**   Turns a positive image into negative image and vice versa.

 ■ **Threshold**   Converts an image to pure black and white and lets you move a slider to determine the dividing line between which pixels turn pure white and which go to pure black, based on their luminance value.

 ■ **Posterize**   Reduces the number of colors in the image to the number you specify. This adjustment reduces the number of color that are available to define detail and render shading. The effect makes the image look more like a poster with broader areas of solid color and less defined detail. The lower the number of colors you enter, the more dramatic the effect.

So how might you go about using an image adjustment layer? Let's do a little exercise to give you the general idea of the basic functions, controls, and functionality of what adjustment layers can do:

1. Click the File Browser tab to open the Photoshop Elements file browser, and navigate to a directory that has several images in it. You might be just learning to use the program, so you might not have many images yet. In that case, you'll find a set of sample images on the program's CD-ROM. Once you've navigated to that directory and opened the program's Samples directory, press CMD/CTRL (to allow you to select multiple images in random order) while clicking on the images you want to highlight. Now just drag them into the workspace, where they will each open in their own window.

2. Pick one of the images to be your background image. Drag it to one side.

3. Click one of the other images to make it active and use any of the selection tools to place a selection around one part of the image. Make the part you select about one-third the size of the overall image.

4. Place your background image's window alongside the window of the file you just selected a portion of. Now choose the Move tool to drag the selected portion of the second image into the window of the background image. Don't bother making this pretty or selecting carefully. That's not the point of this exercise.

5. Repeat steps 3 and 4 for the other images until you have pieces of all the images inside the same image. You can rearrange the composition (such as it is) of these pieces to your heart's content by clicking the layer name bar in the Layers Palette that contains the image you want to move. Notice that the layer name bar turns gray to indicate that this is the currently active layer. Choose the Move tool. Place the cursor in the image window and drag to position that layer. Try doing the same for the other layers. Notice that you can't move the background layer because it's always locked.

6. Now you'll see the difference between applying an image adjustment to a selected layer versus using an image adjustment layer. Click the name bar of the layer in the middle of the stack of image layers (those above the background layer). Choose Image | Enhance | Adjust Brightness/Contrast. The Brightness/Contrast dialog box appears. Drag both sliders so that the change is too extreme to miss. Click OK. It should be obvious that the change you just made affected only one layer. For example, in the illustration that follows, the image on the left was adjusted with an Brightness/Contrast adjustment layer so all the layers were affected; in the image on the right, the Brightness/Contrast adjustment was applied to just the individual portrait layer, leaving all the other layers as they were.

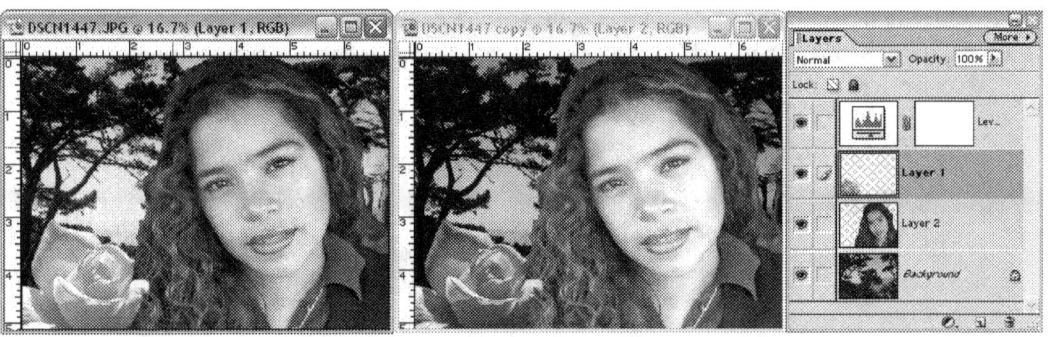

7. In the Layers Palette, click to activate the topmost layer. Click and drag the New Fill/Adjustment Layer icon at the bottom of the palette. Choose Brightness/Contrast. Note that this is not your ordinary Brightness/Contrast command that affects only one layer. True, the Brightness/Contrast dialog box has appeared (just as it did when you chose it from the Enhance menu), but something else has happened: a new layer has appeared in the Layers Palette.

8. Adjust the brightness/contrast sliders in approximately the same way as you did before. This time, the same adjustment affects all the layers equally. Notice that the layer you adjusted individually has been adjusted again by an equal amount, so now it's even darker and has even more contrasted.

Fill Layers

The layer (or any marquee selected area within it) more or less automatically fills with a solid color, a gradient, or a pattern. One of the most versatile and interesting ways to use fill layers is to place one over a stack of layers, then cycle through the Blend modes for the fill layers until you produce a useful effect. See Chapter 9 for specifics on cycling through blending modes. Like adjustment layers, blended fill layers have an equal effect on the visible portions of all underlying layers.

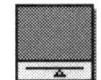 ■ **Solid Colors**   Places a layer above the active layer filled with a solid color. The Color Picker dialog box appears and allows you to pick a color for the fill. You can use this conduction with a selection to fill portions of your image, or you can tint the underlying layers by adjusting the opacity slider or choosing a Blend mode.

 ■ **Gradient Fill**   Places a layer above the active layer and brings up the Gradient Fill dialog box, which allows you to choose the style, angle, and scale of the gradient. You can also pick from a menu of preset gradients by clicking the arrow to the right of the Gradient bar. Click on the Gradient bar to display the Gradient Editor, which allows you to create a custom gradient. You can use this conduction with a selection to fill portions of your image, or you can tint the underlying layers by adjusting the opacity slider or by choosing a blending mode. For more on creating gradients, see Chapter 5.

- ■ **Pattern** Places a layer above the active layer and brings up the Pattern Fill dialog box, which allows you to choose the scale of the pattern. You can also pick from a menu of preset patterns by clicking the arrow to the right of the Pattern thumbnail. You can use this conduction with a selection to fill portions of your image, or you can tint and texturize the underlying layers by adjusting the opacity slider or by choosing a blending mode. For more on creating patterns, see Chapters 5 and 16.

Layer Masks

Traditionally, masking is technique used in painting to cover certain areas of the work with a material that resists the pigment being applied. It is often used in watercolor and airbrushing and referred to as a *frisket*. Masks allow the artist to work freely in the unmasked portions of the image without worrying about maintaining the edge or painting over other areas. The same holds true in the computer world. Masks are electronically produced, but perform the same function.

Photoshop Elements doesn't provide a universal masking tool, but it does give you some ways of working with tools that provide masking functions. Both the adjustment and fill layers come with a built-in masks that you can modify in a number of ways. The second method involves using the Group with Previous command, which we discuss in the "Working with Groups of Layers" section later in this chapter. The third method uses the transparency lock and is discussed in the "Layer Transparency" section. This section focuses on the layer masks that come with adjustment and fill layers.

In Photoshop Elements, layer masks are available for all adjustment and fill layers. As soon as you create one of these layers, a Mask thumbnail appears just to the right of the Layer thumbnail, as you can see here.

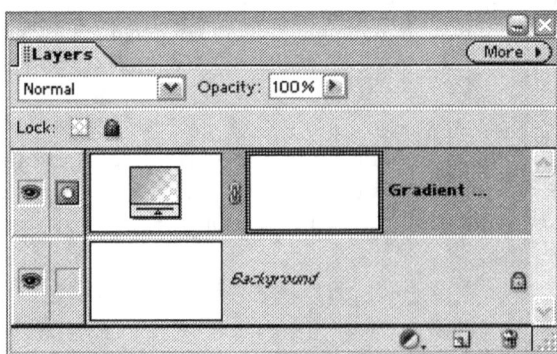

The mask thumbnail appears in its default state, which is completely white. This means that the mask is not blocking anything so that any of the adjustment or fill layer effects affect the entire layers below. The mask is a grayscale image. White is totally transparent, shades of gray represent different degrees of transparency, and black is completely opaque. This means that if the mask appeared totally black, it would block the layer effect completely.

Using Selections to Edit a Layer Mask

If an area is marquee-selected when you create a fill or adjustment layer, a black cutout in the shape of the selection appears in the Mask thumbnail. This indicates that the pattern-layer effect will be blocked in the areas of the selection so the underlying image shows through, as you can see in Figure 8-6.

This allows you to build masks using the selection tools. If you want the layer effect to appear only in the selected area, invert the selection before you create the layer.

You can also create masks with selections after the fill or adjustment layers are in place. You can create selections for each element of your composition and save them (Select | Save Selection) to use later for masks on any number of fill or adjustment layers. There is no direct way to transfer a mask from one layer to another, so saving the selections used to create them is the only practical way to do it.

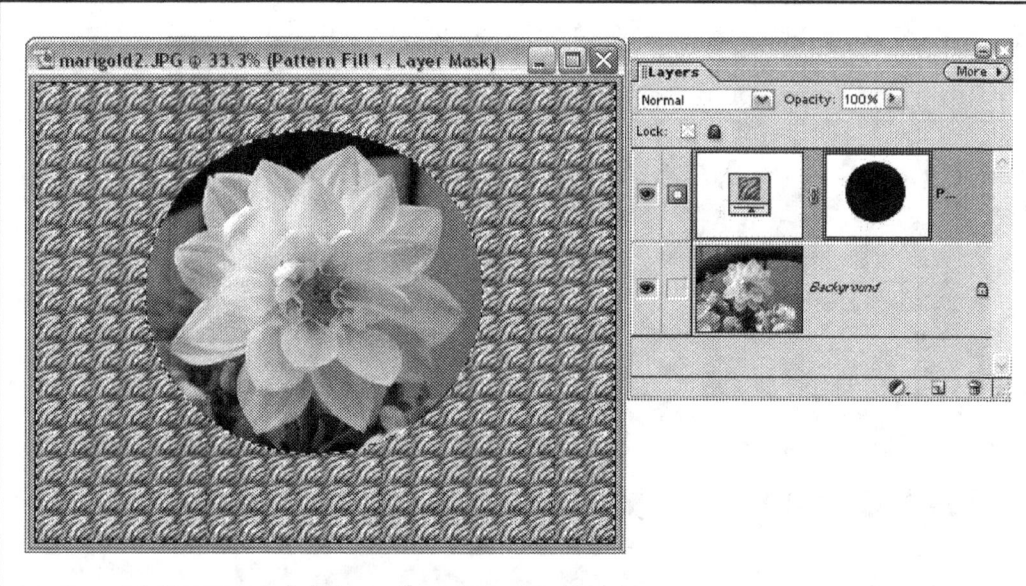

Figure 8-6.   *The round mask in the pattern fill layer blocks the pattern and creates transparency so the underlying image can show through.*

To edit a mask with a selection *before* the fill or adjustment layer is created:

1. From the layers palette, choose the layer where you want to create a new fill or adjustment layer above.
2. Create a selection in the active layer with one of the selection tools and let it remain active.
3. From the Layers Palette, choose a fill or adjustment layer to create from the pop-up menu on the lower Options bar. A new layer, and the dialog box for that layer function, appear. Set the parameters you want and click OK.
4. The Mask thumbnail for the new layer reflects the selection you created, and the layer effect is blocked in the selection area.

To edit a mask with a selection *after* the fill or adjustment layer is created:

1. From the Layers Palette, choose the fill or adjustment layer you want to edit.
2. Create a selection in the active layer with one of the selection tools.
3. If you want a smooth transition at the edge of the mask choose Select | Feather, and enter a numeric value to determine the extent of the feathering.
4. Choose black or shades of gray as foreground colors and then fill the selected area with the background color or pattern. You won't see the color in the image window, just in the Mask thumbnail on the Layers Palette. You can see the effect of the mask in the image window. You can see in the following illustration the effect of duplicating the selection and filling it with different shades of gray. Black blocks the layer effect completely in the selected area, and grays produce varying degrees of transparency.

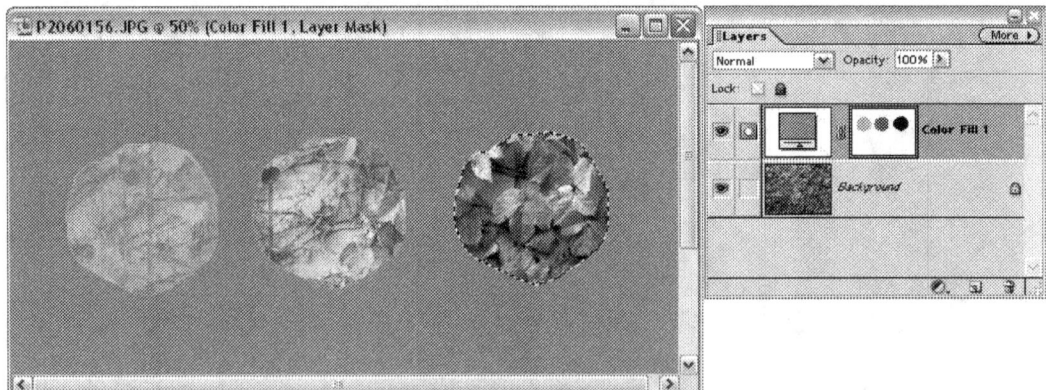

5. You can choose to fill the selection with gradients using the Gradient tool or pattern fills (Edit | Fill | Pattern), as seen in this illustration.

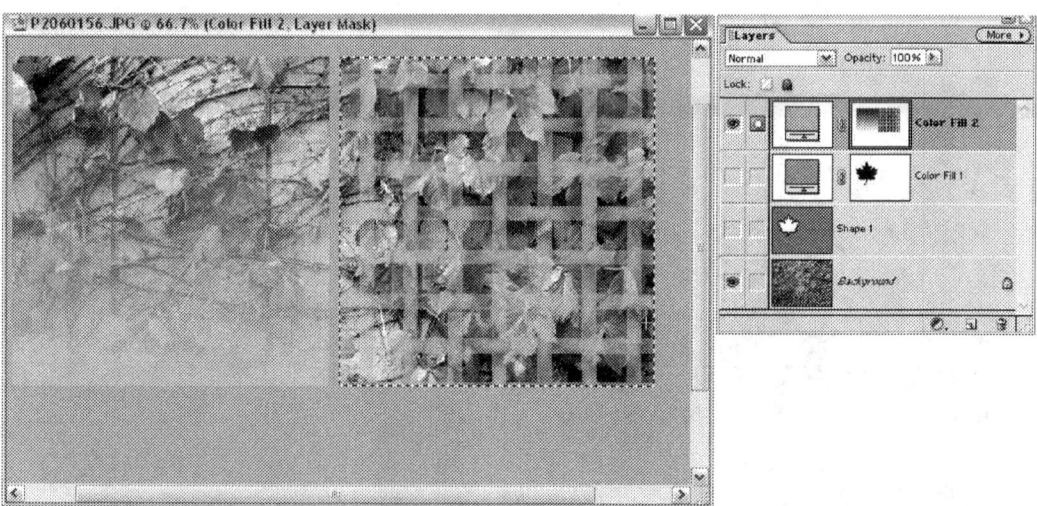

6. You can repeat the process to add or subtract from the mask areas. Filling a selected area with white erases the mask effect.

Here's how to use shapes to create masks:

1. From the Layers Palette, choose the fill or adjustment layer you want to edit.

2. Choose the Shape tool and create a shape by dragging until you have the size and proportion you want. A new shape layer is created with your shape on it.

3. In the Layers Palette, right-click on the new shape layer's thumbnail and choose Select Layer Transparency. This makes a selection out of the shape.

4. Make the fill or adjustment layer that you want to edit active. You will see the active selection you just created form the shape on the adjustment layer. Choose a foreground color of black or shades of gray to block the layer effect by varying degrees.

5. Fill the selection area with the foreground color or pattern to block the effect with in the shape. Invert the selection to have the effect show only within the shape. You can see the effect of using a shape in Figure 8-7.

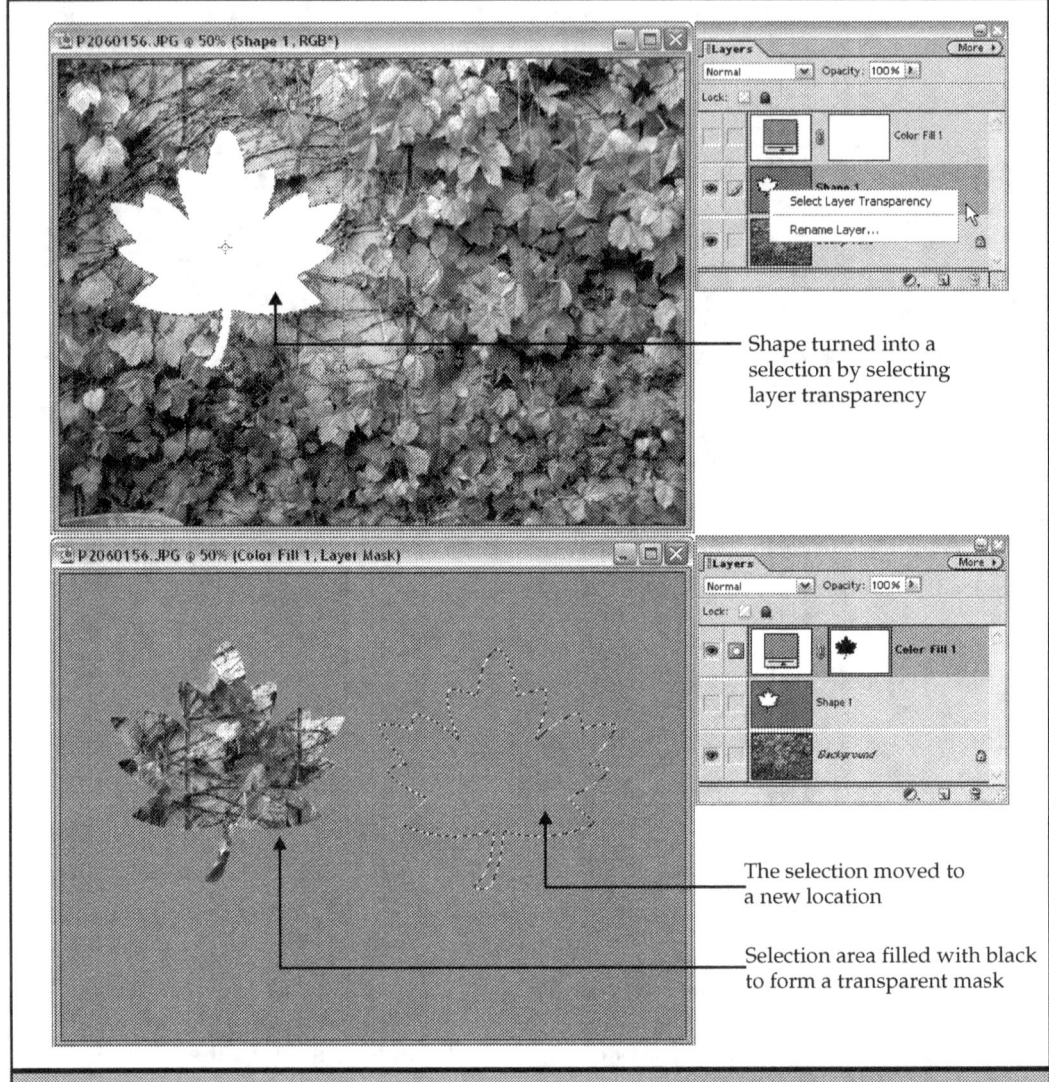

Shape turned into a selection by selecting layer transparency

The selection moved to a new location

Selection area filled with black to form a transparent mask

Figure 8-7. *Use a shape to create a selection and then use the selection to create a mask*

Painting and Filling to Edit a Layer Mask

An alternative is to paint in the mask after the fill or adjustment layer has been created. This works just as well and gives you the freedom to create complex masks from free-hand painting techniques. To edit the layer mask with painting routines as shown in the following illustration:

1. Select the fill or adjustment layer you want to build a mask in.

2. Select a Brush tool. Set your brush options from the Options bar.

3. Use a brush to paint in shades of gray or black in the main image window to designate the areas you want to mask. The mask icon on the layer name bar changes to reflect what you are painting paint. Alter the fill or adjustment layer so the effect on the lower layers is dramatic enough so that when you start painting the mask in, you can see clearly where it is masking the effect.

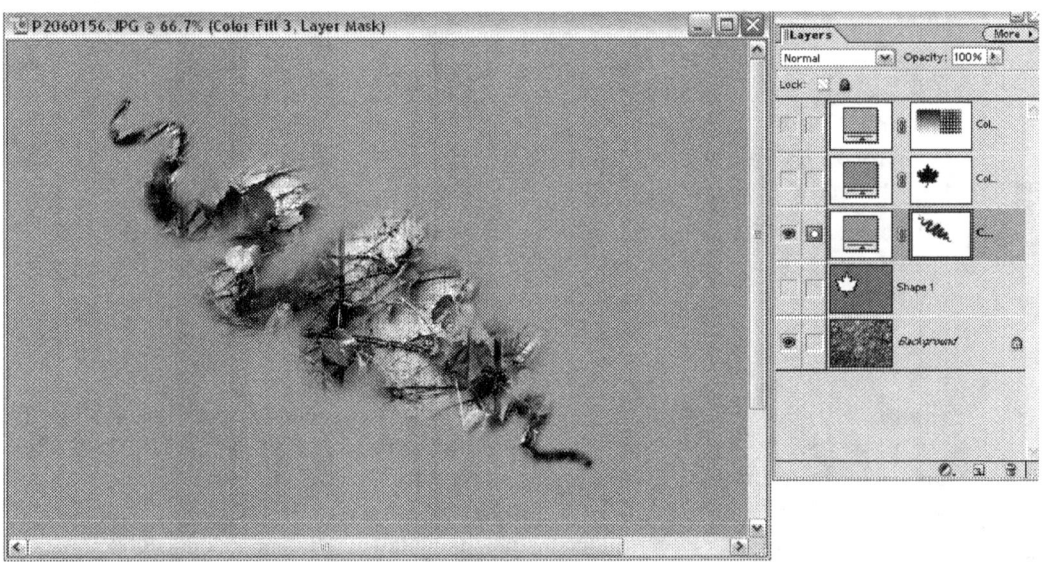

Moving Layer Masks

The beauty of layer masks is that the mask can be linked to the layers it is affecting and moves with it. This means you can then move the combined effect freely without having to painstakingly realign them after the move. This makes them great for applying effects to floating components that you might want to reposition numerous times. This is an incredible timesaver.

Here's how to use a layer mask to keep an adjustment layer aligned with a cutout object. By doing this, you can move the cutout and keep the adjustment aligned with it so that it doesn't affect underlying layers. All you have to do once you've made the layer mask is to link the cutout and adjustment layers so that when one moves or is transformed the other moves with it. You can also readjust the cutout, change the type of adjustment, and turn the adjustment off any time—as long as you keep the layers intact.

1. Open two files, preferably ones shot in different surroundings so that there is a noticeable difference in the color of the general (ambient) light. One of these

files should contain what will be your foreground subject. The other will be the background.

2. Drag the Layers Palette out of the Palette well.

3. Remove the foreground subject from its background. For the purposes of this lesson, it doesn't matter how accurately you remove the subject from its background. However you need to make sure that the background is completely erased. The easiest way to do this is to choose the Magnetic Lasso and quickly make a selection around your subject. (Making accurate selections is covered in Chapters 7 and 17.)

4. Once you've selected your subject, choose the Move tool. Place the cursor inside the selection that surrounds your subject and drag it into the second image window that holds the image you selected for the background. The subject appears on its own layer floating above the background. Position the subject so that it's in the center of the picture (don't worry, it doesn't have to stay there).

5. While the subject layer is still selected, hold the cursor over the Layer thumbnail and right-click. Choose Select Layer Transparency from the pop-up menu. All the transparent area around your image is automatically selected.

6. What you really want selected is the subject, so press CMD/CTRL+SHIFT+I to invert the selection.

7. Choose Fill/Adjustment Layer | Hue/Saturation. The Hue/Saturation dialog box appears, and a new layer with two thumbnail icons appears. The left icon is the Layer thumbnail, the right is the Layer Mask thumbnail.

Note *If you double-click the Layer thumbnail, the dialog box for that layer type appears, and you can adjust or readjust the settings for that layer type.*

8. Click the empty Status button in the subject layer's name bar. A chain-link icon appears to indicate that the currently active layer (in this instance, the adjustment layer) and the layer where the chain-link icon appears are linked.

9. Double-click the Layer thumbnail. This adjustment layer is set to adjust hue/ saturation, so the Hue/Saturation dialog box appears. Carefully drag the hue slider until the overall color tint of the subject matches the overall color tint of the background. You might also want to try the other two sliders. When you're satisfied, click OK.

10. Click the subject layer's name bar to make it the active layer.

11. Choose the Move tool and drag to position the subject as best benefits the overall composition of the image. Notice that the effect of the adjustment layer stays precisely aligned with the subject and, because it is masked, has no effect on the background. In Figure 8-8, you can see in the Layers Palette and that the image of the woman is linked to the adjustment layer above it.

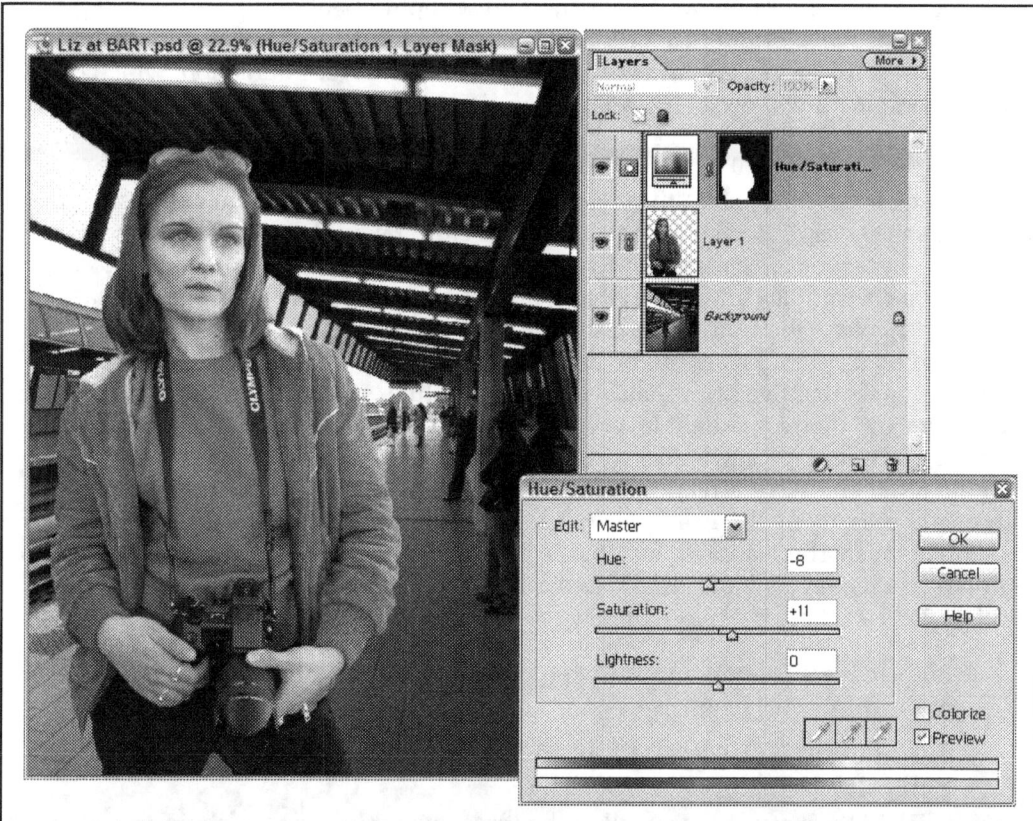

Figure 8-8.   *Finished composite made up of an image of a woman and an image of a train station*

Stacking Order and Layer Interaction

The most fundamental aspect of stacking order is to realize that the topmost layer is always in the foreground; and all successive layers are behind it, in order, until you get to the background layer, which is behind all layers. So it is important to realize as you move layers around that you are also moving them nearer (up in the stack) and farther (down in the stack).

Changing the stacking order of layers is really very easy. With the Layer palette open, just drag the layer whose position you like to change to any other position between existing layers and let go. The layer you dragged automatically inserts itself into the new position, with the exception of the background layer, which is locked in position until you convert it to a normal layer. You can also use the Layer | Arrange command to move the layer you are current on without opening the Layers Palette. This is the easy way to put one object in front of or behind another if they overlap.

The more subtle aspect of layer order has to do with layer interaction, which can be quite complex if you are using adjustment layers, fill layers, and blending modes. Adjustment and fill layers affect all the image, text, and shape layers under them. blending modes affect only the layer directly under them unless there is transparency. The blending effect then passes through to the next layer by the percent of transparency. If you hide the layer under a blending mode, the effect takes place on the next visible layer. Blending mode effects are additive, so if you have a number of blending modes in a row, you get a complex interaction that will not be the same if you change the stacking order. See Chapter 9 for more on blending modes.

Fill and adjustment layers can be built up in an additive fashion too. If you have, for instance, a total of five layers, and you place and hue/saturation layer above the first three layers and then a gradient layer above the next two, the hue/saturation affects just the lower three layers, whereas the gradient affects all five. This is a cascading effect.

If the order and the interactions of cascading effects have become too complicated, you can simplify them. For example, let's take those three layers that are affected by the adjustment layer. You want to simplify the cascade sequence but don't want to lose the ability to edit the layers individually and adjust them as a group. Here is a nice solution. This is where the hide option becomes very useful.

1. In the Layers Palette, duplicate the three layers in question and then hide each of the duplicate layers.

2. Make any layer active except the three you want to modify so you can see the status spaces in those layers clearly.

3. Click in the status space in all of the three layers to select the chain-link icon.

4. Choose Palette | Merge Linked to merge those three layers into one image layer maintaining the attributes set in the adjustment layer.

5. You can now deal with this part of the cascade as a single file, simplifying the interactions. If for any reason you need to go back and change the settings for that subset, you can unhide the original set and readjust it and repeat the merge.

Repositioning the layers is also the easy way to keep a layer from being affected by an adjustment or fill layer. Just drag the layer you don't want affected above the fill or adjustment layer. Of course, that doesn't work if changing the position of the layer suddenly covers something it wasn't covering before. One way to have your cake and eat it too is to drag the layer you don't want affected by the fill or adjustment layer, and then erase through to reveal the part it was covering.

Working with Groups of Layers

Photoshop Elements provides a number of ways to group layers. Linking makes working with them more efficient, and the Group with Previous command provides a means to easily place images inside shapes, text, and drawn shapes.

Group with Previous

The Group with Previous command is found only in the Layer menu. This command is a bit tricky to grasp at first, but once you understand how it works, it can give you some powerful masking capabilities that allows you to create some nice effects. The function of this command is to allow you to use the transparency on the base layer (the bottommost layer in the group) as a mask for the other layers in the group that reside above the base layer. You can combine a number of layers in the group to get combination effects. The following example demonstrates how to fill text with an image:

1. Create a new blank document.

2. Make a new layer.

3. Place some text on the new layer using the Type tool. Make the type large enough so you can easily see images within the text. Bolding the text also helps.

4. It doesn't matter what color the text is because the color will be replaced by images and other effects that are in the group above the type layer.

5. Open an image you want to place inside the text and copy it to a new layer by dragging it onto your image window.

6. With the new image layer active, choose Layer | Group with Previous to group the image layer to the type layer. The image layer thumbnail moves to the right, and a down arrow points to the type layer. The image shows only through the text, and the rest of the image is masked.

7. Now add a level adjustment layer above the image layer. Choose Group with Previous. The level controls were adjusted to get a good contrast range. Now this layer is also grouped with the others. You can see the final effect and the layer configuration in the next illustration.

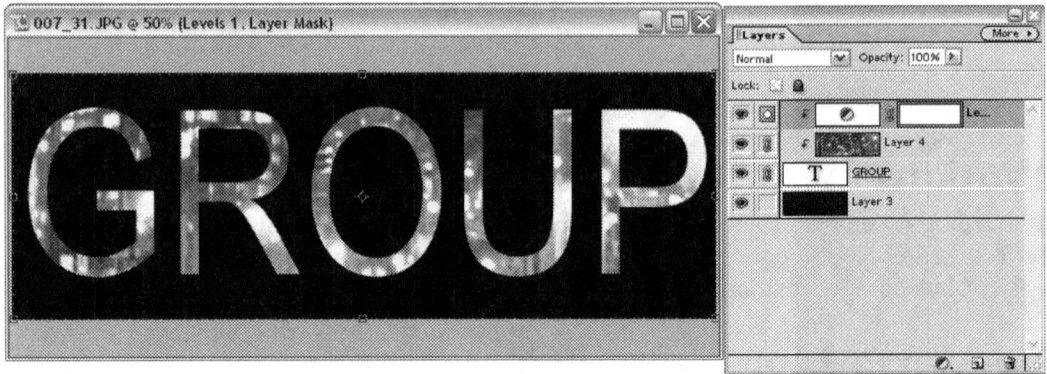

8. To ungroup any of the layers, choose Filter | Ungroup.

You use type, shapes, or any drawn image on a transparent background as a base image in a group. There are obviously many more combinations that can be created with this technique.

Linking Layers

Linking is a powerful tool that can save you vast amounts of time. What linking does is to tie selected layers together so you can perform actions on them at the same time. You can move, copy, paste, merge, and apply transformations to all linked layers at the same time. This is a tremendous help when you have many components on separate layers and need to be aligned. Moving them without a link option would be a major headache.

To link layers together:

1. In the Layers palette, click the Layer Name bar of the layer you want to activate.

2. Now click in the status box next to each layer you want linked to the active layer. The chain-link icon appears, indicating that it is linked.

3. Click in the status box once more to unlink a layer.

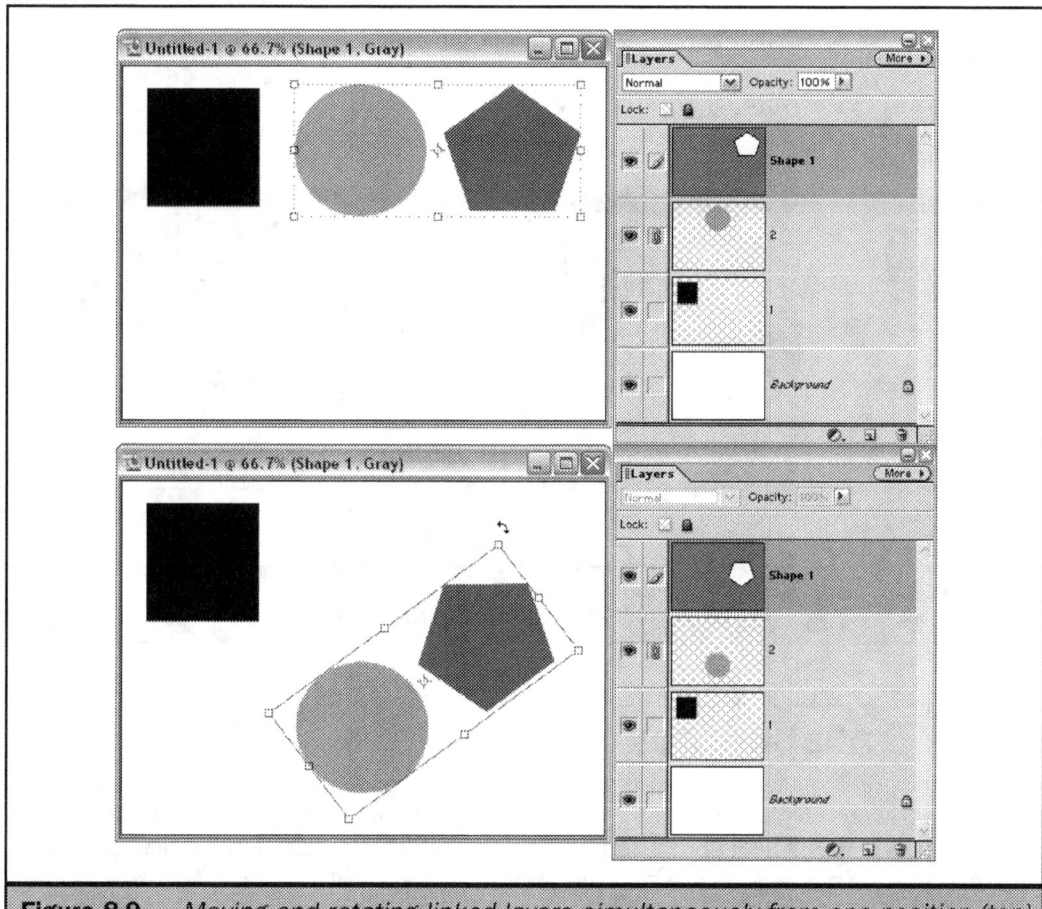

Figure 8-9. *Moving and rotating linked layers simultaneously from one position (top) to another (bottom)*

In Figure 8-9, you can see how the linked layers can be moved and rotated together. Notice that both objects move together, even though they are separate layers.

Linked layers can also moved with linked layer masks, as you can see in Figure 8-10.

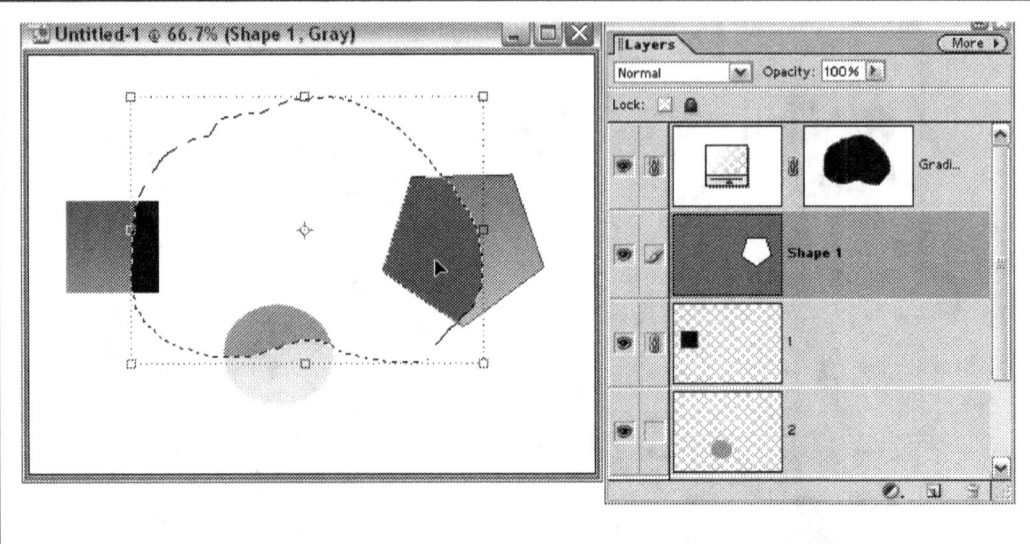

Figure 8-10.   *Here the layer mask is linked to the shape layers and moves with them.*

Layer Transparency

Layer transparency is key to working with layers. The transparent parts of the layers are what allow you to see other layers below and make it possible to assemble the modified layers into a new contiguous whole. There are essentially two basic methods for creating transparency on a layer. The first methods uses the Opacity control found on the upper Options bar of the Layers Palette. This is an overall adjustment that globally changes the transparency of a whole later at once. This means that everything on the layer changes, whether it is selected or has some degree of transparency already. So if a layer were set at 50 percent opacity, painting on it with a 100 percent opaque brush would give you brush strokes that are 50 percent transparent. If you then adjusted the layer opacity back to 100 percent you would see that the brush strokes became opaque once again. The layer opacity overrides the brush.

The second method of creating and adjusting transparency is by erasing parts of the image to reveal layers below or in the case of masks, painting in masks to block the effect of adjustment and fill layers. This can be done in stages by adjusting the opacity of the tool you are using.

Setting Opacity

The Opacity Slider provides you with a way to "fade" the effect of any layer and of any blending mode that's currently in use. One of its most popular applications for opacity is something called *onion-skinning*. Onion-skinning is an animation artist's term for using tracing paper (once called onion-skin paper, hence the name) to overlay one frame of an animation so that the artist could accurately trace the position that objects had moved in each. The very same technique can be used to trace the shapes in photos manually so that you can turn them into drawings or paintings in your own style. You can find out more about tracing in Chapter 16. In fact, if you want to get into doing your own animation, you can use this technique with Photoshop Elements to do so. That is discussed more in Chapter 18.

Setting the layer opacity to a semitransparent level gives you the ability to see underlying layers, which is a great help in positioning objects over background images and also in relationship to objects on separate layers. This is a technique used often in composites, and it is discussed in greater depth in Chapter 17.

The Opacity setting can be used a composite filter of sorts. By making successive layers partially transparent, you are allowing the detail in each to become blended. You also allow blending modes to have an effect on all the layers that are partially visible. By placing different blend modes on successive layers you can build up a complex effect. One very common and useful effect is fog.

1. Open a landscape photograph. One taken on a cloudy day with weak shadows is best.

2. Create new layer.

3. Choose the gradient tool and set the options to linear; the gradient preset color should be white to transparent.

4. While holding the SHIFT key to lock the gradient into a vertical alignment, drag the cursor from the top middle edge of the image to about 75 percent of the way down. You might want a sooner spot, depending on the nature of your image. with your image. There you go: instant fog, as you can see in this example.

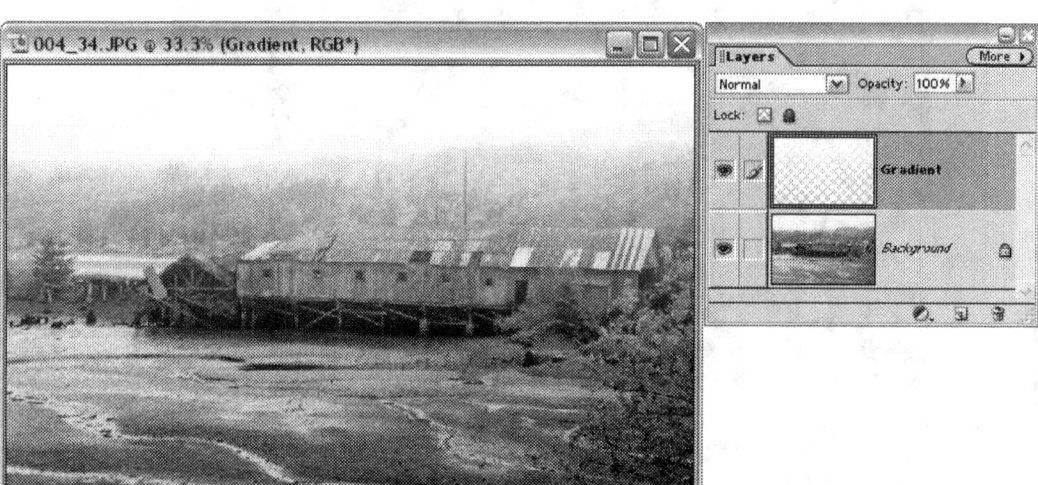

If you want to get fancy with this effect, you can separate out the foreground, middle ground and background and put them on separate layers and interleave gradients in between to get even more depth.

Erasing Portions of Layers

This is a technique that is used widely in composites. What you do is place images on separate layers and then erase portions of the layers away to let layers underneath show through. You can use partial transparency with the Eraser tool to make the effect subtler and blend the images together. You can see the effect of using this technique in Figure 8-11.

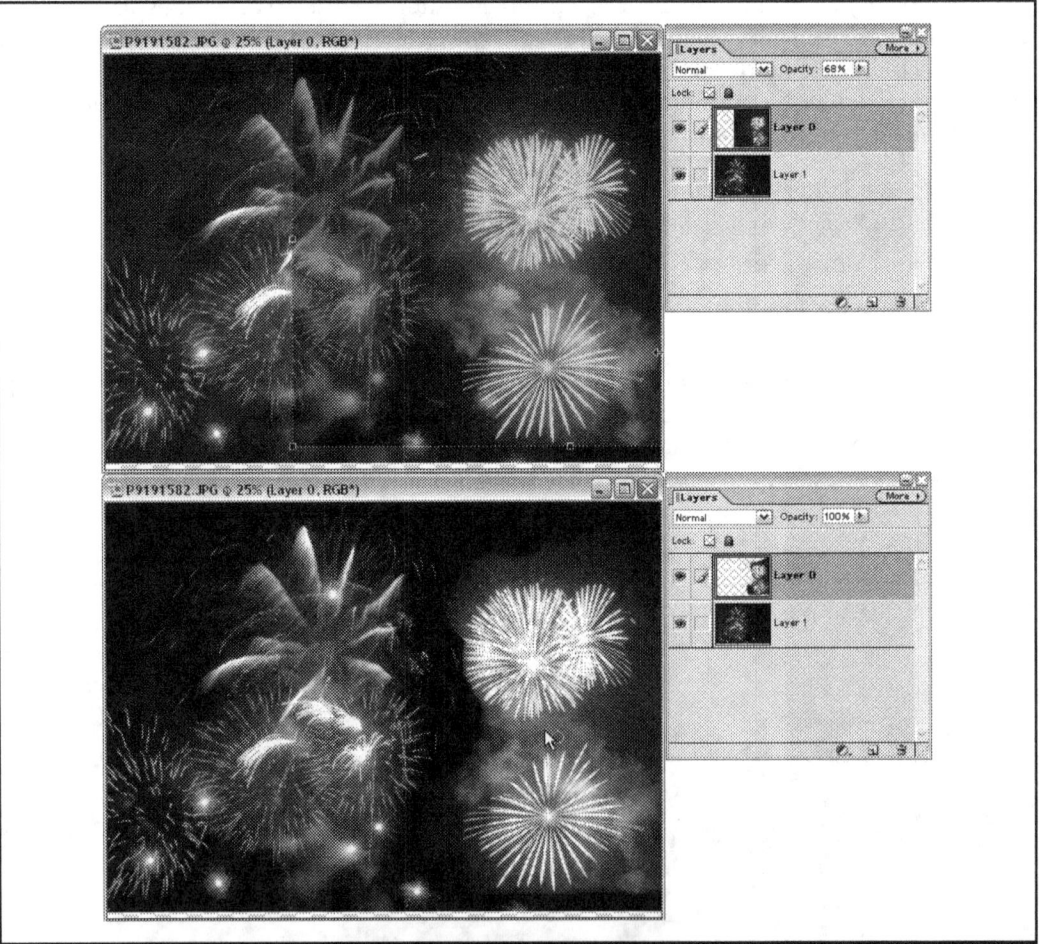

Figure 8-11.   *Moving the upper layer into position (top). After overlapping parts were erased with a soft brush, the images were then combined.*

Locking the Transparency

You can use the Lock Transparent Pixel option, found on the upper Options bar of the Layers Palette, to use the transparency in a layer as a mask. If a layer has transparent areas, you can lock those areas so any editing does not affect the current transparency. Pixels with partial transparency can be edited to the extent of their opacity. This allows you to maintain soft edges on floating while protecting the transparent areas in their original state.

To lock the transparency in a layer:

1. Make the layer you want transparency locked active.

2. Click on the Lock Transparent Pixel icon. A white lock icon appears on the name bar of the layer when the transparency has been locked.

3. Click the icon again to unlock the layer.

This is a powerful feature when you have any number of floating selections with soft blended edges that you need to modify without changing the edge characteristics..

Merging Layers

If you have a set of layers that you know you are not going to be editing anymore, it can be much more efficient to combine them into a single layer so you don't have to keep track of all the and move all the separate layers. The Merge command allows you to combine those layers and simplify the number of layers you need to manage. There are several ways that you can merge layers. Which one you choose to use is a matter of personal preference. A good habit to get into when you are getting ready to merge layers is to make a backup file before you begin, in case you make a mistake in merging or just want to go back and make some changes.

- **Merge Down**   This command allows you to merge an active layer with the layer just below it—*not* all the layers below it.

- **Merge Visible**   This command combines all the files that are not hidden into one layer. Hide all the layers you don't want included in the combined layer.

- **Merge Linked**   Linking also allows you to merge and delete the layers that are linked. This saves a lot of time in doing each one individually. Link the layers you want to merge or delete; then choose the appropriate command from the palette menu.

- **Delete Hidden**   This command is included here because it is closely related to the merge function. As you work through a project, you will find that you create layers that are temporary work layers. These tend to get hidden so they don't get in the way of the actual layers. Saving all those hidden files can take up a lot of disk space, so using the Delete Hidden files when you are ready to save your final version is a good housekeeping habit.

■ **Flatten**   This command merges all layers, no matter what their status. It does not include any attributes from hidden files. You end up with a document with a single Background layer. This erases all layer data from the file, so once you have gone past your history state limit or saved the file, the layer information will not be available when the file is reopened. It is always recommended that you save a version with layers intact.

Converting Layers

Layer types can be changed in two ways: the Simplify command and the Change Layer Content command. These commands give you the flexibility to switch gears in mid editing without deleting creating new layers. Photoshop Elements is very much about options at every level, and this is no exception.

Simplify

Type and Shape layers start out as vector objects. This means they don't exist as pixels yet, rather they are shapes defined by mathematical algorithms. The advantage of having type and shapes in this form is that they are infinitely editable and lose no quality by transforming them. In the case of type, you get the additional advantage of being able to edit the copy, change the font size and style, apply effects, and warp the text. Type is limited to just the scale, rotate, and skew transforms. To apply filter and paint effects to shapes and type, you need to convert them to pixels. This is accomplished with the use of the Simplify command, which is found on all layer menus and even the pop up menu when you right-click on the name bar. After you simplify type and shapes, they are no longer editable in the way they were. You can always make a duplicate layer and hide the Type or Shape layer so you can resurrect it if you need to.

You can also simplify fill layers in the same manner. This turns whatever level of effect you have set at the time you simplify into a fixed image layer that can no longer be changed via a dialog box. You can then affect the gradient, solid color, or pattern layer with normal image-editing tools.

Layer Content

The Change Layer Content command on the Layers menu allows you to change any adjustment layer to a fill layer and also to switch layer types within the same category to another type. This means you can change a gradient fill layer to a level adjustment layer or you can change a level adjustment layer to brightness/contrast adjustment layer. When you use this command, you are presented with a new dialog box so you can pick the settings for the type you're changing to. The effects and settings from the previous layer type are not saved. For example, you might decide that a pattern fill is more appropriate than a gradient in a certain situation or that the Levels command gives you a better adjustment than the Brightness/Contrast command. The Change Layer Content command gives you a quick way to switch gears.

Applying Filters, Effects, Styles, and Blending Modes to Layers

You can apply filters and styles to individual layers and combine them with blending modes to get some very powerful special effects. Chapter 15 gives you a more in-depth view of how to build special effects.

Working with Filters and Layers

You can duplicate a layer and then run any of the special effects filters on one of the layers. You can then use opacity, blending modes, and erasure to combine any of the effect layers with each other or with the original image.

Layers also provide a very handy way to combine two versions of the same image. For instance, fashion and glamour are a specialized area in photography that often combines two layers of the same image so that the model's skin glows and detail is softened, while the eyebrows, eyelashes, irises, and hair are sharpened. The following exercise gives you a good example of how filters can be used in combination with layers to produce a more complex combined affect.

1. Open the image you want to glamorize.

2. Make two duplicates of the background layer. The first layer will be sharpened, and the second layer will be the glow effect to give the halo look.

3. Make the third layer active and use a Diffuse Glow filter on the top layer image. Adjust the sliders until you feel the effect is appropriate for you image. You can always duplicate the background layer again and try out different Diffuse Glow settings on each duplicate. Hide the layers and then show them one at a time to see which settings work the best.

4. Hide the third (glow) layer.

5. Now make the second (sharpen) layer active and apply the Unsharp Mask sharpening filter to the image. Adjust the controls until you feel the image is sharpened enough to be noticeable but not too garish. Once again you might want to experiment.

6. Show the glow layer.

7. Lower the opacity of the glow layer so that the glow is more subtle if necessary; then use the eraser tool to erase through the glow layer to reveal the sharpened areas on the lower level. For example, in the following illustration, the eyes, eye brows, mouth, nose, some of the hands, and foreground hair details were revealed with the eraser. Each layer is shown side by side so that you can see the effect; from left to right you can see the original photo, the top (glow-blurred) layer, the bottom (sharpened) layer, and the finished portrait with the two layers combined.

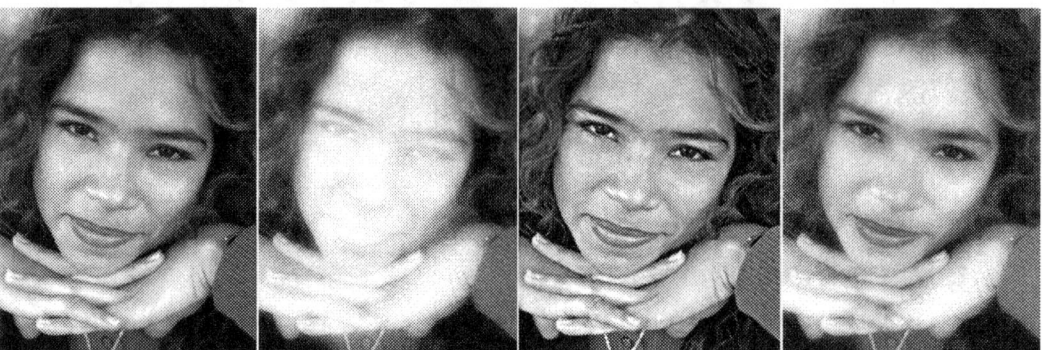

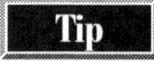

It is best to do the erasing with a pressure sensitive pen so that both the opacity and size of the eraser brush are controlled by pressure. This makes it very easy to blend the sharpened portions of the image with the glow-blurred portions of the image.

Working with Blending Modes and Layers

Blending modes are designed to make layers interact in various was by taking advantage of the differences between the layers. That is why combining the use of blending modes with filters and style changes is so effective. The blending modes are covered in full in Chapter 9.

Basically, what they do is apply mathematical formulas to the interaction of one layer with all the visible portions of any underlying layers. Here's the best way to get a feel for what blending modes do and how they react to an underlying image, and how to run a test mode to quickly walk through each of the blending modes to see how applying a mode to the current layer affects the underlying layer:

1. Open an image, preferably one full of colors and bold shapes.

2. Add a new image in a layer over the current layer. This image can be a duplicate and modified version of the background, a hand-drawn or painted image, or an entirely separate image from another document that was copied in.

3. Hold SHIFT while repeatedly pressing + to select the next blending mode in the Blend Modes menu. Keep the Layers Palette open so you can see which blending mode is active as you cycle through them. Normal mode won't have any effect; neither will Dissolve, unless you change the layer opacity by dragging the opacity slider to the left and watching what happens. When you've seen enough of the variations in grain spattering, drag the slider back to 100 percent. Continue to hold SHIFT while pressing + until you've cycled through the other 22 Blend modes.

Working with Layer Effects

Effects are preset routines that were created by the team at Adobe to provide you with an easy method for applying special effects to layers. The effects in Photoshop Elements are located in the Effects palette. Each effect is accompanied by a before and after thumbnail to show you what the nature of the modification will be before you apply it. You simply drag the name or thumbnail of the effect over the active layer and it is automatically applied. The program might prompt you for certain actions or decisions in the course of applying the effect.

First of all let us explain what an effect really is. In Photoshop, you can create a routine called an *action,* which is a series of commands, operations, and parameters that are recorded into a batch file, which you can run as single command. You can repeat the operation in the same way over and over again without having to enter each individual command. In Photoshop Elements, the effects routines are really actions that have been prebuilt for you. If you watch the status bar when you apply an effect, you can see that the program is automatically running through a series of commands and operations to build the effect. To find out much more about creating and applying special effects, see Chapter 15.

Working with Layer Styles

This section shows you how to add layer styles to you layers. This is a powerful feature that can add dramatic special effects to your images with a few clicks of the mouse. You will be using the Layer Styles palette, which you can access from the Palette well or the Window menu, to move styles to the active layer. The Layers Palette has an extensive library of built-in styles that are separated into a number of categories that are listed in the drop-down menu on the Layer Styles palette. To find out more about the Layers Style palette, see Chapter 4.

Layer styles can be applied to any image, type, or shape layer by simply dragging the style name or thumbnail from the list on the Layer Styles palette over the active layer. The style is automatically displayed (see Figure 8-12). The style automatically updates, reflecting any editing changes to the layer. An F icon appears to the right of the layer name indicating that the layer has at least one style active. One very nice feature of layer styles is the ability to apply more than one style to a layer and have the effect be cumulative. This gives you the ability to create unique combinations that increase the possibilities exponentially. You can reset the active layer and cancel all the applied styles anytime by clicking the Reset icon on the right side of the Layers Style upper Options bar.

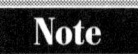

Note   *Unfortunately, when you reset the styles, there is no way to back off the styles one by one, so if you are doing multiple styles, it is good to keep track of which ones you used.*

In addition, you can edit the parameters of the styles by clicking on the F icon and bring up the Setting Styles dialog box that you can see in Figure 8-12. In this case, you can adjust the glow extent and the drop shadow distance. The appropriate sliders appear active, depending on which styles have been applied. You can also adjust the light angle, which affects the direction of the drop shadow and the reflection on the

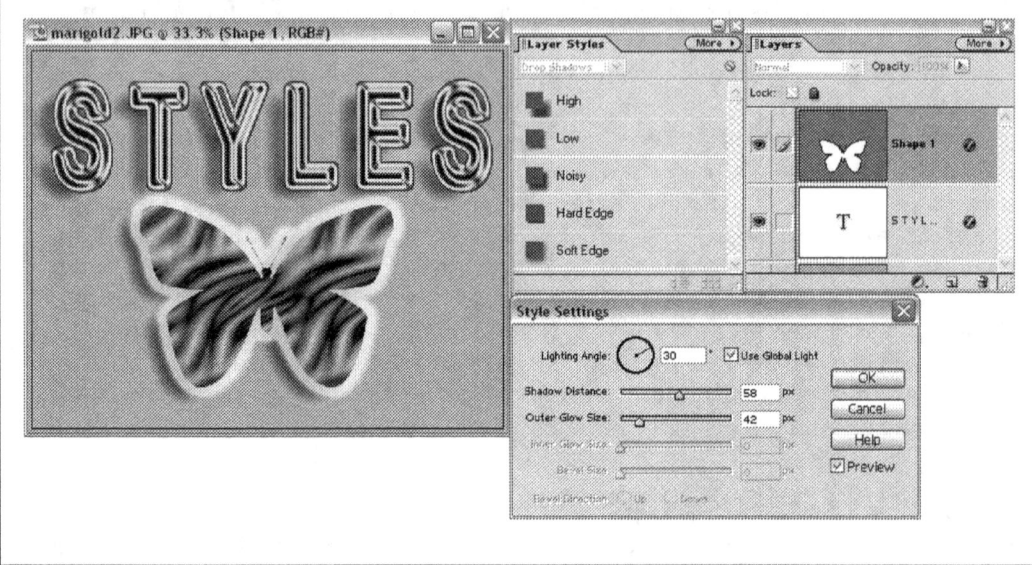

Figure 8-12. *An example of applying multiple layer styles to text and shapes on separate layers*

text. By unchecking the Use Global Light option, you can see a unique lighting angle for each layer.

Integrating Layer Methods

This next exercise demonstrates how you can combine the use of adjustment layers, blend modes, enhancements, and filtered layers to get a very artistic, stylized effect. Working with multiple methods is how most work is really produced. Photoshop Elements is a highly integrated environment and combining methods is usually the name of the game. This exercise gives you opportunity to look at a more typical workflow.

1. Open and image you want to stylize. A picture of a flower or landscape is a good subject matter for this, but anything will do, as long as it has good contrast and edge detail.

2. Duplicate the background layer and call it Base Layer.

3. Duplicate the base layer and name it Outline.

4. In the outline layer, choose Filter | Stylize | Glowing Edges. This filter does the same thing as the Find Edges filter, only it is inverted and gives you more control over the look of the edges. We deal with inversion in the next step. The image changes to a dark background with lighter edges. Adjust the slider controls until you get the detail of the outline where you want it.

5. Choose Select | Invert to make the image positive again, and you have a nicely outlined version of the base image.

6. In the outline layer, choose the Multiply Blend mode to blend the darker outlines with the base image. The lighter portions of the outline layer vanish, while the darker portions overlay the base image.

7. You can go in to the outline layer and selectively erase or enhance any of the detail.

8. Adjust the opacity of the outline layer as necessary to make the effect more subtle.

9. You can adjust the intensity of the outline by using the Levels or Contrast commands.

10. Okay, the outline layer is basically done, so we can turn our attention to the base layer. Make the base layer active and choose Layer | Artistic | Watercolor.

11. Adjust the sliders so that the effect is bold and obvious. You want to push the effect far enough so that the image no longer looks photographic. If it is a high-resolution image, you might have to run the filter a number of times to get the effect you want. When you see the look you want in the preview box, click OK to apply the filter.

12. Now you have a watercolor effect with inked outlines, and you can add the icing on the cake: With the base layer active, choose Filter | Texture | Texturizer. Select the sandstone texture from the drop-down menu.

13. Adjust the scale and relief of the texture so it is clearly evident in the image, and click OK. You can see the combined look in Figure 8-13.

14. You can now apply a hue/saturation adjustment layer above the outline layer (remember layer interaction) and boost the colors to give it a more pigmented look.

You can see from that the power of layers is being able to combine all these operations to get complex effects. The combinations are virtually endless.

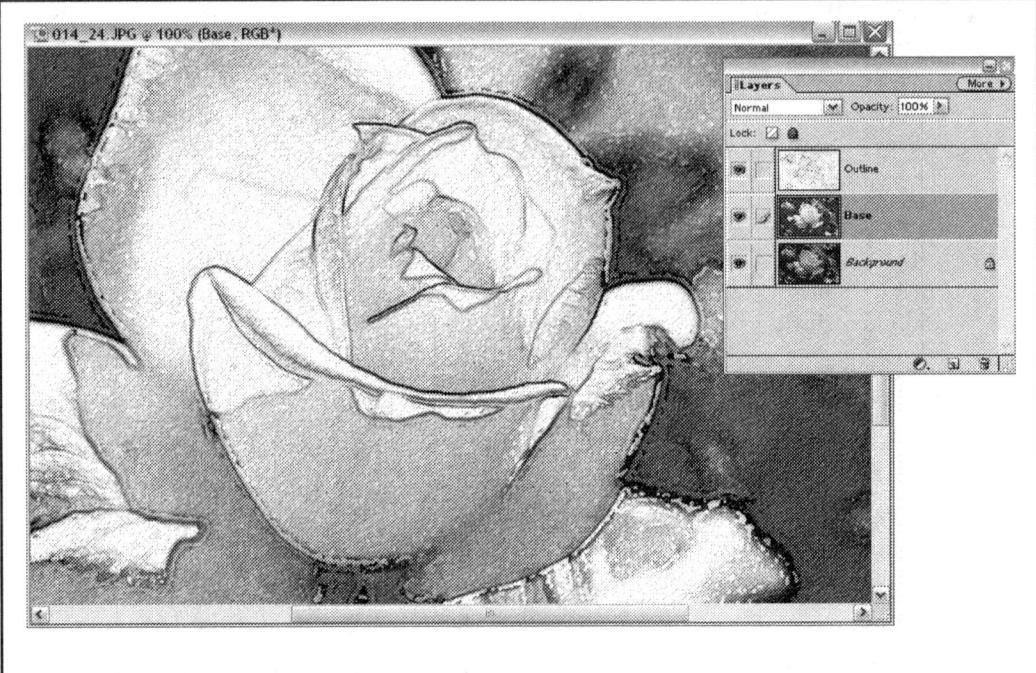

Figure 8-13. *Combine various layer types, commands, filters, and blending modes to get an artistic look.*

The
Complete
Reference

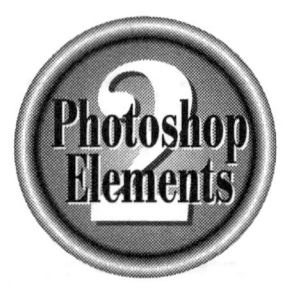

Chapter 9

Blending It All Together

This chapter is all about *blending modes*. There are 23 blending modes in Photoshop Elements, and they are exactly the same as the blending modes in Photoshop Professional. Each blending mode uses a mathematical formula to calculate an interaction with the pixels on the layer below it, which produces some sort of change in the way visible colors below the blend layer interact with the colors in the blend layer, brush, or fill. Although each of these entities has one or two blending modes that are specific to it, most of the 23 modes are held in common with all the commands, tools, and palettes where they apply.

This chapter is a virtual encyclopedia of blending modes: not only what and where they are and what they can do, but some really cool ways they can be used. The ways in which blending modes can be made to affect the image are virtually infinite. This is true partly because each image will react differently, but also because blending modes can be used in combination with one another and because the layers involved can be adjusted from complete opacity to 100-percent transparency. This transparency controls the degree to which either the base or target layer is affected by the blend.

A disadvantage to trying to describe blending modes is that their effects are about the reinterpretation of color, but this is a black-and-white book. So let's try this:

1. From Osborne's web site (www.osborne.com), load Cactus CU and Tangled Leaves.

2. Choose the Cactus CU image to make it active, and then choose Select | Select All (CMD/CTRL+A), immediately followed by Edit | Copy (CMD/CTRL+C). At this point, you have copied the cactus close-up to your operating system's clipboard.

Note *The rest of this exercise works only if you do it before you make any changes to the Layers menu. Especially, do not make a different choice in the Opacity menu. If you do, close the Layers palette and then reopen it. Also, you must drag the Layers palette out of the Palette Well.*

3. Choose the Tangled Leaves window to make it active, and press Edit | Paste (CMD/CTRL+V) to automatically place the clipboard image (the cactus) on its own layer, centered in the picture.

4. Now you can see the effect of every blend mode instantaneously by cycling through them in sequence. This is not only a great way to see what blending modes can do and what their effect is over a wide range of colors and tonalities, but it is a very efficient way to decide which blending mode will work best when you are combining two images for a special purpose or effect.

5. Choose the Move tool from the Toolbox. Do *not* use the tool, or you'll move one of the layers in relationship to the other. We chose this tool only because the

way we're going to cycle through the blends works only when the Move tool is active. Now, each time you want to change to the next blending mode, press SHIFT++ (plus). Repeatedly pressing this combination takes you through each blending mode in sequence, and then loops back to the top and starts over.

6. Once you've narrowed down your choices, it's easier to move between the last two or three blends by choosing them individually from the blending modes menu. The Layer blending modes menu is at the upper-left corner of the Layers palette. If you don't see the Layers palette on your screen or its tab in the Palette docking well, you can make it (or any palette) visible by checking its name on the Window menu.

There are far too many combinations and variations of the blending modes to cover in any book. This is part of the reason they are so useful in the creative process. This chapter is designed to give you the foundation in understanding the ways in which they work and to introduce you to some of the possibilities they offer. We encourage you to explore and experiment to discover unique ways you can use the blending modes to fulfill your individual style. If you're technically oriented and want more detail on how everything works, see the last section in this chapter for a comprehensive set of terms used with the blending modes and associated settings.

Using Blending Modes with Tools and Options

Blending modes are interesting because they are so adaptable to various aspects of digital imaging tasks. Blending modes also work with selected tools and commands differently than the way they work in layers. A blend, when applied with a tool, is tied to the foreground color or pattern, which differs from the Blend layer. This difference allows you to paint and edit your image in a completely different way. Furthermore, you can actually combine the tool and layer methods to get even more diversity.

The tools and commands that allow you to use blending modes are Fill, Stroke, PaintBucket, Gradient, PaintBrush, Pencil, Clone Stamp, and Pattern Stamp. Tools with limited blending mode attributes are Impressionist PaintBrush, Soften, Sharpen, and Smudge. All drawing and painting tools can be used on active layers that have a blending mode already applied to them.

To make a tool or command active with a blending mode:

1. Choose a paint, drawing, or editing tool from the Toolbox or Edit menu. The Options bar will appear for that particular tool.

2. Find the Mode Option menu on the Options bar, as shown next. If you are using paint or drawing tools, choose a color. If you are painting with the Pattern Stamp tool, choose a pattern.

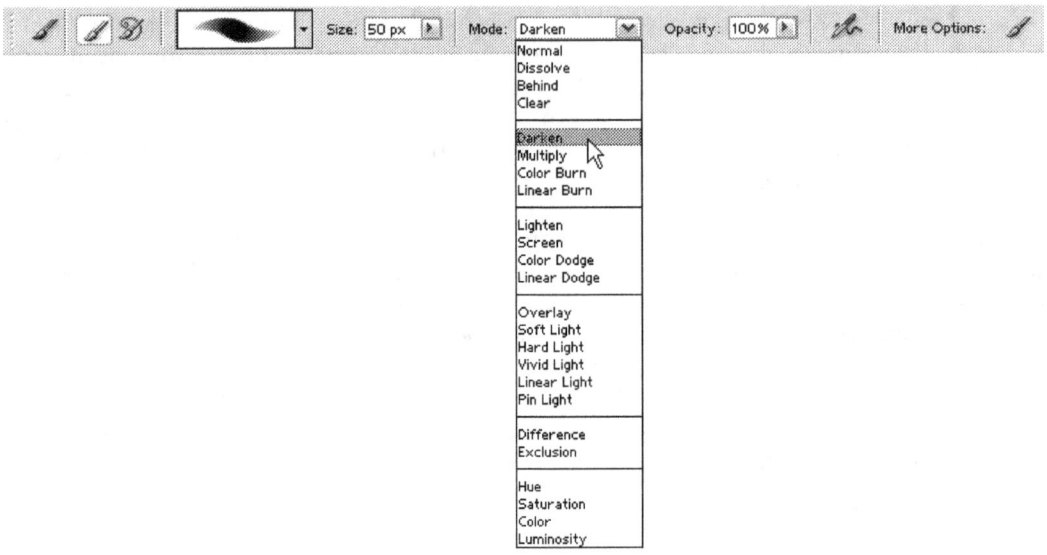

3. Adjust the opacity of the tool to change the effect with some blending modes. The tools maintain all their normal attributes when they are in blending mode.

Painting with Blending Modes

Blending modes can be used to affect the way the currently chosen foreground and background colors interact with colors that already exist in the base image when painting with any of Photoshop Elements' brushes. The Paint tools that are classified as brushes and so can be used with blending modes are PaintBrush, Airbrush, Pencil, Clone Stamp, Pattern Stamp, and Impressionist PaintBrush.

The control you get with paint tools opens up whole new vistas of capability in manipulating images. Tinting, enhancing, dodging, and burning are some of the most common tasks that blending modes can be used for, giving you a greater palette of options to draw from than the standard tools.

When painting with the blending mode options turned on, the brush uses the color or pattern of the tool as the blend source. The advantage of using a paint tool instead of the layers is that you can have all the control that paint tools afford, including brush sizes and styles, flow, opacity, and all the other options normally available to those tools. If you have a pressure-sensitive pen, you also get variations in your strokes according to how much pressure you use in making the stroke. All these features combine to put the control back in the hands of the artist at the pixel level. If you want to be able to control the creation of blending mode effects in a precise manner, then you need to try painting with them.

Another great advantage of using painting tools with blending modes is that you can confine the blend effects to marquee selection areas. This is not possible when you are working on layers alone (unless you simply erase or delete parts of the blend and base layers). Having the advantage of being able to brush into a selected area also gives you the ability to use many different blend effects in different areas of a single image (see Figure 9-1).

By using the Clone Stamp tool, you can draw from a number of images without using layers at all.

1. Open the base image (the image you want to paint other images onto).

2. Open the images you want to paint from (in this instance, these are technically *blend* images).

3. Choose the Clone Stamp tool from the Toolbox. In its Options bar, choose a blending mode from the blending modes menu.

4. Move your cursor into the base image's window and begin painting.

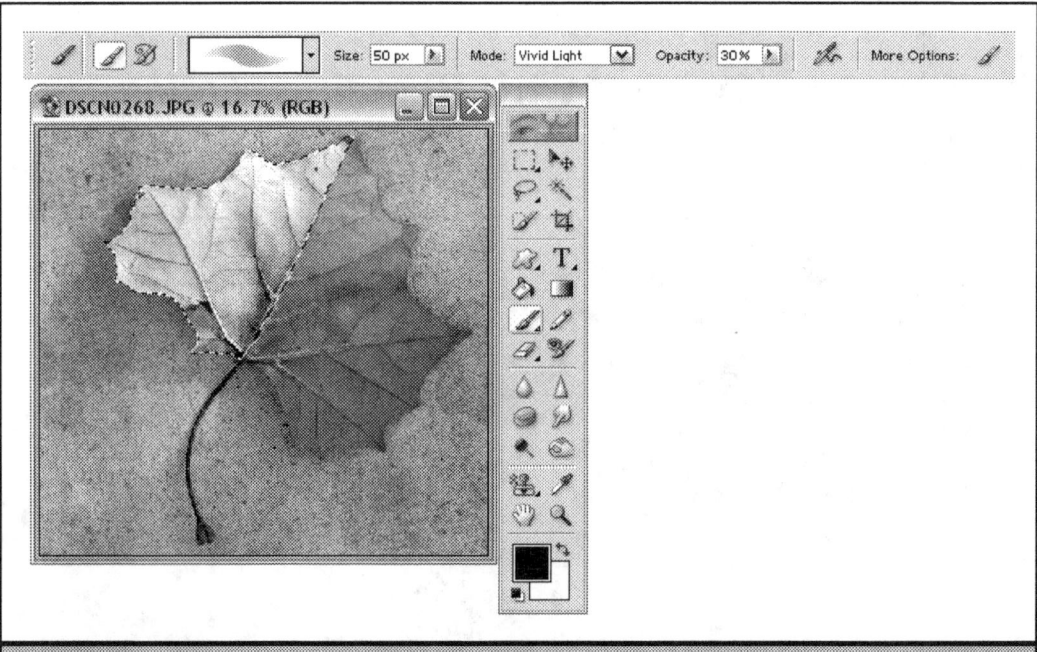

Figure 9-1.   *Using the selection marquee to control the area of blend*

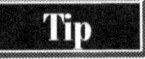

If you have a pressure-sensitive pen, make sure the Pen Pressure command is selected in the More Options section of the Options bar. This allows you to vary the effect of a blending mode with the pressure of the pen.

You can even brush in another image to part of a selected area while using a blending mode. You just have to be a little sneaky about it:

1. Open your base (target) image—the one you're going to paint into.

2. Open your blend image(s).

3. Choose the Clone Stamp tool from the Toolbox. In its Options bar, choose the size and other options you want to use for the brush characteristics. Just as when using the Clone Stamp tool normally, toggle the Aligned box according to your preferences and set the size and opacity of the brush by using the appropriate sliders.

4. In the Options bar, choose a blending mode from the Mode menu.

5. Place your cursor at the point in the base image where you want your strokes to start. While pressing OPT/ALT, click the mouse. This sets the anchor point for picking up the image to be cloned from.

6. Move your cursor into the base image and start painting. The results will look something like what you see in Figure 9-2.

Dodging and Burning with Blending Modes

Two of the most common tasks that are performed with paint tools and blending modes are dodging and burning.

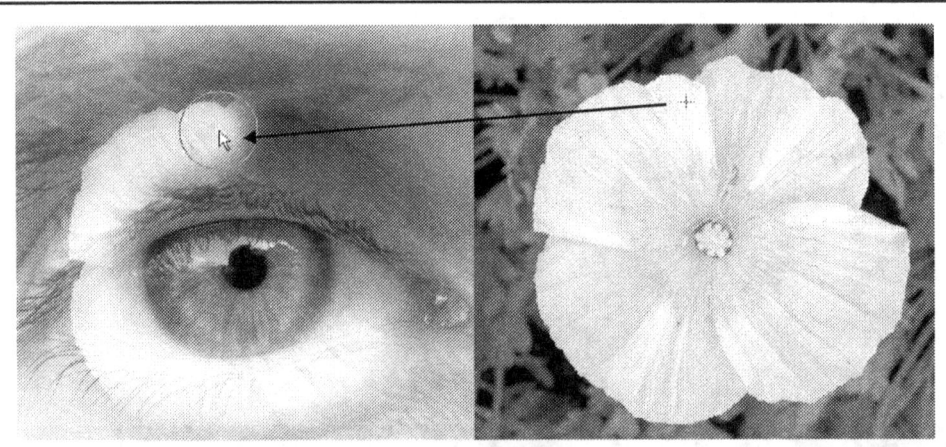

Figure 9-2. *The Clone Stamp was used in screen mode to blend the flower image into the eye.*

By using the blending modes for dodging and burning, rather than the standard Dodge and Burn Toolbox tools, you gain the following advantages:

- You can get a much different and a broader range of effects by using different blending modes that lighten or darken.

- You can get brush effects that aren't available with the conventional burn and dodge tools.

- If you do your painting on a blended layer, you can then turn that layer on and off so that you can compare your effects. If you make a major mistake, you can just paint the layer back to its original color or erase it to transparency, and start working on that specific area again without having to redo all the other little spots of burning and dodging that you've already done.

There are many blending modes that are designed to darken and lighten images with various effects.

Note   *Usually, when you're blending to burn or dodge, you will want to use neutral colors in your paintbrush. However, you can simultaneously tint and burn (or dodge) by experimenting with using colors at the same time.*

As you can see in Figure 9-3, the rocks around the stream were color-burned with a standard paintbrush using middle gray at 50-percent opacity. We used gray to avoid changing the hue while darkening the rocks. You can change the hue if you choose a saturated color, which is something that the standard Dodge and Burn tools can't do. We darkened the rocks gradually as necessary to provide more contrast for the stream.

The Color Burn blending mode maintains the tonal range so the overhanging branches are not darkened at the same rate as the rocks and grass, and the highlights and deep shadows are maintained. This saves hours of time painting around branches and crevices. The Color Burn Blend brush allowed me to darken each area or even each rock separately and adjust it visually as necessary. This is a task that would be next to impossible with layer controls alone. The final step was to lighten the stream highlights using a brush with Vivid Light blending mode.

Here is a method that you can make great use of. It almost seems magical in the way it works because it can draw detail out of shadow areas of an image that you would swear were not there to begin with. The Soft Light blending mode can burn detail into shadow areas that have fallen into near total blackness. In this situation, Soft blend can be a real image saver. For example, if you (wisely) exposed a digital image for maximum detail in the highlights, there's a pretty good chance that shadow detail would fade into blackness. To make matters worse, the areas of shade vary so much in size, shape, and edge detail that it would be near impossible to burn and dodge each by hand so that they blended smoothly with the surrounding highlight areas.

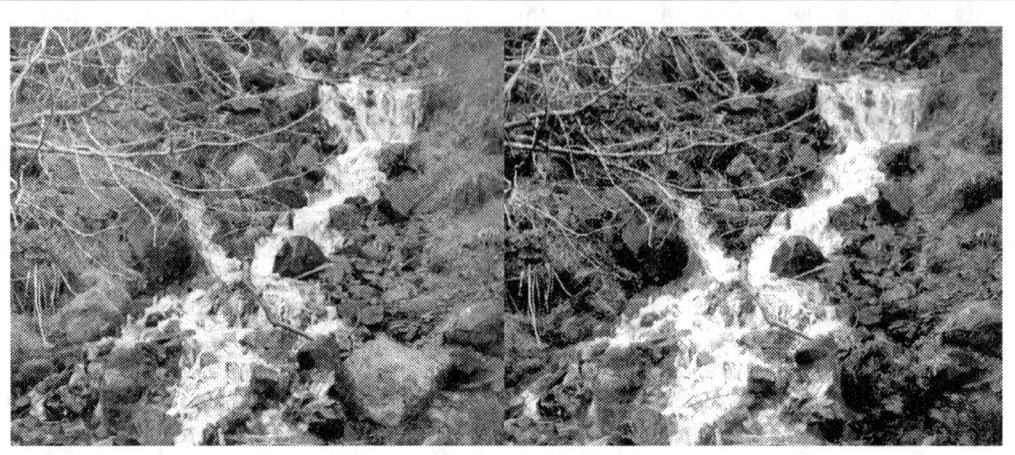

Figure 9-3.   *The before and after of a stream. The image on the right has greater contrast to the surrounding hillside.*

This method combines the use of layers and paint tools:

1. Open the base image that has dark shadows you need to correct.

2. Create a new layer and set that layer to Soft blending mode, but leave the layer opacity at 100 percent so that you can control the intensity of your effect with the fill and brush opacities.

3. Press D to restore the foreground and background colors to the default black (fg) and white (bg).

4. Choose Edit | Fill. The Fill dialog box appears. Choose Use | Background Color. Be sure to enter 20 percent in the Opacity field. We chose 20 percent because it generally lightens the shadows overall, yet leaves some latitude to "customize" specific areas with the paintbrush. The exact number you use on your own projects will depend on the requirements of your individual image and on your personal taste. As soon as the fill executes, you will notice that your overall shadows lighten significantly. The closer you get to midtones, the less the effect. Pure magic!

5. Choose the PaintBrush tool and set the opacity to 10 percent or less (adjust this up or down to your preference). Also, choose a soft-edged brush so that your strokes blend smoothly with their surroundings.

6. Next, set the foreground color to white and the background color to black. Use white to brighten areas and black to darken them. In other words, the black becomes your dodge, and the white, your burn. To switch between black and white, press X.

7. Paint to lighten or darken any areas you feel need to be "customized" beyond the overall effect of using soft blend on the white layer.

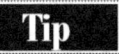 **Tip**   *While you're experimenting with this image, try switching blending modes for both the brush and the layer to the other modes that lighten the image. Lighten, Screen, and Overlay modes are also often used for certain exposure-altering effects, so they're a good place to start.*

In Figure 9-4, you can see the increase in detail in the shadows in the image on the right.

Lighting with Blending Modes

You can create some startling lighting effects with blend modes and gradients that should give you good jumping-off points to go exploring for other ways to light scenes. We need to return to the layers arena because lighting is a more global type of effect; however, do not discount the paint tools for doing subtler localized lighting effects, such as glowing fireflies or embers.

For these lighting effects, the focus is on the blending modes that use the color value of the blend image to reset the luminance levels of the base image. Figure 9-5 uses a gradient adjustment layer with a grayscale gradient from black to white as one of the blend sources. We set the gradient to an Overlay blending mode, which lights the eye with the shades of the gradient. The black branches were set to a Multiply setting to provide a silhouette for the lit background. You can affect both the luminance and the color of the light with the blending modes, giving the power of theatrical gel lighting, if you desire.

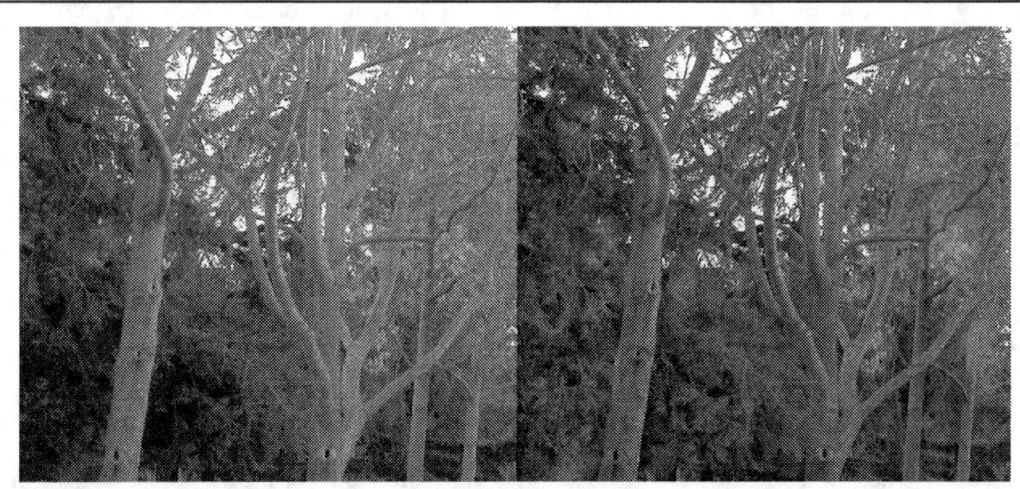

Figure 9-4.   *Bring out shadow detail, shown on the right, with Soft Light blending mode.*

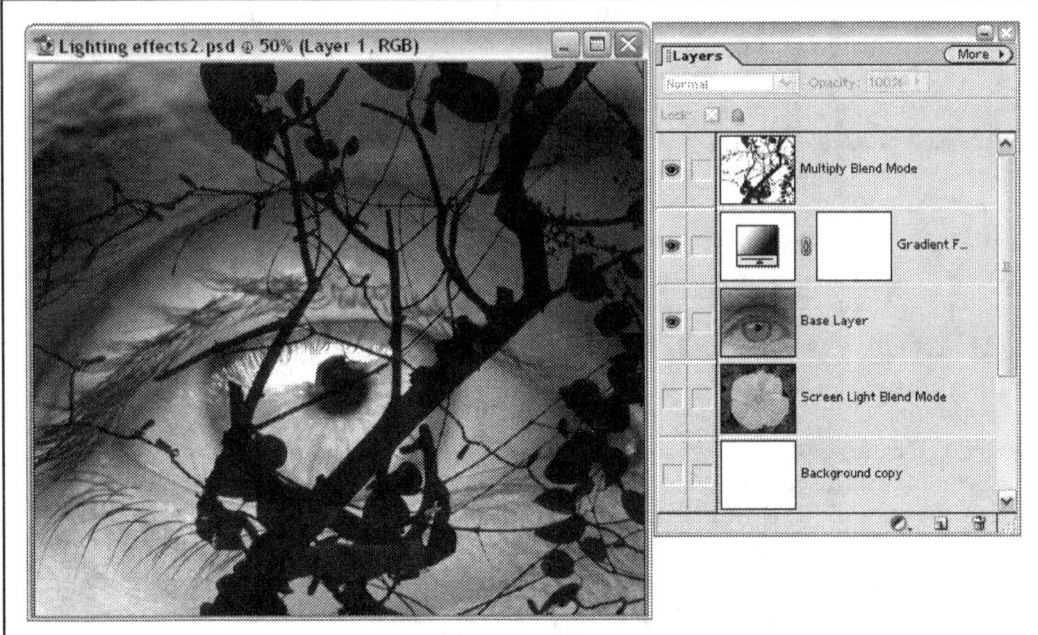

Figure 9-5. *Dramatic lighting using blending modes*

Now just for fun, let's go back to the Toolbox and add some fantasy to the image we just created. Now use the standard gradient tool set at White at one end and 100 percent Transparent at the other. Set the gradient to Radial. Create a new layer above the adjustment layer so it is not affected by the Overlay mode effect, and below the branch layer so the light still appears to come from behind the trees. Now set the new layer to Pin Light blending mode so the lights shine in high contrast over the background. We set the gradient start points on the layer at random locations and varied the distance from the start point to create varying sized lights, as you can see in Figure 9-6. You can add color to the gradients to vary the color of the lights as well.

Creating Special Effects with Blending Modes

One might argue that everything that you do in blending modes is a special effect. The question has always been, Where do regular effects end and special effects begin? There's no hard and fast rule, but we've made one for this book just to make it easier for you to categorize various techniques. "Regular" effects have a practical application because their effect seems natural and believable. "Special" effects create a science

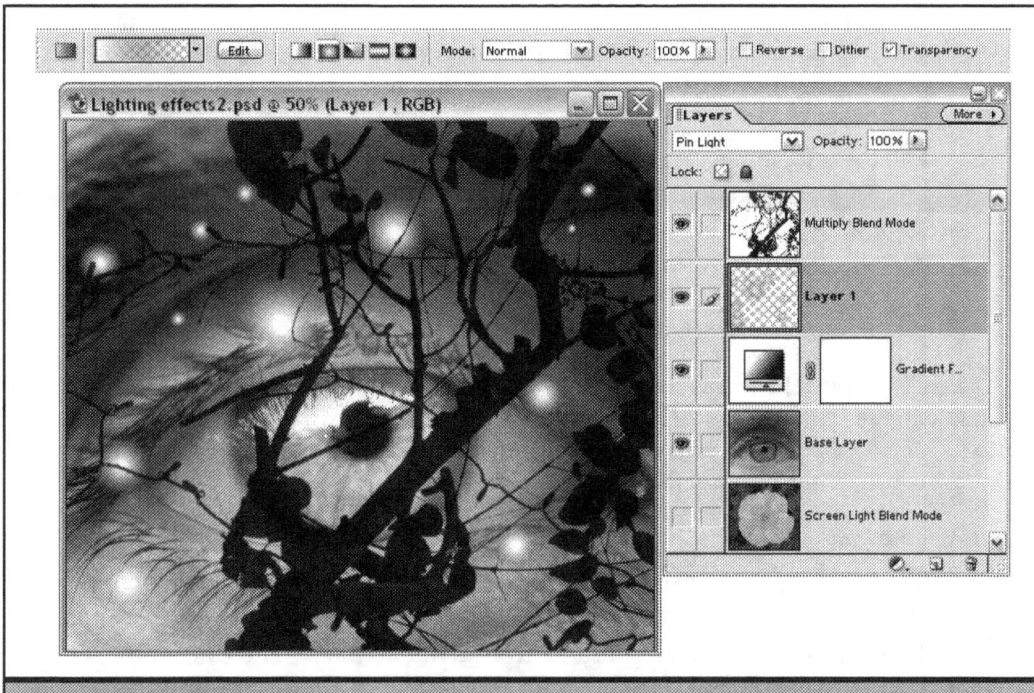

Figure 9-6.   *Add a touch of fantasy with some more blending mode magic.*

fiction, fantasy, or artistic illusion from the combined efforts of the artist and the folks at Adobe.

Going by those rules, this first effect falls into the special category. It involves a feature that photopainters often find very useful. The effect involves using the Filters and the blending modes together. Refer to Figure 9-7 to see the layers that we used to develop this effect.

1. Start by opening Rusty Compressor. You will use this image as the background layer.

2. Make a duplicate. You will turn the duplicate into a layer that looks like a pen-and-ink or charcoal sketch. Make sure the duplicate (top) layer is highlighted in the Layers palette, that is, active.

3. Choose Filters | Styles | Glowing Edges to convert the compressor image on the new layer into light outlines on a dark background.

4. Choose Modes | Difference. This will superimpose the "line drawing" over the original image.

5. Now we create a rusty metal texture with an adjustment layer and tint it rusty orange. Choose Layer | New Adjustment Layer | Hue/Saturation. In the Hue/Saturation dialog box, adjust the Hue to give the image a more yellowish, rusty look.

6. While the adjustment layer is still selected, choose Mode | Difference.

7. For the final treatment, we used a picture of a cat to add an ominous feel. He was photographed on a fairly light background, which works well to drop out the background naturally because we planned to use Multiply blend. We positioned the cat so his eyes picked up lighter portions of the background. We then added some highlights to the eyes, and the image was done.

The second special effect is an easy one, but demonstrates some of the sophistication you can achieve if you manipulate these modes properly. Let's start with a modest photo of Mono Lake in California. Don't you think it needs something surrealistic to perk it up a bit? Enter the special effects team to make it happen.

1. Create a new layer.

2. While pressing SHIFT, use the Elliptical Marquee to draw a perfect circle (see Figure 9-8).

3. Fill the circle with a radial gradient from white to black. The start point is in the upper-right part of the circle (to make it look like reflection from the light source). This will shade the circle to look like a black sphere.

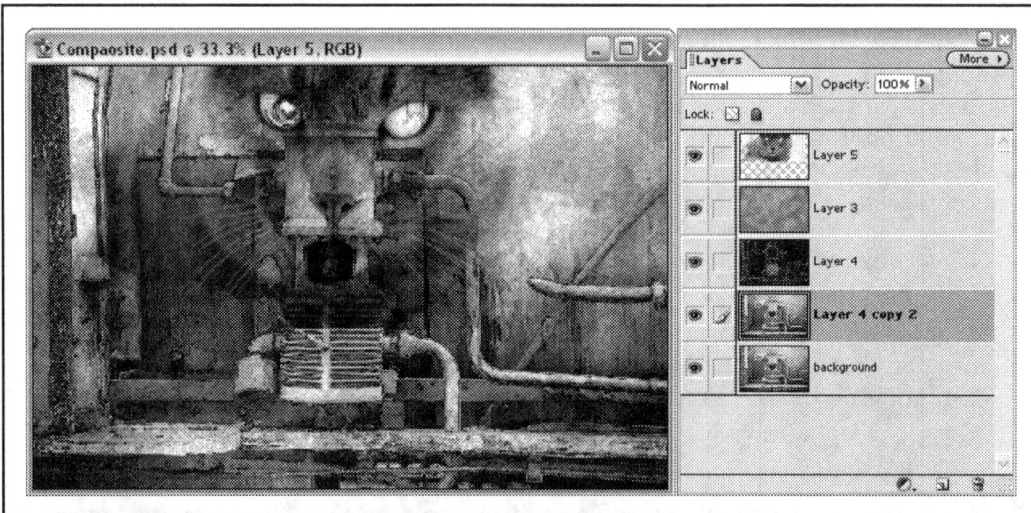

Figure 9-7. *The Cat in the Compressor special effect*

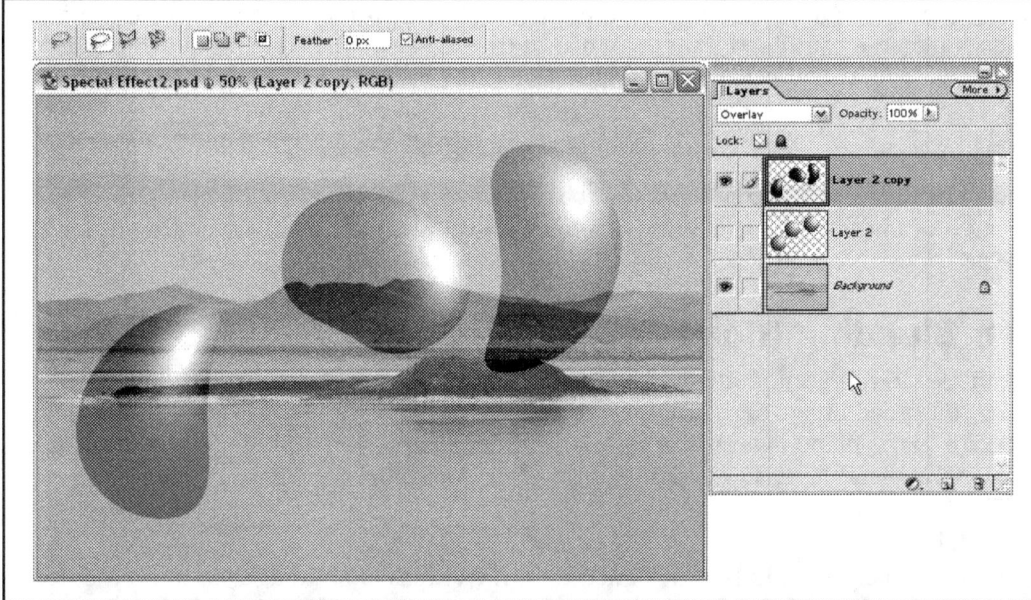

Figure 9-8.   *Aliens at Mono Lake, an easy special effect*

4. Duplicate the circle twice by holding down OPT/ALT while using the Move tool to drag it to two new positions.

5. Choose the Move tool and drag in the appropriate layers to arrange the spheres for composition.

6. Duplicate the layer you just created the spheres on and then make the original sphere layer invisible.

7. Select the visible sphere layer and set the blending mode to Overlay. You now see the spheres magically turn to glass. Nifty trick, isn't it?

8. Choose Filters | Distort | Twirl to bend the spheres into unusual shapes. This is glass-blowing without the heat. You can also use the Liquify filter to distort the shapes.

The Blending Modes

In this section, we will go through each one of the 17 blending modes, and give you an understanding of how they function, and provide you with some insights into how they are used. We have separated the modes into categories that speak generally to their function, and have included an illustration of the combined effect based on the photographs in Figure 9-9 (or later, in Figure 9-10) so you can see how the blending modes affect the combined images. Much of the power in blending modes depends on the way you can affect color as well.

Normal

This is the default blending mode that basically just duplicates the pixels of the Blend layer. You can think of it as having no effect. If you want to cancel a blending mode for a layer, choose Normal.

Darken Blending Modes

The modes in this section are all designed to have an effect that darkens all or portions of the combined image depending on the values of the blend image or color. Wherever the color in the Blend layer is darker than the color in the base image, you will see the color in the Blend layer. Otherwise, you will see the color in the base layer.

Darken

The Darken blending mode is designed to darken areas of an image based on the comparison of the lightness or darkness of the colors in the blend image or tool and base image. If the relative colors in the blend image are lighter than the base image, the blend colors are replaced with the base colors. If the colors in the blend image are darker than the base image, the color in the blend image is left unchanged. This allows you to superimpose darker images into lighter portions of the base image.

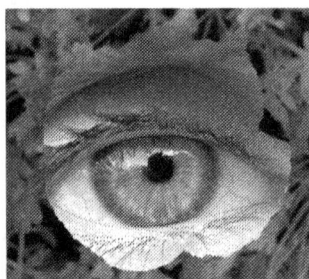

Multiply

The Multiply blending mode darkens all colors in the base image by multiplying the color values of the blend image and base image together to come up with a new color value. Unless the blend image color is pure white, the multiplied value of the two colors will be darker than the original base image. The effect is that lighter colors in the blend image have less darkening effect on the base image, and darker colors have a greater darkening effect. Black produces black, and white has no effect at all. This mode is very powerful for superimposing outlined images that have a large area of very light colors in contrast to areas of dark outlines. It is also very useful in painting. By setting the opacity of a brush or pencil lower, you can darken and colorize areas of an image with

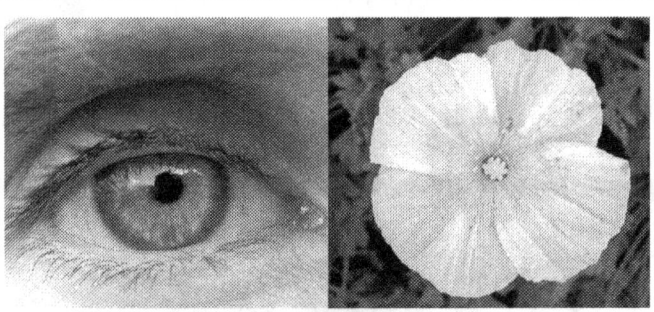

Figure 9-9. *The first set of images that we will be combining to illustrate Blending modes. The image of the eye (left) is the base layer, and the image of the flower (right) is the blend layer.*

successive passes based on the hue and luminance of the foreground color. Each pass over the same area darkens it successively by an equal amount, depending on the darkness of the foreground color. It is referred to as a *buildup* method.

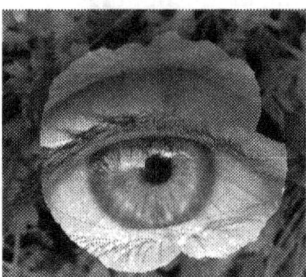

Color Burn

The Color Burn blending mode darkens the base image by increasing the contrast calculated by the color value of the blend image colors. This has a similar effect to multiply with a higher degree of contrast in the result. White in the blend image leaves the base image colors unchanged.

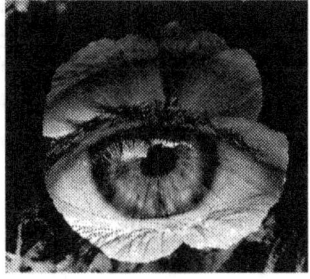

Linear Burn

The Linear Burn blending mode darkens the base image color by decreasing the brightness based on the color value in the blend image. This has is a similar effect to multiply but produces a slightly darker effect overall. White in the blend image leaves the base pixels unchanged.

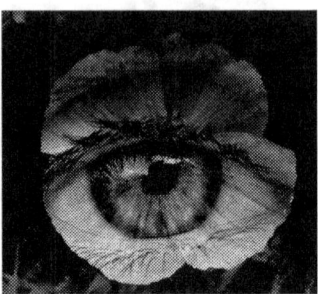

Lighten Blending Modes

The modes in this section are all designed to have an effect that lightens all or portions of the combined image, depending on the lightness of the blend image. In other words, portions of the blend image that are lighter than immediately underlying portions of the target layer will be lighter than the base (underlying) layer.

Lighten

The Lighten blending mode is designed to lighten areas of an image based on the comparison of lightness or darkness of the blend and base images. If the blend image colors are darker than the base colors, the blend colors are replaced with the base image colors. If the blend image colors are lighter than the base colors, the blend color is left unchanged. This allows you to superimpose lighter images into darker portions.

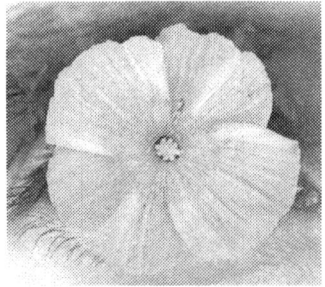

Screen

The Screen blending mode lightens only colors in the base image by multiplying the inverse color values of the blend and base image colors together to come up with a new base image color value. Unless the blend color is pure black, the mixture of the two colors will be lighter than the original base-image color. The effect is that darker colors in the blend image have lesser darkening effect on the base image and lighter colors have a greater lightening effect. White produces white, and black has no effect at all. It is also very useful in painting. By setting the opacity of a brush or pencil lower, you can lighten and colorize areas of an image with successive passes based on the foreground color. Each pass over the same area lightens it successively by an equal amount. It is referred to as a *liftup* method.

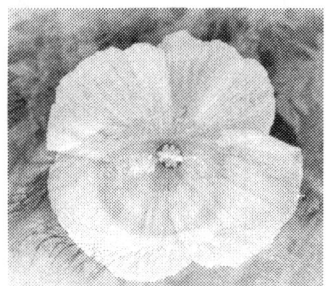

Color Dodge

Color Dodge blending mode lightens the base image by decreasing the contrast based on the color values of the blend image. The effect softens the color as it darkens. This works in a similar way as the Dodge tool but has the added feature of including color in the process. This allows you to dodge and tint at the same time. If you want to just darken without altering color hue, then make sure the brush or blend image is in grays only.

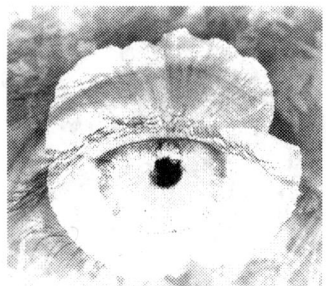

Linear Dodge

The Linear Dodge blending mode lightens the base image by raising the brightness of the colors based on the color value of the blend image. This has the effect of enriching the color as it darkens and also allows you to tint as you darken. If you want to just darken without altering color hue, then make sure the brush or blend image is in grays only.

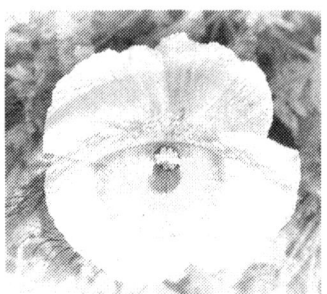

Lighting Effects Blending Modes

This next set of blending modes has the effect of exposing the image to different types and intensity of lighting. We have used a different set of reference images to illustrate these effects more clearly (see Figure 9-10). The Blend layer in this set is a grayscale gradient. Gradients can be used with blending modes to create many interesting lighting effects.

Overlay

The Overlay blending mode is designed to mix two images while preserving the highlights and shadows of the base image. The base image integrates the color patterns of the blend image by using either a multiply or screen blend method, depending on whether the base image color is darker or lighter than the blend image color, respectively. The effect of Overlay blending mode is decreased in the midrange colors of the blend mode image. This mode is ideal for doing tinting because it maintains the tonal range.

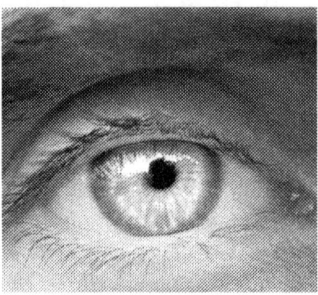

Soft Light

This has the effect of shining a diffused light on the image. The image is either lightened or darkened based on the color value of the blend image. The Soft Light blending mode

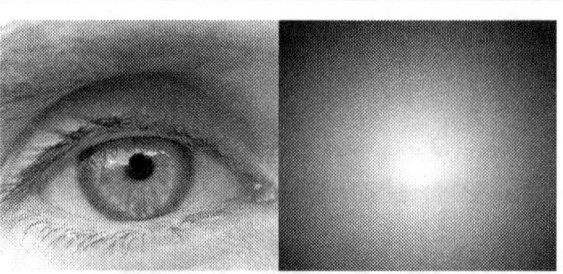

Figure 9-10.   *The image of the eye (left) is the base layer, and the gradient (right) is the blend layer.*

burns in the base image color if the blend image is lighter than 50 percent luminance (middle gray), and dodges the base image if the color in the blend image is darker than 50 percent luminance. This mode is very useful for bringing out detail in dark shadows. You can also use gradients to get soft lighting effects.

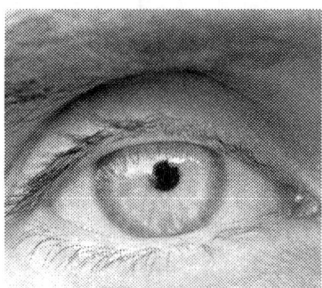

Hard Light

Hard Light mode has a harsher lighting effect than Soft Light mode. It lightens or darkens the base image by multiplying or screening the base-image colors based on the blend-image values. Hard Light mode gives the image a more contrasty appearance and is useful for putting in highlights and shadows.

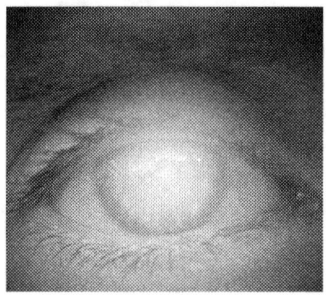

Vivid Light

Vivid Light mode darkens or lightens the base image according to the blend image color values. Vivid Light mode adjusts the contrast to accomplish this. If the blend image color is lighter than 50 percent luminance, it lowers the contrast to lighten the base image; and if the blend image color is darker that 50 percent luminance, it raises the contrast to darken the base image. The look is what the name implies.

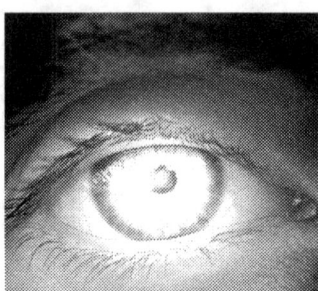

Linear Light

Linear Light mode darkens or lightens the base image according to the blend image color values. Vivid Light mode adjusts the brightness to accomplish this. If the blend image color is lighter than 50 percent luminance, it lowers the contrast to lighten the base image; and if the blend image color is darker that 50 percent luminance, it raises the contrast to darken the base image.

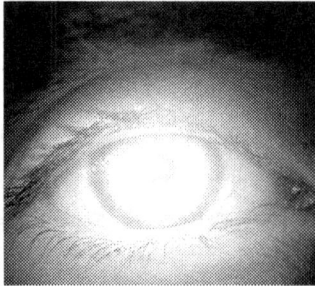

Pin Light

Pin Light uses a method of replacing pixels based on the color value of the blend image. If the color values of the blend image pixels are above 50 percent luminance, then pixels in the base image are replaced with pixels from the blend image if the base image pixels are darker. If the color values of the blend image are below 50 percent luminance, then pixels in the base image are replaced with pixels from the blend image if the base image pixels are lighter. This can produce rather dramatic results.

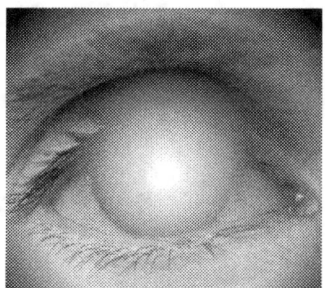

Special Effect Blending Modes

The following blending modes create effects that are so bizarre we don't know how to classify them other than as "special" effects. Try them, and you'll see what we mean.

Dissolve

With Dissolve, each pixel is randomly replaced with either the blend image or the base image, depending on the opacity of the Blend layer. This produces a dithered look. Adjust the opacity of the Blend layer to vary the effect. If the opacity is 100 percent, there is no effect at all.

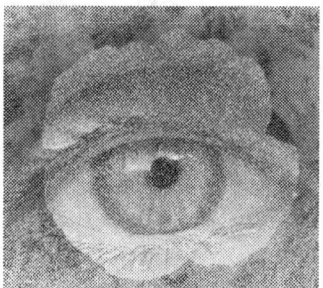

Difference

The Difference blending mode it probably the most visually pronounced of the blending modes. It accomplishes its power effects by analyzing the colors in each color channel in both the blend image and the base image, subtracting either the base value from the blend value, or vice versa, depending on which value is greater. Lesser value is always subtracted from the greater value, which dictates that blending with white inverts the color values, and black has no effect.

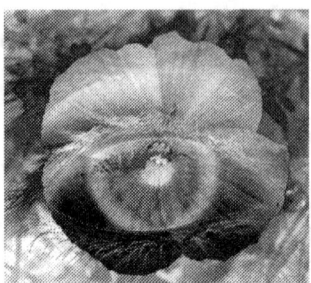

Exclusion

The Exclusion blending mode works in a similar manner to Difference blending mode but has a lower contrast and tends to look more grayed out. Blending with white inverts the color values, and black has no effect.

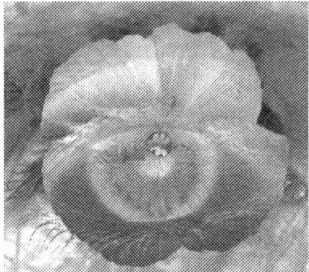

Behind

This blending mode is not on the Layers Blend Mode menu. It's available only through some of the tools. You can paint into transparent areas of a layer as long as the Lock Transparent is deselected. This allows you to simulate the effect of painting on the back of a transparent plastic cell, thus the name Behind. It works with partially semitransparent areas as well. It is an easy way to paint into transparent areas without having to select them with a marquee.

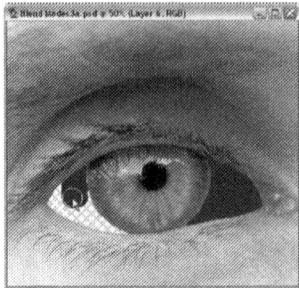

Clear

The Clear blending mode operates in the inverse of Behind mode and very much like the Eraser tool. The Lock Transparency must be deselected in the layer you are working in. Clear blending mode makes the pixels that you paint over transparent, based on the opacity setting on the Options bar. The tools that make use of Clear mode are the Brush, Pencil, Paint Bucket, Line, Fill command, and Stroke command.

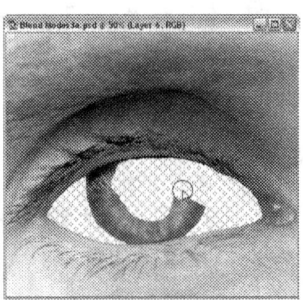

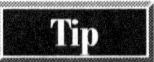
The Clear and Behind modes are very useful in doing composites by allowing you to paint or clone-stamp parts of other images into carefully delineated areas.

Color Blending Modes

These modes are designed to alter the appearance of the color based on the HSL color model, which stands for Hue, Saturation, and Lightness or Luminance. All these blending modes manipulate one or more aspect of this color model to vary the appearance of the color in the image.

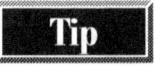
A good way to understand this color model is to go to the Color Picker and select the H, S, or B color modes, and then observe how the color orientation in the Picker changes.

Hue

The Hue blending mode is used to change the colors in the base image without changing the luminance or saturation, so the base image detail is preserved while it takes on the colors of the blend image.

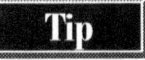
This is good for tinting images and creating washed color effects with gradients and airbrush. This mode works well when you use soft blended colors as the blend source.

Saturation

The Saturation blending mode adjusts the color saturation of the base image according to the saturation values in the blend image. The luminance and the hue of the base image remain constant. This intensifies the colors of the base image. Painting with the Saturation blending mode in areas of the base image that are purely gray (no saturation) has no effect. Painting in Saturation blending mode with a brush that is gray unsaturates the base image by a percentage based on the opacity of the brush or the number of passes over the same pixels.

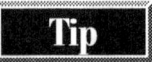

The Saturation blending mode, when used in conjunction with a grayscale image or grayscale paint color, can be used to tone down the color in an image or take it completely to black and white. The opacity option can adjust the degree of the effect.

Color

The Color blending mode changes the hue and saturation of the base image based on the color values of the blend image. Saturation blending mode does not change the luminance of the base image. You can make the effect subtler by adjusting the opacity of the Blend layer or tool.

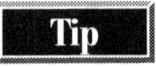

This is a useful mode for color-tinting black-and-white photographs or retouching color photos.

Luminosity

The Luminance blending mode preserves the color and saturation while altering the base image according to the luminance values of the blend image or color. This is useful for superimposing colors onto grayscale drawings, photos, or patterns.

Using Blending Modes with Layers

Now that you understand what the blending modes are, we can go into more detail on how to use them. The first area to look at is using blending modes with layers. This allows you to have the attributes from one or more layers affect the look of a base layer by choosing various blending mode effects. You can do this by orienting separate images on adjacent layers and activating the blending modes on a layer to affect the layer below.

Setting Up Blend Mode Layers

Remember that blending modes use the difference between images to get their effects, so the more dramatic the differences, the greater the effect. If you use a duplicate of an image, you won't get any effect unless you alter it in some way first. You cannot use blending modes to affect the background layer (the bottommost layer) directly.

Most of the time, you will be combining images from separate files, so you can just open the files that you want to use and drag them to the image file you want to use as the base image (the image that receives the effect of the blending mode). If you want the entire base image blended, the sizes of the blend image and the base image need to be the same. Blending modes do not permanently change the image. You can go back and change the blending mode setting at any time. The result does not become fixed in stone until you combine or flatten the layers, or save the image to a nonlayered format.

To set up a Blend layer, follow these steps:

1. Copy or create images on separate adjacent layers.

2. Choose the layer you want to be the Blend layer and place it directly above your base image. Make sure that the layers you are acting on are visible.

3. With the Blend layer active, choose the blending mode from the Mode menu at the top of the Layers palette, just below the Layers tab. You can see it in the next illustration. The default blending mode is Normal. You will immediately see the effect of the mode you chose in the image window. Remember that each Blend layer operates on the layer directly below, so make sure you have the layer you want affected positioned correctly.

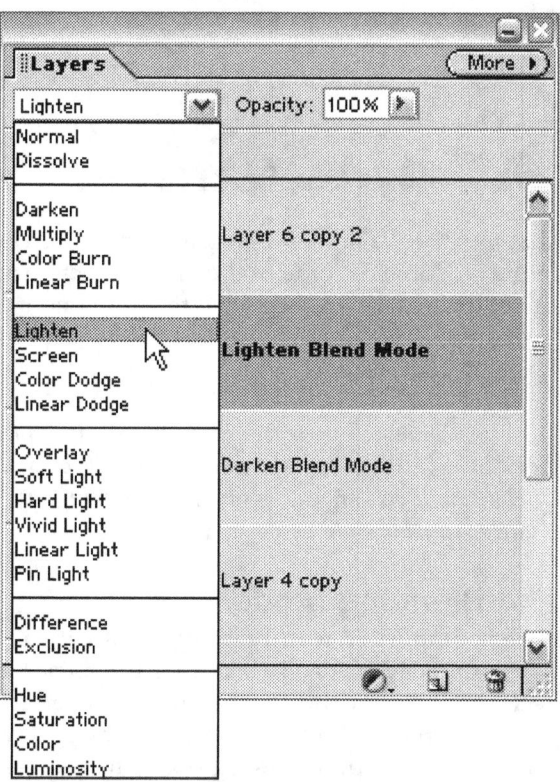

Cascading Layers with Blending Modes

You can choose only one blending mode per layer. You can get around that by cascading a number of layers with separate blending modes on each layer. The blending modes are additive through multiple layers and cascade from one to another until you reach the base image. As you can see in Figure 9-11, we are using a number of layers above the base layer of the eye to generate the image. You can also apply blending modes to adjustment layers, which is a very powerful feature for special effects. The combinations are really endless.

Layer Orientation and Blending Modes

First of all, the layer you're changing needs to be just below the layer or layers with the blending mode, or it won't be affected. You can see the proper orientation in the illustration here, where the flower is being used to blend the eye.

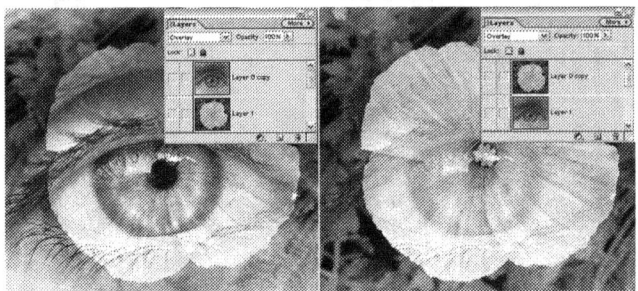

The exception to that are interim layers with transparencies. The orientation of the layers can also change the outcome of some of the blend effects. You can experiment with changing the order of the images and see what the differences are. (See Figure 9-12.) You can also merge layers that have blending modes, but be careful of the method you use because the results are not consistent.

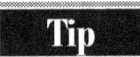

If you Merge Down, the combined layer will have the blending mode of the layer that was above. If you use Merge Visible for the same layers, the combined layer will have a blending mode of Normal. If you are cascading your blending modes, the Merge Visible will cut off the additive cascade affect.

Layer Opacity and Blending Modes

The opacity factor can be an important feature in controlling the intensity of the effect in many blending modes. If the layer opacity is reduced to 50 percent, for example, the total impact of the effect is reduced by the same amount. The opacity can allow you to control the amount of any given layer's effect in multiple blend layers.

Using blending modes on layers produces a global effect across the entire image at once, regardless of whether you have a marquee selection active or not. If you want to have selected areas affected by the underlying image, you need to cut that area out and paste it to a new layer with a transparent background and apply the blending mode to that layer. Transparency in blending mode layers allows the blending mode effect above

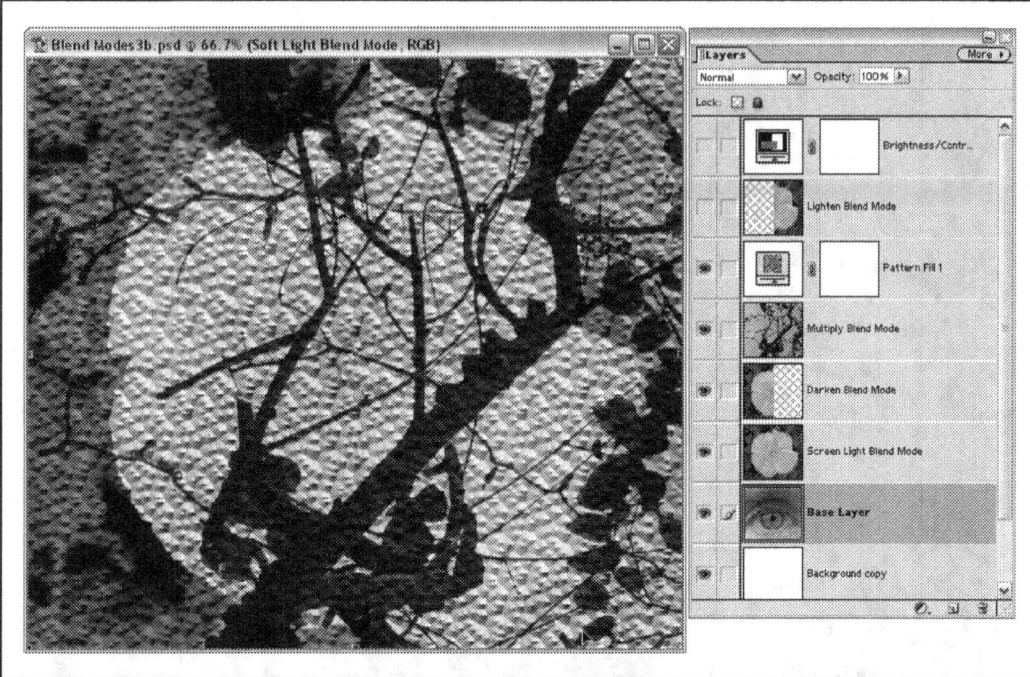

Figure 9-11.   *The effect of cascading blend layers*

a layer to pass to the layer below. (See Figure 9-13.) This is good way to include blending modes in a composite. Opacity options can allow you to build up many layers and have very complex interactions with blending modes.

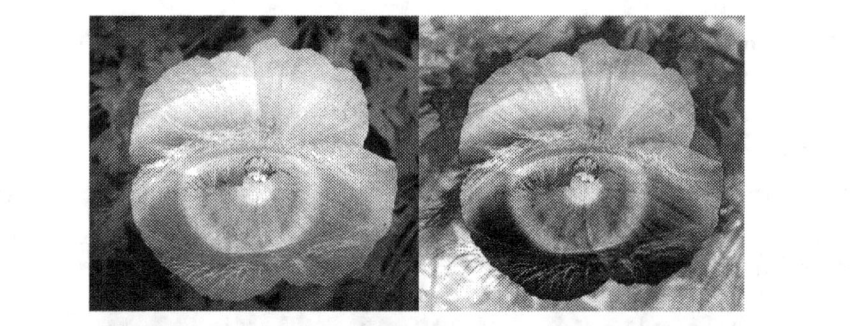

Figure 9-12.   *The effect of reversing the order on the same set of images with the Difference mode*

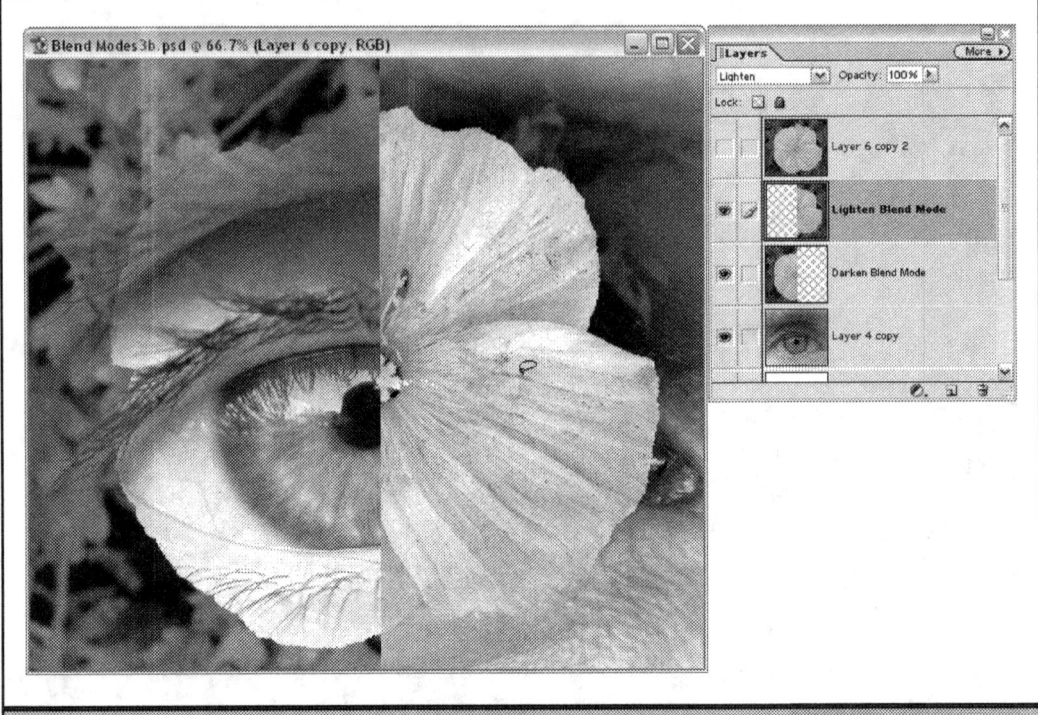

Figure 9-13.   *Pass-through of blending modes*

Definitions

If you're technically oriented and want more detail on how everything works, here's a comprehensive set of terms used with the blending modes and associated settings.

- **Blend color, image, or tool**   This is the color area, image, or painting tool that is used to apply the blending mode.

- **Base color or image**   This is the color area or image that is acted on by the blending mode.

- **Combined color or image**   This is the result of the blending mode operation.

- **Color value**   This is a number derived from the sum of the color channels (red, green, and blue) as measured on a scale of 0 to 255, where 0 is black and 255 is white. Each color channel is measured so that the maximum color value is 765, which would be pure white. This value is used to measure pure intensity (lightness or darkness), not hue. Many colors can have the same intensity.

With some blending mode operations, the individual channel color values are compared separately.

- **Hue**   The perception of color. This is defined as the color that is perceived when a pure white light is reflected from an object. In the computer world of color, it is the perceived color of the pixel when it is displayed. To perceive hue, there must be some level of saturation, or it just appears gray. When hue alone changes, the brightness and saturation of the color does not change.

- **Saturation**   The presence of color. This is any amount of color that moves the color value away from pure gray. Gray is assumed to be the absence of color and is defined as pure luminance or light value. A color is fully saturated when it has reached its maximum color values for its hue. When saturation alone changes, the brightness and hue do not change.

- **Luminance**   The lightness or darkness of any color when measured as a gray value. If you turn a color photograph into a black-and-white photo, you will see that all the colors are translated into shades of gray. The gray values represent the absolute light intensity value of that color with no saturation.

- **Brightness**   The luminance or color value. While maintaining a constant hue and saturation, the brightness determines how light or dark the color can be. It would be the same as putting a dimmer on that white light and turning it up and down. When brightness alone changes, hue and saturation do not change.

The
Complete
Reference

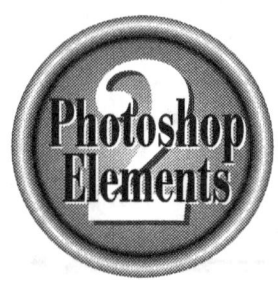

Part II

The Digital Darkroom Workflow

The
Complete
Reference

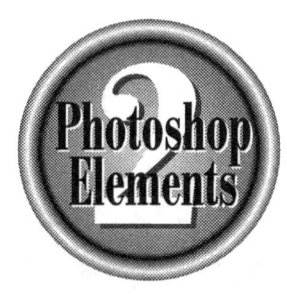

Chapter 10

Collecting, Cataloging, and Managing Images

It doesn't take long to build up a significant collection of images that you might gather from all sorts of sources. If you have a digital camera, scanner, or are a frequent flier on the Internet, you probably have gathered tons of images and are suffering under the weight of trying to find where everything is. It seems to follow the same age-old rule: the more room you have, the more you accumulate to fill it up. Check out any garage. With the large storage capacity of newer computers, you can accumulate thousands of images in no time at all. So what to do? The next step is getting them all in your computer in a form you can work with, organized so you can find what you need when you need it.

This is why this chapter is important to you. The key is in knowing how to handle all these images so you have them in the right form to print. This chapter covers image management, which enables you to capture, organize, and save your images for the best result. You will become familiar with the terms, tools, and techniques necessary to do this task effectively and efficiently. We will show you how to use Photoshop Elements' host of image-management tools that make this endeavor much easier.

Getting the Picture Into Your Computer

This is where it all begins. You have to put something in to get something out, right? There are a number of sources for gathering images including digital cameras, scanners, the Web, and let's not forget the ones you create from your own imagination. This section covers how to use the tools in Photoshop Elements to capture and import images from these sources. Once you accomplish that, you will be ready to begin the process of organizing them so you have easy access for editing.

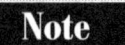
Remember that the information you capture initially is all the information you will ever have, so make sure you don't overwrite the original image with a version of that modified image. Any editing you do deletes some data in the process, so the original always gives you the most data to work with when you decide to re-invent that image.

Transferring Images from Your Digital Camera

There are a number of ways to get images from your camera to your computer. Those that Photoshop Elements supports directly are TWAIN direct transfer, WIA, card readers, and disks. In addition, both Windows XP and Mac OS X have built-in image-capture utilities of their own.

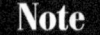
If you're using your camera's software to download and organize your images, check for compatibility with Windows XP and Mac OS X. Not all camera software is up to date enough to work directly with these latest operating systems. Check your camera manufacturer's web site (it's listed in your user manual) for updates.

Image-Management Software

Many digital cameras come with image-management software that was developed by the manufacturer. This software was designed to work with your camera so it has the advantage of being able to remotely control many of the functions of the camera. You can use this software to download images from the camera onto your computer, and also to change many of the settings on the camera that you would normally do from the LCD screen menu. This software also typically provides many editing and image-management functions. You can use the provided software or you can use Photoshop Elements to access the camera directly. The advantage of using Elements is that you can bring the camera's images directly into the Elements editing environment.

Using the Import Option for Direct Transfer

Downloading images directly into Photoshop Elements requires that a TWAIN (Technology Without An Interesting Name) driver be loaded. TWAIN is a specialized driver that is produced by the manufacturer to be compatible with your operating system and image-editing software. You need to load this driver before you can transfer files directly. Check with the manufacturer of your camera for installation and operating instructions for TWAIN drivers. If it is not provided with the software that comes with the camera, you can often get it through the camera manufacturer's web site.

You can access the TWAIN driver for your camera from File | Import, or Window | Welcome | Connect to Camera or Scanner. Make sure your camera is connected and powered up before running the Import option. When the TWAIN interface displays, follow the instructions provided by your camera's manufacturer to download your images to a selected folder. In Figure 10-1, you see a typical TWAIN dialog box for downloading camera files.

Card Readers and Disks

Card readers are external devices that plug into your computer via USB, serial, FireWire, or PCMCIA ports. These readers are designed to accept memory cards of various types that are used to store images from your digital camera. If you have a card reader attached to your system, you can access it from File | Open File (SHIFT+CMD/CTRL+O) | Browser, or Window | File Browser. Card readers do require that you load some software to set them up. Once installed, the card readers are read in the same manner as disk drives, so you do not need a special interface to access them. Just access the card reader through your computer's file browser or finder. Some cameras use floppy disks, which fit in the standard floppy disk drive of your computer and are read in the standard manner.

Using a Scanner

Many people do not have digital cameras yet and still take photographs the old-fashioned way, with film. In order to work with the photographs in an image-editing program such

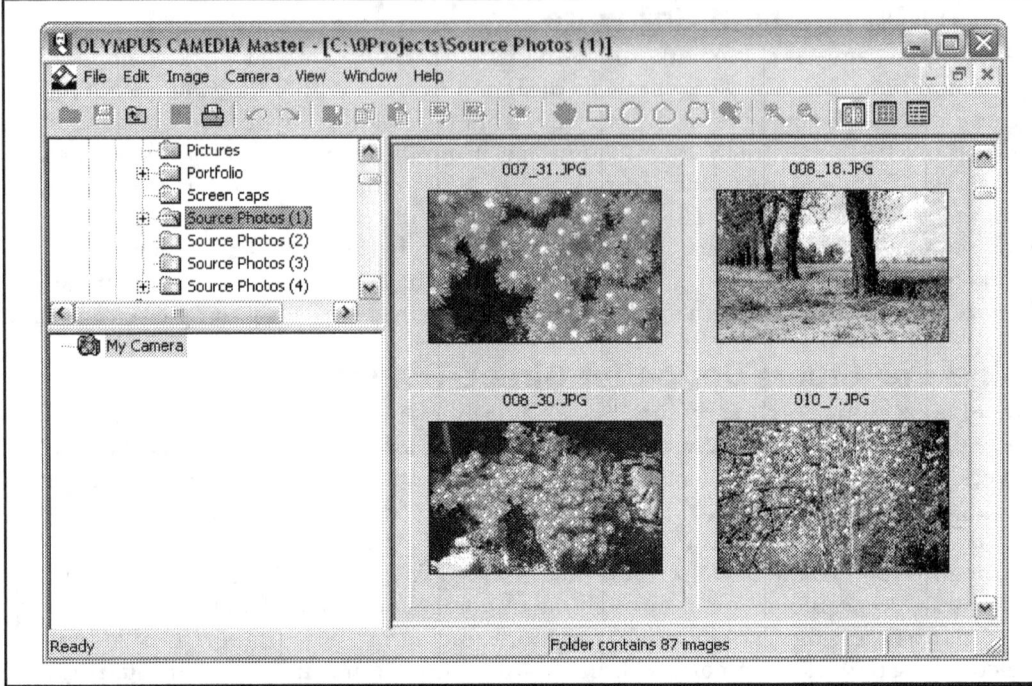

Figure 10-1. *TWAIN dialog box for direct camera downloads*

as Photoshop Elements, the negatives, slides, or prints must be digitized using a scanner. Scanners produce a digital copy of an image from a print, film positive, or film negative by reflecting light off or through the image onto sensor chips, very much like what a digital camera does, but unlike the camera, they are designed to scan only two-dimensional surfaces.

Scanner Types

Scanners come in a number of forms and quality levels. You can purchase a scanner for less than $100 on the low end, and many thousands of dollars on the high end. The difference is in the optics (clarity of focus) and the amount of resolution (amount of pixels) that can be resolved and captured, and in the number of bits of information assigned to each pixel (bit-depth). Speed can also be a factor. The scanner you choose should be based on what kind of output you are aiming for. If you do only web production, then a low-end scanner will suffice. On the other hand, if you are doing professional print production, you need a scanner that can produce very accurate color, the widest possible tonal range (bit-depth), and a high degree of detail. A good midrange ($100 to $300) flatbed scanner with an optical resolution of 600 lines or more will work for most home users.

Film scanners are built exclusively for film and cannot be used for scanning any sort of print or other flat, opaque material. Some flatbed scanners can be adapted to scan film, but very few provide the quality of a dedicated film scanner. If you have a conventional camera or a large collection of slides or negatives, you will find that a film scanner can help make use of your existing camera equipment and collection of photos. You can usually connect directly to a scanner in Photoshop Elements with a TWAIN driver. This allows you to convert your collection of negatives and slides to digital format, so you don't lose your collection by going digital. You might also be able to breathe new life into old photos with a bit of Elements digital-editing magic.

Flatbed scanners are far more common than slide scanners and are a fraction of the cost. Flatbed scanners are designed to scan any flat work, including prints, sketches, art, text, and anything else (regardless of thickness—unlike sheet fed scanners) you can lay flat on the glass platen. They cannot, however, scan transparent film without an adapter, and not all scanners can be adapted. In general, scanned prints do not deliver the quality that scanned film delivers, partly because the print is one generation away from the original film. A lot also depends on how good the print is to begin with. If you are using one-hour photo-development vendors, the chances of getting very high-quality prints are pretty small. The scanner cannot magically make missing information appear.

Flatbed scanners come in varying sizes and quality levels. Make sure you get one big enough for the all the types of material you want to scan, otherwise you will have to scan larger work in pieces and stitch it back together, which is laborious. The TWAIN drivers that are produced by your scanner manufacturer must be loaded before you can access the TWAIN driver for your scanner by choosing File | Import or Window | Welcome | Connect To Camera Or Scanner.

Scanner Resolution

The latest generation of flatbed scanners offers more resolution than most of us will ever use. There is lot of confusion about scanner resolution because some manufacturers want to you to think you are getting more resolution than in fact you are. Advertising interpolated resolution of the scanner, as opposed to *optical* resolution, causes some of this confusion. The optical resolution is the one you need to pay attention to. Optical resolution is the maximum resolution that the optics and electronics in the scanner can capture. Interpolated is a method of expanding the resolution by pixel averaging, which does not increase quality, only size. Interpolated resolution is used to increase the size for output devices such as printers and is better handled by Photoshop Elements or the printer at the time of output.

The resolution you scan at has everything to do with the resolution of the original you are scanning. If you are scanning film, you want to capture all the detail that is in the original slide or negative. Any more resolution does not give you more detail because there *isn't* any more detail. Film has a resolution of about 1800 ppi (pixels per inch). A frame of 35mm film is approximately 1.5×1 inches, so that translates to 2700 pixels of horizontal resolution and 1800 pixels of vertical resolution. If you want to capture the full detail of a frame of film, you need to set the scanner at 1800 ppi to get all the resolution. It is really that simple. When you print a photograph from the same 35mm frame, you are taking that 1800 ppi image and blowing it up to, say, 4×6 inches, a typical print size. The detail is spread out over a larger area, but the detail itself is not increased.

If you then want to scan the print, you need to adjust the scanner resolution to 2700 divided by 6 inches, or 450 ppi. The scanner set at 450 ppi renders the full detail in the print. Today's scanners typically have at least 1200 dpi or more optical resolution, so you will have more than enough to handle any photographic print.

So where to use all that optical resolution? When you scan analogous work such as art or real-world objects such as a pressed flower, for which you have no resolution limit as you do with photos. The more resolution you use on the scan, the more detail you capture.

| Note | *There will be times when you'll need to scan a series of images for a particular print size because you are scanning strictly for a publication or web site and are not concerned with capturing any more information than the medium you are scanning for can resolve. Generally speaking, if you are scanning for the Web, scanning resolution of between 72–96 dpi is adequate. If you are scanning for print, 300 dpi is adequate.* |

Using the Import Command

If you need to move pictures from a camera or scanner, you need to use the Import command. Once you issue the Import command, you'll see a submenu that contains the names of the hardware devices and software programs that you or Adobe installed drivers for. Drivers are programs, usually found on the CD-ROM that comes with a hardware device, that inform the operating system what that device is and how to connect with it. To use the Import command:

1. Choose File | Import, or Window | Welcome | Connect To Camera Or Scanner, and find the listing for your scanner from the pop-up menu on the File menu or the pull-down menu on the Welcome screen. If your scanner is not listed, then the TWAIN driver might not be loaded. The TWAIN driver is an industry standard for communications between computer applications and peripheral devices. Look in your manual or check with your manufacturer to find out if there is a TWAIN driver available. Most scanners are TWAIN compliant and load those drivers when you install the device, so you might just need to read the manual to discover how to load it.

2. To move ahead, we assume that you've installed your TWAIN driver and that your scanner shows on its list. After you choose your scanner from the list, a dialog box appears. See the following illustration for an example. The function of the interface varies from one manufacturer to another, so you need to follow the instructions provided with your scanner.

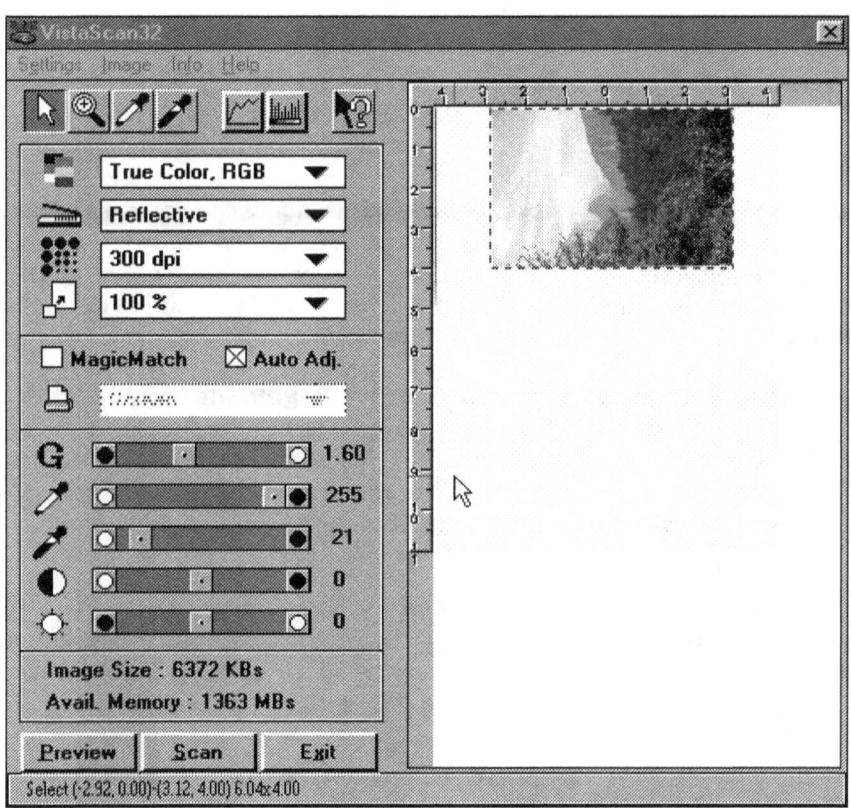

3. Position the print or other flat work on the scanner plate and close the lid.

4. Do a preview scan, if that is an option, to show you how the settings are affecting the scan. You should also double-check your alignment and crop marks.

5. Adjust the crop marks so you just scan the area you want. This keeps the file size to a minimum.

6. Adjust the resolution, exposure, color adjustments, and other options, depending on the scanner you have, and start the scan. You will see lights and hear some motor noises as the scanner proceeds. Typically there is a progress bar that indicates duration.

7. When the scan is complete, you will see the image appear in Elements as an untitled document. It is good idea to save the image before beginning any editing so you have the original scan preserved. If you do successive scans of the same image, it will produce new documents for each scan, which you will see stacked up on the screen. Remember that each scan takes up memory. Keep an eye on the size of the scan before you start to make sure that it is within the size limitations of your system. Most scanner software calculates size for you. If not, you can see the size listed in the Elements status bar after the scan is complete.

Proper Alignment of Scanned Material

When you are scanning prints or other types of images that need accurate orientation, it is important to align them correctly on the scanner platen so the scans are not tilted. Using the edge of the platen as a guide is the most common method, but that is not foolproof. If the scanner cannot scan right to the edge, parts of the image might be cut off. Using a piece of cardboard that is cut absolutely square can act as a guide. Often photos come back from the processor curved because they are cut from rolls, so it can be next to impossible to get them to lie flat and align properly. Do not use tape: it might leave a hard-to-clean residue, and you might scratch the glass tying to clean it off. The easiest solution is to correct alignment with Elements' Straighten Image option.

Using the Straighten Image Option to Correct Alignment in Scanned Images

The Straighten Image option in Elements is a quick way to fix simple problems with alignment. It accomplishes this by finding the edge of the photograph in contrast to the scanned background, which is typically white, and calculating the angle needed for rotation. If there is an abundance of white in photograph you might want to cut a black paper matte and tape the photo inside it. Two options are

- Choose Image | Rotate | Straighten to rotate the image back to a square right-angle orientation. This option leaves a border based on the background color.
- Choose Image | Rotate | Straighten and Crop to rotate the image back to a right angle orientation and crop the excess away.

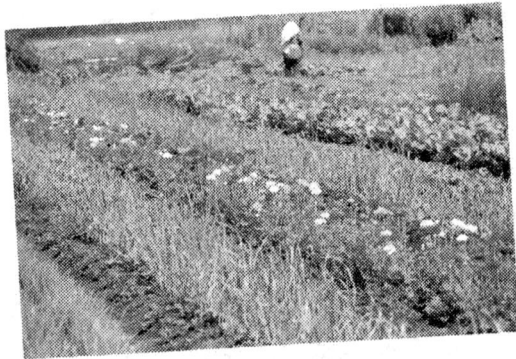 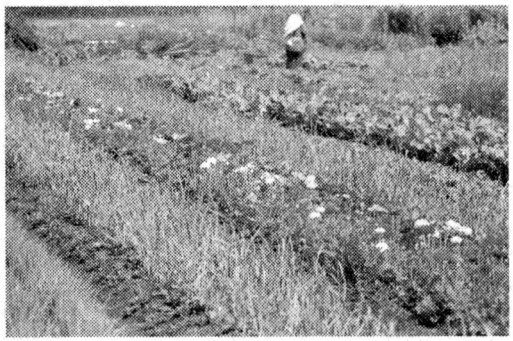

Using the Custom Option to Rotate and Align Scanned Images   A third alternative is to rotate the image with the Rotate | Custom option.

1. Choose Image | Rotate | Custom. The dialog box appears.
2. Enter the angle and the direction you want to rotate the image. You can calculate the angle of rotation by opening the Info palette, choosing the Line Shape Tool from the Toolbox, and drawing a line along the edge of the photo. You will see the angle of the line in the Info palette. Clear the line after you get the reading.
3. Click OK when you are done, and the image will rotate to the proper orientation.

Using the Free Rotate Selection Command to Correct Alignment in Scanned Images   The last alternative is to rotate the image by hand and align it by eye.

1. Choose Select | Select All. You will see a marquee border appear at the edge of the image.

2. Choose Image | Rotate | Free Rotate Selection to begin a rotation transformation. You will see the transformation handles appear. The cursor will change to the rotation cursor as you move it over the handles.

3. Grab a corner handle with the rotation cursor and move it clockwise or counterclockwise to rotate the image to until it looks straight.

4. You can have the Info palette open while you rotate to align the angle of rotation based on the line-shape method mentioned earlier.

5. If the original image used the entire frame, use the Crop tool to trim the borders straight. Choose the Crop tool and drag to establish the approximate boundaries to be cropped. You can then fine-tune the exact crop by dragging the marquee handles until the marquee is positioned in precisely the way you want. If you place the cursor just outside the corner handles, you can rotate the Crop marquee. When you have the cropping marquee aligned as you like, press RETURN to render. The image will be rotated and resized to fit the original frame, as shown in this illustration.

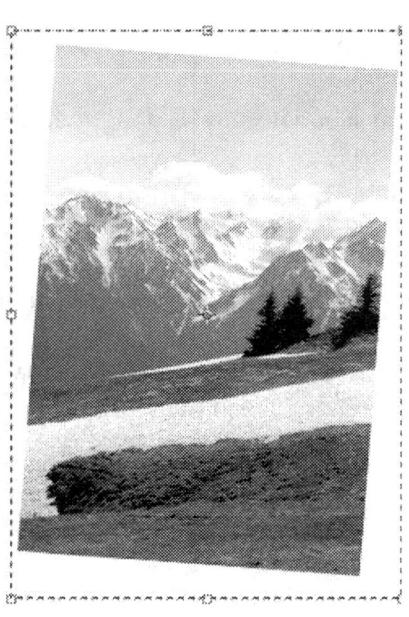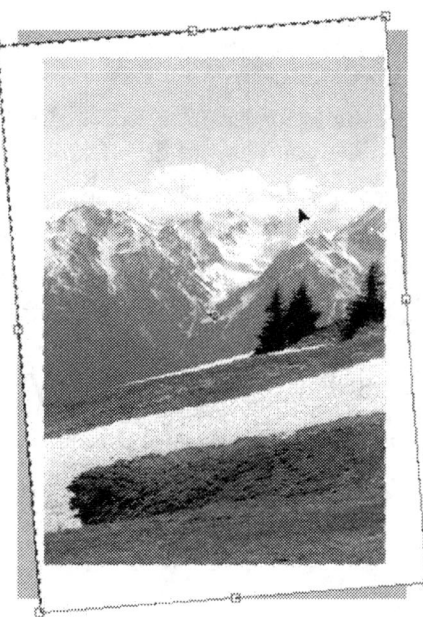

Scanning Material Other Than Photos In addition to scanning photographs, a flatbed scanner can be used as a camera of sorts. You can gather all sorts of common materials and place them on the scanner bed. The scanner does not have a great depth of field but it can do justice to average textures—leather, leaves, fabric, flowers, and the like. This is a good way to add to your texture library. You can use the flatbed scanner to build a collage by placing bits of images along with other gathered items in an arrangement on the platen. This can shortcut the process of making collages and composite images (see Chapter 17).

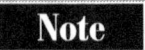
Unless money is no object, it's best to avoid scanning materials (such as rocks) that can permanently scratch the scanner glass. If you must scan such materials, find a sheet of high-quality, very thin plastic (or thick plastic wrap) and place it atop the scanner glass.

Capturing Video

Photoshop Elements enables you to capture single frames from digital video files by using the Import option. This includes video file formats such as AVI (Windows Video), MPEG (Motion Pictures Experts Group), MOV (QuickTime), WMV (Windows Media Video), and ASF (Advanced Systems Format). These are video formats that digital cameras, video capture boards, and video editing software use to create video clips. You can load these clips into Elements and capture individual frames from the clip. The quality of the capture very much depends on the resolution of the original video file. Follow these steps to capture video frames:

1. Choose File | Import | Frame From Video. A dialog box appears, as shown in Figure 10-2.

2. Click the Browse button to open the file system window so you can locate the video file you want to grab frames from.

3. After you select the video, the first frame is displayed in the preview window of the Video Capture dialog box.

4. There is a set of controls directly under the video preview that look like controls on a VCR. You can start, stop, pause, fast forward, reverse, and jump to the end or beginning.

5. Directly below the video controls is the Grab Frame bar. Press this when you want to capture a frame. You can capture a frame when the video is in motion, or use the frame advance pointer just above the video controls to advance the video manually.

6. The captured files will bear the name of the video they are captured from, along with a two-digit appendix.

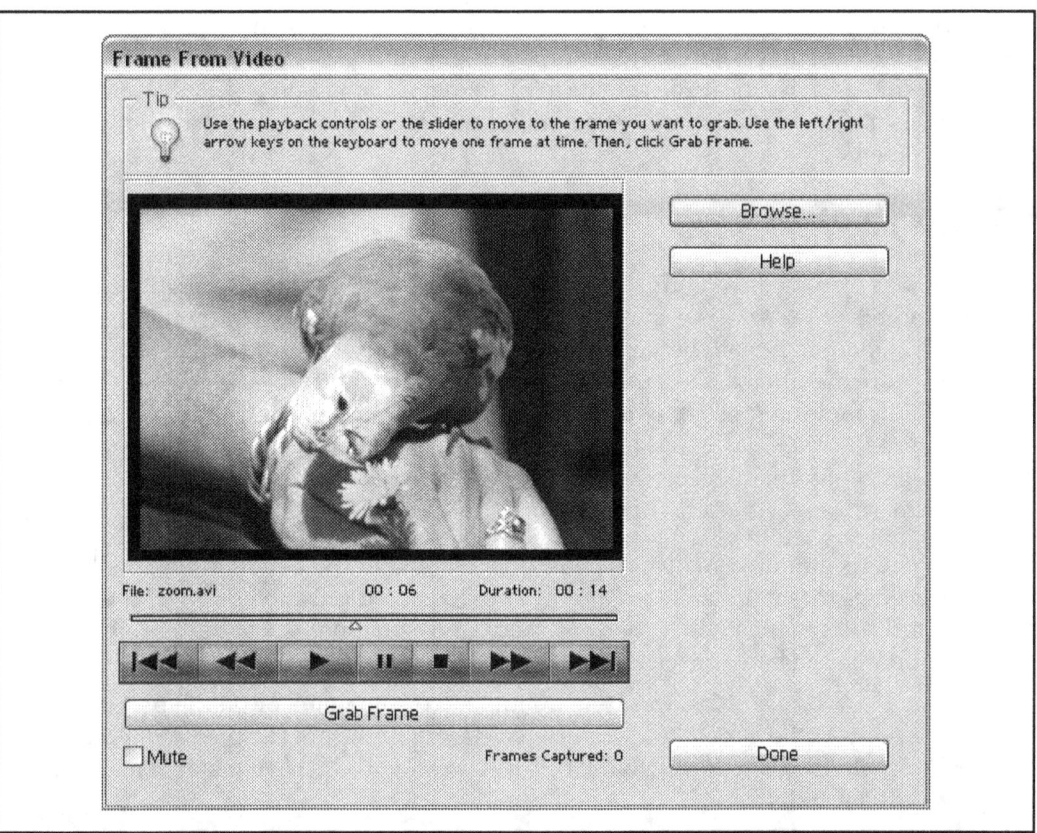

Figure 10-2.   *The Frame From Video dialog box enables you to grab a still image from a digital video file.*

Working with Images from the Internet

The Internet is a rich source of images that can help you in many ways. There are tons of free images that you can download and use to augment your projects or just use as reference. You can also find many online services that can help transfer your film or slides to digital format and print them.

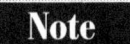 *A word of caution about copyrights. Be sure to check to see if the image you want to download is copyrighted. Downloading images from the Web is so easy that we often take it for granted; but these are the works of others, and taking them without authorization is stealing.*

Online Services

There are many online services that can take your conventional film and process it to produce digital files or prints. This is another way to convert your current collection to digital without purchasing extra equipment. Once you have your slides or negatives converted to digital and sent back to you in hard or soft copy, you can edit them with your computer and use the same service to print them. Using online services allows you to try all this out before you make further investment into peripherals that allow you to do it all yourself.

Images Through E-mail

Got a friend or relative with a scanner? Well if they have e-mail, you might be able to get them to scan some of your photos and e-mail them to you. You might also convince others to use some of the services we mentioned so they can send you photos by attaching them to e-mail. Better yet, if you have a scanner or digital camera, you can scan or capture the photos and send them via e-mail so the recipients can see them on line. E-mail becomes an easy way to transfer images from one computer to another via the Internet.

If you are receiving images via e-mail, here is how to detach and save them to your system.

1. Open the e-mail. Usually a paper-clip icon next to the e-mail in the mailbox indicates that it has an attachment. The exact configuration of attachment notification varies with browser brands and versions. The images might also appear in the body of the e-mail in full display.

2. CTRL+CLICK over either the attachment icon or filename, or on the picture in the body of the e-mail, and choose Save Image As from the in-context menu. This will open a window to the file system so you can save the attached image to you hard disk.

   In addition, most e-mail programs, such as Microsoft Outlook or Eudora, have a default attachments directory. Attachments can be opened from that directly just like any other file. Check your e-mail program's Help files or manual for the location of the attachments directory.

Photoshop Elements lets you send any file you're working on as an e-mail attachment. It can even resize and optimize the image for web transmission if you give the okay.

To attach images to e-mail via Elements:

1. Choose File | E-mail.

2. If the file size is more than the standard limits that most ISPs designate for attachments, a dialog box appears to warn you that the file might be too large to download by the receiving party.

3. Click the Auto Convert button to automatically optimize and compress the file to acceptable limits.

4. Choose Send As Is to send the file without any size reduction.

5. Choose Cancel to halt the send.

6. When you choose Convert or Send As Is, the program automatically attaches the file to your e-mail and brings up the compose window for your default e-mail program so you can enter the address, subject, and message.

7. Choose Send to send the e-mail with attachment to the addressee.

Note   *You can attach only one file to a given message using this method.*

Other Sources of Images

There are a number of other ways to get images into your computer that you should know about. Many of these are very convenient for those who are the occasional user or and don't want get involved with peripherals such as scanning, digital cameras, and printers.

Photo CDs

The Photo CD format was developed by Kodak to provide an affordable means of getting drum-scanner quality in multiple resolutions from each photographic frame. Photo CDs can only be produced by a Kodak-licensed service bureau or film-processing lab that has the equipment required of them by Kodak. Having your images scanned to a Photo CD typically costs from $1 to $3 per scan, and you don't have to spend your time doing it. Furthermore, Photo CDs give you several scans of each image, each at a different resolution.

When you open these files in Elements, you get a choice of a number of output resolutions, as you can see in the following illustration. You cannot save in this format, however, because it is proprietary.

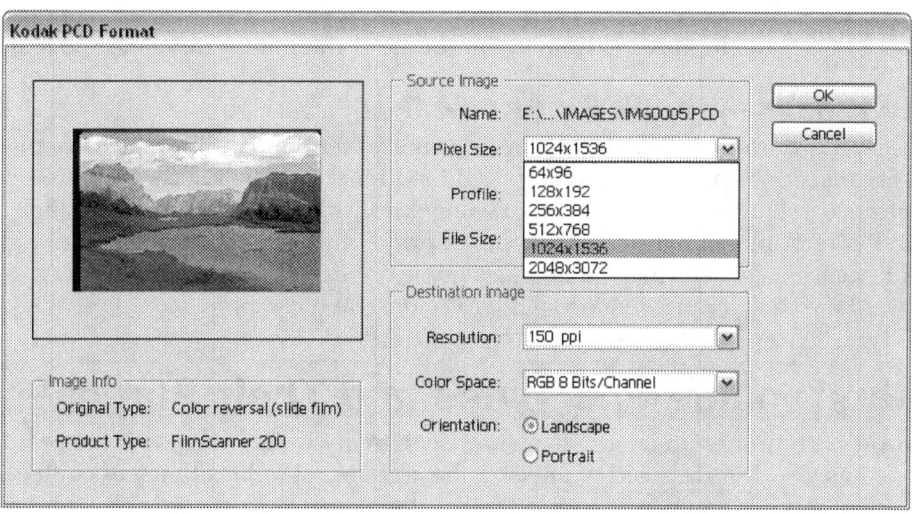

The other choice that's even more popular, also a Kodak product (jointly with Hewlett-Packard), is called Picture CD. Picture CDs are offered by many one-hour snapshot-processing labs as an additional option when you have them process your film. Picture CDs are scanned to JPEG format at only one resolution, which is just high enough for a decent snapshot-sized print. If you are interested only in snapshots or the Web for output, the Picture CD is a good option.

To open files from a Photo CD, follow these steps:

1. Choose File | Open As and then go to the directory on the Photo CD that has the PCD files.

2. Double-click the file you want to load. The Kodak PCD Format dialog box appears.

3. You will see a preview of the photo on the upper left of the dialog box.

4. Choose Pixel Size from the drop-down menu. Photo CD offers you a list of preset resolutions to pick from.

5. Choose a color profile from the Profile drop-down menu. These profiles correspond to the type of film the original image was shot in: K-14 for Kodachrome, E-6 for Ectachrome, Color Negative for standard film negatives, and Standard YCC for no color translation from the original scan.

6. File Size tells you the size of the file in megabytes for the resolution selected.

7. Choose a display resolution from the Resolution drop-down menu.

8. Choose a Color Space from the drop-down menu.

9. Select Portrait or Landscape orientation. This rotates the image 90 degrees counterclockwise.

10. Click OK, and the program processes the resolution you picked and displays the file in an image window in Elements.

Image Info provides information on the source of the photograph and the scan.

Photo Kiosks—Kodak Picture Maker

Another trend started by Kodak once again is the advent of the photo kiosk in places such as malls, photo-processing outlets, and food markets. The kiosks are self-service computer workstations that allow you to scan your prints, negatives, or slides; determine the number to print and the size and layout of prints; and print your digital files right on the spot. You can also take the scanned files home on disk, edit them in Elements, and then take them back for printing on standard photographic paper.

Understanding File Types and Their Purposes

The world of computer imaging has given rise to many file formats over the years, and each one has vied for the position of being the accepted standard that leaves all others behind. The competition has been good in that the newer formats are getting better all the time, but it has left a pile of interim file formats in its wake, which are slowly sifting out of the mainstream.

Essential File Types

There are many graphic file formats that have come and gone over the years, and many new ones emerging every year. It is very important to understand the differences between image file formats because which one you use can make a world of difference to the final outcome.

It's best to stick with the few that have become virtually universal across all image-editing programs and computer platforms. The four most universal are each discussed in the following sections:

- ■ **PSD**   Photoshop document format
- ■ **TIFF**   Tagged image file format
- ■ **JPEG**   Joint Photographic Experts Group
- ■ **GIF**   Graphics interchange format

PSD—Photoshop Document Format

PSD is the Photoshop native format. The PSD file was developed by Adobe Systems exclusively for use with Photoshop, PhotoDeluxe, and now Photoshop Elements. It has become a standard and is accepted by some other image-editing programs, but the cross-application compatibility is not always good. It is primarily used to store images that you might want to re-edit later. The advantage of using PSD files with Elements is that it can store all the image data. PSD preserves layers, modes, styles, text (annotations), and more. The information remains in a fully editable form after you save it. PSD files tend to be much larger than other file formats because they store extra information. Each layer can be equivalent to the background image, so if you have, for instance, an image with 10 layers, the saved image might be up to 10 times larger than a flattened image.

Elements gives you some options when you save an image as a PSD file, as you can see here:

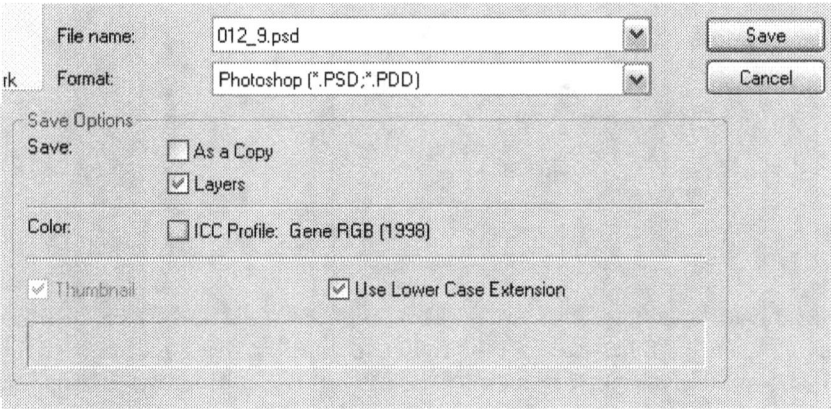

- ■ **Save As A Copy**   Check this option to save a copy of the file under a new name.

■ **Layers** Uncheck this option to flatten the image when saving. Although this saves disk space, layer information is not preserved and will not be there when you reopen the image, so you won't be able to pick up where you left off when re-editing.

■ **Color** Check this option to save the image color profile. This attaches the color profile so other devices, like printers, can interpret your image color properly. See Chapter 1 for more on color calibration.

TIFF—Tagged Image File Format

The TIFF format (or TIF in the PC world) has risen to the top as the number-one standard in cross-application and cross-platform support and compatibility. If you choose Preferences | Enable Advanced TIFF Options, the TIFF format seems to provide every option you might need. You can choose to save in full color, index color, or grayscale; four types of image compression (None, LZW, ZIP, or JPEG); to save layer information; to create an image pyramid (multiple resolutions); and to preserve transparency in layers that have transparent areas. All the options are presented in the TIFF Options dialog box, shown in the following illustration.

Some of the advanced options, such as layers, pyramids, and Zip compression, are useful only in the few other applications that also support those features. In addition, LZW and ZIP are lossless compression formats. That is, nothing but identical pixels are eliminated when the file is compressed. JPEG is a lossy file compression format. Its compressed files are much smaller because the program throws out data that is "close enough" in color and brightness to neighboring pixels.

In Photoshop Elements, TIFF offers three compression schemes:

- **LZW**   This is a lossless compression routine. It tends to be less efficient on photographic images that have complex pixel patterning. Use this if you don't want any degradation when you save a compressed image.

- **ZIP**   The ZIP compression routine is very similar to LZW, and it is the same kind you find in ZIP and WinZIP applications. If you have saved your TIFF files with LZW compression, you will see little gain in compression if you ZIP them up later. Note that few other applications support ZIP compression in TIFF files.

- **JPEG**   JPEG is lossy compression, which means it degrades the image somewhat as it compresses the data to achieve much higher levels of compression. The only advantage in using JPEG compression with a TIFF file is that it can be used in conjunction with saving layers and transparency, which you cannot do with a straight JPEG file. When you select JPEG compression, the slider bar, text field, and drop-down menu just under it activate. All these do the same thing in different ways. They control the quality level of the JPEG compression on a scale of 1 to 10. Slide the bar, enter the value you want in the text field, or choose a preset level from the drop-down menu. JPEG compression is progressive, so it will degrade the TIFF image each time you save.

JPEG—Joint Photographic Experts Group

JPEG is a file format that is widely used on the Internet and in digital cameras because of its ability to compress image data to very small sizes. JPEG compression is lossy, so the image is degraded with each degree of compression and with each successive implementation. JPEG compression does fairly well with complex pixel structures that are typically found in photographs, but does not perform as well with graphic type images that have clear areas of solid color and well-defined edges and shapes. You can set the quality level of the compression at the time you save a file in JPEG format, which will determine the relative amount of degradation in the image quality. When you save a file in JPEG format, the JPEG Options dialog box appears, as shown next.

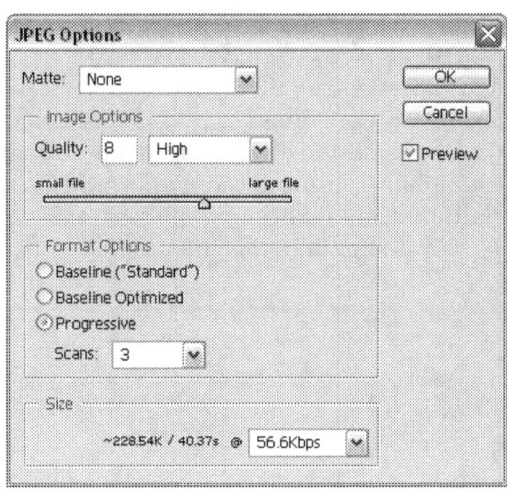

This dialog box offers a number of options for saving:

- **Matte** You can set the matte color to fill in areas of the image that are transparent by selecting presets from the drop-down menu or choosing Custom and choosing a color from the color picker. JPEG does not handle transparency and has to fill it with a solid color. If you choose none, it defaults to white.

- **Image Options** These options allow you to set the compression level with three different controls. You can enter the level value in the text field, select a preset compression level from the drop-down menu, or move the slider from left to right, and you will see the values change in the text field. The value range is from 1 to 10, with 10 being the highest quality but lowest compression ratio.

- **Preview** When Preview is checked, you see the quality changes in the image window as you make your selections.

- **Format Options** There are three format options to choose from. All of them are designed to optimize display of JPEG files on Internet browsers. The Baseline Standard and the Baseline Optimized both display the image from the top down, one line at a time. The Baseline Optimized uses a more powerful algorithm to compress, so it produces a smaller file. Progressive formats the file to display in successive passes or scans adding more detail with each pass. This gives you immediate feedback on the whole image, which makes it more efficient. Choose a scan number, which indicates how many passes you want before the whole image is displayed. Three is good for most, but higher levels might be necessary for larger files.

- **Size** Starting from the right, you have the average connection speed (choose the connection speed from the drop-down menu), next, the time to display the image, and finally, the size of the compressed file at the levels you have picked.

JPEG files can also be saved through File | Save For Web. See Chapter 18.

JPEG 2000, JPX, and JP2 Formats (New)

The JPEG 2000 format is the latest entry into the image format races. We have to say that this one could be a Triple Crown winner, especially for digital camera users. The developers of JPEG 2000 took the best features from many formats such as TIFF, JPEG, PNG (Portable Network Graphics—pronounced *ping*), and Flashpix, and combined them into this new standard that should become the format of choice in the near future. The Save dialog for JPEG 2000 is shown in this illustration.

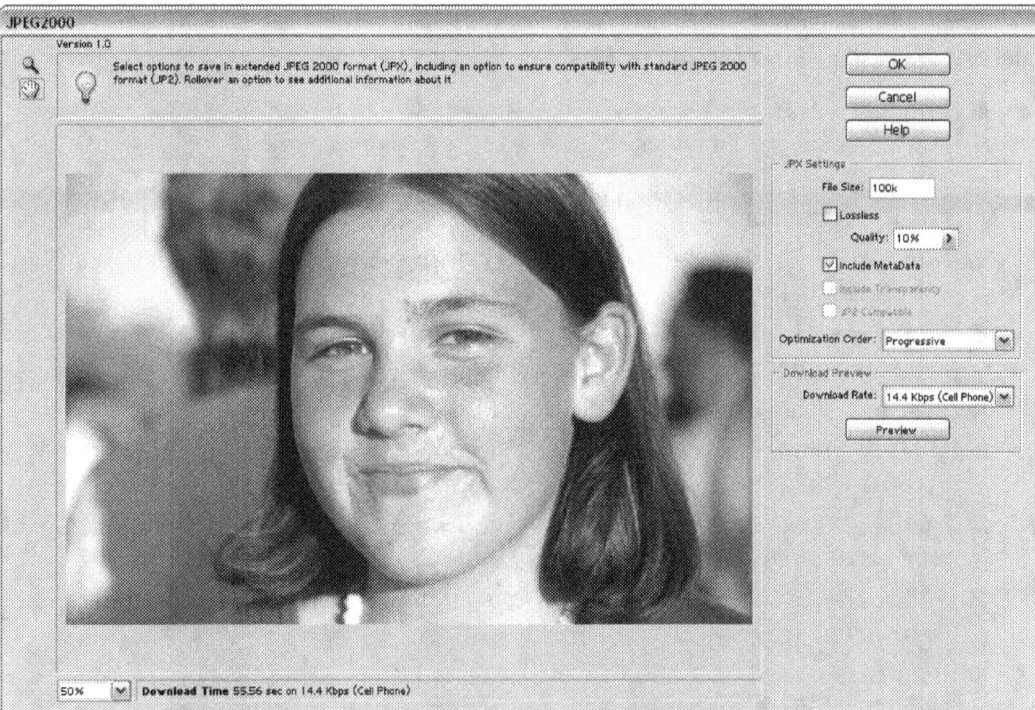

Here are some of the improved features:

- Improved image quality, including Wavelet technology to reduce artifacts
- Lossless compression option, so you no longer have to go to another format to get that capability
- Higher rates of compression without sacrificing quality
- Improved web display options, including new progressive styles and variable resolution display on the fly
- Improved color handling with sRGB color model and the ability to attach color profiles
- Capability of attaching Metadata such as EXIF information or color profiles

THE DIGITAL DARKROOM WORKFLOW

When you save to the JPEG 2000 format in Elements, you have a number of options that appear in the JPEG 2000 dialog box:

- **Preview window**   The preview gives you view of the original file and allows you to see the visual effect of various compression schemes.

- **Zoom tool**   This appears in the upper-left corner of the dialog box. It allows you to zoom in on the preview.

- **Move tool**   This appears in the upper-left corner of the dialog box. It allows you to pan the preview.

- **File size**   You can enter the file size in KB increments, and the program will adjust the other parameters accordingly.

- **Lossless**   Check this box if you want the compression to be lossless.

- **Quality**   Enter the quality level for the compression algorithm from 0 to 100 percent. Click on the arrow to bring up a slider for adjusting this parameter.

- **Include Metadata**   Check this box if you want metadata included in the file when it is saved.

- **Transparency**   Check this box if you want to preserve transparency data from the original image.

- **JP2**   Check this box if you want an extended JPEG 2000 file to be readable on a standard JPEG 2000 reader.

- **Optimization Order**   Choose an option from the drop-down menu that determines how the file displays on a web browser. The options are Growing Thumbnail (progressively larger thumbnails), Progressive (increase detail), and Color (starts as grayscale and adds color).

- **Download Preview**   This is designed to give you a simulated preview of how your file will display on the net.

- **Download Rate**   This sets the simulated Internet connection speed.

- **Preview button**   This button starts the display simulation in the Preview window. You will see the image displayed using the optimization you selected.

- **Zoom Percentage menu**   Select a zoom percentage from the drop-down menu. This allows you see the effect of compression on the image in more detail.

- **Download Time**   This gives you the load time in seconds and the selected simulated connection speed.

GIF—Graphics Interchange Format

GIF files are used for the display almost exclusively for web graphics and animation. See Chapter 18 for more on creating GIF animations and optimizing GIF images. GIF files are in 8-bit color (a maximum of 256 colors out of a total palette of 256,000). When they are displayed on the Web, they are commonly limited to 216 web-safe colors, which are considered safe for the display in browsers and on color cards that display a maximum of 256 colors. When 256 colors is the maximum number of displayable colors, some browsers reserve up to 40 of those colors for their own use. So when we say that 216 is the number of web-safe colors, it means that we can be assured that all of those colors will be displayed in all browsers running on all color displays. As the color capabilities of computers increase, the need for this limitation is fading fast.

To save in GIF format, the image must be converted to indexed color. This means reducing the number of displayable colors in the image to 256 or fewer. This can sometimes produce what is called banding (discrete areas of color that don't blend smoothly), which occurs most frequently when areas of fine gradations are color-reduced. To mitigate the effect of banding, GIF files can be set to employ dithering schemes, which help mask banding.

When you save a GIF image, a dialog box appears (see the next illustration) with several options.

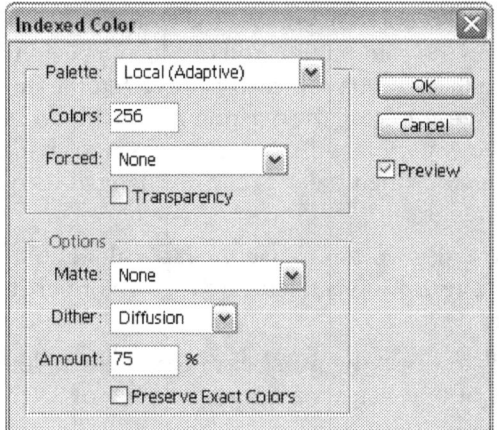

- ■ **Preview**   If you select this option, you see a preview of the changes in palette colors in the image window.

- ■ **Palette**   This is a pull-down menu that gives you a choice of a number of palette options you can use when the file is saved to a GIF format.

- ■ **Exact**   If the image has 256 colors or fewer, you can choose the palette so none of the colors change.

- ■ **System**   You can also choose from the system palettes for Windows and Macintosh.

- ■ **Web**   This palette option reduces the colors to a 216-color palette that web browsers use when displaying in 8-bit color mode. This ensures that colors do not shift when in that display mode.

■ **Uniform**   This palette is derived by selecting evenly spaced colors in the RGB color cube. One of the least-used palettes and has no apparent advantage.

■ **Adaptive**   The Adaptive palette creates a custom palette by choosing the most closely matched set of colors (based on the amount you choose in the Colors option) that most closely matches the original. Adaptive uses all 256,000 colors in the VGA palette to make its choices from, so it has a much better chance at making a close or exact match.

■ **Perceptual and Selective**   This creates a custom palette much like adaptive, only it gives priority to colors that create smooth transitions to make the overall image better resolved.

■ **Selective**   This creates a custom palette while trying to preserve colors that are included in the Web palette and trying to preserve color integrity in general. We recommend adaptive or perceptual over this, unless the image is simple and the areas of color are fairly discrete.

■ **Custom**   If you select custom, you see the Color Table dialog box (see Chapters 3 and 18 for more on the color table). You can load a custom palette and force the image to adapt to it. If you have already converted the image to an 8-bit palette, you can also change colors on the existing palette by double-clicking any swatch and changing its color value with the color picker to change all instances of that color in the image. Modified palettes can be changed using the Save button and reused on other images.

■ **Previous**   Choose this option to use the last palette that was used by the Indexed option. This option is useful if you are converting a series of files to the same palette.

■ **Colors**   Use this to select the number of colors the palette uses for the conversion. This option has a maximum number of 256 and is not available for fixed palettes.

■ **Forced**   This option allows you to lock certain colors on the color table so they are not shifted during adaptive palette conversion. From the pull-down menu, choose

  ■ **Custom**   Locks colors by choosing a color swatch and the using the color picker or eyedropper tool to select a color from the image you want protected

  ■ **Black and White**   Protects black and white only

  ■ **Primaries**   Protects white, red, green, yellow, blue, cyan, magenta, and black

  ■ **Web**   Protects the 216 web-safe colors

- **Transparency**   Check this box to preserve transparency from the original image. Any translucent pixels become opaque because GIF does not support translucency.

- **Matte**   These options determine the color that used to fill in translucent or transparent areas of the image. If the Transparency option is checked, the matte color fills only translucent pixels. If Transparency is not checked, all translucent and transparent pixels are filled with the matte color. Choose the custom option from the pull-down menu to choose a color from the color picker that matches the color of the web page. If there is no transparency in the image, the Matte option is dimmed.

- **Dither**   The Dither options are used to mask the effect of reducing the colors in an image by placing patterns of multicolor dots close together to simulate missing colors.

    - **None**   No dither is used.

    - **Diffusion**   Places pixels randomly in areas of color transition to mitigate the effects of banding. You can control the amount of dithering by setting the Amount percentage. Adjust this by eye.

    - **Pattern**   Pattern dithering works in much the same way as diffusion, only it uses geometric patterns of pixels that do not blend as well. You cannot control the amount of pattern dither because it is a fixed algorithm.

    - **Noise**   The Noise Dither option places random patterns of colored dots over the entire image, producing a grainy effect.

    - **Preserve Exact Colors**   This option is available when the Diffusion option is selected. It preserves areas of solid color that match the original palette by suppressing dithering in those areas.

Less-Common File Types

There are many other graphic file formats available for import to and export from Photoshop Elements, some more useful than others. Many are there in case you happen to run into file in that format but for the most part are not widely used outside very specialized groups. Some of these more obscure formats are TARGA, Scitex, Pixar, and RAW. The other formats covered here all can be useful to you in certain situations, so it is a good idea to familiarize yourself with their function.

EPS—Encapsulated PostScript

The EPS format is based on PostScript coding language that describes everything in the image document in terms of objects. This allows vector objects such as shapes and text to remain resolution-independent and print to their highest quality at output. EPS also allows bitmapped and raster graphics (painted and photographic images) to reside simultaneously within the file to provide the greatest flexibility for composition. EPS is device-independent, so it is commonly used to export image files to other platforms and applications that have PostScript interpreters. Another great advantage of EPS is that it can include font descriptions, so you are assured that the text will format correctly, even if the proper fonts are not loaded on the receiving computer.

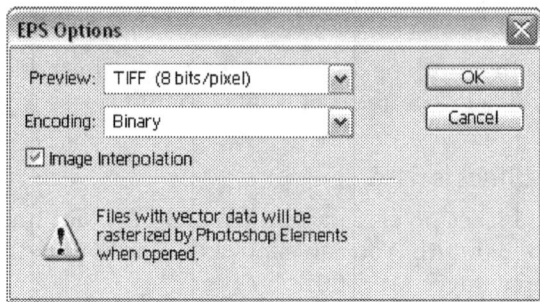

Here are the EPS save options:

- **Preview** EPS gives you two options for creating a preview so you can see what the file looks like when you open it in an application. Choose 1 bit for a black-and-white bitmapped rendition, or 8 bits for an indexed color version. If there is no preview, you will just see a bounding box.

- **Encoding** This is a pull-down menu that gives a number of choices. Binary encoding is the most efficient coding format and is accepted by most up-to-date applications and printers. If the application or printer does not accept binary, then your fallback is ASCII, which writes the EPS file in standard text. The advantage of the ASCII version—if you know how to code PostScript—is that it can be edited in a standard word-processor program.

- **Image Interpolation** When this option is checked it allows the PostScript interpreter to interpolate any images in the file when the file is resized in another application.

BMP—Device-Independent Bitmap

BMP (sometimes designated as DIB) is the native format for Microsoft Windows. It is a standard RGB file that can be saved to a number of color levels from bitmap to true color. It has no advantage over TIFF, but some (mostly Microsoft) Windows applications use this format. 8-bit color levels and lower have the option of RLE (run length encoded) compression. The following illustration shows the save options for BMP format.

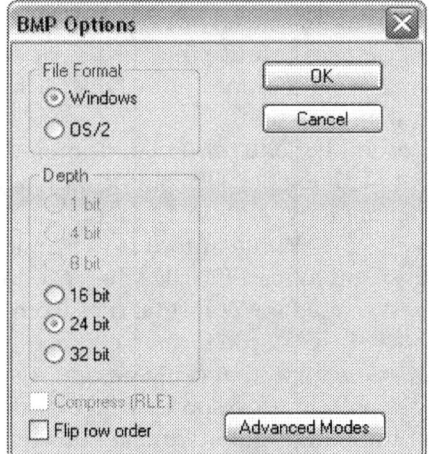

PDF—Portable Document Format

PDF is a file format developed by Adobe based on the PostScript language. It is designed to make formatted documents device and platform independent with the use of a free universal interpreter called Acrobat Reader, which can be downloaded from the Web and is included with all Adobe applications, as well as with graphics and page-layout programs from many other publishers.

PNG—Portable Network Graphics

The PNG format is a true-color format (16.7 million colors) that was designed to provide a better color format for the Web. It has not gained wide acceptance at this time and might be usurped by the up and coming JPEG 2000 format. You can use the Save For Web option in the file menu to PNG files by choosing a PNG option from the Settings menu.

PICT—Macintosh Picture Format

PICT is a native Macintosh format that is an object-based picture format similar to Windows metafile format (WMF). PICT can include bitmapped and vector information in the same file. PICT is a preferred format on the Macintosh because of its versatility. You have two choices when saving PICT files: 16 and 32 bits. The default setting is usually the best setting.

RAW—Raw Binary Data Format

The RAW format saves the absolute binary data with no interpretation or reformatting at all. The file is in the form output by the device creating it. The exact format of a RAW image file is largely determined by the device that is writing it, so it has no universal reader. This kind of file is commonly used in digital imaging devices that need pristine, high- quality, binary picture information. Many midrange to high-end digital cameras are including RAW format files as an output option. The files have much higher color and brightness range (called *gamma*) because they use 12 or 16 bits per pixel color depth in place of the 8 bits per pixel standard with TIFF files. This means RAW files contain more color and detail information.

To display RAW data files in Elements, you need some information about the structure to enter into the RAW dialog box. This information is not easy to come by, so you will have no luck opening RAW files in Elements most of the time. The trend is for manufacturers to provide a RAW file output is to provide TWAIN drivers or reader applications that allow you to read the files they produce. Some third-party applications that are designed to read RAW format files from many cameras are hitting the market. If you want to use the RAW file format, contact the device manufacturer for a recommendation of an application that can read and display the RAW file format. The hope is that RAW images will develop some standard configuration that will allow easy editing and printing of these high-quality images so we all can take advantage of the true digital negative, which is what RAW files have been termed.

SCT—Scitex Continuous Tone

Scitex CT is a full-color format developed by Scitex Corporation for use with its advanced digital prepress systems. Some service bureaus use Scitex format, but it is not common, and TIFF is much more typical. It is a good idea to consult with any service bureau you plan to use to see which format works best for them.

TARGA (TGA)—TrueVision Advanced Raster Graphics Adapter

This format was originally developed to be compatible with TARGA video board, which was one of the first high-color graphics boards developed to work with video applications for overlaying graphics. This very versatile format is still used widely in the video graphics industry.

When you save to TGA format, a dialog box with a number of options appears (see the next illustration). You can save in 16-, 24-, or 32-bit color depth. You can also choose to use RLE compression. The TGA format is one of the few that can save to a 16-bit level, and the 32-bit level supports full alpha-channel support.

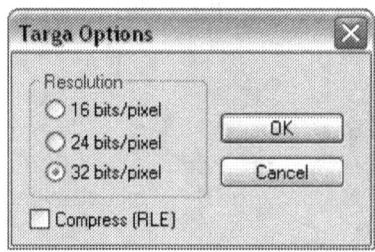

PCX

The format originally developed by Z-Soft for PC Paintbrush on the PC platform. PCX can support multiple bit levels up to 24 bits. PCX is now fading from the scene.

Managing Images

Now that you have loaded your computer with images, it's time to get them in a manageable state so you can find them when you need them without wasting hours opening files one at a time because you have to guess at cryptic filenames. In the past, before the more advanced visual interfaces, it was hard to know which files were which by just looking at the filenames in the open file window. Untold hours were spent hunting through files.

Many of the images you capture, such as those from digital cameras, use cryptic naming systems that tell nothing about the actual image in each photograph, so you end up with a long list of letters and numbers that don't tell you a thing about which one to open. On low-end cameras, you can even end up with duplicate names with each batch you save, which makes it even more confusing. In this section, we help you sort all this out and end up with a managed library of images, where you can find any image you want in the right format in matter of seconds, even if you have misplaced it.

As image-editing applications come of age, they should all take their lead from what Photoshop Elements 2 provides the user to manage files visually. Adobe has always been the innovator, and Photoshop Elements 2 is no exception. The latest version of the file browser is a state-of-the-art image-management tool that allows you manipulate your image collection all sorts of ways and (most importantly) in a totally visual manner. The latest operating systems from both Apple and Microsoft have also improved their visual interface to make it easy to sort through images by looking at small pictures instead of cryptic names such as PDX10005432n. Gone are the days when you need extra specialized software to view thumbnails, run a slideshow, and sort images. With Photoshop Elements, you never have to leave the application to fill all your file-management needs.

Using the File Browser

We cover the basic operation of the file browser interface and components in Chapter 4. In this section, we delve deeper into the image-management operation of the File Browser so you can get a better understanding of how this tool can help with file management. We will go through the various functions of file management and tell you how the file browser can help you perform those tasks. Many of the options in the file browser are duplicated in other menus. We discuss just the File Browser in this section because it's the best place to demonstrate the best aspects of file management in Elements.

Note *The Photoshop Elements File Browser is not a substitute for your operating system's Explorer or Finder. In fact, you can have those browsers open at the same time, so you can actually drag and drop files from several different drives, folders, or computers into the workspace. The biggest difference is that the Photoshop Elements File Browser displays only graphics files. Other documents, such as Word or Excel files, are simply invisible.*

Opening the Browser

To open the File Browser, you have three options:

- Choose File | Browse.

- Choose Window | File Browser.

- If the File Browser is docked in the Palette Well, click on the File Browser tab. Note: If you want it to continue to appear in the Palette Well, you need to choose the Dock To Palette Well option each time you close it (see Figure 10-3).

You can then drag the palette off the Palette Well and float it in the application window, or choose Palette | Show In Separate Window.

The File Browser has two general view states: standard and extended. It saves the state it was in when last closed. The standard view just shows the Thumbnail frame, whereas the extended view shows three additional frames: File Navigation, Preview, and File Information.

Resizing and Extending the Browser

The File Browser palette can be resized by placing the cursor over any of the edges until you get a double arrow icon and then dragging to move that edge in or out. You can also place the cursor over the Resize icon in the lower-right corner of the palette and drag diagonally. Resizing the palette enables you to size the window to your needs.

If you are in extended view (showing all four frames), you can change the frame sizes by moving the cursor over the frame borders until you see a double arrow and bar icon. You can then drag to resize the frame view. Resizing the frames allows you to maximize or minimize the view of any particular frame. For instance, if you wanted to place the emphasis on the Preview Frame so you could see each file preview in more detail as you browsed through the file list, you could maximize the frame for the preview, as you can see in Figure 10-4.

To change the palette from standard to extended view, click the double arrow icon just to the left of Filename on the Shortcuts bar at the bottom of the palette or choose Expand View from the Palette menu. This toggles the display of the three frames on the left side of the palette.

To maximize or minimize the view of the entire palette click the Maximize or Minimize icons in the right side of the Title bar.

Note *When you are trying to locate files, it is best to put the file browser in extended view so you can work with the File Navigation frame for easier navigation through the file hierarchy.*

You can choose to display folders in the Thumbnail frame also. Choose Palette | Show Folders to see folder icons reflecting the directory selected in the File Navigation frame. You can also navigate by double-clicking the folder icons in the Thumbnail frame. Use the Back button on the upper options bar to go up one level in the file system. When you get to the root directory, you can see disk icons in addition to folders. When you double-click on a folder with images, you can see thumbnail displays of each image appear in the Thumbnail frame.

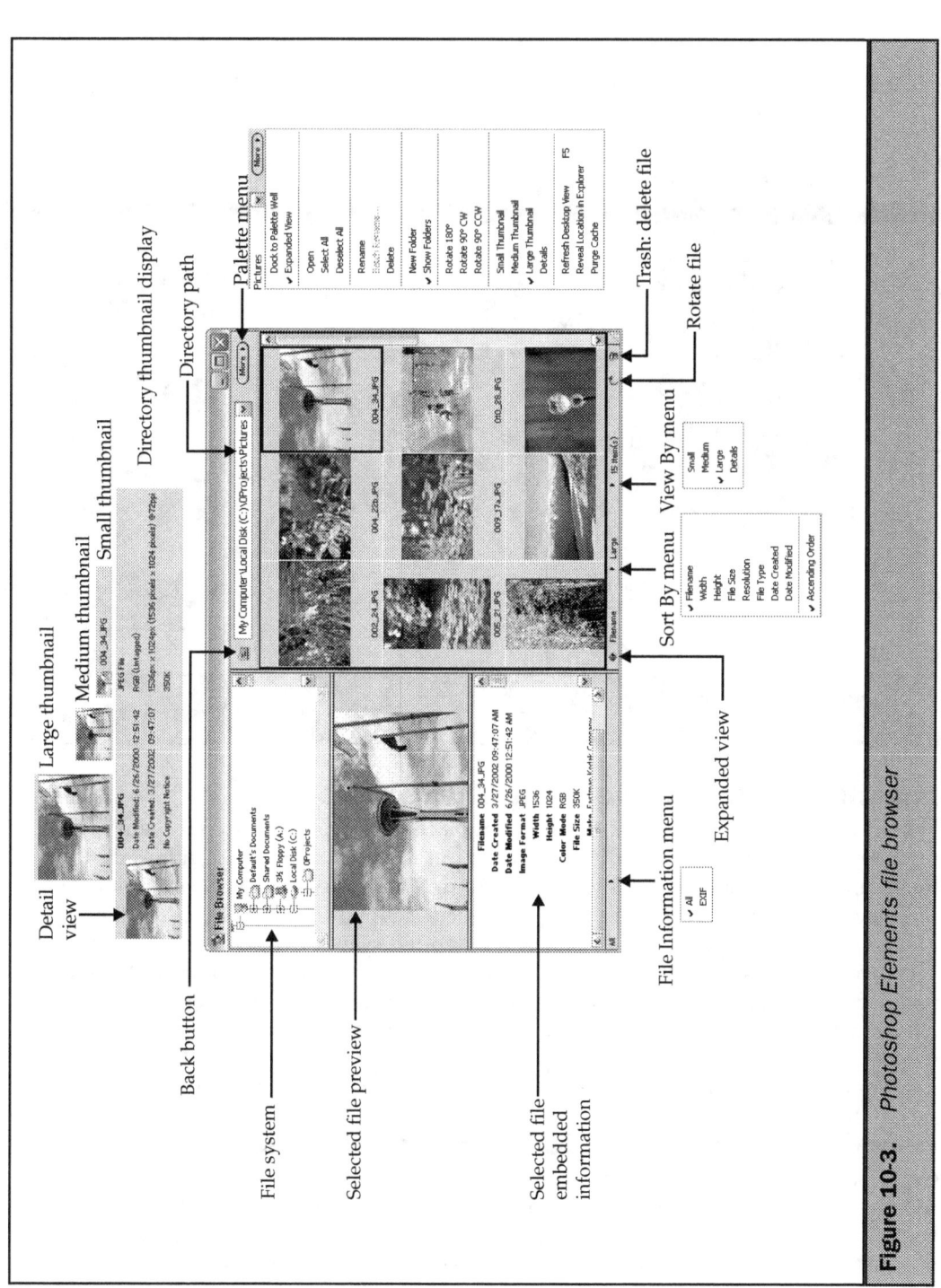

THE DIGITAL DARKROOM
WORKFLOW

Figure 10-3. *Photoshop Elements file browser*

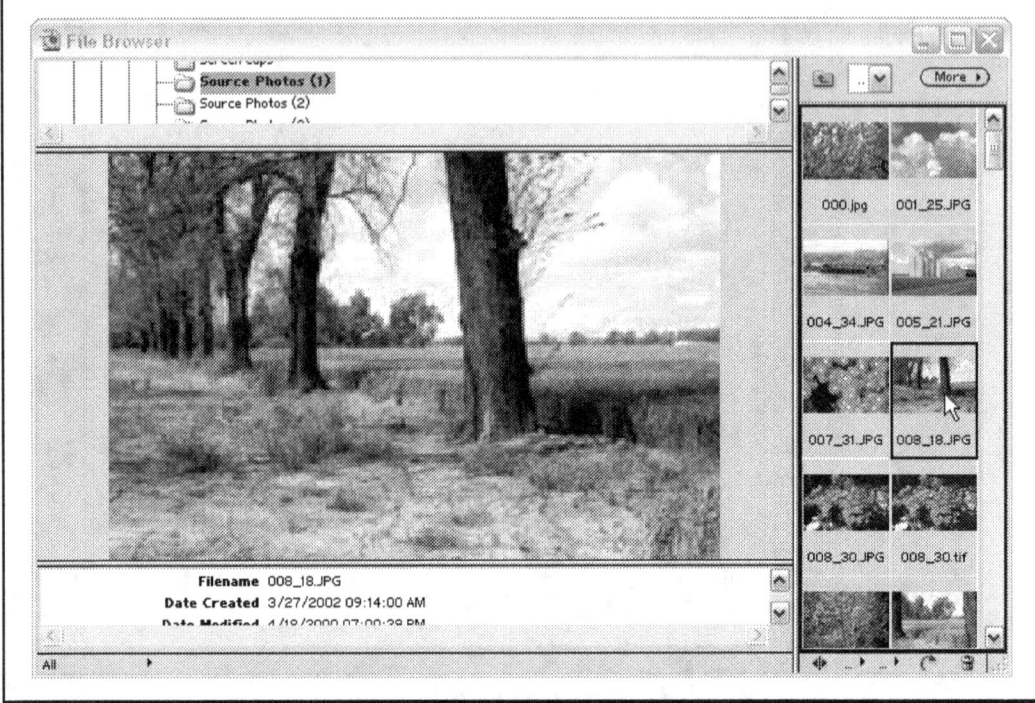

Figure 10-4.   *Maximized preview frame*

Locating Files with the Navigation Frame

When you download images to your system, it is a good practice to put them in a temporary folder and use the file browser to put the images into a working catalogue by sorting, reorienting, renaming, and grouping images so they are easier to locate. First locate the directories where you downloaded all your images by using the File Navigation frame with the file browser in Extended view. This gives you complete access to you file-system hierarchy. As you click on a folder, any images in the folder are displayed in the thumbnails in the Thumbnail frame to the right so you can see exactly what you have in visual form. You can also navigate directly in the Thumbnail frame if Palette | Show Folders is selected. Once you have located the folder and displayed its contents, you can begin working with the images themselves.

Using the Operating System's Search Function

One reason to manage files is to make it easier to locate and individual or groups of files among the hundreds or even thousands you might have on file. There are a few tricks in how you structure your image files and how you access that structure to ensure that your searches yield better results so you can quickly find the files you intended. Here are some pointers on structure:

- **Renaming with categories**   We will go into this in more detail in the "Renaming Files and Folders" section in this chapter.

- **Placing categories in separate folders and subfolders**   If, after you've searched all your directories for a particular file name component, you place the results of the search into its own folder, the search will proceed much more rapidly the next time it is run.

You can also make the search more efficient by following these guidelines:

- **Search on a phrase**   This takes advantage of the naming conventions you have set up by finding unique text phrases in the filename.

- **Search on a file type**   This can narrow the search to the type of files you are interested in. If you wanted to find just JPEG files, you could enter ***.jpg** in the find or search field. The asterisk is called a wildcard, meaning that the search will include anything in the filename that is in the position occupied by the asterisk.

- **Limit the search to a particular disk or folder**   If you keep all your image files in a folder called Artwork, then just search in that area. You can make this very specific if you want. When you have a multigigabyte hard disk, it can take some time to search the whole disk. This limited search can cut the time dramatically.

Viewing Files

The file browser has four options for viewing image files thumbnails in the Thumbnail frame. The fifth display type is the preview. You can choose from Small Thumbnail, Medium Thumbnail, Larger Thumbnail, or Details. You can see examples of the display types in Figure 10-3. The Details view provides the greatest amount of information about the individual files with text that appears along side each thumbnail. The other views provide only the filename. Use the scroll bar on the right side of the Thumbnail frame to view files the complete list of files in the folder if necessary. When you select and highlight an image thumbnail, a preview of the file is displayed in the Preview frame in the extended view of the palette. This allows you to display smaller thumbnails and still get a larger view as you select files.

Selecting Files

Here is how you select files to be opened in Photoshop Elements if you are locating them in the Photoshop Elements Browser:

1. To select an image in the Thumbnail frame, click on its thumbnail. The thumbnail highlights, and if you have the palette in Extended mode, a preview of the image appears in the Preview frame.

2. To select a contiguous group of files, press SHIFT while clicking on the first and last file for the list segment you want to highlight. This selects all the files in between.

3. To select a random group of files, press CMD/CTRL while clicking on the files you want to select in any order.

4. From the Palette menu, choose Select All to select all the files in the current folder.

5. From the Palette menu, choose Deselect All to deselect any currently selected files.

Once the image files are selected, you can then use any number of options or actions to act on all of the selected files at once. This is where the process of image cataloguing begins. As you look through your folders, you can begin selecting images that you want to group together. In the next few sections, you will become familiar with the operations you can perform to begin sorting and moving all your files into a more organized state.

Loading Files into Elements

You can load any selected image file or files into Elements by

■ Placing the cursor over any highlighted image thumbnail (it will change to a hand) and dragging it to the application window and releasing. The image or images selected will open.

■ From the Palette menu, choosing Open.

■ Double-clicking the image file thumbnail. If you have a group of files selected, you can double-click on any highlighted thumbnail, and all selected files will open.

■ Pressing ENTER or RETURN after you have selected the files or folders.

Sorting Files

When you display the images in a folder in the file browser, the images are sorted according to a number of possible criteria that are listed in the Sort By menu found on the Shortcuts bar at the bottom of the File Browser palette. Sorting the files can help organize the images in a way that makes it easier to find the images you want. Here is a brief description of each sort type with the criteria based on the default ascending order. These sorts work well in Details view because all the information the sorts are using as criteria is listed and the file browser is friendly enough to highlight the current criteria data in each file listing.

■ **Filename**   The filenames are listed in alphabetical order by the first letter or number in the filename. Numbers take priority over letters, so the filenames that start with numbers are listed first.

■ **Width or Height**   Lists the files with the smallest horizontal dimension first. Height sort lists the smallest vertical dimension first. If you are trying to find matches or a file that will fit well within a current project, you can actually compare dimensions. Width sort can also tell you if files are appropriate for certain applications. For instance, a file size of 640×480 might work fine for a web graphic but might not be suitable for a photographic print.

■ **File Size**   Lists the files by the total byte size starting with the smallest. This sort can tell which images are taking up the most room and which images are the highest or lowest pixel resolution.

■ **Resolution**   Resolution sort lists the files by the print resolution in ppi, starting with the smallest settings. If you have set your files with different print resolutions that are appropriate for a particular printer, you can sort them so you can see which ones are which.

■ **File Type**   File-type sort lists the files according to their format in alphabetical order. You can see all the JPEG, TIFF, and other formats grouped together, making it easy to act on them in unison.

■ **Date Created**   Date-created sort lists the files by the creation date, with the most recent first. This is good for locating files you created around the same time. It can also tell you the order in which a set of files was created.

■ **Date Modified**   Date-modified sort lists the files by the last date any changes to the file were made with the most recent first. This groups files you worked on in the same period of time.

■ **Ascending or Descending Order**   The default is ascending order. If the words "Ascending Order" are preceded by a checkmark, the files will be listed from the lowest number to the last letter of the alphabet (0–Z). If you click Ascending Order and toggle the checkmark off, the files will be listed from the last letter of the alphabet to the lowest number (Z–0).

Creating New Folders

This might seem like a very simple option, but don't underestimate what it can do for you. Setting up your own hierarchical catalogue or library structure saves more time than you can imagine. You can create folders in the Thumbnail view by choosing Palette | New Folder. An untitled folder will appear in the frame with the text highlighted and ready for a new title. Type a new title for the folder.

Creating folders with unique category names is the first big step in getting your images organized. Make as many new folders as you feel you need to properly categorize your collection: nature shots in one folder, portraits in another, and so on. You can go back once you have set up major categories and further organize them in to subfolders by taking the nature shots folder and breaking down into landscapes, animals, and so on. It is only through visual interaction and manipulating the images into separate folders that you get this kind of power to manage all your images.

You can choose to leave all your images in one folder and just name them so you can sort them into groups. This usually ends up with a folder with too many images, so it takes a long time to display because of all the thumbnails it has to display, and you will find yourself scrolling far too much. Isolating images in folders makes it easier to act on them as a group. The next section tells you how to find images quickly even if they are in separate folders.

Renaming Files and Folders

Photoshop Elements' file browser lets you batch rename any group of preselected images, and you can batch rename by adding information to the existing filename. This and the fact that you can use up to 35 characters (before the file extension) in a filename make it very easy to sort and find images by a wide variety of criteria. Most significantly, it lets you easily name files by category and subcategory.

Renaming individual image files and folders is by far the most important aspect of image management. Developing a system for naming that allows you to sort and search your image collection efficiently streamlines you management tasks. Digital capture devices and camera use a very cryptic method for naming files that does not tell you anything about the image. Often the cameras don't even use unique name from one session to another so you are forced to download them to new folders every time. This leaves with different image files with the same name, which can be really confusing.

Use the file browser to visually sort through you image collection and start renaming all your images with a system that tells you at least the category and a brief description of the contents. As you can see in the next illustration, the name the camera gave the image was changed to a prefix that tells you it is a general category of architecture and the subject is the bay window. We could also add the date, the place it was photographed, and so on. The priority you use is up to you. The example could just have well been named BayArea_Condo.jpg or Residence_ParkStreet_4-4-99.jpg. The folder this file resides in might be called Architecture, Bay Area Homes, or My Properties.

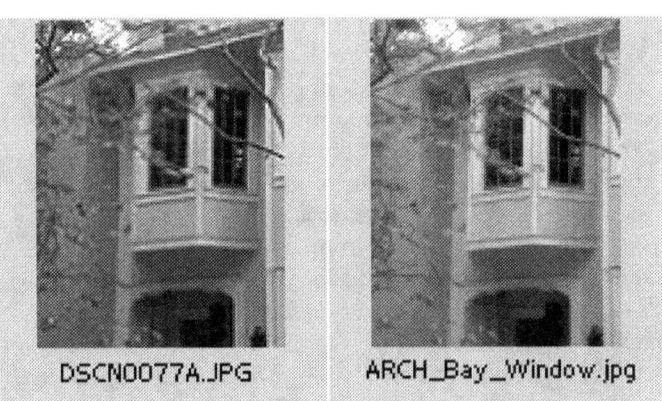

DSCN0077A.JPG   ARCH_Bay_Window.jpg

As we mentioned earlier, you can use the operating system's search function to locate files by entering criteria that isolate certain filenames and types. The naming conventions you use can add greatly to the efficiency of searching by adding categorical information to the filename that can be easily identified. For instance, if you had all images that had to do with structures prefixed with ARCH you could just search on ARCH and get a complete listing of all the files in that category, no matter which folder or disk they reside on. If you misplaced some files but remembered to name them properly, it becomes a trivial task to track them down with a search. On the other hand if you didn't name them by category, you might have a monumental task in finding them, especially given today's gigantic hard disks, CD-ROMs that your kids tend to leave lying all over the house, and detachable drives that can migrate from one computer to another. Files have been know to just get lost in the ozone and never been seen again. Take the time to structure you image names so that doesn't happen to you.

To rename an image file or folder in the file browser:

1. Choose Palette | Rename or place the cursor over the filename in the Thumbnail frame. You will see the cursor change to a text insertion cursor. The name portion of the filename preceding the file extension is automatically highlighted so you can begin typing immediately of you want to change the name completely.

2. If you want to just change part of the name or add to it, click your insertion point and drag to select text or just begin typing.

3. After you rename files or folders you might need to refresh the screen to include the new data. Choose Palette | Refresh Desktop View (F5).

Going through and renaming files one by one can be laborious if you have many files to go through. You can choose to rename a group of files with File Browser Palette | Batch Rename. This option renames the selected files in the current folder with the criteria you select from the Batch Rename dialog box, shown here.

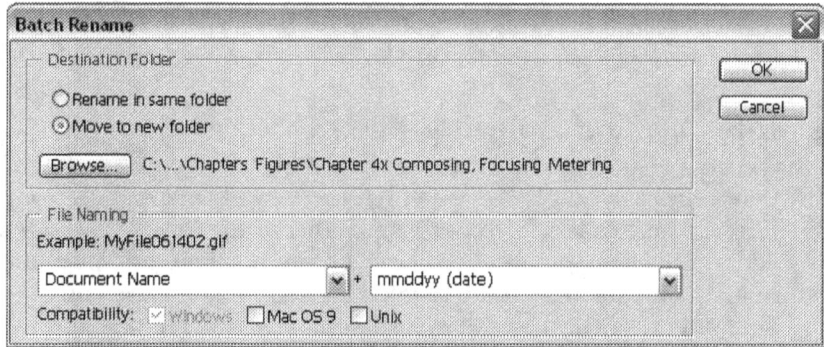

To batch rename your files, follow these steps:

1. In the file browser, open the folder that has the files you want to rename.

2. While pressing CMD/CTRL, click on individual images to select the files you want to rename.

3. Once you have all the images you want to give a common set of naming criteria, choose Palette | Batch Rename, or right-click in the Thumbnail frame and choose Batch Rename from the pop-up menu. The Batch Rename dialog box appears. Set the following parameters:

4. In the Destination Folder section of the palette, choose to rename the files in the same folder that they reside or to move the files to a new folder when they are renamed. If you have created category folders in advance, you can rename and move your files in one operation with this option.

5. Click the Browse button to look for another folder as a destination if you are moving the files.

6. In the File Naming section of the palette, set the parameters in the two fields. There are set of preset criteria that include automatic sequential lettering, numbering, and dating or you can enter your own criteria. One field must have a sequential component, such as a sequential number, to prevent files from having the same names.

7. Choose a compatibility option that assures that the filenames remain compatible with the respective operating system.

8. Click OK to begin the first state of the renaming process.

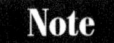

It's important to understand that you can have a potentially unlimited number of sections in a name—even though Photoshop Elements' batch renaming lets you change variables in only two fields. You simply add one field at a time over the course of several batch-renaming sessions. Each time you batch rename, make the first field's menu choice Filename. Then you add whatever you like in the second field. So you can easily end up with filenames like this: People Male Pro 123 C.TIF. Believe it or not, you still have room for 14 more characters if you need to make the scheme more elaborate.

Moving, Copying, and Deleting Files

As part of the process of getting you image collection in shape, you need to move, copy, and possibly delete files as you go. You don't have to leave Elements to accomplish this task. The File Browser makes it easy to perform all these functions. You can move files to category folders. You can copy files to assure you protect the originals while you edit, back up, and archive them. You can delete files that you are sure you not going to use to keep your system lean and uncluttered. If you have archived images to CD or other storage medium, you can delete the files from your hard disk to make more space for new files.

To move files to a new folder from the File Browser:

1. Make sure the file browser is in Extended mode.

2. Navigate to the folder where the files you want to move reside.

3. Select the files you want to move from the Thumbnail frame.

4. Bring the folder you want to move the files to into view in the Navigation frame.

5. Drag the selected files to the folder in the Navigation window until you see the folder icon highlight and then release. You will see the thumbnails disappear from the Thumbnail frame.

6. If you move files to a different disk, they are automatically copied instead of moved.

To copy files to a new folder from the file browser, follow the same steps as moving files, only press CMD/CTRL while you drag the files to a new folder.

To delete files from the file browser:

1. Select the files you want to delete from the Thumbnail frame.

2. Choose Palette | Delete or right-click to get the same option from the pop-up menu.

3. The thumbnails for the deleted files disappear.

Rotating Files for Upright Viewing

When you scan images or shoot digital photos, it is common for files that were shot in portrait (vertical orientation) mode appear in landscape (horizontal orientation) mode when the image is displayed in the file browser. This is easy to correct so you can see all your images in an upstanding manner.

To rotate any image or group of images:

1. Click the Rotate icon located on the right side of the Shortcuts bar at the bottom of the File Browser palette. Each click rotates the selected thumbnails 90 degrees clockwise. To rotate the image counterclockwise, press OPT/ALT while clicking the Rotate icon.

2. Right-click in the Thumbnail frame and choose from the rotate options: 90 degrees clockwise, 90 degrees counterclockwise, or 180 degrees.

3. You can access the same options from the Palette menu.

4. The thumbnails are rotated immediately, but the image itself is not rotated until you open it for the first time in Elements.

Viewing File Information

If you're one of those meticulous types who takes notes on all the technical data that went into every frame you photograph, you should know that you have been replaced. Digital cameras can now do that for you automatically, and you can readily see all the information in the Photoshop Elements File Browser.

Most modern digital cameras, scanners, and the like now add information to each captured image. They do this through EXIF (exchangeable image file), a new standard that allows an image file to store a host of information produced by the originating

THE DIGITAL DARKROOM WORKFLOW

hardware. This type of added information is call *metadata*. Metadata can also include information added by any other means, such as your computer system, application, and in some cases, yourself. We will discuss adding information to metadata in the next section. The file browser can display metadata, and in particular EXIF information, in the Information frame, which appears in the extended view. As of yet, Elements has no metadata search options, but it might in the future. You can choose to display all the metadata or just the EXIF information by choosing the appropriate option from the drop-down menu just below the Information frame.

EXIF information takes a snapshot of the device that created the image, as you can see in the following illustration. This gives you important data on how the device was set up and the image was captured, which allows you to fine-tune the process of capturing images by giving you a visual reference to the settings.

Image Description	
Make	NIKON
Model	E990
Orientation	Normal
X Resolution	300.0
Y Resolution	300.0
Resolution Unit	Inches
Software	E990v1.1
Date Time	2001:02:22 12:27:00
yCbCr Positioning	Cosited
Exposure Time	1/292 sec
F-Stop	6.4
Exposure Program	Normal program
ISO Speed Ratings	400
ExifVersion	0210
Date Time Original	2001:02:22 12:27:00
Date Time Digitized	2001:02:22 12:27:00
Components Configuration	Unknown
Compressed Bits Per Pixel	3.0
Exposure Bias Value	0.0
Max Aperture Value	3.5
Metering Mode	Pattern
Light Source	Unknown
Flash	Did not fire.
Focal Length	9.0 mm
FlashPix Version	0100
EXIF Color Space	sRGB
Pixel X Dimension	2048
Pixel Y Dimension	1536
File Source	DSC
Scene Type	Direct Photographed Image

Adding File Information

You can add to the metadata information to an image file in a number of ways. To add information to an image file in Elements, choose File | File Info. You can see the dialog box for this in the following illustration. Adding personal information to your file helps protect it and also provides information about who created it to other viewers, which is especially handy on the Web.

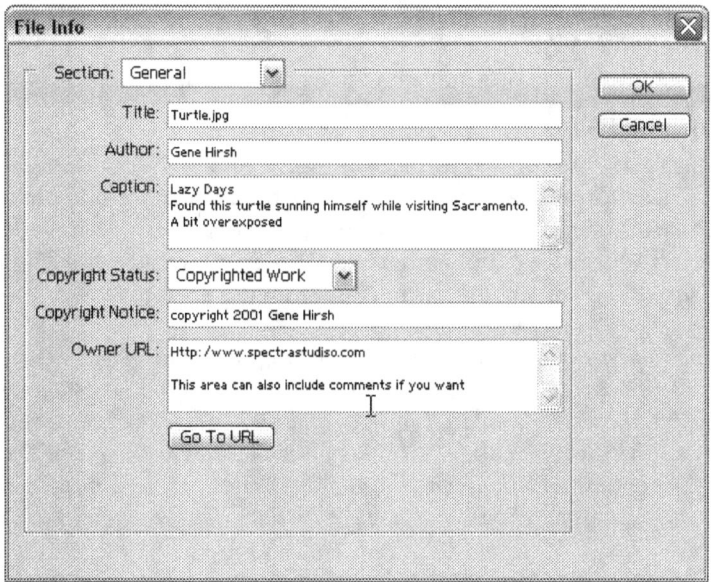

You can also use the operating system information screen, which you can access through the Properties option in Windows and the Show Info option on the Mac. These give you access to windows that allow you to add metadata to you files.

Batch Conversion

The Batch Processing option, which is found in the File menu, is useful when you need to perform a number of operations on a large number of files in a single folder. When you download a bunch of JPEG files from your camera, for instance, and you want to quickly rename for the right category prefix, move to a category folder, resize for the Web, or change the file type to TIFF all in one operation, this is the option for you. You can choose do any or all of these operation in a single pass. Use this option as you download or capture images so you keep your filing system up to date. For more information on using the Batch Processing option, see Chapter 3.

Protecting Your Image Data

You will find that some projects take longer than others, so you might not be able to get them all done in one session. If you find that you need to stop and save the work in progress, it is important to understand how to save it so you preserve all the information, you have accumulated in the course of your work like tool settings, layers, and selections. There are number of important considerations and techniques that can ensure that you don't lose anything (with the exception of the history states).

If you think there is chance you will need to extend your editing into multiple sessions or just might want to be able to modify things later, then you want to put the image into the proper format right from the start:

1. Open the image you want to edit.

2. To make a copy of the original, choose Image | Duplicate.

3. Close the original.

4. Now select Save As on the duplicated image and save it to the PSD or TIFF format. These formats ensure that all your file information is preserved in editable form when you reopen the file in Elements. If you have layers, make sure to check the Layers box; otherwise the image will be flattened when it is saved. The default is to have it checked if layers are present.

 Wondering whether you should save in TIFF or PSD file format? As long as you know the image isn't yet ready for broad dissemination, use PSD. Photoshop will be much more efficient at opening its native format, and there's far less chance of losing changes made by new features. In addition, PSD is not only designed to do all and more than TIFF, but it's optimized to do each as well or better/faster for Elements and Photoshop work. If you plan to share with programs other than these, then TIFF is the better choice.

Using Resolution to Maximize Future Image Quality

Think of the resolution in an image as if it were money in the bank. It is there for you to use when you need it, but let it slip away, and you will not have it there when you need it and you will be left with nothing but a poor-quality image style. Your original image is that bank account, and you want to protect it the same you would if your living depended on it. For some of you, that might very well be the case. You want that original to be as high a pixel resolution (absolute pixel dimensions) as it can be depending on the resolution limits of the creating device and the storage capacity and processing power of your computer.

Always preserve your original and make copies to do your editing with. You never want to risk accidentally destroying resolution because you can't get it back once it is gone.

Saving to a Lossless Format

When a digital camera saves pictures, you are given an option of what file format you can use to save with. Most cameras offer you the choice of TIFF or JPEG formats. JPEG is a lossy format, meaning it always produces some degradation in the image data in the way that it compresses the image, so it takes up less space in the camera's memory card or disk. JPEG files recompress the image every time they are saved, so you can seriously degrade the file if you save it multiple times, which is often the case in the editing process.

If you use JPEG files, convert them to lossless format before you edit them. The lossless format ensures the file will not degrade with each save—and saving often is good thing to do when you are editing. The best format to use currently is TIFF because of its wide compatibility and the range of features. PSD is also a good choice if you are not planning on loading your files to other platforms or applications because it is not as universally accepted as TIFF.

Note *The newest version of the TIFF format, supported by Elements, allows you to use JPEG compression as one of the save options. This degrades the file in the same way as the JPEG format does, so don't use it unless you also have an uncompressed copy you can restore the file from.*

When you open you files for editing for the first time, take note of what file format they are in. The title bar indicates the file type. If it is a JPEG formatted file, choose File | Save As to save the file in another format before you start editing. Get into the habit of doing this, and you will thank us some day.

Making Files Read-Only

Another way to protect original files is to go into the Properties or Information window of you image file (see the next illustration for an example) and change the file to be a read-only file. This allows you to open the file but won't allow you to save over it accidentally. You get a warning if you try to save it to the same name.

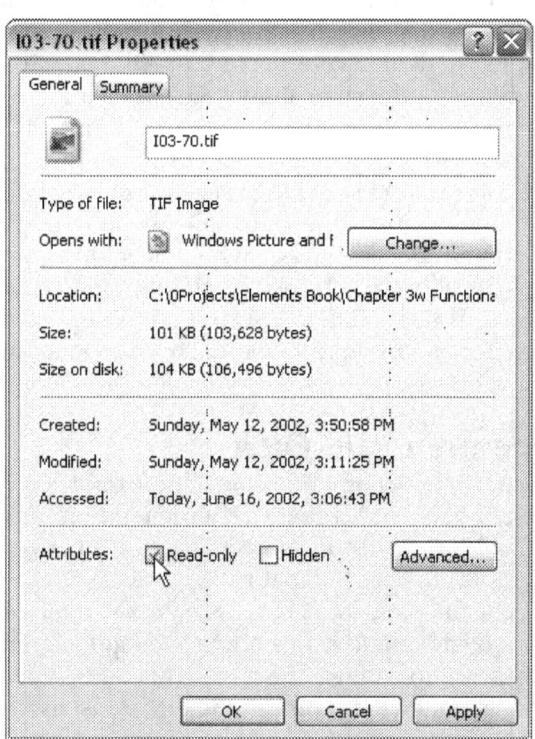

THE DIGITAL DARKROOM WORKFLOW

Backing Up, Archiving, and Using Contact Sheets

One of the most important tasks you can perform as part of your image management is backing up your files. It is something most of us put off and it always catches up with us when we least expect it, so we will nag you one more time: back up those files! Another task closely related to backups is archiving, which is not as imperative, but something you will want to do as your collection grows. You can back up or archive files directly from the file browser if you are going to disk or another computer that is networked.

There is one feature in Elements that can be very useful to archiving you images. File | Print Layouts | Contact Sheet provides a means to print a thumbnail catalog of the images in any folder. This can be filed away with your disks or CDs and be a quick way to review what is on the disks without having to load them. See Chapter 3 for more information on using the Contact Sheet option.

Working with PDF Files

PDF files have a lot of flexibility and portability, and Elements makes good use of them. We will also point out some uses that help with file management.

PDF Slideshow

Slideshows are a wonderful way to share a collection (of any size) of your photos with anyone who has a computer. The recipient doesn't need to know a thing about file formats, image editing, software, or compatibility. You can e-mail the slideshow, put it on a floppy, put a great big one (or several) on a CD. All the recipient has to do is stick the disk in a drive, double-click the slide show's filename, and just sit back and watch. Best of all, anyone can make a slideshow in a matter of minutes.

You can create slideshows by choosing File | Automation Tools | PDF Slideshow. See Chapter 3 for more information on producing slideshows.

The PDF slideshow is really just a standard PDF file that has been triggered to go in slideshow mode. If you hit the ESCAPE key while the slideshow is playing in the Acrobat Reader, it stops the show and brings up the standard Acrobat interface. This means you can use the Multi-Page PDF to PSD option to import images from PDF slideshows that you have created with Elements. This makes an independent, displayable, and portable library.

Capturing Images from PDF Files

PDF files are useful because they maintain a constant format across many platforms. As long as you have a current version Acrobat Reader loaded on the computer, you will be able to read any PDF file. You can use Photoshop's File | Open command to open any PDF file. If the file has multiple pages, a dialog box will ask you which page you want to open. When you choose the page and click OK, another dialog box tells you that the page is going to be rasterized (turned into a bitmap image) and lets you choose the resolution to which you want to convert the page. This time, when you click the page, it is a Photoshop Elements image that you can then treat just as you would any other.

The Complete
Reference

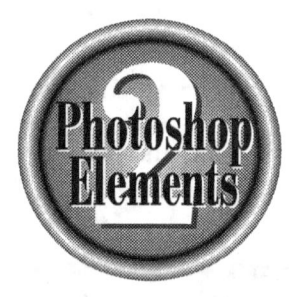
Photoshop Elements 2

Chapter 11

Getting Into Shape: Resizing, Stretching, and Distorting Your Images

This chapter gives advanced techniques for protecting, cropping, resizing, transforming, and distorting images. It not only discusses how to accomplish these tasks, but also points out how to minimize data loss, save time, and develop working strategies that make life easier in the long run.

Image Damage Insurance Strategies

Any time you trim an image or change its size or shape, you *do* lose some image information. Each time you perform another such operation, you lose just that much more information. Just how much image information you lose depends on the degree of your changes. Rest assured, however, that a continuing series of such operations would eventually damage your image to a severe extent. This section points out the strategies necessary to protect you from losing important information any sooner than necessary.

As you start making more radical changes to your images, it becomes paramount to develop procedures to protect the image data from damage or loss. There is nothing more frustrating than finding you can't find your way back from a failed attempt at image editing. You just stare at the screen and kick yourself, realizing that the image data is gone into the ozone forever. If only I had saved, backed up, made a duplicate, right? This section gives you good ways to protect yourself against this nightmare. Learning how to protect yourself from losing image data is a prerequisite to advanced techniques.

Saving the Original File

One of the most common mistakes made is to open an original file, start editing, get all caught up in making changes and additions, and forget that the name on the image file still bears the name of the original. You conscientiously save the file so you don't lose your work—and panic sets in: you have just saved over the original file. It's a photo you took that can never be duplicated, and there's no undo for a save. This kind of disaster is easily avoided.

The first rule is never, never have just one copy of an image. If it is worth keeping, it is worth duplicating. If it's not, why waste any storage space or file-finding time? Put your original files into an archived directory. The only time you should touch them after that is when you need to duplicate them to repurpose or reinterpret them. Then you can always go to the archived version and recover from a mistake.

Here is insurance policy number two. When you open an original file, the first thing you should do *before* you start working is to save the file as a working version with another filename. This assures you do not write over the original file if you save at any point. You can repeat this strategy at any point in the working process that you think you might want to come back to and don't want to lose under any circumstances. You end up with a number of files, which you can review later to determine which you want to keep, but it's more important that you have the choice. Name copies of the original and copies of those copies with version numbers (for example, sally_smile.v2.psd). Then, if you do a search on the first few characters in the filename, the operating system returns all the versions of that file. If you've changed the name of the file itself, it becomes much harder to relocate with a search.

Unless you have a tremendous surplus of memory, your history states will run out at just the point when you need them. The default is 20 states, but you can change this by choosing Edit | Preferences | General and then entering a different number in the History States field. Be warned, though, that adding too many history states could crowd your system's volatile memory (RAM), and thus slow the performance of Photoshop Elements because it has to spend more time writing to disk. A suggestion is to add 10 more states for every RAM increment of 128MB over a 256MB base.

It is the law of edits that your maximum assigned history states will be exactly one less than you need to recover from that last disastrous brush stroke. Get in the habit of pressing CMD/CTRL+S to save your files at regular intervals.

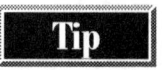

The rule is to save as, never just save. This gives you a moment to think of a distinct filename before you forge ahead to disaster. There is no undo for writing over a file.

File Format Issues

The format you save your file in can actually cause damage to the original if you are not careful. Many digital cameras can write in two file formats: JPEG and TIF. High-end cameras can also write in RAW. TIF and RAW are uncompressed and pose no danger. On the other hand, one of the most popular formats, because it saves space in memory, is JPEG. JPEG is known as a *lossy* format, which means that it sacrifices some image data to get a smaller file size. It is precisely its ability to save more pictures into a given amount of memory that makes JPEG so prevalent as a digital-camera and web-file format.

Unfortunately, you actually lose some picture data every time you save and resave to a JPEG format. See Figure 11-1 for an example of the degradation that occurs when you save to the JPEG format. If you haven't done anything at all except open the file, the computer won't bother to rewrite the file if you close the program, but it will if you choose a Save or Save As command.

If your original file is in JPEG format, there is nothing you can do to get back what was lost when it was originally created, but you can assure that the loss doesn't continue every time you save subsequently. When you open a JPEG original, immediately resave it as a TIF, PSD, Targa, BMP, or any other standard format that supports 16.8 million colors (true color) and does not use lossy file compression. If you know you are going to be creating layers, use PSD or TIF, which support saving layers.

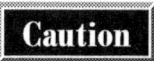

You would not want to save a 24-bit color JPEG (millions of colors) to a GIF (256 colors) format that supports only 8-bit color because you would lose most of the color information in the original. TIF is the most widely accepted standard format.

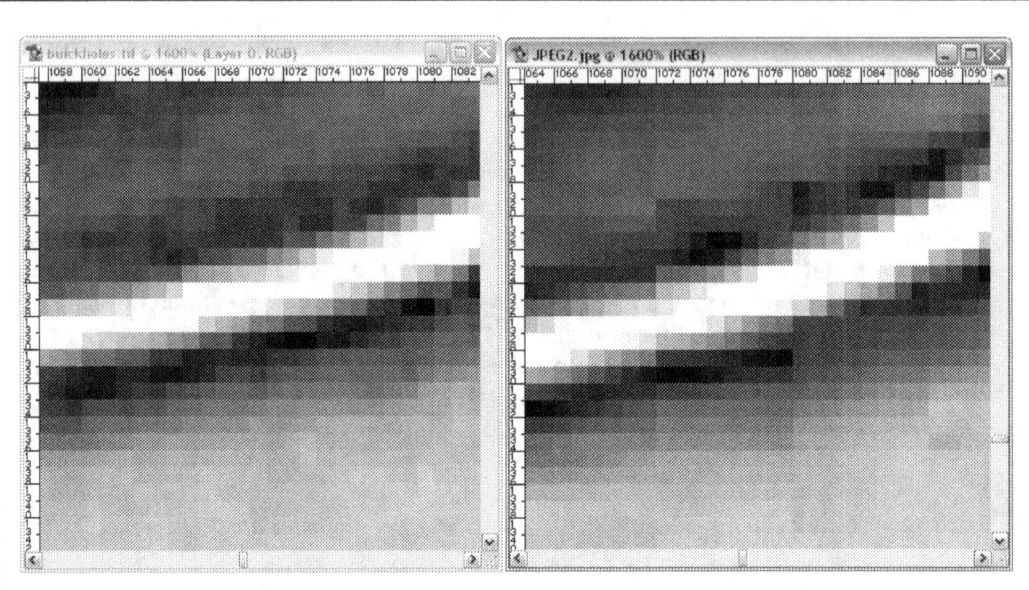

Figure 11-1. *Close-up of original image (left) and JPEG image degradation (right)*

GIFs (graphics interchange format) are indexed color image files. In an indexed color image, each color is *indexed* (assigned) a specific position in the matrix of a color palette that can contain no more than 256 colors. Because GIF files don't have to store as much color information, their file sizes can be even smaller than those of JPEGs. More important, the colors they do display aren't compromised by compressing them and getting artifacts and color shifts as they are with JPEGs. So, for flat-colored art such as text, logos, web buttons, graphic symbols, and simple illustrations, GIFs are a virtually perfect file format. GIFs have two other advantages that can make them invaluable under the right circumstances:

- GIFs can display parts of the graphic transparently by keying a single color in the palette to be transparent when it is displayed, This will allow you to place an irregularly shaped graphic (such as an asterisk symbol) onto a web page without having to frame it as an illustration. The background will show through the transparent parts.

- GIFs can contain a stack of individual files that can animate, flip-book style, any time a web page or presentation is opened.

So, now that you know why you hear so many compliments for GIFs, here's what you should *not* use them for: photographs and other complex or heavily shaded images. True, there is a technique called *dithering* that can intermingle a limited number of pixels so they create the illusion of in-between colors. It can even be a useful technique for creating thumbnail photos because those images contain only a few pixels anyway (often 64×64 pixels, which is 4096 colors—fairly easy to fake with dithering). However, dithered true-color images tend to take on a very grainy appearance, and the lack of fidelity in the colors becomes much more apparent in larger images. For more information on file formats, see Chapter 10.

Duplicating Layers

Another way to ensure against damaging the original image is to duplicate layers to provide you with backup copies before you make changes to a layer. Make the duplicated layers hidden so you can continue to work on the visible layers in the order you set them up—you can't always rely on the History States to be your backup. (Twenty quick little brush strokes will use up the Undo buffer, and then you have no way back.) With a hidden duplicated layer, you can always go back to that point.

The background layer (see Chapter 8) is your original layer, and it is automatically partially protected from certain types of modification—but not all types. It would be nice if Adobe would include a fully protected mode for the background layer, but here is what you can do instead: make a duplicate of the background layer and then make the background layer hidden (click to toggle the eye icon off in the layer's name bar). Now you have a working version of the background layer directly above while protecting the background layer from any inadvertent changes. If you need to replenish the duplicate background layer, you can always Show the original background, reduplicate it, and then hide it again.

Note   *Background layers are not foolproof protection of your original image. Any change to overall size, image format, or color mode will change the background layer also— so if you save it after one of those modifications, you will have changed the original information permanently.*

Labeling Steps

One of the overwhelming aspects of Elements is the shear number of tools you have to work with and all the things you can do at any given point. In the heat of a powerful editing session it is easy to try many things and then suddenly realize that you don't remember exactly what you did to achieve a particular effect. This is especially true when you merge a number of layers that have special attributes into a single layer or when you merge adjustment layers with the underlying layers that they affect.

THE DIGITAL DARKROOM WORKFLOW

You can avoid accidental loss of layer data through layer merging by learning to label your layers with pertinent information about how they were created. Then save a backup version of the file before you do any merging so you will have a record to refer to later. Another method of saving the information is taking screen shots (ALT+PRINT SCREEN on the PC, CMD+OPT+3 on the Mac) of the Layers palette. Better yet, if you're disciplined enough to do it, keep notes on a pad by your keyboard. This way, you can duplicate the effect by referring back to your notes, screen captures, or saved files. Inevitably, you will see the need for this when you become familiar with the shear number of variables that can be set to achieve any particular effect.

You will constantly discover methods and techniques that you will want to use again, and it is totally frustrating when they slip through the cracks because you didn't make some sort of record of how you achieved it. The process used is not always self-evident in the final image. If you use a good screen-capture program such as SnagIt, you can even capture dialog boxes and various screen states if you want to have a detailed record to refer back to. Many digital artists prize the unique styles they have developed; this is a key process in developing and documenting your own.

Tip *You can also type annotations onto your image, even though Photoshop Elements has no official annotation feature. All you have to do is choose a small-enough typeface and a text color that's distinctive enough to let you know that it's a note. When you type the note, Photoshop Elements automatically places the text on its own layer. You can simply hide those layers when you don't want them to be visible or discard them (drag them to the Delete Layer icon at the bottom of the Layers palette), or when you want to pass along your image to someone you don't want to see your notes.*

History States

History states follow you around and record everything you do in case you change your mind and want to go back. If you suddenly realize that you really should go back to what you did seven steps ago and start over, you can open the Undo History palette and select the exact stage of your image editing that you want to return to; however, there are two important limitations: the quantity of memory available and the preference that has set a limit on the number of history states that can be active at a given time.

The default number of history states is 20. After you have added 20 states to the buffer, it eliminates the oldest states as it adds new ones. There is no way to restore a history state once it's been written over in the memory stack. Furthermore, the instant you save the file, all the history states disappear. You can change the number of history states by resetting the value in Edit | General Preferences, as shown in Figure 11-2.

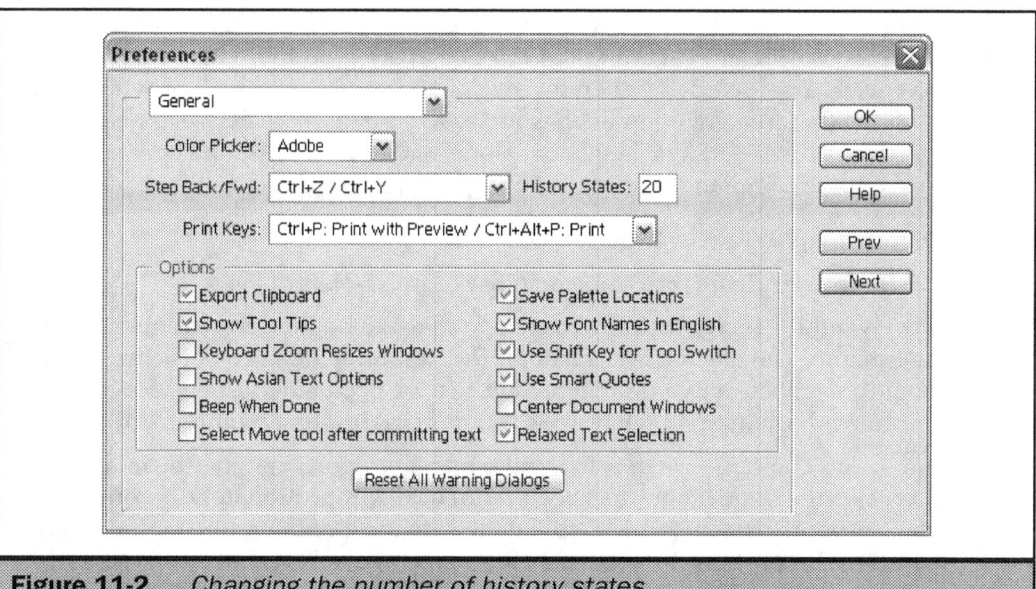

Figure 11-2.   *Changing the number of history states*

THE DIGITAL DARKROOM WORKFLOW

Resizing Strategies

Every time you want to send your image to a new destination (such as a different-size picture frame, another web site, or another publication), chances are excellent that you'll have to crop or resize it. This section takes a closer look at the tools and techniques that Photoshop Elements offers you to resize your images. You might be surprised at how many factors can affect the outcome of resizing. You can't increase the amount of visual information in an image when you resize it, but it's important to maintain the illusion (and it is only an illusion) that you haven't lost any detail.

Tip   *If you want to understand what happens when you enlarge a digital file, try this. Get a deflated balloon and place some dots on the surface in a grid pattern. Start blowing up the balloon and watch what happens to the dots. They all move away from each other as it stretches. This is what happens to the original pixels when you enlarge a digital image. Interpolation fills in the spaces by averaging color between the original pixels, but not more detail.*

Understanding Image Resizing Options

Photoshop Elements 2 (and all other versions of Photoshop) uses the same mathematical formulas for resizing images: nearest neighbor, bilinear interpolation, and bicubic interpolation. The term *interpolation* refers to the process used to determine what is done in terms of coloring and shading the pixels that are used to fill in the gaps when the original pixels are discarded (when the size of an image is reduced) or when new pixels are added (because enlargement has increased the distance between pixels). Each of those options is discussed in this section, along with the other options presented when you select the command to resize an image. Here's how you do that:

1. Choose Image | Resize | Image Size.

2. The Image Size dialog box appears (see Figure 11-3).

3. If you want the image actually to change size and not just resolution, be sure the Resample Image box is checked. If the Resample Image box is checked, you should also choose a resampling method. See the upcoming section, "Resampling," for more information on what these different resampling methods do.

4. You have a choice between resizing the image proportionately (the image maintains the same height-to-width ratio) or disproportionately. If you want to resize proportionately (which will be the case most of the time), make sure the Constrain Proportions box is checked. Then you need enter only one of the two new dimensions. The other dimension will automatically calculate based on the original proportions of the image. You can resize by making an entry in either the Pixel Dimensions area or the Document Size area.

5. Click OK. After a brief pause, your image appears in its new size.

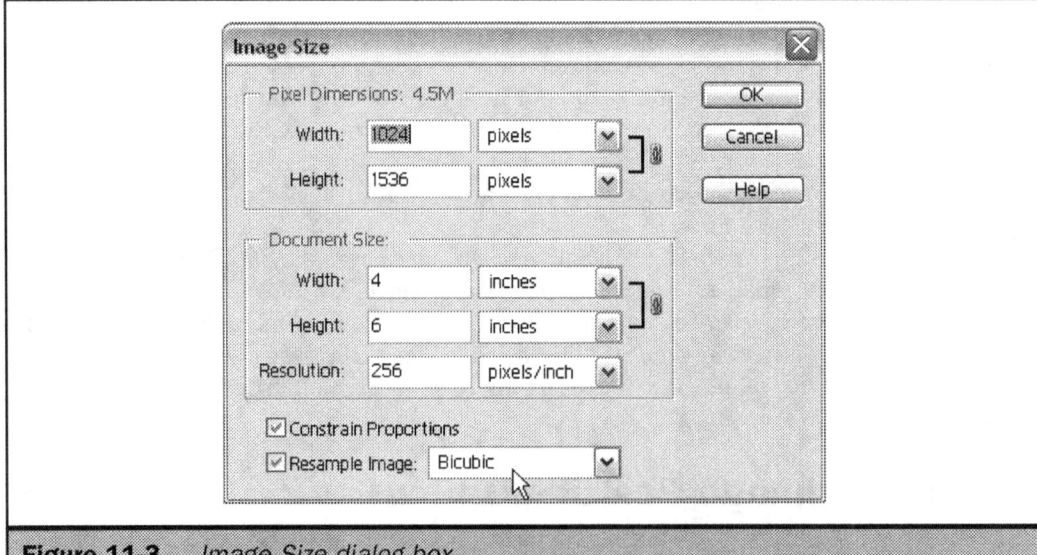

Figure 11-3.   *Image Size dialog box*

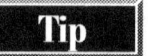

If you want to zoom quickly to a particular percentage of enlargement, just enter that percentage in the leftmost field in the Status bar that appears at the bottom of the workspace. This is only one of many options that Photoshop Elements gives you for zooming, but it is definitely the fastest way to get to a specific level of magnification while keeping the image centered.

Dimensions

The Image Size dialog box gives you all the options you need to choose the best way to accomplish your resizing task. It provides needed information about the dimensions of the document and the methods that can be employed to resize it. The first order of business is to thoroughly understand the difference between document size, pixel dimensions, and resolution (pixels per inch). This seems to be an area of confusion for many users—and if it is not understood properly, it leads to mistakes in sizing images.

Pixel dimensions indicate the absolute resolution of the image, that is, how many picture elements (pixels) are available to define the amount of detail you can see in the image when it is viewed at a given size. If you want to refer to the size of an image, use the pixel dimensions, not the resolution, which is a relative, not an absolute, term. If you combine the document dimension and the resolution, you can calculate the pixel dimension. Let's say an image is 3×5 inches and the resolution is 100. You can calculate the pixel dimension by multiplying the dimension by the resolution, in this case, 100, and get 300×500 pixels. A document of the same physical size, when viewed at a resolution of 300 ppi (pixels per inch) would be 900×1500 pixels.

Resampling

To change the size of an image while maintaining the same output resolution, you need to *resample* (add or subtract pixels). Resampling an image uses a mathematical formula (algorithm) that creates the illusion that the integrity of the visual information has been maintained by ensuring (at the least) that there are no empty spaces between pixels. If the resampling method is the nearest neighbor, it just duplicates the original pixels, thus creating the illusion that the pixels themselves have grown larger. This creates a very rough, low-quality look, with sharp edges zig-zagging like stair steps. It is a look that many refer to as "pixilated" because they can easily discern the square shape of the pixels themselves. If you choose to resample using either the bilinear or bicubic method, the program attempts to keep edges and shading smooth and natural looking. Bicubic gives you the best results.

If you need to push your image resizing beyond a two-times enlargement or reduction, you can buy much more sophisticated programs for doing so from a third-party vendor. Thunder Lizards' Print Shop Pro and Grain Surgery are both excellent choices. Print Shop Pro has the edge in edge sharpness. Grain Surgery is better at imitating the original grain structure and the tonal blending between pixels. These are my personal judgments after using both products on my pictures, and we recommend them both highly. Another great plug-in product is Lizard Tech's Genuine Fractals Pro, which uses advanced wavelet technology to increase details as you blow images up. This product seems to bend the rules.

THE DIGITAL DARKROOM WORKFLOW

If you turn off resampling, you will see that the Pixel Dimensions area is disabled (see Figure 11-4). This allows you to change the relative values between document size and resolution without changing the absolute size of the image. This is important when you print because you want to maximize the detail you can get from your original image without unnecessarily wasting ink. Enlarging or reducing it with resampling activated can actually reduce the quality at the time of output. If the original image is just too small to get a decent resolution for the document size you need, you might have to resample. Just be aware that enlarging it might not give you a much better result. It is better to have a higher resolution image when you begin.

Interpolation

Next to the Resampling option at the bottom of the Resize Image dialog box (see Figure 11-5), there is a drop-down menu that gives you three options on what type of interpolation Photoshop Elements uses when it resamples an image. Interpolation is one of those mysteries that you dare not ask about or someone might actually explain it to you. It is very mathematical, so we will boil it down to make it easier to swallow. As we mentioned earlier, when you enlarge an image, essentially you stretch it out so you create space between the pixels that needs to be filled in. Interpolation is the method of filling these spaces with averaged color, based on the color values of the original pixels. Likewise, when you are reducing an image, you need to remove pixels, which can produce abrupt changes in color where there were smooth transitions before. Interpolation smoothes those transitions to maintain continuity.

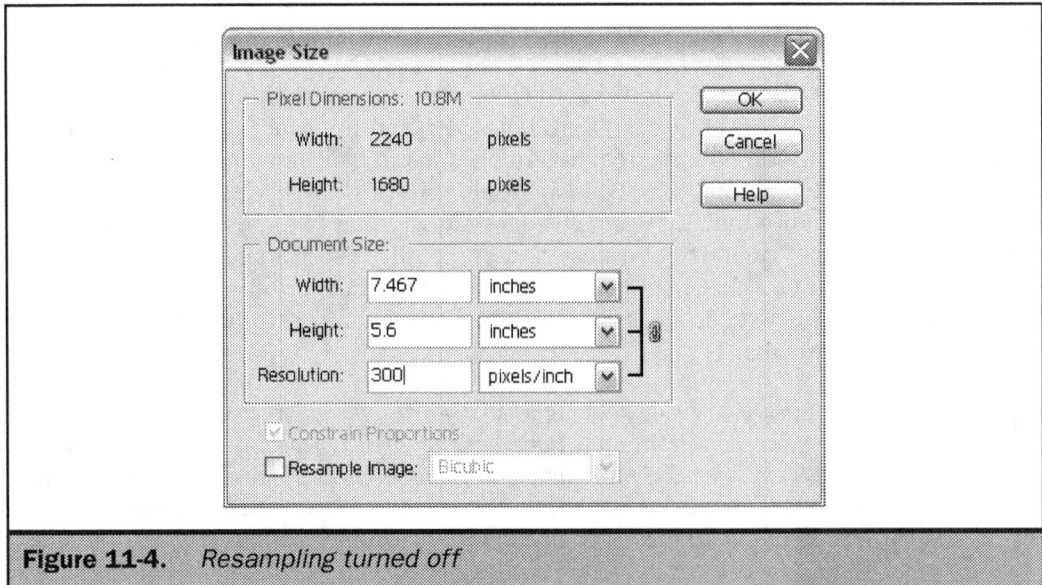

Figure 11-4.   *Resampling turned off*

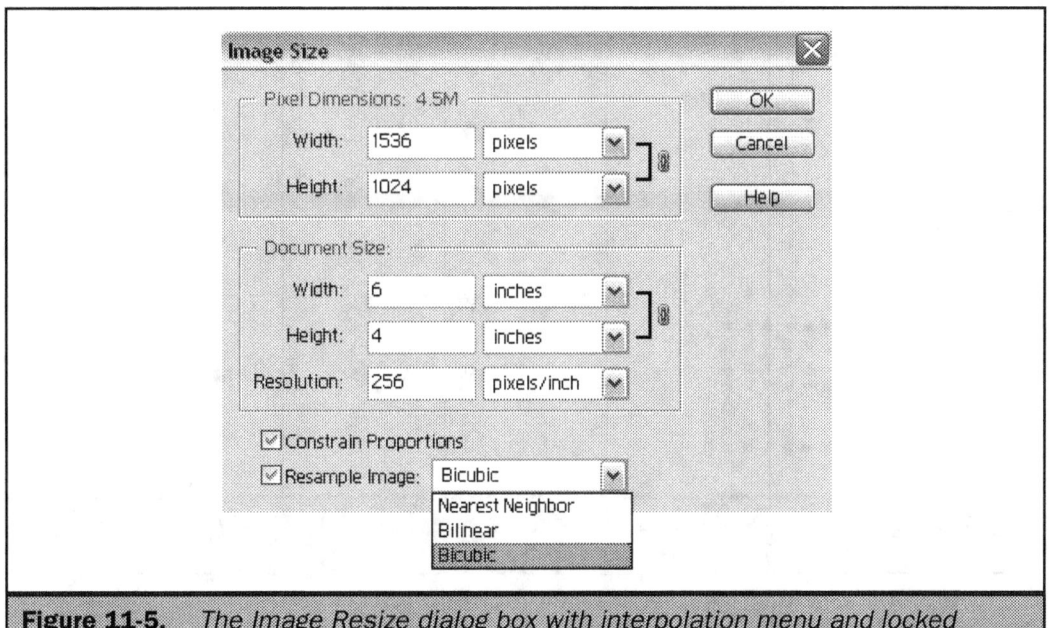

Figure 11-5.   *The Image Resize dialog box with interpolation menu and locked proportion icons*

In both cases, the image is softened and sharp detail tends to be compromised, depending on the degree of resizing. Nearest neighbor interpolation just duplicates the original pixels to fill the gaps, and doesn't do anything to correct reduction errors. Bilinear interpolation uses a linear averaging algorithm that tends to soften more because it does not take the color contrast of adjacent pixels into account. Bicubic interpolation has the highest fidelity and uses Gaussian averaging functions to enhance edge detail, which reduces the softening effect (see Figure 11-6).

There is one more thing to consider when you use interpolation in resampling an image. Because most interpolation routines use color averaging as the method for adding information, it can have the effect of shifting the color of the image. It is a good idea to check the original file to see if you might need to correct the color after resizing it.

Tip   *Resizing an image more than once produces a higher rate of degradation. It is the same as trying to produce another generation of a video from one that was already copied. It goes downhill fast and soon drops off the edge. Try to do all your resizing from a single archived image that has already been fully edited. If your original image is obviously too small for its most likely maximum size output, it might be best to enlarge it before you do any editing, especially if you're going to add elements from other images. Then make an archive copy after you've finished all editing and do any further resizing on that archived copy.*

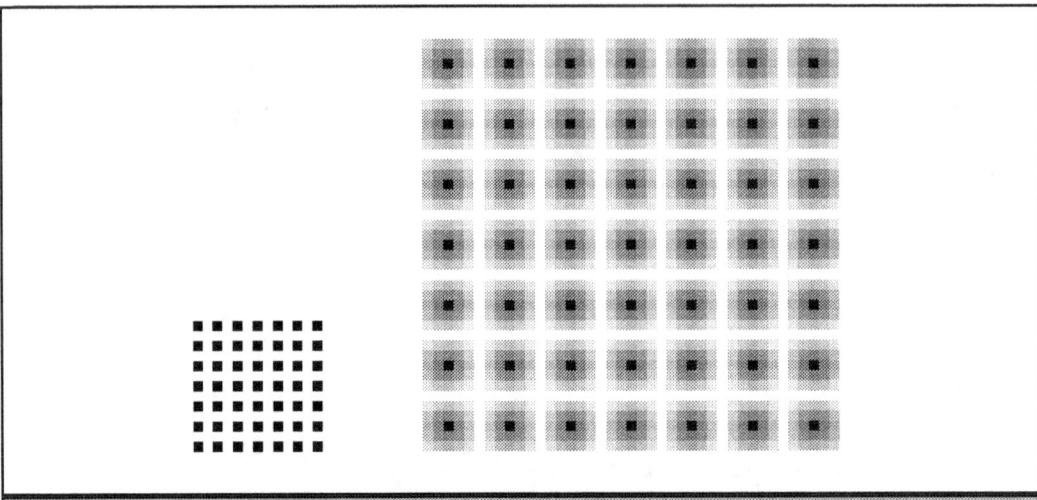

Figure 11-6. *The original image on the left was enlarged 300% with bicubic interpolation, creating the result on the right.*

Proportional and Disproportional Sizing

By checking or unchecking Constrain Proportions in the Image Size dialog box, you can either force the resizing process to keep the aspect ratio of the original image or release the horizontal and vertical dimensions to resize independently. When you resize disproportionately, you are stretching the pixels out of square, which produces distortions in the image that tend to smear the color in the direction of the greatest change. If you keep your resizing at a modest level, it is possible to make minor corrections without many visual problems. When the Constrain Proportions box is checked, you will see a chain icon appear to the right of the Pixel Dimensions and Document Dimensions (refer back to Figure 11-6), which indicates that the two are locked together and will not change independently.

Disproportionate sizing is also used to a great extent in transformations such as perspective, skew, and distort. Any of these transformations can be used to adjust the horizontal and vertical dimensions independently (see the upcoming section "Transformations").

Note *When you know you are going to resize or transform an image more than once, and all those resizings and transformations need to occur at the same stage (for example, before you add additional elements to a composite), try to find methods that combine these operations before final* rendering *(regenerating the image according to the most recently applied commands). In that way, all the pixel changes are made in the same operation, which can save several times the data loss. For instance, when making a transformation, you can enter data for several types of transformations in the Options bar at the same time. Alternatively, you can perform several types of freehand transformations before you click the Commit button to render all those operations at once.*

Resizing the Canvas

So far, we have discussed only resizing the image itself. There is another option that allows you to resize your work area but not the original image. This is the Resize Canvas command (see Figure 11-7). When creating a composition, you often find you want to extend it to accommodate new material outside the boundaries of the original or, inversely, you want to cut it down. The Resize Canvas command allows you to redefine the dimensions of your work area in the horizontal or vertical dimension independent of the original image. The operation is called Resize Canvas because it is like suddenly finding that your original painting has been placed on a larger canvas, with the result that the canvas protrudes beyond the boundaries of the image.

The Resize Canvas command also allows you to orient the image so that the extra pixels get added to specific edges. For instance, if you wanted to add extra area only to the right edge of the image, you would select the box on the left of the orientation array (as in Figure 11-7) and change only the horizontal dimension. Choosing the box in the middle distributes the extra pixels on all edges, or equally top and bottom, or left and right, depending on whether you increase vertical or horizontal dimensions.

Transformations

Transformations allow you to transform the shape and dimension of a selection or layer in a variety of ways. You can scale, rotate, distort, adjust perspective, and skew (see Chapters 7 and 8 for more on transformations). They can also be used to correct common problems with images, and that is the focus of this section.

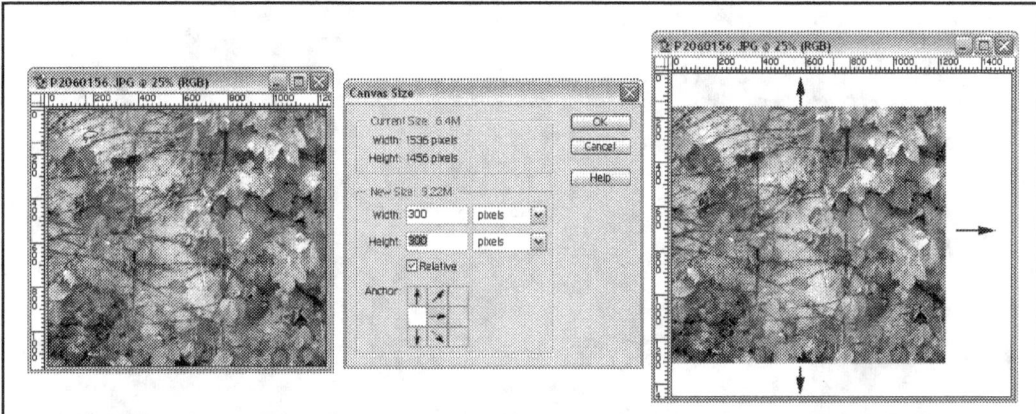

Figure 11-7.   *You can see the original image (left) and the Canvas Size dialog box (center). On the right you can see the outcome and the space that was added according to the way the Canvas Size options were selected.*

THE DIGITAL DARKROOM WORKFLOW

Fixing Perspective Distortion

When you take a photograph and the camera is not parallel with the plane of the subject that is being photographed, it produces a perspective distortion. The distortion basically exaggerates the perspective and gives the image an unnatural look. This is most pronounced in cityscapes where there are a lot of tall buildings and straight lines that can accentuate this distortion. Unless you have a specially designed lens that can correct for this distortion and still capture the extent of the skyscraper without tilting the camera up, you will need to correct it with editing techniques later. You can use the transformation commands in Elements to do this.

The two transformation commands that are most useful for this kind of fix are Perspective and Distort. Both commands provide the means to pull the transformation selection into trapezoidal shapes, which stretches or pinches the pixel dimensions of the selection, counteracting the effects of the lens distortion. First, decide whether you want to correct the wide or the narrow end of the perspective. In the example in Figure 11-8, the narrow end at the top of the picture will be corrected using the Perspective command. The camera was obviously tilted up when the shot was taken so the top of the window is narrower. We want the window to be parallel to the frame, which is the way you would normally see it. Choose | Image | Transform | Perspective. You will see the

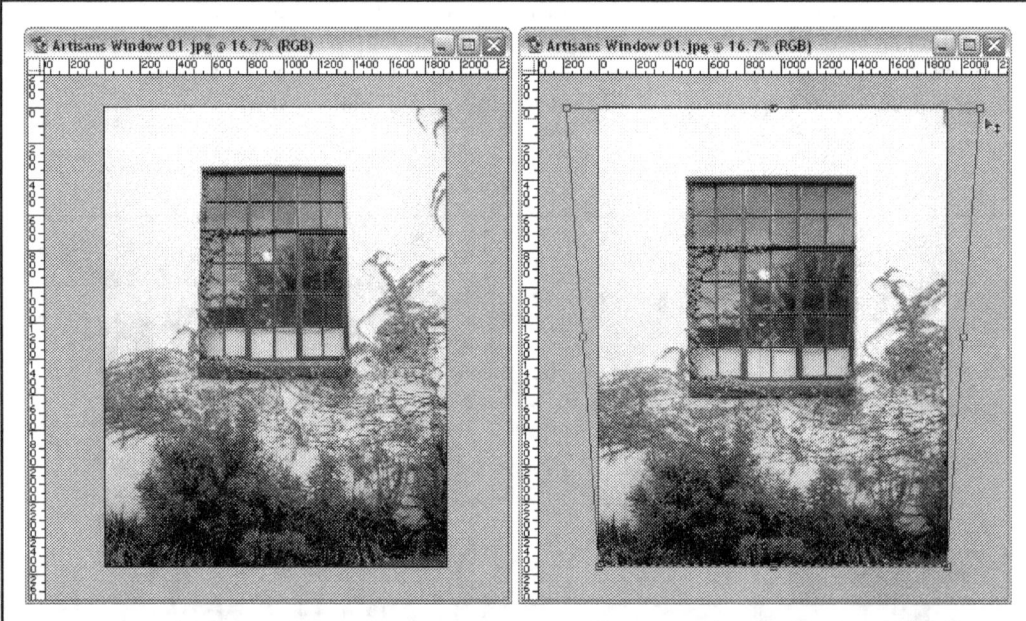

Figure 11-8.   *This example demonstrates how to use the Perspective command to correct perspective distortion. The original is on the left and the correction on the right.*

bounding box and adjustment handles appear at the borders of the image. Adjust either of the upper corners by dragging them. The two upper corners work in unison to adjust the image. If you want to adjust the corners independently, you can use the Distort command. Adjust it until it looks right, and then finalize the transformation. This process can work on some rather severe distortion, as long as you have enough information on the original image. Higher-resolution images return better results.

Correcting Lens Distortion

Not all camera lenses are created equal, and one thing you pay for when you buy an expensive lens is a reduction in the amount of distortion it produces. Distortions are produced by defects in the lens that cause it to bend the light in ways that make the image look bowed out, called *barrel* distortion, or pinched in, called *pincushion* distortion. Wide-angle lenses are more prone to barrel distortion, and telephoto lenses are known to produce pincushion distortion. Elements is not really the best program to deal with these problems, and has no specialized tools to address them directly; however, there are some ways to correct them using the filters Pinch and Spherize. You can see how the Spherize filter can correct this type of lens distortion in Figure 11-9.

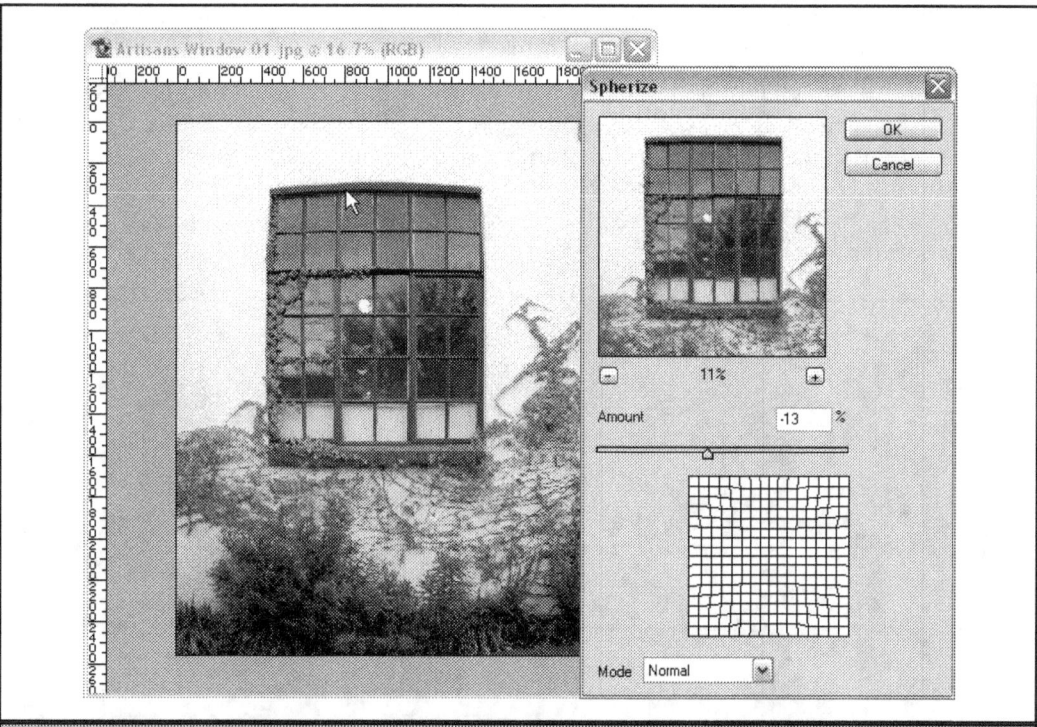

Figure 11-9.   *Correcting the distortion using the Spherize filter*

Resizing by Scaling and Transforming

If you want to resize one layer independent of the rest of the image, you do that by performing a transformation. In Photoshop Elements, the Transform command can be used to do the following: scale (resize), rotate, skew, distort, create perspective (keystone) distortion, and stretch.

Transformations work on either entire layers or the contents of selections when you choose any of the following:

- Image | Transform | Free Transform
- Image | Transform | Skew
- Image | Transform | Distort
- Image | Transform | Perspective

Actually, you can do all these things and more in Free Transform, but you can do perspective distortion only from the Image | Transform | Perspective command.

Here's how you go about resizing with the transform marquee:

1. Choose a layer that has an image you want to resize.

2. Choose Image | Resize | Scale, and you will see a transformation marquee surround the layer, as shown in Figure 11-10.

3. You can stretch any of the handles to resize the box, even beyond the extents of the layer itself. It you go beyond the image boundaries, it effectively changes the total pixel dimension, but that information is kept hidden. It appears as though you have cropped part of the image by transforming it beyond the workspace frame, but, in fact, the resized image is all there—as long as you don't flatten the image.

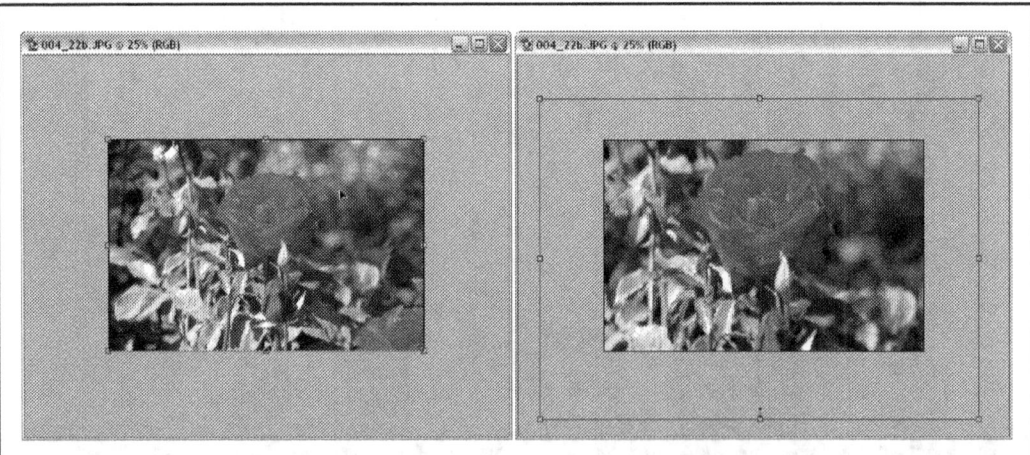

Figure 11-10.   *On the left is the original layer; on the right is the same image scaled beyond the document boundaries.*

If you want to reveal the entire resized image, choose Image | Resize | Reveal. The boundaries will expand to reveal the full extent of the image and adjust the image pixel dimensions accordingly. The Reveal command also works with any other transformations you have performed on any of the layers. The Scale and Transformation commands allow you to adjust the size relationships quickly between layers.

It should be noted that if you enlarge the layer images beyond the current boundary, you are actually resampling the image to a higher resolution, which will increase the file size even though the Image Size dialog box does not report the change in size.

Matching Sizes Between Files

When you are doing composites, you might well be working with a number of image files that come from different sources. This usually means that resolution is uneven between these sources. Some might be scanned photographs, others might be digital stills, and some might be even captured from videotape, film, or the Web. As a result, when you bring them together as layers in a composite image, you need to resize them to adjust the relationship they have to each other. As a result of both original resolution and resampling, it's likely that you will see mismatches in grain structure, color values, and pixelation. You can use filters such as Noise and Grain to help mitigate some of this. There are also some special features of the Cropping tool that allow you to crop and resample based on a referenced image's size and aspect ratio (see the upcoming section "Cropping Your Images"). Of course, it's best when putting together a composite to look for images that need minimal resizing and resampling.

If you are putting pieces together for print, lean toward higher-resolution images and away from images with very low resolution. You don't want to compromise detail when print is your goal. If, on the other hand, you are designing output for the Web, where pixel dimensions are naturally low, you will have more freedom to reduce images to match.

Image Softening and How to Mitigate It

As it was stated earlier in this chapter, linear or bicubic interpolation causes an image to soften very much like using a blur filter on the image. The more you enlarge the image, the more obvious this effect becomes. The way to combat this is to use the Unsharp Mask filter to add more contrast to edges that are softened by the pixel averaging. The Unsharp Mask filter limits its sharpening to high-contrast edges and does not produce noise artifacts in smooth (edge-free) areas, which can be a problem when using the other Sharpen filters.

Here's how you use the Unsharp Mask filter (see Figure 11-11):

1. Open the Image that you have enlarged and want to sharpen.

2. Zoom in on the image so you can get a close look at how the sharpening is actually affecting the pixels. You should be at no less than 100 percent or greater.

3. Choose Filter | Sharpen | Unsharp Mask. The Unsharp Mask dialog box appears.

4. Be sure to toggle on (check) the Preview box so that you can interactively judge the result of changing the settings in the image window.

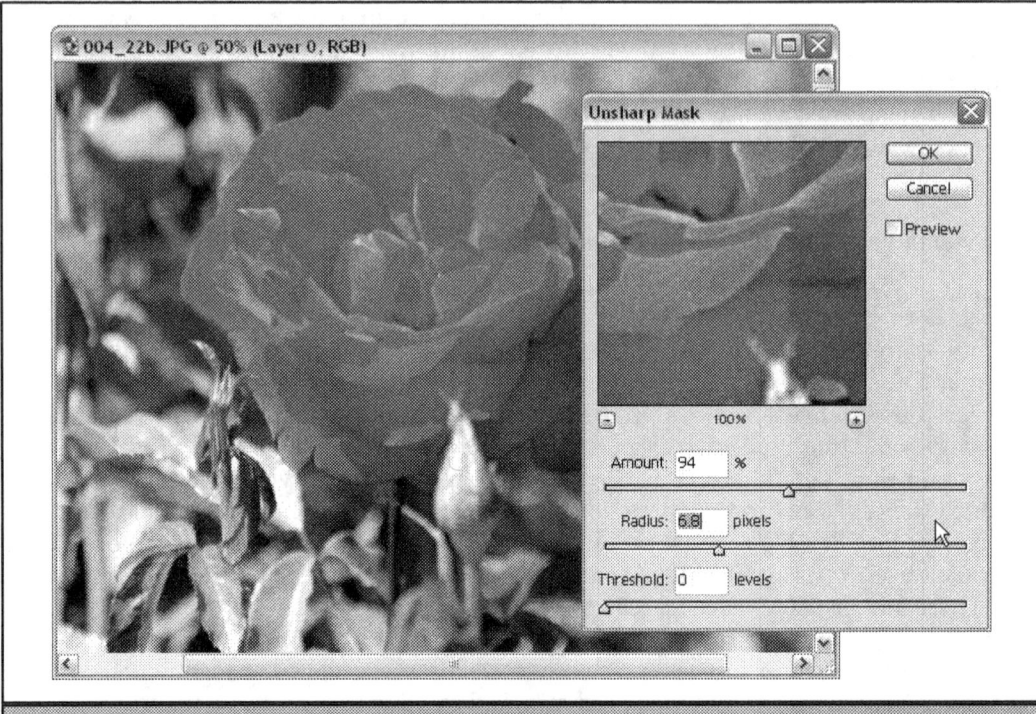

Figure 11-11. *The Unsharp Mask dialog box*

5. Move the Amount slider to indicate the degree to which you want to increase the contrast between the pixels that form edges (any row of similarly colored pixels). A value of 50 is a good starting point.

6. Drag the Radius slider until the thickness of the edges is pleasing. Usually, a very low setting is best, unless you're looking for a "forced" effect.

7. Drag the Threshold slider to determine how much contrast Photoshop Elements must see between adjacent pixels before it will consider them to be an edge. The Contrast slider will apply changes to these edges. We've found the Threshold control to be the most size- and content-dependent setting of the three. Pay close attention to how this control affects the image over a broad area as you drag this slider.

8. When you're happy with the setting for all three sliders, click OK.

This method will help correct some of the softening that occurs in interpolation resizing, but it will never be as good as using a higher resolution image to begin with.

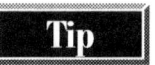

Sharpening, even with the Unsharp Mask filter, should always be the last step you take in editing your image. Otherwise, if you discover later that you have to sharpen again, you're much more likely to see highlight halos along sharpened edges and grainy noise artifacts in areas of the image that would otherwise have been smooth.

Cropping Your Images

Photoshop Elements is chock-full of tools for cropping your images. In fact, there are so many, it makes it difficult to know which one is actually best for a given purpose. We will give you what we believe are the best techniques for accomplishing any number of cropping tasks.

The tools you can use for cropping are the Crop tool, Selection Marquees, Crop command, Canvas Size command, and Scale option. Each one is unique in its approach and offers advantages and disadvantages. We have already covered the Canvas Size and Scale commands, and now we will sort through the rest in this section and give you some pointers on which cropping tool to use when.

Crop Tool

The Crop tool is an excellent choice if you want to

- Rotate the marquee before cropping to straighten the view from a tilted camera.
- Preview the cropped area before executing the crop.
- Position the marquee precisely once you've placed it.
- Crop by the most obvious and versatile method.

Here are the basic steps for using the Crop tool:

1. Choose the Crop tool from the Toolbox.

2. Optional: If you want to crop to a precise height and width, enter the pixel dimensions in the Height and Width fields in the Crop tool's Options bar *before* you start to drag a marquee. When you drag the marquee in step 4, the marquee's shape will be proportionate to the dimensions you entered, but you can make the marquee any size. When you render the crop, the cropped portion of the image is resampled to match the required dimensions (and resolution, if you perform step 3).

3. Optional: If you want the cropped images resampled to a particular resolution (number of pixels per inch), enter that resolution in the Resolution field *before* you start to drag a marquee.

4. Drag diagonally in the image to create a marquee that includes approximately the part of the image you want to retain after cropping.

5. Notice that the area outside the marquee immediately darkens so that you can more accurately judge the composition of the image within the resulting crop.

Resize the marquee as needed by dragging the handles. If you want to resize the marquee proportionately, press SHIFT while dragging a corner handle.

6. If you want to rotate the cropping marquee, place the cursor just outside one of the corner handles. Move the cursor until it turns into a curved, double-headed arrow (just like the one used by the Transform command).

7. When you've got everything just the way you want it, click the Commit icon in the task bar (or press RETURN/ENTER or click the Crop tool in the Toolbox). Depending on which of these you chose, you might see a dialog box asking you to confirm that you want the image cropped. If you clicked the Commit icon, the cropping renders without further ado.

The Crop tool pares down images by deleting all pixels outside the Crop rectangle. The Crop tool always crops all layers simultaneously and in register. Once you've cropped with the cropping tool, you can recover the deleted pixels by stepping backward (CMD/CTRL+Z or Edit | Step Backward), or by opening the Undo History palette and selecting the state before you cropped, or by choosing File | Revert to restore the original image.

If you do rotate the marquee, the image automatically straightens when you render the cropping. After you crop a rotated selection, it reorients itself vertically if the initial rotation is equal to or greater than 45 degrees, or horizontally if it is less than 45 degrees (see Figure 11-12).

There is another feature of the Crop tool that is really quite nice. You can set the final size, proportion, and even resolution of the crop by entering the values into the Height, Width and Resolution boxes on the Options bar, shown next. The Crop tool automatically locks the aspect ratio of the crop to the dimensions you entered, and then resamples the image to the size you specified.

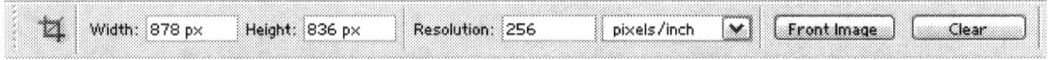

Being able to specify exact numeric dimensions for cropping makes it easy to make unevenly proportioned images fit within a specific frame size. This can be particularly handy for making web image thumbnails a uniform size and proportion, which greatly cleans up the graphic design of the thumbnails page. Wait, it gets better.

Crop Command

The Crop Command, found on the Image menu, is designed to work with any of the Selection tool's bounding boxes. This makes it very handy for quick cropping when you already have a marquee selected or when you don't want the marquee to snap to the size of the workspace window (something that is very annoying when using the Crop tool). More important, you can also use circular and free-form selections to define a rectilinear crop based on the bounding box of that selection (see Figure 11-13). The maximum horizontal and vertical extents of the selection define the bounding box.

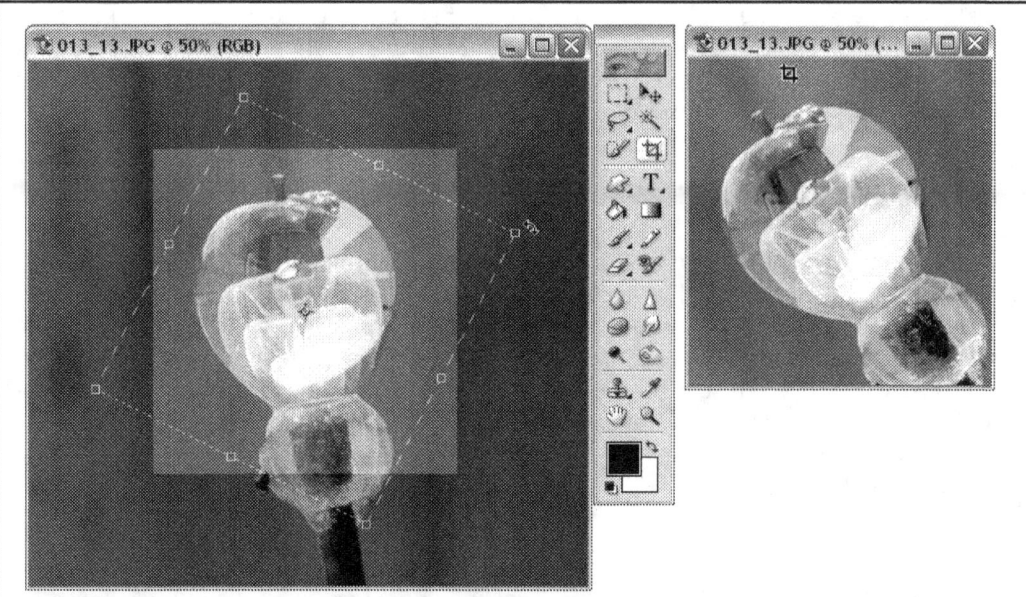

Figure 11-12.   *Positioning and rotating the Crop tool marquee on the left and the final crop on the right*

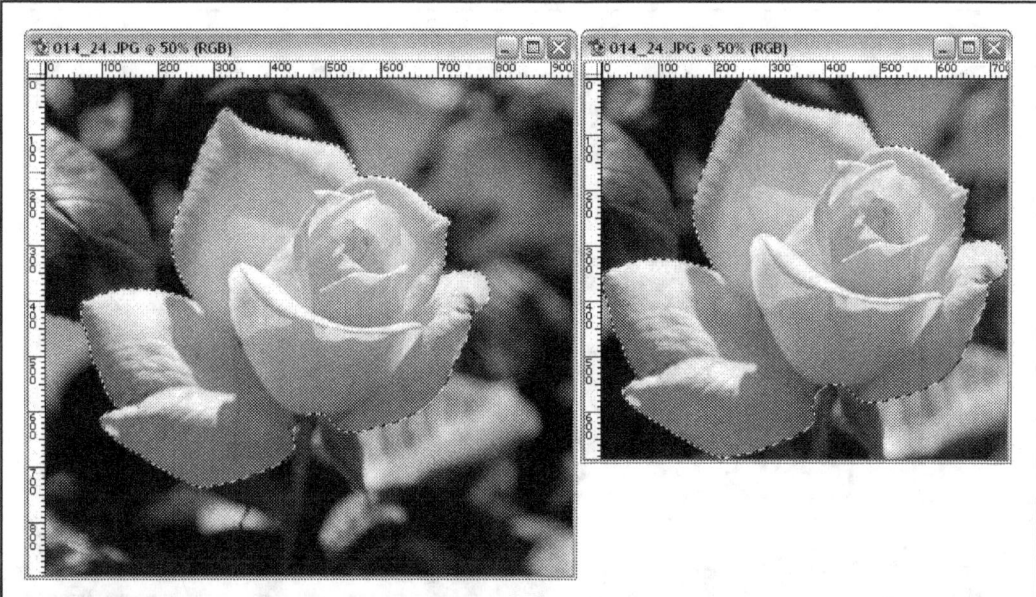

Figure 11-13.   *A free-form selection (left) and the result after the Crop command (right)*

This allows you to define and crop to the smallest space that will contain any selection you might make. This is a good way to make sure you have the minimum sized image to contain the selection you have. This saves disk space when, for instance, you want to save pieces that you have cut out of a background.

Selection Tools

If you want to crop only the image on a single layer, you can use any of the selection tools, but here you will use the Cut command instead of the Crop command to limit the cut to the current layer. When working this way you can even crop to a free-form shape. Of course, in a sense, you're really cheating. The layer you've cropped isn't any smaller—you've just made a portion of it transparent. Still, the effect will be the one you're looking for. This is also a good technique when you want to composite or montage a number of images together over a background, as you can see in Figure 11-14. Selections can be used to perform crops on individual layers.

Here's how to do it:

1. Choose a layer that you want to crop, and use any selection tool to mark the selection.

2. Choose Select | Inverse to invert the selection (press DELETE/BACKSPACE); then choose Edit | Cut to make the inverted selection area transparent.

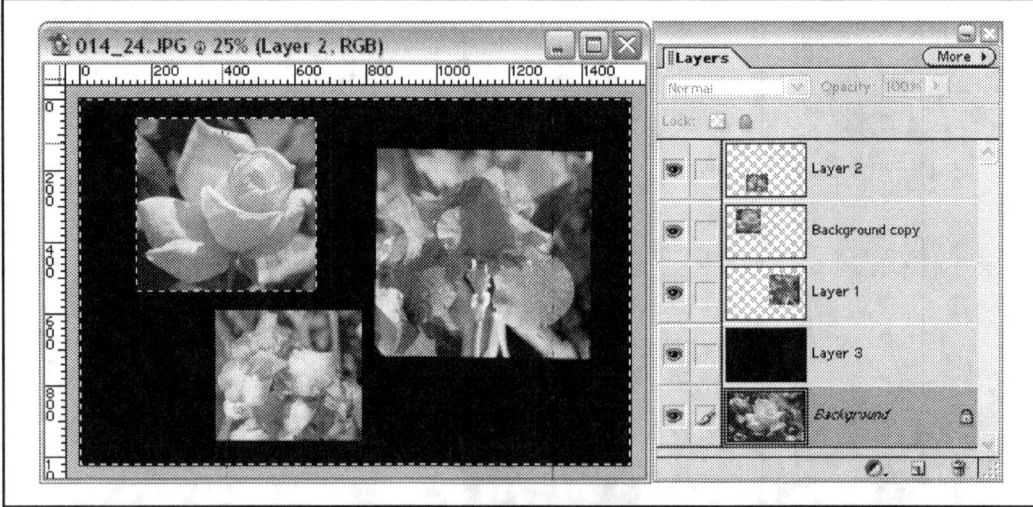

Figure 11-14. Use the Cut command to crop a number of layers so the components can be more easily arranged in their separate layers.

The Complete Reference

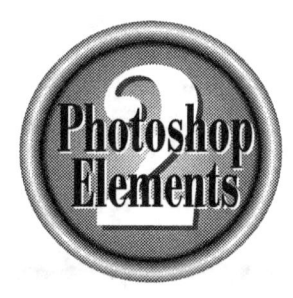

Chapter 12

Correcting Exposure, Contrast, and Color Balance

Given today's cameras, you'll rarely capture an image that's so technically bad it can't be rescued. However, even photographs that appear to be okay at first glance can usually use a bit of tweaking to give the final product maximum impact. The image here shows a good picture (left) made better with a few adjustments (right).

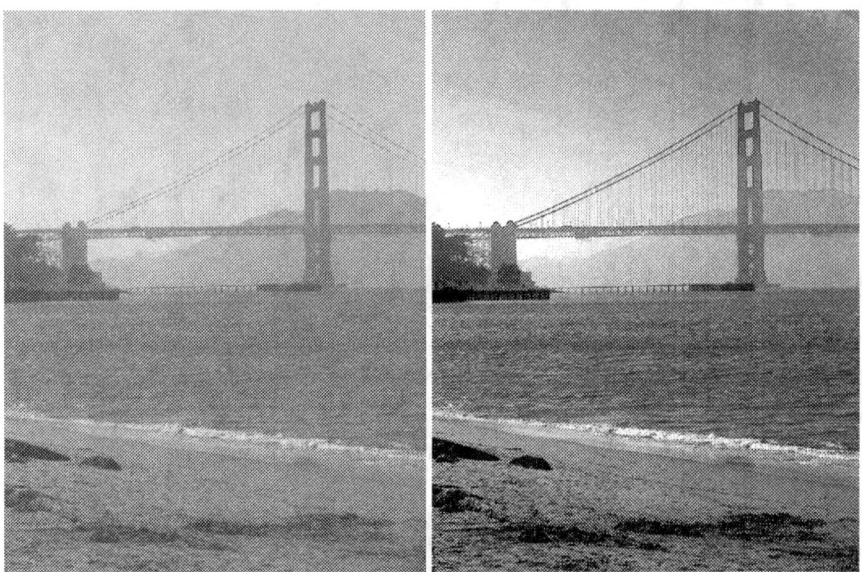

If you are scanning prints or slides, you are at the mercy of the photo lab that is processing them. Some labs use mass-production color balancing, which can compromise the color in many photos. Photoshop Elements can correct for this. The calibration of your monitor can have a big impact on the way you perceive the color and brightness in your images as well. You want to be able to see an accurate representation on your screen while correcting your photos. Color calibration is covered in Chapter 1.

In this chapter, you'll learn numerous techniques for improving the overall brightness of the image, its tonal range, the overall hue of the prevailing light (color balance), and the contrast (difference in brightness) between adjoining areas in the image. It is these three factors—color balance, brightness (exposure), and contrast—that influence the judgment of the viewer as to the quality of the picture. Of course there are other factors, such as lighting, subject matter, and composition, that influence our judgment of the quality of a picture. These factors are not covered in this book, but they are in our other book, *Digital Photography: 99 Easy Tips to Make You Look Like a Pro!* (McGraw-Hill/Osborne, 2002). Methods for making "quick and dirty" image corrections are covered thoroughly in Chapter 2. These are quite effective about 80 percent of the time. This chapter covers the other 20 percent or so of the time you might want to spend correcting images.

Automatic Image Correction

Even if you're not using the Quick Fix interface, all the same one-step image-correction commands are available to you directly through the Image and Enhance menus. If you preview an image thumbnail, either in your operating system or the Photoshop Elements browser, and it's obviously overexposed and the color balance is just plain unnatural, it's probably a good idea to use one or more of these commands.

Note   *Once you execute a one-click command, much of the data in the image is changed, and unless you make a copy, you won't be able to go back again. The best insurance against such data loss is to choose Image | Duplicate Image. The Duplicate Image dialog box appears, and you can name the duplicate to indicate the change you've made to the original.*

There are three one-click commands that instantly make a difference in almost any image: Auto Contrast, Auto Levels, and Auto Color Correction. Each of these usually does such a good job that it is hard to tell one from the other, yet there is a subtle difference. When in doubt, you can perform all three of these commands on an image very quickly.

Auto Contrast works by making the darkest point in the RGB image pure black and the lightest point pure white. It doesn't change the color balance because it doesn't adjust the information in individual color channels at all.

Auto Levels is similar to Auto Contrast in that it does the same thing to each color channel individually as the Auto Contrast command does to the RGB composite channel. The result is usually a bit richer range of tones, but you might find that a color cast has been introduced (though you're actually more likely to find that the color has been corrected). In the "Using the Levels Command to Control Contrast" section later in this chapter, you'll find out how to use Auto Levels command to correct color balance. However, the easy way is to use the third one-click command.

The Auto Color Correction command doesn't use the Levels histograms at all. Instead, it just looks for the pixel closest to a midtone in each color channel and adjusts it to 50 percent gray. This automatically balances the color in the midtones. It then reinterprets the lightest and darkest pixels (not histogram points) in each color channel to be pure white and pure black, which has the dual effect of both adjusting contrast and adjusting color for the highlights and shadows.

As we said earlier, all three of these commands can make such a difference that you might have difficulty choosing among them. The difference is usually subtler than what can be shown in our black-and-white examples. However, the difference between the original image and the one-click-adjusted image can be startling, as you can see in Figure 12-1.

All three of these one-click commands work so well that if you just want perfect color balance and contrast range, there's not much reason to look any further. The exception is those photographs in which you want to introduce a "feeling" or "mood" by taking their brightness range, contrast, or color balance (or all three) out of the

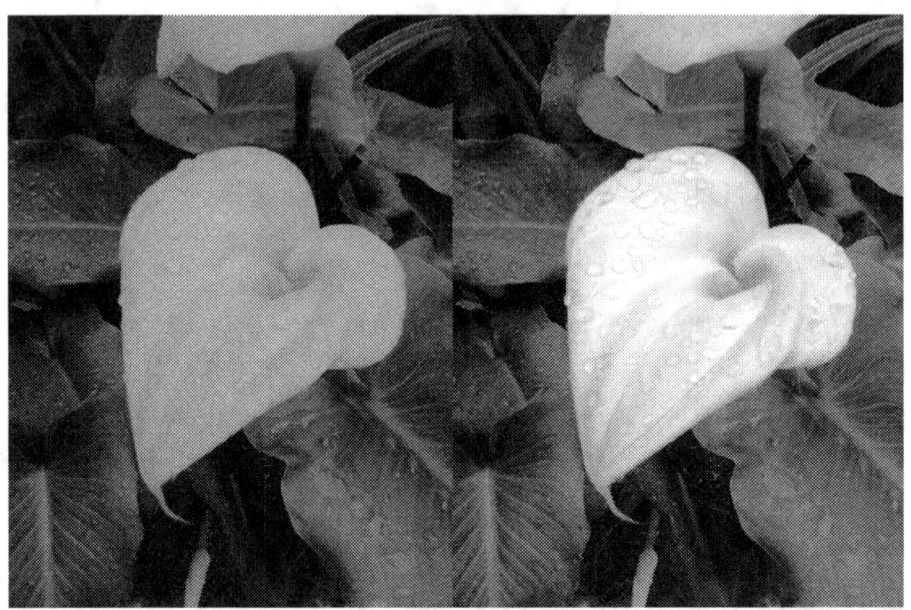

Figure 12-1. *The original image, in which the camera was metered for the whites in the lily, is on the left.*

ordinary. In addition, some of us just like the security of knowing that we are the ones who have control.

Correcting Exposure

Most of the commands that allow you to correct contrast or color balance also allow you some control over the overall brightness or exposure of the image. However, there is one command that is primarily meant to give you a high degree of control over exposure. That command is the Levels command. We'll also show you how to use the Levels command to integrate contrast and color-balance correction. Here's how you'd go about using it to improve an image:

1. Choose Enhance | Adjust Brightness/Contrast | Levels (CMD/CTRL+L). The Levels dialog box appears, as shown next.

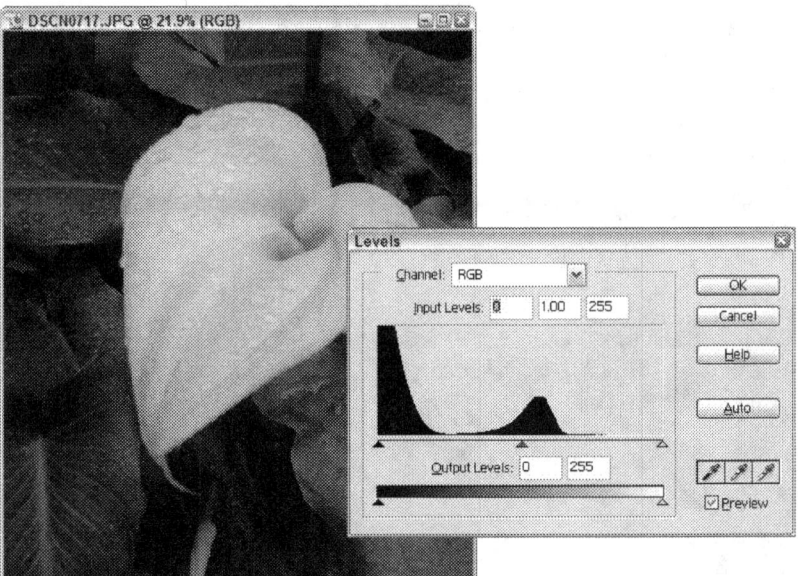

2. The temptation is to start by adjusting the composite (RGB) channel. However, that wouldn't maximize tonal range because the individual brightness range of each color channel has not been taken into account. Press CMD/CTRL+1, and you will see the histogram for the red channel. A histogram is a distribution chart where the base line represents the even distribution of tonal range from black (left) to white (right) and the 253 shades of gray between. It looks like a mountain rising out of a flat plain. Immediately under it are three pyramid-shaped sliders: black, gray, and white. The color of each of these sliders represents the point at which all the colors in the image are at the brightness level of the slider.

Note   *If the histogram for any or all of the channels is cropped at either end, the image is so underexposed (if cropped on the left end) or overexposed (cropped at the right end) that the corresponding shadows or highlights beyond that point reveal no detail or highlights. Photographers would say that the highlights or shadows were* blocked. *Remember that term because we'll be using it throughout this book.*

3. Move the black (leftmost) slider to the leftmost foot of the histogram "mountain." Move the white slider to the rightmost foot of the mountain. Do *not* touch the gray slider. This would prematurely upset the color balance of the image, making it harder to correct later.

4. Press CMD/CTRL+2 to see the histogram for the green channel and adjust the slider in exactly the same way as you did in step 3. Next, press CMD/CTRL+3 and adjust the blue channel in the same way as the other two. Now you have an image in which the brightness and contrast have been adjusted to show a full range of color.

5. Now that you have a maximum range of brightness in each color channel, you can use the RGB composite channel to adjust the overall brightness of the image. Press CMD/CTRL+SHIFT+~ (tilde) to see the histogram for the composite channel. If want the brightness of the midtones to be lighter, drag the midtone slider to the left. If you want a more low-key, moody image, drag the midtone (gray) slider to the right. This adjustment is purely subjective. Just stop when the image looks good to you. You can see how it affects the photo here, with much more detail in the dark green leaves.

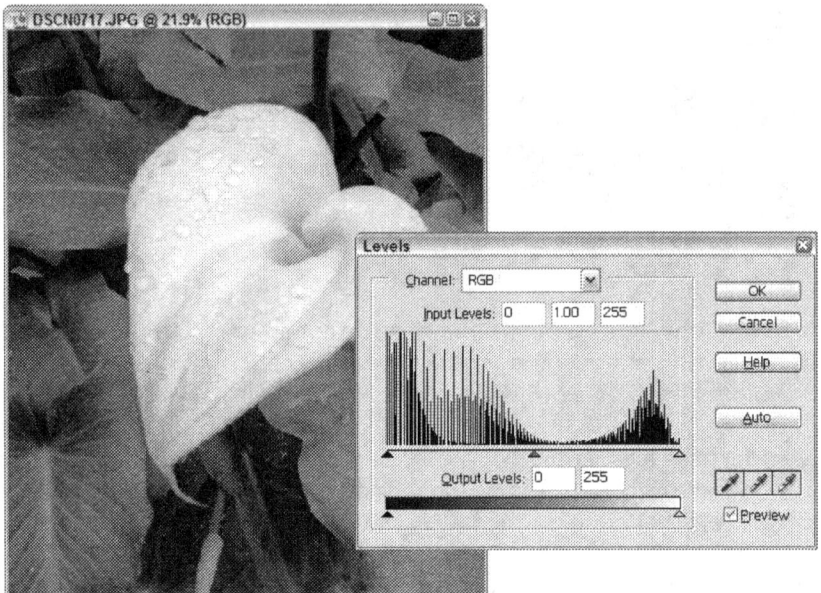

6. This image was shot during a break on a rainy day, so the light was a little on the blue side. Actually, given the presence of the water drops on the lily, that seems appropriate. However, if you wanted it to be a little cooler, you could adjust the midrange slider in the blue channel slightly to the right. If you're familiar with mixing the red, green, and blue colors of light (likely if you've been doing photography, digital imaging, or stage or TV work), this is a very good way to balance color. With a little practice, it quickly becomes easy for most people.

Adjusting Lighting to Correct Exposure

There is a pair of commands that are intended to correct exposure only in highlights or shadows. Photoshop and other image-editing programs have had the means to make such corrections for years. The two Elements commands just make the process easier by making it more direct and interactive. The commands are Backlighting and Fill Flash, and are found on the Enhance | Adjust Lighting menu.

The Backlighting command helps you adjust the blocked highlights that occur when the strongest lighting comes from behind the subject and you've adjusted the camera to expose for the shadow side of the subject because that's the side facing the camera. You get a halo of white (especially if the subject has light-colored hair) that is often so glaring that it, instead of the subject, becomes the center of attention. If you could just get even a little detail into those highlights, they wouldn't be nearly as distracting. The Backlighting command is a useful fix for any image that has scattered, over-bright highlights that are hard to retouch accurately. Cloud photos are a good case in point.

Here's how to use the Backlighting command:

1. Open any image in which the highlights are so light they appear to be (or are) pure white—preferably one in which the highlights aren't completely blocked.

2. Choose Enhance | Adjust Lighting | Backlight. The Backlight dialog box appears.

3. Be sure the Preview box is checked. Drag the slider to the right while watching the highlights in your image. When you get to the point where you like the effect, click OK (see Figure 12-2).

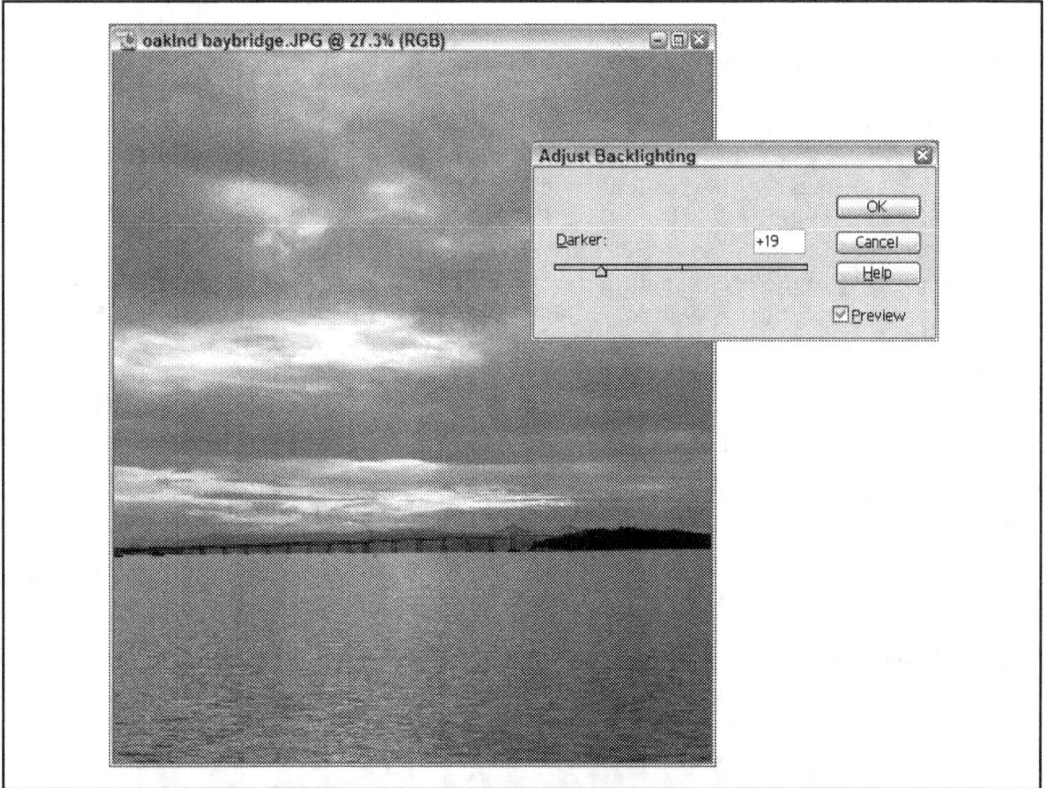

Figure 12-2.   *You can see the Backlight command in action as it brings detail to the washed out clouds in the background.*

THE DIGITAL DARKROOM WORKFLOW

Unfortunately, though the Backlighting command can sometimes help the problem of scattered, over-bright highlights, it's not a panacea. This is not a program flaw; it's because the highlights are blocked, which is to say they're so overly bright, there's really no detail. If that's really the case, then all the Backlighting command can do is turn the white highlight gray. When you encounter that problem, here's a solution for you:

1. Choose the Eyedropper tool and click in the brightest part of the image that still has detail. The color you clicked becomes the foreground color.

2. Choose the Brush tool. In its Options bar, choose Darken as the blending mode. Now the brush can paint only into areas that are lighter than the foreground color because the paint won't show up unless what you're painting onto is actually darker than the color you're painting with.

3. In the Brush Options bar, lower the opacity (drag the slider to the left) just slightly so that the color is just a little lighter than the foreground color. Now brush over the highlights. At least they'll take on a little shade of color.

The other Adjust Lighting command, Fill Flash, is more useful in a wider variety of situations. Fill Flash gets its name from the fact that, like using a flash gun in fill flash mode, the command puts detail into the darker shadows. It produces much the same effect as using a white fill layer in Soft Light mode (see Chapter 9), but with less effort and in less time.

The Fill Flash command also does a better job, in many ways, than the electromechanical technique that it takes its name from. First of all, it doesn't cast any stray shadows, which are often unflattering to the subject. Second, there's no foreground overlighting or background fall-off. With Fill Flash, the distance between the lens and the areas that need to be filled doesn't matter. Fill Flash also gives you complete control over the intensity of the fill. Just about the only fill-flash option most cameras offer is not quite as bright as the prevailing available light. This makes it fairly useless in the kind of dim lighting conditions that often cause deep and unreadable shadows.

Elements' Fill Flash command gets so much more out of a picture, especially one that would be practically impossible to fix with a camera's fill flash (see Figure 12-3).

Here's how you use Fill Flash (it's just as easy as using the Backlight command):

1. Open an image in which you'd like to lighten deep shadows.

2. Choose Enhance | Adjust Lighting | Fill Flash. The Fill Flash dialog box appears.

3. Drag the top slider *slowly* to the right. Most of the time, the adjustment should be slight, so it's easy to overdo it.

4. Occasionally, by the time you've brightened the image enough, the colors start to wash out. That's why this dialog box has two sliders. Should your colors in the brightened areas get overly pale, drag the bottom (saturation) slider to the right until you're happy with the result. That's it. Click OK.

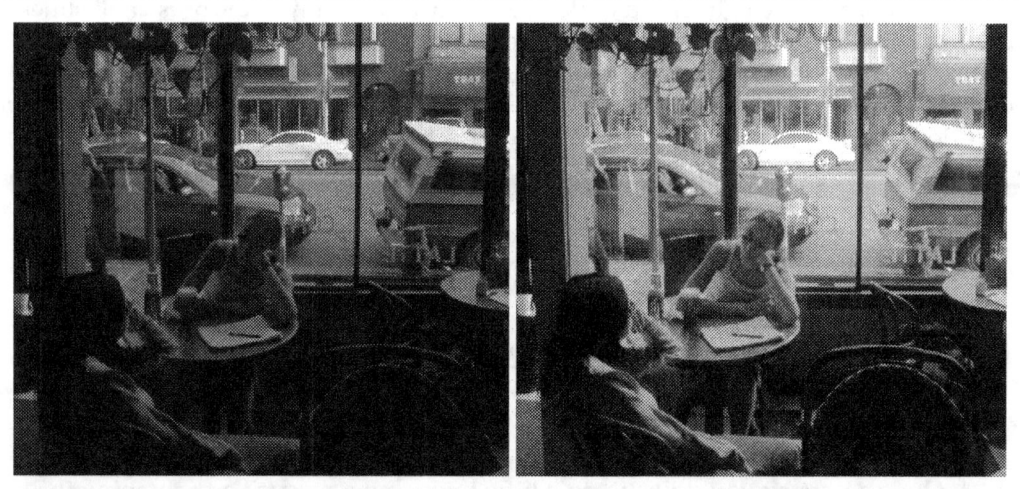

Figure 12-3. *As you can see in these before (left) and after (right) deli shots, the Fill Flash command can bring detail out of the shadowed foreground.*

Correcting Contrast in a Limited Area of an Image

Suppose most of the image has just the brightness range you wanted. If all you've done is make a general correction to the whole layer, it's a pretty good bet that there'll be features and details that are just too light or too dark. As long as those areas aren't blocked, chances are you can make those areas look just as you'd hoped.

There are two basic techniques for changing the exposure in a specific part of the picture: painting and isolation. Painting involves using a tool (usually the Burn or Dodge tool) that's shaped like a brush to stroke the area to be changed just enough to make a difference. Isolation involves either cutting out part of the image and placing it on another layer or placing a selection marquee around it. Then you use one of the image adjustments covered in the first section to "correct" the exposure.

Painting Exposure Corrections

Painting usually works best for quickly adjusting small areas of the image, especially where the lighting is uneven over the area. Perhaps you want to brighten the highlights on waves or remove the crease under someone's eyes.

Though most people think strictly in terms of the Burn and Dodge tools, it can also be beneficial to use a Brush tool in combination with one of the blending modes, such as Lighten, Darken, Soft Light, Hard Light, or Multiply. Lightening and darkening with blending modes can help you avoid the "washed out" or blotchy effects you can get from the Burn and Dodge tools if the change you need to make is too dramatic. If you use purely neutral colors for the brush, you'll simply adjust exposure.

If you use a brush to lighten and darken, you can also use any of the brush adjustments that are available, so you can even introduce textures into the process.

If you use the brush directly on the subject layer, you'll have somewhat less control than if you assign the blending mode to the brush instead of to the layer. You then have the option of also varying the intensity of the effect with the opacity slider. You can also redo a stroked area later by simply erasing it from the layer, so you don't have to erase other strokes.

The following exercise shows you the difference between burning and dodging directly on the image versus using a brush, white as a foreground color for the brush, and painting onto a layer that is set to Color Dodge mode:

Note *Because blending modes affect the visible portions of all underlying layers, you can stack different blending modes on different layers—as long as the strokes themselves don't overlap.*

1. Open a portrait you'd like to do a little retouching on, such as lightening the smile lines under the eyes and brightening the whites of the eyes (two of the most flattering things you can do to a portrait).

2. Open the Layers palette and click the New Layers button. A new, transparent layer appears immediately as the top layer. Drag the opacity slider down to about 15 percent.

3. Keep the new layer active (don't click the other layer) and choose Blend Mode | Color Dodge. You can burn and dodge with the same tool. Just press D so that the foreground and background colors black and white, respectively. Now you can switch colors by pressing X.

4. Choose the Brush tool and click the Airbrush button. This makes paint build up when you hold the cursor over a spot and click the mouse so you can build up the effect of what you're doing.

5. Now gently stroke with the brush to gradually lighten the under-eye smile lines. If the lightness gets too light, press X to switch to black and burn in to compensate or choose the Eraser tool to erase the stroke you just made and then start over.

6. Now you are going to lighten the whites of the eyes slightly to make them seem more wide awake and alive. (Don't overdo this; you'll make your subject look like a zombie.) Turn off the new layer by clicking the eye icon in the Visibility button in the Layers palette.

7. Choose the Zoom tool and zoom in so that only the eyes fill the screen. You want to make sure that the whites of the eyes match from one side of the iris to the other and that both eyes match (unless one side of the face or the sockets of the eyes are in deep shadow).

8. Choose the Dodge tool. In its Options bar, lower the opacity to about 15 percent and choose a brush size that's about a third as large as the whites of the eyes.

9. Now you're going to scrub. Scrubbing is making several quick strokes back and forth, rather than dragging the mouse or pen in a more or less straight line. You usually scrub when you burn and dodge so that the strokes build up in a way that makes them blend with their surroundings. Use this technique to lighten the whites of the eyes.

10. A little judicious darkening of the outside of the iris makes the eyes seem sharper and more focused. Choose the Burn tool. From its Options bar, choose a very small brush diameter. Drag the opacity slider to about 25 percent. Carefully darken the ring around the iris until it's almost black.

Figure 12-4 shows the before and after of the portrait we just lightened and darkened. The difference is subtle, but the person on the right certainly commands your attention more readily.

Isolating Exposure Corrections

There will be times when you have a specific area that you want to correct evenly. For instance, you want to darken the sky, lighten the hair, or place a lighting effect on the background. If you have to correct such a large area, it is usually better to do it all at once so that you can have "streakless" burning or dodging.

If you are going to make several adjustments besides exposure correction, it might be best, after making a selection, to lift the contents of that selection onto a new layer by choosing Layers | Layer Via Copy. You could then make numerous types of changes

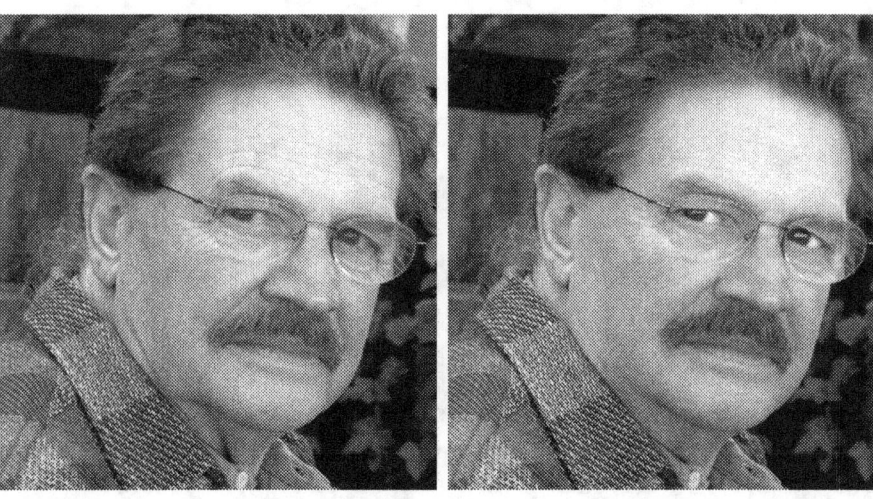

Figure 12-4.   *All the retouching in this portrait was done by lightening or darkening very small portions of the image. You can see dramatic changes in the neck, eyes, and forehead.*

to the contents of that layer without needing to reselect the same area. Of course, you could just save the selection and recall it each time you want to make a change. However, if you have the memory for the extra layer, it's much faster just to activate that layer each time you want to make a change. In addition, because the layer can be visible all the time, you can tell when something you did to the other layers requires that you make a change to that layer.

Having said all that, the following exercise teaches you the basics by using a very simple example: darkening the sky in an image.

1. Open a landscape image that has a clearly defined horizon line.

2. Choose the Magic Wand tool. In the Options bar, enter a fairly high tolerance (around 90). Make sure that the Contiguous box is checked if the horizon line is uninterrupted by tree branches, arches, or other shapes that show the sky through them. Otherwise, uncheck the Contiguous box.

3. Click in the sky at a point that's about halfway through the sky's brightness range. The sky will probably be entirely selected. If not, lower the Magic Wand's Tolerance setting and hold SHIFT while clicking in any areas where the marquee didn't reach. If the marquee overshoots the horizon, lower the tolerance even further, hold OPT/ALT while clicking in those areas to subtract them. If you're still having trouble making the selection properly, see Chapter 7.

4. Once you have the sky entirely selected, choose Layers | New | Layer via Copy.

5. Choose Enhance | Adjust Brightness/Contrast | Brightness/Contrast. The Brightness/Contrast dialog box appears, as shown here.

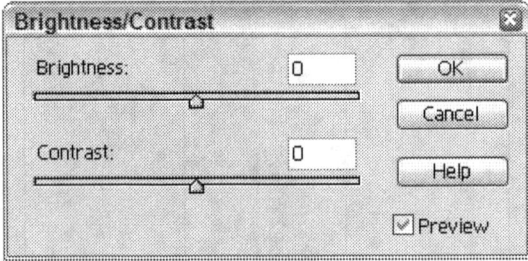

6. Drag the brightness slider to the left to darken the sky. If you want the clouds to pop out a bit more, drag the contrast slider to the right. Figure 12-5 shows the dramatic change.

You could have used the Levels command to make the adjustment. However, for simple changes in brightness, such as the one in this example, it's more efficient to use the simpler Brightness/Contrast command.

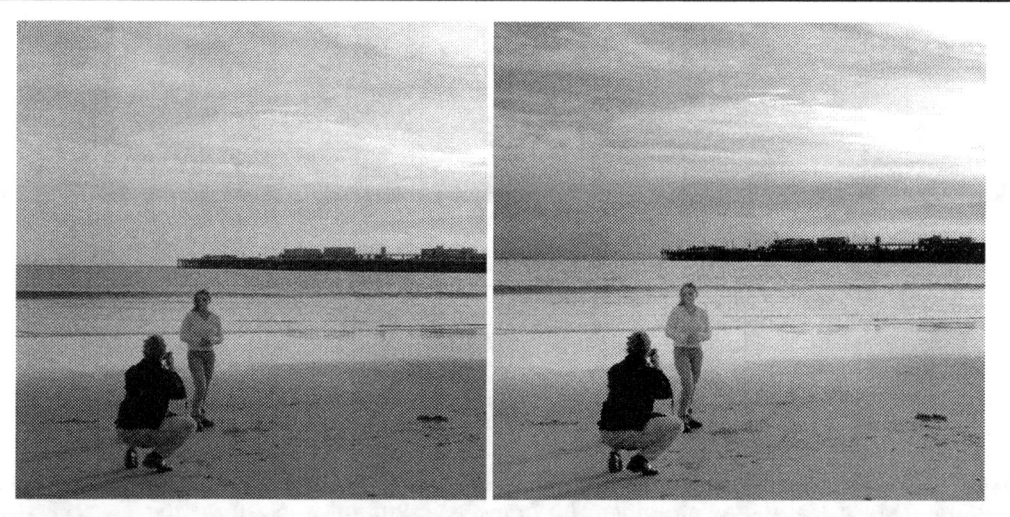

Figure 12-5.   *You can see the difference in brightness and contrast in the sky in this beach scene before (left) and after (right).*

THE DIGITAL DARKROOM WORKFLOW

Correcting Contrast

Actually, the title of this section is a bit of a misnomer. Technically, correct contrast in the image is usually taken care of when you do your exposure correction, especially if you do it as prescribed in the exercise in the "Correcting Exposure" section earlier in this chapter.

Using the Brightness/Contrast Command

If you just want to make a slight adjustment in overall contrast, the Brightness/Contrast command is the path of least resistance. Just choose Enhance | Adjust Brightness/Contrast | Brightness/Contrast. The Brightness/Contrast dialog box appears. Find the contrast you want by dragging the contrast slider to the right to increase contrast and to the left to decrease it. When you have adjusted the contrast to your liking, you can change the overall brightness by dragging the brightness slider. You'll usually juggle these back and forth a few times until you get what you like. When done, click OK. The effect of this type of adjustment can be seen in Figure 12-6.

Using the Levels Command to Control Contrast

When you correct exposure using the Levels command, there is generally a concurrent change in the overall contrast of the image. However, you can also use it to achieve more refined control over contrast than the Brightness/Contrast command provides.

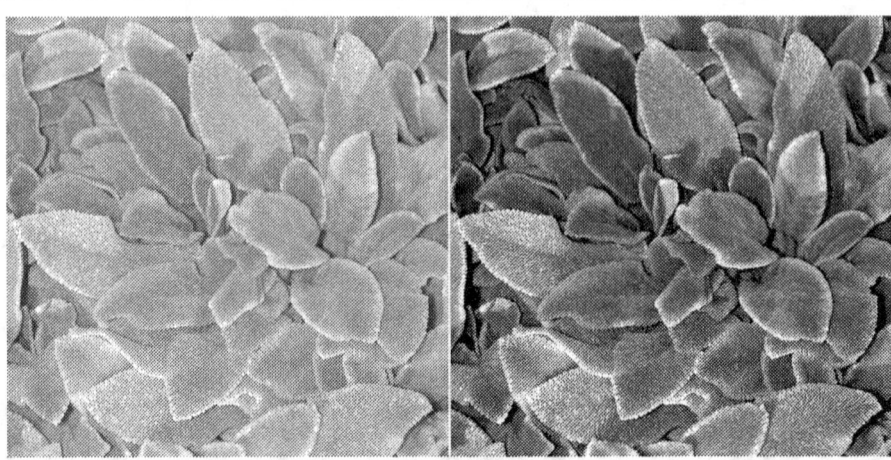

Figure 12-6. *Here is an example of a quick adjustment made using the Brightness/Contrast command that brings out the detail in this image. The adjusted image is on the right.*

The Levels command can give you any degree of contrast and can divide the brightness range between lighter and darker at any point. If you drag the shadows (black) slider toward the center, the tones in the lower half of the darkness range get darker and darker. Conversely, if you drag the highlights slider toward the center, the tones in the upper half of the darkness range get lighter and lighter. You can also drag the midtones slider to change the point at which lighter tones get lighter and darker tones get darker. You can see the effect of level adjustments in Figure 12-7.

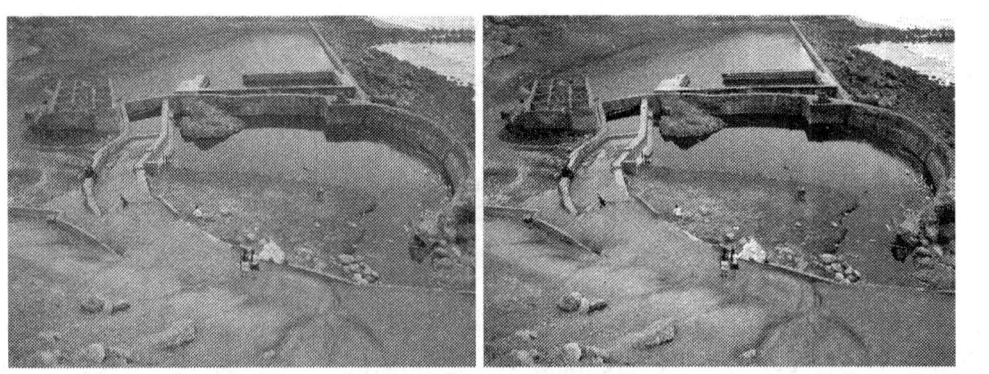

Figure 12-7. *This is the same beach before (left) and after (right) the contrast has been changed with the Levels command.*

Getting Extreme Contrast with the Threshold Command

The Threshold command reduces the image to pure black and white. It is very useful for creating masks and making selections. Simply drag the slider to determine the dividing line between white and black. Once you have the balance you want, you can make a selection that fits either the black or white areas in the image with the Magic Wand tool. You can see the effect of using the Threshold command in Figure 12-8.

Using the Equalize Command

The Equalize command works by finding the lightest and darkest pixels in the image and moving them to the leftmost and rightmost points in the histogram. It then evenly distributes the brightness of those between. Usually, one of the results is an apparent increase in contrast, or higher definition between areas of brightness in the image. The height of the bars represents the percentage of pixels in the image that occupy that tonal value, so if the histogram is higher in the middle than on either end, it indicates that the image is mostly in the middle tonal range, or fairly grayed out.

The Equalize command can be a quick way to really dramatize an image. It's also a great way to preview how much information is in the image. Try using it just after opening an image to get some ideas of where you might want to take that image, or

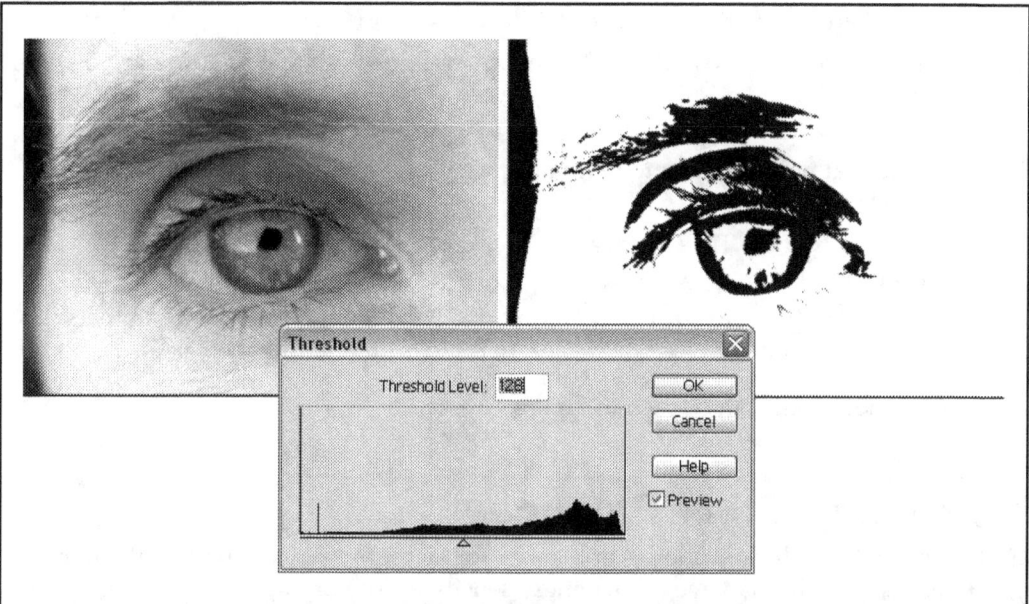

Figure 12-8.   *The effect of the Threshold command reduces the image to a graphic black and white rendition (right). Adjust the slider in the dialog box to get variations.*

THE DIGITAL DARKROOM WORKFLOW

various parts of it, and then immediately cancel the command by choosing Edit | Undo Equalize or pressing CMD/CTRL+OPT/ALT+Z to restore the image to its original state.

You can also run the Equalize command on a duplicate layer and then use the opacity slider, blending modes, and a selection to create an effect on only one part of the image, such as the sky.

Here's an example of how you might use Equalize and Threshold to create an effect in part of an image by creating a mask.

1. Open an image that contains an area that you want to dramatize.

2. Open the Layers palette and then duplicate the background layer by dragging it to the New Layer icon.

3. Temporarily reduce the opacity of the duplicated layer to 50 percent. Now you'll be able to see through to the layer below, so you can see how the Threshold version of the image registers with the original version. This helps you in making an accurate selection.

4. Choose Image | Adjustments | Threshold. The Threshold dialog box appears. Drag the slider until the shape you want to mask is as close to solid black as possible without turning black in areas that you don't want to select. When you like what you see, click OK. Now drag the layer's Opacity slider back to 100 percent.

5. If some areas have turned black or white that you wanted to be the opposite color, hand-paint them black or white as appropriate.

6. Choose the Magic Wand tool. Uncheck Contiguous in the Options bar. Click in either the black or white area of the layer.

7. Choose Select | Save Selection. The Save Selection dialog box appears. Enter a name that will help you to remember what this particular selection is, in case you save others.

8. Hide or trash the Threshold layer. The selection is now active on the background layer.

9. Choose Image | Adjustments | Equalize. The Equalize dialog box appears. Click the Equalize Selected Area Only radio button and then click OK.

The finished result can be seen in Figure 12-9.

Correcting Color Balance

Getting the color right in a photograph is key to the viewer perceiving it in the manner you intended. The human eye is amazingly sensitive to color; the color of light affects

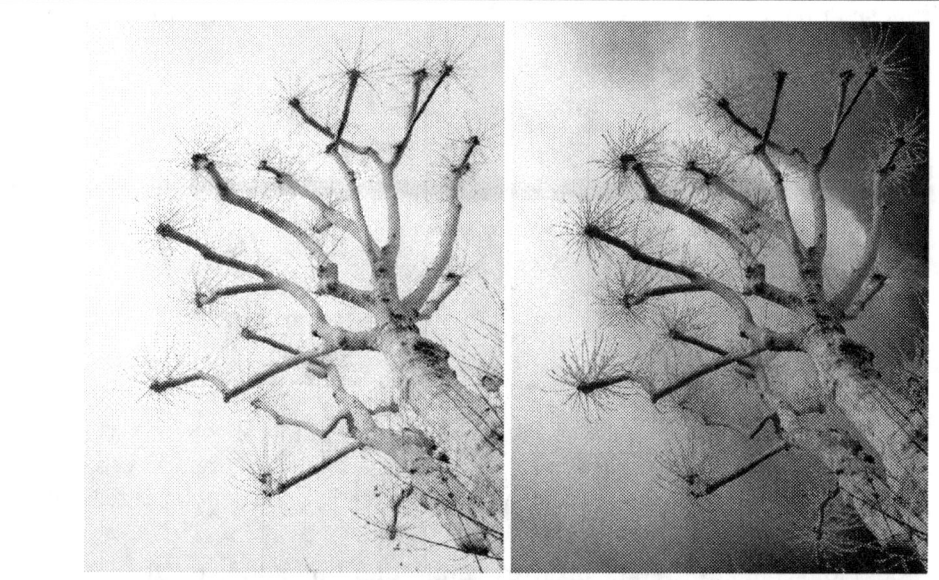

Figure 12-9.   *The original image on the left and the image on the right modified with the Equalize command to bring out important detail and color in the sky.*

the mood, sense of time, and space in dramatic ways. Learning to control how color is balanced in your images will provide you with an important element in good image composition. Photoshop Elements provides you with a substantial set of easy-to-use tools to accomplish color perfection.

Easy Color Correction with the Color Cast Command

It has always been possible to correct color using the eyedroppers in the Levels command, but you needed to place a 50 percent gray card in the picture beforehand and then take the reading from the gray card. Photoshop Elements has a far easier way to go about it. The one big limitation is that you must have something in the picture that's completely neutral in color; shade doesn't matter. It can be any shade of absolutely colorless gray, including pure black or white. Here's how easy it is to get the proper color balance:

1. Open the image in Photoshop Elements.

2. Choose Enhance | Adjust Color | Color Cast. The Color Cast Correction dialog box appears, as shown here.

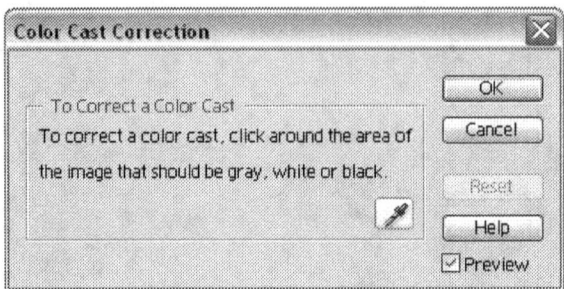

3. Choose the Eyedropper tool and click on anything in the photo that you know or imagine to be purely neutral in color. Some people recommend eyeballs and teeth, but these items are seldom as white as we wish. Black belts, wristwatch bands, and silver jewelry are especially good bets.

4. If the photo changes to some bizarre overall color tint, you know that the object you picked wasn't purely neutral or that you picked the wrong pixel. No problem—just try a different object.

You could make a mistake using this technique. "Close enough" could look good to you without being entirely accurate, and most of the time it's good enough for your purposes. If true accuracy is important, try two or three areas of neutral color. If the color balance is the same in all of them, you've actually found truly neutral colors and your image is perfectly balanced.

Using the Hue/Saturation Command

The Hue/Saturation command brings up yet another dialog box that lets you make adjustments by dragging sliders. In this instance, the sliders control hue, saturation, and brightness. You could use this command purely to control overall brightness, but because you don't have control over contrast in the same interface, the brightness slider is really more useful for making small adjustments in overall brightness to compensate for the results of your adjusting the hue and saturation sliders. Here's the Hue/Saturation dialog box:

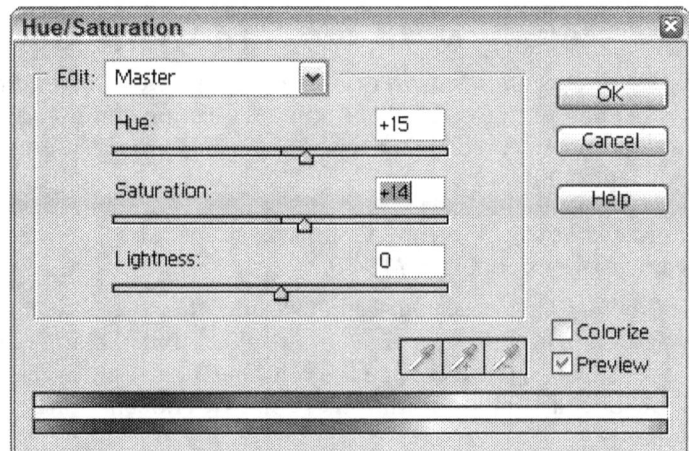

To change the overall color tint of the image:

1. Choose Enhance | Adjust Color | Hue/Saturation (CMD/CTRL+U). The Hue/Saturation dialog box appears

2. Be sure to click the toggle on the Preview box. These sliders are interactive. You stop sliding when the image looks good to you. Frankly, we don't know why Elements even gives you a choice. If you turn preview off, you're totally operating by the seat of your pants.

3. Drag the hue slider until the overall tint of the image looks as you'd like it to look. This adjustment changes the color balance in all three color channels. You might prefer to work within the confines of a specific primary color. If so, choose the color you want to adjust from the Edit menu at the top of the dialog box.

Note   *You can use the Hue/Saturation command to go way beyond merely correcting color balance. Just to see the range of color special effects you can get, experiment with dragging the hue slider across its full range while you have preview turned on. Once you see something you like, try dragging the saturation slider to intensify or soften the effect. If you copy your layer before you apply the hue/saturation effects, you can then use them in conjunction with blending modes.*

You can also use the Hue/Saturation command to convert the image to a grayscale or something approaching a duotone. See the "Converting an Image to Black and White" section later in this chapter.

Balancing Color Visually with the Variations Command

Unless you've had some experience with mixing primary colors to get the color balance you want, color balancing with the Levels or Hue/Saturation commands might seem a little intimidating. For those who feel that way, Adobe has provided an easy and very helpful alternative. Here's how it works:

1. Choose Enhance | Adjust Color | Color Variations. The Color Variations dialog box appears, as shown in Figure 12-10.

2. At the top of the dialog box, you see before and after previews that should be large enough to give you a good idea of the effect that clicking one of the color change buttons has. You can change the color balance in the midtones, shadows, or highlights or change the saturation of color by choosing one of the labeled radio buttons.

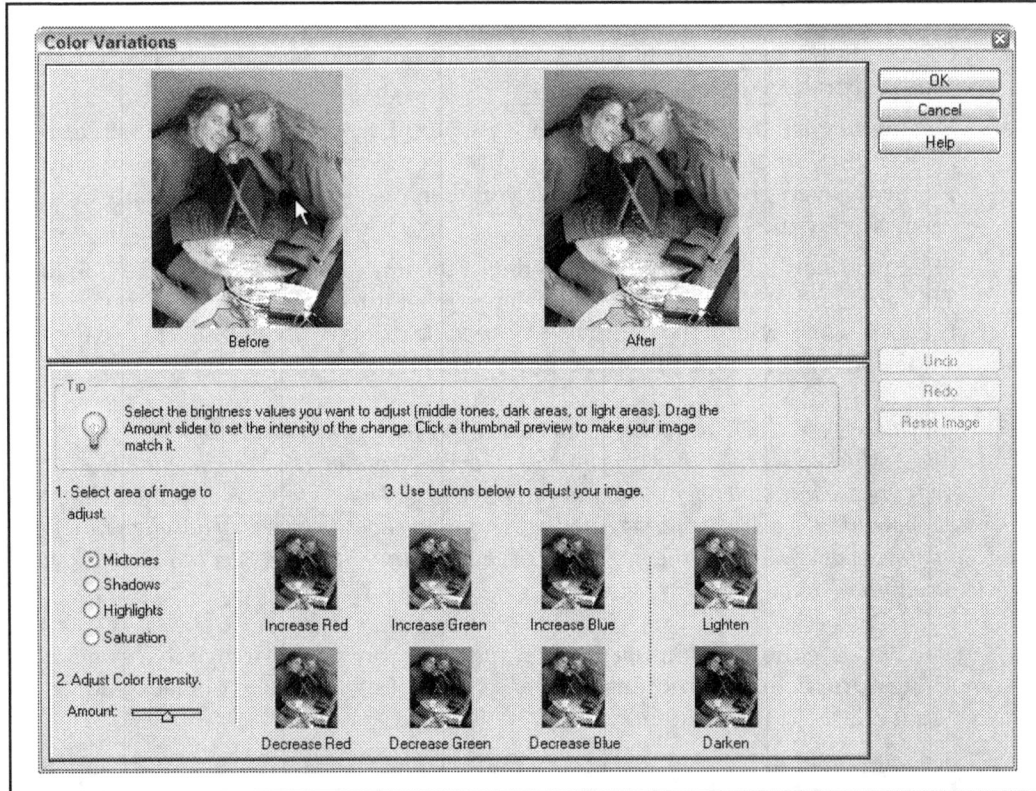

Figure 12-10. *The Variations command interface with a full array of preview boxes that show you the before and after of every adjustment*

3. Start by adjusting the exposure of the image. Drag the amount slider to the left a notch or two and then click the Lighten and Darken buttons until the after preview seems to be about the right brightness.

4. Just to give yourself a good idea of the color balance direction in which you want to head, drag the amount slider all the way to the right, and check out the color change thumbnails. The color changes are very exaggerated, but it's obvious which primary colors give you the most benefit. Now drag the slider back to the middle and click the color button that gets you closest to the color balance you want.

5. Usually you'll want to refine your adjustments a bit. If that's the case, move the Amount slider further to the left (to make the changes more subtle) and click the thumbnail that shows the greatest improvement. Repeat this step until you're happy with the color balance.

6. Optional: Click to toggle on (a dot appears in the center of the circle) the Saturation radio button. Drag the Amount slider until the color saturation you want reaches the intensity you want and then click the More Saturation thumbnail. If the after preview looks good to you, click OK.

Tip *This is a great way to adjust color for a whole series of photographs that have been shot in the same location and under the same lighting conditions. Why? Because the Color Variations command remembers the last collection of accumulated changes you made, so you can load a new image and simply click OK to apply the same setting that you used most recently. If you don't want to reapply those settings, click the Reset button before beginning the rest of the steps in this exercise.*

7. As you click different buttons, their effect accumulates in the image. If you get to the point where you feel you've simply overdone the changes, click the Reset Image button. The original values are restored, and you can start all over.

Changing the Color of a Single Item

Have you ever wondered whether you'd look better in a blue shirt or a red shirt? Wanted to keep the car in the same old bronze or paint it chartreuse? Photoshop Elements gives you an easy way to find out. You just substitute colors for a given object. Here's how:

1. Open an image that contains a subject whose color you want to change.

2. Choose the Lasso tool and make a very loose selection around the item whose color you want to change. The idea is to isolate it from any other items of similar color that happen to be in the picture so that you don't accidentally change the colors in those items as well.

3. Choose Enhance | Adjust Color | Replace Color. The Replace Color dialog box appears. Be sure the Preview box is checked (click the box to toggle it).

4. In the center of the dialog box is a Preview window. Below it are two radio buttons. Choose the button labeled Selections.

5. Just below the Preview box you'll find three eyedropper icons. Choose the Eyedropper tool (the one with no plus or minus sign) and click in the part of the image that best represents the color you want to change. In the Preview window of the dialog box, you will see the areas of the color you selected turn white. You'll also see the colors in your image that correspond to the white areas change to the color that's shown in the sample swatch.

6. If parts of the image outside the shape you've selected also change color, drag the fuzziness slider to the left. It's better to leave too little selected than too much. You can add to the selection in the next step.

7. Choose the Add to Selection eyedropper (the one that has a plus sign attached). In the Preview box, click any areas that are not selected (you could use the image, but it's easier to find what's not selected if it's in the preview box because if it's not black, it's not selected).

8. If you select too much, choose the Subtract from Selection eyedropper and click in the areas that are overselected. Keep switching between the Add and Subtract eyedroppers and the fuzziness slider until you have the area you want to change selected as precisely as possible.

Note *If the object you want to change the color of has a color that's very distinct when compared with its surroundings, this routine should work pretty much without a hitch. If not, be sure to make a careful selection to isolate the object whose color you want to change from the rest of the image.*

9. Now it's time to change the color. The process is just like balancing color with the Hue/Saturation command. Drag the hue slider until the selected area is as close to the color you want it to be as possible. Then adjust the saturation and lightness sliders to make the color precisely what you want it to be. When you're happy with the change, click OK.

Converting an Image to Black and White

There are numerous reasons, both artistic and practical, why you might want to turn your digital images to black and white. Let's face it: some people just like black and white; it looks "artsy" and traditional. If you want to publish your images, there's a greater chance of getting them published in black and white because it's less costly to print them that way. If you're putting images on the Web, they might even have more impact than color images just because today's Web is so color-saturated. Furthermore, grayscale image files are more efficient on the Web because their files are only one-third the size of RGB color images.

You might also want to create an effect that looks more like grayscale than color but that makes a richer or more classic looking image because it uses a limited number of colors. Such images are generally called *duotones,* even though they might contain more than two colors.

Many colors that seem to vary appear almost identical when converted to gray. This can smooth out blotchy skin tones and make for a much more refined-looking portrait.

Finally, you might want to reduce an image to grayscale or duotone because it's a good start for digitally "hand-coloring" an image. This section shows you techniques that are appropriate to all these purposes.

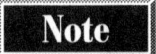 *Some of the most beautiful black-and-white images can come from photos that have been "dramatized" before converting them to grayscale by using the techniques described in the foregoing sections of this chapter. For instance, try using the Equalize command before converting to grayscale.*

Using Grayscale Color Mode

By far the quickest way to reduce a color image to grayscale is simply to change the color mode of the image to Grayscale. Choosing this route, however, generally produces a somewhat flat and lackluster image. That is because no adjustments are made in the brightness and contrast of the image. The program just subtracts the hue and saturation information from the image.

The big advantage of Grayscale mode is that it's true monochrome, so the file is smaller because only 8 bits of data per pixel are required to show all 256 shades of gray. The big disadvantage is that you can't add anything to the image that's in color without first converting it back to a 24-bit RGB image.

If you are submitting color images to a publisher that will print them in grayscale, it is not a bad idea to duplicate them and reduce them to grayscale yourself. Then you can use the Enhance commands discussed earlier (particularly the Brightness/Contrast command) to bring out form and detail. Better yet, use the Levels command as prescribed earlier.

To convert a 24-bit RGB color image to grayscale, choose Image | Mode | Grayscale. That's it. There are no dialog boxes or options. In the blink of an eye, your image is in grayscale mode.

Removing Color All at Once

If you are going to add color back into your image after you convert it to gray, then you should use the Remove Color command. Just choose Enhance | Adjust Color | Remove Color (SHIFT+CMD/CTRL+U). That's it. Your image is in grayscale while still in RGB mode.

If you want to tint the image, you can do that quite easily with a fill layer. After using the Remove Color command, follow these steps:

1. Open the Layers palette. Click the Fill/Adjustment layer button at the bottom of the Layers palette and choose Solid Color. The Color Picker appears.

2. Choose the color you want to tint the image with and click OK.

You can also use many of the other layer blend modes to tint the grayscale image in a number of ways. If you want to hand-color the image, try using the Screen mode or the Soft Light mode.

Removing Color with the Hue/Saturation Command

Tinting an image produces a look that was quite fashionable in black-and-white photography just after the turn of the century. That doesn't mean that it can't still be quite effective. As we've already shown, there are several ways to accomplish such an effect. However, the most versatile of these is using the Hue/Saturation command.

1. Choose Enhance | Adjust Color | Hue/Saturation (CMD/CTRL+U). The Hue/Saturation dialog box appears.

2. Click the Colorize box to toggle it on. The image becomes a blue/green monochrome. To change the tint, drag the hue slider and watch the overall tint change as you do so.

3. Once you've found a tint that pleases you, you can change the intensity of its color by dragging the saturation slider.

4. Adjust brightness until you get the exact range that pleases you.

5. When you're pleased with the result, click OK.

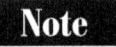 *There will also be times when you want simply to reduce the color in the image to "near black and white." You also do that with the Hue/Saturation command by dragging the saturation slider to the left. You could then select isolated areas and make them either completely grayscale or full color. You can even exaggerate the color in some areas and make it very subtle in others.*

Hand-Coloring a Monotone Image

Once you've used any of the above techniques to reduce the color in an image, you can add color in a number of different ways.

Paint Over the Color

One very nice way of doing that is to use some of the brush options that give you "natural media" brush styles (see Chapter 16). You can press OPT/ALT to change the brush to the Eyedropper tool, click in the image to pick up color, and then paint over the image.

Another technique is to do the painting on a separate layer. This gives you several additional options. You can

- Discard the layer if you mess it up.
- Change the transparency of the layer so that the original image shows through to some extent.
- Use the blending modes to "melt" the brush strokes into the original image.

Paint Over the Image

You can use the Color blending mode for the Brush tool and then just paint back over the image. Here's how that's done:

1. Load your image and duplicate the image layer.

2. Make your background layer an image layer by renaming it.

3. Click the Show/Hide button on the top layer to hide that layer.

4. Activate the bottom layer.

5. Choose Enhance | Adjust Color | Hue/Saturation. The Saturation Dialog box appears.

6. Drag the saturation slider to the left until there's just the barest hint of color in the bottom layer.

7. Hide the bottom layer and activate the top layer. Choose Enhance | Adjust Color | Hue Saturation. This time, click the Colorize checkbox to turn it on. Move the hue slider until you get a tint you like.

8. Place the layer you just colorized in Soft Light blending mode. Some of the color in the background image will come through, but it will be heavily influenced by the tint from the colorized layer.

9. Click the New Layer button to place a new, clear layer at the top of the stack. Choose Blend Mode | Multiply.

10. Choose Window | Color Swatches. The Color Swatches palette appears. This allows you to quickly choose different colors for the brush.

11. Choose the Brush tool, and in its Options bar, choose a brush style and size that's to your liking. Paint color into whatever areas in your image you would like to make more vivid. That's all there is to it!

The Complete Reference

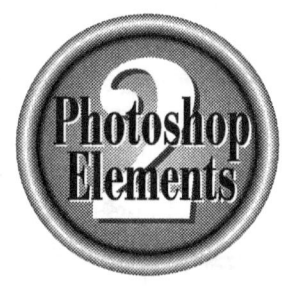

Chapter 13

Retouching and Repairing

This chapter is all about fixing whatever ails the picture. Most books on this topic tend to concentrate almost solely on using the Clone Stamp tool for retouching. Granted, the Clone Stamp tool is the most useful single tool for retouching, but the fact is that nearly every tool in Photoshop Elements is useful for retouching something sometime. This chapter doesn't cover every possibility—that would take a whole book—but it does cover a whole lot more than just using the Clone Stamp tool. We should mention up front that using a pressure-sensitive pen and tablet adds a level of subtlety and control to retouching that really improves your results.

Including the Clone Stamp tool, here's a list of the Photoshop Elements tools that are most frequently used for retouching, accompanied by the problems each is most useful for solving.

- **Clone Stamp tool**   The best tool for removing small defects by copying a nondefective part of the image over them.

- **Layers**   If you place your retouching strokes on a layer above the image, you can then adjust their transparency or change their brightness level for a better match with the picture. In addition, you can erase one stroke without affecting the other strokes or the underlying image.

- **Dust and scratches filter**   Excellent for removing fine but populous blemishes, such as the namesake dust and scratches.

- **Burn and Dodge tools**   Excellent for making stains and discolorations blend with their surroundings and for lightening shadows and darkening highlights that might over-emphasize something such as eye bags.

- **Selection marquee**   The best way to make sure that your retouching strokes don't extend into details that you want to keep. Also invaluable for selecting multiple areas for changes in tonality, intensification of color, or for replacing with the background layer.

- **Pattern Stamp tool**   The best tool for painting with texture and pattern to match surroundings or cover an architectural feature.

- **Noise filters**   Can be used for matching the grain structure of the original image in those instances whenever the most effective way to cover a defect is to over-paint or over-blur.

- **Blur tool and blur filter**   Can smooth an existing texture (such as skin) to give it an airbrushed look.

- **Sharpen tool**   Excellent for crisping edges and bringing out detail to draw the viewer's attention.

- **Liquify filter**   The best way to reshape parts of the picture.

- **Compositing**   A combination of these tools that lets you integrate objects from another image into the present image. Perhaps your technically perfect photo needs an object that can become the center of attention, or you need to cover a defect with a plant, or you want to replace a boring sky.

Each of these tools is featured in one of the solutions exercises that compose the remainder of this chapter.

Replacing One Part of the Image with Another

The Clone Stamp tool is easily the most frequently used tool for retouching. You can copy the texture of grass on the lawn over the little bits of litter the environmentally dysfunctional have left behind. You can cover up all sorts of skin imperfections that make everyone from teenagers to seniors appear to be in their twenties.

There are several things you should remember when using the Clone Stamp tool:

- Whenever possible, clone to a transparent layer. Then you can always make changes to your cloning or start over again if you mess up.

- Keep the Clone Stamp tool feathered. It makes the retouching strokes blend better with their surroundings.

- Don't make the Clone Stamp tool any larger than it needs to be to cover up the problem.

- Don't use the Clone Stamp tool to cover large areas. You can probably do the job faster by selecting one area and then placing it on a layer above the original. You can then clone to cover up any seams.

Here's how you'd use the Clone Stamp tool to retouch a portrait:

1. Open the image you want to retouch. Before you start retouching, make all the exposure, contrast, and color corrections you think this image is likely to need. Otherwise, you might find that your retouching strokes don't blend as well as you need them to because the adjustments have exaggerated the differences between those strokes (or the areas those strokes were cloned from) and their surroundings.

2. Double-click the Zoom tool in the Tools palette. This enlarges the image to 100 percent.

3. Open the Layers palette and click the New Layer button to add a new layer above the background layer. Be sure to drag the Layers Palette tab away from the Palette docking well because you will need to constantly activate one layer to place your pickup point, and then the other to clone it.

Note *Any time you have to constantly switch back and forth between layers, here's a way to save lots of time: Choose the Move tool. Place the cursor over an element in the layer you want to switch to and hold CTRL while right-clicking to see an in-context menu of all the nonactive layers. Then you can just click to activate the layer you want to switch to. Of course, it helps if you've disciplined yourself to give names to your layers that make them easy to identify.*

1. Choose the Clone Stamp tool.

2. Find a defect, such as a mole, that you want to cover up. In the Layers palette, click the image layer's (probably the background layer's) name bar to activate it.

3. Place the cursor over an area that has the same color, texture, and brightness as the mole (or other "defect") that you want to cover up. Press OPT/ALT so that you see a cross hairs in the center of the brush shape. Click to specify your target area.

4. In the Layers palette, click the new, transparent layer's name bar to activate it. Brush to paint over the defect that you're eliminating.

5. Repeat steps 3 and 4 as many times as necessary to get rid of all the little, annoying stuff. The finished result should look like the picture on the right in Figure 13-1.

What you see here is not a finished job of retouching (even though we think you'll agree it's an improvement), but simply what we've been able to do with the Clone Stamp tool. In fact, we could have done more by taking out the smile lines. If that were done, it would be better to do it on yet another layer. Then you'd have the option of reducing that layer's transparency so you could at least get a hint of where the smile lines were. Then you'd get a younger look, but not a phony look.

More important, versatile as it is, the Clone Stamp tool isn't the tool for all reasons. For instance, the sun-burned nose (the model is from San Diego) is better lightened and recolored than cloned-over. We'll do that in the next section.

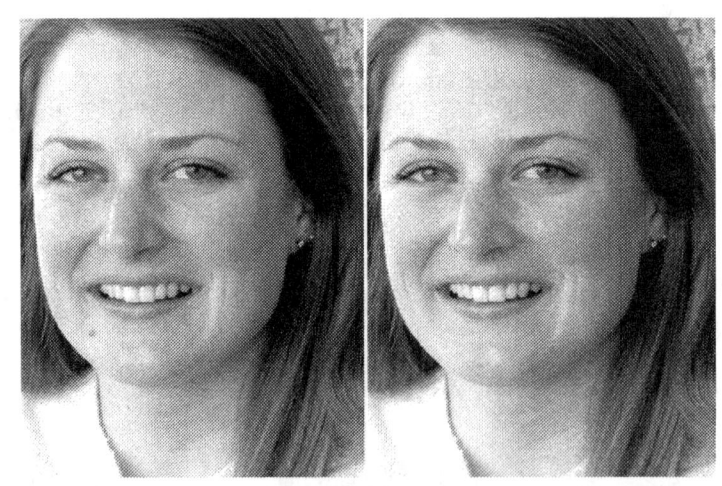

Figure 13-1.   *The Clone tool was used to eliminate small moles.*

Note

About the Align check box: It's usually best to leave it on when you're cloning from one layer (or image document) to another. The pickup point then moves to the same distance and angle from the cursor each time you click, so you don't have to constantly switch to one layer to pick up and then to the other to clone. However, be sure to switch layers whenever you need to set a new pickup point. Check the Align check box when you need to reproduce a large area in a completely different part of the picture. Be sure you don't release the mouse button until you've cloned as much area as you like.

Putting Your Retouching on Layers

In the case of the portrait in the preceding section, there were at least three instances in which, no matter where the pickup point was positioned, the clone would not match the brightness of the surrounding area. As long as your clones are on layers, clones that are too dark or too light are very easy to fix. You just lighten or darken them with the Dodge and Burn tools—dodge to lighten, burn to darken. Those tools are covered in the next section, "Eliminating Shadows, Stains, and Blotches."

There might also be times when you need to rematch the color of a cloned area. You can do that easily by choosing the Brush tool and setting the foreground color to a local color with the Eyedropper tool. Set the opacity of the brush at about 25 percent. In the Brush Options bar, choose Color from the Blend Mode menu and then paint over the retouched area to add the local color in gradually. To add diversity and avoid the colorized look, resample the foreground color with the eyedropper as you paint.

Finally, as mentioned earlier, if you make a mistake, instead of having to start all over again or undo dozens of strokes to get back to the ones you don't like, you can simply use the Eraser tool to remove the bad strokes from the retouch layer and then redo them. The History palette can also provide an easy way to go back a number of steps with a simple click—as long as the step wasn't outside the limit set by Preferences. For this kind of operation, you could temporarily raise the history states limit to give you more of a buffer.

Eliminating Shadows, Stains, and Blotches

Often (especially when restoring old photos), you'll find that lightening, darkening, or tinting an area so that it removes a stain or surface discoloration looks much more natural than cloning or painting over the area. This is especially true when working on portraits. We're so used to seeing people that we very quickly pick up on anything that looks artificial.

Lightening and Darkening Areas

Much of what we perceive as information in an image is defined by how light or dark one area is in comparison to another. In fact, in the case of monochrome (black-and-white) images, that's all the information there is. If you want to maintain the original texture and at least some of the contrast information, it's better to lighten or darken that area than to paint or clone over it. There are several ways to lighten areas. Following is a list of each of the tools that can be used and the situation in which they're best:

- **Dodge tool**   This is nothing more than a brush that causes whatever you stroke over to be lightened. It's best for changing the brightness of small areas (less than 1/25th of the overall image area) that are best blended gradually and with multiple strokes.

- **Soft Light**   This is a blending mode that can be used as a Brush option or as a Layer blending mode. It works best when you want to simply lighten a shadow, rather than trying to make it match its surroundings. If you need to lighten several areas to an equal extent, it is best to use a separate layer, fill selected areas, and then use the Opacity slider to adjust the brightness of the layer. This technique is discussed at some length in Chapter 12.

- **Image adjustment in a selected area**   There are times when using a fill layer over-brightens the shadows and changes the contrast of the area you want to match. In those instances, it is better to use the Levels command to control the brightness within selected areas. Better yet, do this with an adjustment layer so that you can adjust brightness for all the underlying layers at once.

- **Moving selected areas to a new layer**   If you select several areas of the image at once, you can lift them to a new layer. You can then make several types of adjustments and do retouching within a retouched area with all the advantages that retouching on a separate layer affords.

   In the following exercise, we use several of these techniques for changing the brightness and tint of specific areas. You can use any image in your library for this exercise, but we suggest you continue with the same image used in the previous exercise so that you can better visualize how the effects help one another.

1. Choose the Dodge tool. In its Options bar, drag the exposure slider to about 15 percent. Choose Brushes | Soft Round Brush. Zoom in to 100 percent (double-click the Zoom tool or enter 100 percent in either the Status bar or in the lower-left field in the Navigator palette).

2. Dodge the small blotches and discolorations first by scrubbing lightly with the Dodge tool until they match their surroundings. You can use the same technique on any small lines or edges that seem too pronounced.

3. Enlarge the brush slightly to brighten slightly larger areas that you want to clean. If your image is a portrait, these would likely be the whites of the subject's eyes and the subject's teeth.

4. If there's a larger area that's stained or too light or dark, choose the Freehand Lasso tool and drag a marquee around the area. Choose Select | Feather. In the

Feather dialog box, enter a feather radius that's wide enough to let your adjustment blend. Now choose Layers | New | Layer Via Copy (or hold CTRL while right-clicking inside the selection to bring up the in-context menu and then choose Layer Via Copy). Then choose Enhance | Adjust Brightness/Contrast | Levels or Brightness/Contrast to lighten the new layer so that it comes as close as possible to matching the brightness of the surrounding area. This is seldom a perfect match because there's shading within the area you lifted, but you've saved a lot of time retouching tiny areas within the large area.

5. If necessary, repeat step 4 on any small areas within the new layer until the whole area is a reasonably smooth match.

6. Merge the layers that you lifted with the layer the main image is on (see Chapter 8). Then use the Burn, Dodge, and Clone Stamp tools to blend any smaller areas or any visible borders between what were the selection marquees.

7. In the example image, the model's sunburned nose was quite a bit redder than the rest of her face. To fix any similar problem, choose the Brush tool. In the Options bar, choose Color as the blending mode. Lower the opacity slider to about 50 percent. While pressing OPT/ALT, click an area of the skin that most closely represents the overall area surrounding the off-color portion of the image. Now just brush over the discolored area. Because you have set the opacity to a fairly low percentage, you can brush over the area several times to increase the intensity of the color change, thus blending the color change with its surroundings.

The image in Figure 13-2 picks up where Figure 13-1 left off. All the retouching was done using the processes in the preceding exercise. You can see the result in Figure 13-2.

Tinting Areas

You tint areas for one of two reasons: to add some glamour or pizzazz to the image, or to "color balance" the area to match its surroundings. This section gives you a couple of ways to correct both instances.

In addition, there are several ways to tint areas. The following list describes each of the tools you can use and the situations in which they're best used:

- **Brush tool in Color or Hue mode**   Best for color matching relatively small areas of an image with their surroundings. We already used this method in the retouching exercise in the previous section.

- **Fill layers**   An excellent way to tint an image for effect. It's not often used for retouching, but you can create a layer mask for specific areas of the image. This technique can also be used in conjunction with blending modes to create some useful illustrative effects—provided you don't overdo it. You can also use the layer's opacity slider to minimize the effect and make it subtler.

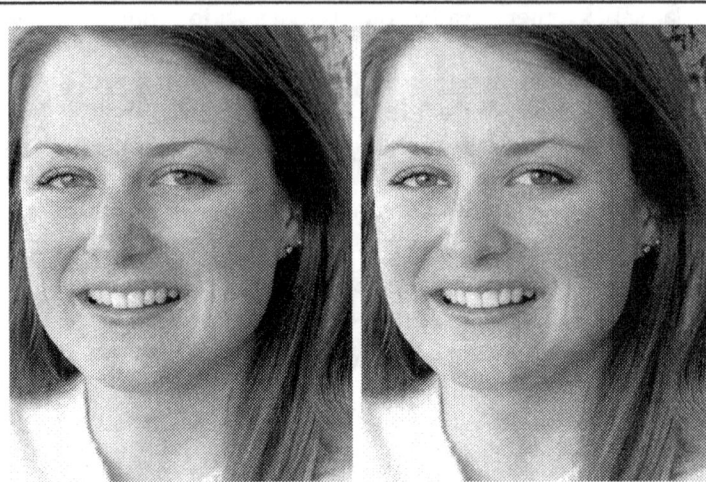

Figure 13-2. *The improvement to skin tones can be seen in the image on the right.*

■ **Hue/Saturation command**   Using this command in a selected area is a quicker (and often more precise and more subtle) way to adjust a selected area.

The following exercise demonstrates one way of adding tints to large areas of a photograph to create a mood illusion:

1. Open an image with a large area of sky, water, or reflection. These aren't the only subjects you can treat with the methods used here, but they make the demonstration easy to follow.

2. Place a selection around the areas you do not want to tint. This can be a fairly tight and precise selection or (depending on your subject) a very loose, highly feathered free-form. Press CMD/CTRL+SHIFT+I to invert the selection.

3. Open the Layers palette. Choose New Fill/Adjustment Layer | Solid Color. The Color Picker dialog box appears (see Chapter 3). Choose the color you want to use as a tint, and click OK. A new color-fill layer appears, with a layer mask created by the selection you made (see Chapter 8).

4. Choose Layers | Blend Mode | Overlay. The unmasked portion of the image will be tinted with the color you chose.

5. If you need to make the original image match the brightness and contrast of the tinted area better, click the name bar of the image layer and choose Enhance | Adjust Brightness/Contrast | Levels (or press CMD/CTRL+L). The Levels dialog box appears. Adjust the sliders until you like what you see.

6. If you want to tint the masked portion of the image, click the image layer's name bar to make it the currently active layer. Choose Enhance | Adjust Color | Hue/Saturation. The Hue/Saturation dialog box appears. Drag the hue and saturation sliders until you like the effect they create when seen with the effect created by the Overlay blending mode imposed on the solid-color fill layer. You can see the effect in Figure 13-3.

Getting Rid of Dust, Scratches, and Other Unwanted Artifacts

If you've scanned your images or are restoring old "shoebox" photos, you've undoubtedly collected some dust and fine-line scratches (especially with scanned film). To save time and do the best possible job of getting rid of such schmutz, do it in two stages. First, use the dust and scratches filter to get rid of the tiny specs and scars. If you use settings that are high enough to get rid of the larger defects, you'll just blur the

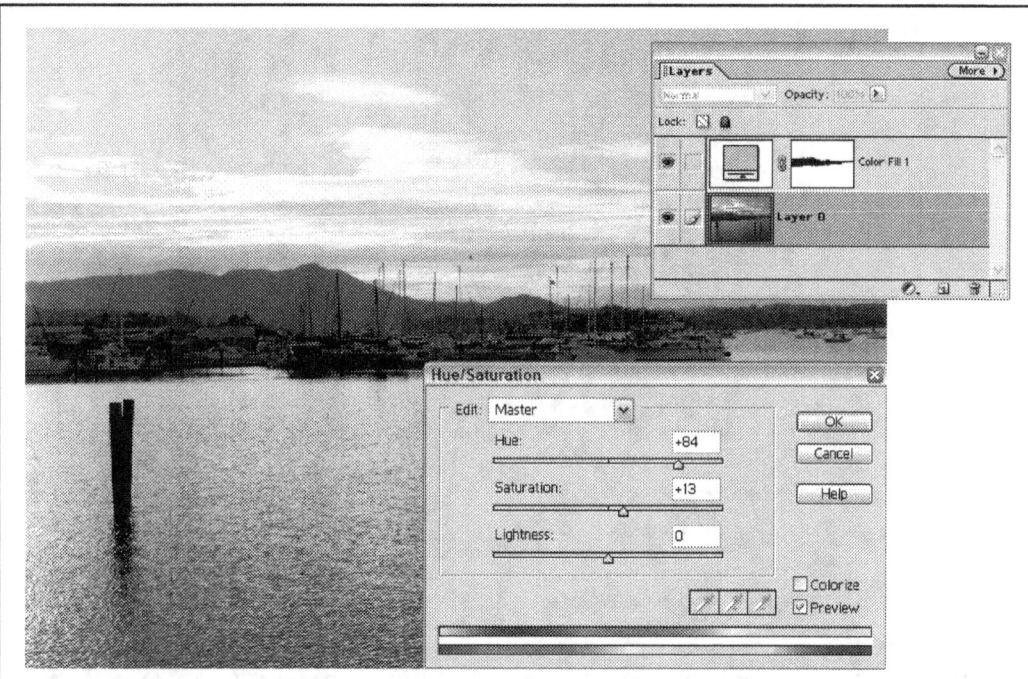

Figure 13-3. *You can't see the full effect in black and white, but you can see the mask in the solid-color fill layer and how the hue and saturation were adjusted.*

image too much. Then you can use the Clone Stamp tool and a very small brush to stamp out the larger (and less frequent) problems.

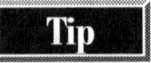

Keeping your equipment clean is the first line of defense against an image full of unwanted artifacts. Taking time to clean your lens, scanner, negatives, prints, and slides before you digitize saves you from heaps of work later.

Let's assume you want to restore an old photo:

1. Scan the print and then open it in Photoshop Elements. Choose Enhance | Auto Color Correction. Most of the time, this automatically color-balances the image, turns the blacks to true black (old photos have usually faded), and keeps the highlights from being totally washed out.

2. Use the Burn and Dodge tools to minimize any stained or faded areas in the image.

3. Now, all you're left with are the scratches, folds, and dust. Duplicate the background layer and leave it selected. We're going to run the dust and scratches filter on the duplicated layer.

4. Choose Filter | Noise | Dust & Scratches. The Dust & Scratches dialog box appears, as shown here.

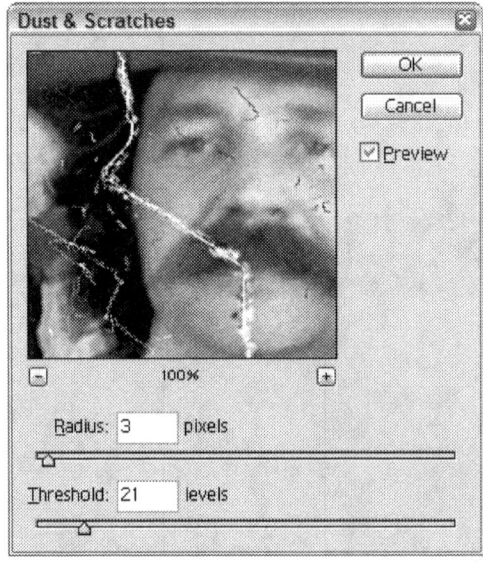

5. Drag the radius slider to a maximum of 3 or 4 pixels. You will see that the image becomes quite blurry, which is why you don't want to overdo it. The instant the majority of specks and scratches disappear, stop increasing the radius.

6. Drag the threshold slider to the point where the picture regains most or all its sharpness. Click OK. Most of the specks disappear.

7. Now you're going to give the image back just enough of its original sharpness to fool the viewer into thinking that the picture is sharp. We tend to look for areas, such as the eyes and hair, that tell us that the image is sharp. If we see that they are, we seldom look any further. Choose the Eraser tool. From its Options bar, choose a small, soft-edged, round brush. Enter 80 percent in the Opacity field. Now, erase through to the original layer to expose the sharper detail of the original in areas that need to have a sharp look—for instance, along the edges of lips, eyes, and eyebrows. It might take a little practice, but you'll get the idea quite quickly.

8. Choose Layer | Flatten Image to merge the two layers.

9. Create a new layer by clicking the New Layer icon at the bottom of the Layers palette.

10. Choose the Clone Stamp tool. You are now going to remove the remaining spots and scratches. This is much easier if you first remove the smaller spots because you're not as likely to find yourself cloning small spots over larger ones. Choose a small brush that just covers the spots. Make sure the Aligned box is checked in the Options bar. Clone from the image layer to the new transparent layer (see the section "Putting Your Retouching on Layers," earlier in this chapter).

11. When you've finished removing the spots and scratches, again choose Layer | Flatten Image. Now all you have left to do is to remove any scars from folding or crumpling the photo. You do this with the Clone Stamp tool. Choose a larger, soft brush and then repeat step 10. To paint over the lines this time, however, drag the brush rather than clicking it. Be sure to change your brush size if the fold changes width. Also, keep resetting the anchor point so that you blend the retouching by cloning from different areas close to the crack.

Most of the time, that will do it. You might have to do some burning and dodging if there are stains or discolorations. You can see the before and after results here.

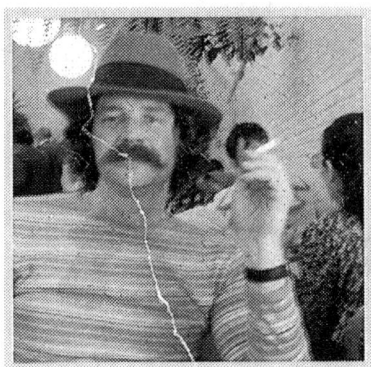 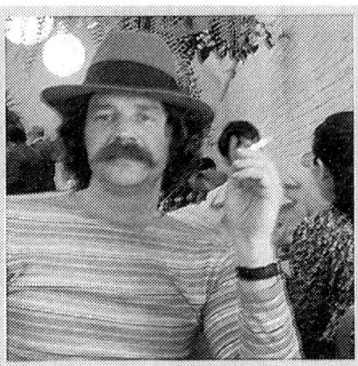

Red Eye Removal

Red eye is almost always the result of using a camera with built-in flash. The brilliant light fires directly into the iris of the subject's eyes (especially if the photo was taken at night and the irises are dilated) and is then reflected back into the camera's lens. The result is an eerie "monster movie" effect. Ironically, Photoshop Elements can do a much better job of this than your camera's red-eye shooting mode (so don't bother to use it). Here's how you get rid of the red eye:

1. Open the image that has red eye.

2. Choose the Red Eye Brush tool (Y). Make sure the brush is just about the same size as the iris of the subject's eyes (this works for pets, too).

3. In the Options bar, you will see two color swatches: Current and Replacement. If you aren't sure of the real color of the subject's eyes, click the Default Colors button. Otherwise, choose Sampling | First Click and click the brush first in the red portion of the iris. The current color swatch turns red. Then click in the replacement color swatch. The Color Picker dialog box appears. Choose the iris color you want.

4. Place the cursor over the center of the iris and scrub until the iris is the color you want it to be. Notice that the color does not change outside the iris, even if the brush is larger than the iris or if you scrub outside the iris.

Do Fence It In

Don't forget the power of using selections to restrict the retouching you do to the exact area you want it to apply to. This can be especially helpful if you're cloning from one area to another or want to place content from one layer inside a specific location in another.

In Figure 13-4, the image of the hugging couple was placed on one layer and scaled so that it fit inside a specific group of windowpanes in the image of the warehouse window. That layer was then hidden, and the panes in the warehouse window were carefully selected. The selection was then inverted (CMD/CTRL+SHIFT+I), the layer with the couple activated, and the Show/Hide button toggled to Show. The inverted selection now appeared on the couple's layer, so pressing BACKSPACE/DELETE was all it took to completely erase everything outside the chosen windowpanes. Layers | Blend Mode | Screen was then chosen and the couple's opacity lowered to 32 percent so the couple appeared to be behind the window glass.

Adding Shadows and Highlights

Retouching isn't just a matter of fixing the little things. Sometimes it can change the entire mood and dynamic of the photograph. You might add highlights and shadows,

THE DIGITAL DARKROOM
WORKFLOW

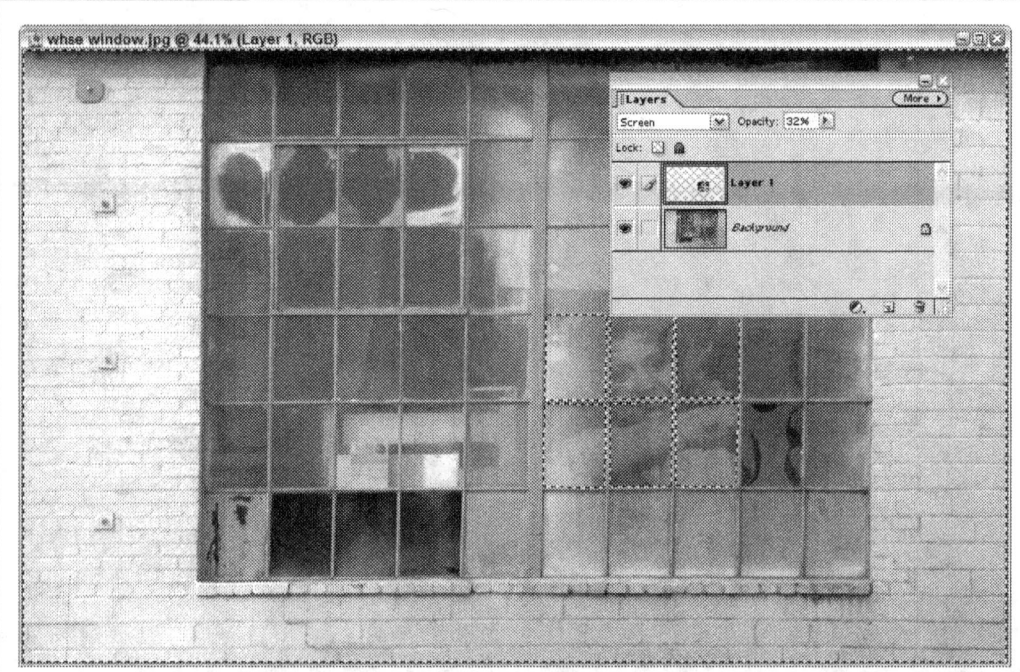

Figure 13-4.   *In this image, you can see how the selection marquee was used to superimpose the image of the couple onto the panes of glass.*

change the sky, and darken or blur the background in relation to the subject, as seen in Figure 13-5.

Here's what we did to the cheerleaders picture to create an image with so much more impact:

1. Open a single-layer image that has a prominent foreground object as the focus as well as a part that could be replaced with something more interesting. In the case of this image, the boring part is the sky.

2. Duplicate the background layer. Then, in the Layers palette, click the eye icon in the Show/Hide button of the background layer's name bar to turn it off temporarily. Then click the duplicated layer to make it active.

3. To remove the sky and knock out the cheerleaders from the background, begin by choosing the Background Eraser. In the Options bar, enter about 15 percent in the Tolerance field. Choose Limits | Contiguous (unless you are extracting flying hair or leaves that show small areas of background colors behind the foreground). Choose a brush size that is large enough to reach into the foreground far enough to pick up any "holes" that contain the background color.

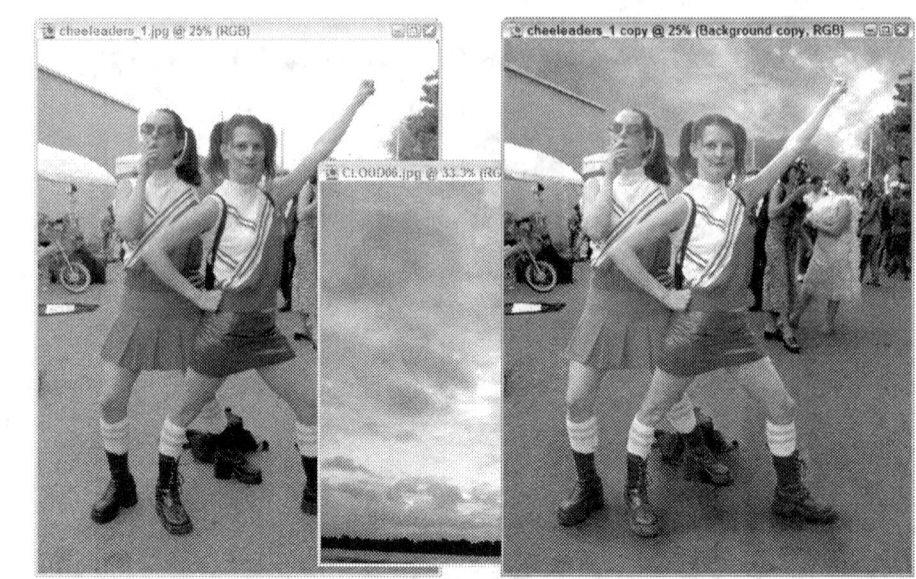

Figure 13-5. *The photo on the left was combined with the sky image and some retouching magic to produce the much more dramatic image on the right.*

4. Drag the cursor so that the cross hairs are touching the colors you want to erase, and then start erasing along the border between the foreground and the sky. Make sure you haven't left any blotches of color or fringing along the edges. If you have, you might have to zoom in extremely close and remove them with the eraser. Take a look at Figure 13-6.

5. Erase the sky in a border that stretches all across the horizon. Then choose the Lasso tool and make a selection through the erased border so that the marquee encloses all of what's left of the sky. Once the marquee is all set, press BACKSPACE/ DELETE. You should see nothing but the transparency checkerboard where the sky once was.

6. Duplicate the layer with the erased sky, hide the erased sky layer, select the duplicate layer, and repeat step 5 to continue erasing the foreground subjects (in this case, the cheerleaders) from their environment.

7. When the background and foreground colors get too similar, you'll start erasing parts of the foreground. There are two things you can do about that: either go back later and clone in the accidentally erased parts from the original layer, or undo your erasure and lower the tolerance in the Options bar.

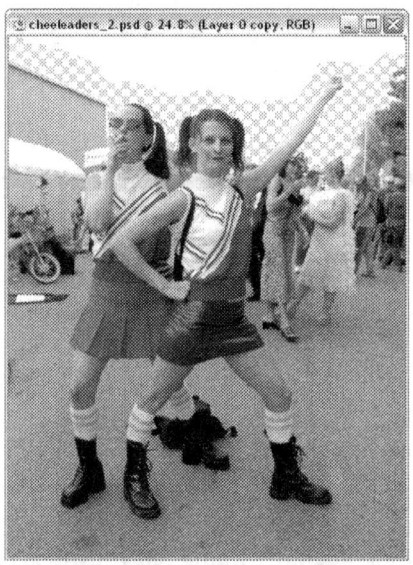

Figure 13-6.   *First, erase the sky border with the Background Eraser tool, as shown here.*

8. Alas, some borders are so complex or so close in color that only the human eye can tell the difference. In those instances, you just have to painstakingly erase with the Eraser tool. Do so, very carefully, at about 200-percent zoom. The result should look like this:

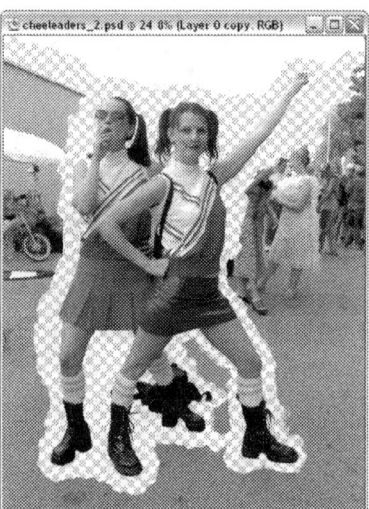

9. Choose the Sharpen tool and enter about 40 percent in the Strength field in the Options bar. Choose a brush size that is about the same as an area in the foreground object that needs sharpening, and brush over it until you get the degree of sharpness you want.

10. Open an image that contains a more interesting sky. Press CMD/CTRL+A to select the entire image, and then click the image you are putting together and press CMD/CTRL+V to paste the image.

11. In the Layers palette, drag the sky image's name bar so that it is between the layer with the knocked-out sky and the layer with the entire original image. If the sky needs to be scaled to fill the open sky area, press CMD/CTRL+T. A Transform marquee appears around the sky. Drag the handles until the sky fills the area you knocked out for the sky.

12. Press CMD/CTRL+L to bring up the Levels dialog box, and use it to give the sky the brightness and contrast needed to match its new surroundings. When you like what you see, click OK. The Levels dialog box disappears.

13. In the Layers palette, click all the Show/Hide buttons to make sure all the layers are turned on, and then click the name bar for the layer with the knocked-out sky to make it the active layer. Now darken the scene behind your subjects so that they stand out more (in another image, it might be more appropriate to lighten or blur the background to make the subjects stand out).

14. Okay, we're almost done. Now we want to add a little lighting direction so that this photo seems to have been taken on a brighter and more cheerful day. Choose the Dodge tool and burn in the ground so that a deeper shadow seems to have been cast by the subjects. The easiest way to detect the lighting direction in the scene is to look at how the objects in the scene are lit and on which side the shadows appear. Here, the light is coming from a high angle and to the left, so the shadows are cast under the subjects and slightly to the right, as you can see here.

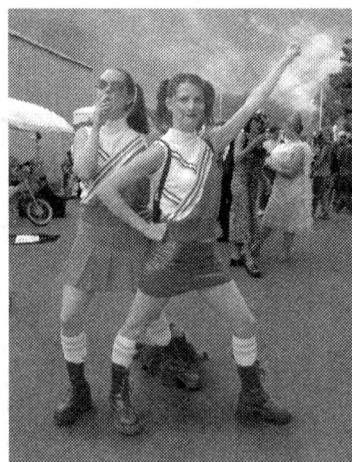

15. When you've finished casting the shadows, activate the subject (top) layer. Choose the Dodge tool. If your subjects were part of the image, you'd select them first to make sure that the highlights didn't extend into the background. However, because your subjects have been knocked out, they are isolated from the background anyway. Carefully dodge the top edges of your subjects so that the light seems to be coming from above and behind them.

Adding Texture

Sometimes you really need to replace part of the image with the texture that surrounds that part. For instance, in the scene used as the example for this section, part of a tree and some unsightly plumbing break up the otherwise pleasant texture of the brick wall. You can see the original image in Figure 13-7.

Photoshop Elements has a tool that's similar to the Clone Stamp (and occupies the same slot in the Toolbox) called the Pattern Stamp tool. Unlike the Clone Stamp, the Pattern Stamp doesn't require that you set an anchor point. Instead, the Pattern Stamp lets you paint with whatever pattern you've defined or with any pattern you have in your pattern library. If you want to paint the texture of a fabric or a person's hair into an area that has been blocked by over- or under-exposure, you first define a pattern for

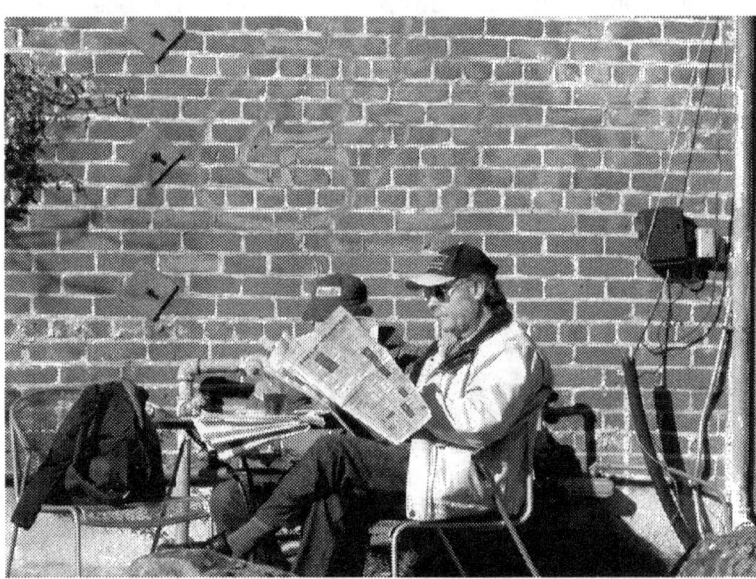

Figure 13-7. *This is the original photograph that you want to add a brick texture to in order to eliminate unwanted details in the background.*

that texture. Then you choose the Pattern Stamp tool and paint into that blocked area with the pattern you defined.

Here's how you define a pattern. We'll use the brick wall as an example:

1. Open an image you want to repair by painting in texture.

2. Choose the Rectangular Marquee tool. Drag diagonally until the selection includes as large an area as possible that is evenly lighted and in which the highlights, shadows, and colors that make the shapes in the textures are as uniform as possible.

3. You can now define a pattern if you like. To do so, choose Edit | Define Pattern. The Pattern Name dialog box appears.

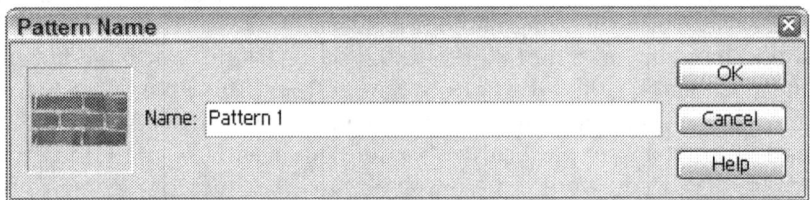

4. Enter a name that will make it easy to identify the pattern verbally and click OK. That's all there is to it. If you look in the Pattern Presets drop-down palette, you'll see an icon that pictures this pattern, so you can choose it anytime from the current library of presets.

Ah, but we have a problem. We picked this brick pattern intentionally to illustrate that problem and its solution. When we paint with this pattern, it doesn't look like a smooth texture but like a series of repeating tiles with a "seam" between each, like this:

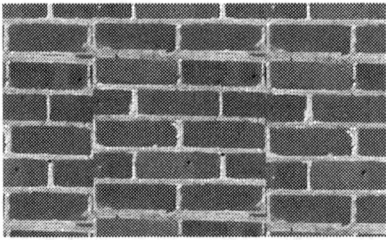

Here's how we turn a tiled pattern into a seamless pattern:

1. While the selection is still active (that is, the marquee is still there), press CMD/CTRL+C to copy the contents of the selection to the clipboard.

2. Choose File | New From Clipboard to open a new file with the contents of the clipboard that will be the same size as the brick selection you copied.

3. Before you start the process of creating a seamless tile, you will need to make a note of the dimensions of the selection because we want to wrap both horizontally and vertically by entering the proper pixel values in the Offset command dialog box to move it by exactly 50 percent. Press CMD/CTRL+A to select all, and then choose Window | Info. The Info palette appears (see the next illustration). In the lower-right corner are the width (W) and height (H) of the selection. If these dimensions aren't stated in pixels, choose Edit | Preferences | Units and Rulers. The Units and Rulers dialog box appears. Choose Rulers | Pixels, and click OK. The height and width of the marquee are now shown in pixels.

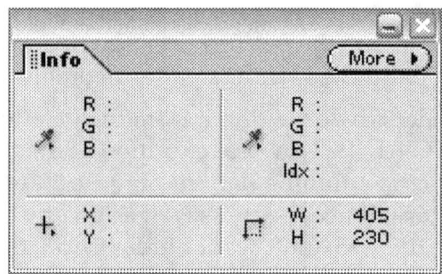

4. Now you need to align and blend the edges of the image so it will tile seamlessly. The way you do that is to slide the image over so the matched edges are in the middle of the image. There is a clever command called the Offset command that can do this in such a way that when you slide and push the pixels off one edge, they will wrap around the other so that the pixels on opposite edges will now match perfectly. First, you do it in the horizontal direction, and then in the vertical direction. When the seams have been moved to the center, you can use paint tools to camouflage the seams.

5. Choose Filter | Other | Offset. The Offset dialog box appears. Enter half the number of pixels shown in the width dimension in the Info dialog box in the Horizontal Pixels Right field. Click OK. The image looks like the picture on the left in the following illustration. Use the Clone Stamp tool to cover the seam in the middle and any characteristics in the pattern that make it obvious it is repeating. The result should look like the picture on the right.

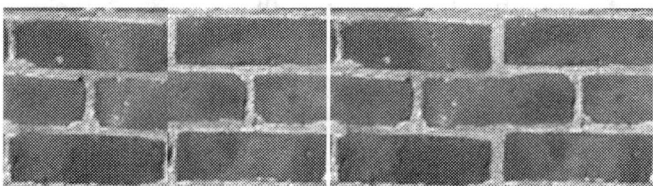

6. Now you want to do the same trick from top to bottom. Enter half the number of pixels shown in the height dimension in the Info dialog box in the Vertical

Pixels Down field. Click to toggle on the Wrap Around radio button. Then fix the seam with the Clone Stamp tool.

7. When you've finished, press CMD/CTRL+A to select all, and then choose Edit | Define Pattern. The Define Pattern dialog box appears. Enter a name for the pattern, and click OK.

Now you have a perfectly seamless pattern that you can use to paint a texture pattern over an area to cover up items that you don't want to include in the picture. We'll use the picture of the outdoor coffee drinkers to show you some of the best techniques for doing that:

1. Open the image you made the pattern from (or, in any case, an image into which you want to paint the seamless pattern you just made).

2. Open the Layers palette by dragging it from the Palette Well or choosing Window | Layers. Click the New Layer button at the bottom of the Layers palette. We are going to paint the pattern onto a separate layer. That way, we can realign the pattern, if necessary, as well as do any erasing needed to let parts of the picture that we don't want hidden show through.

3. Make a selection to contain the areas that you want to paint into, and feather it by about 10 pixels so that what you paint in blends better than you could otherwise.

4. Choose the Pattern Stamp tool. If you'd rather not look under the Clone Stamp in the Toolbox, just press SHIFT+S until you see its icon appear in the Toolbox. In the Options bar, choose the pattern you just made. Also, uncheck the Aligned check box. Now, just paint into the area you want to cover.

5. When you're reasonably happy with how you've used the texture to cover the clutter in the background, choose the Move tool and drag until the pattern you painted in matches the seam as closely as possible. This will take some experimentation, and with a pattern such as these bricks, it will never be a perfect match; but when you're satisfied, press CMD/CTRL+D to deselect the selection. From the Palette or Layers menu, choose Flatten Image.

6. Double-click the Zoom tool to zoom in to 100 percent. Now choose the Clone Stamp tool and clone out the seam between the painted-in pattern and the original pattern. This will take some time, and you will have to relocate your pickup point several times to get a smooth blend. Nevertheless, it will go much faster than if you had to clone the entire area in. In the case of the brick wall, our end result can be seen in Figure 13-8.

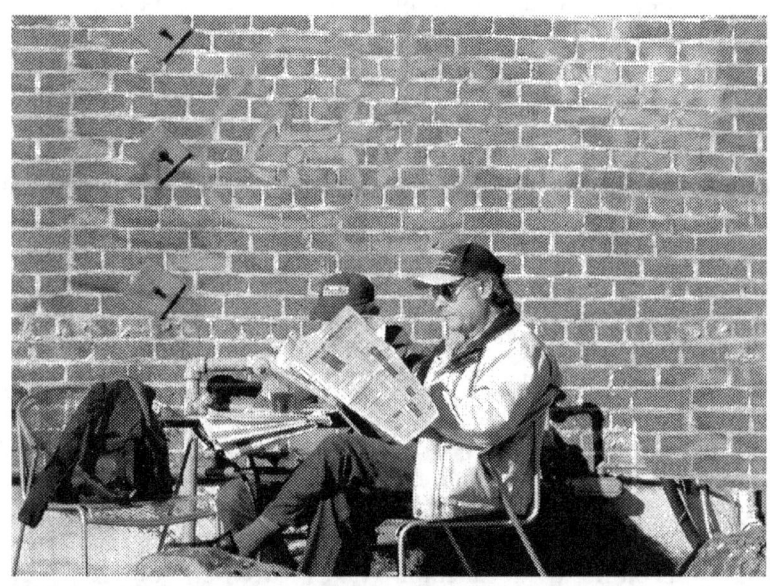

Figure 13-8. *This is the final scene where the unwanted details have been painted out using the Pattern Stamp tool.*

Smoothing Over the Rough Spots

There are times when an edge is just too sharp and harsh to look natural. This often is the case when you made an unfeathered lasso selection to remove an image from its original background and then pasted it into a new background, or when there is a hairline defect in an otherwise perfectly smooth surface. In either case, you can correct the problem with a slight amount of blurring. There are two tools appropriate for the job: the Blur tool and the Smudge tool. As you will see, each uses a slightly different method for softening what they brush over.

The Blur Tool

The Blur tool "defocuses" whatever you brush over. It does this by scattering the pixels it brushes over and by lowering the color contrast of adjacent pixels. If you want to soften edges of an image you're going to composite, it is best to do it when the image that's being composited is on its own layer; this is so that when you use the Blur tool, it doesn't affect the background image. Of course, you also have to be sure to toggle off the checkmark in the Use All Layers check box.

In Figure 13-9, a flower was selected with the Magic Lasso and dragged into another image containing leaves. You see most of the edges as they were selected and cut, but the lower edge of the front-left petal has been blurred slightly with the Blur tool.

The Smudge Tool

The Smudge tool softens edges by smearing pixels into one another to mix them up. If you've seen artists mix adjoining colors in an oil painting by pushing and pulling the paint-laden tip of the brush against a different-colored paint on the canvas—you get the idea. The Smudge tool produces a somewhat different effect from the Blur tool. Instead of smoothing and softening, it pulls pixels that it grabs either from local color or, if the finger painting option is selected, from the foreground color, and smears them in the direction of the brush stroke. In Figure 13-10, the Smudge tool was used with a 100-percent strength setting and with finger painting deselected to make the repair to the petal, as shown in the middle image. The cursor was placed in the petal area near the edge to choose the local color, and then the color was pulled to rebuild a clean edge.

The Smudge tool was then placed in finger painting mode with the percentage at around 80 (adjust this to your own needs) to make the brush stroke color fade slowly from the foreground color to the local color. The Eyedropper tool was used to pick a color from the flower's darker areas that would work for the striations in the petal. The brush was placed where the darkest part of the striation begins and then painted in with one continuous stroke, following the contours of the petal. The stroke automatically fades out as the stroke is painted. The result can be seen in the image on the right in Figure 13-10.

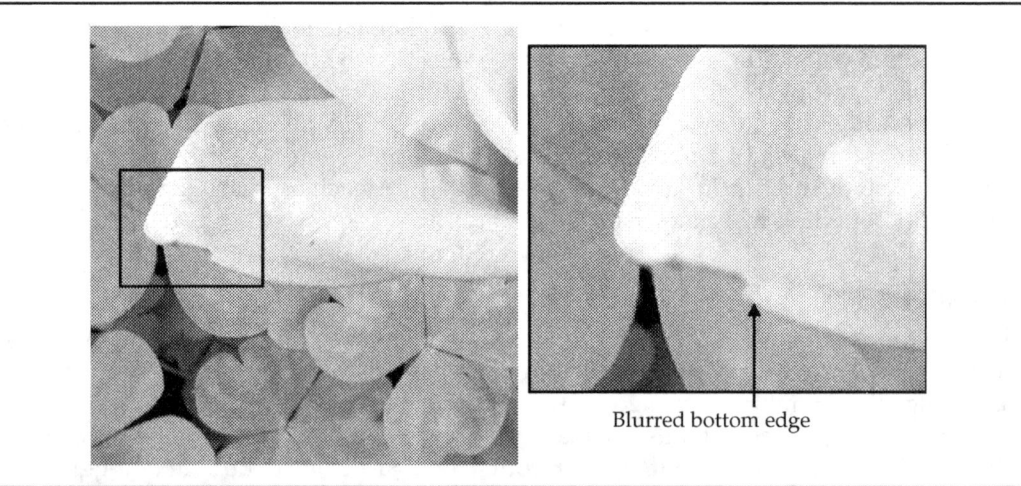

Blurred bottom edge

Figure 13-9. *Blurring is often subtle, but it's effective. You can see clearly how the sharper edge comes forward and the blurred edge recedes in the detail to the right.*

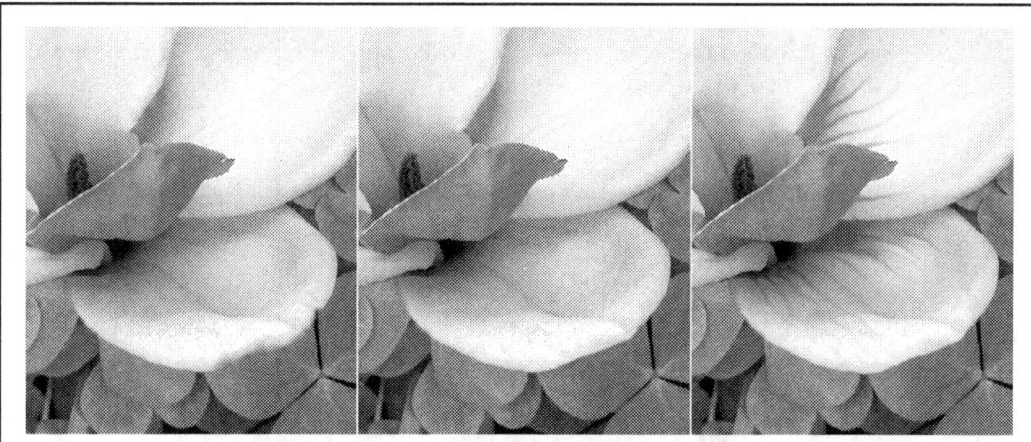

Figure 13-10.   *The original flower with a damaged lower petal on the left, the repair done with the smudge tool in the middle, and the petal striations put in with the Smudge tool set to finger painting mode on the right*

If in doubt about whether to use the smudge or blur tool, use the rectangular marquee to select a part of your image and raise it to a new layer by choosing the New Layer Via Copy command (found on the Layers menu and in-context menu). You can then experiment without affecting the original image. When you get the result you like, click the Status button of the original layer. A chain-link icon appears. Choose Layers Palette | Merge Linked.

Sharpening the Focus

When you need to "pop," a term used for sharpening and enhancing an area so it visually pops out of the background, the edges of an important part of the subject, such as eyelashes, or a feature item (such as a diamond ring in an engagement photo), the Sharpen tool can be handy—as long as you don't overdo it. However, we prefer the method in the following exercise, which uses filters to blur and sharpen an image.

The Diffuse-Glow Effect

It has long been a favorite trick of portrait, glamour, and wedding photographers to use filters that blur skin tones while actually increasing contrast in darker areas, such as hair, eyes, and eyebrows. You can do this automatically with the diffuse glow filter:

1. Open a portrait.
2. Use the Clone Stamp and Dodge and Burn tools to retouch any prominent defects.

3. Duplicate the background layer. Press D to reset the foreground/background colors to the default black and white. Choose Filter | Distort | Diffuse Glow. The Diffuse Glow dialog box appears.

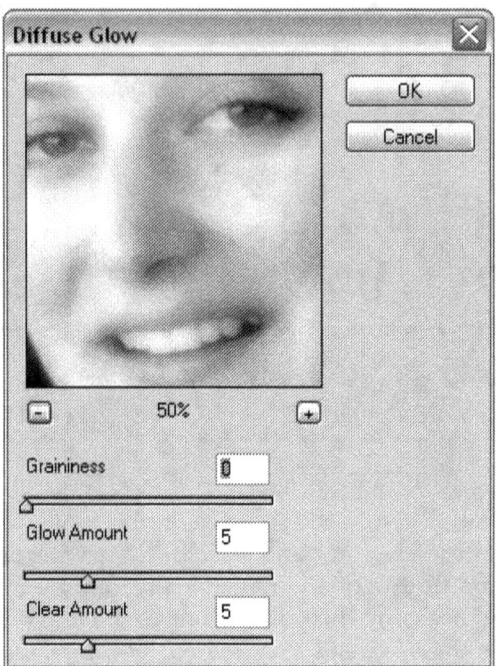

4. Click the minus button under the preview window until you can see most of the image. Drag the graininess slider all the way to the left (you can add noise later if you want grain—but if you introduce it now, you'll have a harder time matching the overall effect after you've finished retouching).

5. Enter 5 in both the Glow Amount and Clear Amount fields. Now play with adjusting the sliders until you like what you see, and click OK.

6. This filter often takes too much color out of the image. If that's the case, choose the Sponge tool. From the Options bar, choose Mode | Saturate, and drag the flow slider to about 50 percent. Now scrub in small areas to bring out the color. In this case, the model's eyes became greener and her lips became redder. You can see the effect of using Diffuse Glow in Figure 13-11.

THE DIGITAL DARKROOM
WORKFLOW

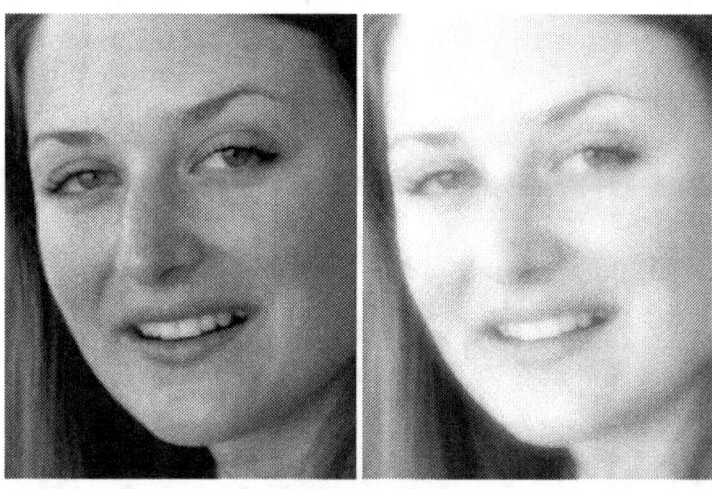

Figure 13-11.   *The before and after (right) images after using the Diffuse glow filter to give the model a soft light ethereal appearance.*

Airbrushing a Portrait

Some portrait subjects want to look natural but glamorous, too. Here's an easy way to retouch out all the small stuff:

1. Make a duplicate layer of the main image.

2. Double-click the background layer's name bar. The Layer Properties dialog box appears. Enter a new name, or just accept the default Layer 0 name, and click OK. You've converted the background layer to a normal image layer.

3. Click the top layer's Show/Hide button until the eye icon disappears. This layer is now temporarily hidden.

4. While the bottom layer is still active, choose Filter | Blur | Gaussian Blur. The Gaussian Blur dialog box appears (see next illustration). Drag the blur slider until the image is so fuzzy that all the freckles and small wrinkles disappear.

What we've done is eliminated the details but maintained the brightness and color of the skin tones.

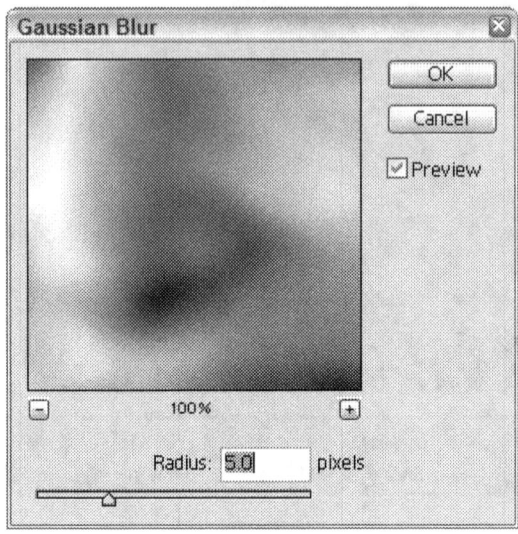

5. Toggle the top layer back on, and then click in the name bar to make it the active layer.

6. Choose the Eraser tool. From the Options bar, choose Mode | Brush, and drag the opacity slider to (or near) 100 percent. Finally, choose a soft round brush so that the strokes don't create a hard-edged seam.

7. Now just erase over any part of the face that isn't as smooth as a baby's. Instant retouching!

Here's the final result we got:

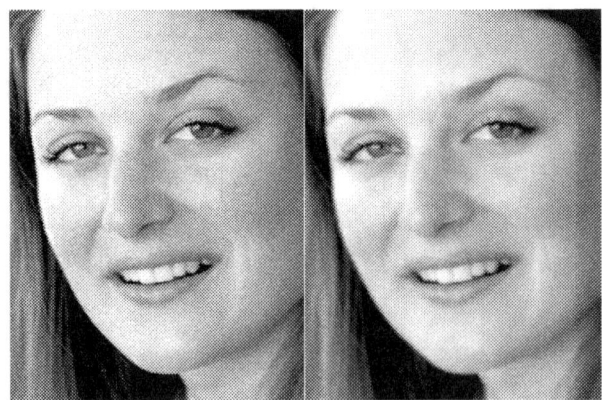

Changing the Shape of Things

There are times when you need to slim a waistline or thigh, make eyes bigger and more expressive, or take a bump out of a nose. All these are within reach when you use Photoshop Elements 2.0. We almost said "within easy reach," but the truth is that making it look realistic takes considerable practice—as is the case with most retouching. One thing that especially takes some practice is learning to draw smooth curves when making selections.

Three basic techniques account for the vast majority of reshaping work done by accomplished Photoshop retouchers:

- Select, clone, and light
- Liquify
- Layer, transform, and clone

Note
Rarely does it make sense to reshape a whole subject. You almost always get better results if you shape parts of the whole one part at a time. Whenever possible, reshape the parts on layers. Then you can go back to shape one part to make it match another, control the exposure of parts individually, and light them individually.

Select, Clone, and Light

To use the select, clone, and light technique:

1. Make a selection that defines the shape you want that part of the image to become.

2. Feather the selection just enough so that the shape blends believably into its surroundings

3. Clone in from the outside of the shape to make it smaller or from the inside of the shape to make it larger.

4. Once you have cloned in the data needed to reshape the item, you need to add highlights and shadows that make the new edges look appropriately three-dimensional.

Liquify

There are times when you could add appeal to an image by reshaping small portions, but when you try, you have to do a lot of cloning and retouching to make the reshaped portion of the image blend back in. Fortunately, Photoshop Elements has a secret weapon. It's called the Liquify filter.

This section doesn't give you the whole rundown on using the Liquify filter. You'll find that in Chapter 15. Here, we cover a special application for it: reshaping objects in an image. There can be all sorts of reasons to want to reshape objects in an image. You might even want to use this to completely redesign a product or create a caricature. However, the application that uses reshaping the most by far is retouching, especially in the portrait and fashion fields. You can use it to arch eyebrows (we show you how in this section), make eyes larger (you'll learn how to do that, too), slim waistlines, or stretch legs.

Note *The most important thing to know about reshaping for retouching is that you should select the area you want to reshape so that you don't accidentally reshape portions of the image you don't want to. It's also a good idea to feather that selection just enough so that when the area surrounding the reshaped area stretches or shrinks, it does so gradually. Otherwise, you might have to further retouch a hard-edged, unnatural-looking border.*

In the following exercise, we enlarge my friend Janine's eyes and arch her eyebrows slightly. At the end of the exercise, you'll see the image we started with and the end result.

Caution *Don't overdo it when you're using the Liquify filter for retouching. This tool is so powerful and modern computers are so fast that you really have to be careful not to end up with something that looks like a caricature or just plain bad.*

1. Open a portrait. The techniques in this exercise are probably more appropriate for retouching a woman, but you can use a picture of a man if you like.

2. The first thing we want to do is arch the eyebrows. Because you want to change separate (and in this case, adjacent) areas of the same image, you'll get the best results by using the Liquify filter twice. Choose the Lasso tool and draw a very loose selection around each eyebrow (use the Add mode in the Options bar so that you can make two separate selections).

3. Choose Filter | Distort | Liquify. The Liquify dialog box appears. Actually, this is more than a dialog box (although that's what Adobe officially calls it). Liquify is really a whole plug-in application within an application, with its own tools and user interface. To find out more about this interface, go to Chapter 15.

The following is an illustration of what you should see now.

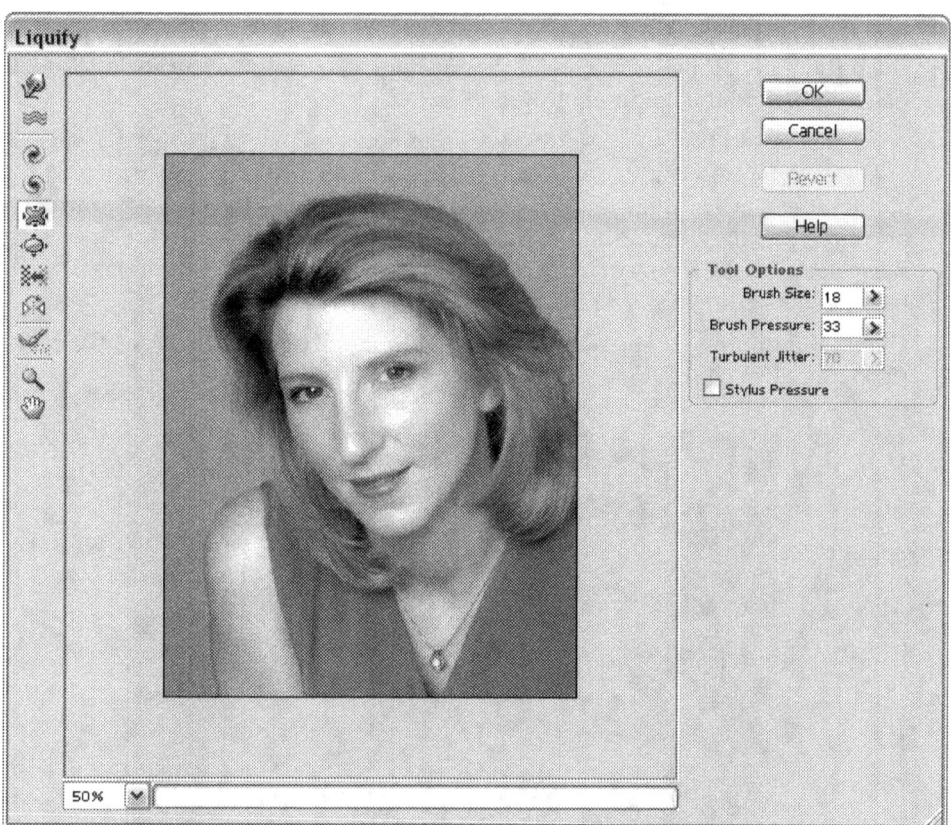

4. Choose the Warp tool (the very top icon). Use the bracket buttons to size your brush so that it moves just enough of your image. There are no strict rules for brush size, so be prepared to press CMD/CTRL+Z to undo immediately if you don't like what you see.

Caution *You can't do multiple undos or use the Undo History palette while working in the Liquify filter.*

5. Use the brush shape to push the eyebrows up slightly. You won't be able to push them past the unprotected (red-masked) area. When you're satisfied, click OK to return to the original image.

6. Now make selections around the eyes and choose Filter | Distort | Liquify again. The Liquify dialog box reappears. Choose the Bloat tool. Size your brush so that it is a little larger than an eyeball. Center it directly over the pupil, click, and hold just long enough to see a very slight bulging of the eye. Position is very critical to how the shape gets interpreted, so undo and try again if you don't get exactly what you're looking for.

7. Click OK and you'll return to the original image. Here, you can see the before (left) and after (right).

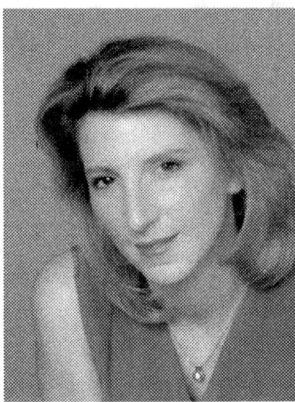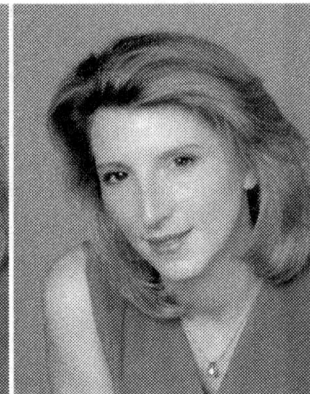

Layer, Transform, and Clone

If you just want to make an item a little larger in one direction, or to reposition the item, or both, here's the easiest routine:

1. Place a loose selection around the item and use the New Layer Via Copy command to lift it to a new, independent layer.

2. Press CMD/CTRL+T to place a free transform marquee around the item. If you need to make the item thicker or thinner in one direction, place the cursor outside a corner handle so that it becomes a curved double-headed arrow, and drag to rotate the item so that it's either vertical or horizontal. Then press RETURN/ENTER, or click the Render checkmark in the Options bar. You can see the selection with handles in Figure 13-12.

3. Now, to rotate the item, again press CMD/CTRL+T to place a free transform marquee around it. If you need to make the item thicker or thinner in one direction, place the cursor outside a center handle and drag to squeeze or stretch the item. If that's enough, you can render now.

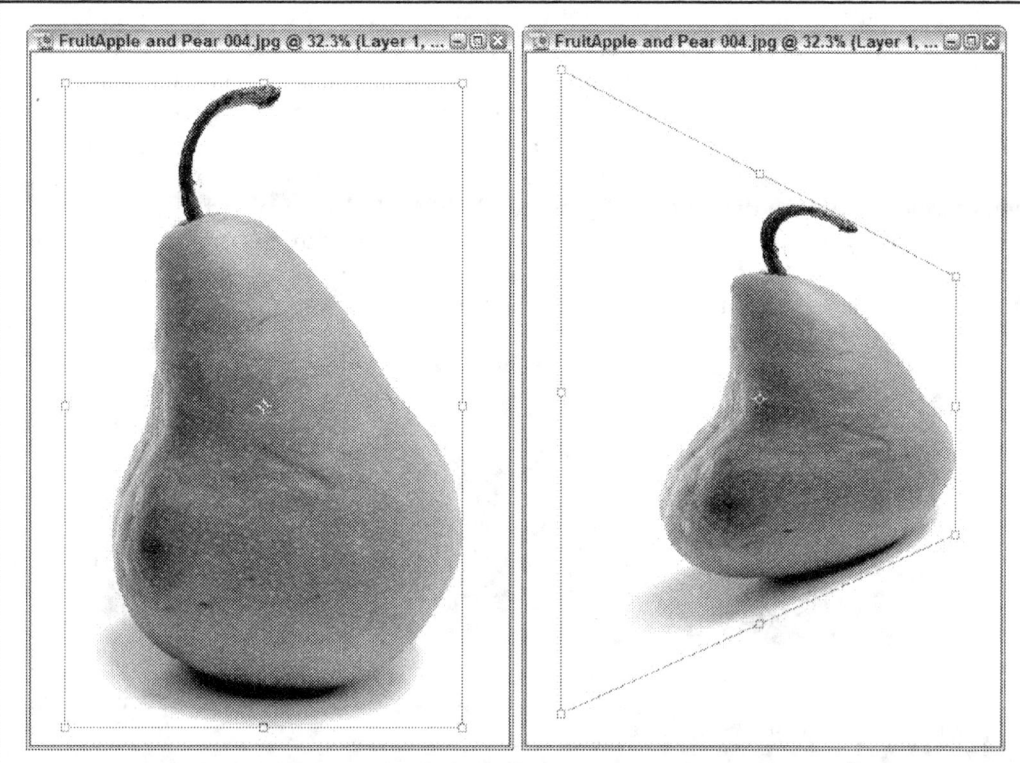

Figure 13-12. *The pear is selected with transformation handles visible after choosing the Transform command (left). The handles can then be manipulated to reshape the object (right).*

4. If you want to distort the item, press CMD/CTRL and drag a corner point in any direction you like.

5. If you want to skew the item, press CMD/CTRL and drag a center point.

6. If you want to slant the item, press CMD/CTRL+OPT/ALT, drag a center point, and then press RETURN/ENTER or click the Render checkmark in the Options bar.

Note *You can also enter exact numbers for height, width, and angle of rotation in the Options bar.*

If you want to make the image look as if it were painted or projected on a flat surface and then viewed from an angle, you can do a perspective transformation. Choose Image | Transform | Perspective, and then drag a corner handle horizontally simultaneously to move both corner handles in the direction of the drag. You can also change the point of view from top to bottom or side to side by dragging the center handles. You can get the idea from Figure 13-12.

If transformation doesn't reshape the item exactly as you'd like, you can then "tune by trimming." Use the Lasso tool to draw a marquee that reshapes only part of the object. For instance, if you'd made lips thicker, you could trim to bring the lips to a point at the ends where they'd been made unnaturally thick. They're on their own layer, so you could then erase the area you didn't want. Then you light with the Burn and Dodge tools (or with another layer in soft-light mode) to create any needed dimensional highlights and shadows. In the following illustration, you can see the result of using this method to thicken the model's lips. The image on the right is after thickening.

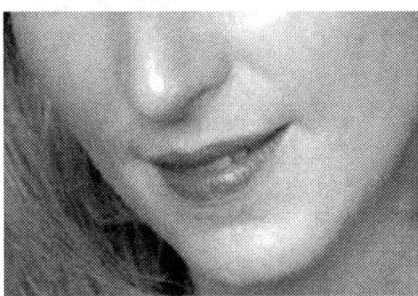 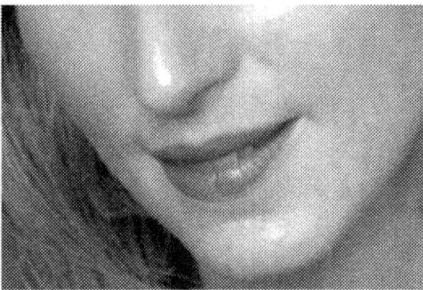

Putting It All Together

One retouching technique that is frequently used is compositing. Compositing is the business of combining objects that originated in a different photo (or that were duplicated from the current photo) with the base photo. For instance, putting a photo of your favorite puppy on the sidewalk leading up to your house might be just the touch that's needed for a photo for your house-warming invitation. Compositing can be a great way to add atmosphere or interest or to cover something that you'd rather not include. Chapter 17 is devoted to compositing.

The
Complete
Reference

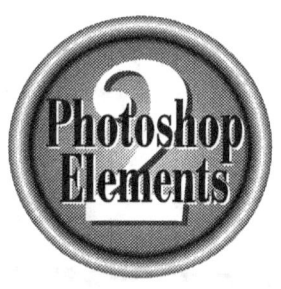

Part III

The Special Effects Workflow

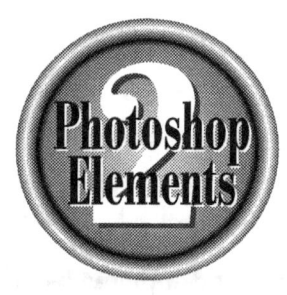

The
Complete
Reference

Photoshop
Elements
2

Chapter 14

Filter Effects

473

Filters, also known as plug-ins, are one of the cornerstones of special effects production in Photoshop Elements. Filters are routines that use mathematical algorithms to alter all or parts of an image in unique ways. These effects can be preset or they can be user controlled by changing the settings in dialog boxes that appear when you issue some of the filter commands.

Within the wide range of filters available in Elements, some are simple to access and apply with one click of the mouse—such as Blur, Despeckle, and Facet. Others— such as Liquify, 3D-Transform, and Lighting effects—are basically mini applications that make infinite variations possible.

This chapter details the fundamental characteristics of the filters included in Photoshop Elements. Chapter 15 discusses how you can integrate filter effects into a wider scheme of creating special effects.

Using Filters

Elements' built-in filters are distributed in submenus by category. If you have loaded plug-in filters, they will appear at the bottom of the Filter menu after you've placed them in the designated plug-ins folder and restarted the computer. The built-in filter categories are Artistic, Blur, Brushstroke, Distort, Noise, Pixelate, Render, Sharpen, Stretch, Stylize, Texture, Video, and Other. All the filters in each category have certain traits in common—for instance, all the Artistic filters produce some sort of painting or sketching simulation such as watercolor or pastel, and Distort filters all bend and warp the image into different shapes.

To apply any filter, choose Filter | *Filter Category* | *Filter Name,* or use the Filter palette from the Palette Well. (See Chapter 4 for more on the Filter palette.) When you choose filters from the Palette Well, a small thumbnail shows you what each effect does. If you are unfamiliar with the effects, the Filter palette helps by providing thumbnails that show a visual approximation of each filter effect. When using the Filter palette, applying a filter can be a simple drag-and-drop operation.

Figure 14-1 shows the basic anatomy of a filter dialog box—in this case, the Add Noise filter. Of course, the controls vary depending on the filter chosen. Some filter dialog boxes allow you to preview the effect in the preview window in real time as you adjust filter settings. You can click the plus or minus button to zoom in or out, respectively, on the preview. Adjust the filter's controls until you see the effect you want in the preview window. Click the OK button to initiate the filter effect, or click Cancel to exit without making any changes.

Before applying a filter to a layer, make the layer active in the Layers palette. To apply the filter, choose it from the Filter menu. Some filters will apply the effect immediately, whereas others require that you fill in fields in a dialog box first.

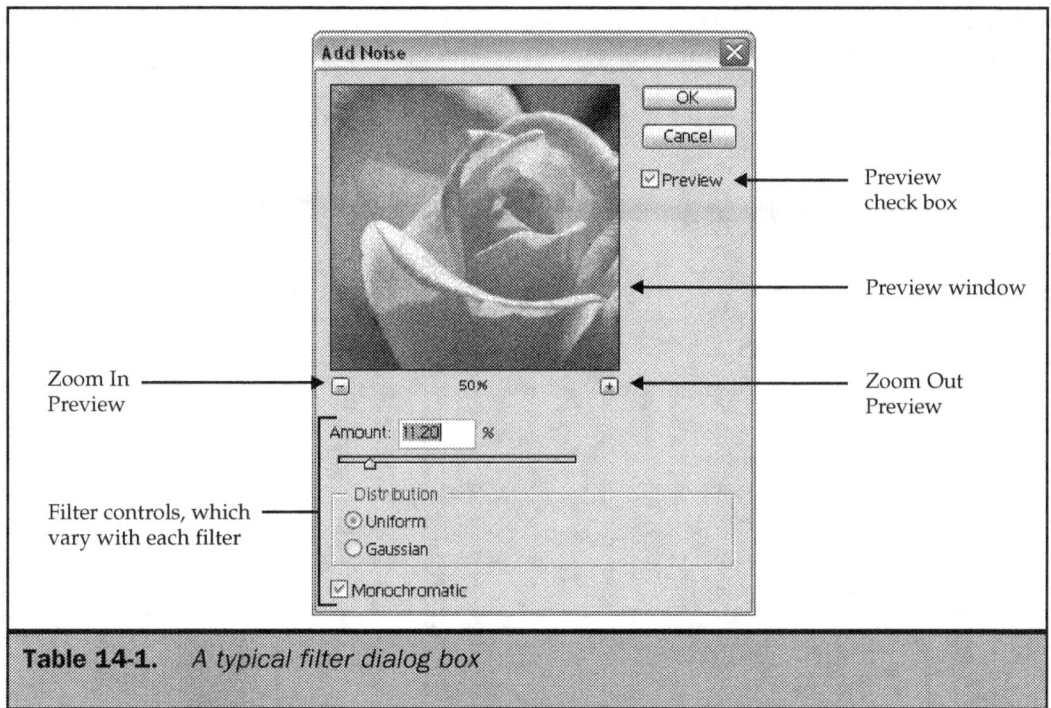

Zoom In Preview

Preview check box

Preview window

Zoom Out Preview

Filter controls, which vary with each filter

Table 14-1.   *A typical filter dialog box*

THE SPECIAL EFFECTS
WORKFLOW

To apply a filter to a selection, make sure the selection is active on the layer in which you want the change applied. After you have used a filter, its name will appear at the top of the Filter menu for easy reselection, or you can press CMD/CTRL+F to reselect the last filter you used. Some filters can be selected multiple times in succession to create additional effects. Plug-in filters may vary more in their function and operation, so make sure you follow the filter manufacturer's instructions.

Now let's discuss these filters in detail, by category.

Artistic Filters

Fifteen Artistic filters are designed to simulate some aspect of painting styles and techniques. A few filters, such as Neon Glow and Plastic Wrap, lean a bit more toward special effects, but, in general, you can classify these as painting effects. Artistic filters are useful for photo painting and for producing quick, stylized illustrations.

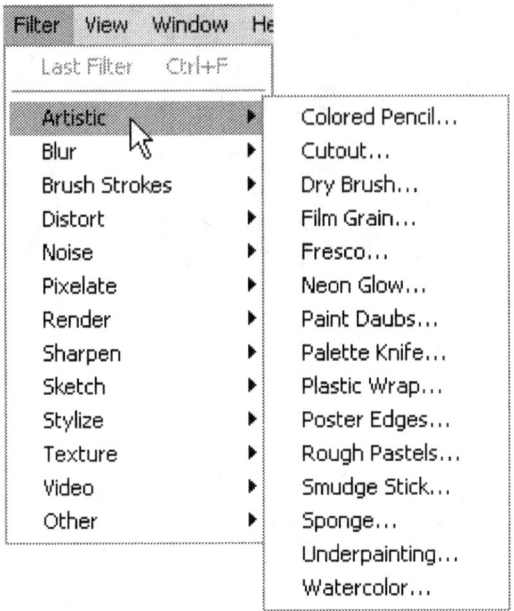

Colored Pencil

The Colored Pencil filter is designed to simulate drawing with colored pencils over a rough-textured, colored paper, such as charcoal or pastel paper. The Background color shows through in the smoother parts of the image and the highlights and edges are given a rough, crosshatched look using the colors of the image as reference.

In the Colored Pencil dialog box, shown next, you can vary the thickness of the crosshatched lines with the Pencil Width slider. The Stroke Pressure slider varies the intensity of crosshatching. The Paper Brightness slider varies the brightness of the background color. To get good results with this filter, make sure your background color has good balance and contrast in terms of color and value relative to the colors used in your image. The resolution of your original image can also have a big impact on the final look. The more detail and edge contrast in the image, the more realistic the outcome.

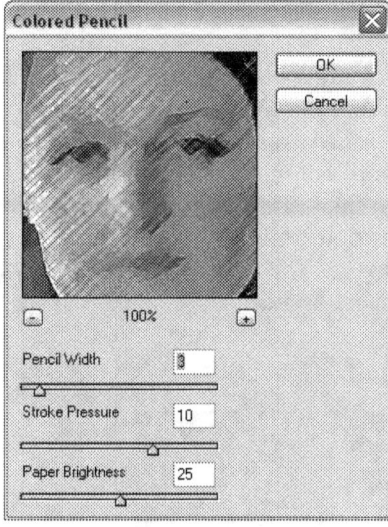

Cut Out

The Cut Out filter is designed to reproduce the look of tracing simplified shapes and then cutting them out in different shades of colored paper. The program simplifies the image and reduces the number of colors to one of eight levels. Each level adds more color variations. In the Cut Out dialog box, shown next, use the No. Of Levels slider to vary the number of colors. The Edge Simplicity slider reduces edge detail. The Edge Fidelity slider suppresses the edge smoothing effect of the Edge Simplicity and maintains edge detail in the shapes. When the Edge Fidelity slider is set high (to the right), the Edge Simplicity slider will drop shapes but not smooth edges to simplify the image. This filter is good for creating stylized illustrations, such as those often seen in posters.

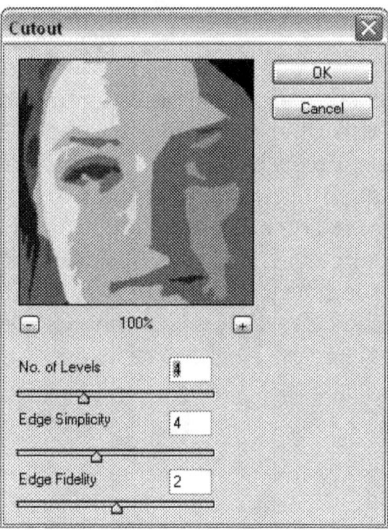

Dry Brush

The Dry Brush filter simulates the style of painting that uses a brush with paint and not much water or solvent (thus the name) to produce coarse-textured brush strokes. The filter simplifies the color, averages areas, and then creates a rough look with coarse edge detail and areas of smooth color. The effect works best if texture is added. In the Dry Brush dialog box, shown next, the Brush Size slider affects the size of the averaged areas. The Brush Detail slider determines how much of the original detail of the image is blended into the filtered image. The texture slider adds a simulated texture (such as canvas) to increase the dry brush look.

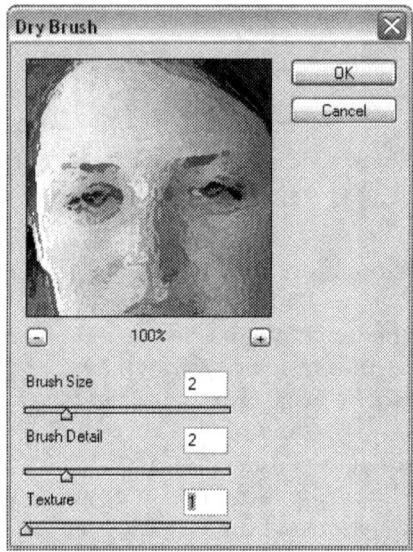

Film Grain

The Film Grain filter is designed to simulate or exaggerate the grain that is normally found in conventional film. This filter is commonly used to match image elements taken from different original sources. In the Film Grain dialog box, the Grain slider affects the density of the grain pattern. The Highlight Area slider affects the spread of the lighter areas of the image. The Intensity slider affects the contrast. If you have combined images with different levels of grain, or your images have color banding, applying this filter can be a good way to mitigate these visual problems. This filter is also used to make an image look like a blown-up photograph.

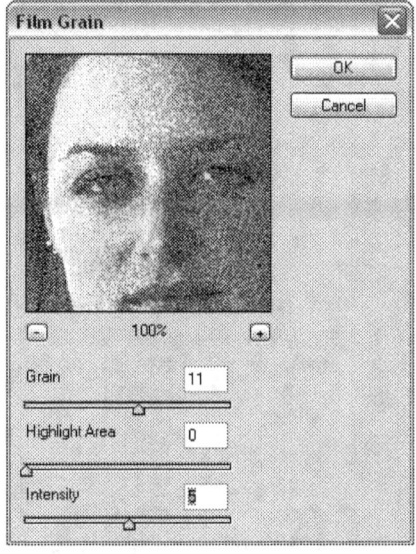

Fresco

The Fresco filter is designed to simulate fresco paintings, which are a type of painting created by embedding paint in wet plaster walls by daubing on color quickly (think Michelangelo). The filter produces a coarse, daubed look with a lot of contrast, similar to the Dry Brush filter. In the Fresco dialog box, the Brush Size slider affects the size of the averaged areas. The Brush Detail slider determines how much of the original detail of the image is blended into the filtered image. The Texture slider adds a simulated texture to increase the dry-brushed look.

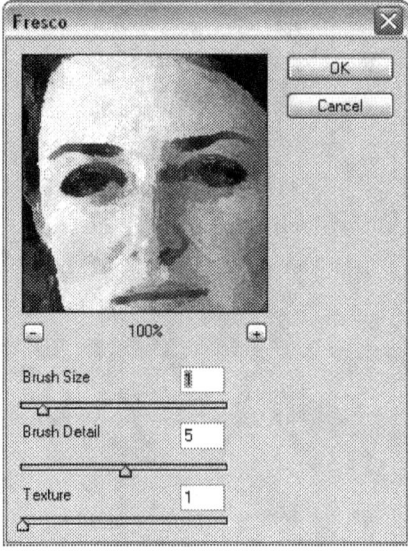

Neon Glow

Neon Glow is a unique filter that produces the effect of a light glow around highly contrasted edges, simulating the effect of neon lights. The glow is created by combining three colors—the foreground color, the background color, and a third color you choose from the dialog box. The glow is produced by a combination of the glow color and the background color. In the Neon Glow dialog box, adjust the Glow Brightness slider to vary the intensity of the glow effect. The foreground color will colorize the image. Adjust the Glow Size slider to change the area of effect for the glow. Click the Glow Color box to change the color of the glow. The Glow filter is commonly used for text effects. When you use it on more complex images, they must be images that are on transparent backgrounds because the glow emanates from the edges of the shape. When applied to images rather than text, the effects are less predictable but still interesting.

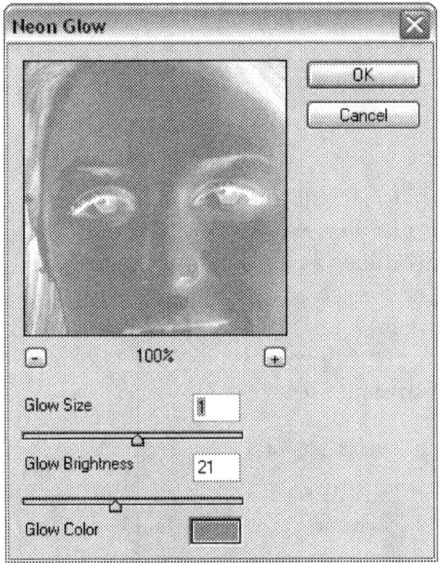

Paint Daubs

The Paint Daubs filter simulates placing daubs of paint from varying brush sizes and style to create an impressionistic effect. The filter offers a wide array of brush types including Simple, Light Rough, Dark Rough, Wide Sharp, Wide Blurry, and Sparkle, as shown in the Paint Daubs dialog box in the following illustration. The Brush Size slider determines the size of the daubs. The Sharpness slider sets the amount of edge contrast. This filter gives you a lot of variation in the range of effects.

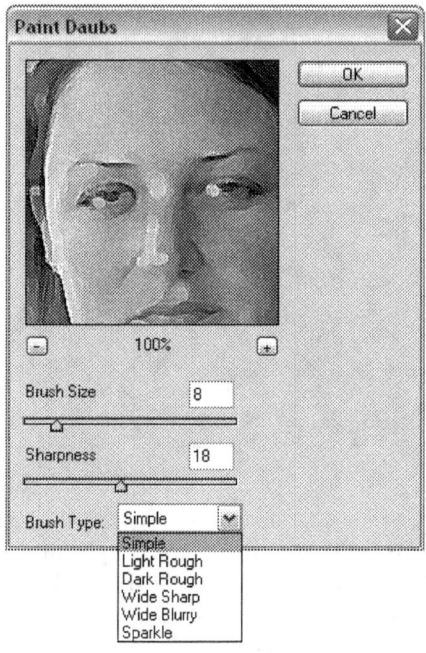

Palette Knife

The Palette Knife filter is designed to simulate the effect of spreading paint with a palette knife in wide strokes across a canvas and letting the texture show. This effect doesn't quite live up to its name, but it's still a nice effect if you want to create a rough, blocked-in look. In the Palette Knife dialog box, the Stroke Size slider determines the size of the averaged areas, which are basically large daubs. The Stroke Detail slider determines how much of the detail from the original image will be blended in. The Softness slider lets you smooth the edges of the Strokes.

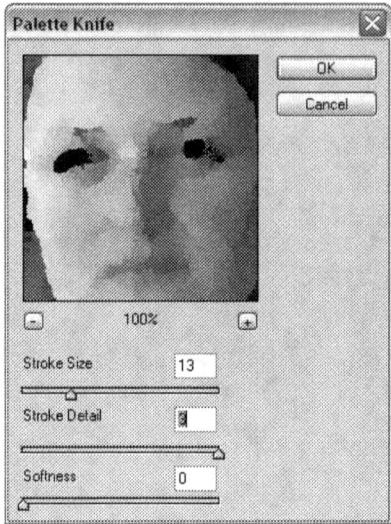

Plastic Wrap

The Plastic Wrap filter is a favorite. It simulates the appearance of wrapping the image in clear plastic—think of the image as being vacuum-packed. In the Plastic Wrap dialog box, the Highlight Strength slider determines how much of the lighter parts of the image will read as highlights on the plastic. The Detail slider lets you increase the modeling in the effect. The Smoothness slider lets you soften the whole effect so the simulated wrinkles have a smoother transition.

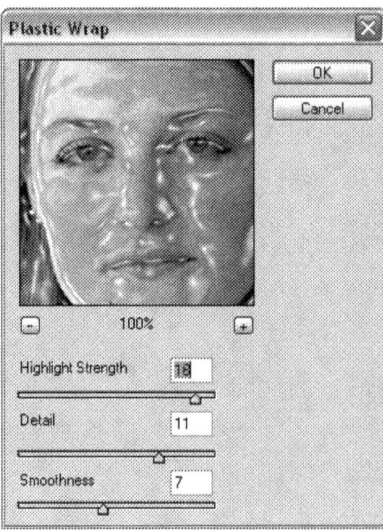

Poster Edges

The Poster Edges filter is another popular filter. The filter "posterizes" (reduces the number of colors) in the image. It then finds the high-contrast edges and paints the edges with thick, black lines. The color becomes solid, rather than shaded, while the black lines accentuate the detail. In the Poster Edges dialog box, the Edge Thickness slider determines how thick the outlines will be. The Edge Intensity slider determines the level of contrast at which an edge will be drawn. The Posterization slider lets you set the amount of color reduction.

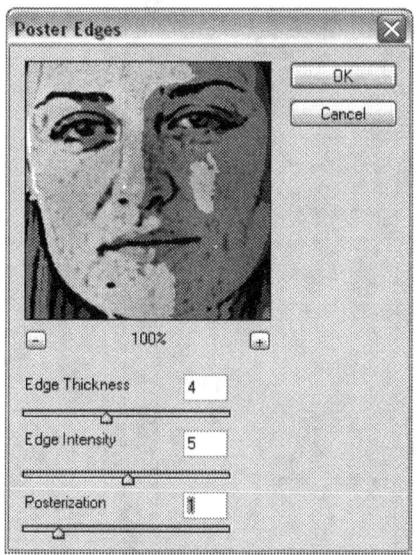

Rough Pastels

The Rough Pastels filter simulates the look of soft pastels or chalk on a textured surface. The texture is more pronounced in the darker areas of the image. The strokes are rendered on the diagonal, from upper right to lower left. In the Rough Pastels dialog box, the Stroke Length slider determines whether the strokes are short, rapid strokes or long, drawn-out strokes. The Stroke Detail slider sets the amount of edge and highlight detail that is detected. The Texture slider is the same slider found in the Texturizer filter. (See the section "Texturizer" under "Texture Filters," later in this chapter, and also Chapter 15 for more on using textures.)

Choose a texture from the drop-down menu, and then set the scale of the texture with the Scaling slider. The Relief slider determines the intensity or depth of the texture. You can change the light source direction on the texture from the Light Direction menu. Check the Invert box to invert the texture pattern. This filter works fairly well at simulating pastels, but it looks a bit mechanical. Try experimenting with different textures to achieve a more realistic look.

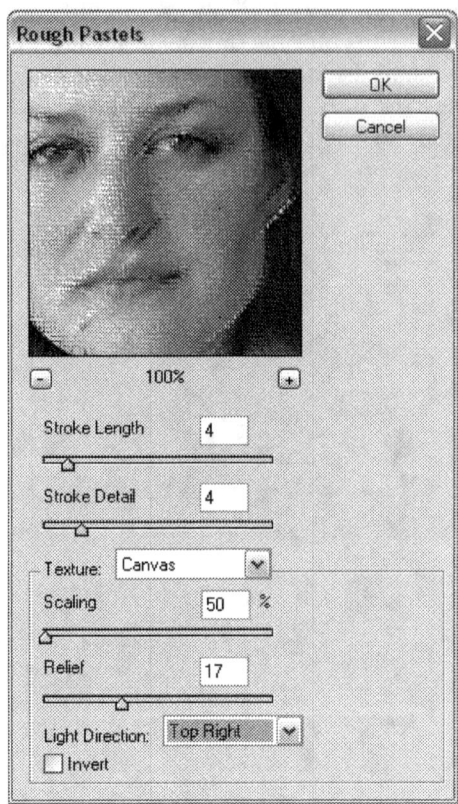

Smudge Stick

The Smudge Stick filter alters an image to have a soft, loosely drawn appearance, where the darker areas are smeared with diagonal strokes. This filter would be equivalent to using your fingers or a smudge stick to smear paint or chalk on a drawing. The highlight areas are dodged. In the Smudge Stick dialog box, the Stroke Length slider determines the amount of smearing. The Highlight Area slider spreads the area of highlight. The Intensity slider brightens the highlight area. This is a nice effect, similar to Rough Pastels. It is useful when you want a softer, more ethereal look. You can also use this filter when you want to create a rainy weather effect.

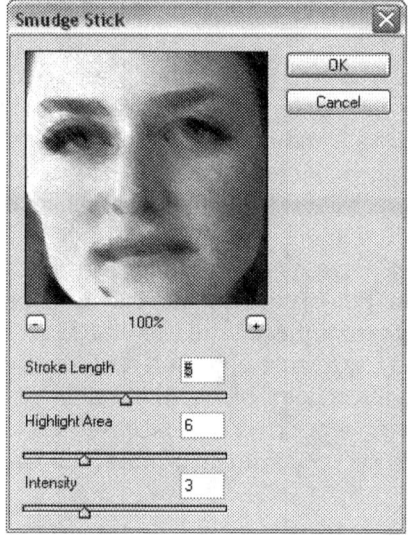

Sponge

This filter can create a rough, aged, or beat-up look. It's also good for adding texture. The Sponge filter attempts to simulate the look you would get if you used a sponge to daub on paint. Unfortunately, it falls far short of that effect. Instead, it produces a mottled look. In the dialog box, use the Brush Size slider to set the size of the mottled areas. The Definition slider determines the level of area contrast. The Smooth slider softens the edges of the mottled areas.

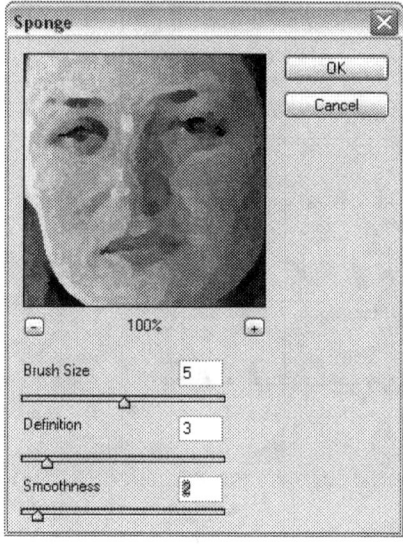

Underpainting

Traditionally, underpaintings were used as a painting surface that blocked in general shapes and tonal ranges to act as a base for the finished painting. The Underpainting filter works in reverse. It takes an image and blurs it to simplify the shapes, and it roughs the edges of a textured ground to give the image the appearance of a preliminary paint sketch. In the dialog box, the Brush Size slider determines the level of detail that is rendered. The Texture Coverage slider sets how much of the shadow areas will be textured. Choose a texture from the Texture drop-down menu, and then set the scale of the texture with the Scaling slider. The Relief slider determines the intensity or depth of the texture. You can change the light source direction for the texture from the Light Direction drop-down menu. Check the Invert box to invert the texture pattern. This filter is useful for creating paint sketches from composite images. It helps blend all the elements together, and then abstracts the shapes and edges so you can work over it more easily. It's also useful for creating a washed effect, which can be combined with an outline of the image (which can be made with the Find Edges filter).

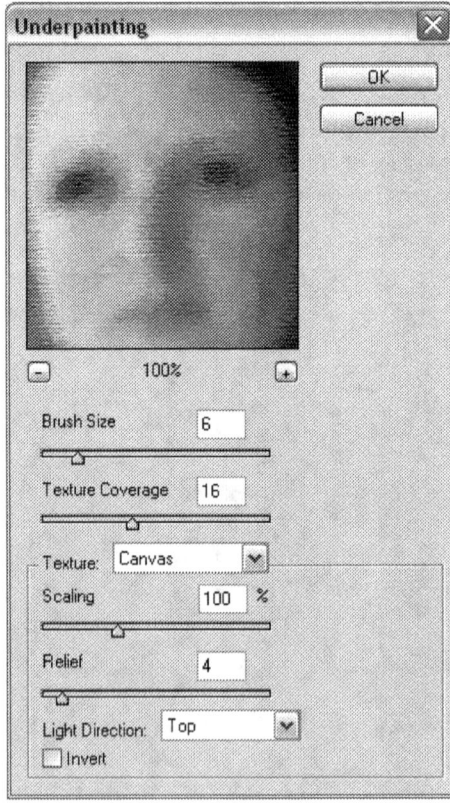

Watercolor

Graphics software companies have been trying for years to come up with a filter that will believably simulate watercolor. The problem has been that watercolors use complicated physics to achieve the watercolor look, which has a lot to do with weight and solubility of pigments, the viscosity of water, and the texture and absorption of paper. All that said, this Watercolor filter doesn't come close to fitting the bill. The filter simplifies details and creates areas of color based on details in the original image. The colors are more saturated at the high-contrast edges in an attempt to simulate the pooling of pigment at the edges of a wet area. In the Watercolor dialog box, the Brush Detail slider determines how much of the detail is maintained from the original image. More detail means smaller brush strokes. The Shadow Intensity slider darkens the shadow areas of the image. The Texture slider creates more contrast at the borders of the brush strokes. The type of watercolor this simulates is the type you would create by making individual strokes with a brush. It offers no blends or washes. If a simple brush-stroked look is what you're after, this filter will be fine, but don't expect a genuine simulation of a watercolor painting.

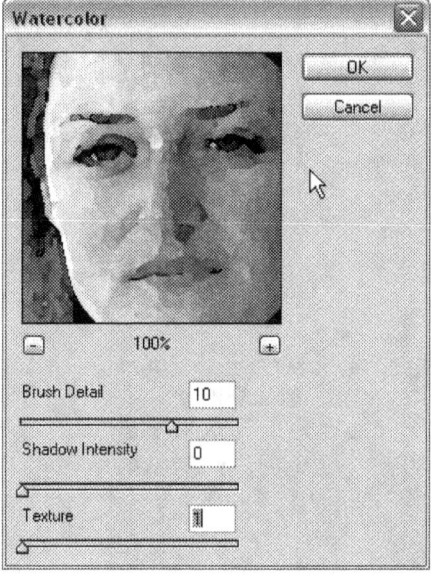

Blur Filters

The six Blur filters shown in the following illustration are all designed to soften all or parts of an image. Blurring is used to soften the look of an image, blend textural elements, drop out backgrounds or foregrounds, produce special effects, and simulate motion. Almost all softening in digital images is accomplished by a system of averaging the pixels of high contrast to smear the edges and produce a softening effect. An example would be an edge with pure black on one side and pure white on the other—this is the sharpest edge you can achieve. When an edge is blurred, it is "spread out" so it becomes a series of gray pixels that transition from black to white, reducing the sharpness of the edge. Some Blur filters allow you to control the range of contrast that gets blurred so you can maintain the most important sharp edges while blending everything else.

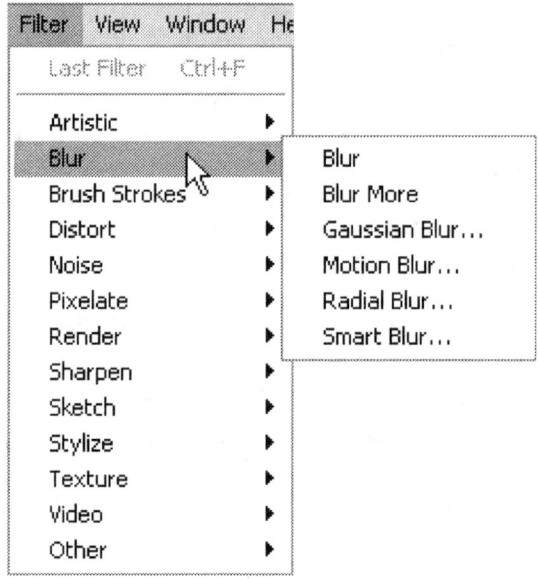

Blur and Blur More

The Blur and Blur More filters perform simple pixel averaging on high-contrast edges and individual pixels. Blur uses the adjacent pixel for averaging. Blur More looks out three or four pixels and averages over a broader range to produce a more powerful effect. Both filters can be applied repeatedly to increase the effect. The most common use for these filters is to soften texture or noise in the image.

Gaussian Blur

The Gaussian Blur filter is a more versatile blurring tool than Blur or Blur More. It allows you to control the level of blurring over a wide range. In the dialog box, set the Radius slider to determine the spread of the averaged pixels. Gaussian blur weights the averaging to produce a more even transition on all edges. (See Chapter 15 for more on using blur filters for applying special effects.)

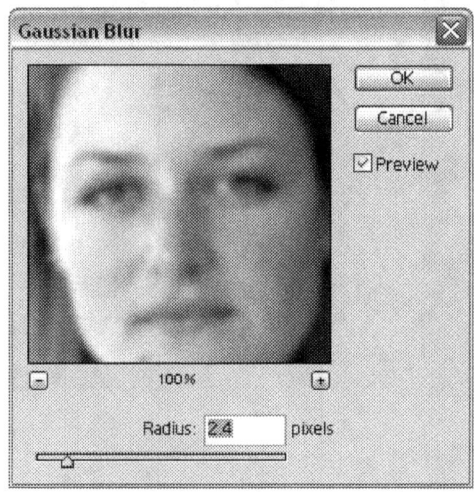

Motion Blur

The Motion Blur filter is designed to simulate the effect of perceptual blurring of objects when moving at a high rate of speed. This blurring becomes more evident in freeze-frame photography. The filter can control the direction of the blur through a 360-degree range. To adjust the angle of force in the Motion Blur dialog box, click and drag on the directional line on the Angle dial until you get to the angle you want or until the preview looks the way you want. You can alternatively enter an angle between –360 and 360 degrees. Set the Distance (1–999) in pixels to determine how far the image is blurred in the direction you have indicated. The Motion Blur filter can add a kinetic dynamic to an image by triggering your perceptual reaction to fast-moving objects. It can also be used to create rain or wind effects, blur backgrounds, or create

THE SPECIAL EFFECTS WORKFLOW

special effects such as the burst of exhaust from a rocket engine. See Chapter 15 for more on using Motion Blur as a special effect.

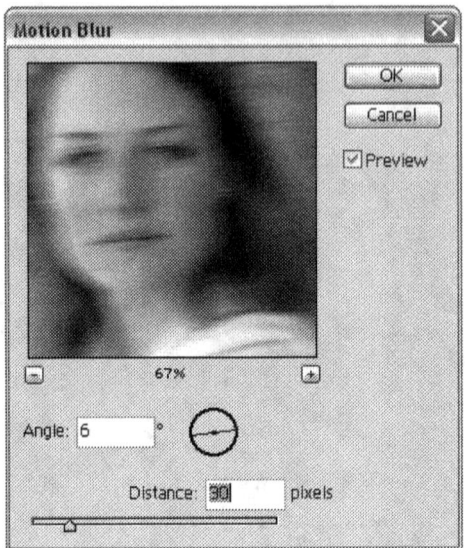

Radial Blur

The Radial Blur filter is designed to simulate the blur created when you spin the camera or rapidly zoom in or out while the camera shutter is open. In the dialog box, you can drag the center of the blur in the preview window to the approximate location of the center of the image. Unfortunately, this preview isn't superimposed on the image itself, so you must place the center by trial and error. In the Blur Method area, choosing the Spin radio button will allow you to set the Amount (1–100) of rotation around preset concentric circles indicated in the preview window. The Spin setting can be used on anything that spins, such as a propeller, turbine, or wheel. The Zoom setting can be used effectively to achieve a dreamlike quality to portrait shots, to create bursts of light, or to enhance an explosion effect. Choosing Zoom will blur the image along radial lines indicated in the preview window. You can set the Amount (1–100) the image blurs. You can set the output Quality by choosing Draft, which renders quickly but produces a grainy look, or by choosing Good or Best, which renders more slowly and blends better. To change the blur point origin, click the preview window and drag the target pattern to a new location. The Radial Blur filter is used mostly as a special effect.

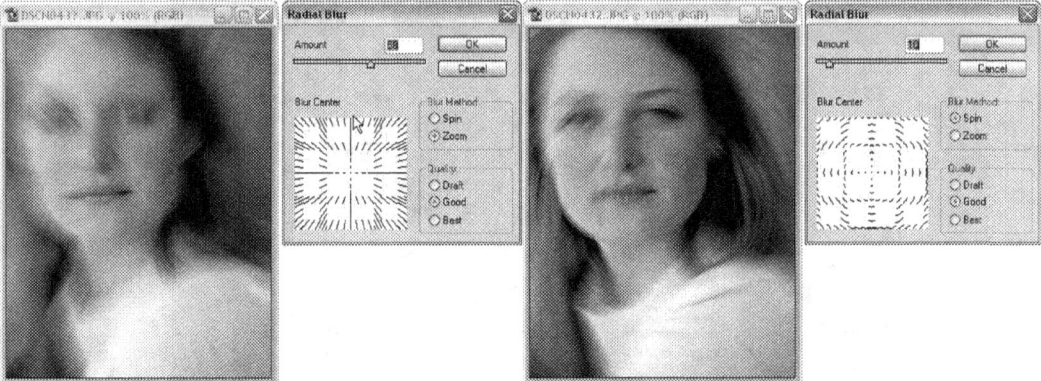

Smart Blur

The Smart Blur filter is by far the most versatile blur filter in this set. It provides a number of controls that provide a wide range of results. The Smart Blur filter lets you blur selected areas of the image while preserving sharp edges where necessary. In the dialog box, the Radius slider sets the distance the filter will search to find pixels with differing values. The Threshold slider determines how different the values must be before they are blurred. The lower the Threshold value, the more edges it will find and the less blurring will occur. You can set the filter Quality to Low, Medium, or High. The Mode menu allows you to change the way the filter works. Normal uses the entire image to designate areas of blur and edge detail. Edge Only mode renders the edges only in white over black. Overlay renders the edges of the original image in white.

Use the Smart Blur filter when you want to smooth out areas in which only minor variations in value occur, but you want to preserve the sharp detail with higher contrast edges. This is an easy way to smooth the complexion of skin without losing

THE SPECIAL EFFECTS WORKFLOW

the details in the face, for instance, or to blend the color in an object while maintaining a sharp highlight.

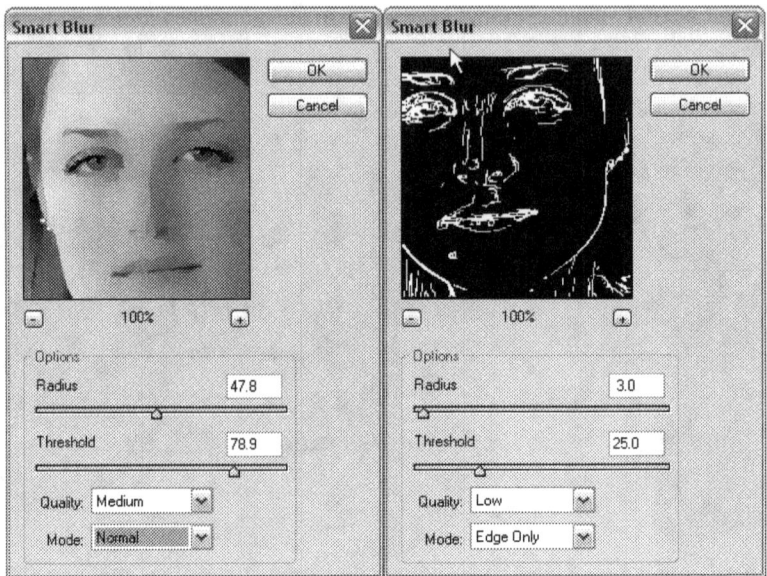

Brush Strokes Filters

You could call the Brush Strokes filters an extension of the Artistic filters. This set of eight filters creates more simulations of painting and drawing styles.

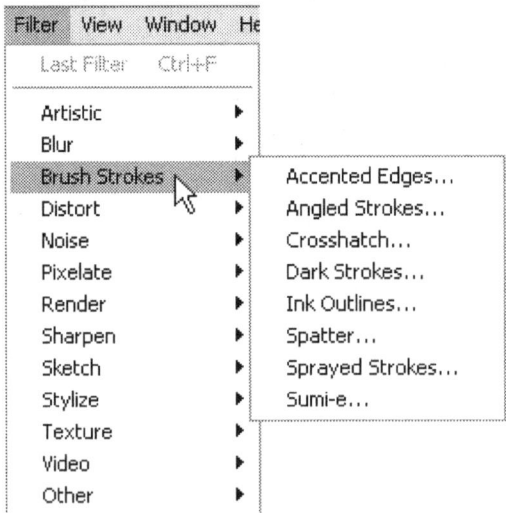

Accented Edges

The Accented Edges filter is designed to accentuate the edges in an image by either brightening or darkening the edges. The brightening effect gives the appearance of light-colored pencil or chalk, and the darkening looks like ink, dark pencil, or charcoal. In the dialog box, the Edge Width slider varies the width of the edge effect. The Edge Brightness slider makes the edges brighter or darker. The Smoothness slider blends the edge transitions to give a softer look. This is a good filter to use if you need to increase the visibility of edges in the image. With the Brightness and Width sliders set to higher values, you can get a glow effect.

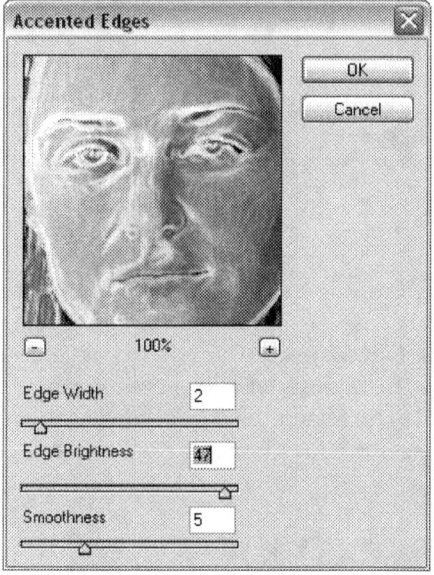

Angled Strokes

The Angled Strokes filter is designed to simulate a drawing style with parallel diagonal lines and smeared details. The diagonal lines can be set to have opposite directions based on the luminance value of the colors in the image. In the dialog box, the Direction Balance slider determines which values get which direction stroke on a scale of 1 to 100. If you slide the Direction Balance above 50, more dark areas will be stroked the same direction as the light areas. A value of 100 makes every stroke run the same direction. A value of 0 will cause strokes in the image to run in the opposite direction. Values in between will provide varying degrees of mixed-direction strokes. The Stroke Length slider determines the length of the stroked lines and the amount of edge smearing. The Sharpness slider affects the contrast in the stroke detail. This filter provides a quick-sketch look.

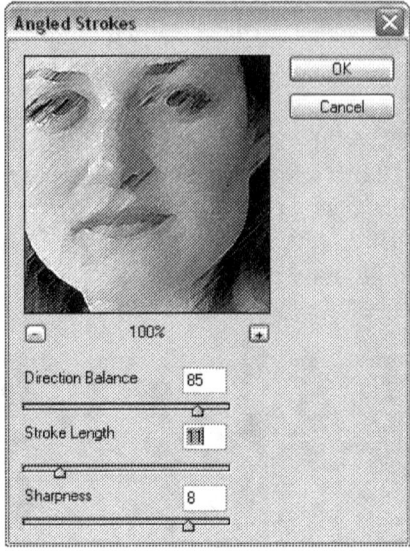

Crosshatch

The Crosshatch filter is similar to the Angled Stroke filter. The Crosshatch filter uses criss-crossing lines instead of just diagonal lines running in a single direction. This produces a more evenly sketched look and tends to suppress more edge detail. In the dialog box, the Stroke Length slider determines the length of the stroked lines and the smearing of the edge detail. The Sharpness slider affects the contrast in the stroke detail. The Strength slider sets the number of stroke passes (from 1 to 3) to affect the stroke detail.

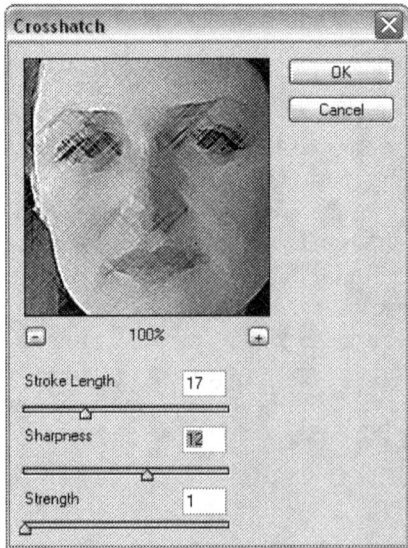

Dark Strokes

The Dark Strokes filter is designed to make the image look like a sketch made with short, quick strokes, with a lot of contrast between darks and lights. Dark Strokes works similar to Angle Strokes, except that the strokes are darker and have somewhat harder edges. Because the effects of the Dark Strokes and Angled Strokes filters are so closely related, and because both have variable controls, there may even be some overlap in their effect.

In the dialog box, the Balance slider determines which values get which direction stroke on a scale of 1 to 10. If you move the Balance slider to a value above 5, more dark areas will be stroked the same direction as light areas. If you push the slider all the way to 10, every stroke goes the same way. A value of 0 will cause the strokes in the entire image to appear in the opposite direction. Values in between will give varying degrees of mixed strokes. The Black and White Intensity controls determine the brightness in the dark and light areas of the image. Use this filter when you want a more contrasted sketched appearance.

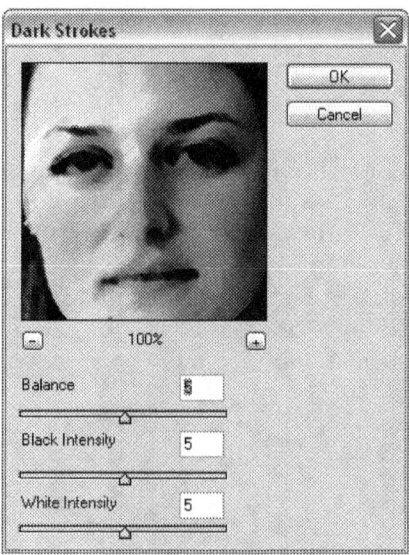

Ink Outlines

The Ink Outlines filter is supposed to simulate the look of an inked drawing with color washes. It does a moderate to poor job of accomplishing that. It does produce some interesting effects, though. This filter uses the diagonal stroke system technique, as do many of the filters in this category. In the Ink Outlines dialog box, the Stroke Length slider controls the length of the stroke. Shorter strokes tend to produce more accurate results. The Dark Intensity slider increases the stroke intensity in the dark areas of the image. The Light Intensity slider increases the lighter areas of the image. The effect of this filter depends on the detail and contrast present in the original image. It works better on images in which the detail is clearly delineated and the patterns and textures are not too complex.

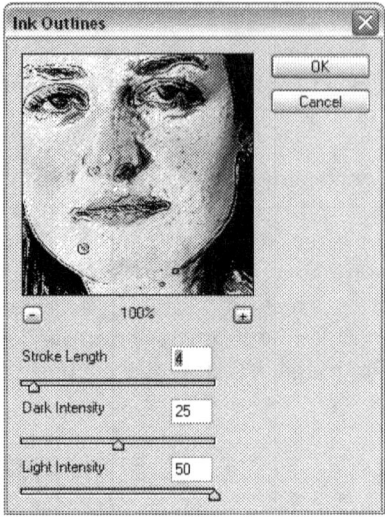

Spatter

The Spatter filter is designed to simulate the effect of a spatter airbrush. It does a fairly decent job. In the Spatter dialog box, the Spray Radius slider determines the amount of diffusion in the strokes. The Smoothness slider controls the amount that the spatter strokes are blended together to form lager areas of a spatter. In addition, a higher Smoothness setting gives you better sponge effects than the Sponge filter provides. This filter can be used to add noise or grain to an image, and it can be used to create a blotchy image that appears as though the paint was daubed on.

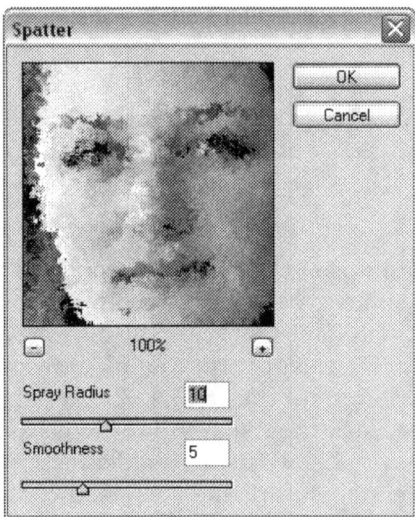

Sprayed Strokes

The Sprayed Strokes filter produces an angled stroke effect that smudges the edge detail with an oscillating stroking pattern. In the dialog box, the Stroke Length slider determines the stroke size and the Spray Radius slider determines the area of effect. You can choose one of four directions from the Stroke Direction drop-down menu: Left Diagonal, Right Diagonal, Vertical, and Horizontal. This filter produces a painterly look with a good deal of variation. It can be used as a decent pastel filter with the addition of texture.

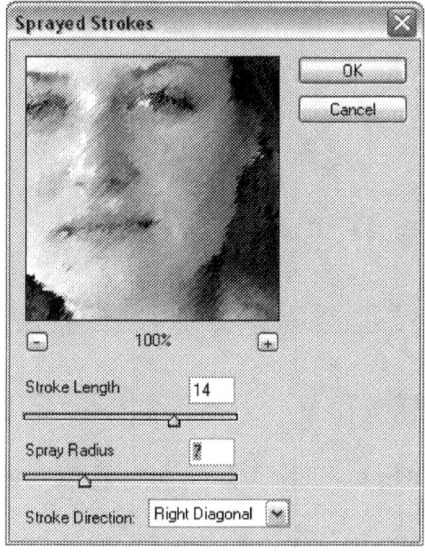

Sumi-e

The Sumi-e filter attempts to simulate Japanese brush painting on paper. It doesn't do a convincing job, however. The filter smoothes out color and places soft, dark lines at the higher contrast edges. In the Sumi-e dialog box, the Stroke Width slider sets the thickness of the edges lines. The Stroke Pressure slider determines the amount of detail found in the edges. The Contrast slider affects the contrast between light and darks in the image.

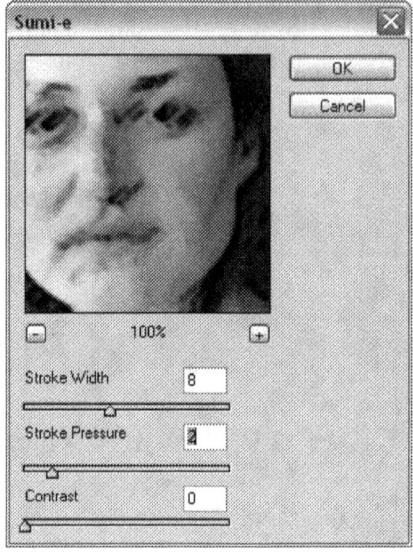

Distort Filters

The Distort filters are designed to alter the geometry of the image through mathematical manipulation. This is a somewhat misleading definition because all filters distort the image's geometry in some way. These filters are set apart because they are not trying to simulate any real-world painting or drawing styles. They are purely distortion filters that will allow you to bend, warp, stretch, and reshape images in a variety of ways. The effects can be dramatic. Many of the Distort filters use a fair amount of memory and can take a few minutes to render on larger images because they calculate a large amount of mathematical manipulations. The Diffuse Glow, Liquify, Pinch, and Spherize filters all have important roles to play in retouching and special effects, which are discussed in greater detail in Chapter 15.

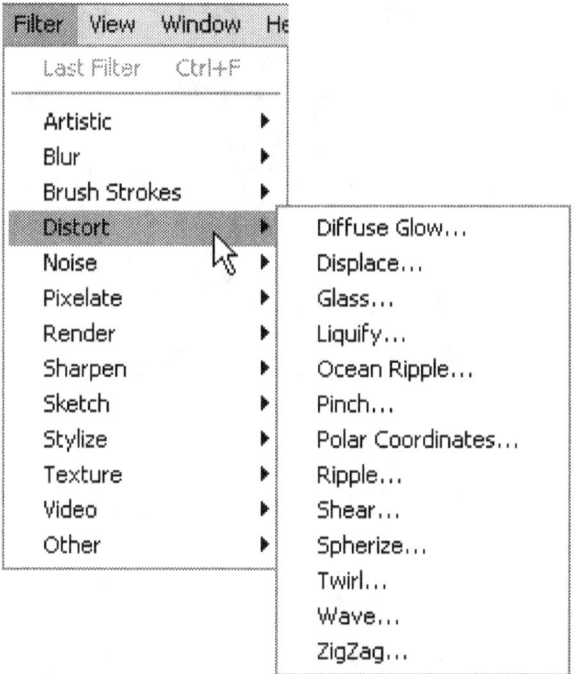

Diffuse Glow

The Diffuse Glow filter produces a halo effect around lighter areas of the image. You can also fade the original image to produce a more ghostly effect. In the Diffuse Glow dialog box, the Graininess slider adds grain to produce a more textured look. The Glow Amount slider determines the extent of the glow effect. The Clear Amount slider fades the image behind the hazy glow. This filter produces an ethereal effect that's often used in glamour portraits. If you want to accentuate the glow of light in a scene or add a hazy look to a summer day, this filter can be a good choice. See Chapter 15 for more on using this filter for special effects.

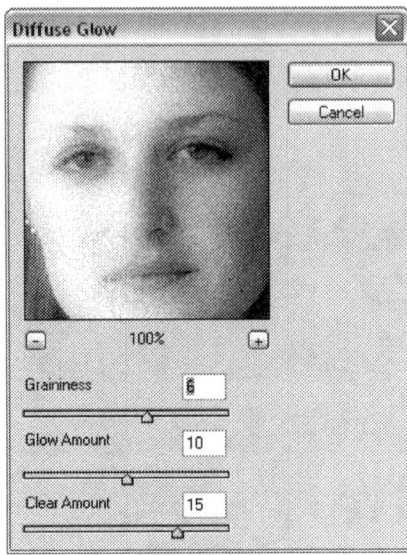

Displace

The Displace filter is a complex filter that works in a unique fashion. This filter uses the brightness values in a displacement map as a reference to shift pixels in another image. A displacement map can be any standard PSD format image saved with no layers.

To use this filter to its best advantage, you need to understand how it works. The filter uses the brightness values in the displacement map to offset the pixels in the original image. (The brightness values in any image are measured from 0 to 255, where black is 0 and white is 255.) The offset is increased as the values move away from the midpoint, which is 128 (middle gray). This means a value of 128 in the displacement map will produce no offset in the original image, and the value 255 will produce the maximum offset, which is 128 pixels from the original pixel position. Darker values below 128 cause the image's pixels to move down and to the right, and lighter values above 128 cause the pixels to move up and to the left.

In the dialog box, the Horizontal and Vertical Scale fields add another degree of control on the amount of displacement the map dictates. You can set the offset in the horizontal and vertical directions as a percentage of the amount set by the displacement map. This will reduce all offsets by that percentage. Enter a value of 0 to have no offset in that direction, or enter 100 to render the maximum offset set by the displacement map. In the following illustration, you can see an example of a displacement map (left), the displaced image (middle), and the Displace dialog box (right). Notice how the image is offset as it corresponds to each shade of gray in the displacement map.

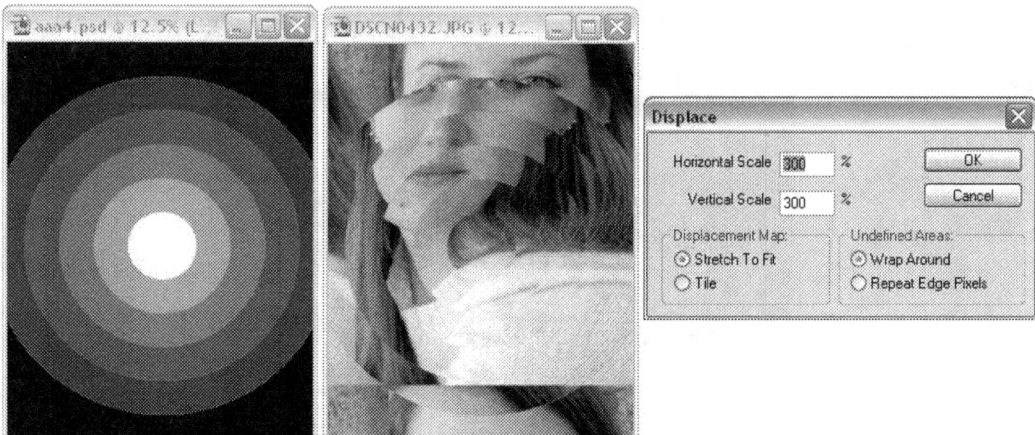

If the displacement map is not the same size as the image you are manipulating, choose the Stretch To Fit option in the Displacement Map area. This will expand or contract the displacement map to fit the dimensions of the original image. If you choose Tile, the displacement map image will be repeated in a tile pattern to fit the image area. As the image distorts, parts of the image will be pulled away from the edges. The Undefined Areas parameters will tell the program how to fill those areas. If you choose Wrap Around, pixels that have been pushed over the opposite edge into the gap will be pulled. If you choose Repeat Edge Pixels, the pattern of pixels that were at the edges in the original image will continue to fill in the edges.

Note   *The Displace filter is complex and its results are difficult to predict when it's used with complex displacement maps. Try using gradients and simple geometric shapes to get warping and shattered effects. Displacement map images with scattered pixel values will produce rather chaotic results.*

Glass

The Glass filter convincingly simulates viewing of an image through different types of textured glass. You can use the preset texture maps found in the Texture drop-down menu of the Glass dialog box, or you can load your own maps by choosing Load Texture from the same menu. The filter uses the values in the texture map to simulate high and low undulations in the glass, which warps the image in much the same way as real glass would.

The Distortion slider sets the amount of depth and warp. The Smoothness slider reduces the contrast in the texture map and makes the transitions more gradual. The

Scaling slider enlarges or reduces the texture map by a percentage. Check the Invert box if you want the lights and darks in the pattern inverted. This filter can be used to cause the effect of peering through translucent glass, such as stained glass, to view an image, and you can even get some interesting water effects. The Glass filter is also good for simulating ice or viscous substances such as honey. You can also create striking backgrounds. The ability to add your own textures adds a whole new dimension to this filter.

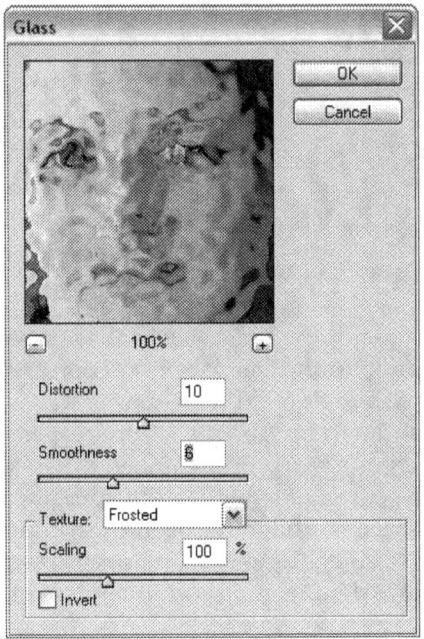

Liquify

The Liquify filter is one of the filters that qualify as a mini application. It has a unique interface and an extensive set of interactive tools, which provide a wide array of ways to distort your image. The image will appear in the center preview window of the Liquify dialog box. The controls for the brush are at the right of the preview window and the Liquify tools are on the left. For a complete description of the Liquify filter and how you can use it for special effects, see Chapter 15.

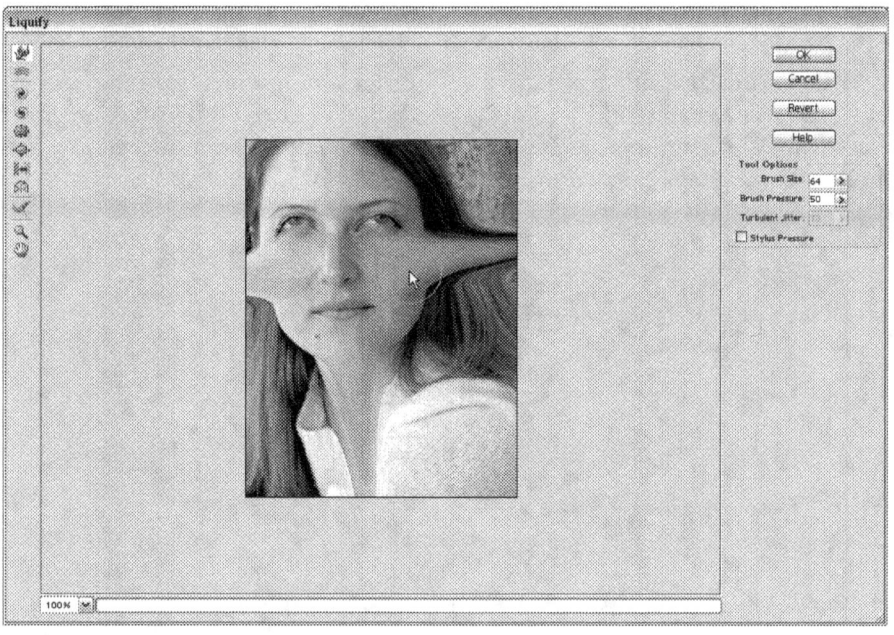

Ocean Ripple

The Ocean Ripple filter is similar to the Glass filter, but it's not quite as versatile as the Glass filter. It is designed to simulate an image reflecting in a ripple on a liquid surface or under water. In the dialog box, the Ripple Size slider determines the distance between highs and lows in the ripples. The Ripple Magnitude slider determines the simulated depth of the ripples.

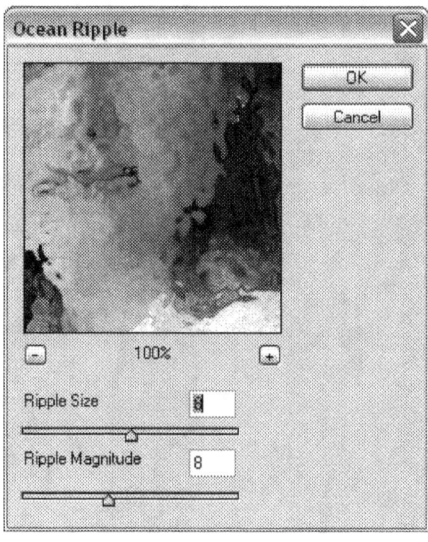

Pinch

The Pinch filter squeezes the image inward or bulges it outward from the center. In the dialog box, use the Amount slider to move the bulge in or out. Positive percentages move it outward and negative percentages move it inward. For more on how the Pinch filter can help correct lens distortion, see Chapter 11.

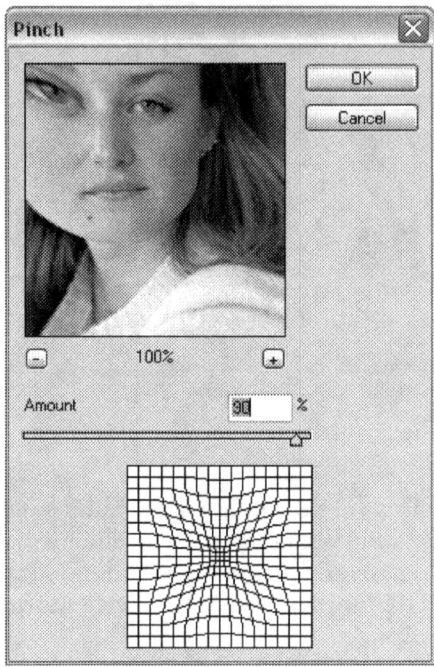

Polar Coordinates

The Polar Coordinates filter is used to convert an image from rectangular (Cartesian) coordinates to polar coordinates and from polar coordinates back to rectangular. Polar-to-rectangular conversion is much more useful, in general. It has the effect of wrapping the picture elements around a sphere. You can use these filters in conjunction with geometric shapes and patterns to create interesting results.

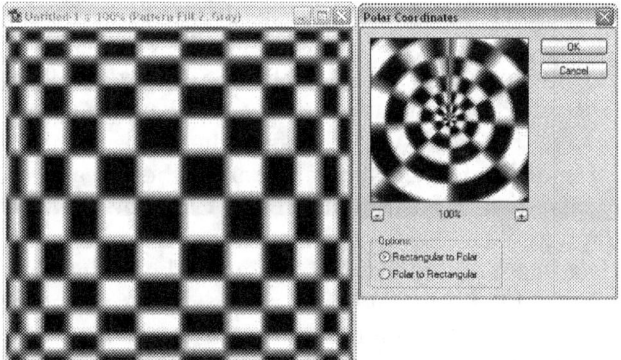

Ripple

The Ripple filter is similar to the Ocean Ripple filter, except the ripples are much more uniform. In the dialog box, adjust the Amount slider to set the amplitude of the ripples. You can choose between Small, Medium, and Large ripples from the Size drop-down menu.

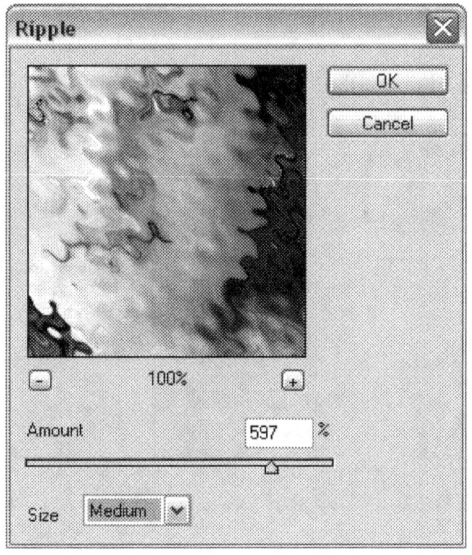

THE SPECIAL EFFECTS WORKFLOW

Shear

The Shear filter bends the image along a straight line or curve as indicated in an interactive graph. The line represents the center vertical axis in the picture. When you apply a slope or curve to the axis, it will rearrange the pixels in the image according to the new centerline coordinates. Click on any part of the line and then drag the control handle that appears to reposition the curve. Click the Defaults button to reset the values in the graph to normal. Select Wrap Around if you want the image to be continuous, and select Repeat Edge Pixels if you want the undefined areas to be filled with a repeating pattern of the original line of pixels at the edge of the image. If you choose the Repeating Edge Pixels option, parts of the image may be truncated as the image warps. This filter can be used to straighten lines that are curved, or curve lines that are too straight. You can use it to create the effect of trees bending in the wind, for example.

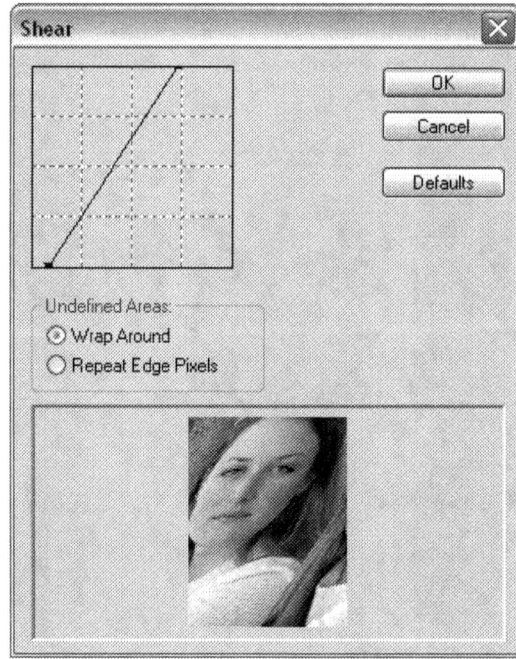

Spherize

The Spherize filter uses a 3-D effect to make the image look as though it is being viewed through a convex or concave circular lens. It will also simulate looking through a horizontal or vertical convex or concave rectangular-shaped lens. In the dialog box, adjust the Amount slider to make the image more convex or concave. This filter can be used to adjust or simulate lens distortion. See Chapter 11 for more on correcting lens distortion.

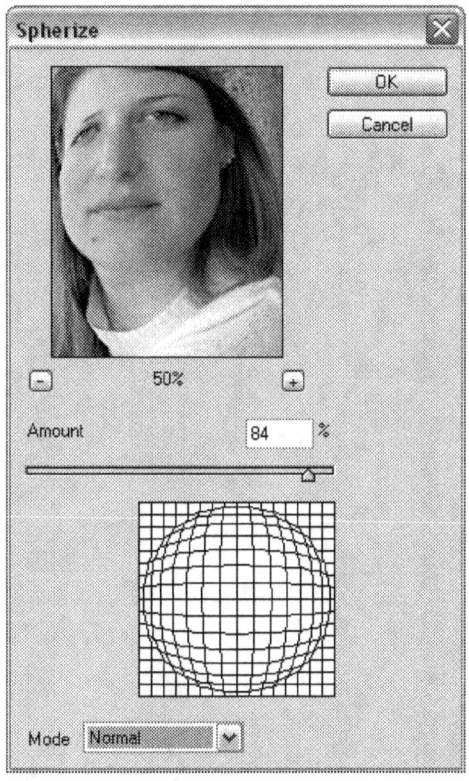

Twirl

The Twirl filter produces a twisted rotational effect by rotating the pixels more toward the center of the image. In the dialog box, moving the Angle slider to the right of center rotates the image clockwise and moving it to the left rotates counterclockwise. This filter can be used to produce a whirlpool or rotating galaxy effect.

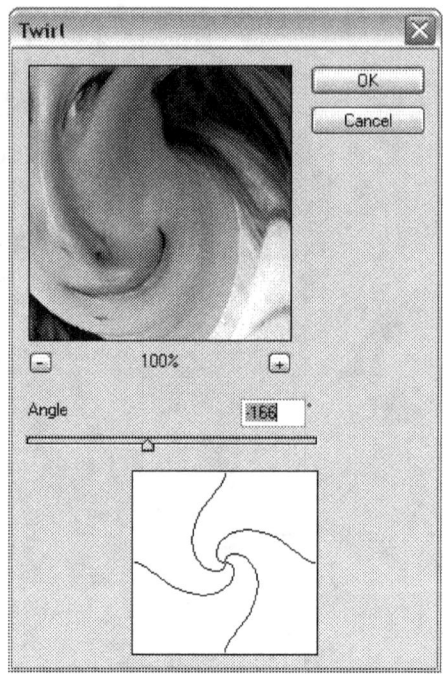

Wave

The Wave filter offers a great deal of control over how you generate undulating distortions that simulate waves in the image. This filter is basically a more complex version of the Ripple filter. In the Wave dialog box, the Number Of Generators slider sets the number of waves that will be created in the image. The higher the number, the more complex the wave pattern becomes. The Wavelength slider (1–999) lets you set the distance between crests and valleys of the waves. The Amplitude slider (1–999) lets you set the rise and fall of the waves. The Scale slider (1–100%) enlarges the horizontal or vertical effect of the wave distortion. In the Type area, you can choose among three types of waves: the Sine wave produces a smooth rounded wave, the Triangle wave produces a jagged sharp wave, and the Square wave produces a banded effect. Click the Randomize button to generate random values for the Wave filter. Choose Wrap Around or Repeat Edge Pixels to fill the undefined areas that are the result of distortion, revealing areas with no pixels.

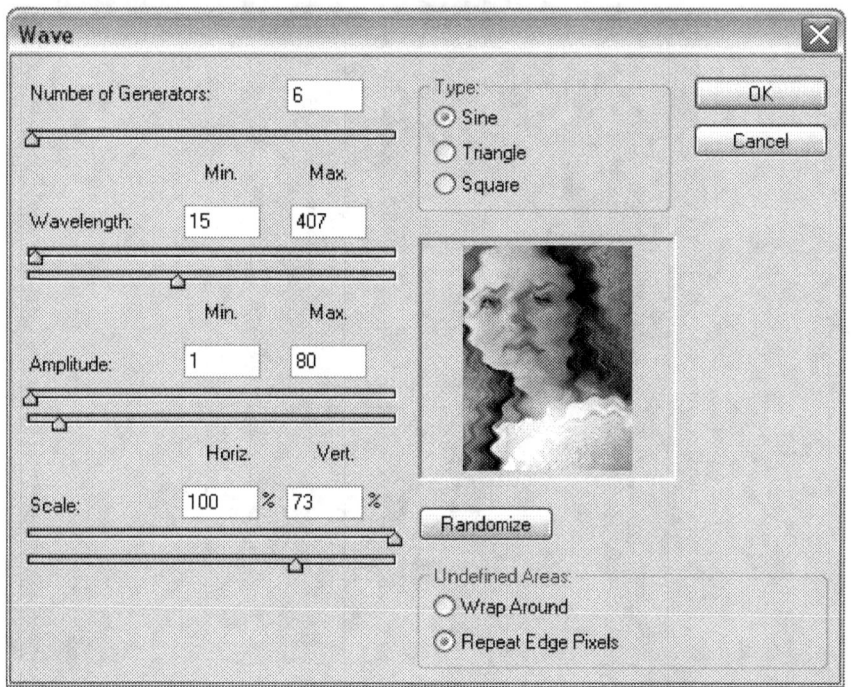

ZigZag

The ZigZag filter displaces pixels in a radial manner while alternating the displacement between the clockwise and counterclockwise ripples on regular intervals—thus the name ZigZag. In the dialog box, three separate style schemes can be used for displacement. Pond Ripples displace the pixels to the upper left or lower right; Out From Center displaces pixels from the center out; and Around Center displaces pixels in a rotational manner on a center axis. The Amount slider determines the intensity of the ripples, and the Ridges slider determines the number of ripples. This filter produces a convincing ripple that would come from dropping a stone in a smooth body of water, for example.

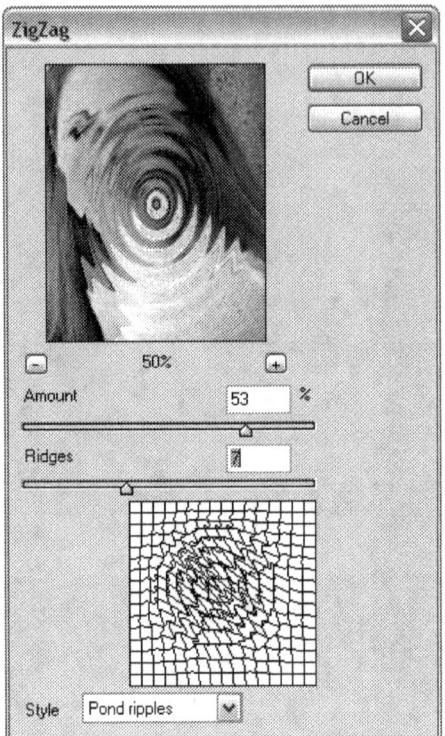

Noise Filters

Noise filters are designed to deal with areas of pixels that have random color fluctuations so they are perceived as being noisy, with no perceptible repeating pattern. These filters can add a random pattern to help blend areas together or remove noise and other unwanted visual elements such as dust, speckles, and scratches. Noise filters are helpful in the process of photo retouching. The subject of retouching is covered in more depth in Chapter 13. They are also used as an alternative to the Film Grain filter to match grain or digital camera noise when compositing photos. If you need to do this, you might want to experiment with both.

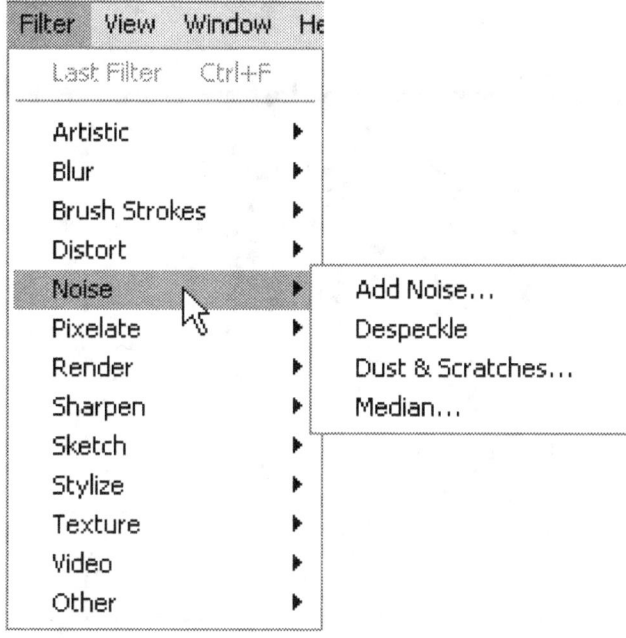

Add Noise

The Add Noise filter is designed to introduce random pixels with varying tonal fluctuations to an image. The effect is similar to that created when shooting a photo with high-speed, grainy film. This filter is used to blend areas of an image that have been reworked or composited. In the dialog box, the Amount slider sets the degree of noise that is added. Two types of patterns can be chosen from the Distributions area: Uniform and Gaussian. Uniform distribution uses random numbers between 0 and plus or minus the amount set with the Amount slider. Gaussian uses a bell-shaped curve, which produces a weighted distribution resulting in a more speckled effect. Checking the Monochrome check box will force the added pixels to maintain the hue range of the original image—otherwise, the filter will vary hues also. The Add Noise

THE SPECIAL EFFECTS WORKFLOW

filter is useful in photo retouching and compositing. See Chapters 13 and 17 for a more in-depth view on these subjects.

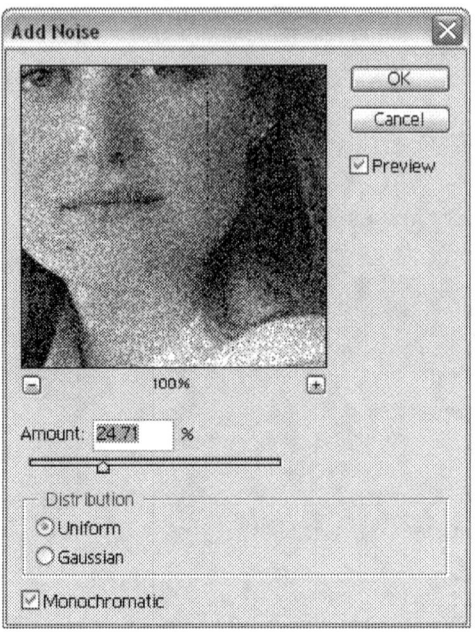

Despeckle

The Despeckle filter is similar to the Smart Blur filter discussed earlier in the chapter. It is designed to maintain edge detail where there is a high degree of color contrast, and it smoothes random detail in the rest of the image. Despeckle is good for removing random spottiness or excess graininess from photos. This is a one-shot filter with no dialog box. It can be run multiple times in succession to increase the effect. See Chapter 13 for more on retouching.

Dust & Scratches

The Dust & Scratches filter allows you to clean your slides, negatives, or scanner bed after the fact. It is designed to remove unwanted detail from an image by blending dissimilar pixels in a given radius. In the dialog box, use the Radius slider to set the area to clean. The Threshold slider determines the level of difference that pixel values must be before they are deemed dissimilar. See Chapter 13 for more information on repairing photos.

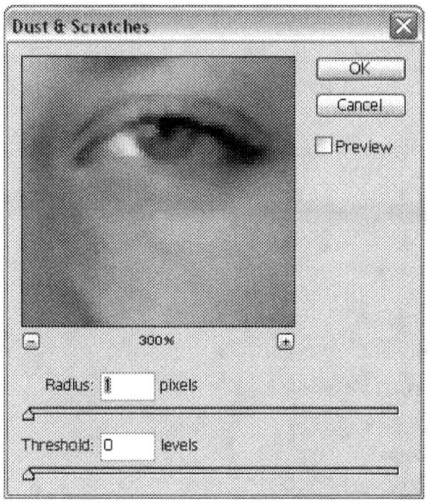

The Dust & Scratches filter is also popular as a means of smoothing small defects in the surface of the subject, such as minute skin wrinkles and blemishes. If you use it for that purpose, be sure to isolate the area you are retouching so that it doesn't blur the entire image. Also, be sure to add noise (with the Add Noise filter) to match the grain in the retouched area with the grain (noise) in the rest of the image.

Median

The Median filter is similar to the Dust & Scratches filter, without any edge preservation effect. It searches the radius around each pixel and resets the value of the center pixel based on the median value of all the pixels searched. This reduces random fluctuations in value. It's a good filter to use for removing noise and random imperfections.

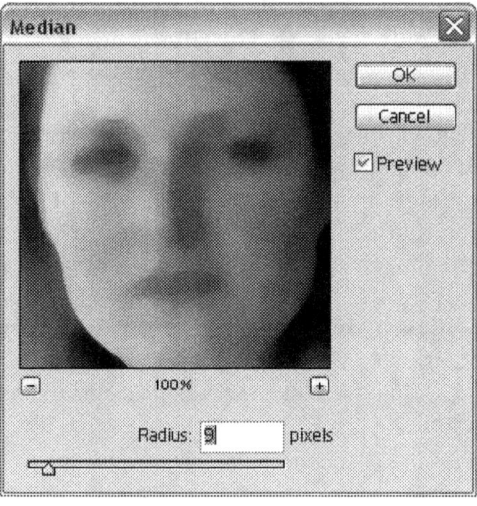

Pixelate Filters

Filters in the Pixelate set perform routines that gather pixels of similar color values and use algorithms to manipulate the pixels in a cellular fashion. These filter effects all simplify and alter the color attributes of the image in some way.

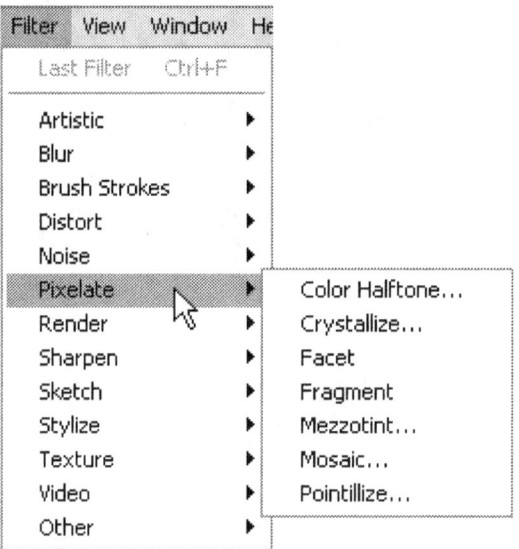

Color Halftone

The Color Halftone filter simulates the effect of a color-offset print with interlacing dot patterns of Cyan, Magenta, Yellow, and Black. You should be aware that this filter does not create a true CMYK file—just a simulation of a halftone (Photoshop Elements doesn't currently support CMYK color format). The filter builds an array of color-averaged rectangles that then define the color and size of the dots for each area based on the color and tonal values. The dots are placed on grids rotated at different angles so they are offset from each other to produce an intermixing of color. Experiment with different angles to change the look of the image.

In a black-and-white image, this filter varies the sizes of dots of black and white. In the dialog box, the Max. Radius field sets the maximum size (in pixels) of the dots (1–127). The channels represent the angle of the grid for each color. Channels 1, 2, 3, and 4 are Cyan, Magenta, Yellow, and Black, respectively. However, note that Channel 1 is the only channel that will be active when you are creating a halftone from a grayscale image. Click the Default button to reset the default values for all the fields. The Color Halftone filter produces a stylized effect that was popular in the 1960s, when pop art in advertising was all the rage.

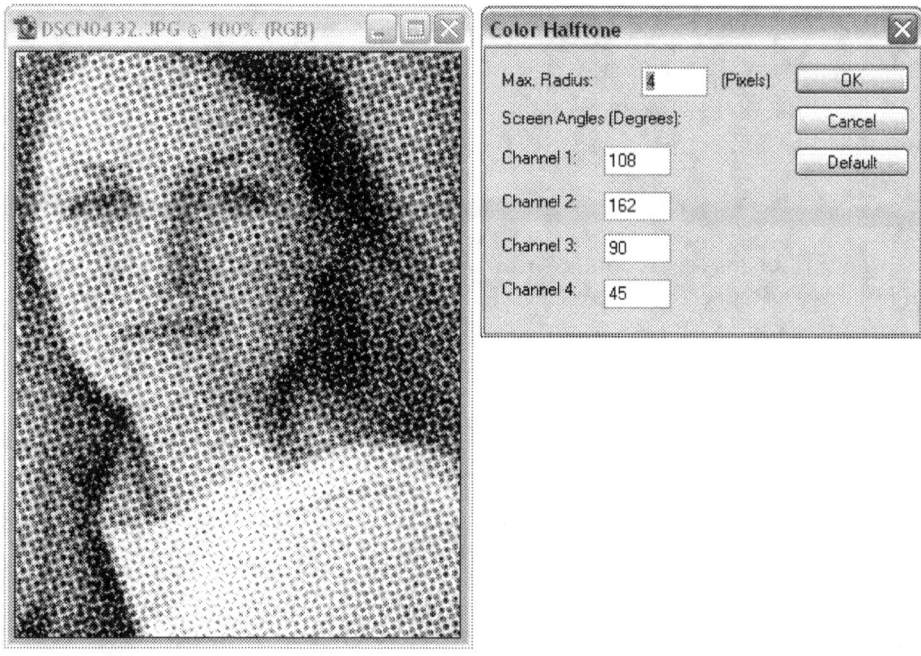

Crystallize

The Crystallize filter produces polygon-shaped cells of designated sizes and then finds the color average within each shape and fills the polygon with that color. This produces a faceted look that simulates crystal surfaces. In the dialog box, the Cell Size slider enlarges the polygon cells (in values from 3 to 300).

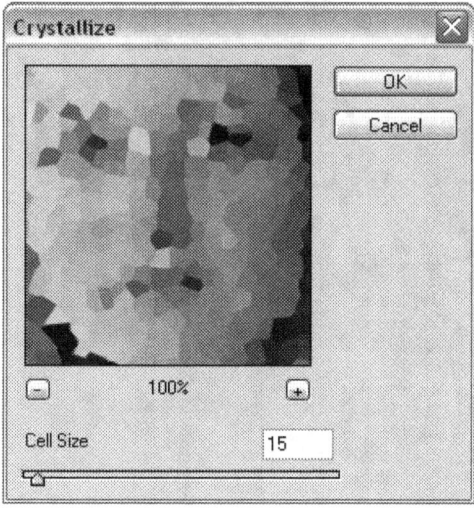

THE SPECIAL EFFECTS
WORKFLOW

Facet

The Facet filter simplifies the color variation in local areas of the image, producing a more daubed-on look to the color. The Facet filter produces the feel of hand painting by providing a more abstract look. Run the filter multiple times to intensify the effect.

Fragment

The Fragment filter makes the image look out of focus. It accomplishes this effect by copying pixels and offsetting them by a fixed amount, and then blending them back into the image. This produces a toned down duplication of the image at an offset. You can run the filter multiple times to increase the effect.

Mezzotint

The Mezzotint filter produces a random pattern of dots or lines on the image. The density of the pattern will vary according to the luminance of the original image. If the image is in color, the dots or lines will consist of fully saturated color based on the hues of the original image. You can change the nature of the pattern by choosing different patterns from the Type menu in the Mezzotint dialog box. This filter falls short of more advanced methods of producing a mezzotint, which involve dithering each separate color channel and recombining them.

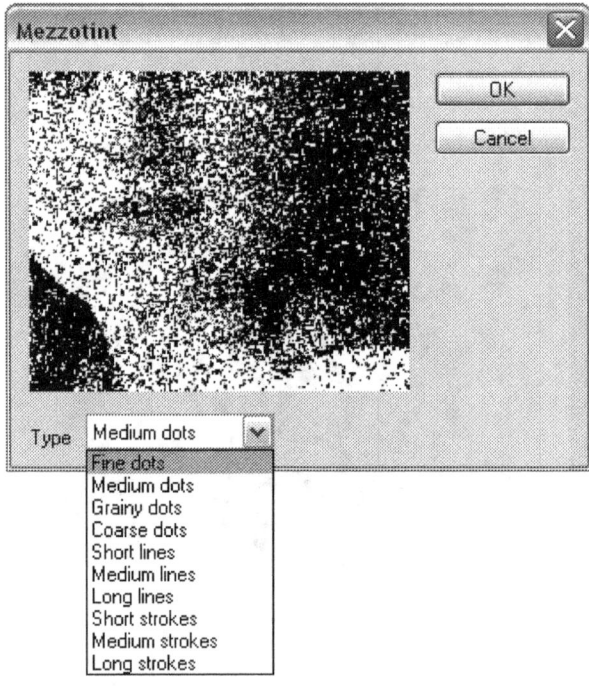

Mosaic

The Mosaic filter is a simple pixelation routine. It takes the average color of a designated cell range and creates larger blocks with the averaged color. This process produces an abstraction of the original that's similar to that produced by mosaic tiles. Use the Cell Size slider in the dialog box to set the level of abstraction.

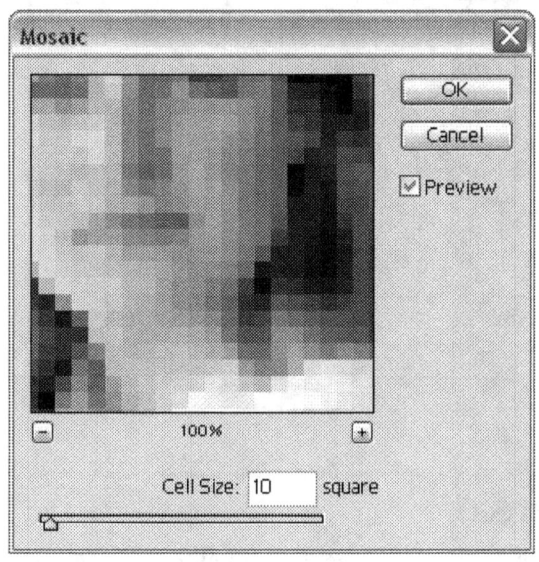

Pointillize

The Pointillize filter attempts to simulate the style of a pointillistic painting. This is accomplished by placing small, uniform circles of color with small, random fluctuations in position. The dots are placed so that some space is left between them where the current background color is used to fill in. The dot colors are based on the color values of the original image. The smaller the dots, the more detail rendered. In the dialog box, use the Cell Size slider to vary the size of the dots. This filter does a fair job, but it really fails to get the true feeling of pointillistic painting. It can be good for backgrounds and adding a grainy look, however, or for stylized illustrator looks.

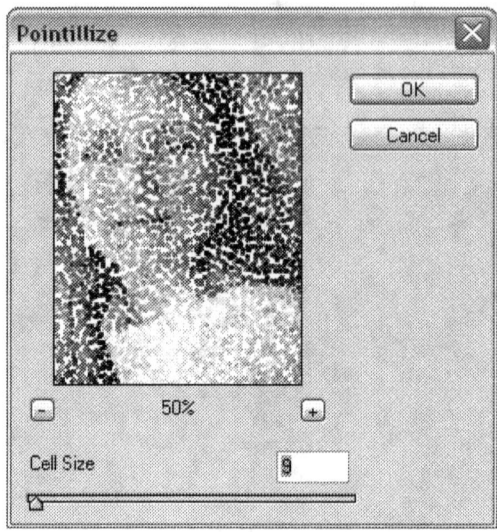

Render Filters

The Render filters provide more complex manipulations of the images to produce dramatic special effects. These include transformations to 3-D surfaces, creating lighting effects, and producing cloud patterns. Lighting effects will be covered in more detail in Chapters 15 and 17.

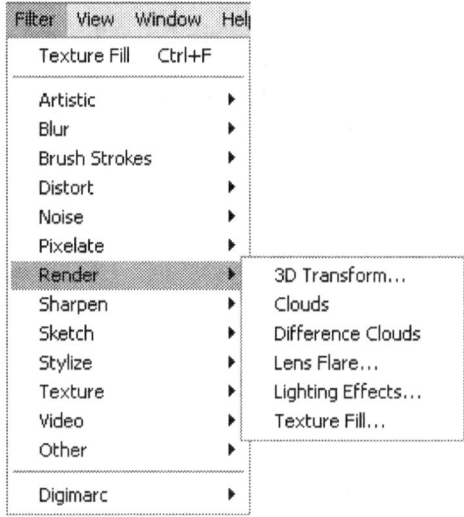

3D Transform

The 3D Transform filter is another filter that could be called a mini application. This filter is useful if you want to render an image to appear to conform to the surface of a 3-D object such as a box or vase. 3D Transform allows your image to conform to basic geometric shapes: a cube, cylinder, and a sphere. You can also modify the cylinder to create custom shapes, such as the shape of a vase or pitcher. Click a shape tool from the 3D Transform Toolbox in the dialog box, and click and drag the shape into the preview window. You will see the wire frame of the shape you selected with handles for transforming and rotating the 3-D shape.

Use the Selection tool to move the wire frame as a whole, or grab the handles to resize the shape to how you want it. Click the Trackball tool to see the image mapped to the shape. With the Trackball tool still selected, click and drag on the shape to rotate it in three dimensions. The Pan Camera tool will move the shape left, right, up, or down. The Field Of View and Dolly controls on the right side of the dialog box allow you to zoom in and out on the shape. Click the Options button to open the Options dialog box, and adjust the rendering quality levels and whether you want the image outside the shape to display or not. If you choose not to display the background, the area outside the shape will be transparent, allowing you to superimpose it over another layer.

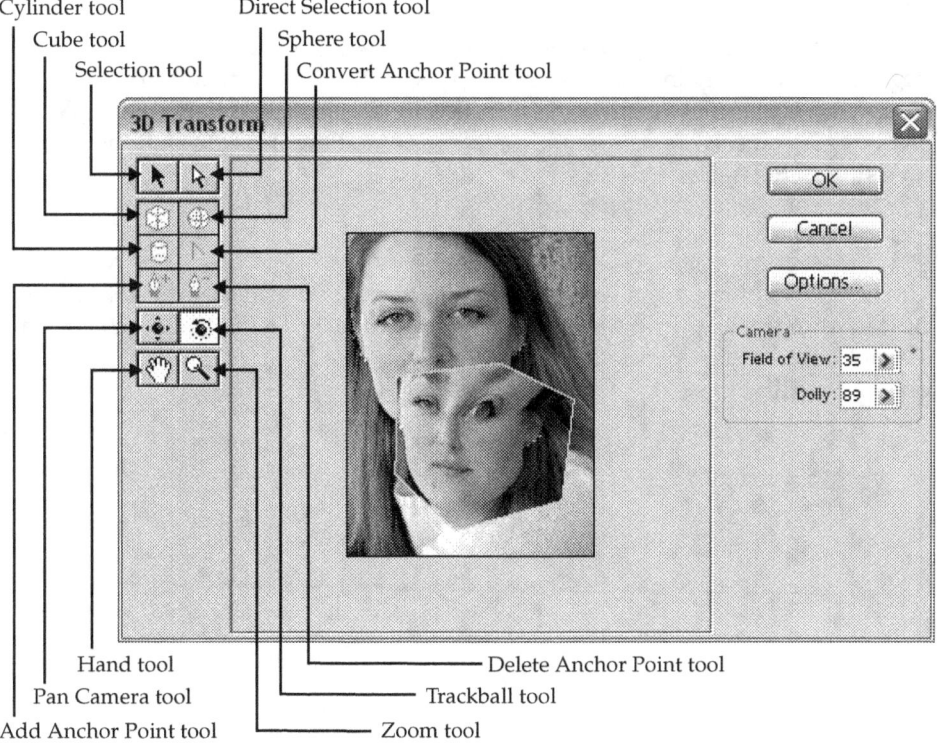

THE SPECIAL EFFECTS WORKFLOW

Clouds

The Clouds filter is a simple one that uses the foreground and background colors to mathematically generate a cloud pattern from random numbers. Every time you run the filter, it will generate a new pattern. To raise the contrast of the cloud pattern, press OPT/ALT while you select the filter.

Difference Clouds

The Difference Clouds filter works the same way the Clouds filter works, but, in addition, it uses the same method of adding the cloud pattern to the image as the Difference blending mode (see Chapter 9 for details on difference calculation). The Difference method causes a color inversion effect. The filter can be run multiple times, increasing the complexity of the pattern. This filter is good for producing highly colored and complex smoky patterns.

Lens Flare

The Lens Flare filter is designed to simulate the flare that occurs when a bright light shines directly into the lens. It is used to add a spectral highlight to the image. You can choose from among three types of lenses that will alter the size and intensity of the flare: 50–300mm Zoom, 35mm Prime, and 105mm Prime. In the Lens Flare dialog box, click anywhere in the preview window to change the position of the flare. Adjust the Brightness slider to increase the light intensity (10 to 300%). This filter is also good for adding bright highlights to shiny objects and for placing a corona around points of lights, such as candles. By increasing the brightness in even increments on multiple copies of the image, you can create animation frames of flaring light. See Chapter 15 for more on using flare effects.

Texture Fill

This filter fills the current layer with a repeating tile of a saved grayscale PSD image that you choose from the File Browser pop-up. It is useful for placing tiled textures on layers above an image and using blending modes to composite them. See Chapter 15 for more on Texture fills.

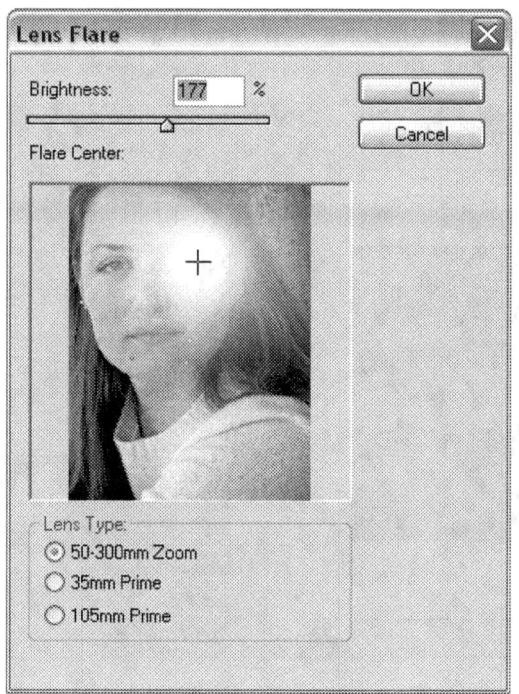

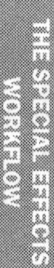

Lighting Effects

The Lighting Effects filter is a mini application that is designed to add simulated lighting effects to an image. It includes 17 preset light configurations that can be modified and saved as new presets. Three light types can be chosen from the dialog box: Omni creates an even light over the entire image, as indirect lighting would produce. Directional is general lighting with a definite directional component that is similar to sunlight or flood lamps. Spotlight has an area effect and a directional component. You can also adjust lighting properties and ambient lighting, which determines the color and intensity of the general light levels. You can add multiple lights and control them individually. In Chapter 15, you'll find out more about using lighting effects to add mood and focus.

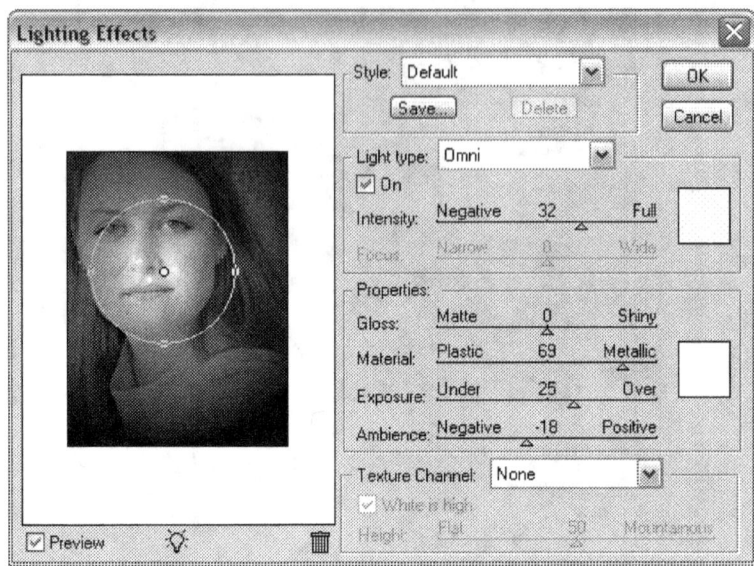

Sharpen Filters

The Sharpen filters are designed to sharpen the detail in an image by increasing the contrast among pixels. The more sophisticated filters like Sharpen Edges and Unsharp Mask provide much more control by limiting their contrast enhancement to areas of higher contrast, which would indicate edges. Unsharp Mask offers controls that adjust how it finds edges and the degree of contrast applied.

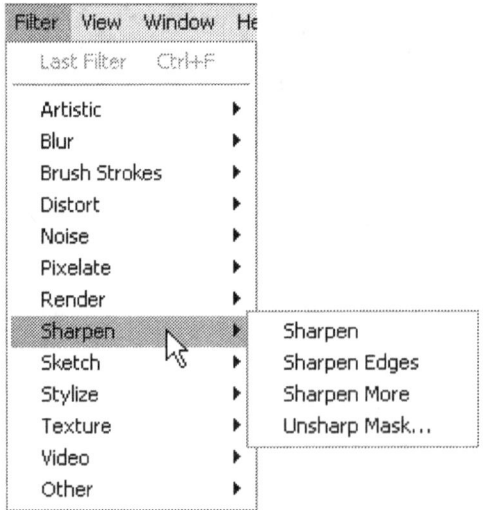

Sharpen, Sharpen Edges, and Sharpen More

The Sharpen filter is a simple one-shot filter that increases the contrast among all pixels in the image. It produces a minor focus improvement. The Sharpen Edges filter uses a built-in algorithm to determine the difference between edges and smooth areas, and it sharpens only the edges. The Sharpen More filter applies the same effect as Sharpen filter, but it's a number of times stronger. Sharpen and Sharpen More can be run multiple times to increase the effect. However, because the effect is global, with no consideration of edges, applying the effect too many times can oversharpen unwanted detail and cause the image to become objectionably pixelated. See the following illustration for an example of an image before sharpening (left) and after sharpening (right).

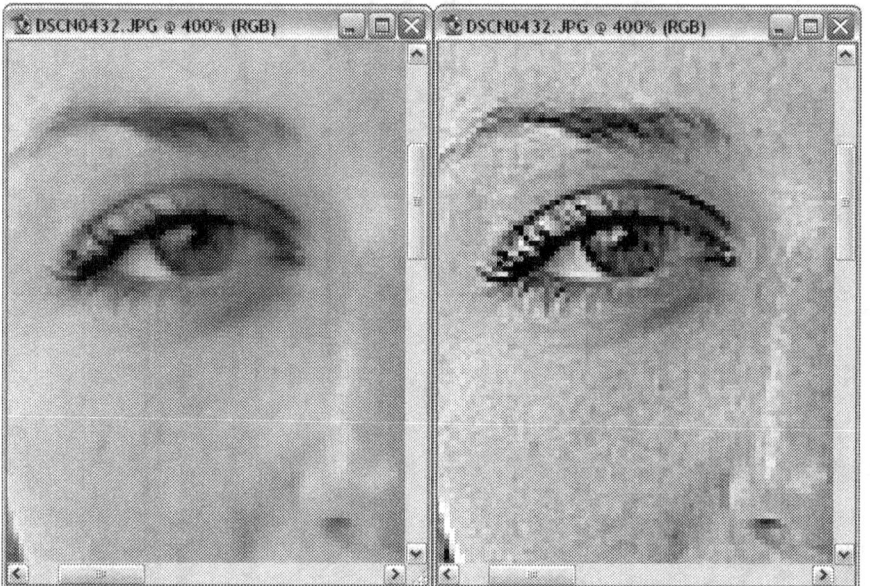

Unsharp Mask

The Unsharp Mask filter is the most powerful filter in the set. In this filter's dialog box, you can set the Radius slider to determine how many pixel searches should occur to find an edge. The Threshold slider sets the contrast value required for edges to be identified. The Amount slider determines the amount of level adjustment that will occur on either side of an edge to increase the edge contrast. This filter gives a broad range of control over what gets sharpened and what doesn't. To increase your control even more, use selections to isolate areas of the image in which you want to use different values. See Chapter 13 for more on sharpening techniques.

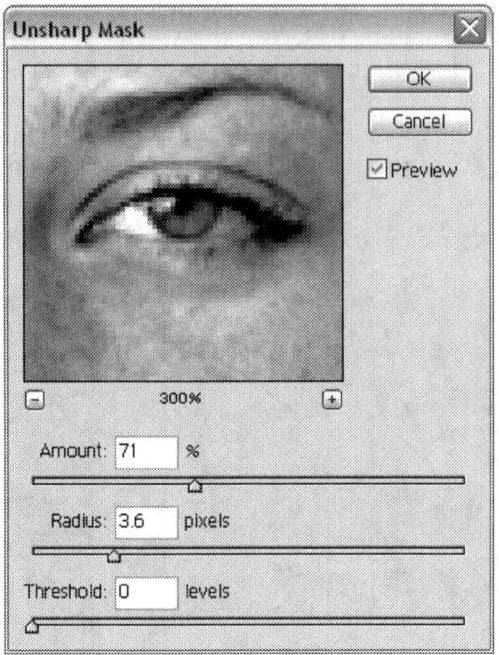

Sketch Filters

The Sketch filters are designed to simulate the look of sketching tools such as pencil, chalk, and charcoal. Some of these filters also make heavy use of textural effects and effects that simulate certain processes and surfaces such as Chrome, Bas Relief, Plaster, Stamp, Photocopy, and Water Paper. Because many of the filters in this set use the foreground and background colors as part of their routine, you can achieve a range of results by varying the foreground and background colors.

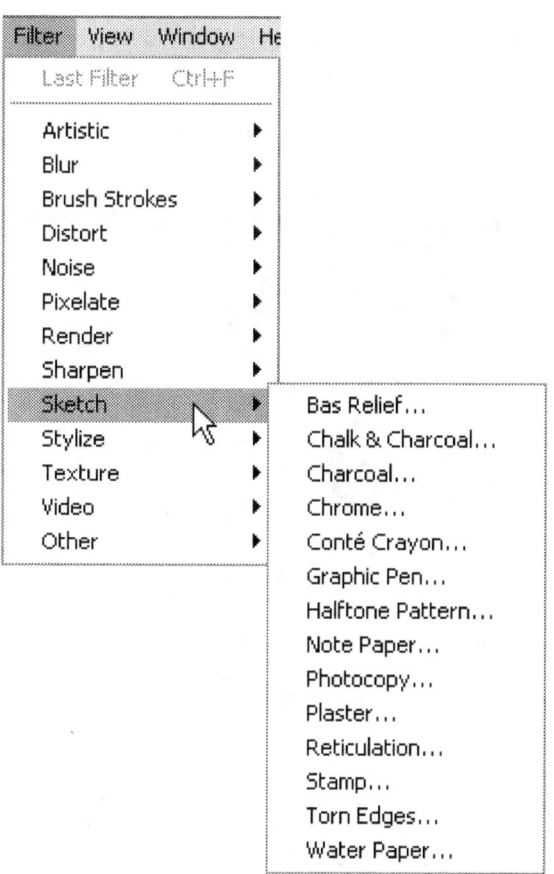

Bas Relief

The Bas Relief filter is designed to simulate a carved relief design. The filter uses the light and dark areas of the image to simulate depth and height with pseudo lighting. In the dialog box, you can choose the lighting angle from the Light Direction drop-down menu. The Detail slider (with values of 1 to 15) determines the amount of contrast that defines a raised relief detail. The Smoothness slider (1 to 15) softens the edge detail.

You can use this filter to get the look of a carving in wood or stone, or to create a textural effect. Vary the foreground and background colors to change the look.

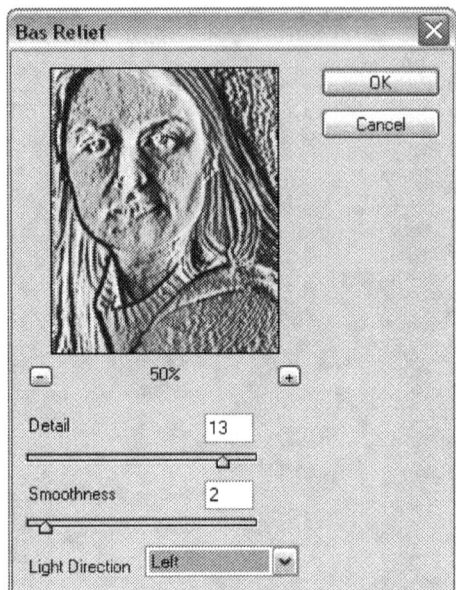

Chalk & Charcoal

This filter simulates drawing with light chalk and dark charcoal on a rough surface. It uses the foreground and background colors as it renders the image. To stay true to the chalk and charcoal look, you need to set the foreground color to black and the background color to white or light gray. The foreground color is used for the shadow areas and the background color is used in the highlights. The midtones are filled with middle gray. By varying the colors, you can switch to a colored chalk look. In the dialog box, adjust the Charcoal Area slider to expand the area of effect. Adjust the Chalk Area slider to expand the area of highlights. The Stroke Pressure slider increases the contrast between shadow and highlight and reduces the midtones. This filter is an effective simulation and can produce a nice sketched look.

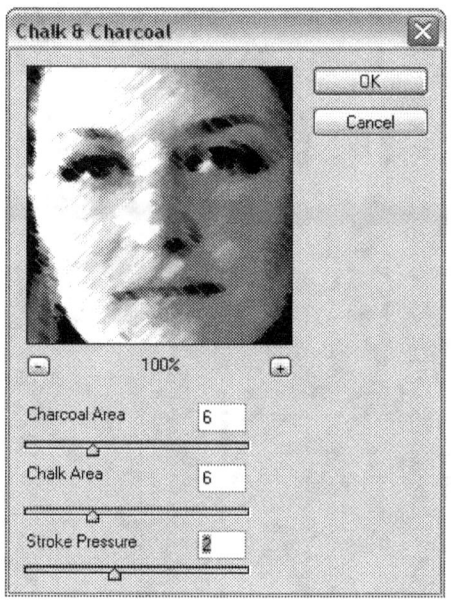

Charcoal

The Charcoal filter is designed to simulate a loose charcoal drawing. It reduces all the colors in the image to two: the current foreground and background colors. The filter demands a high degree of contrast in the edges it chooses to render, so subtle images will produce weak results. You can set the foreground and background to different colors for this filter. White background and black foreground will render the best, however. The foreground color will be rendered to the darker areas with strong outlining at the edges and loose diagonal strokes in the midtones. In the dialog box, the Charcoal Thickness setting makes the strokes wider and darker. The Detail slider determines how much gets rendered as an edge. The Light/Dark Balance slider determines the contrast. Reducing the Light/Dark Balance value will gray out the darker areas of the image to create a lead pencil sketch effect. Depending on the subject, this can be a good filter to use for a preliminary sketch for a digital painting or a black-and-white illustration.

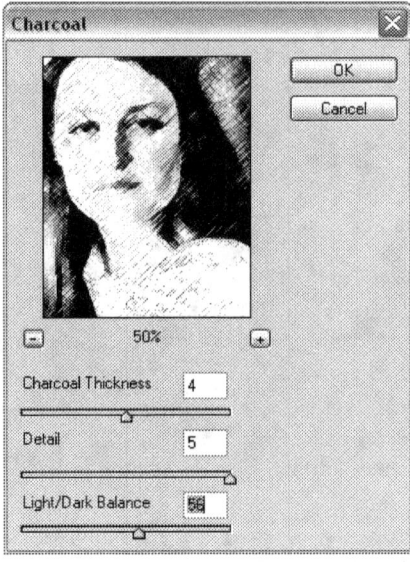

Chrome

The Chrome filter is designed to simulate an undulating reflective chrome surface. The light areas of the image will be the raised areas on the chrome and the darker areas will be the lower areas. The filter works best with simple shapes with gradual value transitions. In the dialog box, the Detail slider (1–10) determines how sensitive the filter is to changes in value. A value of 10 will create the most detail. The Smoothness slider softens the transitions between high and low areas. Increasing the brightness and contrast after applying the Chrome filter can enhance the effect.

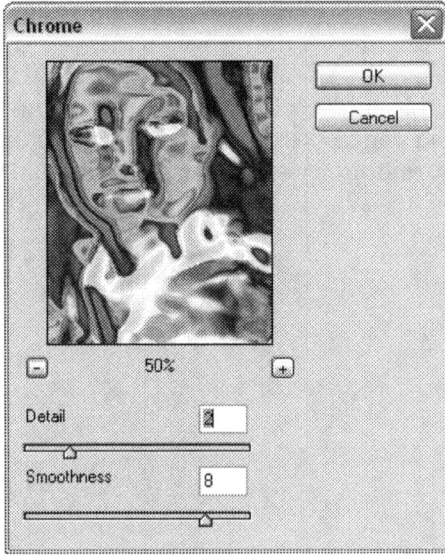

Conté Crayon

The Conté Crayon filter is designed to simulate the look of bright white, sepia, and sanguine Conté crayons. The filter is much the same as the Chalk & Charcoal filter in how it works with color. The major difference is the addition of texture controls in the dialog box. The texture controls allow you to add and adjust preset textures or load your own (see the "Texturizer" filter section, later in the chapter). The foreground color renders the shadows, the background color renders the highlights, and the midtones are filled with middle gray. The Foreground Level and Background Level sliders, respectively, enhance the shadow or highlight regions in the image.

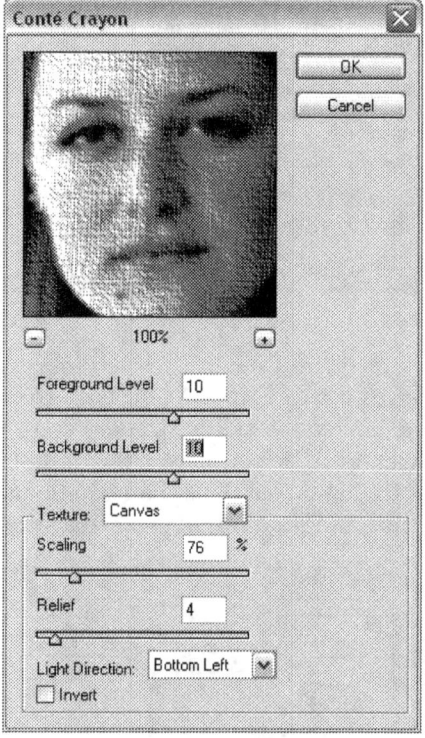

Graphic Pen

The Graphic Pen filter simulates a drawing style that uses diagonal ink strokes to render the detail in the image. This is a two-color process in which the foreground color is the ink color and the background color is the color of the paper. Darker areas and edges are rendered with ink strokes and the lighter areas are filled with the background color. In the Graphic Pen dialog box, the Stroke Length slider determines the length of the strokes. The Light/Dark Balance slider determines how much of the image is rendered with ink. You can choose to angle the stroke in one of four orientations from the Stroke Direction drop-down menu. This filter produces a nice pen-and-ink sketch style that makes a good black-and-white illustration. If you select the background color with the Magic Wand, feather the selection slightly, and press BACKSPACE/DELETE to let the original image show through, you get a nice sketch-like outlined effect.

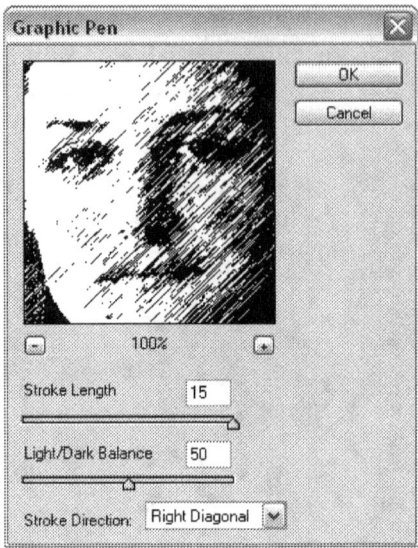

Halftone Pattern

The Halftone Pattern filter uses the foreground and background colors to produce a halftone screen of the image. You can vary the size and contrast of the screen elements, which can be dots, circles, or lines. The controls in the dialog box work similar to the same controls in other filter dialog boxes. This filter can be used to produce a quick halftone of a grayscale or color image so it will print in a single color.

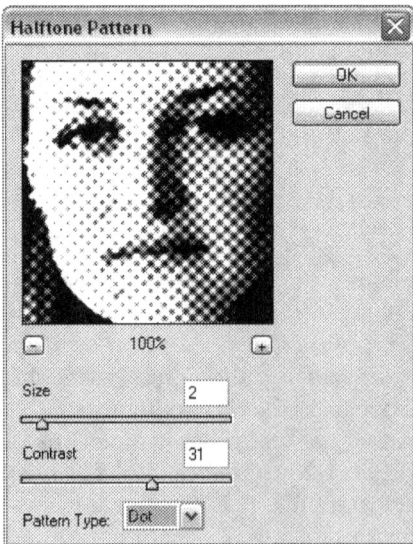

Note Paper

The Note Paper filter attempts to simulate the look of handmade paper, where the lighter parts of the image are rendered in the background color and the darker regions are rendered in the foreground color. The areas are then embossed and textured to accentuate the thickness of the "paper." In the dialog box, the Image Balance slider will determine the proportion of light or dark areas that are filled. The Graininess slider adds texture. The Relief slider determines the amount of embossing that occurs at the edges. This filter will work well when the image is designed to take advantage of a particular paper's texture. Under normal circumstances, it produces a nice embossed image that looks similar to a cutout. If you run the filter multiple times and adjust the controls, you can achieve some interesting textural effects.

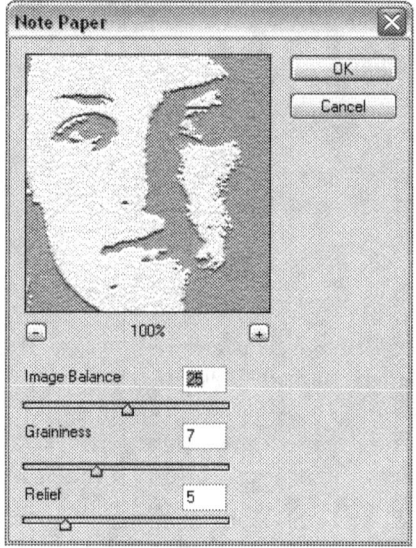

Photocopy

The Photocopy filter simulates the effect of photocopying an image. This is basically the same as posterizing the image into two colors. The edges are maintained while large, darker areas drop out away from edges. Midtones will threshold to either black or white. In the dialog box, the Detail slider affects the amount of edge detail that is rendered. The Darkness slider changes the threshold to push more midtones toward the foreground color. This filter uses the foreground and background colors as it renders.

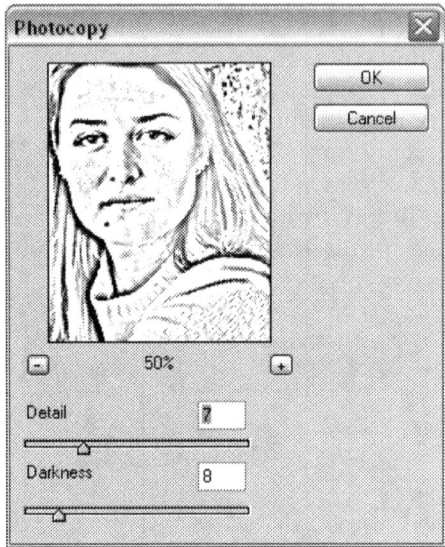

Plaster

The Plaster filter effect is similar to that of the Note Paper filter. This filter is designed to simulate the look of raised plaster or stucco. It uses the foreground and background colors to replace light and dark areas of the image with solid color. The areas with foreground color are embossed to look raised. In the dialog box, the Image Balance slider determines the proportion of light or dark areas that are filled. The Smoothness slider determines the amount of detail that's maintained at the edges. You can select the direction of the light source from the Light Direction drop-down menu. This filter is good for producing a prominent raised texture.

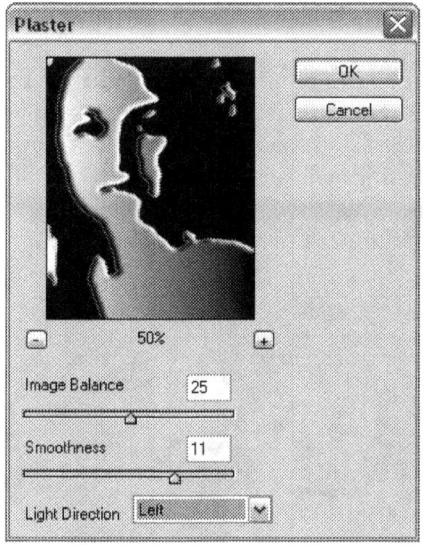

Reticulation

The Reticulation filter produces a clumped, grainy effect where the clumping is denser in the darker areas. This filter uses the foreground and background colors, where the foreground fills the darker areas of the image. The Density slider (0–50) in the dialog box increases the overall graininess. The Foreground Level and Background Level (0–50) controls increase the effects of their respective colors. This filter produces some interesting grain patterns, and when combined with other filter effects, it can be quite dramatic. It would be more powerful if it had a grain size control, but you can control the relative size of the grain by changing the document size.

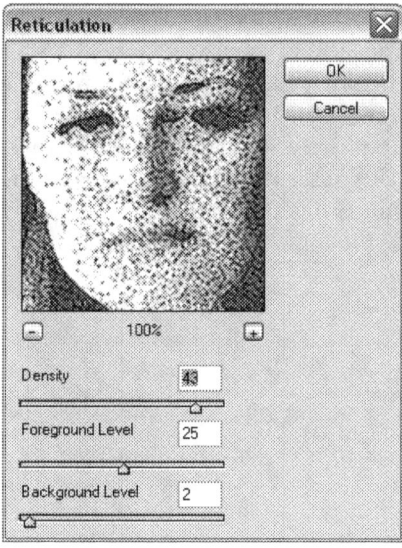

THE SPECIAL EFFECTS WORKFLOW

Stamp

The Stamp filter simulates the kind of image you would see when using a rubber stamp. This filter works best with high-contrast color or black-and-white images. The filter simplifies the image to areas of high contrast using the foreground and background colors. In the dialog box, the Light/Dark Balance slider (1–50) adjusts the proportion of the contrasting areas. The Smoothness (1–50) slider adjusts the edge detail. This filter is nice for a achieving a linocut or woodcut look.

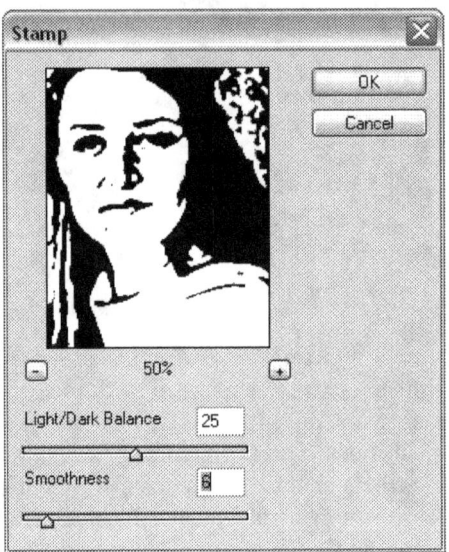

Torn Edges

The Torn Edges filter simplifies the image into "fuzzy" areas of high contrast using the foreground and background colors. The filter creates rough edges in the contrasting colors that simulate torn paper. The Torn Edges filter works best on high-contrast images. Text and simple shapes are good candidates for this filter. In the dialog box, the Image Balance slider (1–50) determines the proportion of contrasting areas. The Smoothness slider (1–15) determines the roughness of the edges. The Contrast slider (1–25) sets the overall contrast levels.

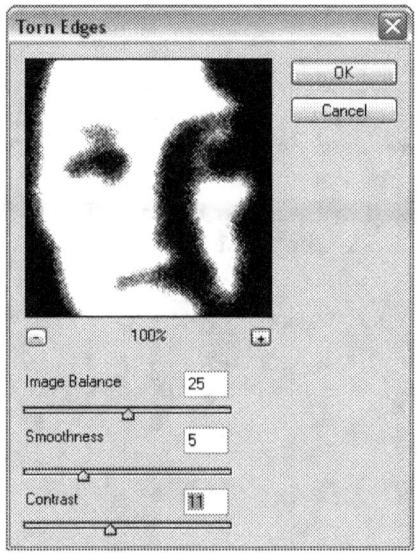

Water Paper

The Water Paper filter simulates wet watercolor diffused into an evenly woven fibrous paper. High-contrast areas are diffused and stroked with a vertical and horizontal crosshatch pattern, while the rest of the image is daubed and blended to look wet. In the Water Paper dialog box, the Fiber Length slider (1–50) determines the length of the strokes. The Brightness slider (0–100) sets the overall brightness of the colors. The Contrast slider (0–100) adjusts the contrast, which affects the area that will be stroked.

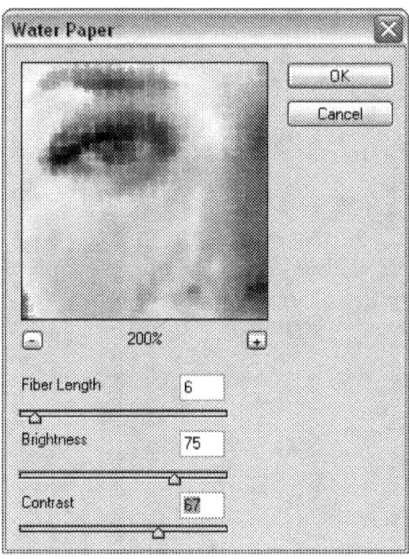

Stylize Filters

The Stylize filters are a collection of unique filters that deal with finding and modifying edges, such as Diffuse, Find Edges, Glowing Edges, Wind, Emboss, and Trace Contours. Extrude and Tiles filters create rectangular cellular effects. The filters with outlining capability are useful in conjunction with blending modes and layers to produce line drawings that can be colorized in a number of ways. The Diffuse and Wind filters can be used to create blur effects. See Chapter 16 for more on using outlines in painting.

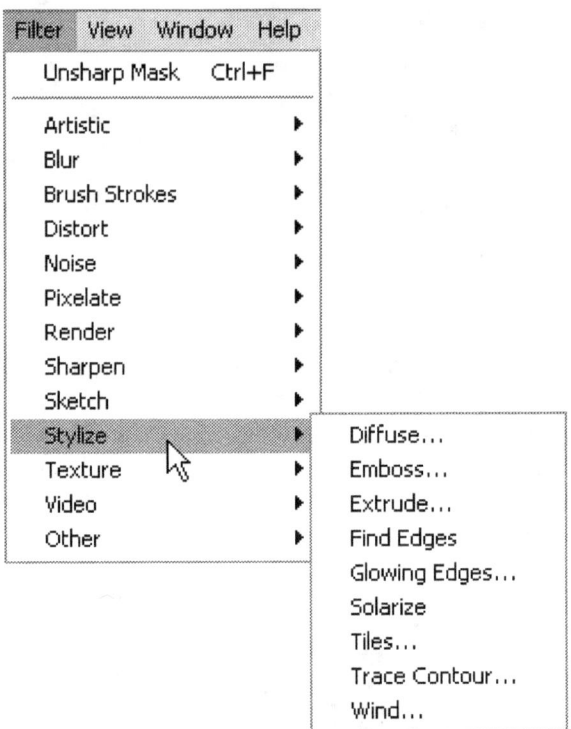

Diffuse

The Diffuse filter has the effect of "bleeding" the edges in the picture in various ways. The first three modes that you can select in the dialog box, Normal, Darken Only, and

Lighten Only, produce coarse edge diffusion that makes the image look textured or frosty. Normal moves edge pixels in a random fashion with no regard for color values. Darken Only replaces lighter pixels with darker pixels, and Lighten Only replaces darker pixels with lighter ones. The fourth method, Anisotropic, creates a look as though water were poured on the image and softly diffused the color in the paper. Anisotropic can be dramatic with multiple passes, and can also be used to smooth noise and reverse some pixelation effects of JPEG compression (it's best to do this in carefully selected areas of the image so that you don't diffuse the entire picture).

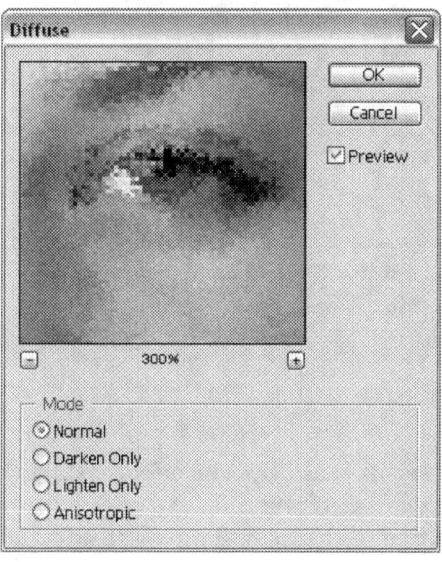

Emboss

The Emboss filter highlights the edges in the image and fills everything else with middle gray. The edges are traced with the original image colors. Edges are highlighted and darkened to make the image look embossed or stamped. You can change the angle of the light source with the Angle dial or input field in the Emboss dialog box. Changing from positive to negative degrees will invert the look of the embossing from raised to lowered, respectively. The Height slider sets the depth or height of the embossed edge. The Amount slider determines the intensity of the edge effect.

Embossing can create sophisticated patterned textures that can be used for backgrounds, lettering effects, and creating textures to use in the Texturizer filter.

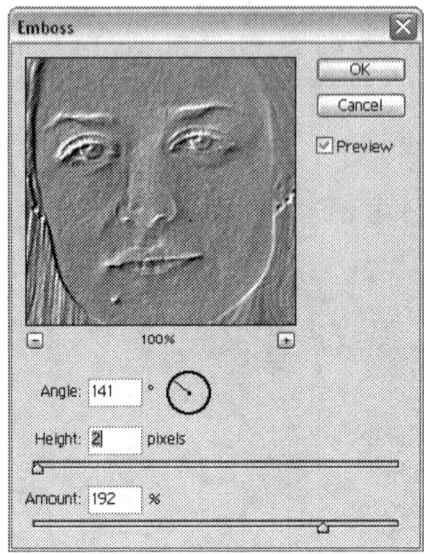

Extrude

The Extrude filter can be classified as a special effect that has limited applications. It divides the image into a square grid and then extrudes rectangular or pyramidal solids using the average color in that grid square. In the Extrude dialog box, the Type buttons let you choose Blocks or Pyramids. The Size input field sets the size of the grid in pixels. The Depth input field sets the depth of the solids. Choose Random if you want the blocks' heights to be placed randomly, or choose Level-Based to have the height of the blocks be higher for lighter color values. The face of the rectangular solids can be a solid color (Solid Front Faces) or a remap (Mask Incomplete Blocks) of the detail in the original image. This filter can be useful for some illustrator and poster effects, but it is rather cliché.

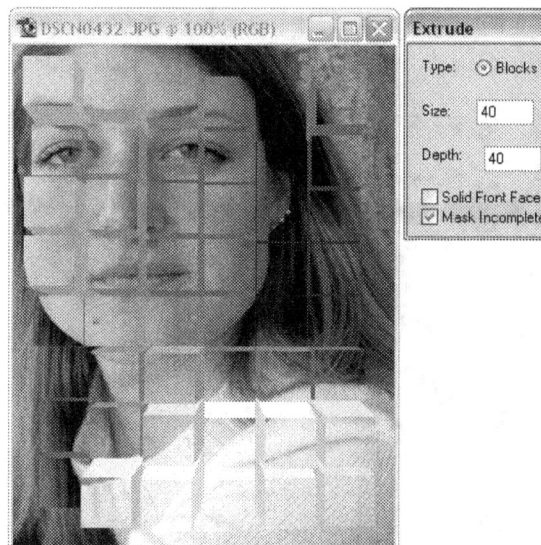

Find Edges

The Find Edges filter uses a built-in algorithm to find edges based on the contrast of adjacent pixels. Because no controls are available for this filter, images with higher contrast detail will have a better result than softer images. Lower contrast pixels are lightened and higher contrast pixels are darkened more. This produces an effect of dark outlines on a lighter background. The filter can be run multiple times to intensify the effect. You can produce edge masks to help in protecting the quality of edges when you refocus an image.

Glowing Edges

The Glowing Edges filter works similar to the Find Edges filter, but Glowing Edges inverts the color values of each pixel so you end up with light outlines on a darker background. The inverted effect gives the appearance of glowing neon. The Glowing Edges filter also provides some controls that let you modify the effect. You can use the Glowing Edges filter in place of the Find Edges filter if you are willing to invert the pixels after you run the filter by choosing Image | Adjustments | Invert. In the dialog box, the Edge Width slider expands the areas that are lightened around edges. The Edge Brightness slider raises the color value of all edges. The Smoothness slider smoothes edge detail and tends to reduce the amount of noisy, low-contrast edges.

The controls provided by the Glowing Edges filter make it a better choice than the Find Edges filter for getting the kind of edge detail you want.

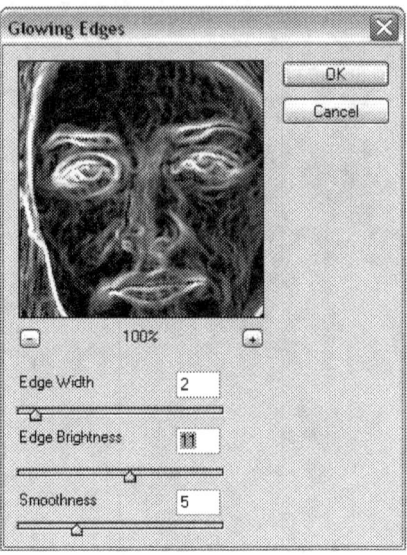

Solarize

The Solarize filter builds a composite of the original and its inverse using the Darken blending mode (see Chapter 9 for more on blending modes). You can see an example of the Solarize filter's results in the following illustration:

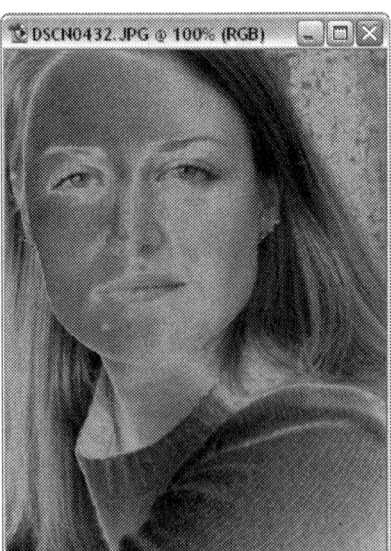

Tiles

The Tiles filter breaks up the image into a specified number of square tiles that are randomly offset within a set range, leaving space between the tiles. In the dialog box, the space can be filled with the foreground color, background color, the original image inverse (Inverse Image), or just the original image (Unaltered Image). The Number Of Tiles value sets the amount of tiles (1–99) into which it will fragment. The Maximum Offset value sets the maximum distance of the offset. This filter produces a quick mosaic tile look. If you combine it with an embossed layer blended with Hardlight blending mode, the illusion becomes amplified. You can achieve an interesting composite by selecting the space between the tiles and clearing it to a transparent color and then layering a second image into the spaces between the tiles.

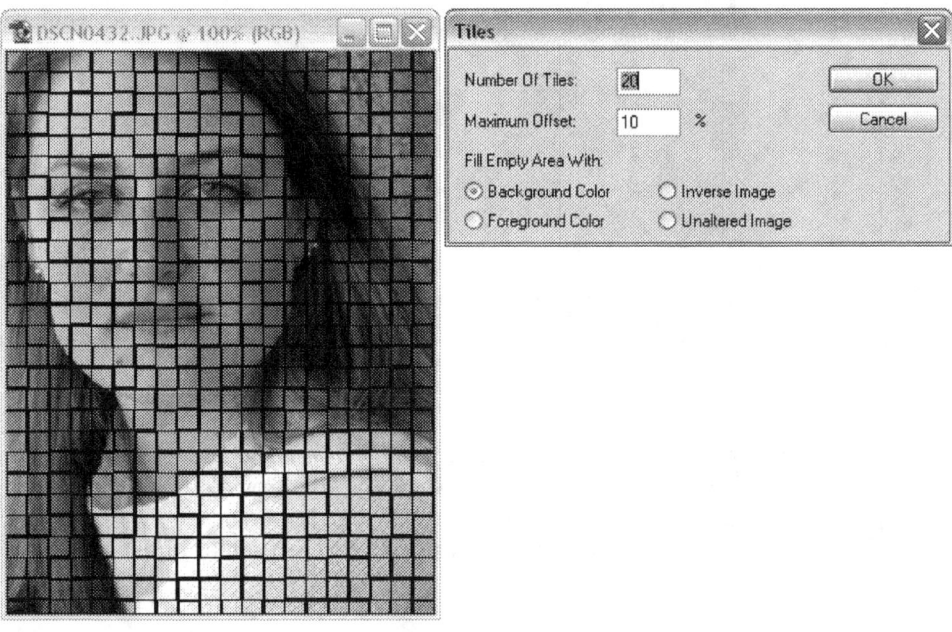

Trace Contour

The Trace Contour filter uses the luminance mapping of an image to define areas to outline. In the dialog box, you can set the Level slider (1–255) to the level of luminance that will be used to find edges. The filter sets up a contour line that outlines areas with the same level of brightness. This is useful for isolating and outlining shapes with stark differences in value—such as a light-colored flower with dark foliage.

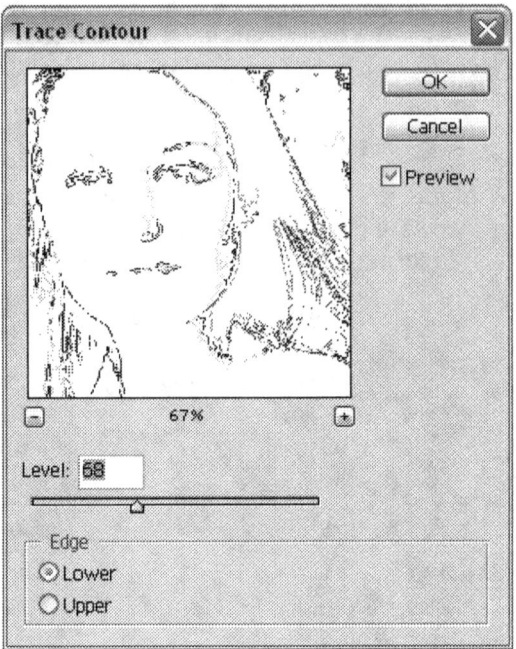

Wind

The Wind filter is designed to simulate the blur effect of wind. It accomplishes this by introducing a series of horizontal, smearing lines that move from either the left or right, depending on which radio button you choose in the Wind dialog box. Wind Method choices are Wind, Blast, and Stagger. Blast gives you an accentuated effect. Stagger randomly offsets the lines to give a more chaotic effect. This filter can be used to achieve a variation on the Motion Blur filter.

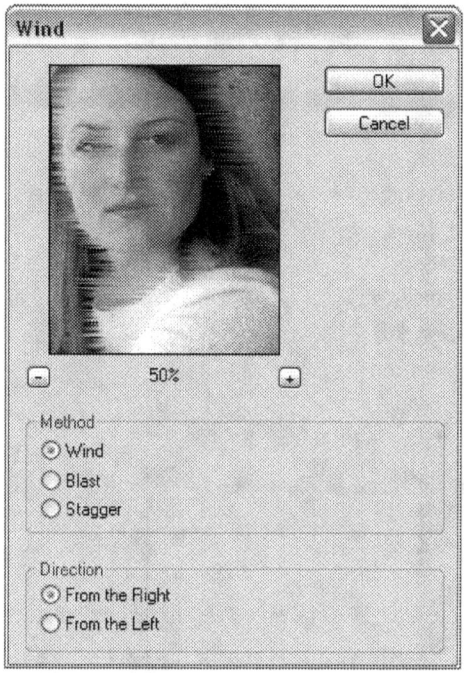

Texture Filters

The Texture filters are all designed to add a textural effect over the image. These effects are pseudo effects that create the illusion of texture by creating highlights and shadows that indicate peaks and valleys. Some simulate organic textures, and others have a more abstract look. The Texturizer filter allows you to build your own textures and add them to the built-in preset list.

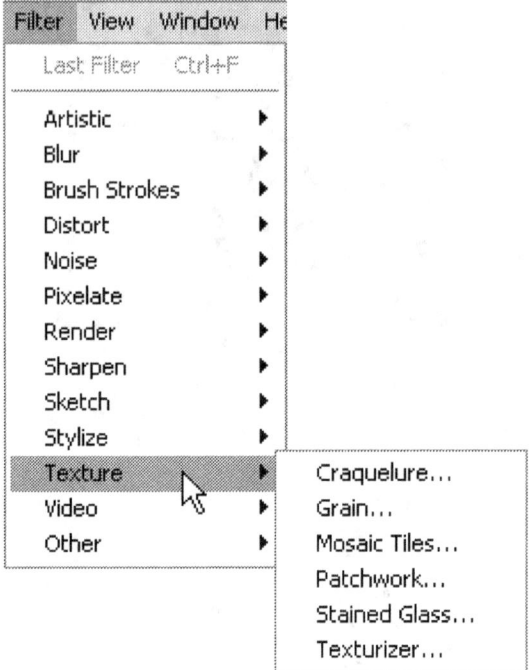

Craquelure

The Craquelure filter is designed to simulate a cracked, rough plaster look. The filter creates an embossed appearance and then applies random cracks to the embossed pattern. The Crack Spacing slider (2–100) in the dialog box determines the separation between cracks. The Crack Depth slider (0–10) determines the depth of the cracks. Crack Brightness (0–10) affects the shadow color of the cracks.

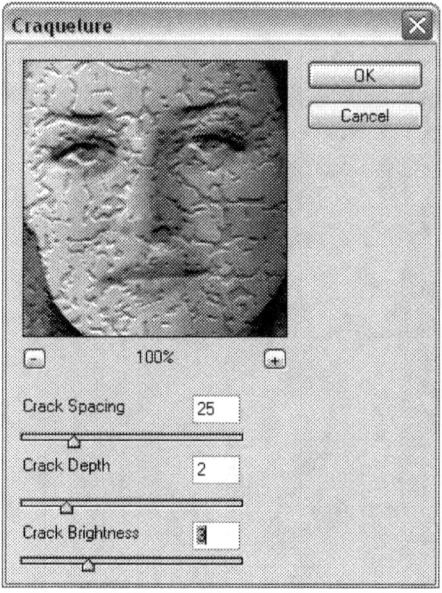

Grain

The Grain filter is designed to add multiple grain patterns to the image. You can choose from among 10 grain patterns from the drop-down menu in the Grain dialog box: Regular, Soft, Sprinkles, Clumped, Contrasty, Enlarged, Stippled, Horizontal, Vertical, and Speckle. Stippled uses the foreground and background colors, whereas Sprinkles uses only the background color. The Intensity slider determines the density of the grain pattern. The Contrast slider makes the image higher contrast, which affects how the grain is placed. See Chapter 15 for more on using textures for special effects.

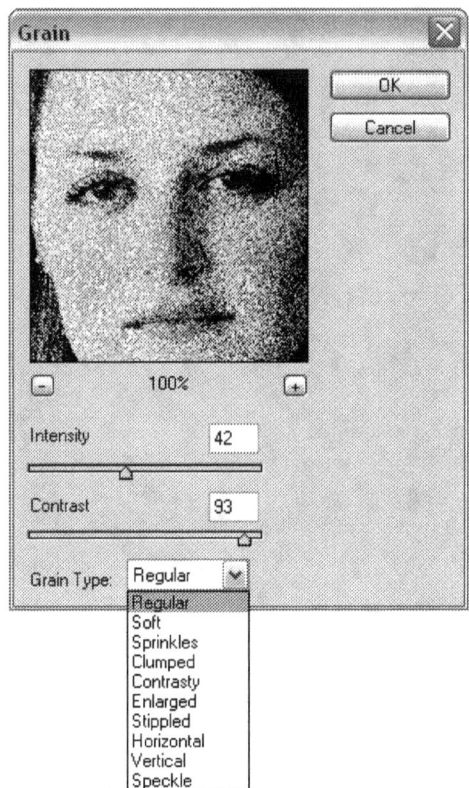

Mosaic Tiles

The Mosaic Tiles filter simulates rough-cut tiles that have been grouted in an even grid pattern. The filter randomizes the border designs to look more natural. The tile pattern is embossed to look dimensional with the grout spaces appearing to be deeper. In the dialog box, the Tile Size slider (2–100) determines the size of the tile grid. The Grout Width slider (1–15) determines the size of the space between tiles. The Lighten Grout slider (0–10) lightens the color of the grout.

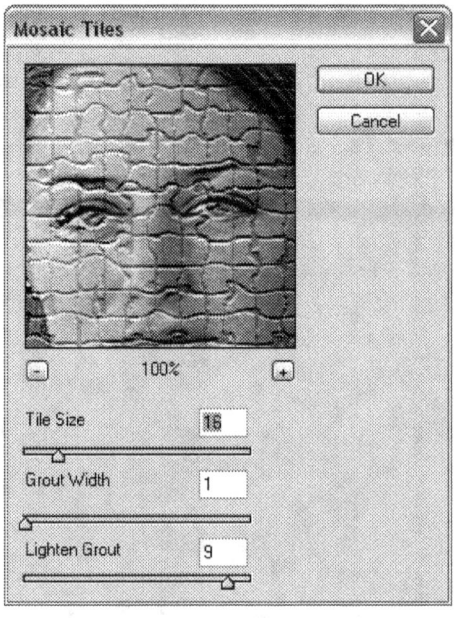

Patchwork

The Patchwork filter simulates a tiled wall on a square grid, where the height relief is based on the lightness or luminance value of the average color in each grid square. In the dialog box, the Square Size slider (1–10) changes the size of the grid. The Relief slider (0–25) increases the depth effect.

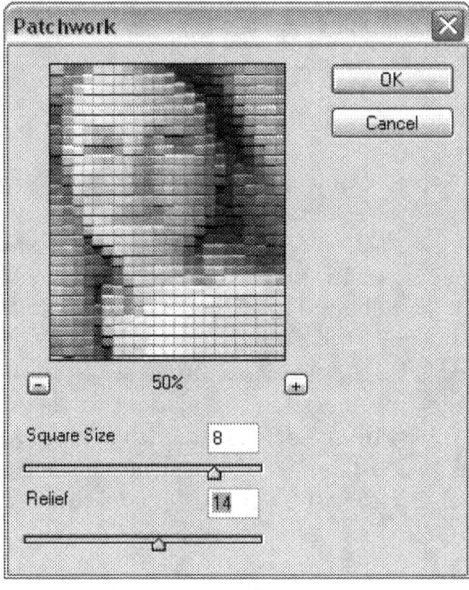

Stained Glass

The Stained Glass filter repaints the image with irregular polygon cells that are filled with the average color of the pixels in that cell. The cells are outlined with the foreground color. The filter simulates the effect of a light shining through glass panes when you adjust the Light Intensity slider (1–10) control higher in the dialog box. This creates a gradient brightness effect from the center out. Use the Cell Size slider (2–50) to increase the cell area. The Border Thickness slider (1–20) increases the thickness of the outline around each cell. This filter does not create a very believable stained glass effect, but it is a nice effect for simple illustrations.

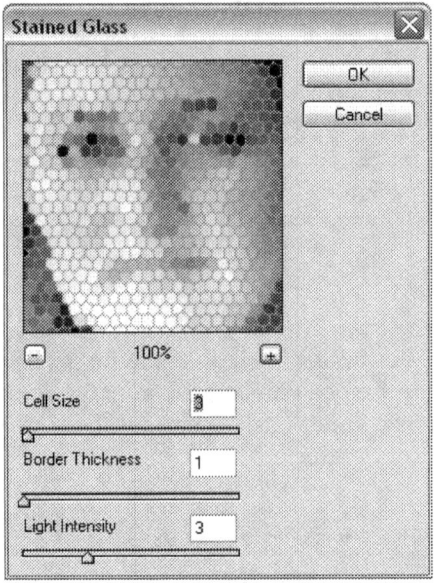

Texturizer

The Texturizer filter offers a level of user control that makes it a versatile tool. You may already recognize this interface because it is integrated into many other filters that use texture as part of their scheme. This filter uses luminance maps, which are Photoshop (PSD) files, to alter the luminance of the original image by overlaying it with the texture map. This will change the lights and darks in the image to align with the texture map.

In the Texturizer dialog box, choose a texture preset from the Texture drop-down menu. Choose Load Texture from the menu to load a texture you have created. You can create a new texture from any Photoshop file that has been saved with no layers. The Scaling slider (50–200 percent) will enlarge or reduce the scale of the texture pattern. The Relief slider (0–50) will increase the depth of the texture. The light source can be changed by selecting a direction from the Light Direction drop-down menu. Checking the Invert check box will invert the texture's luminance. Find out more about creating and applying textures in Chapters 15 and 16.

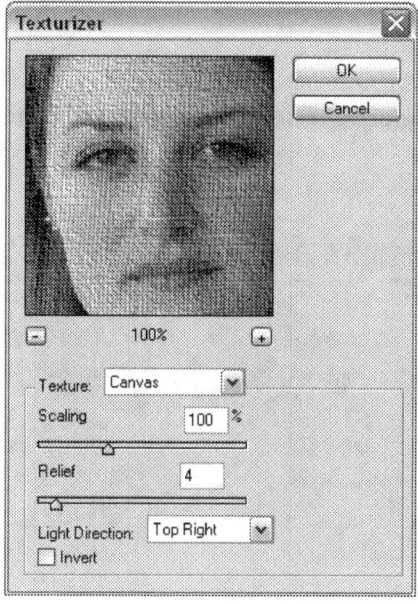

Video Filters

The Video filters contain special routines that deal with captured video frames and with color limitations imposed by displaying images on a television.

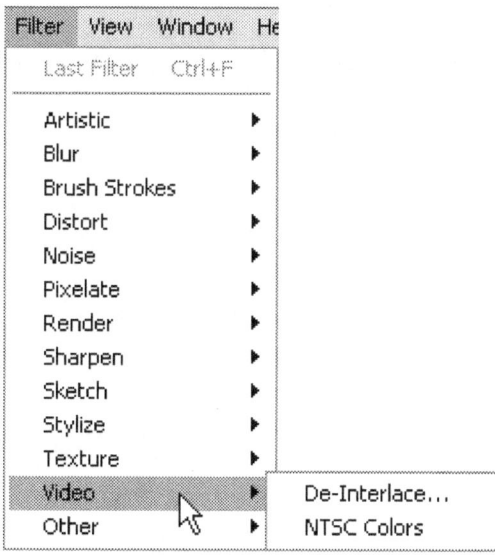

De-Interlace

Standard video frames use a system of interlacing two frames together to reach the display resolution. This means that one frame has even scan lines and the next has odd scan lines. The interlaced frames are not displayed at the exact same time, so when you capture a frame of video, you see a smearing effect caused by the way interlaced frames display. This filter removes one of the interlaced frames, fills the gaps with a duplicate of the remaining scan lines, and then interpolates the colors between those lines. The result is a clearer image.

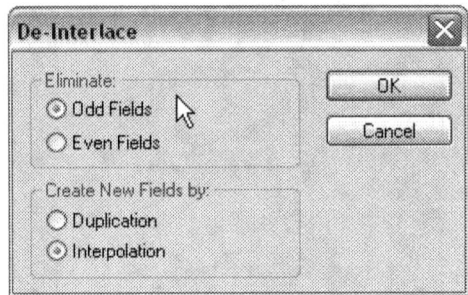

NTSC Colors

The NTSC Colors filter simply restricts the colors in any image to the colors that can be properly displayed on a standard television. This will help prevent bleeding of colors that are too intense for that kind of display.

Other Filters

This is a collection of filters that Adobe has not otherwise categorized.

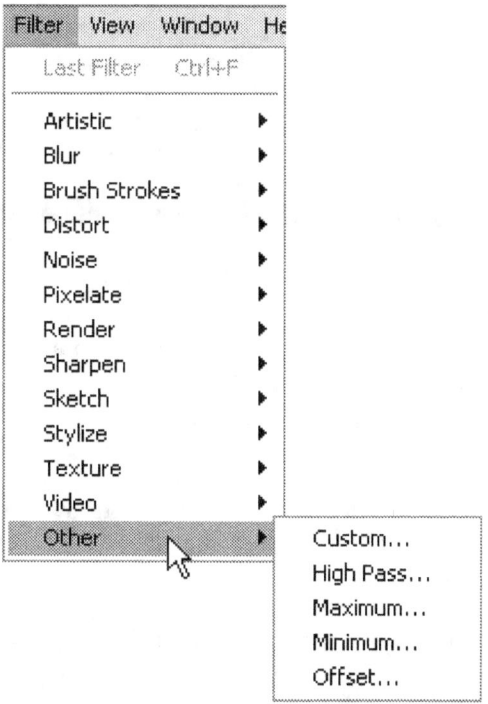

Custom

The Custom filter lets you design your own filter within a limited range. You can create filters that adjust brightness, sharpen, and emboss your image by manipulating numbers in the matrix in the Custom dialog box. The text boxes in the matrix represent pixel positions. The field in the center represents the pixel that is being evaluated. The adjacent fields represent adjacent pixels, 24 in all. The numbers you enter into these fields represent the values by which you want to multiply each pixel's brightness. You can enter positive or negative values: positive numbers will lighten the pixels, and negative values will darken them. The Scale input field will reduce the effect by dividing the Scale factor into the sum of all the pixel brightness values in the matrix to darken the effect. A scale factor of 3, for example, will yield one-third the values, a value of 5 will yield one-fifth, and so on. The Offset value will add to the sum of the brightness values to lighten the effect. Maintain the sum of the matrix values at around 1 to prevent excessive darkening or lightening.

In general, you can achieve these kinds of effects from these manipulations:

- You can get a sharpening effect by placing negative numbers symmetrically around the center pixel.
- A softening or blurring effect can be achieved by placing positive numbers symmetrically around the center pixel.
- Embossing is achieved by placing positive and negative numbers in a symmetrical arrangement around the center pixel.

Thousands of combinations can be derived using this system. You can download many combinations that others have created from the Web to see how they configured them to achieve certain effects.

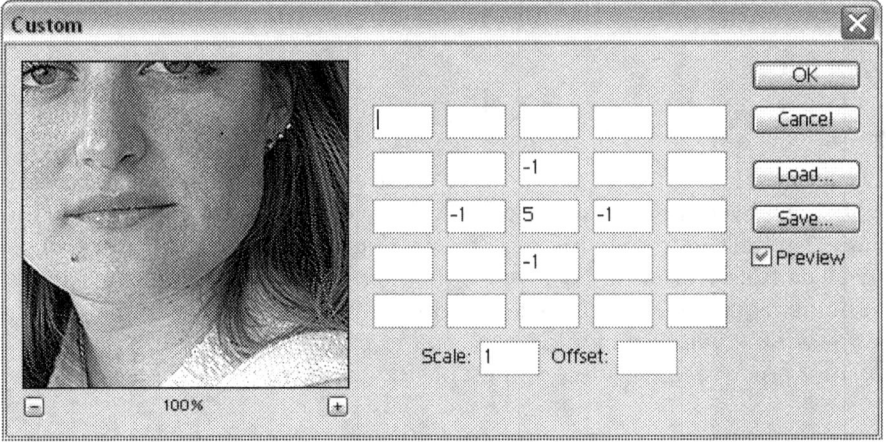

High Pass

The High Pass filter is designed to accentuate areas of high contrast transitions in the image. It also suppresses detailed areas of the image with gradual transitions. In the High Pass dialog box, the Radius slider is used to adjust the amount of area around the high-contrast edges that are not suppressed. Lower values accentuate the edge. This filter has its greatest power when used in conjunction with color channels, so its scope is limited in Photoshop Elements (which doesn't support channels).

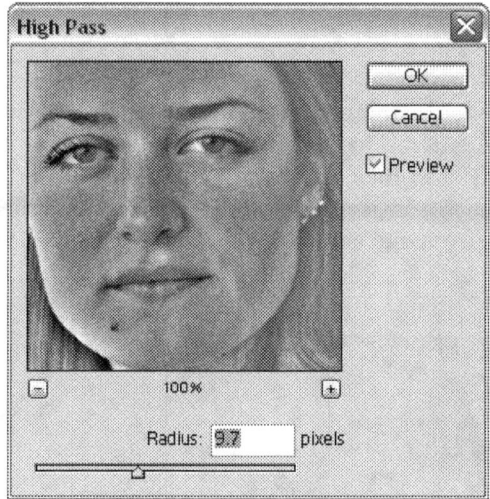

Minimum and Maximum

The Minimum filter is used to reduce the highlight areas and spread out the darker regions. The Maximum filter does the opposite. Both filters measure the highest or lowest color value in the radius around the current pixel and replace the current pixel with that value.

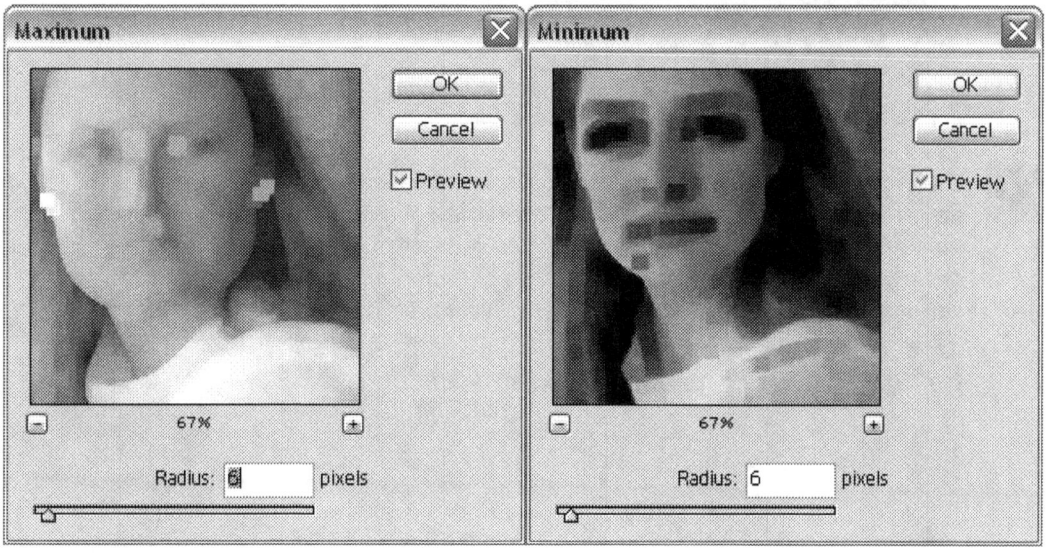

Offset

The Offset filter is used to make seamless tiles. See Chapter 13 for more on creating tiles. The Offset filter shifts the image down, to the right, or down and to the right, depending on the values entered in the Horizontal and Vertical fields of the dialog box. The area revealed by the offset will be Set To Background (filled with transparent background), Repeat Edge Pixels (single line of edge pixels are repeated), or Wrap Around (pixels of offset from the opposite edge are placed in the fill area).

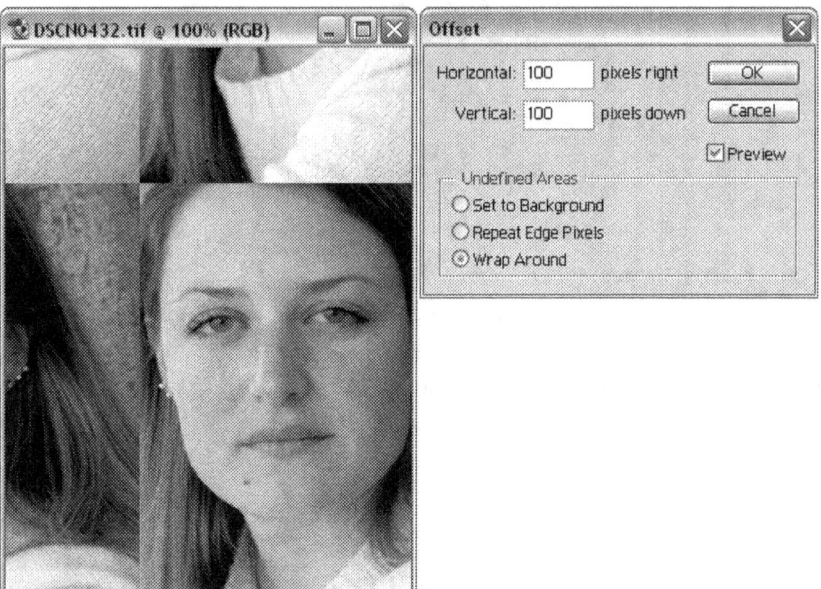

Note   *An often overlooked and useful characteristic of all filters that require a dialog box is that the settings stay the same as they were set the last time you used them. If you rerun the same filter twice, the effect is collective. You can return the filter to its original or default settings by pressing OPT/ALT and clicking the Cancel button (it toggles to the Reset button when you press OPT/ALT). PS: The Zoom filter cannot be reset. Go figure.*

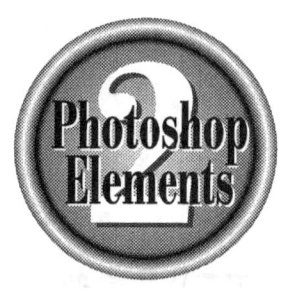

Chapter 15

Creating Special Effects, Text, and Shapes

This chapter isn't going to teach you how to create aliens or to make cars crash through buildings with the driver and passenger smiling as they emerge on the other side. Perhaps we should call Photoshop Elements special effects "visual effects" instead. These processes set a mood, add lighting and texture, make text and buttons stand out from the page, and overcome some of the limitations of today's digital cameras.

We've already covered a number of special effects in the course of explaining how to use certain aspects of Photoshop Elements, such as using layers or making composites. There wasn't room in those chapters to explain all the special effects provided by Photoshop Elements, and there isn't room in this chapter, either. In fact, special effects in Photoshop Elements should be the subject of a book unto itself. What you will learn from this chapter are some special effects that are most frequently used, as well as how to accomplish certain special effects with the click of an icon.

Creating Special Effects with Filters

Special effects can be accomplished by any number of means (and, more important, many combinations of means). Most Photoshop Elements special effects, however, are the result of the use of plug-in programs called *filters*. Hundreds of these filters are available for purchase and download, but Photoshop Elements comes with the same 99 built-in filters that are included with big brother Photoshop. Many of these filters are used to achieve painterly effects, and those won't be discussed here because they are discussed in Chapter 16. The filters discussed here help you create visual and photographic special effects such as texturizing, 3-D warping, lighting effects, and photographic effects (such as lens flare).

Filters and Effects Palettes

The Filters palette and Effects palette work in exactly the same way. However, unlike filters, effects may combine any number of filters and Photoshop Elements commands so that they execute in a single application. We'll discuss the effects that are built into the current version of Photoshop Elements later in this chapter, starting in the section "Adding Effects." The following information pertains to the Filters palette, but almost all of it applies equally to the Effects palette.

You access a filter in one of two ways: you can either choose a command from the Filters menu or double-click an icon in the Filters palette. The Filters palette is the quicker option, and the thumbnails give you a visual approximation of a particular filter's effect on the image. Figure 15-1 shows the Filters palette in both List and Thumbnail modes.

- To choose which category of filters will be seen in the palette, choose the category from the Filters menu.

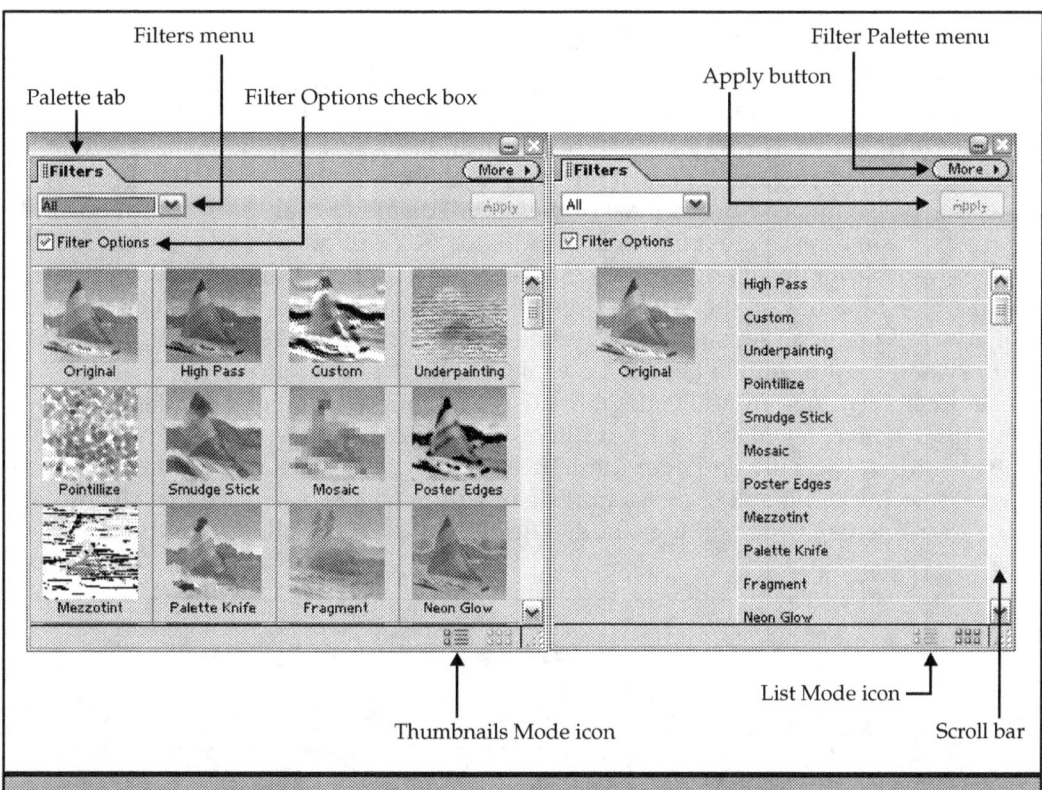

Figure 15-1. *The Filters palette, showing Thumbnail mode on the left and List mode on the right*

THE SPECIAL EFFECTS WORKFLOW

■ To bring up the filter's dialog box, which will allow you to set options before the filter is rendered, click the Filter Options check box to toggle on the check mark. Not all filters have dialog boxes, so those that don't will render immediately. The Find Edges filter is an example of this. In the case that a filter does not have options, the Filter Options check box will be disabled.

■ To switch from Icon to List View mode, click the icon in the lower Options bar that is not grayed out or select it from the Palette menu by clicking the More button.

■ To see more filters in a long list, drag the scroll bar.

■ To apply the filter on a layer or selection, do one of the following:

   ■ Click the Apply button.

   ■ Double-click the filter's name or thumbnail.

   ■ Drag the filter's name or thumbnail onto the image.

Customizing the Look of Filters

It is important to know that you have many options in how you apply the filters to your images. You will notice that there is a check box entitled Filter Options just below the Filter menu in the Filters palette. It might seem like a small item, but it opens up a world of possibilities that are almost limitless. When this is checked, all the filters that have optional settings (which is most of them) will display a dialog box after you apply the filter, as you can see in Figure 15-2. This dialog box will present you with the set of options available for the filter you chose. Adjusting these options can dramatically change the effect the filter has on the image. This is especially true because the adjustments will generally depend on such variables as an individual image's size, brightness, contrast, and most prominent colors (in typical order of importance).

Another very good reason to display the Filter Options is to get a preview window of the filter's effect (available on most filters) because many of the filters can take some time to render, especially on larger files. The preview gives you a more immediate view of what the effect will look like on a portion of your image before it renders so you can make adjustments to your settings more efficiently. You can scroll around the preview

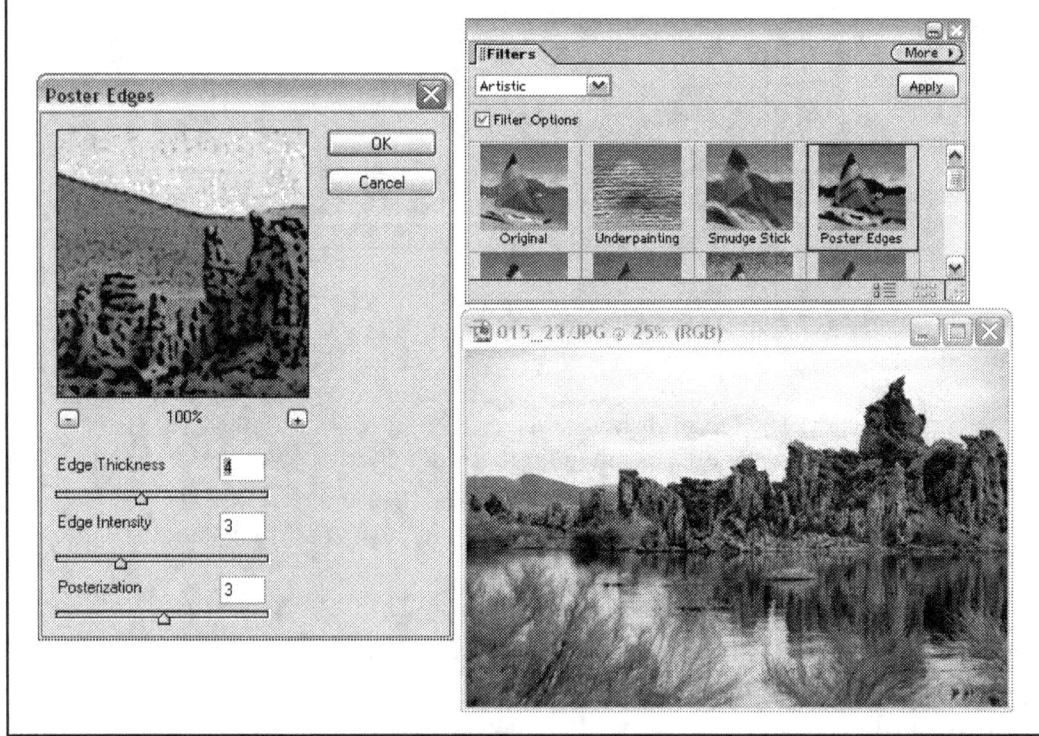

Figure 15-2. *A typical Filter dialog box*

image by dragging the cursor inside the preview window, and zoom in and out by clicking the plus and minus icons just below the preview window.

You also have the choice of turning Filter Options off by unchecking it. When you do this, you can apply the default settings of the filter to multiple images without having the options dialog box appear each time. If you want to use custom settings and be able to modify the look of your filters, you will need to have the Filter Options checked.

Lighting

The Lighting Effects filter allows you to aim any of three types of light sources (spotlight, omni, and directional) at the surface of your image and then change the source's apparent intensity. You can use Lighting Effects to make an image look as though it has been hung in a gallery, projected on a wall, or made from an old-fashioned daguerreotype. You can also combine these effects with texture effects to make the effects of texturing even more dramatic.

You'll find Lighting Effects in the Render group of filters. Take a look at Figure 15-3 to get a quick overview of how versatile and powerful the Lighting Effects filter can be.

You can dramatize an image through the use of this one filter in four different ways.

- Lighting a portrait
- Emphasizing geometry
- Lighting a background
- Adding and accentuating textures

If you try these methods on images that are similar to those used here as examples, you'll quickly realize that millions of other possibilities exist.

Lighting a Portrait   We're often forced to shoot portraits on the run. These quick shots are often the only portraits available for use when a person's image is needed for a book cover, resume, or rock-and-roll album. We can darken, blur, and remove the background to make the subject stand out and to make the image look a bit more formal. In Figure 15-4, we removed the background and added some filters and effects to focus more on the woman.

Now we're going to make this portrait much more dramatic by using the Lighting Effects filter to give it a studio lighting appearance. You might want to use this technique on simple still-life photos, too, especially if you don't have an elaborate studio lighting setup. Here's how we fixed up the portrait.

1. After opening the informal portrait, the image was knocked out using the Background Eraser. (Find out more about using the Background Eraser for knockouts in Chapters 5 and 17).

2. Window | Layers was chosen to open the Layers palette (you can also drag the palette from the Palette Well if its tab is there). We needed a new layer to

Drag to change
direction of light

Drag to move
hotspot of light

Style menu

Light Type menu

Light color

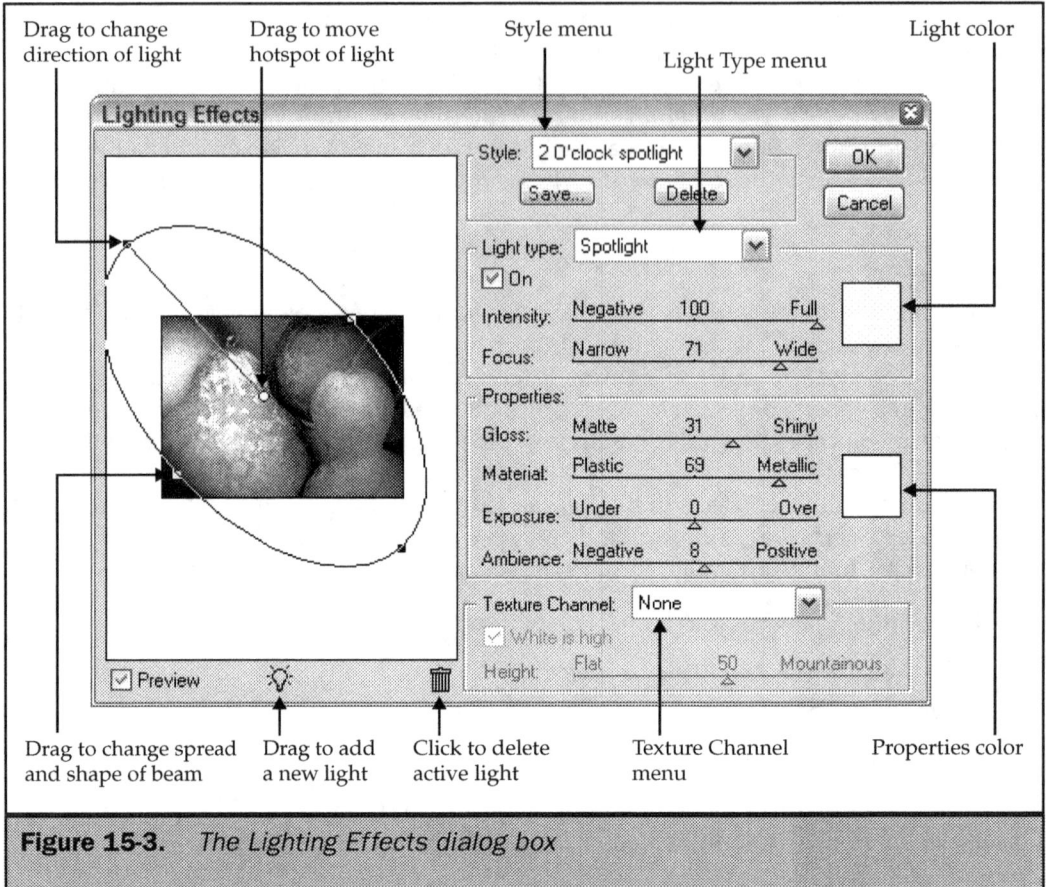

Drag to change spread
and shape of beam

Drag to add
a new light

Click to delete
active light

Texture Channel
menu

Properties color

Figure 15-3. *The Lighting Effects dialog box*

fill for the new background, so we clicked the New Layer icon at the bottom of the palette.

3. Then we chose Edit I Fill. In the Fill dialog box, we then chose a color for the background and clicked OK to create a solid-color background.

4. To light the portrait, it was necessary to de-emphasize the white sweater and emphasize her face. Filter I Render I Lighting Effects was chosen for this purpose. (You can also use the Filters palette by choosing the Render filters from the Palette menu and then choosing Lighting Effects.)

5. In the Lighting Effects dialog box, to make the lighting on the woman's face look a bit more hard-edged and high key, we chose Spotlight from the Light

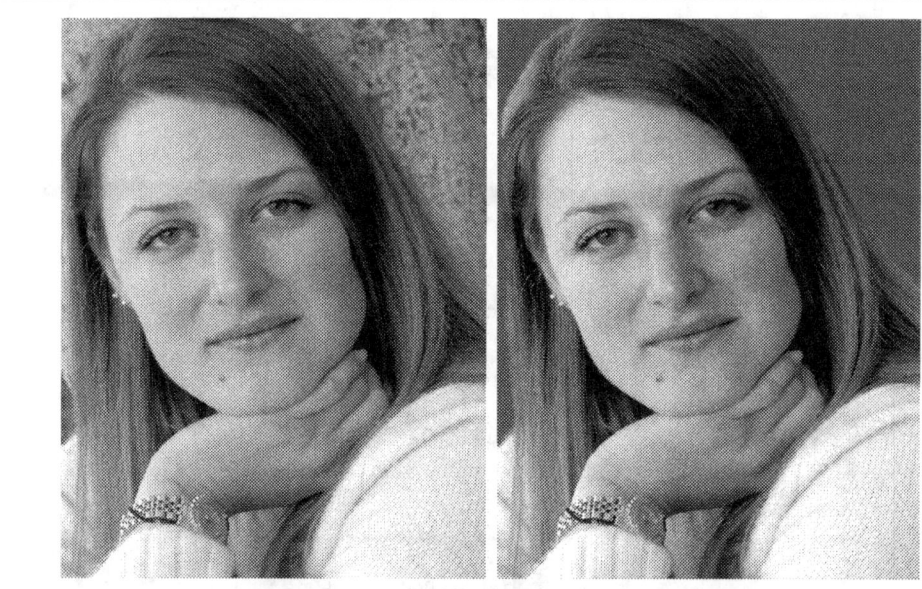

Figure 15-4.   *Before (left) and after (right) the background was removed and some filters and effects were added*

Type menu. In this instance, it wasn't necessary to adjust the sliders, but we reshaped the spread of the light by dragging the side handles and repositioned the light by dragging the hotspot. You can see the exact settings that were used in Figure 15-5.

6. To show a bit more detail in the sweater, we moved up the Ambience slider. To be even more dramatic, we added another light (recall that you can add any number of new lights) by dragging the light bulb icon into the preview window to place a new light.

7. We then added a softer light that still had some direction. We chose Directional from the Light Type menu. (When light is added, the overall brightness in the image is enhanced, so don't be alarmed when this happens for you.) We dragged the directional handle so that shadows were cast in the same direction as the light coming from the spotlight.

8. We adjusted the ambience and exposure levels for the two lights so that they balanced with one another. (You can tell which light will be affected because its marquee and handles are showing. To switch lights, click the hotspot of the light you want to activate.) The final settings are shown in Figure 15-6.

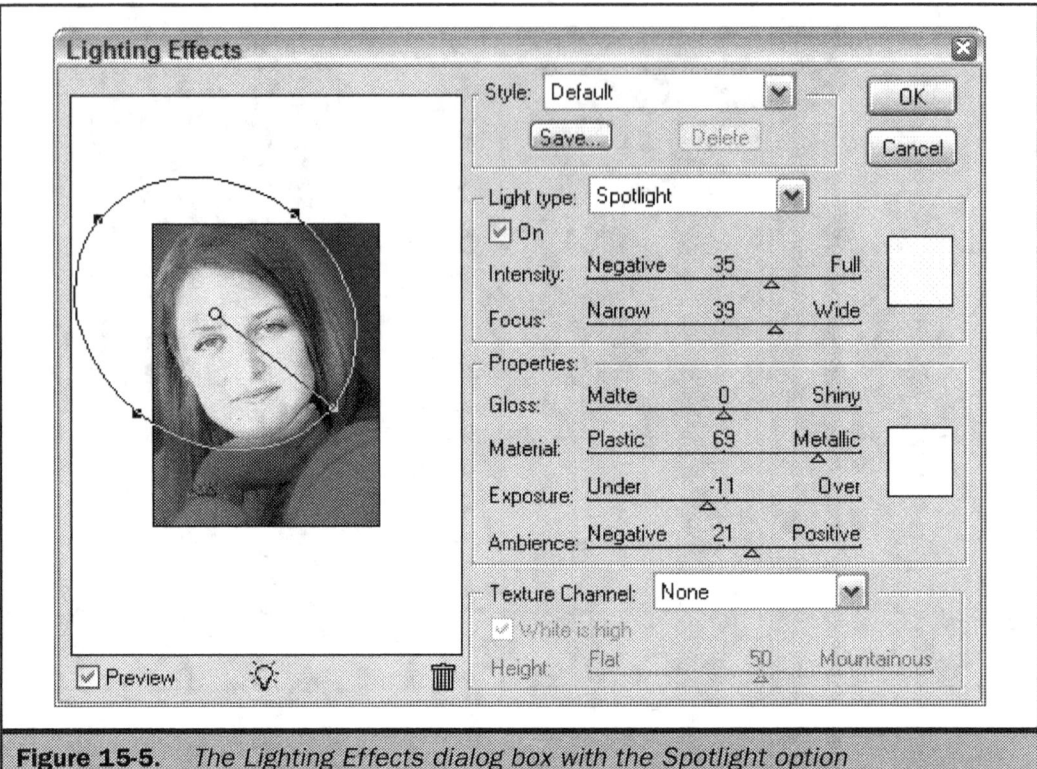

Figure 15-5. *The Lighting Effects dialog box with the Spotlight option*

Emphasizing Geometry   Lighting effects can give depth and shape to geometric forms in a photograph. Adding lighting effects to geometric forms is a bit similar to lighting the portrait in the preceding exercise. See how darkly lit the gourds are on the left in Figure 15-7. Here's how to add this effect:

1. Choose Filter | Render | Lighting Effects. The Lighting Effects dialog box appears. The spotlight is the default light type. For the purposes of this exercise, just leave this setting at the default. Spotlights are usually best for making geometry pop.

2. Adjust the spotlight's marquee so that it vignettes the shapes in the photo and lights them so that your eyes travel to the center of interest.

3. You probably need to adjust at least the Intensity, Focus, and Ambience sliders in the dialog box. As a rule, do what looks good to you. Remember that each

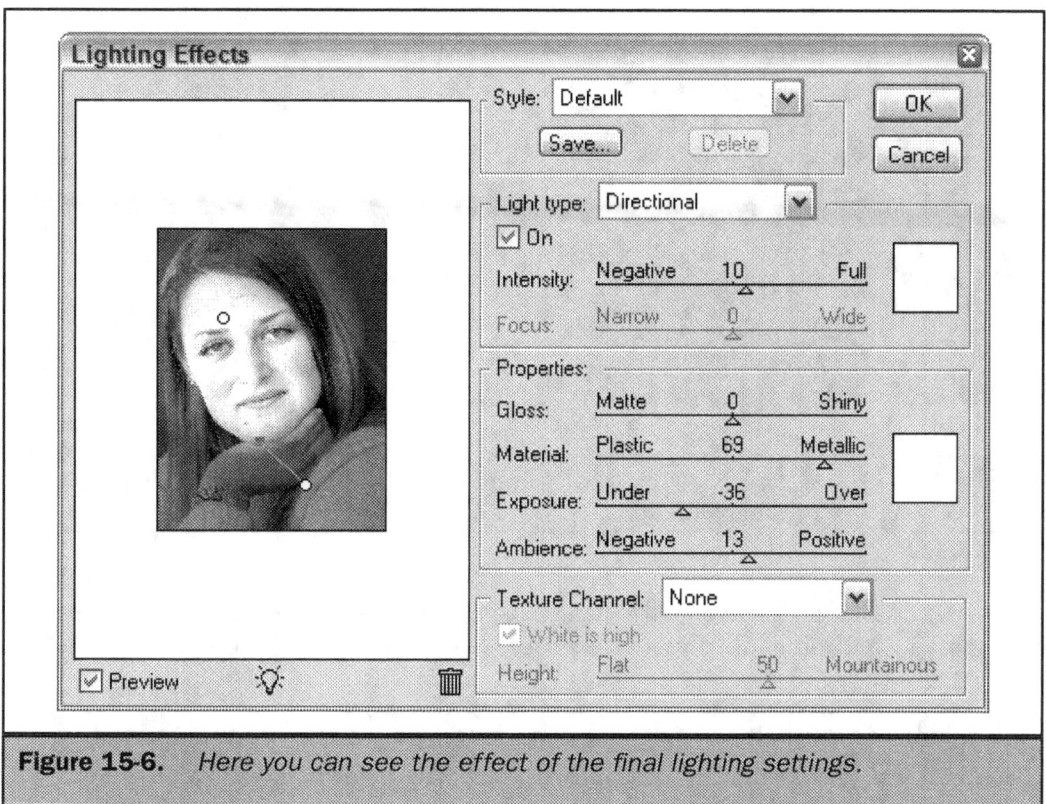

Figure 15-6.   *Here you can see the effect of the final lighting settings.*

new light source will change the overall brightness of the image, and you should rebalance the exposure and color of each light as new lights are added. You can see how our settings and the preview window looked in Figure 15-7 just before we clicked OK.

Adding Background Lighting   You can add a lot of depth and interest to background layers by using the Lighting Effects filter to light a solid color or textured background. You can add even more interest by coloring the lights that are used in the background lighting effect.

Tip   *You can create some backgrounds and light them, and then save them in a folder full of backgrounds to use later. Make sure the file sizes are large enough to cover the highest resolution your camera or scanner is likely to produce. You can always reduce a background to fit a smaller image, but if you try to enlarge it, you'll lose definition.*

THE SPECIAL EFFECTS
WORKFLOW

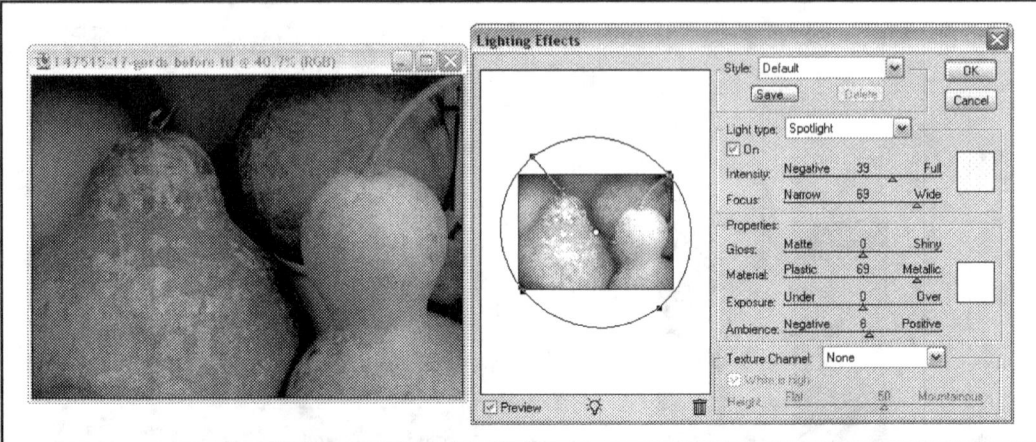

Figure 15-7.   The lighted gourds (right) suddenly convey a much greater feeling of
dimension and focus.

For this example, we'll reopen the file in which we created the front lighting for
the woman's portrait in the previous exercise. Assuming the background was saved,
follow these steps:

1. In the Layers palette, click the background layer's name bar to activate it.

2. Choose Filter | Render | Lighting Effects. The Lighting Effects dialog box
   appears.

3. From the Style menu, choose Circle Of Light. Four lights, each a different
   color, appear automatically. Drag the hotspot of each light into position and
   experiment with the options sliders for each. Figure 15-8 shows the placement
   of the lights.

4. When you've finished experimenting with the settings and want to see the results,
   click OK. You can see the final result of adding the lights to the background in
   Figure 15-9.

Adding Texture with Lighting   The Lighting Effects filter lets you use the image
itself as a texture. Let's take a brief look at how you can use this filter to texturize a
subject. The photo in Figure 15-10 was texturized with the Lighting Effects filter using
the following steps:

1. Open the image you want to texturize.

2. In the Filters palette, make sure the Filter Options check box is toggled on.
   From the Filter Palette menu, choose Render, and then double-click Lighting
   Effects. The Lighting Effects dialog box appears, as you can see in Figure 15-10.

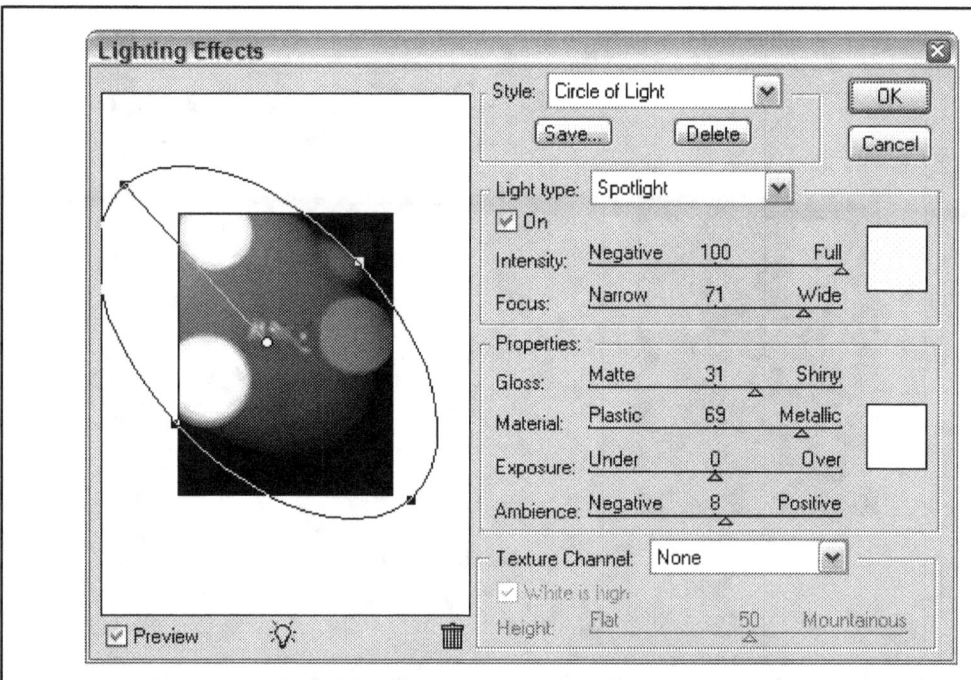

Figure 15-8. *Here you can see the position of the three different lights that will be placed in the background.*

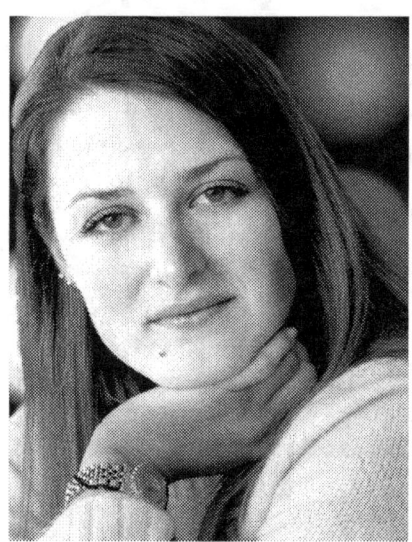

Figure 15-9. *Placing the lights in the background adds depth to the scene.*

THE SPECIAL EFFECTS WORKFLOW

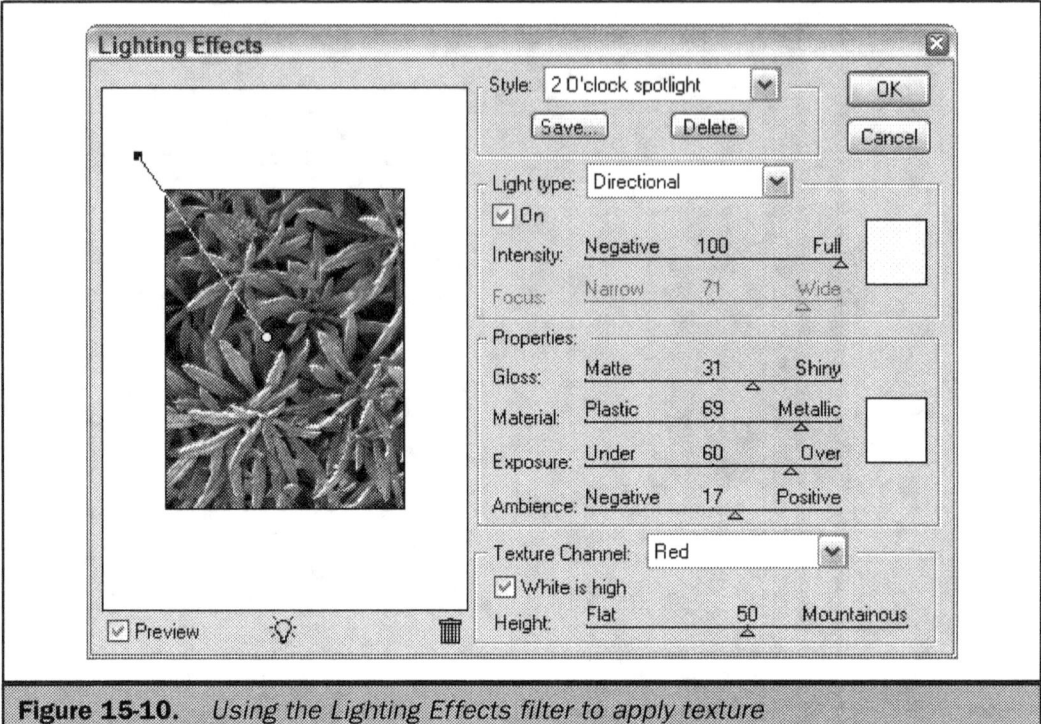

Figure 15-10. *Using the Lighting Effects filter to apply texture*

3. Near the bottom of the dialog box, you will see the Texture Channel menu. Because a preview window appears in this dialog box, you can see the effect that the channel you choose produces. Texture mapping from an image works on contrast and brightness. Try each of the color channels to see which produces the effect closest to the one you want. For the image in the leaves illustration, we chose the red channel. The red channel will usually produce the most dramatic effect because it is usually the highest contrast channel, but this is not an absolute rule.

4. In the next section, you will learn quite a bit about how to produce a variety of lighting effects, and these are almost always more dramatic on a texturized image. For now, choose Directional from the Light Type menu and make sure the On box is checked.

5. You might want to experiment with the other lighting settings. However, you'll probably find this image quite dark. Drag the Exposure slider to the right to lighten the image.

6. Because we are working with a directional lighting source, the highlights become quite bright, whereas the leaves (shadow areas) are still too dark. One way to solve this problem is to add another light source. Drag the light bulb icon from below the preview window into the preview window until its hotspot circle is in the center of the window. From the Light Type menu, choose Omni. Adjust the exposure and ambiance to suit your tastes. You can also adjust the spread of the light by dragging one of the handles in the outside circle of the light.

7. You're encouraged to experiment with all the settings. When you're ready to apply the results, click OK. You can see the effect of this procedure in Figure 15-11.

Blurring for Effect

Several blur filters, particularly the Motion Blur and Radial Blur filters, are useful for creating special effects.

Motion Blur   The Motion Blur filter is useful for making the foreground object look as though its been frozen in motion by panning the camera in parallel with a slow shutter speed, as you can see in Figure 15-12.

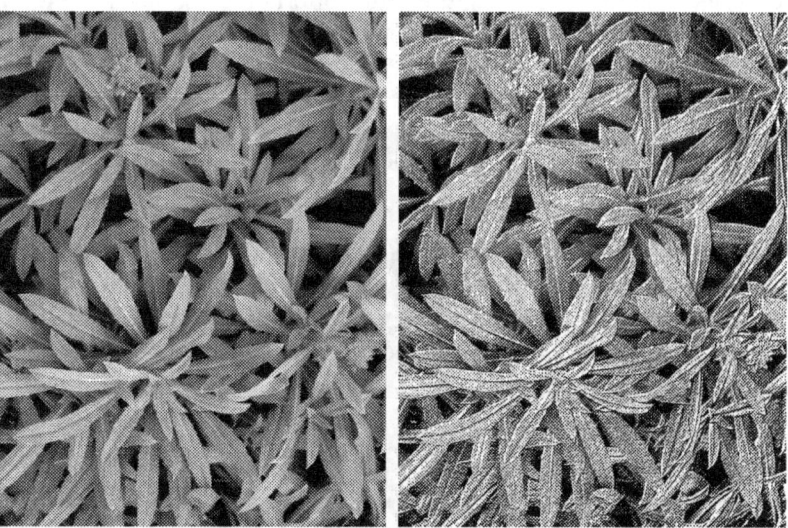

Figure 15-11.   *Before (left) and after (right) applying a texture with lighting effects*

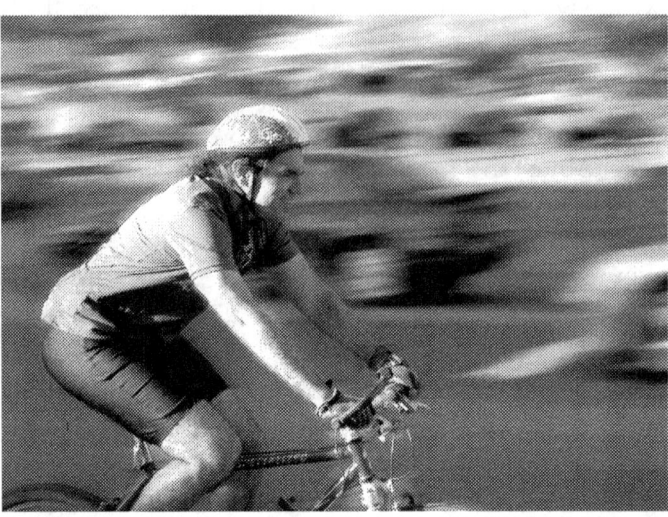

Figure 15-12.   *The background was blurred with the Motion filter to make it look as though the camera followed the motion of the bicyclist.*

The filter is also useful for making the foreground object look as though it were moving too fast to cause it to freeze, as you can see in Figure 15-13.

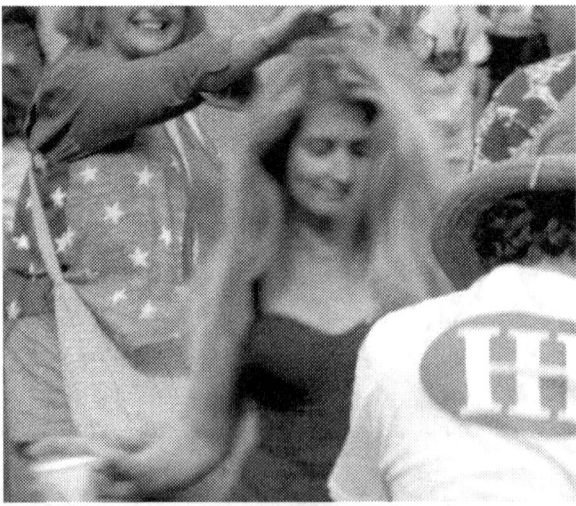

Figure 15-13.   *The dancer is isolated and blurred to give the appearance of rapid movement.*

Whether you use motion blur on a whole layer or on the contents of a selection, you take the same steps:

1. Make sure that you have either selected the area you want to blur, or, if you are blurring a whole layer, that it's that layer that has been activated in the layer's palette. (To activate a layer, choose Window | Layer to reveal the layer's palette, or drag it out of the Palette Well if its tab is there.) Then click the name bar of the layer you want to activate.

2. Either choose Filter | Blur | Motion Blur, or from the Filters palette choose Blur from the Filter Type menu. Then click the Filter Options check box to toggle it on, and choose the Motion Blur thumbnail. Click Apply, or drag the Motion Blur thumbnail onto the image. The Motion Blur dialog box appears (see Figure 15-14).

3. The effect of a motion blur doesn't preview in the image itself, so you can use the preview window in the dialog box. By default, the preview window is zoomed to 100 percent, so it's a good idea to drag the image around until the most important part of the image shows in the window.

4. Set the direction of the motion blur, either by entering an angle in the Angle field or by dragging the line that crosses the Angle icon just to the right of the field.

5. Finally, drag the Distance slider so that it shows the number of pixels across which the blur should occur.

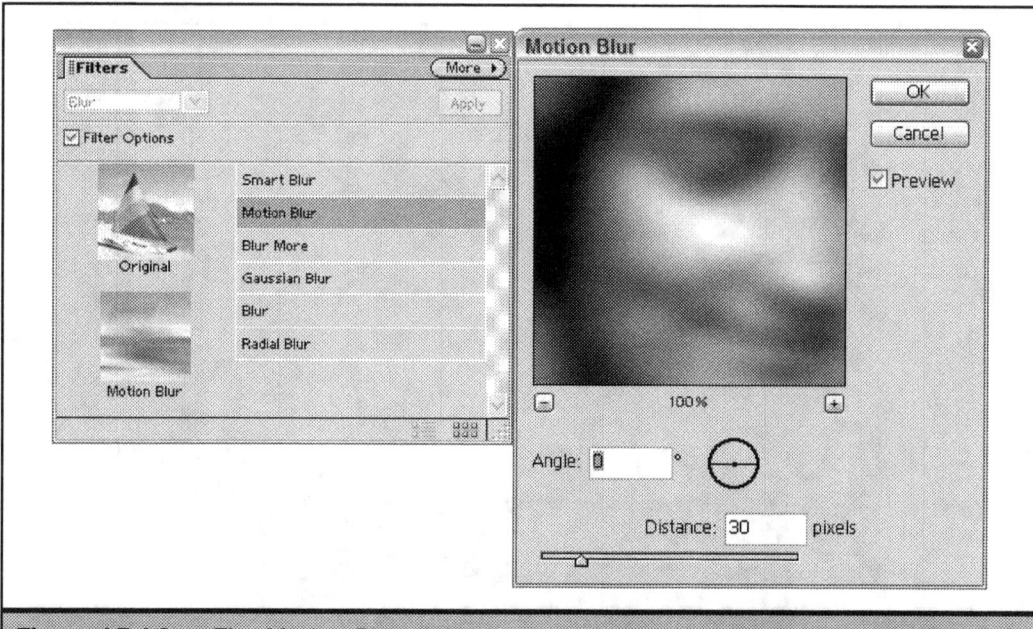

Figure 15-14.   *The Motion Blur dialog box*

6. When you think you like the effect, click OK. If you have misjudged the blur distance or the angle of the blur, press CMD/CTRL+Z to undo, and then change the settings and reapply the filter.

Radial Blur A radial blur creates blurs in two kinds of circles: spinning and zooming. Here's an example of a couple of spinning motion blurs—both on the same motionless model helicopter. You can see one radial blur on the main rotor and another on the tail rotors in Figure 15-15.

Zooming is an effect that makes a shot look as though it was taken at a slow shutter speed while the lens was being zoomed. It is a dynamic technique for forcing the viewer to focus on one particular point in the image. In Figure 15-16, a spooky eye image was created using a radial blur in Zoom mode.

Applying a radial blur isn't much different whether you're spinning or zooming. Here's how an image like the spooky eye is created:

1. Open an image that has a central point on which you want the viewer's attention to focus.

2. Make a loose selection around that point. The Elliptical Marquee tool is usually best for this, but feel free to experiment with other tools and methods.

3. Feather the selection about one-quarter the number of pixels of the diameter of the selection. Choose Select | Feather, and then enter the number of pixels in the Feather Selection dialog box's Feather Radius field. Then click OK.

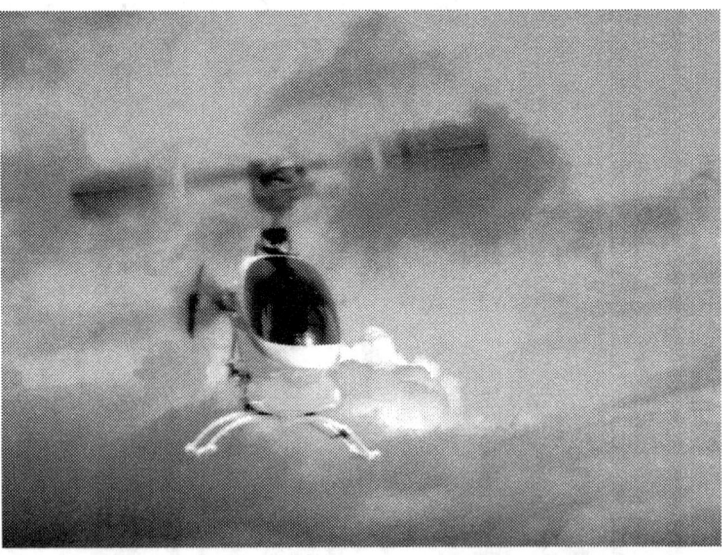

Figure 15-15. *The radial blur applied to the rotors adds a motion dynamic to this shot.*

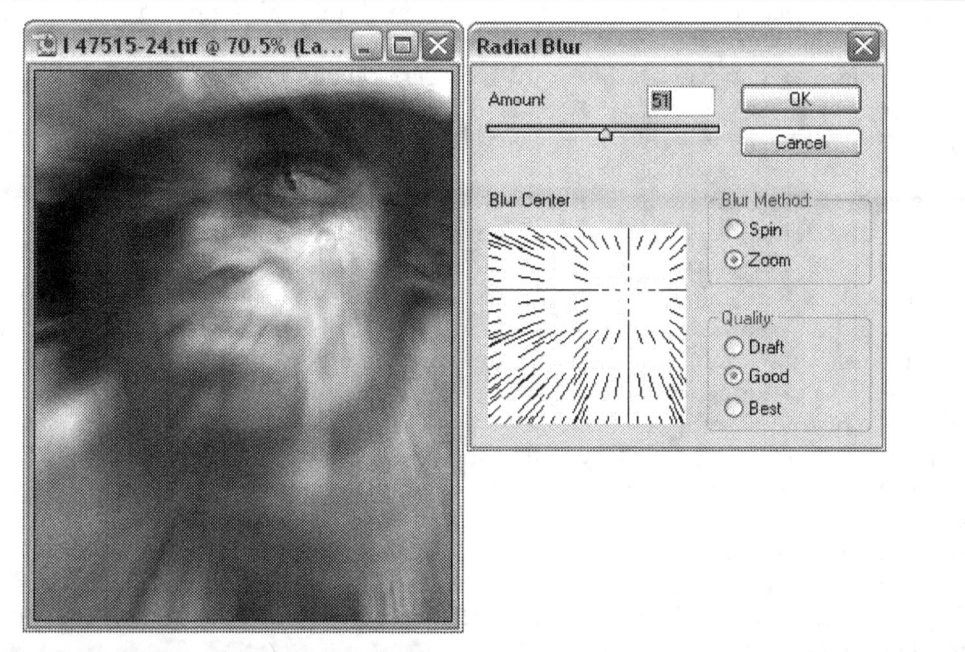

Figure 15-16.   *This already spooky photograph takes on a new dimension when you add this radial blur that draws you to his eye.*

4. Choose Select | Inverse (SHIFT+CMD/CTRL+I). The selected area will become the area *outside* the original selection.

5. Choose Filter | Blur | Radial Blur. The Radial Blur dialog box appears (refer to Figure 15-16).

6. Click the Zoom radio button under Blur Method, and drag the Amount slider to indicate the amount of blurring you want to see in the image.

7. Note that the Radial Blur dialog box neither previews the effect in a window nor sports a preview window of its own. That is because radial blurs take quite a bit of recalculation and rendering of the image, and taking the time to preview each adjustment could make you crazy with waiting. You can use the Blur Center window, however, by dragging the center of the blur to the approximate image coordinates where you want the blur to be centered. Because there is no exact method for placing the center, you'll have to use the trial-and-error method (that is, apply the filter and press CMD/CTRL+Z if you don't like the result).

Distorting

Several filters that are useful for creating special effects live on a submenu under the Distort command: Displace, Spherize, and Polar Coordinates. A variety of waves and ripples also appear here. Although you can be much more flexible and inventive with your image distortions by working within the Liquify filter, these distortion filters can come in handy when you need to apply a single effect with as little fuss as possible.

Displace   The Displace filter is so called because it is used to push pixels in certain directions and to a certain degree according to the settings you use. The result can look like anything from a finger painting to a flag blowing in the breeze. If you get really proficient with the Displace filter, you can make just about any two-dimensional image look as though it's wrapped around any three-dimensional object.

The results of this filter are really difficult to visualize—at least without a lot of practice or the mind of a mathematical genius—before you try the filter on a combination of two images. That's right, you need two images: the image to which you want to apply the effect and the one that is the *displacement map*. A displacement map is an image whose levels of brightness tell the program how to interact with the pixels in the displaced image. The result of using a Displace filter is shown in Figure 15-17. As 256 levels of brightness are used in either a true-color or grayscale image, your displacement map will move the pixels in one direction if they are darker than middle gray, or level 128, or in the other direction if they are lighter than middle gray. For more on displacement mapping, see Chapter 14. In Figure 15-17, you can see the original image, the displacement map, and the result when both horizontal and vertical displacement are set at 100 percent.

Spherize   The Spherize filter also has dual personalities: positive and negative (or as some like to say, "innies and outies"). In other words, you can use this filter to make either a bubble or the inside of a bowl. To illustrate, look at the checkerboard pattern

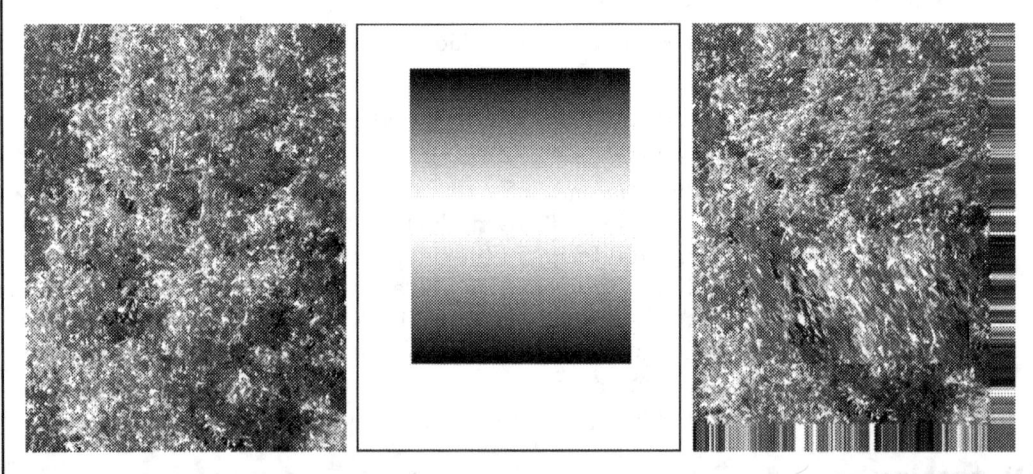

Figure 15-17.   *The original image, the displacement map, and the result of using the Displace filter*

on which we used the Spherize filter to make both a globe (left) and a bowl (right) in Figure 15-18.

Most of the time, you won't want to use this filter without first selecting the area you want to spherize. When you make your selection, save it. You might want to use other images, gradients, or patterns and superimpose them on your spherized area with blending modes. This can enhance three dimensionality, provide texture, or create reflections. The following exercises show you how to do these things while making a bubble.

1. Open the image you want to spherize.

2. Choose the Elliptical Marquee tool. In the window of the image you just opened, press SHIFT to constrain the marquee to a circle and drag diagonally until the circle covers the portion of the image you want to spherize. If it's not an exact match, place the Elliptical Marquee cursor in the interior of the selection and drag to move the selection until it's correctly positioned. For this exercise, we filled the circle with a checkerboard pattern using the Edit | Fill command so you can easily see the distortion.

3. Save the selection by choosing Select | Save Selection so that you can recall it if you accidentally drop it. Choose a unique name for the saved selection and click OK. The next several steps assume that the selection has not been dropped.

4. Choose Filter | Distort | Spherize. The Spherize dialog box appears, as shown in Figure 15-19.

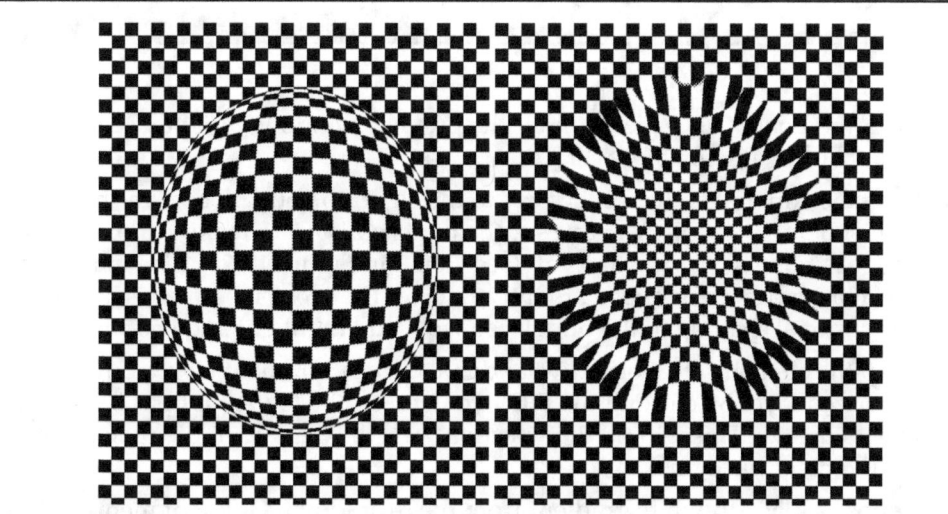

Figure 15-18.   *The bow-out and bow-in effect of the Spherize filter*

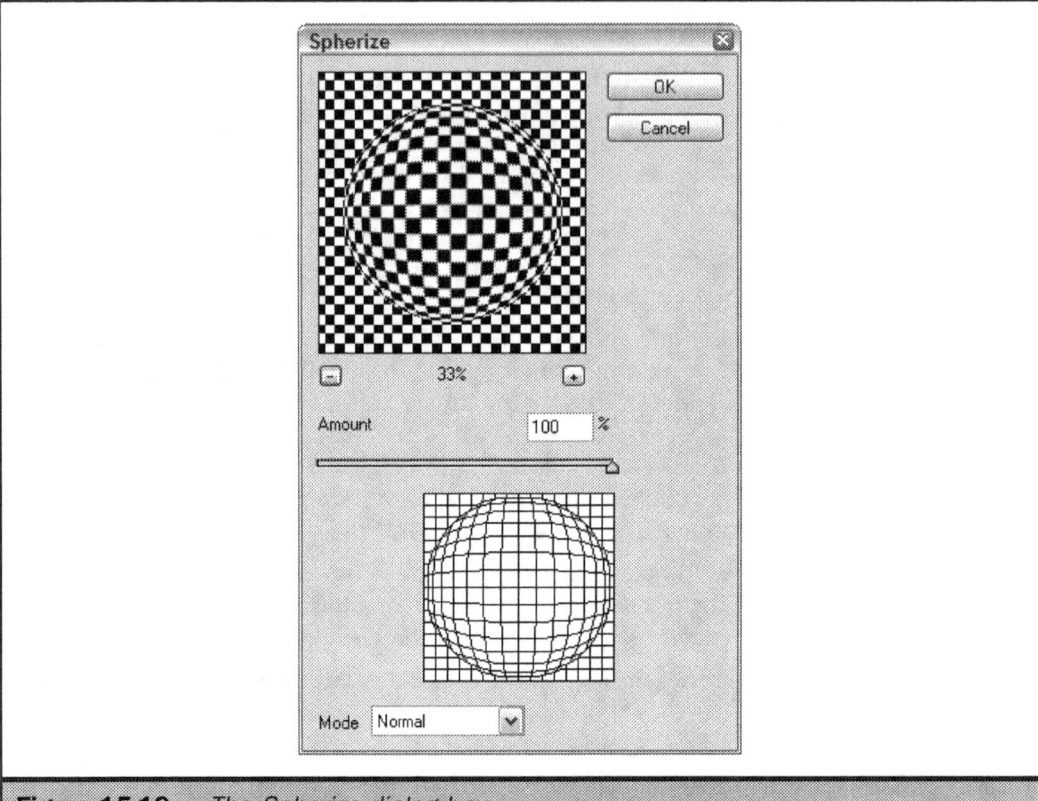

Figure 15-19.   *The Spherize dialog box*

5. Click the Zoom Out (–) icon under the preview window until you see the entire area that the sphere will cover.

6. Drag the Amount slider all the way to the right, so you will be creating a perfect hemisphere. Click OK. You can see the pattern distort to make it look as if the image is bowing out toward you (see step 2 in Figure 15-20). The image now resembles a pattern wrapped around a bubble. The problem is, there's no apparent dimensional shading to the bubble, so we'll add highlight and shadows.

7. Keep the circular selection active and make a new gradient layer above the spherized layer by clicking the Fill layer icon on the lower Options bar of the Layers palette. This will fill the selection with the default gradient and open the Gradient dialog box.

8. Choose a black-to-white gradient from the drop-down Gradient menu. Set the type to Radial. You want the gradient to be lighter toward the middle, so if it is

not, check Reverse to correct it. Use the Scale option if you want to spread the light and reduce the shadow area.

9. The next step is to put the highlight in a more natural position. Place the cursor within the light part of the gradient inside the selection, and drag it up and to the left to position, as you see in step 3 of Figure 15-20.

10. Now let's put this gradient and the patterned bubble together for the final effect. With the gradient layer active, choose the Hardlight blending mode to superimpose the gradient on the pattern. Adjust the opacity of the gradient layer until it looks how you want it. Now the patterned bubble takes on a believable three-dimensional appearance, as seen in step 4 of Figure 15-20. If you want to put the crowning touch on, place a lens flare on the highlight area to make it look like a shiny object.

Now you can take this concept one step further by using a Lens Flare and a reflected image that has also been Spherized. You can see the result of this in Figure 15-21. You

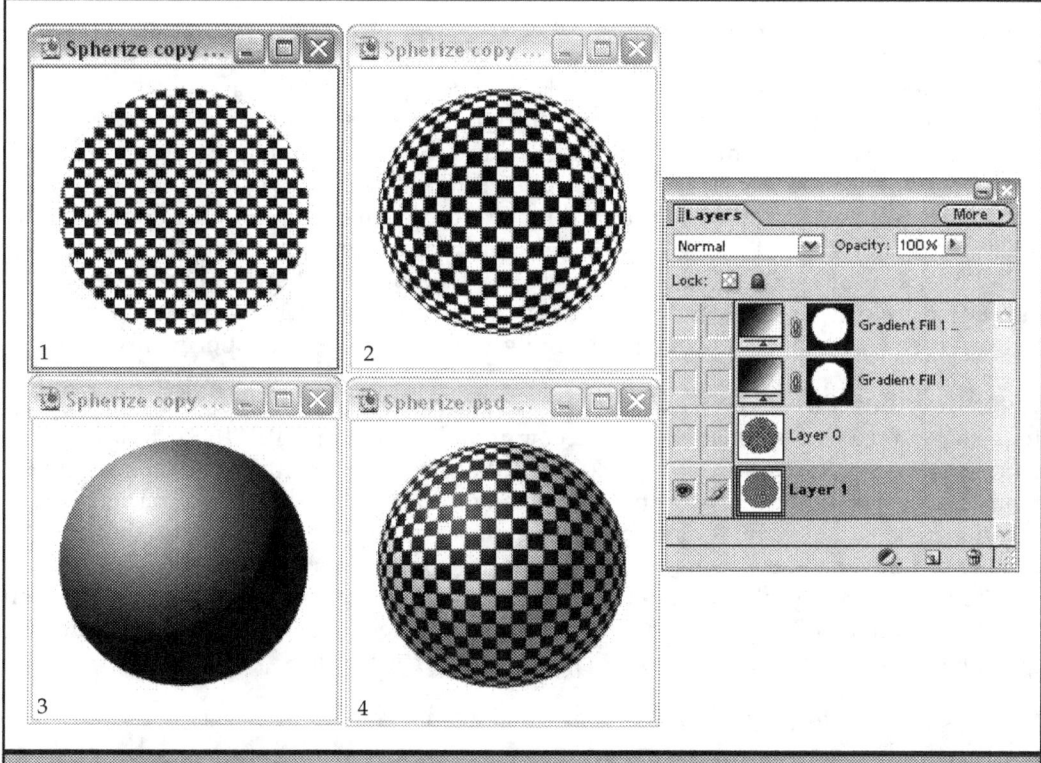

Figure 15-20. *(1) The marquee filled with pattern, (2) the Spherize filter applied, (3) the gradient shading layer, and (4) shading applied with blending mode*

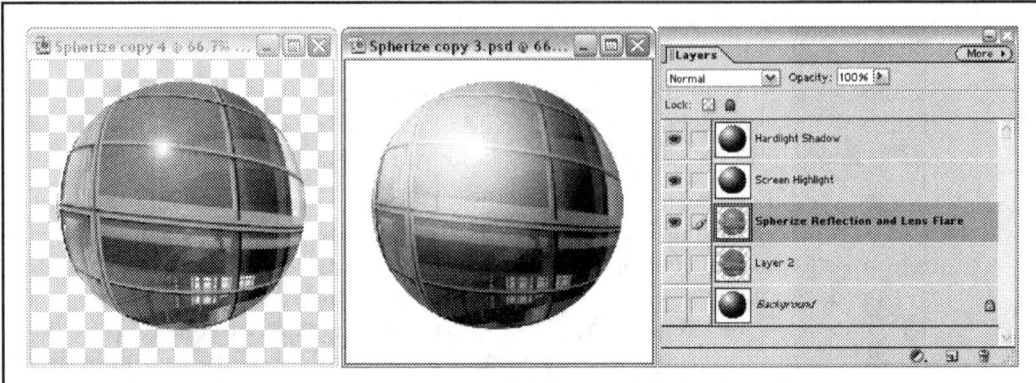

Figure 15-21.   *The Spherized reflected image and lens flare (left) combined with the blended gradient on the right to produce a mirrored surface ball*

can also flatten all the layers and then adjust the Opacity so it becomes partially transparent. This will give the appearance of a glass ball with reflections when you place it over a background.

Believe it or not, you have just opened a world of possibilities. That one little bubble (or Christmas tree ornament, push-pin top, or wide-angle rear-view mirror— get the idea?) can have a million variations within the routine you just learned. You can also use it to produce glass or plastic push buttons like the ones in Mac OS X. You can put the sphere through the Liquify filter (see the "Full Court Liquification" section, later in this chapter) and change its shape to that of a million other objects. You can then knock out and scale these objects (especially bubbles) so that you can use them as recurring elements in a composite photograph or as the background for interactive buttons on a web site. That ought to be enough to get you to start experimenting.

Polar Coordinates   Polar Coordinates is another of the Distort filters that can be used to produce two different effects: Rectangular To Polar or Polar To Rectangular. To be honest, we can't imagine why you'd use either effect. You could create images that made people feel either claustrophobic (Rectangular To Polar) or as though they were coming apart at the seams (Polar To Rectangular). Figure 15-22 shows you what happens to the image on the left when you use the Polar Coordinates filter.

Here's how you go about rendering to polar coordinates. The only difference between whether you render Rectangular To Polar or Polar To Rectangular is which radio button you click, so we'll just describe how to get one of the two results:

1. Open the image you want to make look really weird.

2. Choose Filter | Distort | Polar Coordinates. The Polar Coordinates dialog box opens, as you can see in Figure 15-23.

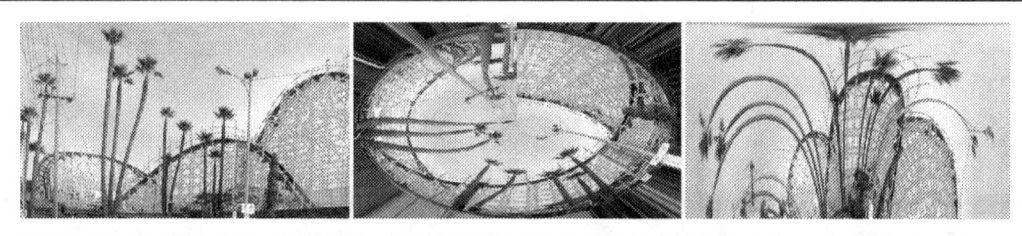

Figure 15-22.   *The original image (left), rendered Rectangular To Polar (middle), and Polar To Rectangular (right)*

3. The preview window will instantly display the result. Click the Zoom Out (–) button until you can see the entire image (or selection) that you want to distort.

4. Click the radio button for the variation button you want, and then click OK. The image will render.

Adding Surface Distortions

The filters discussed here are a part of the set of filters under the Distort filter category and can be found in the Filter menu or Filters palette. They are grouped here because

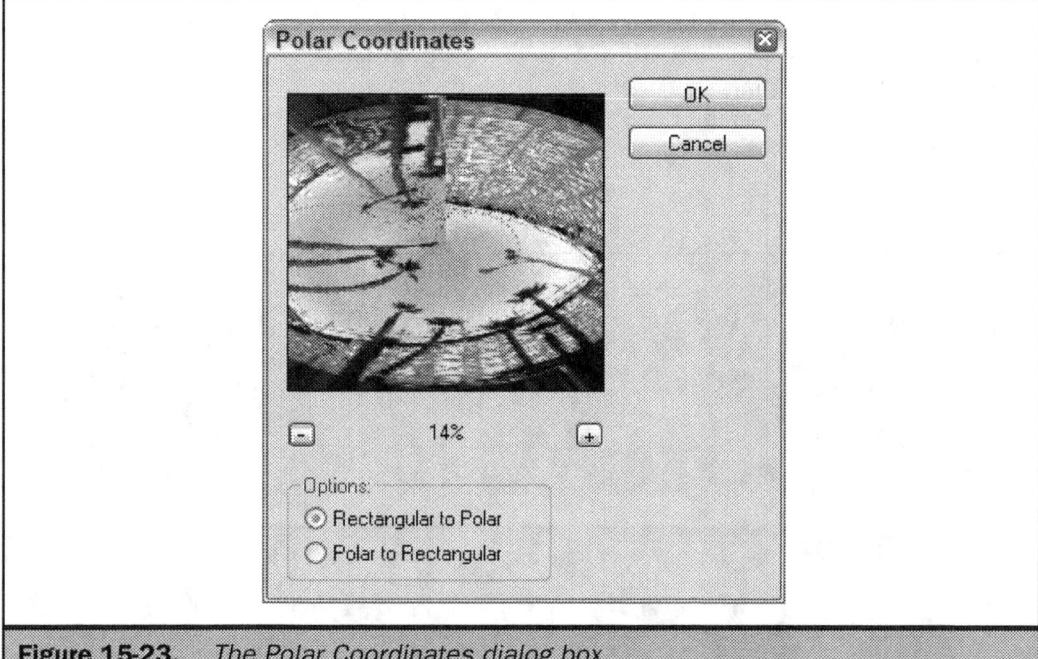

Figure 15-23.   *The Polar Coordinates dialog box*

they all deal with various ripple effects that we mentioned at the beginning of the preceding "Distorting" section. They create surface distortions that can simulate the effect of waves, puddles, shower glass, and so forth.

Zigzag   The Zigzag filter produces various types of circular ripples: pond ripples, ripples that move out from the center, and ripples that move around the center (like water going down a drain). In Figure 15-24, you see all three of these variations on the same image.

Twirl   The Twirl filter should probably be called the Twist filter. It twists the image around the center, as if it were projected on water going down the drain. You can use it to create a special illustrative effect that looks like "it's all going down the drain." You can see this effect, as well as the Twirl dialog box and its options, in Figure 15-25.

Using the Twirl filter is about as easy as it gets. Once your image is loaded, do this:

1. Drag in the preview window to center the twist on the area that you want to be the "drain hole."

2. Drag the Angle slider to the right to twist in a clockwise direction or to the left to twist in a counterclockwise direction. The farther you drag the slider, the more "ripples" appear and the more severe the twist.

3. When you like the look of what you see in the preview window, click OK.

Shear   The Shear filter makes things lean or wiggle. It's a great way to create a dreamscape or sine-wave distortion. You can create this effect only in a vertical orientation; but if you plan ahead a bit, you can always rotate your image, run the filter, and then rotate it back. Seeing the Shear dialog box and the original image should be the best way to get the idea, as you can see in Figure 15-26.

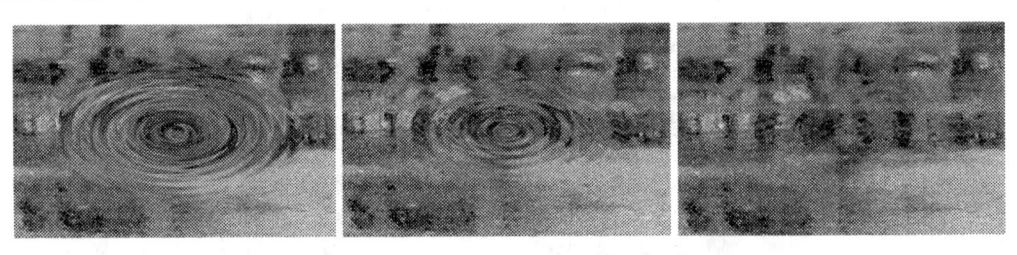

Figure 15-24.   *Here are three types of the Zigzag filter simulations demonstrating different ripple patterns in liquids: pond ripples (left), ripples emanating from the center (middle), and ripples moving around the center (right).*

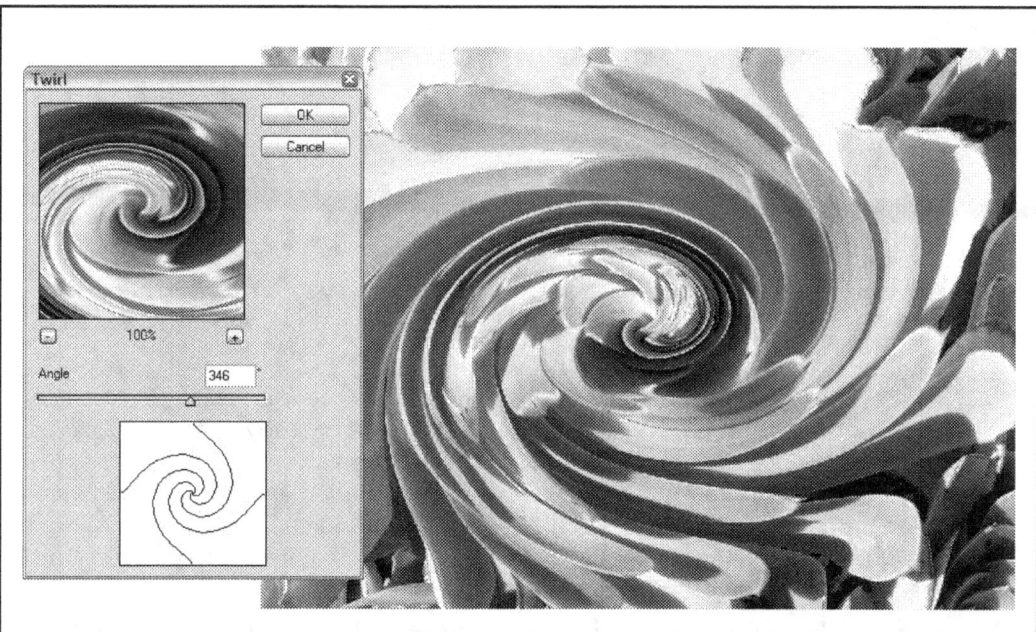

Figure 15-25. *The Twirl filter dialog box—you can clearly see the power vortex effect created by this filter.*

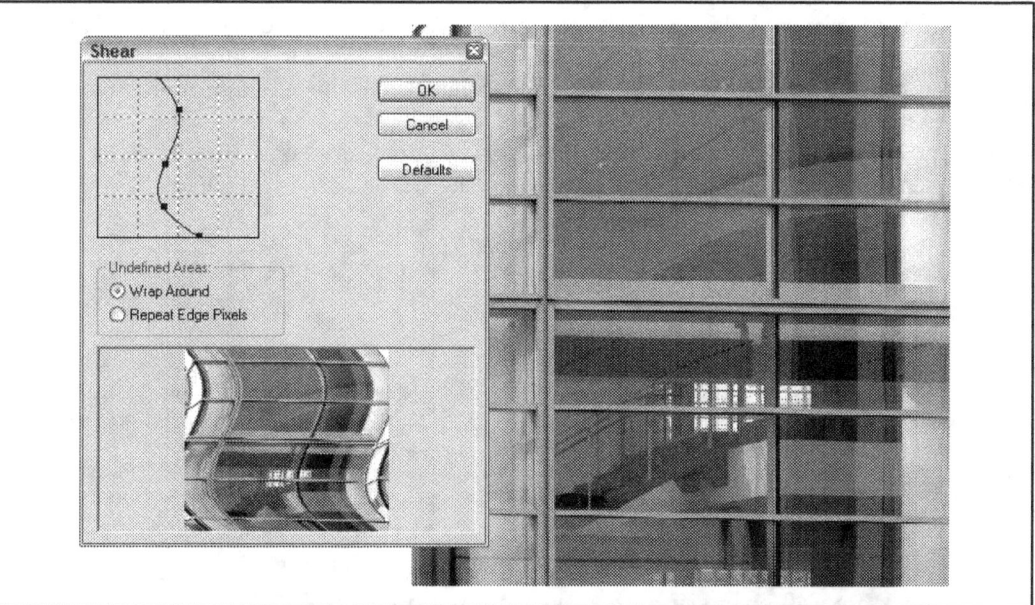

Figure 15-26. *The Shear filter was used to warp this window into a nice undulation.*

Here's how you go about using the Shear filter after choosing an image that you want to make lean or undulate vertically:

1. To slant the image, drag the curve point at the top of the grid window in the direction you want the picture to lean.

2. If you like, you can make the picture lean even more drastically by moving the bottom curve point in the opposite direction from the center grid line. The preview window always shows you how far you've gone.

3. You can create a sine-wave distortion by clicking any point on the line to place a curve point. Then drag the curve point in the direction you want the wave to move.

4. When you distort the image, it pulls away from its outer borders. Rather than leave that space empty, Photoshop Elements lets you choose whether you want to have the pixels you pushed out on one side wrap around to the other side or whether you want to repeat the edge pixels you pulled away until they extend to the border. (It would be good if Adobe also let you choose whether you'd rather just fill with black, white, or the background color—but that's for some version farther down the road.)

5. When you've finished leaning and curving, straighten out before you hit the shoulder and roll the car…oops. Sorry. That's another experience. Just click OK.

Glass   Of course, if the Glass filter were "clear as glass," it would have no effect at all. This filter gives you the choice of having glass blocks (but with no grout, which doesn't exactly ring true), frosted glass, or canvas-textured glass (oh, sure), or you can load any PSD file as a texture pattern. Any seamless tile works well. We find the frosted glass filter most useful and believable. Using your own textures can also produce some surreal surface effects—especially if the image you texture is on a semitransparent layer above another image, and especially if you use blending modes. Daydreaming aside, the "shower door" frosted-glass effect and the Glass filter dialog box are shown in Figure 15-27.

To use the Glass filter:

1. Select the area of your image you wish to turn to glass (unless you want the effect to apply to the entire image layer).

2. Choose Filter | Distort | Glass. The Glass dialog box appears.

3. From the Texture menu, choose the type of glass you'd like to use; or, if you want to use another texture that's already a PDF file, choose Load Texture, and then navigate to the texture file you want to use.

4. Drag the sliders until what you see in the preview window (at 100 percent) is the final effect you want to achieve.

5. If you want to make the highs lows, or vice versa, click to select the Invert check box. When everything looks right to you, click OK

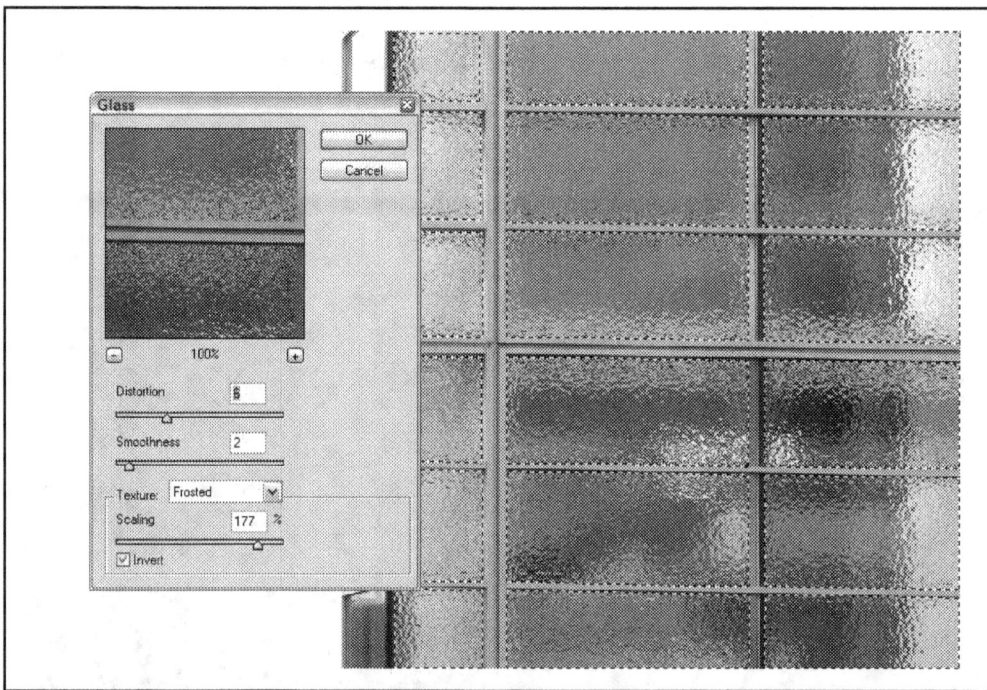

Figure 15-27.   *The Glass filter was used to change this clear glass into frosted glass by first isolating the glass panes with multiple selections.*

Wave   The Wave filter is wonderful for creating the illusion of a sudden gust of wind blowing across the water at the instant the picture was taken. The Wave filter is much more versatile and powerful than either its name or this description might imply. You can shape the waves with smooth-curved peaks (sine waves), or jagged sharp-cornered peaks, or as squares that make the image look as though it's being viewed through some custom frosted-glass pattern. In Figure 15-28, we used a picture of sailboat masts reflecting in the water, and then we used the Wave filter to intensify the effect of the waves.

To use the Wave filter:

1. Open an image to which you want to add a wavy distortion. You might want wind ripples, as simulated in Figure 15-28, or you might want to create the illusion of a desert mirage.

2. Choose Filter | Distort | Wave. The Wave dialog box appears. (Did you ever see so many sliders in your life?)

3. Adjust the sliders until you like what you see in the preview window. Click OK.

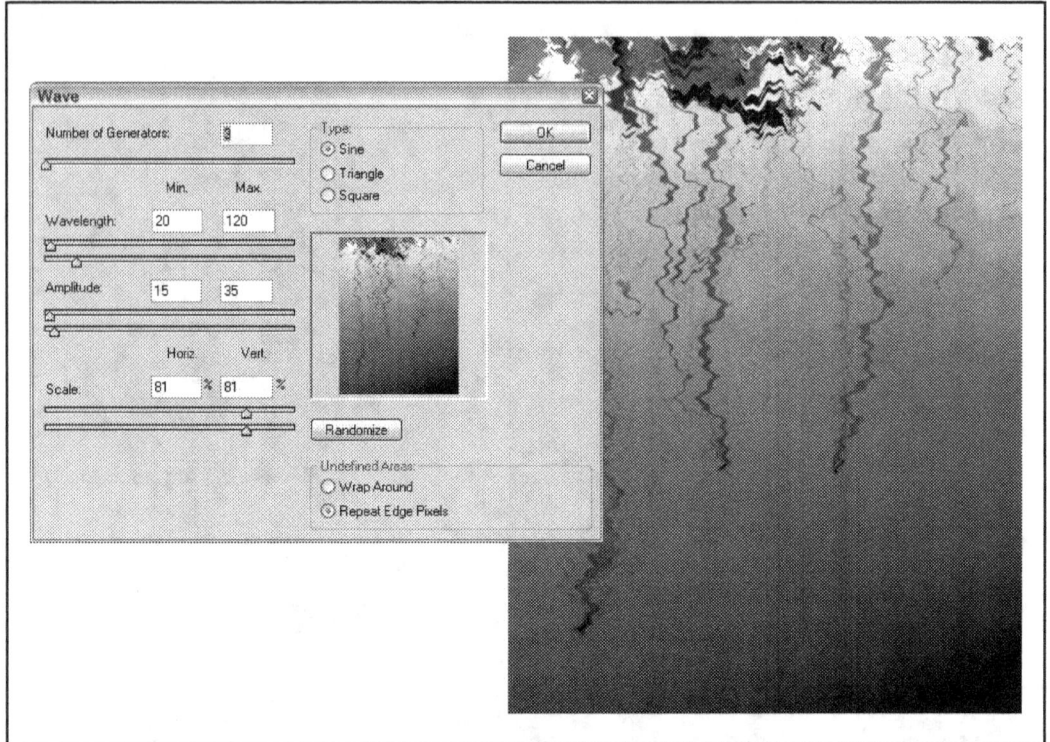

Figure 15-28. *Use the Wave filter to create the look of a gentle ripple in this water reflection.*

Ripple The Ripple filter is another "breeze on the water" effect. It can also be used to create glassy or crumpled textures. We've often used it to give a street or other paved area a wet effect (but to do that, you should also create a layer that looks like a reflection of whatever's on the "shoreline" of the paved area, and then merge the reflection layer with the paved area so that the ripple filter affects both images).

Anyway, you can choose from three sizes of reflections—small, medium, and large—and you can drag an Amount slider that makes the ripples (or the sine wave) longer or shorter. It's so simple it doesn't even deserve an explanatory exercise. You can see the Ripple dialog box and what the application of the filter does to water in Figure 15-29.

Ocean Ripple The Ocean Ripple effect differs from the Ripple effect in that the shape of the ripples is a little different and because two slider controls, Ripple Size and Ripple Magnitude, are available. Might as well cut to the chase and refer you to

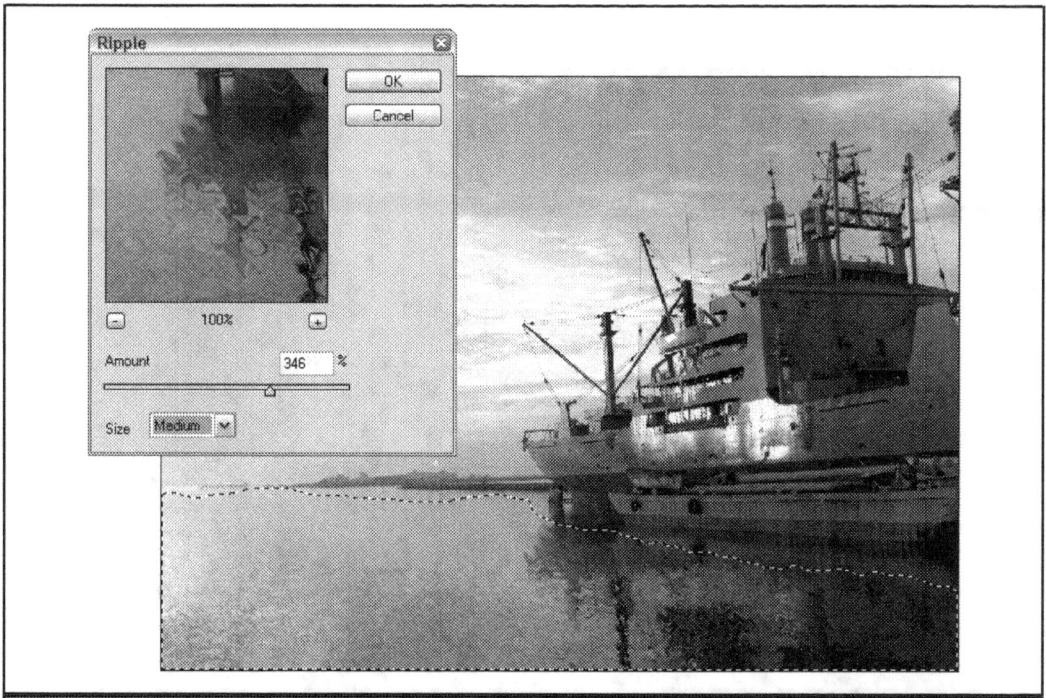

Figure 15-29.   *The Ripple filter was used to create a choppier surface to the water.*

Figure 15-30, which shows the Ocean Ripple filter dialog box and the same battleship image that we used with the Ripple filter, so that you can compare the effect directly. Once again, we won't waste your time with an exercise.

Pinch   Pinch is another "down the drain" effect, in a sense. However, it doesn't swirl. It just pulls all the pixels toward the center point that you designate, so the closer shapes are to the center, the smaller they become. If you drag the Amount slider all the way to the left, the center of the image becomes larger than it originally was while the outer edges remain the same size as they originally were. Figure 15-31 gives you an idea of how you might put this filter to good use.

Rendering

The Render filters place a variety of photographic effects into your image. They are classified under the name "Render" because, in computer graphics, the term refers to

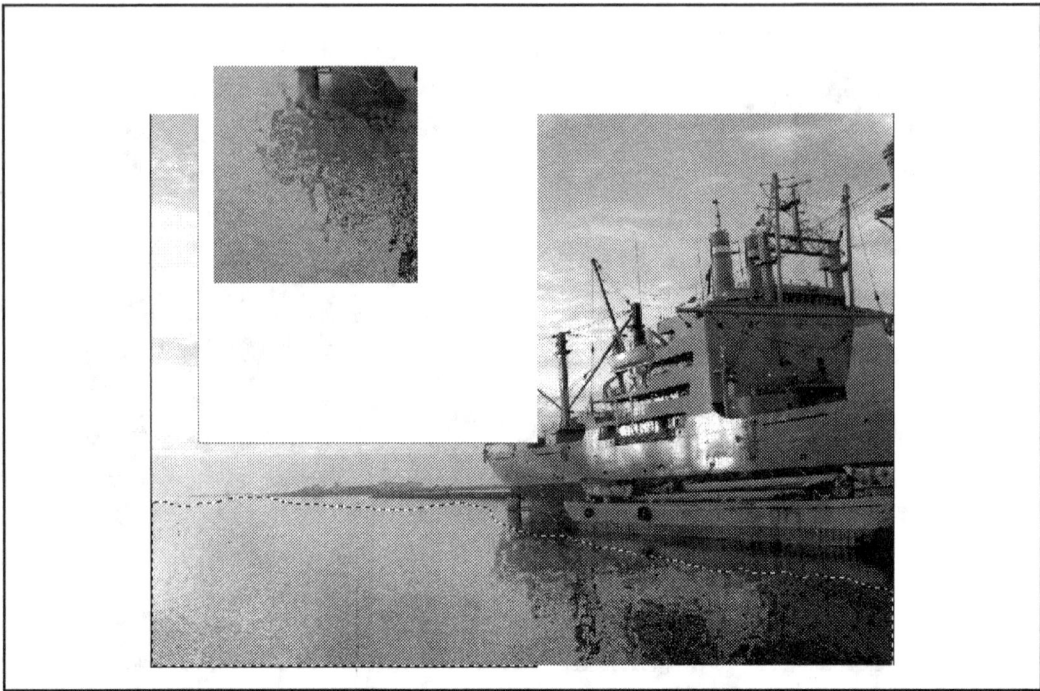

Figure 15-30. *The Ocean Ripple effect is more complex than the Ripple filter.*

using mathematics to create an item or effect from scratch. In the loosest sense of that definition, that is what these filters do.

3D Transform   The 3D Transform filter lets you project, or paint, two-dimensional images onto the surface of three-dimensional objects. The two applications for which we've often seen this filter used are for package design and for compositing (the process of combining multiple images into one). The filter is nice for package design because you can place the illustration that will be on the can or the box by using the 3D Transform filter to project the image onto a cylinder for the can or a cube for the box, rotate the geometric shape to the angle and perspective from which it will be seen in the final design, and then knock out the projection and paste it onto the art for the product. You could also use such techniques to place a reflection on the iris of an eye or a leopard skin on a torso (perhaps with a little additional shape-shifting help from the Liquify filter).

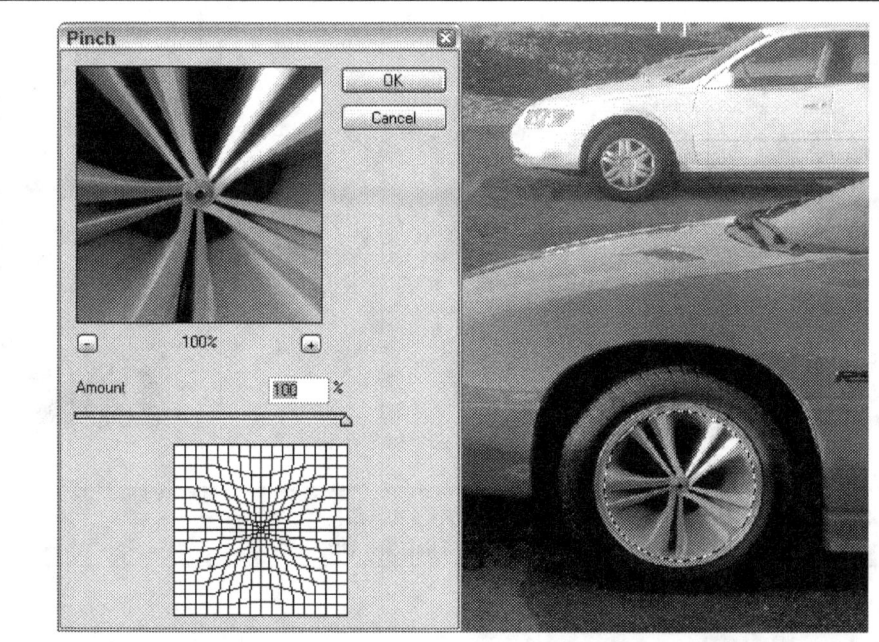

Figure 15-31.   *The Pinch filter was used to create a one-of-a-kind look for the wheels on this sports car.*

The big problem with using the 3D Transform filter for projecting an image is that it doesn't light the projected shape, which results, even after it's been projected, in the image still looking flat. If you do a lot of this kind of work, you may want to look into a more sophisticated filter like the one made by Andromeda software. Having said that, there's a benefit to not having these projections lighted: The photographs on which you're going to place the projections have already been lighted. If you use a Multiply blending mode to composite the projection and the image you're projecting onto, the result will probably be more realistic because you don't have to try to match the lighting for both layers. In Figure 15-32, you can see how the 3D Transform filter was used to place a label onto a wine bottle. With a few gradients and some airbrushed highlights, you get a nice illustration. For more on the 3D Transform filter, see Chapter 14.

Clouds and Difference Clouds   If you need a sky that's more interesting than anything currently in your own library of cloud photos (something you should definitely collect if you haven't started already), or a faux-finish texture for a wall or portrait background, one of these two filters will do the job for you.

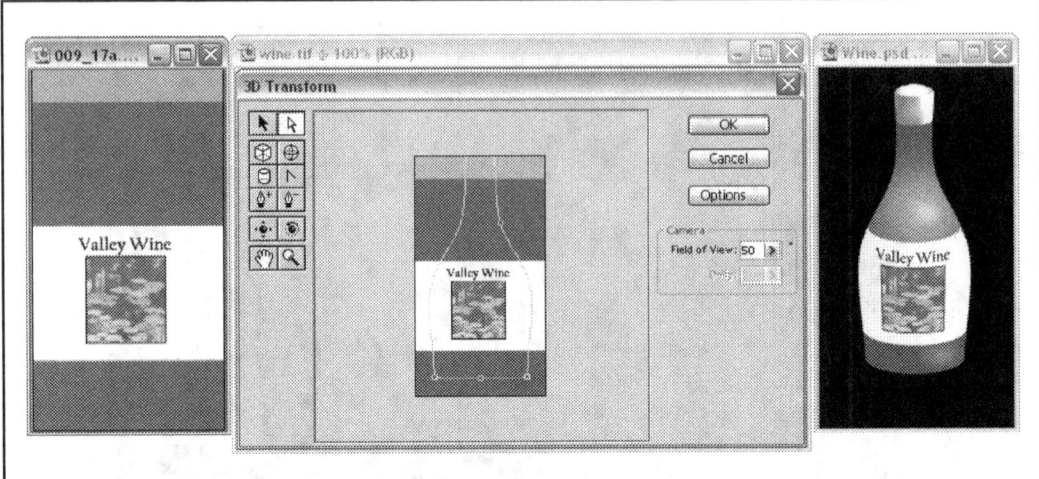

Figure 15-32. *The original label layout (left), the 3D Transform dialog box with the bottle wire frame (middle), and the final look (right)*

To create a cloudy sky:

1. Open an image that needs a new sky.

2. Place a selection around the sky. A Magic Wand tool selection, edited with the Magnetic Lasso tool, is usually the best combination of tools for this task (see Figure 15-33).

3. Open the Layers palette and click the New Layer icon at the bottom of the palette to create a new layer. If necessary, drag the Layers palette out of the Palette Well so that it stays on screen.

4. Choose Filter | Render | Clouds. No dialog box opens. The clouds simply appear, as shown next. You can't adjust these clouds, so hopefully you'll like what you see.

5. In the Layers palette, choose the Overlay blending mode. See Figure 15-33 for the before and after. If you find this a bit much, you can either change the opacity of the layer, or, if your selection is still active (as it should be), you can choose Enhance | Adjust Brightness/Contrast | Brightness/Contrast.

Lens Flares   Lens flares can be an extremely effective way to dramatize a portrait or landscape, especially if the lighting already implies that the sun (or the backlight in a studio portrait) could have been striking the surface of the camera lens.

In the cityscape of San Francisco shown in Figure 15-34, the afternoon sun was, in fact, just to the right of the camera lens (which was shaded with a hand to avoid lens flare). However, the result was that the light and the sky were much brighter on the

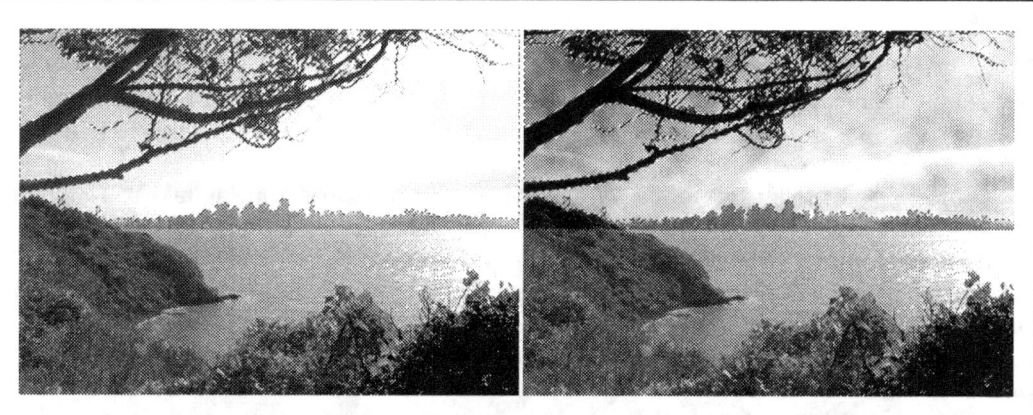

Figure 15-33. *The sky is selected with the Magic Wand (left), and then a new sky layer is created with the Clouds filter and blended with the original sky using Overlay blending mode (right).*

right than on the left, and, without a visible apparent light source, the picture just doesn't look quite right. The next illustration and the Lens Flare dialog box settings show how the problem was solved.

THE SPECIAL EFFECTS WORKFLOW

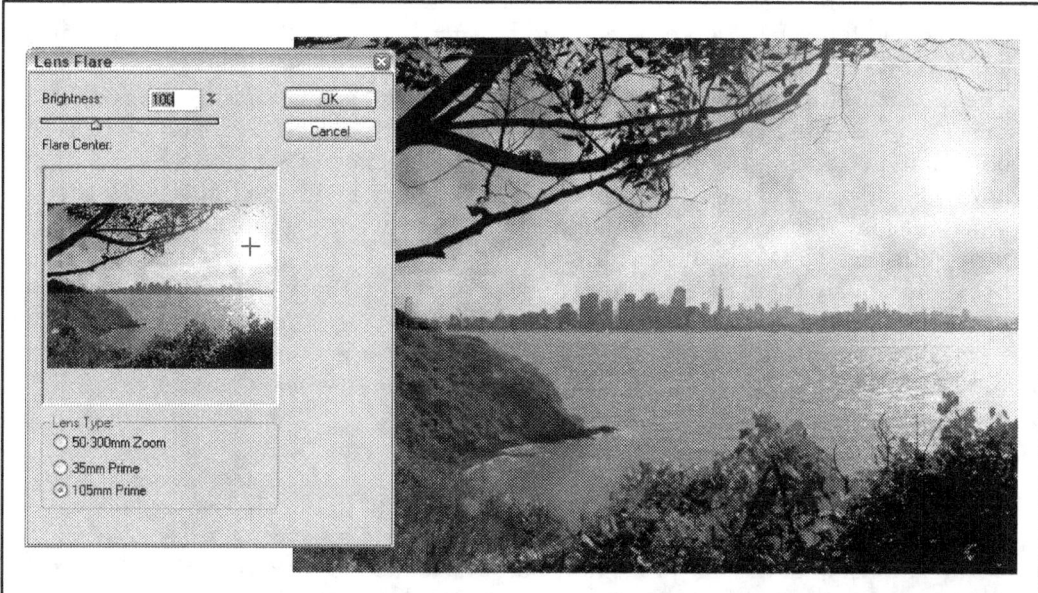

Figure 15-34. *Adding a Lens Flare effect to this scene gave it a credible light source that pulled the light reflection into the composition.*

Adding Textures

Textures such as rust, canvas, stucco, and concrete are more often used to make text or flat-color graphics look more photographic or have more character. However, you can also texturize a photo so that it looks as though it were printed on some natural surface or so that the objects in a photo seem to have three dimensions.

Photoshop Elements provides several ways to make textures. You can take a section of an image that has a texture area in it, re-create it as a new image, and then use the Offset filter and the Clone Stamp tool to turn it into a seamless tile. Step-by-step instructions on how to make seamless tiles are included in Chapter 13. You can then choose the Edit | Fill command to fill any layer or selection with the seamless textured pattern. Many such texture patterns come with Photoshop Elements. They can be found in any of the pattern preset libraries that ship with the program. You can view the patterns by choosing Edit | Preset Manager | Preset Type | Patterns. You can then view different preset pattern libraries by clicking the More button to view the Palette menu.

The next way to apply texture is to use one of the texture filters or effects. So that you can see one of the effects filters at work as a means of applying a texture, we'll take a look at one of the built-in effects routines in the Effects palette.

Texture Fill

The best use for the Texture Fill filter is to place a pattern or texture on a layer above the main image, and then use the Opacity slider and the blending modes to incorporate that texture into the overall image. The end effect is much different than that produced by the Texturizer filter found in the Filters | Texture submenu.

Texture Fill fills a selection or layer with any grayscale file (that is, the image must be in grayscale *mode*—not just a completely desaturated RGB file). The texture file can be any size. If it is larger than the target image, it will be overlaid starting at the upper-left corner. If it is smaller, it will be tiled. When making a texture fill file, it is a good idea to make it seamless, in case you have to tile it later. We made the preceding texture fill by defining a pattern and then filling a new file with the pattern. We then cropped the new file in such a way that the borders between symbols were even on all sides, effectively making the texture fill file seamless.

To define a pattern, make sure you are *not* working on the background layer. If you are, turn it into a regular image layer, either by copying it or by renaming it. If the pattern is part of a photograph, just place a rectangular selection around it and choose Edit | Define Pattern. When the Define Pattern dialog box appears, be sure to name the pattern.

Here's how to create this peace symbol pattern.

1. Open a new file the same size as the file you want to fill. Size isn't an absolute determinant; however, make this one the same size because it's easier to see the relationship of the size of the new pattern element to the size of the image that you're going to place it into later.

2. Use a combination of the Circle and Line Shape tools to make the peace symbol, simplifying each shape as you draw it and adding one shape to another by using the Darken blending mode.

3. When the shape is finished, place a rectangular marquee selection around it. Press CMD/CTRL+T to free-transform the selection. Press SHIFT to keep the transformation proportional as you drag a corner handle to rescale the symbol to a much smaller size. Press ENTER/RETURN to render the transformation.

4. Place a rectangular marquee around the symbol, pressing SHIFT while dragging to make sure the selection is square. Once the selection is made, make sure the Rectangular Marquee tool is still chosen, and use the arrow keys to precisely center the symbol in the square.

5. Choose Edit | Define Pattern. In the Define Pattern dialog box, name the pattern Peace and click OK. This new pattern is now a part of the default patterns file—even if you change files or turn off the computer.

6. Press CMD/CTRL+D to make sure all selections are dropped. Choose Edit | Fill. When the Fill dialog box appears, choose Pattern. Also, from the Pattern Presets palette, choose the thumbnail of the peace symbol. Click OK. What you see in Figure 15-35 is the result.

Here's how you would go about using a grayscale image as a texture fill. So that you have a basis for comparison, we're going to use the same photograph of a

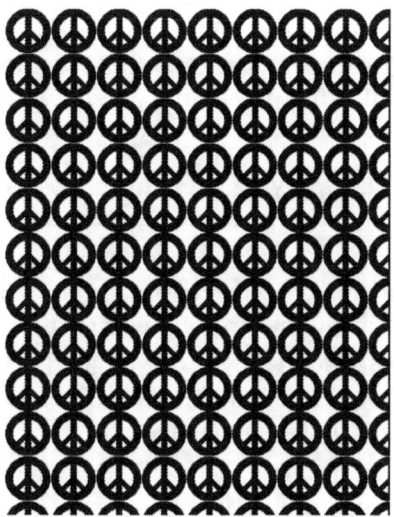

Figure 15-35. *Here you can see the repeating pattern created by filling with the peace symbol.*

motorcycle parked on San Francisco's Haight Street and the same peace symbol that we use to demonstrate what the Texturizer filter does in the next exercise. Make sure you have a grayscale texture file handy.

1. Open the file you want to fill with a texture.

2. Drag the Layers palette out of the Palette Well. Click the New Layer icon to create a new layer, and then fill it with white by choosing Edit | Fill and choosing White from the Use menu when the Fill palette appears. Click OK, and you will have an empty white layer. (Actually, another color might work better for other blending modes, so you might want to experiment with that later.)

3. Now you will use the Texture Fill filter. Choose Filter | Render | Texture Fill. The Texture Fill dialog box appears. This is merely a file finder/explorer. Use it to locate the grayscale texture file, and then double-click its filename. The texture will automatically fill your new layer.

4. When the new layer fills, you'll see only the texture pattern. Make sure the Layers palette has been dragged out of the Palette Well, and, in the Toolbox, choose the Move tool. Now press SHIFT++ to cycle through the blending modes until you find an effect that suits your vision for what the combination of the pattern and the image layer should look like. The combination that worked best for us was the Lighten mode with the Opacity slider set at about 40 percent. You can see the results in Figure 15-36.

Pasting in Textures

In this section, we will show you how a texture can be applied to a surface that isn't parallel to the film (or image sensor) plane by pasting a perspective-corrected texture into a selected area. In the following procedure, we show you how to change a street in a photo from asphalt to sandstone.

1. Open the image. (When applying a texture, choose an image that has a flat surface, such as a wall, pavement, or even a beach.)

2. Create a new image that is roughly twice the size of the current image. Because you are going to apply perspective to this second image, you want the most distant parts of the plane to be large enough to fill the area you want to cover.

3. Open the Effects palette by dragging it from the Palette Well or by choosing Window | Effects. Double-click the Effect thumbnail named Sandstone. This texture will be used to fill the new image.

4. Choose Image | Transform (CMD/CTRL+T). The Transform marquee appears around the image. Zoom out just enough to make the image window larger than the image and give yourself room to drag the handles so that the perspective of the texture is approximately the same as the perspective of the

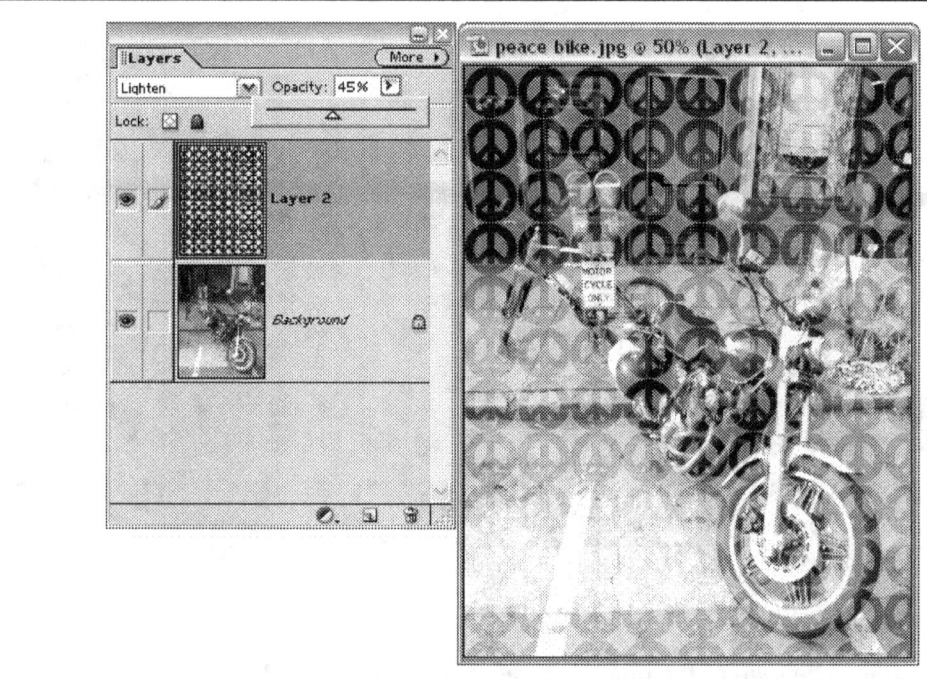

Figure 15-36. *The motorcycle with a grayscale pattern texture applied with the Texture Fill filter and then modified with a blending mode*

image you're going to place the texture into—as shown in the center image in Figure 15-37.

5. In the sandstone image, choose the Magic Wand tool and select the white area that isn't textured. Then invert the selection (SHIFT+CMD/CTRL+I) so that the textured area is selected, and press CMD/CTRL+C to copy the selection to the clipboard.

6. Go back to the car and street image. To select the street, you can use the Magic Wand tool, and then edit the result with the Lasso tool's Add To Selection and Subtract From Selection buttons. See the image on the left in Figure 15-37.

7. Add a new layer to the image you're going to texture. The street selection will be in effect on the new layer.

8. Choose Edit | Paste Into. The texture appears inside the selected area. Because you want the color changes, shadows, and stains that would be on the street to be a part of the texture, you use a blending mode to merge the two.

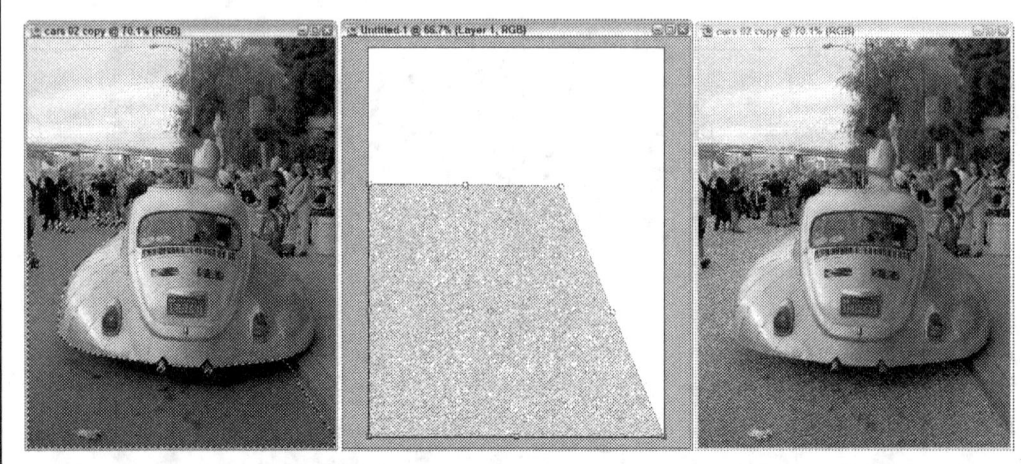

Figure 15-37. *The area selected for paving (left), the gravel texture adjusted for perspective (middle), and the combined final image (right)*

9. From the Blend Mode menu in the Layers palette, choose Overlay. The final result can be seen in the image on the right in Figure 15-37.

10. Finally, Texture filters include several premade textures that can be adjusted in several ways. This type of filter can make a texture map of any Photoshop (PSD) file—though black-and-white files work best. You can make a seamless tile (see Chapter 13), and then, instead of saving it by defining it as a pattern, you simply save it as a file (or, better yet, do both).

Using the Texture Filters

The Texture filters are a group of filters specialized for texturing the image or a selected portion thereof. All but one of these use standard texture-type dialog boxes similar to those you've seen throughout this chapter.

The Texture filters impose a texture on whatever layer you choose. To give you a more concrete idea of the effect of each filter shown in the following list, see the results of applying them in Figure 15-38.

Note *Most of the built-in textures have been around for so long that they can make your art look trite. However, you can combine these texturing effects with one another in an infinite variety of ways: blend layers (any number of them) with one another, run different filters on the same image, duplicate layers and place different filter effects on them, and then erase through them. Such techniques allow you to create unique and highly professional-looking textures. See the next section, "Combining the Look of Filters," for more information on blending effects.*

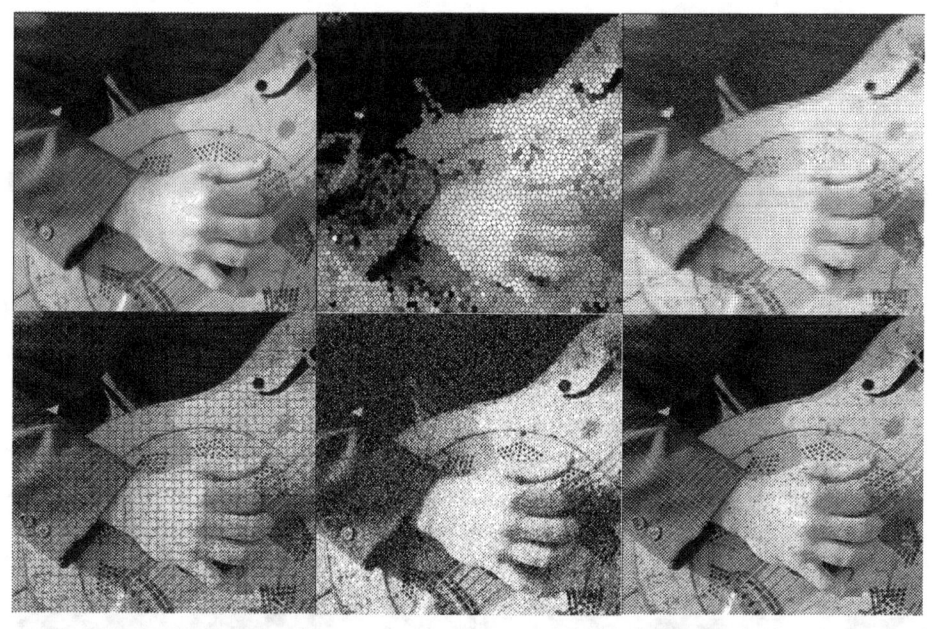

Figure 15-38.   *Top row from left: Original Image, Stained Glass, and Patchwork. Bottom row from left: Mosaic, Grain, and Craquelure.*

The Texturizer filter lets you use any PSD file as a "bump map" for giving a textured appearance to the image itself, rather than overlaying a texture file on the image. The result creates the illusion that the print was made on textured material. Figure 15-39 shows the dialog box and the result the settings produced when we used the peace file as the texture file.

You can also use the built-in textures by simply choosing them from the Texturizer dialog box's Texture menu. Your choices are brick, burlap, canvas, and sandstone. We have found that the sandstone texture is very good for simulating the texture of watercolor or pastel paper, which adds an authentic look to watercolor type illustrations and paintings. Use the Scaling and Relief sliders to adjust the texture to the size of your image and to control the intensity of the effect. A good way to build up a library of useful textures is to photograph or scan in textures from real life and then save them as grayscale images. Find out more about painting effects in Chapter 16.

Combining the Looks of Filters

You can create the most interesting and least trite special effects by combining several filters using layering techniques and blending modes.

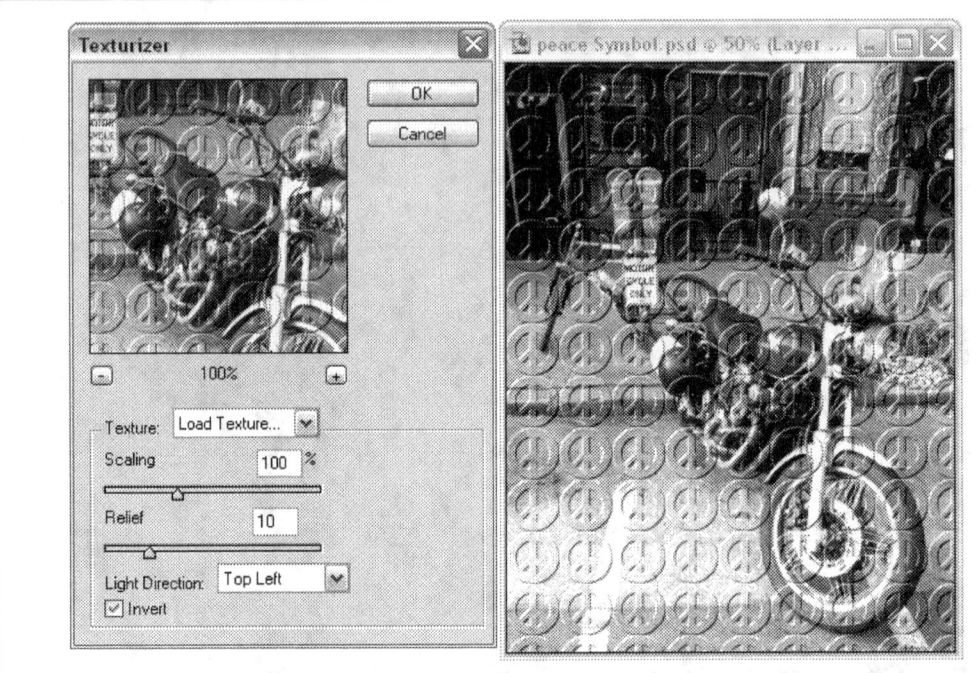

Figure 15-39.   *The result of using the saved peace symbol pattern as a custom texture in the Texturizer filter*

Layering Techniques

One of the problems with using filters is that they are applied uniformly across the image. You can make the results of your filtering look more professional by selecting only portions of the image on which to run different filters. If the filters are texture oriented, you might find it better to run the same filter at several different options settings. Then you can make the texture larger and more pronounced on objects that are in the near foreground or distant background, and tighter and more detailed on objects that are of greater interest. An example of such a technique is shown in Figure 15-40.

The example in Figure 15-40 was created by making different cutout layers of the background, the flowers, and the artichokes. Then each layer was filtered with the Craquelure filter set with different options for each. The flowers are the most prominent objects—and the most detailed, closely followed by the artichokes. For the background, the cracks have been set very far apart, so we have a more "out of focus" feel here.

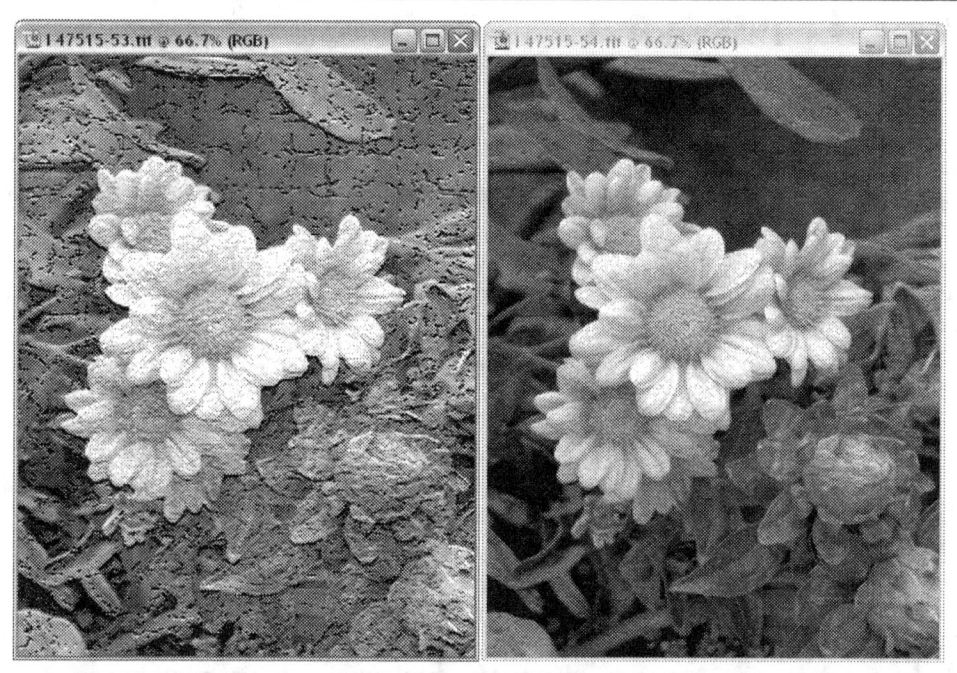

Figure 15-40. *On the left, a multilayer technique was used to vary the texture filtering for various parts of the image. On the right, the original image was used with a blending mode layer and then erased in key areas to control the area of effect.*

Blending Mode and Opacity Techniques

You can create an interesting combination of techniques when you apply filtering techniques that help you highlight some detail from the original photograph. To accomplish this, a photograph was pasted into a layer overlying a photograph treated with the Craquelure filter. Lowering the opacity of the pasted in (top) layer to about 50 percent and using the Multiply blending mode had the effect of darkening the shadow areas. Then we used the Eraser in Brush mode and set at a low opacity (about 25 percent) to bring up even more detail in the center of the sunflowers by partially erasing through the top layer. Refer to Figure 15-40.

Note   *The "blended and erased-through multiple-layer technique" works well for such special-effects filters as lighting effects, lens flares, and motion filters. It is the key to giving your images a personal and professional touch that turns them into true art and commanding graphics.*

Full Court Liquification

One "filter" in the Photoshop Elements 2 arsenal is so powerful that calling it a filter is almost misleading. The Liquify filter is more like a special-purpose application. That special purpose is the seamless reshaping of parts of the image. You can use this filter for anything from shrinking the bridge of someone's nose to putting a smile on their face. Movie studios use software like this to create the archetypes for galactic landscapes, monsters, and alien creatures. We're still waiting for someone to use it for creating comic-strip characters from photos of live actors.

For more practical, everyday applications, you can use the Liquify filter to reshape text or to change a shaded bubble into a shaded raindrop that can then be used to create a splash or reshape to make a sweat bead on a glass of beer.

The Liquify filter provides tools (see Figure 15-41) that let you brush to warp, make turbulence, twirl clockwise, twirl counterclockwise, pucker, bloat, shift, reflect, reconstruct, freeze a portion of the image, or thaw a portion of the image.

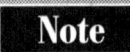 *If you want to liquify a foreground object and leave the background alone, it is best to knock out the foreground object first. Then you can just liquify its layer and composite it back with the background. If any areas left when you cut out the foreground object still show, you can use the Clone Stamp to fill them in.*

Refer to Figure 15-42 to see the effects of the following Liquify filter tools.

Warp   Pushes pixels ahead of the brush, or pulls pixels that are behind the brush.

Turbulence   Causes the pixels that you push or hover over to wave and bubble, much as if you blew air on a reflection in water.

Twirl Clockwise/Counterclockwise   Spins the area covered by the brush in a clockwise or counterclockwise direction, depending on which of the two tools you choose. As with all of these tools, the visual effect can be dependent on the size of the brush.

Pucker   This is a great tool for making noses and waists smaller. It pulls the image in toward the center of the brush. You can make a whole area of the image thinner by dragging slowly in a line as you watch the image move.

Bloat   This is a great tool to use for making eyes and ears larger. Be very careful, though, as you can easily overdo it and end up with a cartoon character.

Shift   Pushes the image to the brush's left, or, if you press OPT/ALT and drag, it pushes pixels to the right. It's best to practice with this one a bit.

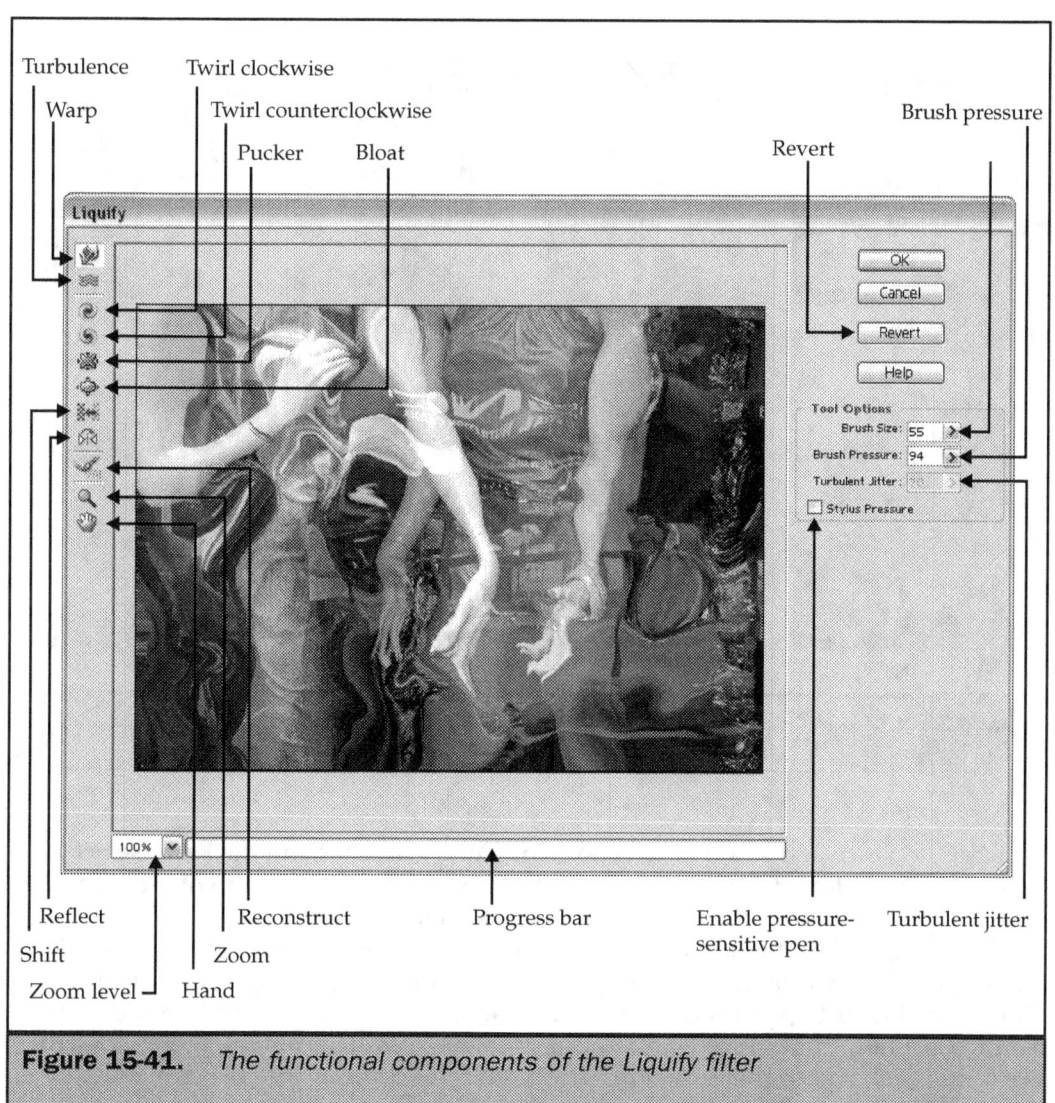

Turbulence Twirl clockwise

Warp   Twirl counterclockwise   Brush pressure

    Pucker   Bloat   Revert

Reflect   Reconstruct   Progress bar   Enable pressure-   Turbulent jitter
                                                        sensitive pen
Shift   Zoom
Zoom level ⌐ Hand

Figure 15-41. *The functional components of the Liquify filter*

THE SPECIAL EFFECTS
WORKFLOW

Reflect   Flips an area the size of the brush in a given direction, depending on which direction you move the brush. Refer to Figure 15-42 to see what happens when you move the brush down.

Reconstruct   Adobe saved the best for the last. If you mess up, you can use this brush to undo gradually what you've done. It would be wonderful if pressing X

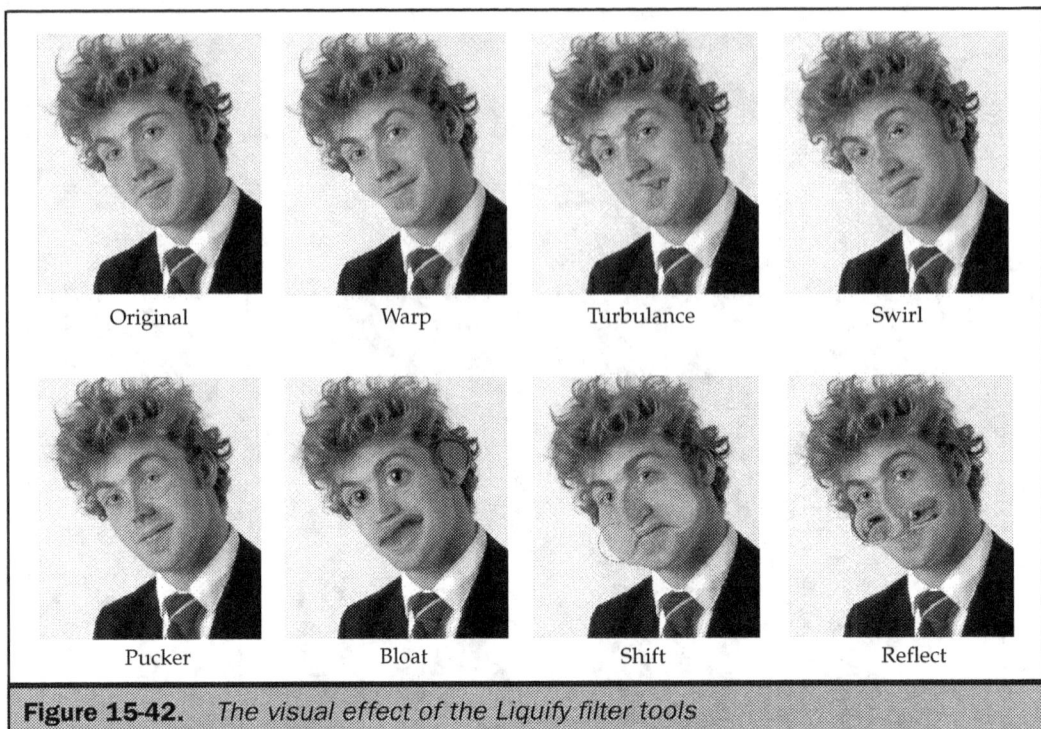

Original   Warp   Turbulance   Swirl

Pucker   Bloat   Shift   Reflect

Figure 15-42.   *The visual effect of the Liquify filter tools*

switched you between your current choice of Liquify brushes and the Reconstruct tool—but even without that convenience, the Reconstruct tool lets you fine-tune all the distortions until you've "fingerpainted" the exact image you want.

At the right of the Liquify window, an area called Tool Options contains three fields that let you specify brush size, brush pressure, and turbulent jitter. *Jitter* is the term that Adobe Photoshop products use to describe random variations. So Turbulent Jitter controls just how "turbulent" your Turbulence strokes will be. Finally, there's a Stylus Pressure check box. If it's turned on (checked), you can vary the brush size, and therefore the degree of the effect, by applying more or less pressure to your stylus. Of course, choosing this option does nothing at all if you don't have a pressure-sensitive stylus and tablet.

If you use the Liquify filter, once you click OK, the liquified image will be rendered and will appear in the Photoshop Elements workspace. You can't use Undo—so if you mess up so badly that you need to start over, do it before you click the OK button. Click the Revert button instead.

Adding Effects

This section is about using the Effects palette, which Adobe has been kind enough to give us as a partial substitute for the fact that you can't create your own automated routines (called *actions* in Photoshop). The effects in Photoshop Elements use the same fundamental process, though, which is to run a series of routines in succession to create a single effect. You just can't create new routines. You are limited to the library that comes with the program. This may sound restrictive; but when you discover the control you have over mixing and adjusting them, it expands the possibilities quite a bit.

In the Effects palette, Adobe has created pre-programmed routines for certain series of Photoshop Elements commands that are used to implement some of the most commonly used special-effects routines. The Effects palette and Layer Styles palette have a lot in common in this regard, but they also have some key differences. The differences are in the types of results you get and in what those results are used for. Although layer styles are primarily used for text and shapes, the effects in the Effects palette tend to be applicable to the full range of bitmapped graphics—including simplified text and shapes. See Chapter 4 for a complete description of all of the Effects palette functional components. In this chapter, we will concentrate on how to create special effects with the options offered with this palette.

The Effects palette will show you all the categories at once if you select Category | All. The menu is then subdivided into four categories:

- Frames
- Textures
- Text Effects
- Image Effects

The Effects palette includes thumbnails of each effect that give you a visual of what the routine will do to an image. The thumbnails are so nicely designed that it is easy to tell what the effect does—including the fact that some of the effects (mostly, those in the texture category) will completely cover the original image. When that is the case, you'll see only the texture or other effect in the thumbnail, rather than the sailboat image.

There are four ways to apply an effect, all of them nearly instantaneous:

- Drag the thumbnail from the palette onto the image and release.
- Double-click the thumbnail.
- Click the thumbnail to highlight it and then click the Apply button.
- Choose Apply from the Effects palette menu.

Each of the sections below will give you a brief example and illustration of what you might use each of the categories for.

Frames

Using frames presents a lot more possibilities than you might expect because clicking on your choice of frames causes Photoshop Elements to create all the elements of the frame on separate layers. You can then go into each layer and texture it, create another frame around it, or use any of the Enhance commands on it. Figure 15-43 shows a still-life photo that is framed with a number of frame effects. Notice that the bottom photos combine the frame effects from the images above to construct a more complex frame. You can combine any amount of individual frame effects. Some of the frame effects also allow you to adjust options to vary the look. An effect will be variable when the *f* icon is visible in the name bar. The number of combinations possible is vast. The photo was also textured with the sandpaper texture and the Multiply blending mode.

Textures

Textures are created on a layer above the image to which you apply the effect. You can then use the blending modes in the Layers palette to incorporate those textures into the surface of the image. Alternatively, you can cut out a portion of the texture and make a frame (or matte board) of it by using the selection tools to cut out a portion of the texture layer, and then applying one of the bevel-edge and drop-shadow layer styles to the texture layer. You can see the use of texture in conjunction with blending modes in Figure 15-44.

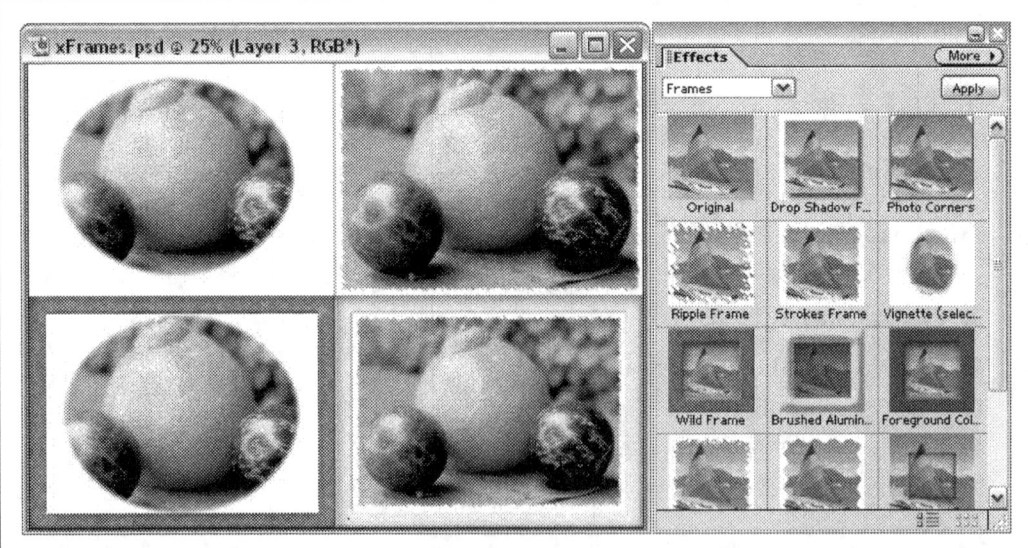

Figure 15-43. *The frames in the top row were combined with a second frame to form the framed images in the bottom row.*

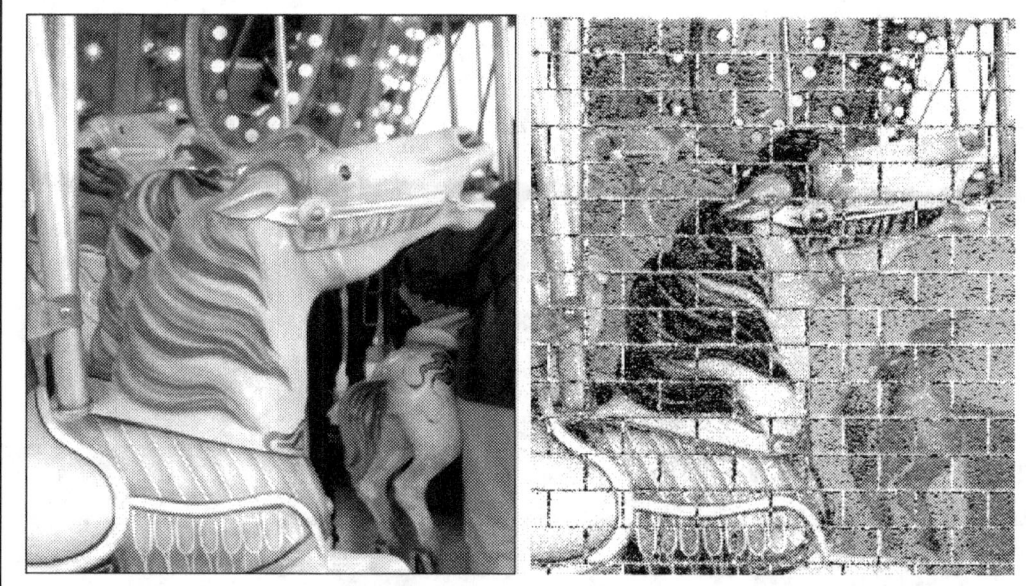

Figure 15-44.   *Using the brick texture effect and a blending mode on this carved horse transforms it into a painting on a brick wall.*

Text Effects

This category of effects is limited to text. The results are generally more complex and more pictorial creations than those generated by the Layer Styles palette. The effects are bold outline, brushed metal, cast shadow, clear emboss, confetti, medium outline, running water, sprayed stencil, thin outline, water reflection, and wood paneling. Brushed metal and wood paneling work especially well with graphics that use the frame effects bearing the same names. You can see some examples of this type of effect in Figure 15-45. We will go into text functions in more in depth the "Text and Shapes" section, later in this chapter.

Image Effects

The image effects can be very useful for texturing text, frames, and shapes as well as images. Text and shapes, however, need to be simplified first. Most of these effects are the result of using a combination of one or more filters and blending modes. Their names alone will give you some idea of what you can do with them: blizzard, colorful center, fluorescent chalk, horizontal color fade, lizard skin, neon lights, oil pastel, quadrant colors, soft flat color, soft focus, vertical color fade. In Figure 15-46, you can see the effect of applying multiple image effects to the iris photo. The fluorescent chalk effect was used twice to texture the flower, and then we created the frame by using a circular selection to knock out a transparent hole to show the first effects layer.

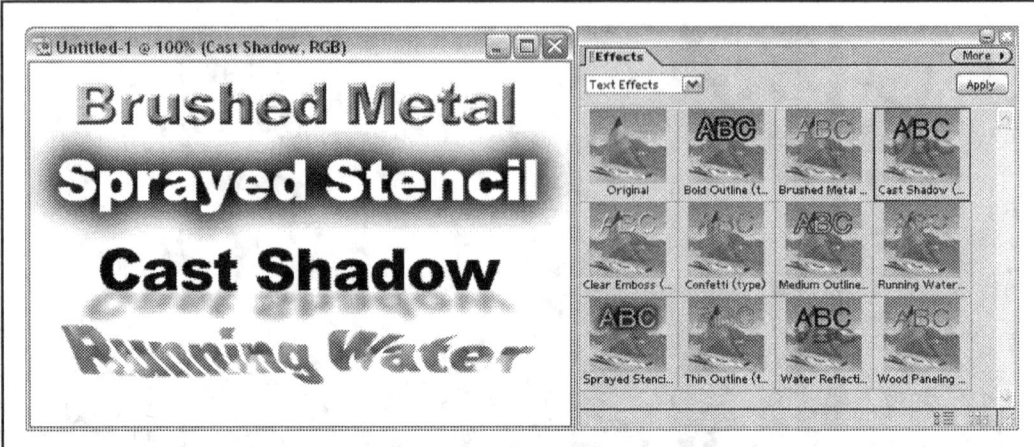

Figure 15-45.   *Some text effects that demonstrate the power of the Effects palette*

Note   *When using the Effects palette, it will often be necessary to make adjustments to such parameters as the width of a bevel or a shadow. That is because Photoshop Elements doesn't automatically modify these adjustments according to the size of your image. Go to the Layers palette and look for the layer to which the effect has been applied. If there are adjustable parameters, there will be a small f icon on the right side of that layer's name bar. Double-click the icon and the Style Settings dialog box will appear. The purpose of the adjustment options are clearly labeled and you will instantaneously see the result of any adjustment you make, so all you need to do is experiment until you like what you see. Any adjustments that are not available will be grayed.*

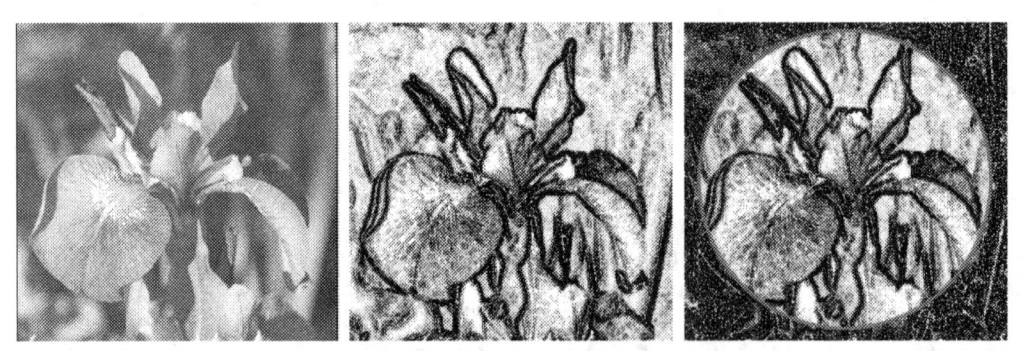

Figure 15-46.   *The original photo (left), the first use of the Fluorescent Chalk effect (center), and the same effect applied again to a layer copy and the selected circular area knocked out (right)*

Layer Styles

Like effects, you can apply multiple layer styles to the same image, text, or shape. Also like effects, the styles in the Layer Styles palette are themselves often the result of multiple applications of the different individual styles. The Layers Style palette can be accessed from the Window menu, the Palette Well, and the Shape tool Options bar. It uses thumbnails to let you see what the style does. You can apply the styles in the Style palette in the same manner as the Effects palette (see the preceding section). Layer styles let you add effects to the nontransparent portion of any layer. A complete rundown on the Layer Styles palette's functional components is included in Chapter 4.

There are 14 categories of layer styles. All of them apply instantaneously when you have a layer selected and click a layer style, or when you already have a shape or text selected. Rather than try to reproduce all the layer styles in this chapter, you'll find out a lot more by selecting a shape or text layer and then trying various layer styles and combinations of styles. Remember to press CMD/CTRL+Z or click the Clear Style button in the upper Options bar of the Layer Styles palette to undo each style you apply when experimenting. Otherwise, if you apply a style to a layer that's already been selected, the effect will be cumulative, which can produce interesting results, as you can see in Figure 15-47. You see the result of applying a number of layer styles to a layer that started out with a simple oval shape.

You can apply layer styles to any layer, as long as there's some transparency in that layer. With the lack of transparency, the edge of the layer will be the boundary for the style effect. Some styles will not work when they have only the layer boundary to work with; they require some areas of transparency within the image to have an effect. It is

THE SPECIAL EFFECTS WORKFLOW

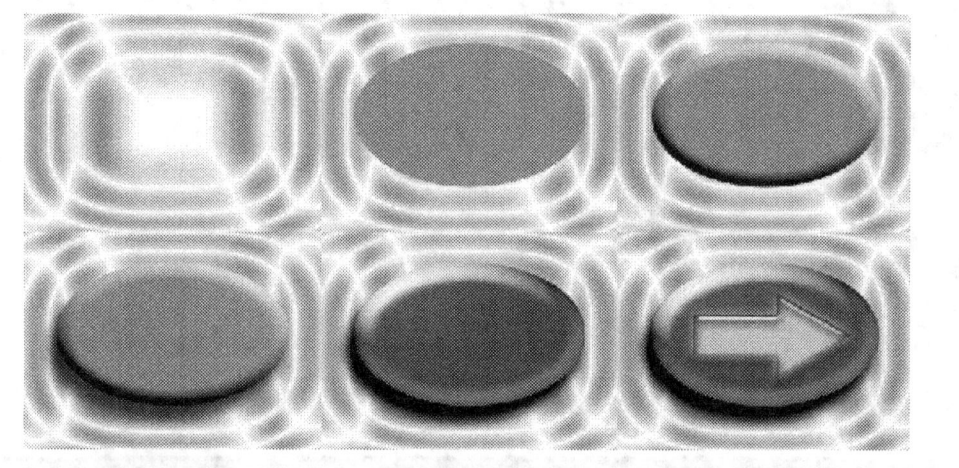

Figure 15-47.   *Top row from left: Water Reflection, Oval Shape, and Simple Inner Bevel. Bottom row from the left: Drop Shadow, Glass Button, Custom Shape, and Glass Button.*

the transparency that is considered to be the "edge" of the layer by the layer style. When you create a text or shape layer, the area around the shape is automatically transparent. In other words, if you have chosen a bevel style, for example, the dividing line between any level of opacity and any amount of transparency will be beveled. If the layer is completely opaque, the bevel will be rendered on all four edges of the layer frame.

Unlike most of the other effects, you can make adjustments to the layer styles. When you can make adjustments to Effects, it is because there are layer styles included in the routine. In the Layers palette, when you apply a layer style, a Layer Style icon appears on the left portion of the layer name bar, which is noted by an *f* in a black circle. You can double-click that icon and open a Style Settings dialog box for that layer style. A few layer styles do not have options. Figure 15-48 shows the Layers palette when a Layer Style icon is present and what the Style Settings dialog box for that layer style looks like. The layer style effect shown was achieved by applying a Wow-Plastic style to an image and then using circular selection to cut holes in it. As you can see, the beveled edge appears where transparency is created. The settings available for adjustment will vary with each style you apply and will often increase as you add multiple styles to one object. The settings that are not available will be grayed out.

Let's go over how the style settings work. The Lighting angle dial at the top of the dialog box sets the angle of the lighting sources. You can also enter a degree value in the text filed to the immediate right. Use this to adjust the lighting on text or a shape to match the lighting in a background image, for instance. The Use Global Angle button will link this setting to all other styles that have it selected so when you change

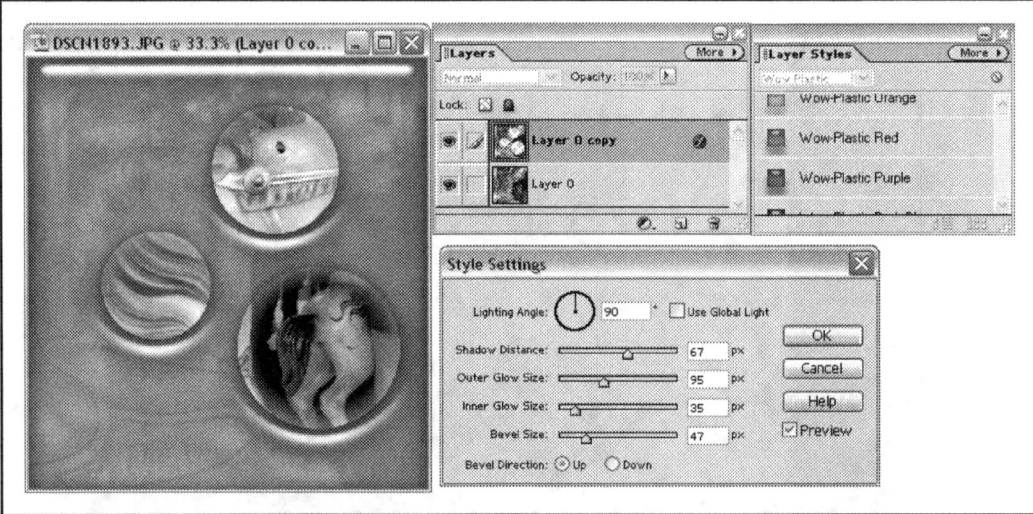

Figure 15-48.   *Here, you can see the Layer Settings Options dialog box, which allows you to adjust the bevel, glow, light-source angle, and drop shadow on this shiny plastic effect.*

the lighting angle of any one of them, they all change. If you want each style to have a separate angle, uncheck this option.

All the styles use the same Style Settings dialog box. The options that are available will vary from one to another. There are four sliders, which represent four possible attributes that can be changed:

- **Shadow Distance**   This adjusts the distance in pixels the drop shadow falls from the object in the direction of the lighting angle. This gives the appearance that the object is closer or farther from the image plane.

- **Outer Glow Size**   This adjusts the amount of glow effect in the transparent portions of the object or image. This produces an effect that gives the appearance of light emanating from the object.

- **Inner Glow Size**   This adjusts the amount of glow effect in the opaque portions of the object or image. This produces an effect that gives the appearance of light inside the object.

- **Bevel**   This setting determines the extent of the bevel edge.

Remember that many of the styles have hidden features that are built in and cannot be varied. The sliders that are not grayed are the attributes you can change for any particular style. The Bevel Direction Up and Down buttons reverse the effects so, for example, a bevel that looks raised will look sunken. The Preview check box allows you to see the style on the actual object immediately.

Using the Layer Styles Commands

In addition to the layer style options, you can also find a set of commands on the Layer | Layer Style menu. The layer style commands affect only a selected layer to which layer styles have already been applied. These commands are not available from the Layer Style palette menu or the Layer palette menu. To use the layer styles commands, choose Layer | Layer Style. The choices are

- **Style Settings**   Displays the Layer Styles Options dialog box.

- **Clear Layer Style**   Removes all style settings from the current layer so that you can apply new ones without adding them to the old ones, and scale effects.

- **Copy Layer Style and Paste Layer Style**   Allow you to copy a style from an existing layer and paste to any other layers. The layer you copied the style to will take on all of the style attributes from the source style layer. Select the layer you want to copy from, choose the Copy Layer Style command, choose the layer you want to copy it to, and choose the Paste Layer Style command.

- **Hide/Show All Effects**   Temporarily hides the effects of any style that has been applied. This is handy when you want to make changes to the object or layout and do not want the visual interference as you do.

■ **Scale Effects** Brings up the Scale Effects dialog box, which provides you with a value field and slider to adjust the percentage (1–1000) by which the style effect is scaled larger or smaller. Make sure the Preview check box is selected so that you can visually and interactively choose the exact result you want as you drag the slider. When you find it, just click OK.

Text and Shapes

The balance of this chapter is devoted to showing you how to create and manipulate text and shapes in Photoshop Elements, and also how to apply special effects. For the most part, the same effects are applicable to both text and shapes, with the exception of the Effects palette's text effects, which are applicable only to text and a few transformations.

Creating Text

Photoshop Elements lets you place text anywhere you want in an image using any PostScript or TrueType font on your system and at any font size. All you have to do is choose the Type tool. All the possible options can be found on the Type Tool's Options bar, shown in the following illustration. For detailed descriptions, see Chapter 5.

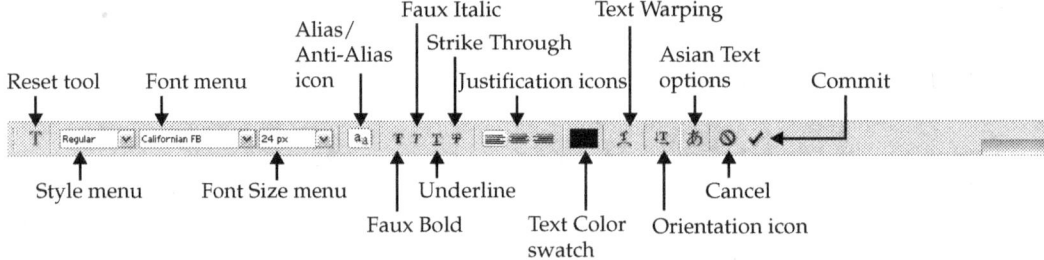

Photoshop Elements deals with text in a very simple manner and does not provide any advanced text handling capability, such as text boxes, line spacing, tabbing, and kerning. Text is entered one line at a time, and, if you want to create a paragraph, you will have to place line breaks by pressing RETURN/ENTER when you want the text to wrap. This is bare-bones text input. What is nice is that text is placed on its own layer and remains editable so you can always go back and make changes, even after you have applied many special effects. If you have simplified the text or if the effect you are using simplifies the text, you will no longer be able to edit it in Text mode. This is because simplifying the text converts it to bitmapped form, which means it has become a pixel image and is not in vector form.

The following steps take you through the basic operations for entering text:

1. Select the Text tool from the Toolbox. You will see the Text Options bar appear and the cursor will change to a vertical bar indicating the current vertical size of the current font.

2. Set your font style, family, size, and any other options you might want to use from the Text Options bar. Be aware of the justification because the type will position itself and flow from the place you first click according to the justification selected. For instance, the text will move to the right of the original entry point if you have left justification selected. Don't panic if your text isn't positioned perfectly the moment you type it in. You can reposition it later.

3. Now you are ready to enter some text. Click where you want to start entering, and the program automatically creates a new text layer. The new text layer will be indicated by a capital *T* in a square icon. You will see a blinking cursor in the form of a vertical bar that indicates the start position.

4. Begin typing in text or paste in text that you copied from another source. You enter text continuously and press RETURN/ENTER when you want the text to wrap to a new line and form a paragraph. If you have pasted text, you will need to go in and add line breaks by hand because Photoshop Elements will not hold on to the line breaks from other programs. The text might run off the edge of the frame, but it is all there. Just keep placing line breaks until it is all visible on the screen, or reduce the size. All the text that is entered with one placement of the text cursor remains in a single line or paragraph that can be acted upon as a single object and will occupy its own layer.

5. You can change the font style, family, or size any time while typing, and the text will change accordingly while maintaining the attributes on the text already entered. This allows you to mix type looks within one line or paragraph. You can see that the 2003 in Figure 15-49 was reduced in size to align with the lowercase letters in May.

6. If you want to start a new line or paragraph. Click the Commit checkmark on the right side of the Text Options bar to accept the current text, and then click somewhere else in the layer and type. A new layer will appear each time you do this.

7. You can copy text from one document to another by dragging from the source to a layer in the new document. You can also copy or cut it to the clipboard and then paste it to the new document. Finally, you can select the text by placing the text cursor at the point you want to start selecting text and drag to highlight the text. You can select the whole line or paragraph by double-clicking its layer icon. After the text is selected, right-click the text and choose Copy from the pop-up menu to place the highlighted text in the clipboard; and then, in the new document, paste it by right-clicking at the text cursor position and choosing Paste.

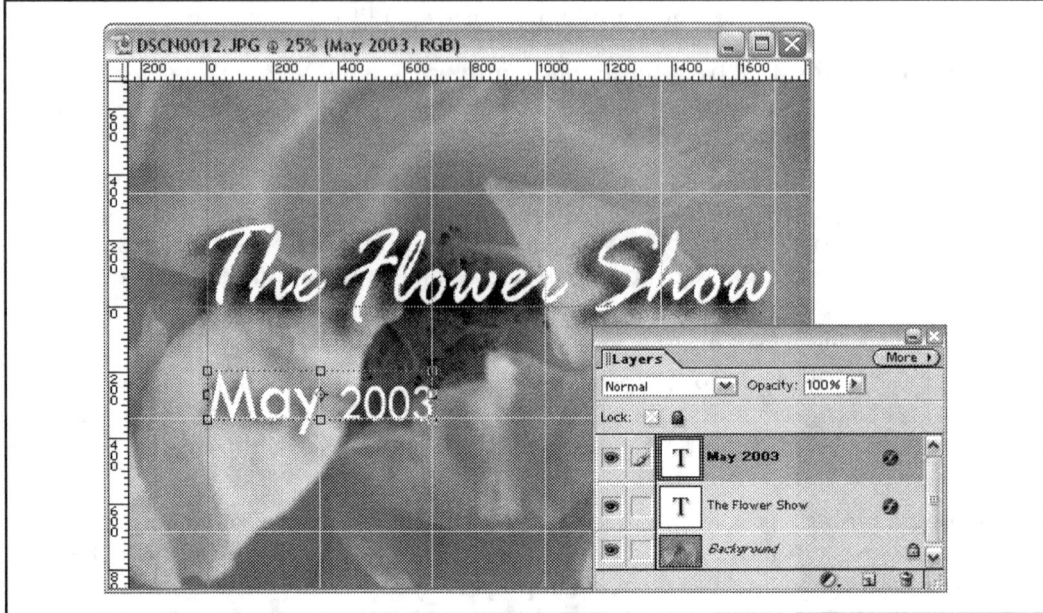

Figure 15-49.   *You can see each separate text line is aligned to a grid line both horizontally and vertically.*

If you want to align the text in a paragraph or a list, set the justification to the orientation that you want. As long as you are entering text in the same paragraph, it will maintain alignment and line spacing. It gets a bit trickier when you have to align separate lines or paragraphs of text.

For this, we recommend that you turn on the grid or set up guidelines on a temporary layer. To do this:

1. Choose View | Grid to show the grid lines, and then choose View | Snap To Grid to force the text object to align exactly with the grid. Be aware that the snap alignment is with the bounding box, which will include descenders. Make sure the Layers palette stays open so you can recognize which line of type is on which layer.

2. Choose the Move tool, select each text layer in turn, and drag it so that the starting points for all the lines are at the same vertical grid line and so that the bottom of each line of type rests on a horizontal grid line.

3. Choose Edit | Preferences | Grid to change your grid spacing for the size text you want to place. You can realign the grid vertices by resetting the zero points on the ruler. See Chapter 3 for more on setting up a grid and resetting the ruler. In addition, you can see an example of using the grid to align text back in Figure 15-49.

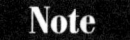 *You can enter paragraph text by pressing RETURN/ENTER at the point where you want the text to align according to the justification. However, you then have no control over the spacing between lines. Not every placement of text makes it imperative to control spacing between lines, but at least the grid procedure gives you a way to do it manually.*

Editing Text

The fact that text stays on its own layer and is in vector form gives you the ability to edit the text content anytime. You can change the content, position, size, orientation, font style, and font family of any portion of a text line or paragraph. Editing text is amazingly easy. Special effects always affect the entire line or paragraph.

1. Select the text layer to make a limited number of editing options available. The available options will be active on the Options bar.

2. For more options, double-click the text layer icon in the name bar to select and highlight the text in that layer. You can also insert the text cursor at the beginning of the line and drag it to select all the text. This method selects the whole line or paragraph of text. While the text is selected you can then change any of the parameters on the Options bar or in the Layer | Type menu.

3. Click the text icon in the active layer again, or choose the Cancel option on the Options bar to deselect the text.

4. To select a portion of the text, use the text cursor insertion method just mentioned, but insert it anywhere within the line or paragraph where you want to begin selecting text. You can then drag the cursor to select a string of text or you can click in another part of the line while holding SHIFT, and the text between the first and second insertions will all be selected and highlighted.

5. After the string of text is selected you can delete text, retype new content, or change any of the options for that string of selected text exclusively. You can see that the color of each letter in Figure 15-50 was changed individually to create a gradient effect.

Orienting Text

Photoshop Elements allows you to orient text in a number of ways. There is the standard method, which we all know as the convention horizontal left-to-right orientation. You can also force the text to orient in a vertical manner, which has the appearance of stacking the letters vertically, one on top of the other. You read this as vertical text from top to bottom unless you type it in backward. To orient type so it is rotated, you will use a transformation (covered in Chapters 7 and 11).

You place vertical type by using the Vertical Type tool, which is one of the sets of type tools in the type slot on the Toolbox. When this tool is selected, the text cursor will change to a horizontal bar and the text justification will change to top, middle, and

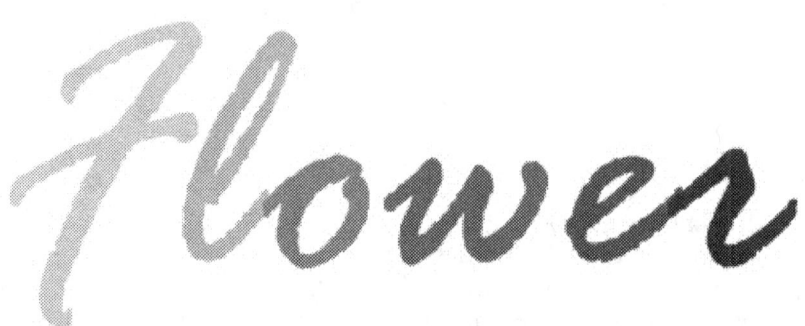

Figure 15-50.   *Each letter was selected individually and the color was changed.*

bottom. Otherwise, all the same rules apply for entry of text as with the standard type tool. You can choose to type in your text in standard format and change it to vertical by selecting the Text Orientation icon on the far right of the Options bar. It will toggle the text between Horizontal and Vertical. You can edit the type in either orientation.

Type Masking

Type masking is another means of entering text that gives you unique options. Instead of creating type, it creates selections in the shape of the type, so the areas of the image that the type covers are automatically made into a selection and then can be manipulated in all the same ways a selection can (see Chapter 7). There are two type mask tools, which correspond to the Standard and Vertical Type tools in terms of their orientation.

When you enter a type mask, the layer will turn translucent red and the type will appear in the form of a knockout. As long as the red is visible, the text is editable. You can also use the warp function at this time. Once you commit the type, the red will disappear and the type will be outlined as a selection and no longer editable as type.

Tip   *You can achieve similar results and give yourself the option of maintaining editing capability by placing your text that you want to convert to a selection with the standard Text tool. Then edit or transform the text any way you want. Create a duplicate layer so you can come back and edit the original text later, if you need to. Simplify the duplicated text and use the Magic Wand tool set on noncontiguous to select the type. Now you have essentially the same selection as you created with the Type Mask tool with all the advantages of being able to edit the original text and re-create the selection as many times as necessary.*

With text in the selection form, you can cut it out of the image layer to reveal layers underneath or fill the selection with patterns and gradients. Fill the selection with images by using the Paste Into command. You can see an example of type masking in Figure 15-51.

Another interesting way to mask with text is to use the Group with Previous command found in the Layer menu. This allows you to let layers stacked above the text layer show through when linked a special way. You can fin out more about this in Chapter 8.

Bending and Warping Text

Photoshop Elements provides 15 different styles for warping type. Because pictures are far more useful than words, take a look at the examples in Figure 15-52.

To warp selected text, choose the Warp icon on the Type Options bar, or choose Layer | Type | Warp Text, and the Warp Text Options bar appears, as shown in Figure 15-53. You can select a warp style from the drop-down Style menu. Each style is accompanied by a small illustration indicating the topological effect of the warp.

Choose the Horizontal or Vertical button to determine if the warp bends up and down, or from side to side. All of the warp styles have the same three slider controls to adjust the look of the effect: Bend, Horizontal Distortion, and Vertical Distortion. The Bend control determines the extent of the curvature. The Distortion control adjusts the perspective effects. The zero point in the middle of the slider is a neutral position. Moving the slider to the left or right of the zero point will toggle the direction of the effect. You will need to try out the controls on the warp style you have selected because the effect of the sliders can vary widely from one style to another. Once you have warped text, you can still edit it in same manner as regular text and apply layer styles to it.

To unwarp text, make the type layer you want to unwarp active. Choose the Type tool and then click the Warp text icon in the Options bar or choose Layer | Type | Warp Text. When the Warp Text dialog box appears, select None from the Style menu. Click OK.

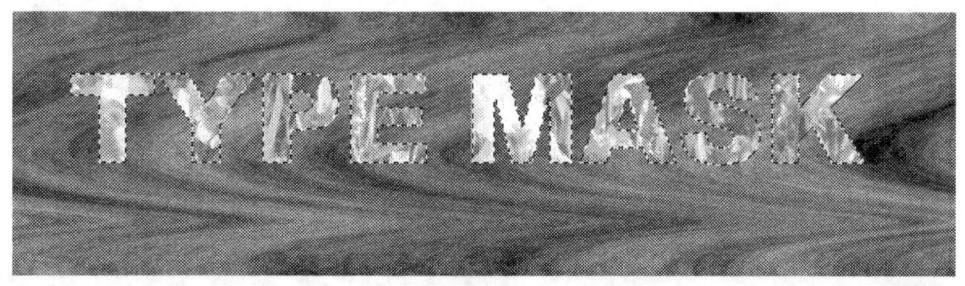

Figure 15-51.   *The type mask was used to create a selection that was cut to reveal the layer underneath.*

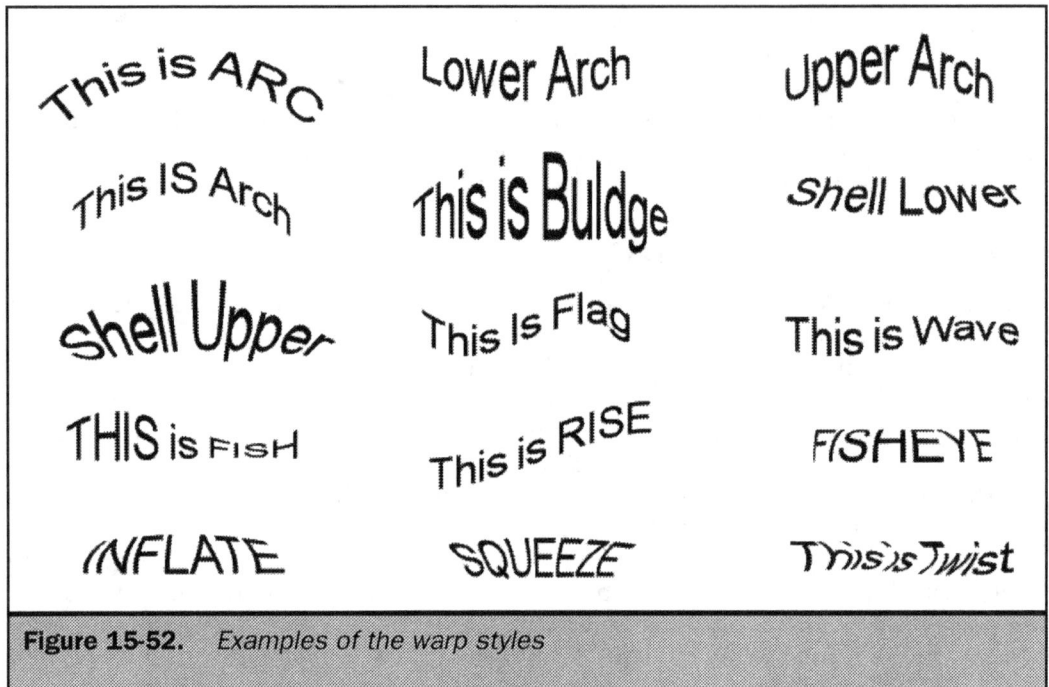

Figure 15-52. *Examples of the warp styles*

Photoshop Elements doesn't provide a way to let text follow a vector path that you create yourself. To approximate that process, create an empty layer above the image or

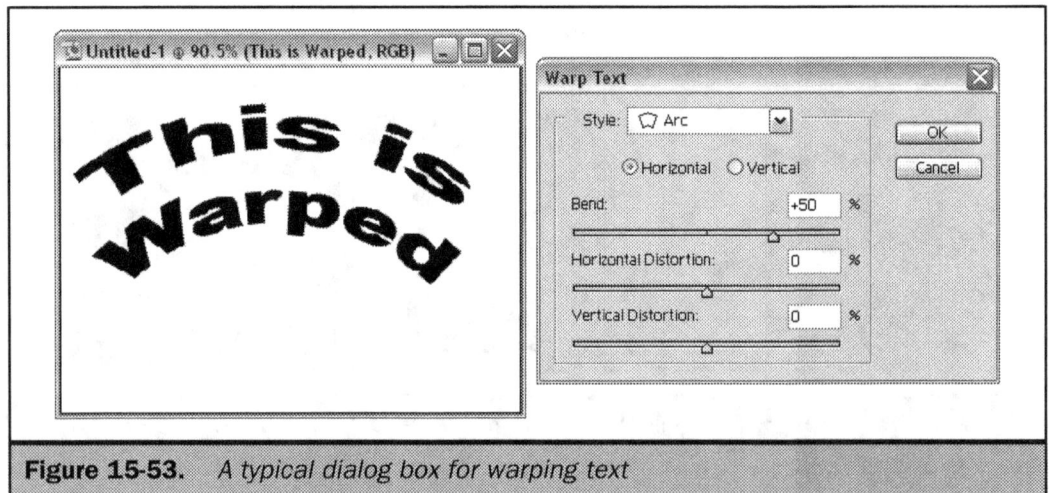

Figure 15-53. *A typical dialog box for warping text*

shape you want the text to conform to. Find a part of the image that has the curve or area you want to follow and use that as a guide as we did with the bananas in Figure 15-54. If you need to, trace the edge in a contrasting color to make it easier to align to. Then warp, scale, position, and transform the text as necessary until it fits the shape. When it does, delete the layer that contains the shape tracing.

Creating Shapes

Shapes are vector drawings. Vector shapes and their applied effects and styles are defined by mathematical algorithms, which means you can scale and shape them to any size without changing that shape's resolution. Photoshop Elements comes with a number of libraries of prebuilt shapes that you can choose from. The libraries have a total of 497 shapes that include arrows, symbols, speech balloons, flora and fauna, and much more. Layer styles can be applied to shapes in exactly the same way as they are with text.

The Rectangle tool is the first in the set of shape tools that you can access from the same slot in the Toolbox. The set includes Shape Selection, Rounded Rectangle, Ellipse, Polygon, Line, and Custom Shape tools. You can see an illustration of each in Figure 15-55, with a variety of layer styles applied. You can draw a shape in Photoshop Elements just by selecting the shape type you want and then dragging diagonally in the layer until the shape has the desired dimensions and proportions. Shapes are great for creating graphical elements, such as buttons and picture frames that will be used on web pages.

THE SPECIAL EFFECTS
WORKFLOW

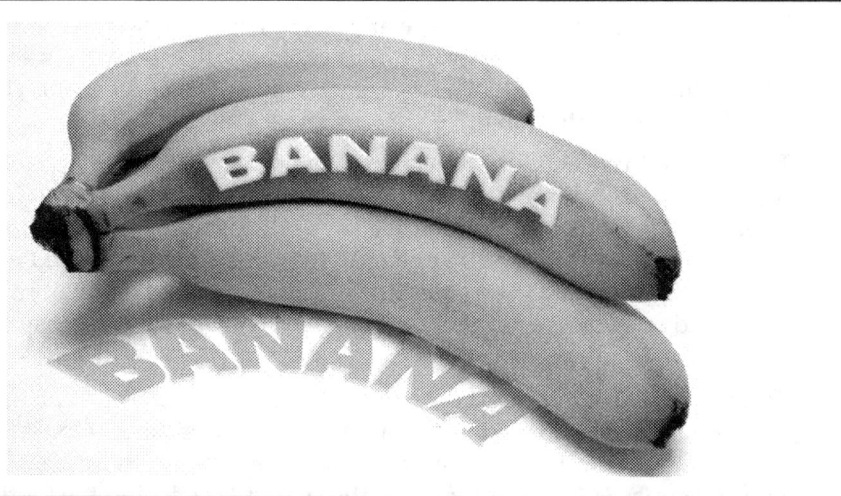

Figure 15-54.   *The text was warped to fit the curve of the bananas, and then some style effects were added.*

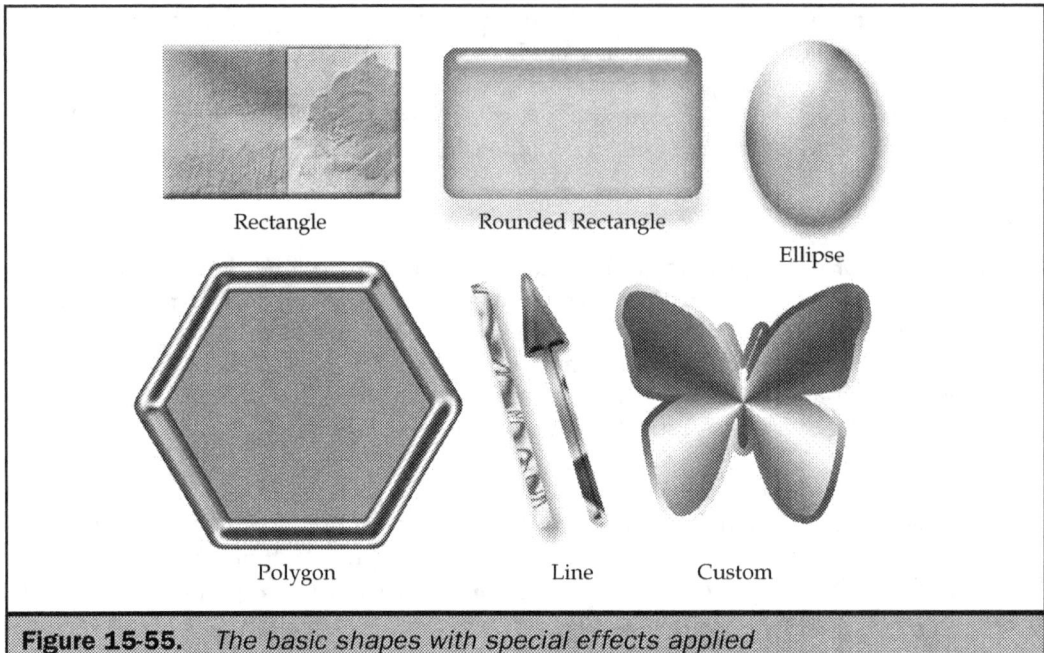

Rectangle   Rounded Rectangle

Ellipse

Polygon   Line   Custom

Figure 15-55. *The basic shapes with special effects applied*

To place a shape into an image:

1. Choose any shape tool. If the specific shape isn't showing in the Toolbox slot, drag across the box, and a drop-down palette will appear, from which you can choose the appropriate tool—or you can choose the exact shape you want from the Shape tool Options bar.

2. If you want to choose a custom shape, choose the Custom Shape tool (the default icon is a speech balloon). Then choose the exact shape from the Custom Shape Picker by clicking either the shape icon or the down-arrow icon to its immediate right. The Shape Picker will appear. If, from the Custom Shape Picker Palette menu, you choose All Elements Shapes, all the shapes in the library will be displayed at once. This is generally the best choice if you're unsure of which shapes you might want to use.

3. To place and size the shape once you've chosen it, place the cursor where you want one "corner" to start and drag diagonally until the shape is the size and proportion you want. In addition, just as is the case with the Marquee tools, you can choose options for most of the shapes by clicking the Options button in the Shape Options bar. The Options button is highlighted in the following

illustration. Immediately below the Options button, you see the dialog box for the Rectangle Options. A similar dialog box pops up for any of the shape tools.

Shapes are always drawn on their own layer automatically. You can use the Free Transform command to transform any shape by pressing CTRL while right-clicking the shape. A context menu appears that lets you make a selection from the shape, simplify the layer, or transform the shape.

Each shape type has a set of custom options that appear in a pop-up palette that can be accessed by clicking the down arrow just to the right of the Custom Shape icon on the Options bar. The custom options give you more control over how your shape is drawn, and provides for the enabling and adjusting of any special attributes for that shape type. See the following illustration of the Shape Options bar. If you want detailed information about each shape type and its options, refer to the sections for individual shape tools in Chapter 5.

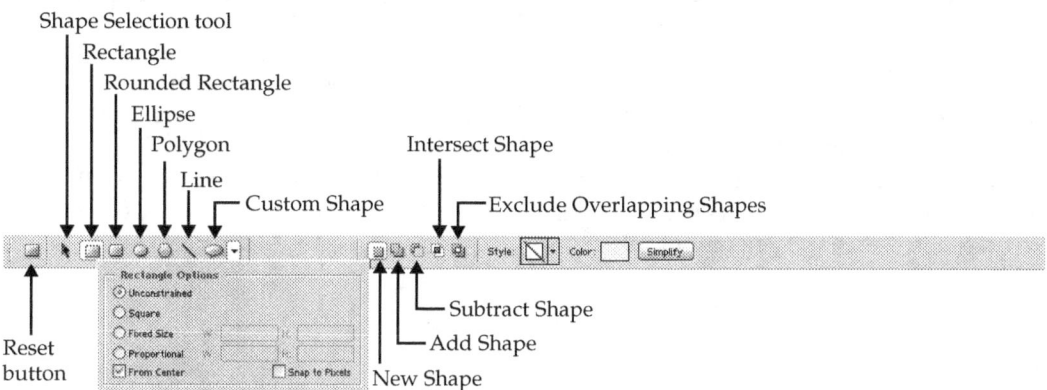

Photoshop Elements does not allow you to edit the vector shapes directly by manipulating the object's vertices, but you can augment the shape by using transformations and the modes for combining shapes by adding, subtracting, or intersecting multiple shapes. You can change these modes by clicking the appropriate icon on the Options bar. You can see how the circular shape in Figure 15-56 was changed by using the Subtract From Shape option as other shapes were placed. It is a cookie cutter–like process. You can also add shapes on, and overlap shapes to leave just the areas that intersect or everything that doesn't intersect. Use the Shape Selection tool to move or resize any of the shapes on the current shape layer. Use the Move tool to move or transform all the shapes at once. Using one shape to modify another gives you a great degree of freedom in developing new shapes. You can place these shapes in PSD files as layers and create your own custom shape archive.

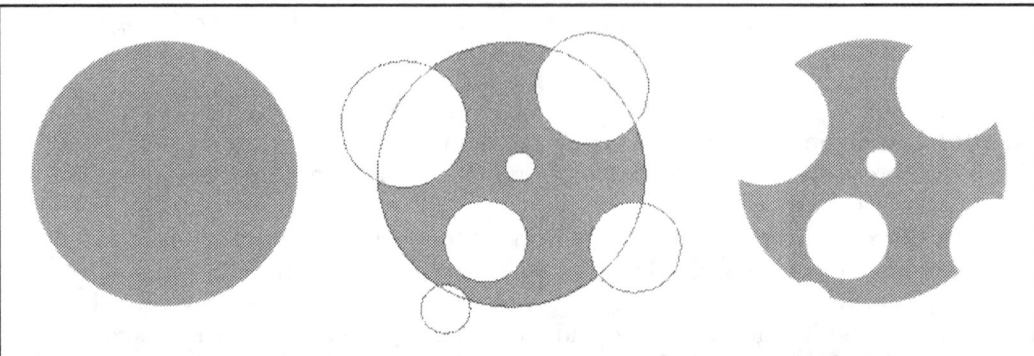

Figure 15-56. *A number of smaller circular shapes (middle) were used to cut portions of the larger circle (left) away, leaving a much more complex shape (right).*

When you try this, notice that when you use these modes, the extra shapes all end up on the same layer as the original shape. This is a clever way to get multiple shapes on one layer because they do not actually have to overlap. Use the Add To Shape option, and then place shapes anywhere on the layer. When you select one with the Move tool, all of the shapes are selected as a group. If you want to move individual shapes, use the Shape Selection tool.

The
Complete
Reference

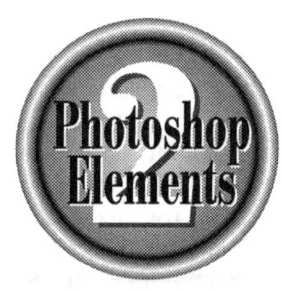

Chapter 16

Painting in Elements

617

Let's begin by defining what we mean by digital painting as opposed to many of the other techniques that Elements supports. Digital painting is defined as any manipulation of an image by any of the painting tools with the hand-eye coordination of an input device. So the use of automated filters, blending modes, or fills, for instance, would not qualify strictly as painting, even though you can create wonderful effects with those tools, and they can be used in conjunction with painting techniques to expand the effect of painting. Creating digital images often involves integrated techniques, so there is no absolute line where painting ends and special effects begin. The integration of tools and techniques is at the heart of digital art. This chapter covers a number of techniques that involve using Elements for digital painting. This involves a wide range of tools and commands, so you get a good look at the integration of Elements' functions.

This chapter places special emphasis on the Toolbox as the core of using Photoshop Elements in a painting mode. Photoshop Elements is not technically a paint program, but it can perform many painting tasks with the tools Elements provides. We reveal how to unleash the side of Elements that goes beyond mere image editing and into the more subjective world of painting, ranging from photo painting (mixing photo-editing and painting techniques) to sophisticated illustrations and works of fine art.

Using a Pressure-Sensitive Tablet Versus Using a Mouse

Part of what makes painting different from other types of graphic activities is the free-form nature of it. The mouse was not designed to be a painting tool. To get the kind of interaction a painter does with a brush or pen requires a different kind of input device. The digital tablet and pressure-sensitive pen allow you to interact with the graphic application environment with many levels of dexterity. Photoshop Elements takes advantage of the pressure sensitivity of digital pads such as those made by Wacom.

When you use a pressure-sensitive pen instead of mouse, a whole new world of possibilities opens up through the Photoshop Elements interface. Many of the brush preset styles support pressure sensitivity, which allows you to vary their parameters by the pressure you apply when you move the pen. For instance, you can vary the line width or jitter in a brush stroke interactively as you paint, much as a real brush would. You also get complete use of your fingers, which increases your ability to control brush strokes immeasurably. If you are serious about producing spontaneous, dynamic digital painting, then the pressure-sensitive pen and tablet is an absolute must.

To activate the pressure-sensitive capability of Elements, select the Tablet Support check box at the bottom of the More Options pop-up on the Paintbrush Options bar. Notice in the next illustration how the dynamics change in the course of one stroke.

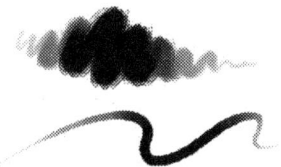

Preparation for a Painting

Paintings can range from a very realistic rendition of something in the real world to something totally abstract and a work of pure fantasy. We leave that subjective choice to you. Our job is to give you the tools and knowledge to use Photoshop Elements 2 to accomplish your goals. You bring the inspiration and the talent.

You should know what the composition is going to be so you can size your image document accordingly. Make sure the image size and print resolution are correct for the final output. See Chapter 19 for more on setting up images for print. It is also always a good idea to decide on a palette of colors as a theme for your piece. The Color Swatches palette is a good way to set up your base palette of colors, which we discuss in more detail in the "Swatches Palette" section, later in this chapter. The following are some other basic startup techniques that will help you be more successful in digital painting.

Laying the Groundwork

When you open a new document for painting, you have some choices that you need to make right off the bat.

1. Choose File | New to open a new document. The New File dialog box appears, as shown here.

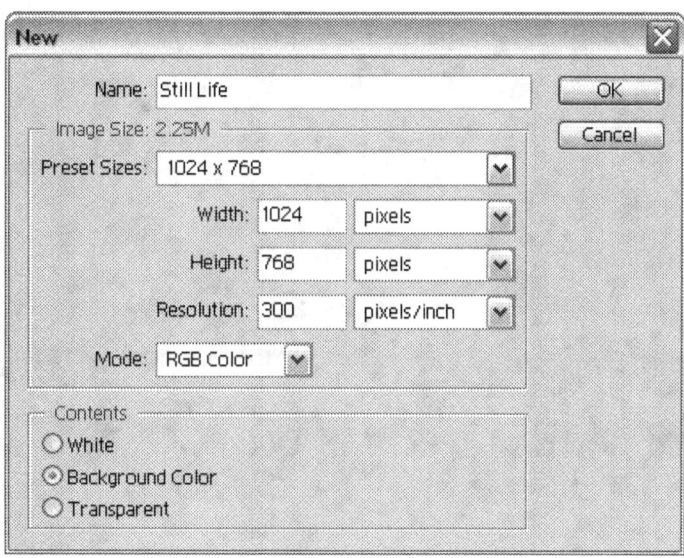

2. Set the image size by choosing a preset size from the drop-down menu, or enter custom values in the text fields for width and height. Understand what your subject matter is going to be and set the proportions of the document to suit the composition. You can adjust it later, if you need to, with the Canvas Size command.

3. Set the print resolution for the printer you will be working with for final output. This ensures that you have the right amount of pixel information in your original so output resizing won't lose your detail.

4. Set the color mode (RGB for full color).

5. Choose a background from the three options. It is often good to start a painting with a midtone background color that sets the theme for the painting or acts as a base color for an underpainting of tonal values.

Sketching

Making some preliminary sketches can help you work out compositional issues before you start applying more finished brushwork. Using a small brush or pencil tool set on a light gray or another color if you prefer, sketch in the basic shapes. By keeping the opacity of the drawing tool around 50 percent, you can build up the density gradually. Adjust the opacity to your preference. Some digital pens allow you to use the reverse tip as an eraser so you can easily change portions of your sketch until you get it the way you want. You can also work with a conventional drawing and scan or photograph the sketch as a starting point. You can see a quick sketch of a landscape in the following illustration, which was done with a digital pen and some standard preset brushes that come with Elements. The background color was set to a medium brown, and the lights and darks were blocked in quickly to get a sense of form and space. You can also use View | Grid to help get the shapes in the right place.

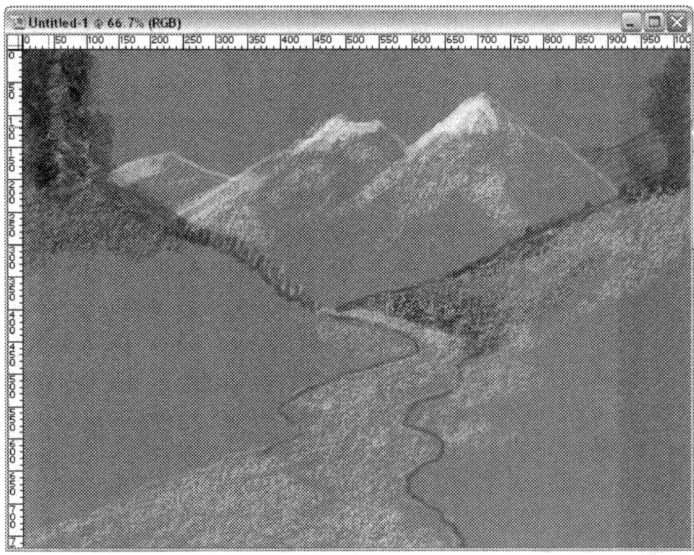

Tracing

For those of you that were not born with a built-in gift for drawing, there is always tracing. Elements makes it easy to trace from any captured image with the use of layers. Here is an easy way to trace an image:

1. Place the image you want to trace on the background layer.
2. Create a new layer with 50-percent opacity and fill that new layer with white.
3. A ghosted image of the background image shows through the new layer.
4. Set the foreground color to black or dark gray and trace over the important lines in the image. You can erase a mistake by drawing with white.
5. When you have finished tracing, return the layer to 100-percent opacity, and you will see the traced image by itself, as in the following image that was traced from a photograph of a cat.

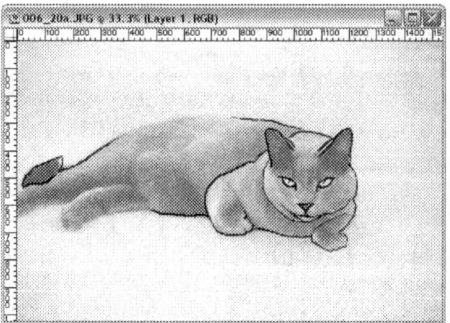

You can trace images from a number of sources on separate layers and then combine them into one composition.

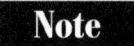 *Use the Find Edges filter to produce a quick sketch of a captured image, as shown in the following illustration.*

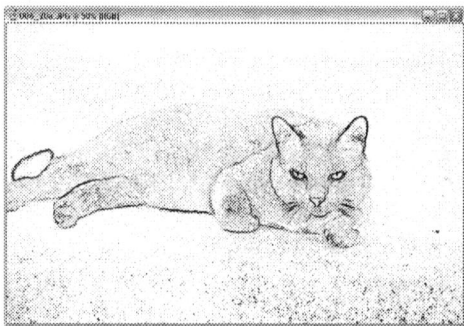

Source Material

Source material for digital painting includes anything that can be photographed, drawn, scanned, collected, or made to sit still long enough, which means pretty much anything, so there is no lack of material! Don't think that everything needs to be scanned in, either. You can set up a still life on your desk, or have someone sit for a portrait and paint it from real life. The most important ingredients, as always, are your imagination and your knowledge of Photoshop Elements 2. We can help you with the second one.

Using the Brush Tools for Painting

At the heart of painting in the digital environment are the Brush tools. Brush tools vary in their degree of sophistication from one paint or editing application to another. Photoshop Elements provides adequate paintbrush capability, which allows you to produce illustrator-level paintings, but falls short of being able to easily render fine-art–quality work in the pure painting mode. It does, however, have great capability in the photo painting realm. Photoshop Elements was not designed to be a full-blown paint system, but it has more punch than you might think once you dig in.

We now take a closer look at the aspects of the Brush tools that are useful in digital painting, and show you how to control them to fit your style. The Brush tools in Photoshop Elements that are classified as brushes and, therefore, can be used in painting are Paintbrush, Impressionist Paintbrush, Airbrush, Pencil, Eraser, Red-Eye Brush, Blur, Sharpen, Sponge, Smudge, Dodge, Burn, Clone Stamp, and Pattern Stamp. These Brush tools come with a host of options that are displayed in various icons, menus, and palettes in the Options bar for each tool.

Brush Tool Options

The Brush tools have a number of options in common that appear on the Options bar when you choose one of these tools from the Toolbox. You can see the Options bar for the Paintbrush tool in Figure 16-1.

In addition, most individual Brush tools have unique options found only on that tool's Options bar. We go over the common elements and specific features as they relate to the painting techniques we cover here. For more on specific features of each tool, see Chapter 5.

Preset Palette

You can choose from a large variety of brush shapes and sizes by opening the Preset pop-up palette. An array of icons shows you a representation of the brush shapes and a number that indicates the default pixel size. The brush shape is always indicated in shades of gray, with black being totally opaque and white being transparent. Any gray areas have degrees of transparency based on their luminosity. This allows paintbrushes to have rough edges and a textural quality by laying down color in varying degrees of

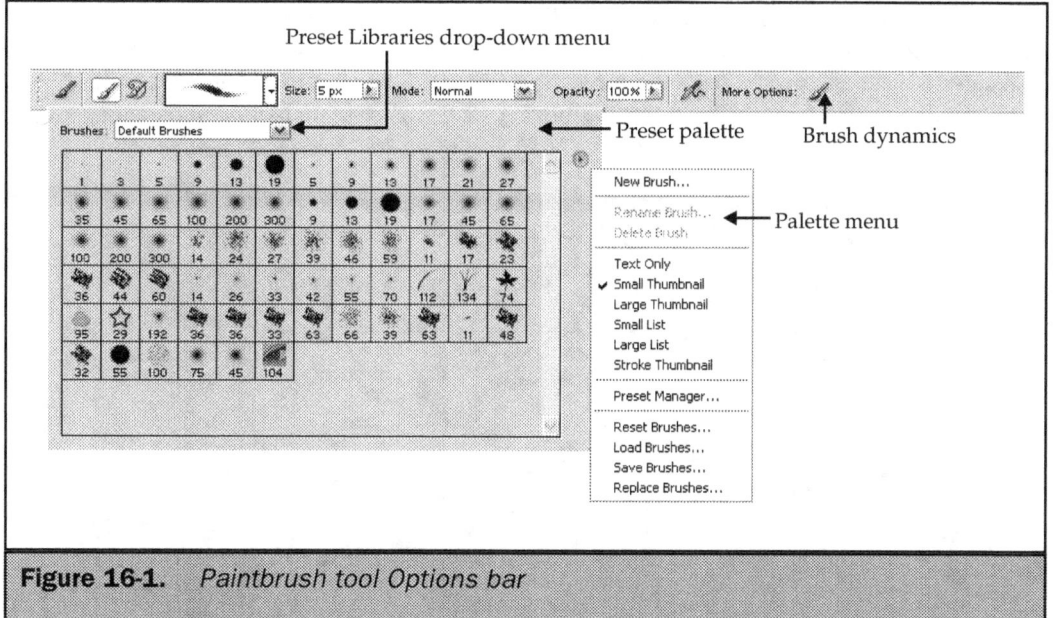

Preset Libraries drop-down menu

Preset palette

Brush dynamics

Palette menu

Figure 16-1.   *Paintbrush tool Options bar*

opacity. You can see a small stroke preview of each paintbrush shape in a window on the Options bar. Just a few samples of the hundreds available are demonstrated in the following illustration.

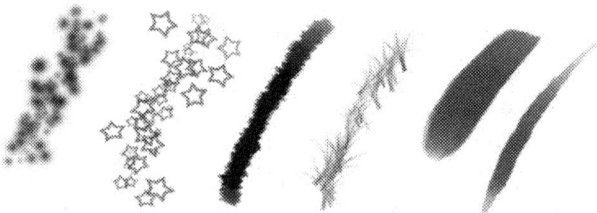

Photoshop Elements includes a number of preset libraries that can be loaded from the pull-down menu at the top of the Preset pop-up menu. Choose a library from the list and you will see the array of paintbrush icons change, as you can see in the Paintbrush Option bar back in Figure 16-1. All the Brush tools have this Preset pop-up palettes, so you can change their brush shapes as well.

Each Preset originates with user-changeable attributes that give it unique characteristics such as texture, pressure-sensitive variability, scatter, and color jitter, to name a few. The names of the brushes give some indication of the behavior of the brush. Choose a List mode from the Palette menu so you can see the names of the brushes displayed. Take time to look through the libraries and see what's available. Try them out on a blank document so you get an idea of each one. You can use the Preset Manager to move your favorites to a single library and rename them to make it convenient for you. To make a personal library of your favorite brushes, do this:

1. Choose Edit | Preset Manager. The Preset dialog box appears.

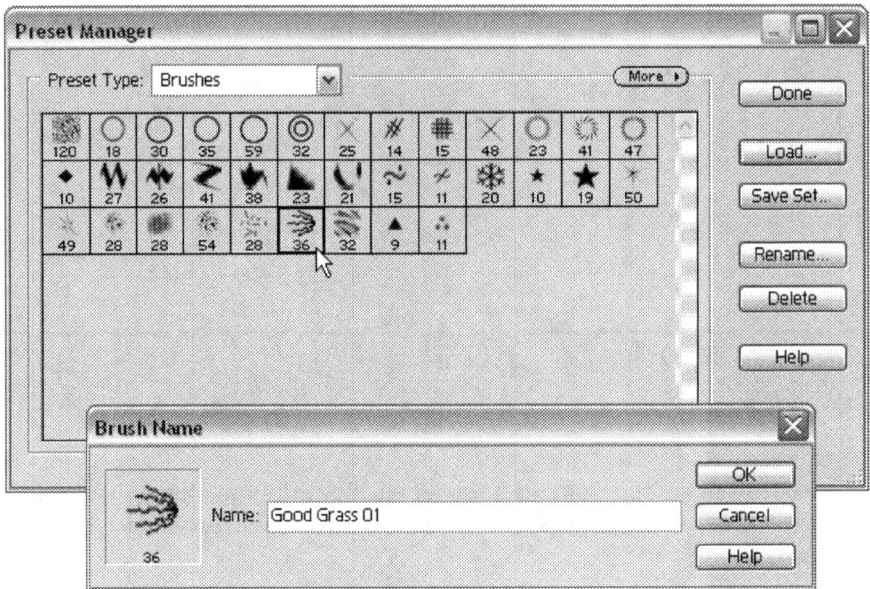

2. Select Preset Type | Brushes. The current library of brushes appears.

3. Load each of the other brush libraries from the Palette menu in succession. The brushes will be appended to the display. When you have finished loading all the libraries, you will have a complete thumbnail list of all the preset brushes.

4. Save this library with a new name, such as "My Brushes," in the Preset/Brush folder in the directory where Adobe Photoshop Elements was loaded.

5. Now go through and sample each one, and discard the ones you don't want by right-clicking and choosing Delete Brush. When this is complete, you will have a personalized list.

6. Save the library again, and it will appear on the Palette menu the next time you open Photoshop Elements.

You can create custom brushes with custom settings. Custom brushes can also be saved to your personal library or added to existing libraries. We cover creating custom brushes in the "Making Custom Brushes" section, later in this chapter. You can create a brush library for each project if you want. There are already some indications that add-in brush libraries will soon be available from a number of sources. Keep your eye on the Adobe web site's Photoshop Elements page.

Brush Size

Each paintbrush shape in the preset libraries was created at a certain size, which is indicated by the number just below the thumbnail. The number represents the diameter, in pixels, of a circle that would encompass the brush shape. You can change the size of any brush by entering a new pixel value in the Size field on the Options bar or by clicking on the arrow to the right of the Size field to open a slider. You will see the cursor representation of the brush change accordingly. Be aware that large brush sizes take much more processing power to paint with and might lag in their operation, depending on the processing power of your computer and the refresh rate of your graphics card.

When using a pressure-sensitive pen, be sure to follow the tablet manufacturer's instructions for calibrating the pad so that it responds to your touch the way you expect it to. It's also always a good idea to make sure that the tablet's drivers are up to date so that they cover any improvements you might have made in your system, including the graphics card you are using. Once you've calibrated your tablet, a change in brush size changes the size range affected by the pen pressure. Do some tests to judge the effect of changing sizes before you start painting. You might need to adjust the setting in your tablet's software to get the look you desire.

Blending Modes

The Mode menu gives you a complete list of all the blending mode options available in most of the Brush tools in Photoshop Elements 2. Some of the Brush tools have mode limitations. You can apply any of the blending modes to your brush and paint with them, which alters the current image using the blending mode algorithm, based on the foreground color, pattern, or clone source you have selected. See Chapter 9 for more information on using blending modes in painting.

Opacity

Type in a value or use a slider to change the Opacity field percentage value. Values lower than 100 percent make the brush transparent by varying degrees. Using a pressure-sensitive pen allows you to vary the opacity by pressure as you paint with presets that have pressure-sensitive attributes. Light pressure is more transparent. The Opacity value limits the maximum opacity you can achieve by maximum pressure on the pen. Working with semi-transparent brushes allows you to build up color gradually in layers, like using watercolors or pastels. The soft-wash effect in the following illustration was accomplished by using a soft paintbrush set to a dark color with Opacity set at 20 percent. The washes were put on successively, starting a little lower each time so the color built up in steps, resulting in a more natural-looking gradient.

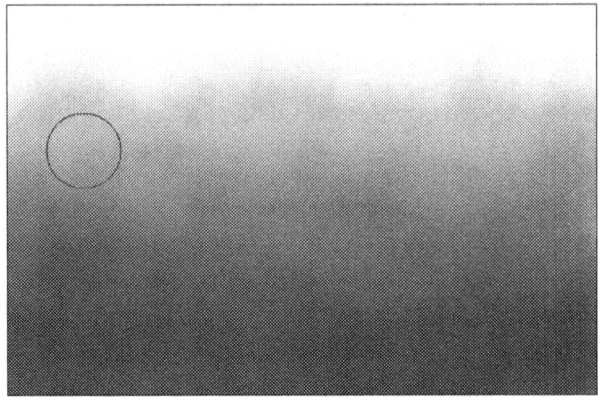

Using Brush Dynamics

Brush dynamics are a set of controls that tell the brush how to behave. Brush dynamics have such names as texture, scatter, jitter, rotation, opacity, spacing, and the like. Many of these dynamics are built into Photoshop Elements' brushes and are not available for modification. The names of the brushes give some indication of their fixed attributes, and the stroke preview shows you a sample of the effect. We have found that there is no substitute for actual testing of each brush to see what it really can do. If you are using a tablet, make sure you have the Tablet Support box checked in the Brush Dynamic pop-up menu so you can see if a brush reacts to pen pressure. You have the option to rename any of the brushes to be descriptive of what you feel are its built-in dynamics.

Now let's look at what we can modify. You can view the dynamics of a brush by selecting a brush shape from the Preset pop-up menu and then clicking on the More Options icon on the Options bar. The Brush Dynamics pop-up menu appears, as you can see in the following illustration.

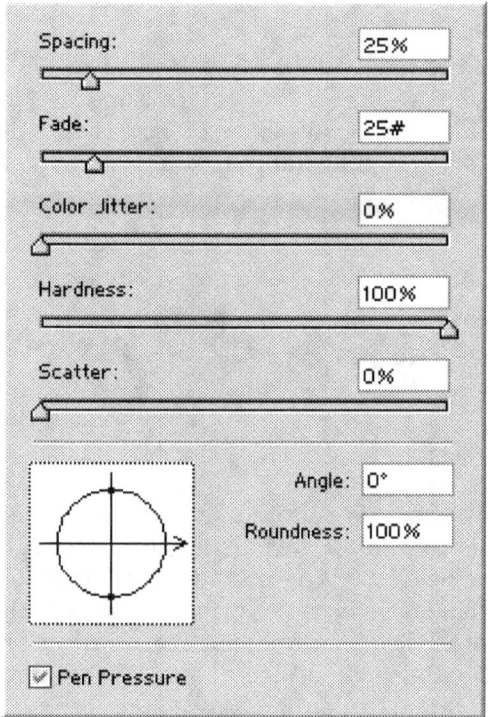

The pop-up menu presents you with a number of fields, sliders, and diagrams to alter the way a brush lays down color. Here is a description of each control in Brush Dynamics pop-up.

Spacing

This control sets the distance that individual paint dabs are set apart. If the spacing parameter is set to zero, the brush has a smooth, continuous flow of color. The higher you set the value, the more space is inserted between each dab, producing a dashed-line effect with the brush shape. Use this if you want a more staggered look to the brushstroke, as the illustration shows.

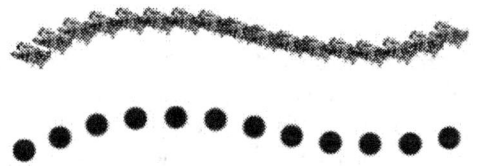

Fade

The Fade control determines how fast the flow of your brushes tapers off. This gives you the ability to make your strokes all taper at the same rate, producing a uniform look and a soft end to the stroke. See the effect of increasing fade values in the strokes from left to right in the following illustration.

Color Jitter

The Color Jitter control is a very nice addition to Photoshop Elements 2. One of the drawbacks of most paint programs is the inability to produce good color variation within a single brush stroke, which is one of the reasons that computer painting has always been so recognizable from its real-world counterpart. This is not to say that Photoshop Elements is at the level of producing realistic brush strokes, but color jitter takes us a step closer to getting a varied color blending that is much more interesting.

Color Jitter forces the brush to alternate between the foreground and background colors as you paint. The higher the Color Jitter values, the more intense the fluctuation between colors. If you are using a textured brush and a third color for the background and you set opacity below 100 percent, you can get some very complex color mixing as you paint. It is hard to show you the subtly of this because it is an effect that has mostly to do with color. The following illustration gives you some idea of the variation in a brush stroke that has a Color Jitter value applied.

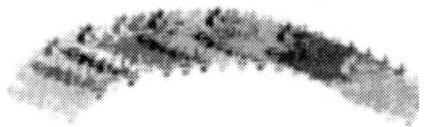

Hardness

The Hardness control determines how hard the edge of your brush stroke is. When you set the control to the left, it softens the brush; to the right makes the edges sharper. The effect is similar to feathering; it blends the soft edges into the surrounding image. You can see the look of soft and hard brush strokes in the next illustration. Soft brush strokes give you the quality of airbrush or wet media. It is much easier to blend brush strokes together if the edges are soft.

Scatter

The Scatter control places the paint dabs in a random distribution within a range around the brush path. The range is set by the Scatter value you enter. The higher the value, the wider the distribution. This can give the brush a randomly rough-edged appearance or a spattered look if the distribution of dabs is wide enough to produce separation. Some of the preset brushes have built in scatter as part of their look. In the following illustration, you can see a number of brush strokes with different degrees of scatter applied to them.

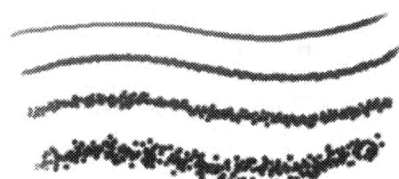

Brush Roundness and Angle

The Roundness control consists of a text-entry field where you can type in the percentage by which you want to reduce one axis of the circular footprint of the current brush. The resulting elliptical shape is reflected in the diagram at the bottom left of the palette. This alters the profile of your brush shape by squashing it in one direction so it draws more asymmetrically.

You can also change the angle of rotation by either entering a value in the Angle field, or dragging the elliptical diagram around until you see the angle you want displayed in the Angle field, or clicking around the circumference of the circle or ellipse. The rotation will not be visible on round brushes until you alter the roundness. You will see the rotation of all other brushes reflected in their cursor profile.

Altering angle and roundness can produce calligraphy-type strokes and strokes that have built-in width variability, as you can see in the following examples. Accentuate the directional aspect of your stroke patterns by having the brush mimic the direction, or create a more chaotic pattern by changing the angle often.

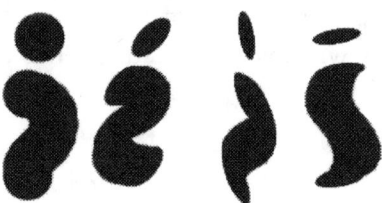

Tablet Support

Check the Tablet Support box to enable the use of your pressure-sensitive pen with the brush presets that support pen pressure.

Color and Brushes

Now that we have taken a close look at how to shape, size, and set brush dynamics, let's talk about paint color. This is when all your preparation and setup finally get to express themselves as you apply the color and render the image you have in your mind to the screen. So much of the computer process is exacting and precise, which makes letting go and expressing with abandon one of the hardest things to do when painting on a computer. Remember, Photoshop Elements has user-definable levels of undo capability (the default is 20), so you can do some experimenting and then back up if you don't like the effect you're getting. Just remember that each stroke is a complete undo step and 20 strokes isn't much. You might want to set the levels higher when you're painting.

To change the number of available undo levels:

1. Choose Edit | Preferences. The Preferences dialog box appears.
2. Choose Preferences | General.
3. In the History States field, enter the number of undo states you'd like to have and then click OK.

Regardless of the number of undo history states you have set, there are two ways you can move backward and forward in the undo history states: You can issue the Edit | Step Forward (CMD/CTRL+Y) or Edit | Step Backward (CMD/CTRL+Z) commands, or you can simply choose a state in the Undo History palette.

If you get to a certain stage and know you want to go back before you resume work, go back to where you want to start before you close the file. That's because when you reopen Photoshop Elements, you always start with a blank Undo History palette.

Applying Color to Brushes

The foreground and background color swatches in the Photoshop Elements Toolbox display the foreground and background colors. The default colors are black as the foreground color and white as the background color. You can always restore these defaults by pressing D, and you can swap them by pressing X.

Clicking either color swatch opens the Color Picker, which allows you to use a number of color models to select colors from the RGB color space. See Chapter 5 for more information on using the Color Picker. This is a very capable system but one that gets in the way of spontaneity when you are painting. It is cumbersome to have to open and close the Color Picker every time you want a new color. Conventional artists use hand-held palettes, which they dab into repeatedly to alter the colors often as they paint. Can you imagine having to open your paint box every time you want to put another color on your brush? The alternative is to just use the two colors on the Toolbox, which makes for a pretty boring painting unless you are doing a black-and-white sketch. For full-color renditions, you need a robust palette.

Swatches Palette

This brings us to the purpose of the Photoshop Elements Swatches palette. The Swatches palette lets you place virtually any number of colors right next to where you are actually painting. All you have to do to choose one of those colors is click in its square. Any time you want to create a new color, you just change the foreground color by clicking it and choosing a new color from the Color Picker, and then clicking the New Swatch icon at the bottom of the Swatches palette. A new swatch (square) will appear, and its color will be that of the current foreground color swatch.

The only advantage a conventional artist's palette has is that you can dab and mix the colors interactively. The paintbrush takes one color at a time, with the exception of the Color Jitter control, which we cover in more detail in the "Color Jitter" section, later in this chapter. The key to mixing and blending colors as you paint has a lot to do with overlaying textures; transparency; and varying the placement, color, thickness, and density of your brush strokes with pen pressure. Access to a diverse palette as you paint is also an important consideration. The following sections go into detail about how to get color onto the brush from a variety of sources and with a number of techniques.

Note
Here is way to approach the feeling of a mixed palette. If you want to get a range of colors from mixing two colors together, create a new, small (1×2 inches is usually large enough) document with a white background. Create a small rectangular selection. Create a linear gradient between the two colors you want to mix and fill the selection with the gradient. Then you can pick any color by placing the brush in the gradient document's window and pressing OPT/ALT while clicking to select colors from anywhere in the gradient. The gradient represents all the possible colors that could occur as a mixture of the two original colors. Create as many gradients as you want, and save the document as your palette.

The Swatches palette provides a wider selection and easier access than the color control boxes in the Toolbox. For a complete rundown on the Swatches palette functions, see Chapter 4. You can access the Swatches palette from the Palette Well or the Window menu. The Swatches palette provides you with a number of preset palettes that give you a pretty good range of basic colors along with a range of tints. Most of these palettes were designed for use with web production and not specifically with painting in mind. You can choose to modify the existing palettes or create whole new palettes from scratch

THE SPECIAL EFFECTS WORKFLOW

using the Preset Manager. Before we discuss customizing, let's see how to use the Swatches palette while painting. You can see the Swatches palette in the following illustration.

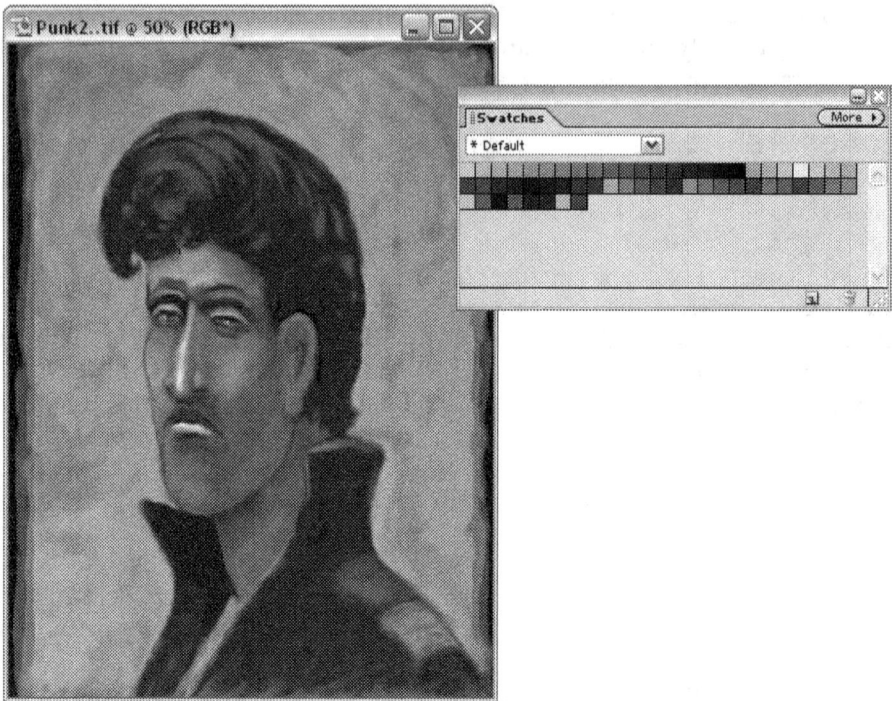

Using the Swatches Palette While Painting   Open and drag the Swatches palette from the Palette Well so it floats freely in the application window alongside the image window. If you need to, you can minimize it to a very small screen profile by clicking on the dash icon on the title bar. If you leave it in the Palette Well, it automatically closes every time you start painting. This is just what you want to avoid. Floating the palette allows you quick access to a whole host of colors just by moving your cursor over the palette and clicking on the color swatch you desire. Click to set the foreground color, and press OPT/ALT while clicking to set the background color. You will see the foreground or background color change as you make selections.

Building a rhythm in painting is very important so you want to set things up to be easily accessible. Keep the Swatch palette open while you are painting so you can dip into it and get a color without breaking the flow of your brushwork.

You can choose to view the color thumbnails in the Swatches palette as just an array of color squares or with names showing. These options are accessed through the Palette menu. The default swatch names for the preset Swatches palettes, except for the default palette, are in hexadecimal format, which is commonly used by web editors but doesn't mean much in terms of easily finding a color that you used before. The default palette uses more subjective naming, which makes it easier to find a color later. You can also rename any colors to be more memorable to you. If you don't see the colors you want within the preset palettes, you have the option of creating custom colors in the existing palette or creating new palettes entirely. You want the palette to include all the basic colors you want to use in your painting. Just remember that if you make changes to the current palette, you need to save the palette to a new name or it will automatically revert to the default when you close Photoshop Elements or reload the palette. We discuss other methods of extending the color palette's capability in the next sections.

Customizing Your Color Swatch Palette for Painting   Sooner or later you will want to move beyond the preset palettes and set up palettes that are uniquely yours. In this section, we take a look at how to customize various features of the Swatches palette to give you complete flexibility.

To add a new color swatch (the current foreground color) to an existing palette:

1. If the color of the new swatch isn't already the foreground color, click the foreground color swatch. The Color Picker appears. Choose the color you want to use in the new color swatch.

2. Choose Palette | New Swatch, or right-click on any swatch and choose the New Swatch command, or move the cursor to the first open swatch position (you will see the cursor change to a Fill icon) and click. The New Swatch dialog box appears.

3. Type in a new name or accept the default name and click OK. The new color swatch appears at the end of the palette. This addition is temporary while you are in an active work session unless you save the palette.

If you prefer to choose colors by name, you can add unique names when you create new swatches or edit the existing names by double-clicking to open the Rename dialog box directly or right-clicking on a swatch and choosing Rename Swatch.

To delete color swatches, right-click any swatch and choose Delete Swatch.

You can keep adding and deleting colors until you have the set you want for the painting. This is akin to the conventional artist setting his colors by squeezing colors from the tube onto the palette in preparation for painting.

To save the modified palette:

1. When you have finished editing your palette, choose Save Swatches in the Palette menu and enter a name for the new palette.

2. Save the swatches to the folder called Preset/Color Swatches in the program directory for Photoshop Elements 2. This ensures that they appear on the Palette menu.

Note   *There is no undo for most of these palette editing functions, so if you delete a color by mistake, you have to create an identical swatch or reload the original palette and start over.*

THE SPECIAL EFFECTS WORKFLOW

Using the Preset Manager to Customize Your Palette

The Preset Manager, found in the Edit menu, has another set of tools for customizing and managing your Swatches palettes. The Preset Manager palette interface is covered in detail in Chapter 4. The Swatches palette allows you to add, delete, and rename swatches, and then save them to unique libraries files. What it doesn't do is allow you to create new swatches. Swatch creation is unique to the Swatches palette. The Preset Manager, shown here, allows you to rearrange the colors on the palette, combine two or more palettes together, and then save them to new library files. You can also choose a set of colors within any Swatches palette and save it to a separate library.

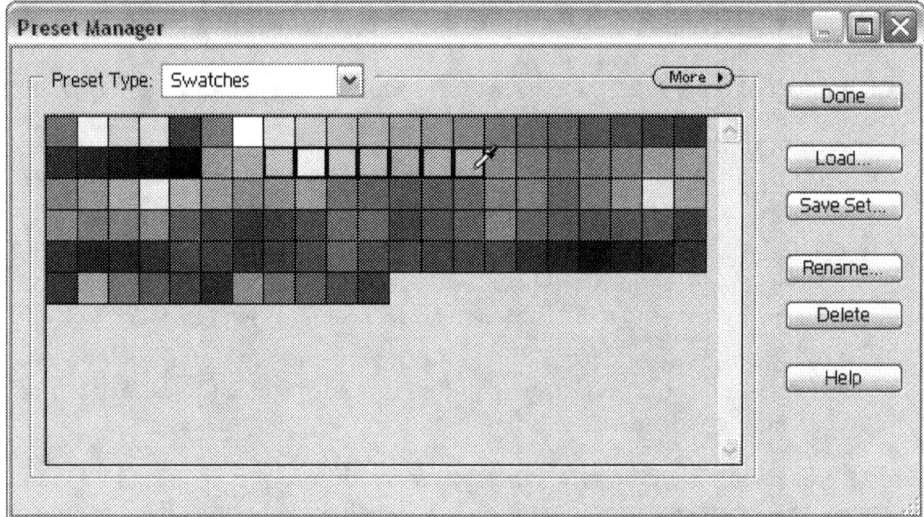

Rearranging the colors allows you to reorder colors into more logical groups. You can group all the reds together and put them in ascending order according to luminance, or group colors by where you are going to use them in the paint—flesh tones in one area, and sky colors in another. How the colors are organized is really up to you.

To rearrange the color swatches:

1. Place the cursor over the color you want to move. Click and hold and you will see the Eyedropper cursor turn into the grabbing hand.

2. You can then drag the swatch to a new location.

3. An insert icon appears between two swatches to show you the point at which you can insert the swatch as you move it over the palette.

4. Release the mouse button to insert the swatch in the new location.

5. Repeat the operation to move more swatches.

To move a set of swatches:

1. Select a group of swatches by holding SHIFT while clicking the swatches you want to move. You will see the swatches highlight to indicate they are selected.

2. Follow the same steps as you did with a single swatch.

You can create subsets of any palette by saving selected sets to new palette library files, and then reloading those in a modular fashion to mix and match as you need them. For instance, you can create a palette that has just flesh tones and load it only if you are doing a portrait, or save another palette that has only earth tones or bright colors. The Preset Manager allows you to load palettes and append them to the current palette, so you can add these sets as you need them.

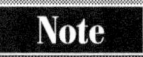 *In the Preset Manager, only the Load button loads and appends palette files. If you load palettes from the Palette menu, they will replace the current palette. Be sure you have saved before you load a new palette.*

To save a set of swatches on a new palette:

1. Choose Edit | Preset Manager. The Preset Manager palette opens.

2. Choose Preset Type | Swatches.

3. Load the palette(s) you want to select your set from. You can load multiple palettes, including ones you have created using the Load button.

4. Select the swatches you want to include in your set by holding SHIFT while clicking the swatches. You will see the swatches you have selected highlight with a dark border, indicating they are selected. You can deselect a single swatch in the set by holding SHIFT and clicking any highlighted swatch. To deselect the whole set, click anywhere in the swatches.

5. When you have completed your selection, click Save Set and enter a name for the new palette that will contain the set you selected, or save over an existing set. Save the swatches to the folder called Preset/Color Swatches in the program directory for Photoshop Elements 2 if you want the palette to appear in the Palette menu.

Eyedropper Tool

This tool is very handy little device that has more of a role in digital painting than you might think at first glance. In fact, a technique we discuss here might make this one of the tools you use most as you paint. Use the Eyedropper tool to select the color of any pixel in an image just by placing the Eyedropper cursor over the pixel and clicking to set the foreground color or holding OPT/ALT while clicking to set the background color. What is especially nice is that you can hold down the OPT/ALT key to temporarily switch from the Brush tool to the Eyedropper tool. In other words, you can pick a color without having to switch tools. This keeps the painting flow continuous, making this one of Adobe's more brilliant additions. As soon as you release OPT/ALT, you are back to the Brush tool you were using.

Because you can easily pick colors with the Eyedropper tool from other open images, you can use another image as a palette to dab or push colors—just as you would mix paints on a conventional artist's palette. You can accomplish this by using gradients; blends; transparency; smudging; and the motion blurring, radial blurring, and liquify filters. This "palette image" becomes a source for selecting colors with the eyedropper as you paint. You can see an example of a mixed-palette image here. With grabbing colors from the painting itself, a palette image, the Swatches palette, the Color Control boxes, and the Color Picker, you have quite a selection to choose from.

Color Jitter

The Color Jitter brush dynamic allows the Paintbrush tool to alternate between the foreground and background colors as you paint. You can control the intensity of the alternation by adjusting the Color Jitter values in the Brush Dynamics pop-up menu, which is found on the Paintbrush Options bar. You can change the color effect by changing or flipping the foreground and background colors. When you use the Color Jitter control in conjunction with textured brushes and transparency, you can get very complex color mixing and patterning and a more natural-looking brush stroke.

The Color Jitter control is a new addition to Photoshop Elements 2. and a very welcome one, indeed. One of the great drawbacks of digital painting in many paint programs is the inability to load the brush with multiple colors to increase the complexity and natural look of brush strokes. The technique of loading brushes in this manner goes back to the beginning of painting, yet, in this most modern of mediums, it seems to have been often overlooked. The Color Jitter control is a step in the right direction. We encourage experimenting with the Color Jitter control with various styles of the Paintbrush to fully appreciate its range of capability.

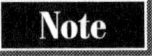   *Color Jitter is especially good for creating loosely painted backgrounds, which work especially well in portraits and still-life paintings. See the still life in the section "Painting from Scratch," later in this chapter.*

Blending Modes

Blending modes are another way to affect the way in which color is laid down by the Brush tools. By selecting a blending mode from the Brush Options bars, you apply the selected blend algorithm to your Brush tool, which alters the color in unique ways as you paint. The intensity of the effect is affected by all the other options available for the tool you selected—color, brightness, pattern, opacity, and so on. To get in-depth information about painting with blending modes, see Chapter 9.

Making Custom Brushes

Photoshop Elements provides a rather extensive library of preset brush libraries to choose from. Before you venture out into the world of creating custom brushes, be sure to peruse the existing sets provided with the program. Choose the Paintbrush tool, and then open the Preset menu from the Options bar. Select a library from the Brushes drop-down menu. Choose Palette | Large List so you can see the shape and the text description of each brush, which gives you an idea what each brush can do. For instance, if the brush name is Pastel Rough Texture, you can surmise that it will be a chalky (soft edges) and textured (as if it was done on rough paper) stroke. Many brushes have built-in characteristics that you cannot change, but you can still apply any of the options, such as size, opacity, and brush dynamics.

If you have seen what Photoshop Elements has to offer in the way of preset brushes and you are still not satisfied, here is a breakdown of how you can build your own brushes to suit your unique needs. There are two brush customization methods, and it is important to understand the distinction:

■ In one method, you take an existing preset, apply new options and dynamics to it, and then save it as a new brush. The reason for using this method is to preserve the built-in attributes that come with many of the preset brushes, which can be a real asset. For example, when you build a brush from scratch, you cannot add things such as texturing and stepped rotation.

■ In the other method, you define your own brush from scratch by rendering or capturing it using the Define Brush command and then adding it to a brush library.

You can change the attributes on any brush from the Options bar, and the brush will hold those changes while the current work session is active. If you want to hold onto the changes for a longer period of time, you must save the brush to a preset library. Now let's take a look at the steps for making a custom brush.

How a Brush Shape Works

Brush shapes are confined within a circular area that is defined by the initial brush size. That size represents the diameter of that circle. Brushes are strictly grayscale. The opacity of the brush is defined by the luminosity of the pixels in the brush shape with white being transparent and black being totally opaque. Shades of gray produce all percentages of transparency. This is how you can get soft edges, for example. The fact that white can be transparent is what allows for the very complex shapes within the circle. White essentially acts as a transparency mask for the brush shape.

You can build brushes by painting the shapes on a white background, using black where you want the color to be solid and grays where you want some level of transparency. Try making some shapes that are solid and others with separate elements so you can see the difference when you paint with both. Separating the elements into a number of dots, for instance, has an effect similar to spreading the bristles on a real brush so you can see the individual bristles, giving the brush stroke a hairy or fuzzy look, as you can see in the illustration here.

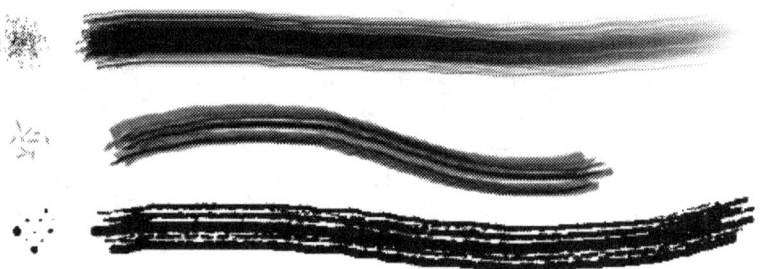

Defining a Brush

Defining a brush is very easy, as shown in Figure 16-2. Here is how it works:

1. Use a marquee tool to define the area you want to capture as a brush.

2. Choose Edit | Define Brush. The Define Brush dialog box appears.

3. You will see a thumbnail of the brush you just captured. If it is not to your liking, try changing the defined area and repeat step 2. Enter a name for your brush or accept the default name.

4. The new brush is displayed in the last position of the current brush's preset palette. The size indication corresponds to the largest dimension of the marquee selection you used to define the brush.

You have a lot more control if you draw your brush shapes from scratch, or you can choose to capture any part of any image and turn it into a brush. Just remember the rules about luminosity and transparency. Even though the part of the image you are capturing might look interesting as an image, this doesn't mean it will translate well to a brush. Areas of high contrast work best. Ideally, brush shapes have an area of white separating the shape from the marquee border so the brush does not take on the shape of the marquee. Use the Lasso tool to get more free-form shapes.

Just as with the Swatches, you might want to move your custom brushes you just created to unique libraries so they are more convenient.

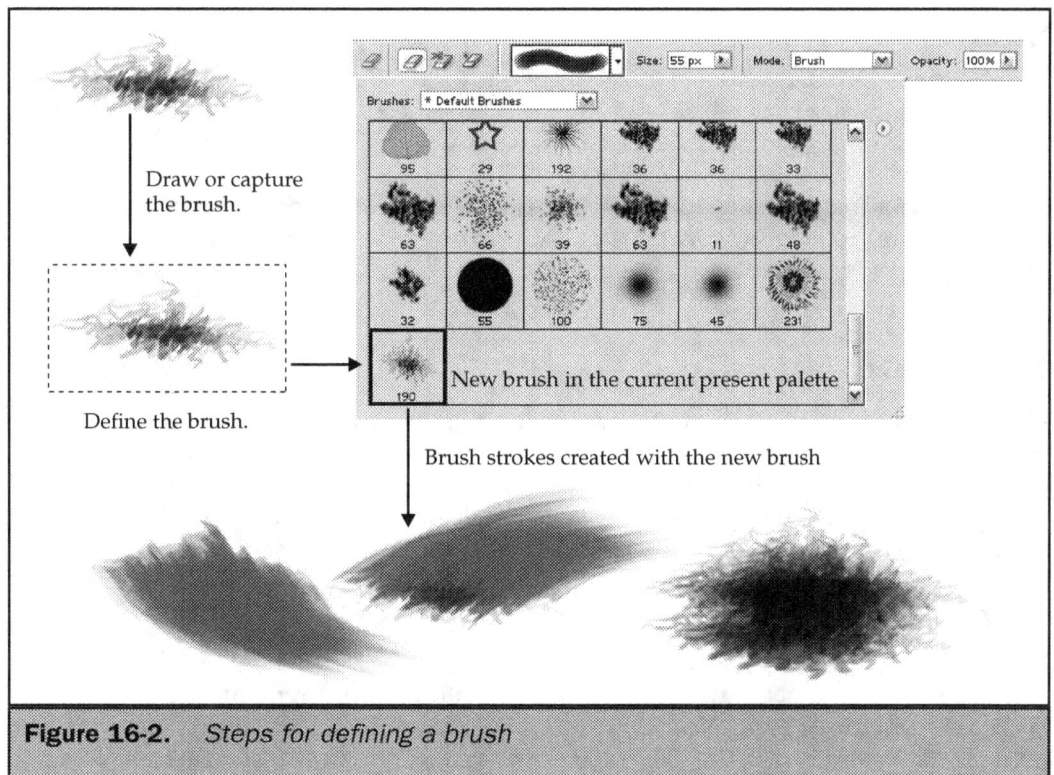

Draw or capture
the brush.

Define the brush.

New brush in the current present palette

Brush strokes created with the new brush

Figure 16-2.   *Steps for defining a brush*

To save a set of brushes to a new library:

1. Choose Edit | Preset manager. The Preset Manager palette opens.

2. Choose Preset Type | Brushes.

3. The current preset palette will contain the brushes you just created.

4. Select the brushes you want to include in your set by holding SHIFT while clicking the swatches. You will see the swatches you have selected highlighted with a dark border, indicating they are selected. You can deselect a single swatch in the set by holding SHIFT while clicking any highlighted swatch. To deselect the whole set, click anywhere in the swatches.

5. When you have completed your selection, click Save Set and enter a name for the new palette that will contain the set you selected or save over an existing set. Save the swatches to the folder called Preset/Color Swatches in the program directory for Photoshop Elements 2 if you want the palette to appear in the Palette menu.

Airbrush

The Airbrush option appears on the Options bar for the Paintbrush tool. This option simply places a paintbrush in a buildup mode. This means the color will continue to build up as long as you hold the mouse button down or apply pressure with the pen without moving the brush's screen position. This mimics the constant flow of paint from a real airbrush. The airbrush effect works best on soft-edged brushes with a lower opacity setting. You can get great effects with Airbrush by using selections as masks. The next section goes into masking with selections.

Masking with Selections

Photoshop Elements doesn't provide any built-in general-purpose masking capability other than the masks that come with the adjustment and fill layers, but that should not deter you from using the selection tools to create homemade masks that really work very nicely. In this section, we show you some selection techniques that help you have more control over which areas of your painting get special treatment.

Isolating Areas

Use selections to isolate areas of your painting so you can work more freely without the fear of messing up other parts of the image. This allows more dynamic brush strokes and specialized brushes in selected areas while other areas are protected. You can also invert the selection, which flips the masking effect so you can work in adjacent areas while protecting the area you just painted. Selections can be saved to use later and even merge with other selections expanding the selection area. Saving your selections allows you to move between selected or masked areas over and over again as you build the painting. For more information of using selections, see Chapter 7.

Here is a good example of using a selection to mask one area of painting, allowing you to paint in dynamic brush strokes to achieve a nice painterly effect in the selected area. We are going to paint in a sky through the branches of a tree, as shown in Figure 16-3. Under normal conditions, it would be very difficult, if not impossible, to get a broad brush stroking pattern to the sky if you had to draw between each individual branch. By selecting the sky area as the active painting area, however, it becomes easy.

Here is how to paint in the sky:

1. Use the Magic Wand tool to select the sky portion of the image. Some trial and error is necessary to determine the best tolerance setting for preserving the detail in the tree branches, and still get all the sky selected.

2. Uncheck Contiguous so all areas of the sky are selected even though not adjacent.

3. Check Anti-Aliased to maintain a smooth transition at the edges of the selection.

4. Choose the Paintbrush tool.

5. Choose a spatter-type brush from the Wet Media Preset Library, and size it to 200. Adjust the size of the brush based on the image you are working on.

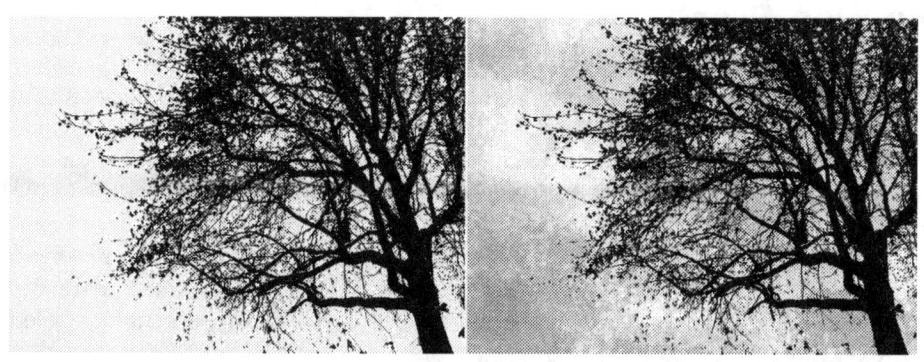

Figure 16-3. *Starting out with the image on the left, it's easy to add a sky. Use a selection to mask the tree, and then paint in a sky to create the image on the right.*

6. Bring up the More Options Brush Dynamics pop-up menu, and adjust the Color Jitter control to 50 percent.

7. Select the foreground and background colors for the sky.

8. With the sky area still selected, paint in the sky using broad, rapid brush strokes. You don't have to worry about the tree because it is masked. You will see the brush alternate between the foreground and background colors as it paints. Build up the color as needed. Press X to alternate the foreground and background colors to get variations.

9. Repeat the previous step with lighter cloud colors to get the final effect.

Conventional airbrush painting methods have always made great use of friskets to mask parts of the painting as the paint was sprayed on the exposed portions. The process is not too different in the digital world. You can create some wonderful airbrush effects with the use of selections, which act as digital friskets. As you can see in this illustration, selections maintain defined edges as you spray the color into the interior of the selected area and, if you invert the selection, the exterior. If you want softer edges, choose Select | Feather.

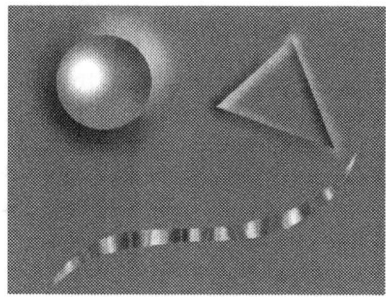

The Selection Brush

The Selection brush is a new tool in Photoshop Elements 2. This unique selection tool combines the best of marquee selection tools with a paintbrush. The Selection brush allows you to paint in selections in the same technique you use with a Paintbrush tool. This is ideal for freehand painting, when you want to create selections that have complex shapes. You paint in a selection and then use the Paintbrush tool to color the selection in, as we did with the sky example back in Figure 16-3. The really exciting part of the Selection brush is that it can take on the attributes of a normal brush. That means that every brush preset can be applied to the Selection brush and, instead of the brush shape placing color, it places a selection. Even textured presets make a selection out of the texture, as you can see in this example.

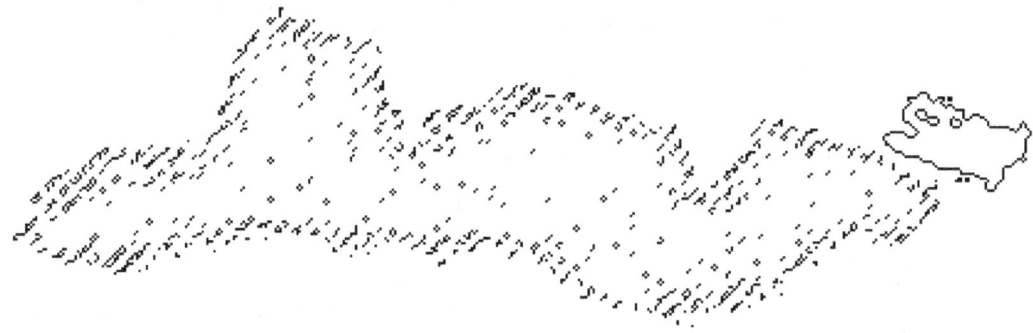

Painting with the Clone Tool

The Clone Stamp tool is known for its ability to do retouching, but it is also a very useful tool for painting. With the Clone Stamp tool, you can use any image area, including separate layers and documents, as a source. The Clone Stamp tool can use a reference point you set manually as the source for its paint. This means that if you want to paint in some grass, you can open an image with pictures of grass and use that as a source to paint with. Of course, you can also apply blending modes, brush shapes, opacity, and other brush options to the mix. You could call this compositing with a brush. To learn more about composites, see Chapter 17.

Brush Styles and the Clone Stamp Tool

You can apply any of the brush shapes and styles to the Clone Stamp tool, giving you a broad range of capability on how you blend the cloned images into the target area of the image. By using a soft brush, for instance, you can blend the clone source into the image with soft edges. Use a coarse textured brush to let some of the original image show through. A hairy bristle brush allows you to feather the edges in a more random or coarse manner, controlled by your stroking pressure and direction. Take a look at the next illustration to see the examples of various brushes, modes, and option settings and how they affect the target image.

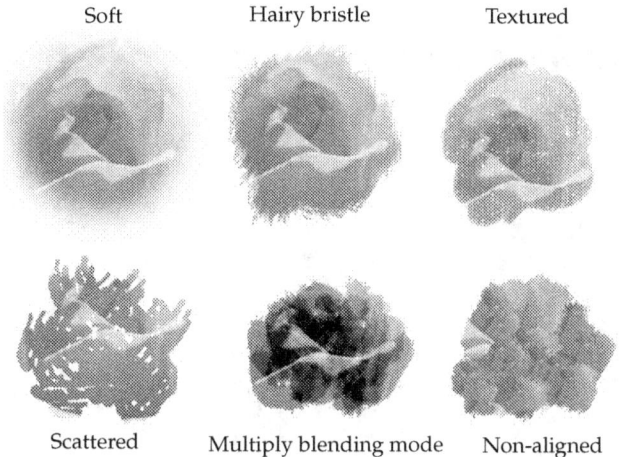

Soft   Hairy bristle   Textured

Scattered   Multiply blending mode   Non-aligned

Cloning Between Layers and Documents

One of the most powerful features of the Clone Stamp is the fact that you can set the anchor point to clone from an entirely different layer or document than the one that you're cloning to. You can use this as a technique for painting in a detail from another image.

Say you had a photograph of a windowless building and you wanted to see what a certain style of window looked like on it. Of course, you could cut the window out of one photograph and paste it onto the photo of the building, but painting it in from another layer can be a little more flexible. If you first put the window on a separate layer, you can lower the opacity of that layer and scale the window to just the right size to fit the photograph. You can also use adjustments (see Chapter 13) to match the exposure, contrast, and color balance of one of the images to match the other. Finally, it can be easier to blend images from two sources if you paint them in.

For instance, in the case of the window, there might be a tree or a lamppost in front of the position you want to put the window in. Especially in the case of the tree, it might be much easier to paint the window into the areas between the tree branches and even selectively paint over some branches that you want to eliminate. Painting it in gives you ultimate control on how the images are integrated. You can blend edges more precisely because you can temporarily change the transparency of one of the layers so that you can "onion skin" the positioning and blending of the edges as you paint. When you return to 100-percent opacity in the layer you're painting on, the object you've painted in will be at 100-percent opacity as well. Of course, if you want it to be a lower opacity when you paint it in, you can change the opacity of the Clone Stamp tool in its Options bar. When you are using a pressure-sensitive pen, the opacity changes with the amount of pressure you apply, so you can blend as you paint.

The following illustration shows the Clone Stamp tool capturing its source from a second document.

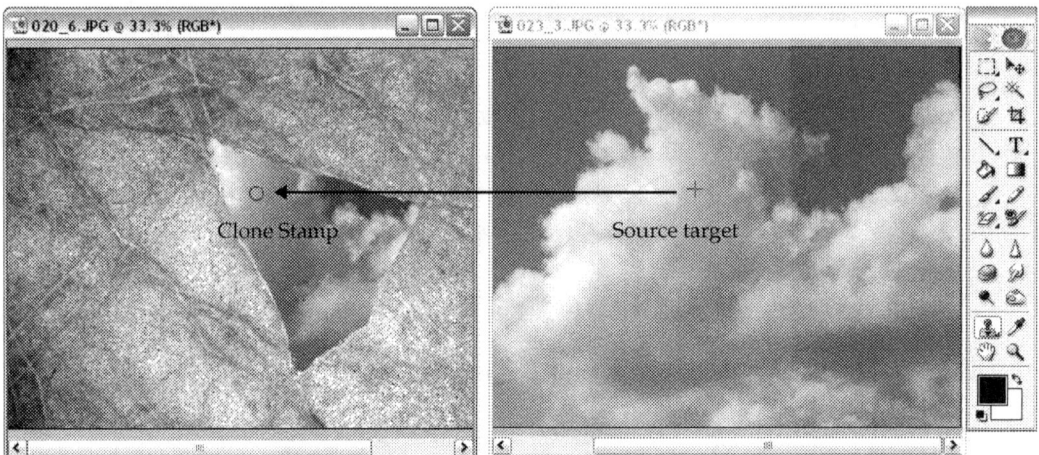

Here are the steps for painting with a Cloning tool from one layer or to another:

1. Open the source and destination images. The destination image can be a new blank document if you want to paint from scratch.

2. Open the Layers palette by dragging it from the Palette Well.

3. To move portions of the source image to layers in the destination image, loosely select the area of the source image you want to paint from. Next, choose the Move tool and drag the selected source image area into the target image. It automatically appears on its own layer.

4. Create a new transparent layer above your target layer to clone onto. This gives you editing flexibility later on.

5. In the target layer's name bar, click the eye icon in the Visibility button to temporarily hide the target layer. Now you can see the source image clearly.

6. Choose the Clone Stamp tool and, in the Options bar, check the Align box and then move the cursor to the exact position you want to start cloning from.

7. Hold OPT/ALT and click to set the cloning source point for the layer you are cloning from. Pick a starting point that gives you a clear reference in positioning the clone source in your target.

8. In the target layer's name bar, click the Visibility button to temporarily unhide the target layer. The eye icon reappears.

9. Start clone-painting in a new transparent target layer while viewing the original target layer underneath. Keep painting until your image looks as you intended it to look. If you need the edges to blend, adjust the brush feathering to blend.

10. Move to other source layers and add new image elements to clone more images to your target image. You can create new transparent layers for each source.

11. Adjust the size and location of any of the target layers and merge them together for your final image. You can also save the file with layers intact so you can go back and edit the individual layers later. See Chapter 8 for more on editing layers.

Here are the steps for cloning from one document or to another. If you are using only one source image, then cloning directly from that image without copying to a layer is faster.

1. Open the source and destination images.

2. Open the Layers palette by dragging it from the Palette Well.

3. Make a new layer in the destination image to paint onto before you start cloning so you don't alter the original as you paint onto it. This gives you flexibility in editing it later.

4. Choose the Clone Stamp tool from the Toolbox. Hold OPT/ALT while clicking to set the clone starting point in the source image document. This location should be something easy to reference in the target location so you can position it as close as you can. You can move and size the cloned image later if you need to.

Note *If the source image has multiple layers, you can choose to clone from any of the layers in the source image by making that layer active and the only one that is visible.*

5. Make sure the Aligned box in the Options bar is checked.

6. Start painting the source image onto the target layer in the destination image until you have all the detail you want.

7. You can open other documents and repeat the process as needed.

Note *Unchecking the Aligned box on the Options bar resets the clone source to the original position you selected every time you start a new brush stroke. This allows you to use one location as a source for cloned brush strokes anywhere in the target area so it becomes more like painting with a pattern, which is the subject of the next section.*

Painting with Textures and Patterns

One of the things that makes painting exciting is the use of textures and patterns to produce a more dynamic mixture of color and form. Computer paint programs were notorious for allowing the application of only flat color, which is rather boring and limiting, to the artist. It also earmarks the work as mechanistic computer-generated work. the introduction of more sophisticated brush algorithms that allow for texturing and patterning has opened the door for a new level of expressive freedom in Photoshop Elements. Let's take a look at what textures and patterns can do.

Textured Brushes

There a number of ways that brushes can apply texture to your paintings. The first aspect of brush texturing lies in the brushes themselves. Photoshop Elements includes a large library of preset brushes. Many of the brushes have built-in texture algorithms, which are designed to simulate various mediums on textured surfaces. You can see a small sampling of some preset brushes in the following illustration. These textures are built so you can't modify them. If you find some brushes you like in particular, you can use the Preset Manager to move your favorites to a separate library so you have easy access to them. The second method involves the use of the Pattern Stamp tool, which we go into in the next section.

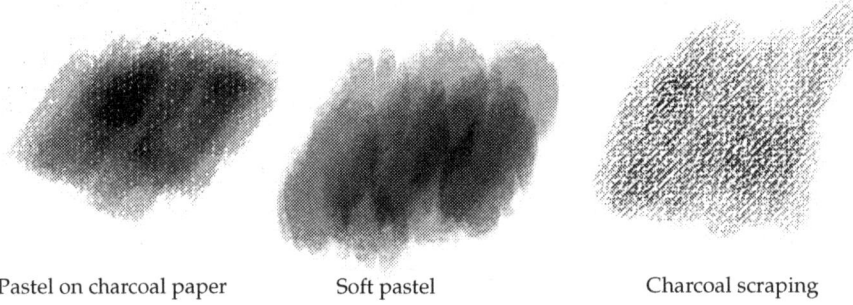

Pastel on charcoal paper   Soft pastel   Charcoal scraping

Pattern Stamp Tool

The Clone Stamp tool has a cousin called the Pattern Stamp tool. The Pattern Stamp tool works in a different way because it uses only preset or defined patterns as its source, and not a targeted image area as the Clone Stamp tool uses. You could say the Pattern Stamp tool is cloning from a special source, which is the library of stored patterns. Patterns produce a repeating tile pattern. The size of the tile depends on its size when it was created. Pattern tiles will have a noticeable border unless they were created in a seamless manner. See Chapter 13 for more on creating seamless tiles.

The library of preset patterns can be accessed from the Pattern Stamp Options bar by clicking on the Pattern pop-up palette. You can select preset categories from the Palette menu. There are two categories that are dedicated to textures, but you will find many more in other categories also. The difference between a pattern and a texture is sometimes subtle. Textures simulate a three-dimensional surface by the way the pattern is shaded, whereas patterns are two-dimensional. Textures are illusion patterns, so they are all listed in the same palette.

When you select a pattern from the preset palette, the Pattern Stamp brush paints with the pattern. If you check the Aligned box, you will paint a fixed tiled pattern no matter where you paint in the image. If you uncheck the Aligned box, the pattern will start anywhere you start painting, so you will get overlapping patterns, which produces a more random appearance.

Patterns may be color or grayscale. The Pattern Stamp tool uses the Brush Preset palette to apply brush styles, which changes the way the pattern is painted. You can also change opacity and brush size to produce very complex overlapping patterns as you paint. If that was not enough, Photoshop Elements includes an Impressionist option, which appears on the Pattern Stamp Options bar. The Impressionist option cycles through the colors in the pattern while placing spaced dabs to produce an impressionistic effect. This is not the same as the Impressionist Brush tool, which uses the colors in the image.

Creating Custom Patterns

Life is full of wonderful patterns. It is really very easy to capture patterns and textures from everyday life and use them with the Pattern Stamp tool to add a whole new feel to your work. Your camera (conventional or digital) and your scanner are essential tools in this process. If you lack the camera, you can always bring the texture or pattern to the scanner and scan it directly, or you can consider doing a rubbing or sketch to capture a pattern on paper. If you are without any scanning capability, you can search the Web for free textures and patterns. You might be surprised by how much is out there for free. Patterns and textures appear in many average photographs, which can be a rich source. And last but not least, you can create textures and patterns by drawing them directly in Photoshop Elements with, you guessed it, the paint tools!

Once you have some image files with textures or patterns you want to keep, it is time to learn how to define a pattern:

1. Open the image file that has the texture or pattern you want to capture.

2. Locate the area of the image that has the detail you want.

3. Use the Rectangle Marquee tool to select the area you want to make a pattern.

4. Choose Edit | Define Pattern. The Pattern Name dialog box appears with a thumbnail of the pattern you just captured. If it is not to your liking, close the dialog box and try again. When you are satisfied, enter a new name for the pattern or accept the default and click OK.

5. You can use the Preset Manager to gather your collection of custom patterns into a unique preset palette library or add them to existing ones. Be sure to save the preset palette with your custom patterns or they will be lost when you load another preset palette or reload the current one.

Painting Textures with a Pattern

Another method for applying textures to brushes involves an integrated approach. The integration of tools and commands is where you gain the next tier of capability with

Photoshop Elements 2. This method involves using the Pattern Stamp tool in conjunction with the blending modes to create a brush to paint a textual effect over an existing image.

1. Open the image you want to add texture to.

2. Choose the Pattern Stamp tool from the Toolbox.

3. Select a pattern from the Pattern Preset pop-up palette. For the best result, choose a texture pattern that has good contrast range.

4. Choose one of the blending modes that makes use of contrast to alter color. Multiply, Screen, Overlay, and Luminosity modes all work well. See the next illustration for examples of how these modes affect textures' appearance.

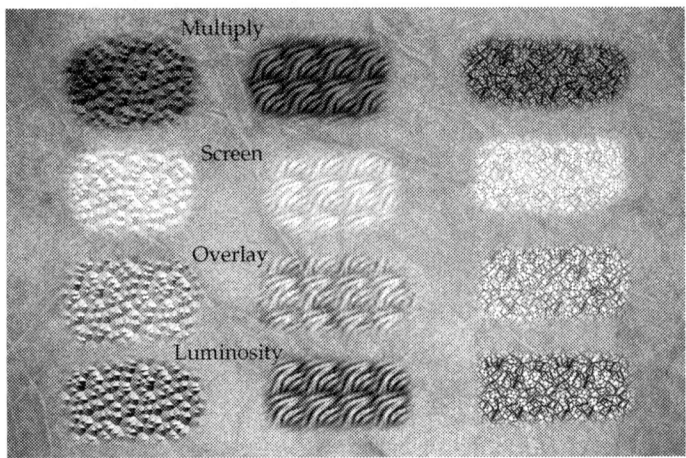

5. Adjust the opacity setting to control the intensity of the effect.

Moving Digital Paint Around

So far, we have dealt with brushes that alter the color and brightness of pixels, but pretty much leave them in one place. Now let's take a look at two tools that allow you to move the pixels around, giving the look of real paint: the Impressionist Brush tool and the Smudge tool. The Liquify filter is also very good at moving digital paint, and Chapter 15 goes into its function in detail.

Painting with the Impressionist Brush

The Impressionist brush tool was designed to produce an impressionist style by placing a randomized pattern of various-shaped paint dabs around at a certain radius from the brush position. The colors used are based only on the local color in proximity to the brush, so the Impressionist brush is best used on existing images. You can get a wide range of painting effects with this brush, especially when you add in the brush shapes and styles, opacity, blending modes, and brush size into the mix. Brush size makes a big difference, so be sure to experiment with that. You can see some of the hundreds of paint effects you can achieve with the Impressionist brush in Figure 16-4.

To paint with the Impressionist brush, follow these steps:

1. Open an image you want to modify.

2. Choose the Impressionist brush from the Toolbox.

3. Click More Options to set the basic parameters for the Impressionist brush.

4. Pick a style from the Style drop-down menu. This determines a basic shape and spacing of the brushstrokes.

5. Set the tolerance value to determine which pixels within the Area get affected. Lower values demand that adjacent pixels be very close in value to the reference pixel before they are affected. Higher values are more liberal. If you want all pixels to be affected, slide the value to 100 percent.

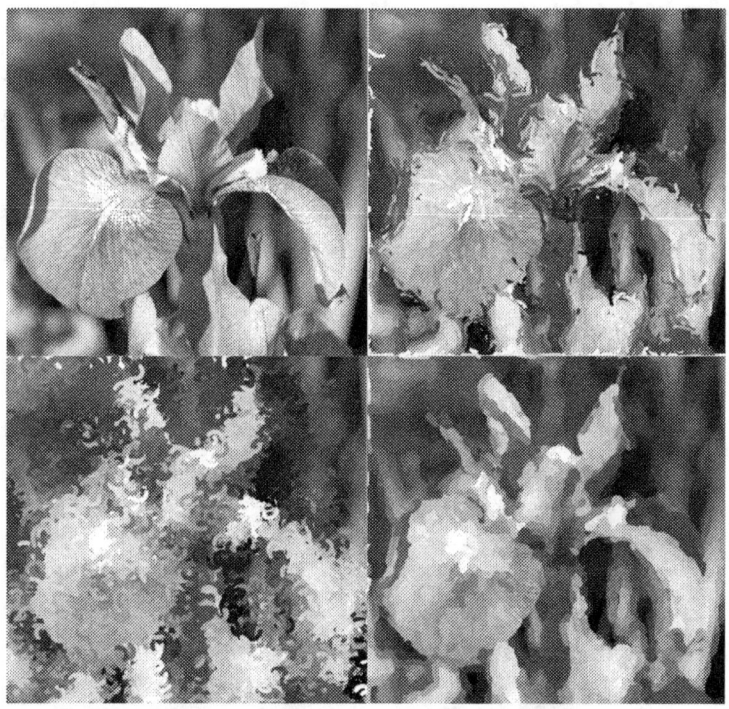

Figure 16-4.   *Some examples using the Impressionist brush*

6. Set the area to determine the range of affect in pixels. A value of 100 means that the brush effect covers an area with a 100-pixel radius from the reference pixel.

7. Pick a brush shape from the preset palette. Brush shapes can have a big influence on the characteristics and final appearance of the Impressionist brush. Experiment with various shapes and styles to see the result. There are literally thousands of possible combinations.

8. Paint over the image with the brush. The Impressionist brush changes the image directly, so you might want to make a copy of that layer so you can go back if you want.

9. The flow of paint from the brush is constant, like an airbrush, so if you hold it in one position, it continues placing paint dabs.

10. Hold SHIFT while dragging the brush to constrain the effect to just horizontal or vertical lines.

11. Hold OPT/ALT while dragging the brush to override the tolerance option.

Smudging

The Smudge tool allows you to push pixels around as though you were using your finger. The effect is very much like dragging your finger through wet paint or dipping your finger in paint and smearing over an image, depending on which parameters you choose. Use this tool to make minor corrections to brush strokes or just as a stylized method of spreading or applying color. You can see some examples of Smudge tools with various brush shapes in the following illustration. One handy use is to feather out edges much as a conventional painter would do with a fan brush. Feathering lets you use the Smudge tool to blend colors together when you overlap strokes of different colors.

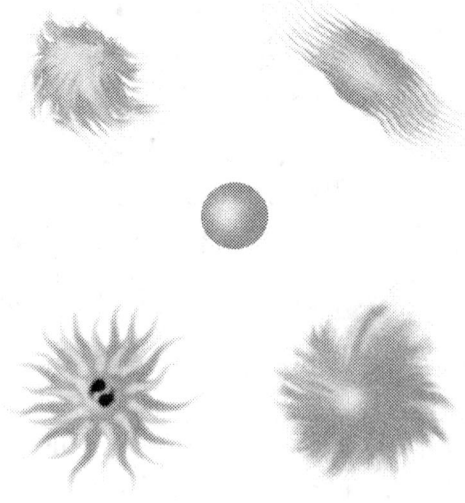

To move color with the Smudge tool:

1. Open the image you want to modify.

2. Choose the brush shape and style you want from the Brush Preset palette. Each brush style gives unique results with the Smudge tool, so experiment to find combinations that work for you.

3. Set the strength percentage to determine how far the brush pulls the color before it fades out. Use any of the pen pressure brushes to control the strength with the pressure-sensitive pen. Set the strength to 100 percent when using pen pressure.

4. If you want to use the foreground color as the start color you smear out, check the Finger Painting box.

5. If you want to smear all the color from visible layers at one time, check Use All Layers.

6. Set the mode to further affect how the brush changes color.

7. Place the brush pointer where you want to start pulling color from. The first click sets the color you drag—unless you have Finger Painting selected; then it uses the foreground color. Drag the brush in any direction as it smears the color until it fades out or you release the brush. If you have the strength set to 100 percent, it does not fade at all.

Editing Tools

Photoshop Elements 2 has a whole class of Brush tools that are primarily used for editing image content and not creating it, even though some can be used for both. For example, the Eraser tool can be used to erase parts of an image so you can go in and re-create in those portions of the image. It can also be used on a "pull out" color in a technique where you start with a dark-colored background and pull color out in stages to produce highlights. You can also use the Eraser tool to erase through to an even-darker color so you can accentuate shadow areas, too. This technique was used by the Flemish painters, such as Rembrandt, for their underpaintings.

The tools used for editing are the Eraser, Sponge, Dodge, Burn, Blur, and Sharpen tools. This section focuses on the editing aspects of these tools. You can fine-tune your images with the control of a brush and pen pressure, which enable you to tweak the finest details. One of the marvelous things about digital painting is that the image can be edited at any time and to any degree—no drying time, no painting over, no throwing it away and starting over because it was overworked. You see something you want changed, you change it. It is really that straightforward. This frees you to explore and experiment without the worries or restrictions of other mediums, which can make you pay a high price in terms of time and money if you make a mistake. With digital painting, there are no real mistakes, just things that occasionally need more work, right? On the other side of the fence, though, is the temptation to be less disciplined and not work efficiently, knowing that it can always be undone or tweaked. The other problem is that because the possibilities are endless, you can easily spend far more time than you can afford on a digital painting because it's much too tempting to try "just one more thing."

Erasing

The Eraser tool is a very handy device that you will most likely make use of on numerous occasions when you want to eliminate some stray brush strokes, rework a portion of the painting, or erase through to underlying layers. The Eraser tool has a number of modes that give you different options for how you erase the image. You have the basic Eraser tool, the Background Eraser tool, and the Magic Eraser tool.

Basic Eraser Tool

This tool removes the current pixels, based on brush size and opacity, and replaces them with the background color. You can set the brush size, shape, and style from the Preset palette. Set the opacity lower to erase partially with each pass of the brush. You have a choice of three modes: Brush, Pencil, or Block. The Brush mode gives you all the options of the Brush preset palette. Pencil also lets you choose from the preset palette, but doesn't allow any transparency in the brush. Block just gives you a fixed-size square brush.

Background Eraser Tool

This tool removes a range of colors, limited by the tolerance value, in an area based on the brush size and opacity, and replaces it with transparency. This allows you to remove color ranges selectively with the control of a brush. In erase-through painting techniques, which we go into in the "Painting with Filters and Layers" section, later in this chapter, this eraser can be useful.

Magic Eraser Tool

This is not really a painting tool, but it's mentioned here to give you the complete view of the Eraser functions. This tool works very much like the Magic Wand selection tool. It erases any similar-colored pixels limited by the tolerance value relative to the pixel you first click with the tool. You can set opacity and choose Contiguous if you want to contain the erasure to only adjacent pixels.

Blurring

The Blur tool is used to subtly blend the pixels affected by the brush shape by reducing the contrast between the adjacent pixels. This allows you to use a brush to soften harsh edges and make the transition more gradually. The effect can be seen in the following illustration. When you are painting with many effects and tools, you can get harsh transitions in certain areas of the image. You can adjust the intensity of the effect by adjusting the strength value. If you want to blur all the layers at once, choose Use All Layers.

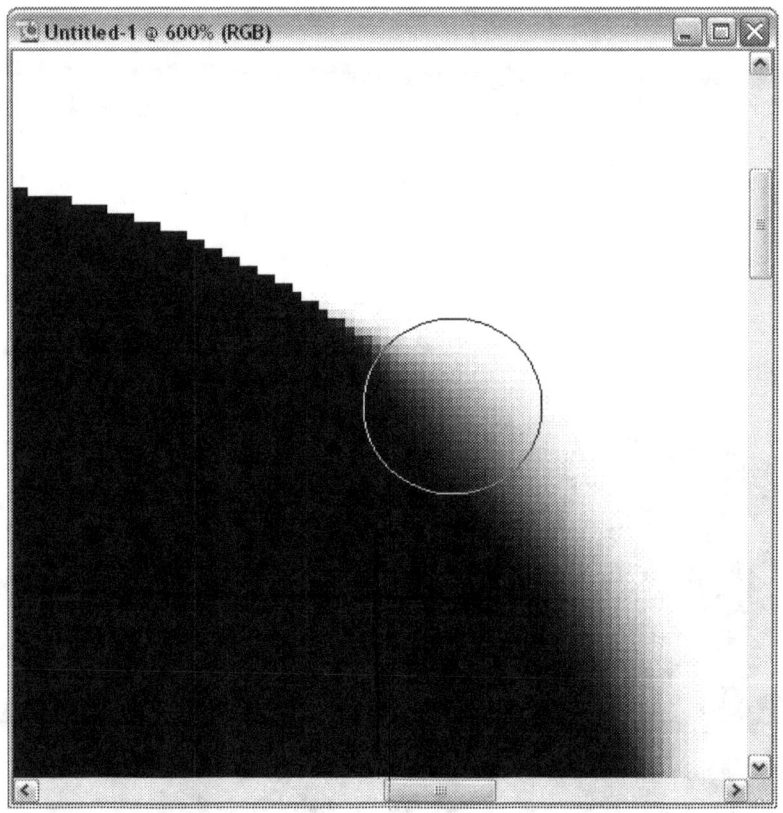

The Blur tool helps blend those areas together to unify the look of the work. This tool can also be used to adjust focus in parts of the image so you can control the focal point precisely. Perhaps you just want a dreamy quality to the image, and softening parts of the image will give that effect. Using the Blur filter affects the entire layer, whereas the Blur tool gives you pixel precision. There are a number of modes you can choose from. We find the most useful of the modes to be Darken and Lighten. Darken spreads the darker pixels into the lighter side of the edge and Lighten spreads the lighter pixels in the dark areas.

Sharpening

The Sharpen tool does just the opposite of the Blur tool. Where there are soft, unfocused areas in your image, the Sharpen tool increases the contrast and brings more clarity to the transitions. Use the Sharpen tool where you want to accentuate some details so they stand out a bit more and to add more crispness to the edges. The next illustration shows how the edge becomes starker when you apply the Sharpen tool. You can adjust the intensity of the effect by adjusting the Strength value. If you want to sharpen all the layers at once, choose Use All Layers.

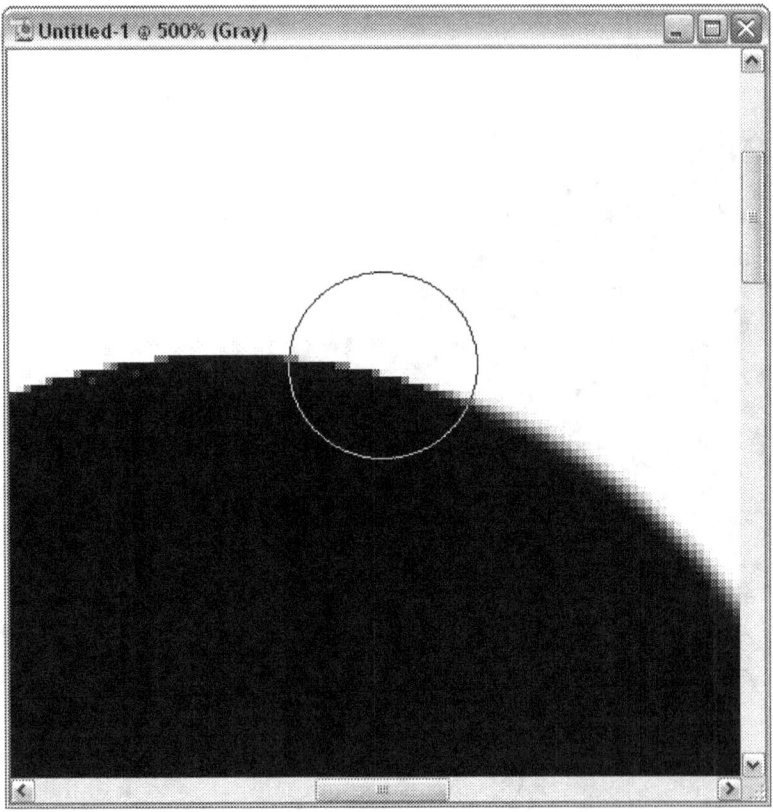

Note   *There is a word of caution here. Overuse of the Sharpen tool produces color artifacts and causes line edges to look jagged (stair-stepped), so set the strength low and work it up gradually. If it starts to look overdone, go backward with the Step Backward command.*

Controlling Saturation

The Sponge tool is designed to let you paint to increase or decrease the color saturation. This can be a good way to add a bit more punch or tone down a brush-sized area of color. You can change the shape of the brush in the Preset palette and adjust the size of the brush on the Options bar.

You have two modes: Saturate and Desaturate. Select Saturate to add more color intensity and Desaturate to reduce the color intensity. The Flow option determines the rate at which the effect changes the image area.

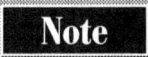 *One easy way to make a photograph look hand colored is to decrease the overall saturation to the point where there is very little color, and then use the Sponge tool in Saturate mode to brighten the color of one or two items, such as a model's eyes and lips or a rose.*

Dodging and Burning

These two tools are very important in the final stages of any image creation. This is the time when you adjust the tonal range of the image to encompass the broadest range applicable for the subject. Adjusting highlights and shadows plays a big part in the power of how light plays in your image and the visual impact it has on the viewer. It is often hard to judge that precisely until you see the relationship of all the parts. When you view all the relationships, you can make informed choices about where to tweak the details to push it that one step farther.

The Dodge tool lightens the pixels as you paint with the brush and the Burn tool darkens pixels, in much the same way as a photographer uses these tools in the dark room to lighten or darken parts of the print. The modes allow you to choose between three ranges to make your adjustments more controlled. You can choose highlights, midtones, and shadows, which confine the effect—respectively, the upper, middle, and lower part of the image's tonal range. The exposure control determines the intensity of the effect.

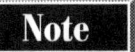 *When using the Dodge and Burn tools, it is usually a good idea to keep the Exposure setting low (about 10–15 percent). Then you can gradually build up the lightness or darkness in the area you want, so it seems seamless.*

Photo Painting

Photo painting is really a very new form of art that is now taking a foothold in the art world. It merges two disciplines, photography and painting, into one medium via the integrated world of digital imaging. Photo painting can transform your photographs into unique works of art with an extended subjective flare that wasn't possible before interactive digital painting came of age within this last decade. Adobe has been at the forefront of this revolution, and Photoshop Elements 2. has opened the door to this new integrated art form with high-quality tools the average user can understand, use, and afford.

Photo painting starts out with a digitized photograph. The fun begins as you use the painting tools to transform the photo into something that it can't be through photographic means alone. Generally speaking, turning a photo into a photo painting makes the subject more abstract, and allows you to believably add elements to the picture so that it makes the

THE SPECIAL EFFECTS WORKFLOW

statement you intended. Photo painting is its own art form, and, at its best, is not an attempt to fool anyone. It also provides the tools for expanding the artist's vision beyond what could be expected from the use of traditional media.

Photo painting goes well beyond the bounds of dodging and burning or adjusting exposure and color, and gets more deeply into the art of moving pixels and reinterpreting reality with a subjective interpretation of the subject, with the only rule being to follow your imagination and use any tools you want.

In this chapter, we focus on changing photographs with painting techniques, but many other tools (especially the built-in painting filters in Photoshop Elements) can be used as well. The rules for photo painting have not been determined or even well explored yet, so have fun discovering new ways to interpret your photographs. We will now explore a number of the most popular techniques for producing photo painting, but, again, nothing is set in stone. The following examples just give you a starting point and basic understanding of the process.

Painting with Filters and Layers

One technique that is used by many photo painters involves using layers as the image source for the brushes. With this technique, you literally open up the brushes to every effect, filter, texture, fill, gradient, and pattern available in the program. Remember when we said that using fills, filters, and other effects at the command level didn't qualify strictly as painting? Well, here's a way around that rule. In fact, throw out that rulebook.

In this technique, you erase through to various layers that are duplicates of the original photo with various effects and filters applied. This gives you a palette of layer clones altered only by different effects. The goal is to erase parts of the original so the effects show through, creating an effect composite, so to speak. As you paint, you expose underlying layers and replace the original pixels with altered ones. You rotate the layers to get different effects in different areas you paint into. By using opacity, you can also mix the effects.

Now that you have a general understanding of how this technique works, let's take a look at a particular example to get a closer look at the specifics.

1. Open the photo you want to work with and make any adjustment to color or exposure that you feel is necessary. It is often helpful to punch up the saturation and contrast a bit with a photo painting, just to give it a more artificial painted feel from the start. Paintings tend to exaggerate color as a subjective tool.

2. Open the Layers palette by dragging it out of the Palette Well or choosing from the Window menu.

3. Duplicate the background layer several times so that you'll have one for each effect you plan to add. These duplicates will become the source images for this technique.

4. Now, one by one, make the duplicate layers active and the only ones visible by deselecting the eye icon on all the other layers. Apply any effects you want to each layer. These can be artistic filters, Effects, blending modes, or anything else you can think that will alter the look of the image. Try to pick looks that will easily blend together in the final piece. It is hard to tell exactly which effects to use because that is something that will vary with each piece and there are many to choose from. We recommend that you take a close look at the filters as a rich source. Charcoal, Dry Brush, Rough Pastels, and Cross Hatch were used to create the image in Figure 16-5.

5. After you have applied the effects to the separate layers, we can begin the process of painting them in. Make sure you have one extra duplicate of the original image without effects. You will use this as a way of adding back in original detail if you need to.

6. There are two ways to combine the layers you have created effects on to the original photo. The first is to place the effects layer right under the photo layer and make the photo layer active so you can erase parts of it with an Eraser brush and let the effects show through. The second way is to place the effects layer right above the photo and apply a blending mode to combine the two layers; then erase out parts of the effects layer you don't want in the photo painting.

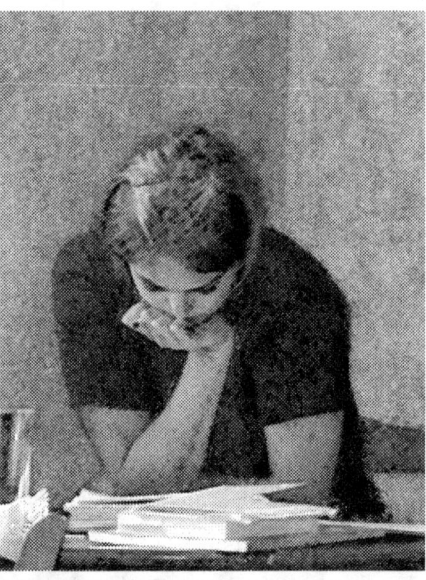

Figure 16-5.   *This painting of a student uses the erase-through technique with multiple effects layers.*

THE SPECIAL EFFECTS
WORKFLOW

This works well with lined images, like those created by the Find Edges filter, for instance, and then blended with the Multiply filter. You can then erase the outlines you don't want and even paint in new ones. In Figure 16-5, the Charcoal layer was applied in this top-down manner. All the other effects were erased, though, from a lower layer.

7. Move the effect layer into position under or on top of the photo layer, depending on which method you are using, by dragging it into position on the Layers palette.

8. Choose the basic Eraser Brush tool from the Toolbox.

9. Select a brush style and shape, and then set the opacity lower if you want to erase gradually (often a very effective technique).

10. Begin adding detail from the effects layer.

11. When you have finished adding that effect, make a duplicate of the effects layer you were using. If the effects layer is below the photo layer, select the photo layer. If the effects layer is above, make the effects layer active.

12. Choose Palette | Merge Down to combine the effects you just added with the original photo. This sets the stage for the next effect to be added. You don't want any transparency showing when you put the next effects layer in place.

13. Drag the next effects layer into position and continue the process until you have completed the painting.

Painting-Over Techniques

Painting over is a method of laying digital paint right into the photograph. You are directly affecting the look of the photograph within the same layer or a layer above (as opposed to erasing, which can take its information from layers below in more of a composite mode). Painting over is related to photo retouching, but it goes much further. With photo painting, you are not trying to fix a photograph, as you do with retouching; you are instead pushing the image beyond the purely photographic into the world of interpretive painting. As you can see in the before and after portrait in Figure 16-6, there is dramatic change to what was less than a good photograph.

There are two ways to approach this technique. You can place the original photo underneath a new blank layer or paint right in the photo layer, depending on whether you are feeling lucky. Using the layer above gives you a lot more leeway for corrections.

As far as the tools for this technique, the whole suite of Photoshop Elements tools is available. There are no real restrictions.

One handy method is to use Image | Duplicate Image to make a copy of the photo in another open window. Use this duplicate as a color source where you can pick colors with the Eyedropper while pressing OPT/ALT. Alter the color map of the duplicate to set up a palette for the new painting, and you automatically have the colors mapped to the tonal range image.

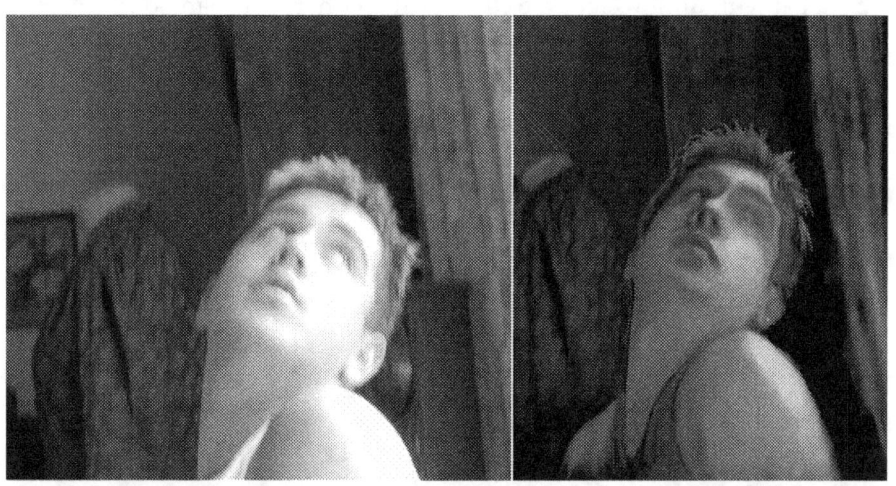

Figure 16-6. *The image on the right was painted right on top of the original photo (left).*

The use of textured brushes and varying degrees of opacity allow you to build up color in complex ways. Using selections helps isolate areas of the painting to work on with different techniques. This is the photo painting process that is closest to conventional painting, so, if that is your background, you might want to dive right in and work directly. How much of the original photo you care to leave or how much you choose to paint in is entirely up you.

Painting from Scratch

For those of you who are purists, we saved the best for last. This section focuses on techniques for painting totally in the computer environment, with only the tools Photoshop Elements provides and the painting talents you bring with you. This is truly digital painting in its most pure state. For an example, a still-life painting was created so you could see the steps that were taken to paint it from real life. We wanted to demonstrate that the digital painting and Photoshop Elements could be used in the traditional way.

1. The first step in the process was to sketch the composition and the basic shapes of the objects in the scene, as you can see next. A white background was used in this case, but you can choose to use any color. We used a thin, round paintbrush

to sketch with until we got the composition where we wanted it. Take time to adjust things at this stage because it is a lot easier to make changes.

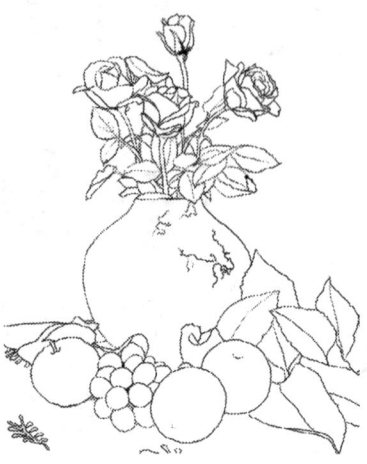

Note *Many traditional artists who have adopted the computer as their painting medium do their sketching on paper and then scan the sketch on a flatbed scanner (you can buy an adequate one for scanning sketches for less than $100).*

2. The next step was to set up the palette with the Swatches palette. Refer to the "Swatches Palette" section earlier in this chapter.

3. A broader brush was chosen to block in the colors and shapes using midtone colors. The highlights, shadows, and details will be added later. You can see the blocked-in painting next.

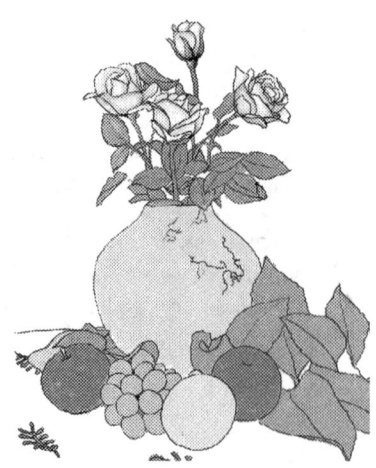

4. The Magic Wand was used to select the background.

5. A large textured brush was chosen and Color Jitter was applied. Two dark shades of green were picked for the foreground and background colors so that, when the background was painted, it would have a mottled look.

6. The details were painted in one shape at a time, using various paintbrushes and degrees of opacity. The Tablet Support option was turned on in the Brush Dynamics palette so we could get more subtlety and variation in the brush strokes with pen pressure. Color Jitter and Scatter were often used to add randomness and color variation to the strokes, as evidenced in the vase. Opacity was set lower to build up detail gradually in layers to add depth and complexity. You can see the final painting in the following illustration (you can see the color version in the color insert).

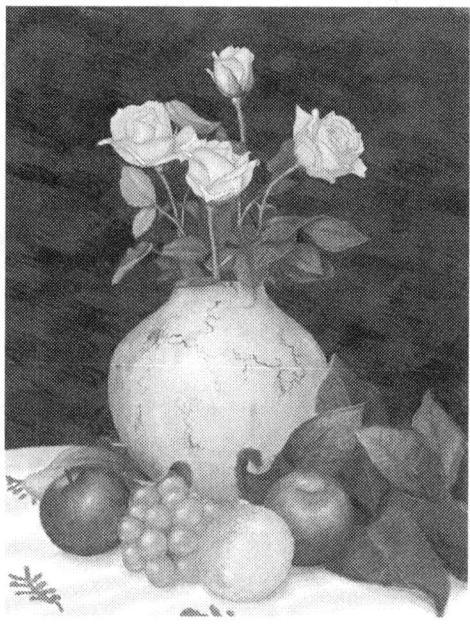

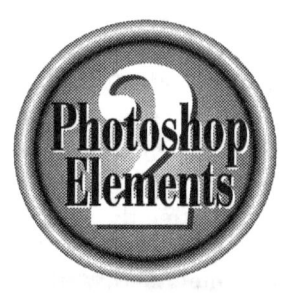

Chapter 17

Making Composite Images

This chapter is about putting it all together. To be more specific, it's about creating a new image from two or more existing images. There are really two categories of images that result from combining images: collages and montages. In a collage, images are put together in such a way as to communicate a message or feeling without making the individual images appear to be a cohesive part of a whole. In other words, there is no need to make the juxtaposition of the various images appear to be seamlessly integrated. You can see an example of a collage in Figure 17-1.

A montage (in still-image terms) is a composite image in which two or more elements are seamlessly and imperceptibly combined to create a fictitious illusion of reality. This is the type of compositing you will probably do most often, not because you want to misrepresent reality, but because you want to add that extra dimension and create the drama or romance you experienced at the scene. For instance, you saw moonlight glimmer; but had you waited until the moon was in the right position, it would have been too dark to capture any landscape detail, so you shot two pictures: one just a little after sunset, one later in the evening after the moon was fully risen. Then you put the moon into the sky. In another instance, just for shock value, you wanted to show a cow grazing on a sandy beach. You can see a sample of a montage in Figure 17-2.

This chapter is concerned primarily with the creation of photomontages. The process is fairly demanding. This chapter encompasses all the technical procedures needed for making a a montage, and then shows you how to precisely blend all the components so viewers will be unlikely to think they weren't that way to begin with.

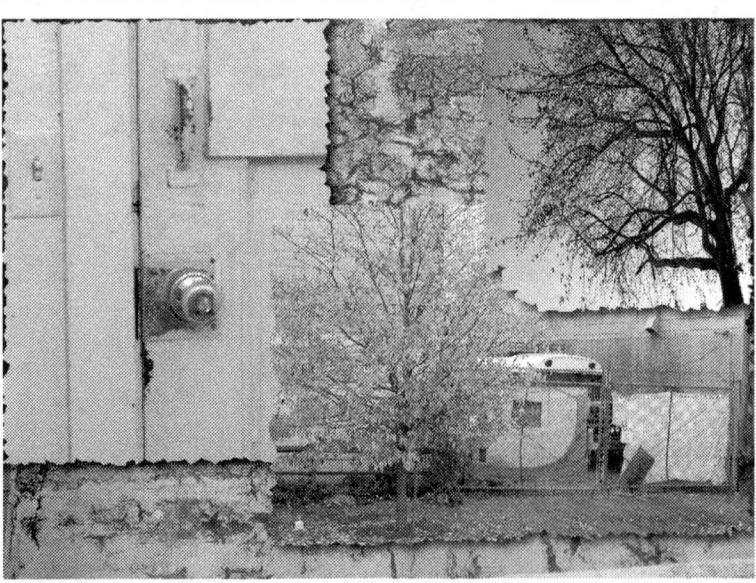

Figure 17-1.   *Here is an example of a collage with elements arranged in a stylized, abstract manner.*

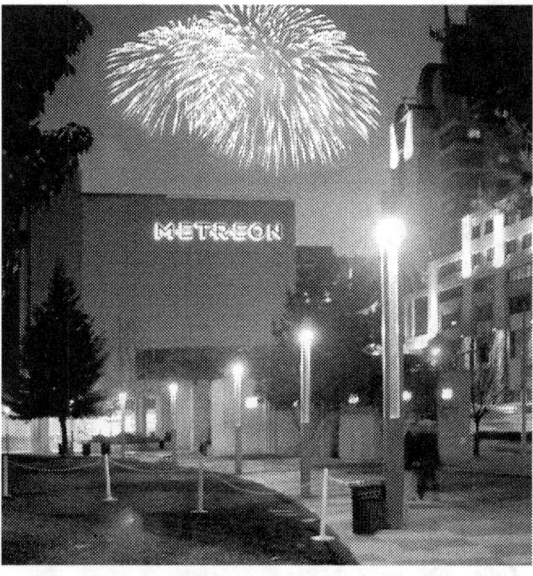

Figure 17-2. *An example of a montage where the fireworks and night scene have been blended together to look natural*

Taking the Right Pictures for a Composite

If you plan to make truly realistic photomontage images, you should ideally plan them from the beginning. If you're pretty good at making sketches, it's a good idea to sketch out your idea in advance. If not, shoot or find "sketch" photos that you can paste together and annotate. It really helps to have a concrete concept of what you're planning to produce so that you can make a list of what's needed to get the job done. This helps even if you're not going to take your own pictures. We'll talk about how to gather pictures from outside resources and what the pros and cons of that approach are. All other things being equal, though, it's best to shoot original pictures for what you plan to turn into a composite. It simply gives you more control over the final result.

Make a List of the Pictures You Need

The most important thing to decide is exactly what your background image is to be. Once you've done that, go take the picture (unless you have to wait for a particular time of year to get the right foliage, action, or whatever). Having the background picture usually makes it plain what you have to do to get matching pictures. You can also record the time of day when you took the picture so that you can take the other pictures.

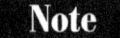

Often, you just want to enhance a picture you've just taken by adding elements to it. If, for instance, you've taken what you expect to be a nice scenic shot, look to see if there are more interesting cloud formations farther down the coastline, a tree that would frame the foreground nicely, or people and animals that might populate the scene nicely. It's always better to have the "props" you might need when you get back home than to have to find them later.

Keep the Light Source Constant

It's important to know what time of day you took the background picture because you are much more likely to get the subjects you plan to add to the composite lighted with the same angle and color of lighting. In addition, silly as this might sound, you're much more likely to be in the same state of mind when you shoot each of the component subjects.

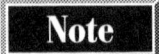

If you use a late-model digital camera, there's a good chance that you can find out the date and time of a shot, even if you didn't write it down at the time of shooting. Most of these cameras record meta data that appears in the lower-right corner of the Photoshop Elements file browser. That meta data (EXIF file) shows you the date and time that all the pictures were shot.

If you don't happen to be there at the exact right time of day, it may be possible to change your shooting position to match the light angle of the background picture. If you shoot from a different position, the light falls on the subject from a different angle. For a stationary subject, move to where the angle of light matches the light in the background picture (make sure you have a print of the background with you for reference). If your subject is animated, wait until it moves to a place where the lighting matches, or just chase it around until you get the right lighting angle. This is good for your physique, too. If your subject is fixed and can only be shot from a particular position, you are stuck with having to be there at the right time or using artificial light sources, if possible, to create the right lighting. Figure 17-3 shows an example of two photos that were shot at different locations with lighting angles that closely match, which allowed them to be composited believably.

Get the Distance and Angle Right

Just because the lighting angle is right doesn't mean that you're in the right position to take the picture. You also have to keep in mind how close or far away you want that subject to appear to be in the final composite picture. Subjects that are closer to the camera show more perspective distortion than subjects that are farther away. They also show more detail; so if you plan to have the image in the near foreground, you need to get a closer, more detailed initial shot. Remember that whenever you snap a shot, the view of the camera will be the view in the composite. You cannot rotate the object later to expose the top or another side. If you change your position and orientation significantly from one shot to another, you will produce images that do not blend together well. If

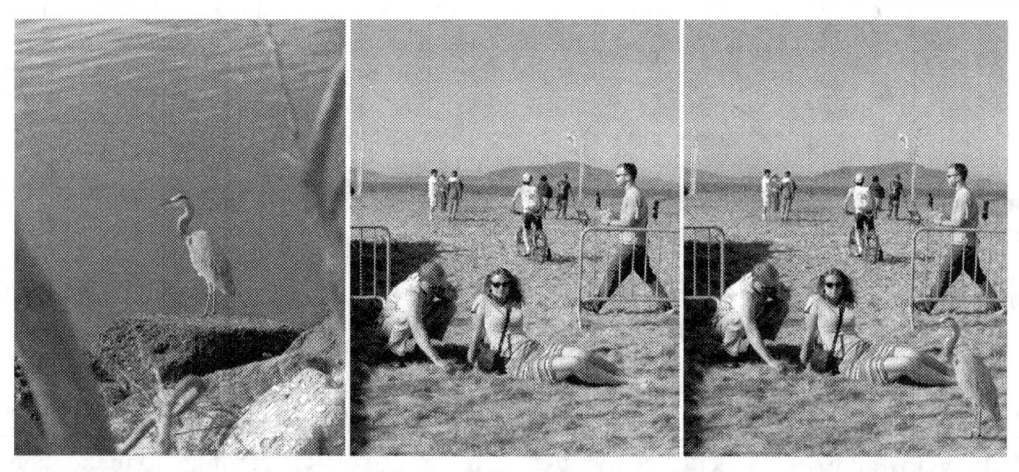

Figure 17-3.   *The composited scene on the right shows how two photos with similar light sources can be combined with credibility.*

you are looking down on one image and up on another, it's impossible to resolve this visually—unless you're a fan of surrealism!

Use Lenses of the Same Focal Length

When taking photos for use in a single composite, using lenses of different focal lengths produces a different perspective distortion for each type of lens. If you try to blend these images together in a composite, it is very difficult to make it look believable. Your brain is very sensitive to the subtle queues of spatial relationships. Keep to one type of lens and make your life much easier.

Shoot on Cloudy Days

Sometimes you just can't get the subjects you need from the same lighting angle. If that's really the case, the next-best alternative is to take the picture in conditions in which the lighting is as nondirectional as possible. It is then much easier to use Photoshop Elements' lighting tricks to control the apparent direction of light. We give you step-by-step instructions on how to accomplish these lighting tricks in the "Matching the Direction of Light" section, later in this chapter—and if you've read Chapter 13, you've already gotten a pretty good idea.

Get Add-In Objects from Your Local Environment

If your composite consists of small, easily available, and accessible objects, use your local surroundings to help fill in missing details. Always look for images that would be interesting to add to your composites and keep them in a folder for later use. Taking pictures of small objects around the house, office, or other places you frequent can be a rich source of add-on visuals. Remember, you will be cutting them out of their background much of the time, so all you need to do is concentrate on getting the part you need, not a perfectly composed photo overall. Cutting objects from their backgrounds and then storing them on layers in archived files keeps them ready to be moved right into your composite. Think of it as more like clipping out and filing images so you can piece them into a scrapbook later.

You can also make good use of your scanner to capture objects that can be placed on the scanner glass. Be careful not to use anything that can scratch the glass surface. Once again, be aware of the source lighting direction and color so you can closely match the other components of your composite.

Combine Pictures of the Same Size and Resolution

You don't want to have to enlarge pictures more than a small percentage to make them match, but reducing them is okay. If you enlarge the pictures beyond the resolution of the background image, they appear to be too soft in focus and to have too little detail in comparison with the background. Actually, if you have to enlarge something, you might be better off to enlarge the background. In fact, if the subject is fairly close to the camera, you might even want to intentionally throw the background out of focus by blurring it. That would certainly obliterate any difference in detail lost through enlarging.

The issue of resizing also comes into play with the perceptual size relationships of the objects. A car is bigger than a chair and a house is bigger than a car, right? Well, only if you ignore perspective. A chair can be much bigger than a house if it is placed in the foreground. Things that are closer also allow you to see more detail and need to have higher resolution. For instance, if you are placing a tree over the background, it needs to be big enough to be perceived as a tree in relation to the objects around it. If it is in the foreground, it needs to show more detail in the bark and leaves. If you start out with a small low-resolution image, you will not have the pixels to pull it off. The safest method is to always capture images that have as much resolution as you can achieve so you can size them down to whatever you need. If you can put every image in the foreground and maintain the same clarity and detail, you are home free.

Use Royalty-Free Stock

You might think that, if you have to follow all these suggestions to make a successful photomontage, it's just not worth the effort. The fact is, if you look carefully through your photo collection, you can probably find skies, props, and people that will work when composited into another scene. At least you now should know what to look for.

Of course, your image collection might not yet be all that large, or you might really need a shot of a Polar bear and just don't feel like driving to Alaska. Take heart. There are dozens of suppliers of very affordable royalty-free images—in fact, far too many to mention here. Type **royalty free images** into your web browser's search engine. There is no end to the images you can find and download for a nominal fee. Just do your best to make sure that they meet the lighting, angle, size, and perspective criteria described in the preceding paragraphs of this section.

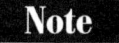

Many of the photo stock sites allow you to use the photos free only under certain conditions. It is common for royalty-free stock to be limited to only private noncommercial use. Be sure to read the terms of use on any site you are downloading images from.

Making Drop-Dead Knockouts

A knockout is much more than just a pretty face or a way to win a boxing match. It is the professional photographer's term for a photograph that has been removed from its background. You see many examples of knockouts used in product advertising and pedagogical illustration, where the subject of the photograph simply appears isolated on a solid-color background. You can see an example of a knockout in Figure 17-4. The original image is on the left.

Knockouts are essential to the art of compositing because you have to remove the various components from their original backgrounds to seamlessly place them into the new background photo. *Seamless* is the key word here. The knockout really has to look as if it belongs where you put it. If it belongs, it has the same color tint as its surroundings. It might need to reflect the colors of nearby walls or, if its surface is really reflective, to reflect the images of nearby objects. If you put a woman in a billowing white wedding dress on the shore of a lake, you'll probably want to see a reflection of her in the water

THE SPECIAL EFFECTS
WORKFLOW

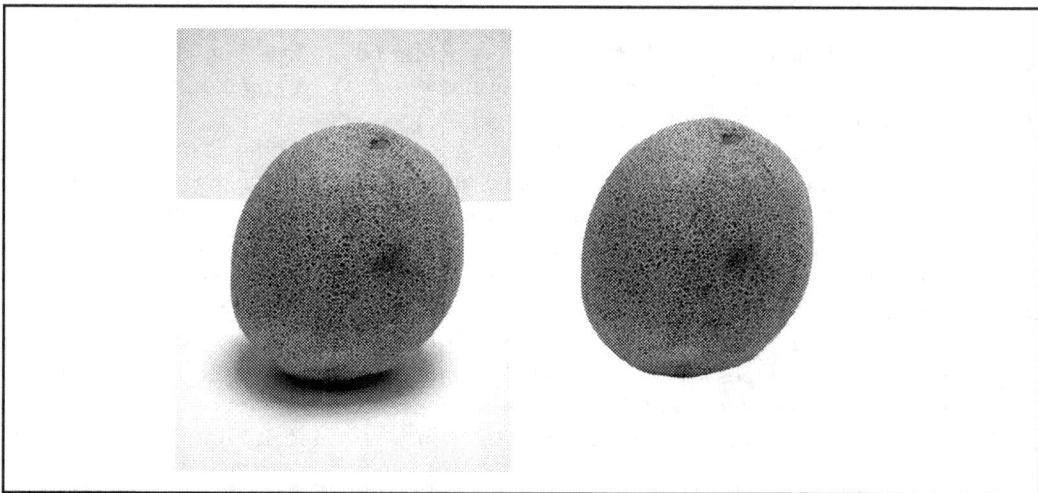

Figure 17-4.   *The image on the right is a clean knockout from the background.*

of the lake. If the subject in the knockout was really on the scene, it's probable that it would cast its shadow onto the scene itself.

Finally, in composites, knockouts must have transitional edges. What's a transitional edge? Put simply, it's an edge with pixels that blend with the pixels in the background. The closer the subject is to the viewer, the wider the edge transition needs to be. Here's why transitional edges are essential to making the placement of a knockout into a composite look believable: People have two eyes, each of which focuses independently and sees the scene from a slightly different point of view (POV). One eye is going to look slightly past the subject while the other focuses directly onto it. If the subject is relatively close to you (roughly within 10 feet) the difference becomes even more noticeable. The human brain then overlaps the image seen by the eye that focuses on the subject and the image seen by the eye that focuses on the background. As a result (though we're not usually conscious of it), the images along the edges overlap. So regardless of how you select the edges of the knockout, you then need to make the edges of that selection transition from fully opaque to at least partially transparent.

All edges in a knockout that is used for compositing must be more or less transitional; exactly how transitional depends on

- The apparent distance (in the composite) between the camera and the subject.
- The materials the subject is made of. Highly transparent materials are transitional throughout, with less of a transition in extreme shadows and highlights. Highly reflective materials are also highly transitional.
- Whether the subject (or something attached to the subject, such as wind-blown hair) is moving.
- Edge complexity (explained next).

There are two kinds of edges that you must consider when deciding what techniques to use to make a knockout or a selection you will use to make a knockout: smooth (hard or geometric) and complex.

Smooth edges are most commonly found on machine-made objects (such as irons or automobiles). They are most likely to be best knocked out by making a selection (at least, in Photoshop Elements) with a combination of marquee selection tools. You can see two smooth-edged objects that are *not* machine made in Figure 17-5.

Complex edges are those that have mixed foreground and background. For instance, tree branches that reveal little bits of sky between the leaves, or flying hair that reveals little bits of background between the strands. A complex edge might also be a transitional edge, but transitional edges are not necessarily complex. Complex edges are generally best knocked out by using either the Background Eraser or the Magnetic Lasso, or a combination of both. You can see an example of a complex edge in Figure 17-6.

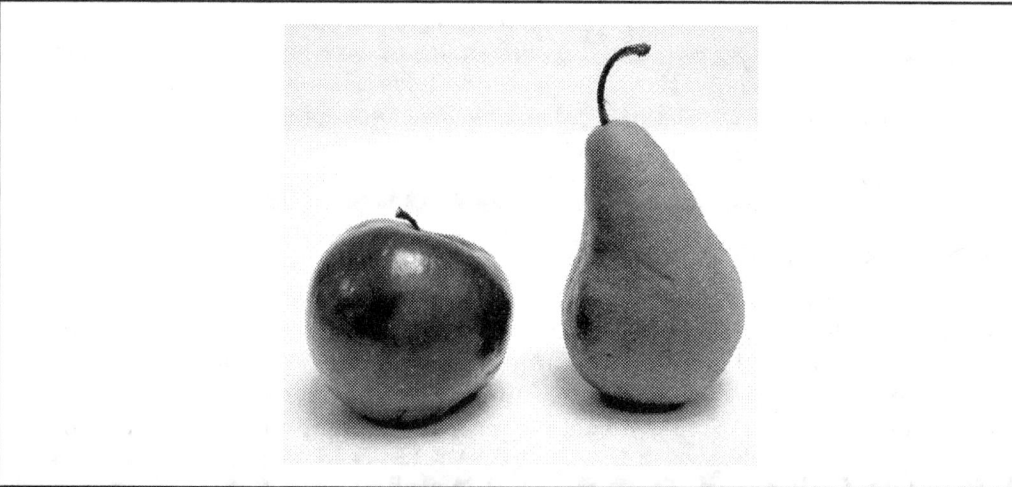

Figure 17-5.   *These fruit images have smooth images with clear, simple boundaries between interior and exterior space.*

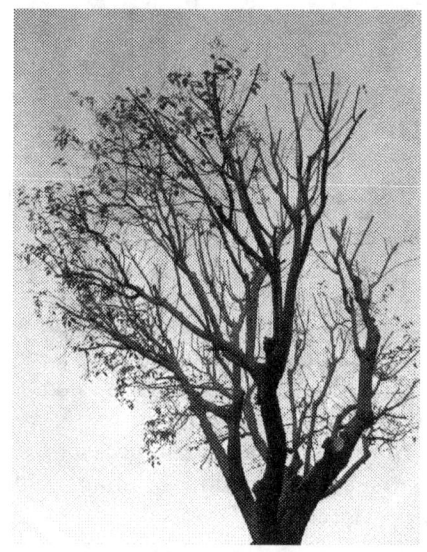

Figure 17-6.   *Images with complex edges, such as this tree, contain many areas of interior and exterior space that make it harder to select the object.*

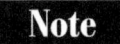**Note** *Some edges, such as wedding veils or stained glass windows, are so complex that it's almost mandatory that you shoot them in a studio using very even lighting and against a background of knockout blue or green. Knockout blue and green are specific mixtures of those colors that are least likely to be found in foreground objects and also dark enough to make it unlikely that they will reflect back onto the subject of the knockout. Using this technique really cuts the time you spend editing edges.*

Selection Versus Extraction

Perhaps the first thing you should decide when you set out to make a knockout is whether to first duplicate the item's layer and then knock it out with the Background Eraser, or to make a selection with the marquee tools and then use the Layer Via Copy command to place the contents of that selection onto its own layer. Either technique is valid, so choose the one that's most likely to require the least post-knockout editing.

Match the Selection Technique with the Subject

If the edges are complex or there needs to be unevenness in the amount of transparency required along the edge to make the transition, your best bet is the Background Eraser.

If the edges are smooth, you definitely want to use the Selection tools. We suggest starting with the Magnetic Lasso, and then editing with the other selection tools as required.

If the edges are a combination of complex and smooth, use the marquee tools first. When you've finished making the selection, edit it so that it's broadened in areas where the Background Eraser would be a better choice. Then invert the selection (CMD/CTRL+SHIFT+I) and press DELETE/BACKSPACE to erase everything outside the selection. Finally, use the Background Eraser wherever you need it to make the edge transitions you need.

Make Your Own History Brush

Photoshop Elements has an Undo History palette (see Chapter 4) so that you can back up by multiple steps in the development of your image. These past history states, as they exist within the Undo History palette, cannot be used as a direct source for a brush as they can in Photoshop. With some clever maneuvering, however, you can create a workable facsimile of a history brush, which can have a useful application as a clone source. At any stage of the image, you can choose Image | Duplicate Image. When the duplicate image's window opens, choose Layers | Flatten Image.

1. Press CMD/CTRL+A to select all, and then CMD/CTRL+C to copy the selection to the clipboard.

2. Immediately activate the original image's window, and then choose CMD/CTRL+V to paste the clipboard contents into the original image as a new layer.

3. In the Layers palette, drag the new layer to the bottom of the stack. While it's still active, click the New Layer icon at the bottom of the Tools palette. Fill the

new layer with black, and then double-click it to bring up the Layer Options dialog box; enter **Divider** as the name of the new layer.

4. Activate the bottom layer and double-click its name bar. When the Layer Options dialog box opens, name this layer **Snapshot**.

You now have a hidden layer that you can clone from should you over-erase and need to paint certain areas of the image back in. Just remember to anchor the Clone brush in the Snapshot layer after you've chosen the Clone tool and before you attempt to stroke the clone.

The Select and Delete Secret

Here's one technique you should keep in mind if you are going to remove large portions of the image: start by making a very loose selection around the areas you know you're not going to keep and where there are no transitional or complex edges. Then just press BACKSPACE/DELETE to make that area transparent. You'll be surprised how much easier it then becomes to focus on any problems you might have in doing the rest of the work it can take to make a clean knockout.

Secrets of Using the Background Eraser

The Background Eraser works by removing everything that's within a certain percentage of tolerance of the colors on the edge of the object you want to knock out. If conditions are ideal (meaning you've shot your foreground subject in a studio with an evenly lit and highly contrasting background), the Background Eraser can do an almost perfect job almost instantly. The trouble is, 90 percent of the time, it isn't that easy. If you want to make knocking out an object that was shot outside a studio as quick as possible,

- Erase at 100-percent magnification so that you can see when you've erased too much.

- Start by duplicating the layer you're going to erase from and then hiding it. Later, you'll be able to use the original layer as a history snapshot (something Photoshop Elements doesn't directly support).

- Make a loose selection around everything you want to erase, and then press DELETE/BACKSPACE to get rid of it. It is much easier to see what you have to erase in the critical areas.

- In the Options bar, enter a relatively low range of tolerance and a fairly large brush size. The exact numbers depend on the colors in your image and the size of your image, but 5-percent tolerance and a 30-pixel brush size are a good start.

- Start erasing at a low tolerance, go all around the object, and then move up to a higher tolerance. Keep moving up the tolerance each time you erase around the image until everything you want to erase is gone.

- There are often background areas with so many colors that they end up blotchy or smudgy. The fastest way to get rid of these is with the Magnetic Lasso. Once you've used the Background Eraser, there's a lot more contrast between what was the background and what is the foreground. This makes it much easier for the Magnetic Lasso to follow the edges. In addition, if you have a halo (dark or light) along some of the edges, once you've used the Magnetic Lasso, you can choose Select | Modify | Expand to get rid of the halo. Once you've expanded, it's a good idea to feather by one or two pixels so that you have a slight transparency along your edges.

■ End up by zooming in to about 200 percent and moving along all the edges. Use a small brush eraser to clean up and reshape any rough edges.

The Magic Eraser Secret

Probably the most frequent application of compositing techniques is in changing the sky. The challenge is that the horizon line is often very complex, and there's often a fringe area along the horizon line that makes it difficult to knock out the sky without a light-colored fringe dividing the sky from the horizon. The technique that seems to work best most often involves making a very fast selection with the Magic Eraser, and then using the Background Eraser to get rid of the fringe.

Note   *This technique also works well if you want to keep the same sky but just want to enhance it by using the Equalize or other Image and Enhance commands to give the sky a more alluring appearance. Duplicate the image layer and hide the top layer so that you can see the layer below it. Make your image adjustments with the sky as the only consideration. Then make the top layer active and use the technique described next to knock the sky out of the foreground. The new sky immediately appears.*

Here's the step-by-step procedure for making this work:

1. Open an image in which you want to replace the sky.

2. Choose the Rectangular Marquee tool and select that part of the image that contains the sky.

3. If there are areas of color below the horizon line that are approximately the same as those in the sky, choose the Lasso tool, and then choose the Subtract From Selection button in the Options bar. Select those areas that might be mistaken for the sky color, and they will be removed from the Rectangular Marquee selection.

4. Making sure you don't drop the marquee for the selection you just made, choose Layer | New | New Layer Via Copy. The contents of your selection are lifted to a new layer.

5. Now you can use the Magic Wand to select the sky with a fair degree of accuracy and speed because you've isolated the sky and horizon on its own layer. This makes it impossible to accidentally select areas that are reflections or colors similar to the sky. Choose the Magic Wand tool. In the Options bar, make sure

that Contiguous is not checked. Also in the Options bar, enter **60** in the Tolerance field as a good starting number. You need enough tolerance to cover most of the tones in the sky without accidentally selecting tones in the horizon. Click an area that appears to be a midtone. The selection marquee should cover most of the sky without covering much—preferably any—of what should be below the horizon line.

6. If there are areas above the horizon line that are still unselected, reduce the tolerance to a smaller number (try between 15 and 20), click the Add To Selection button on the Options bar, and click the areas that haven't been selected yet. If the selection jumps over the horizon, press CMD/CTRL+Z to undo your last selection, reduce the tolerance, and repeat that loop until your overall selection comes right down to the horizon line.

7. If there are still marquee holes in the sky, click the Magic Wand inside those holes until they all disappear.

8. When you've got a selection that's very close to what you want, choose Select | Save Selection. The Save Selection dialog box appears (see the illustration that follows). Enter **Sky** as the name for the selection, and click OK. Now, if you should accidentally drop the selection or should want to use it later to contain something else, you won't have to repeat steps 1 through 7.

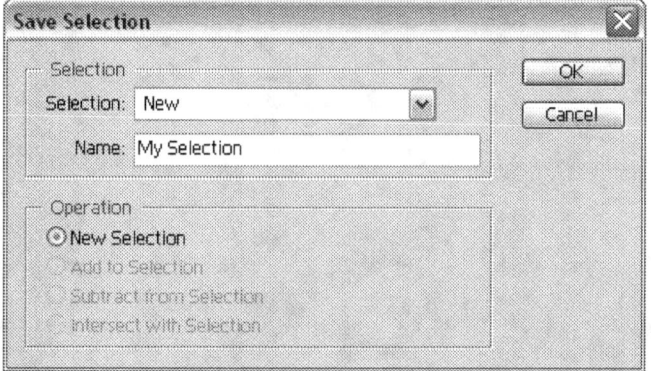

9. Now zoom in to about 200 percent. The fastest way to do that is to enter **200** in the Zoom field at the far left end of the Status bar. Press SPACEBAR to temporarily choose the Hand tool, and then drag until the horizon line is in view. Choose the Lasso tool, and use SHIFT to add and OPT/ALT to subtract from the selection along the horizon line until it matches as perfectly as possible.

10. In the Layers palette, select the sky layer and delete it.

11. In the Layers palette, double-click the original image's name bar. The Layer Properties dialog box appears. Enter **Foreground** as the layer name, and click OK.

12. Open an image of a sky you like better that's roughly the same size as your original. Press CMD/CTRL+A to select all, and then CMD/CTRL+C to copy the sky image to the clipboard.

13. Click your original image's window to make it the active workspace, and then press CMD/CTRL+V to paste. The sky image is centered in the target window and on its own layer. Choose the Move tool to drag the layer so that the new sky is positioned exactly where you want it.

14. In the Layers palette, drag the new sky's layer to a position below the original image's layer.

15. Click the original layer's name bar to make it active.

16. If the sky selection is still active, press DELETE/BACKSPACE. The old sky disappears and you see the new sky (see the image on the right in Figure 17-7).

Tint the new sky to match the old foreground, or vice versa. The "Matching Color Balance for Each Layer" section, later in this chapter, shows you how to do that.

Make a Knockout Selection with the Threshold Command

If the object you want to select is silhouetted against a plain and contrasting background, you can select the edges by making a copy of the background layer and then choosing

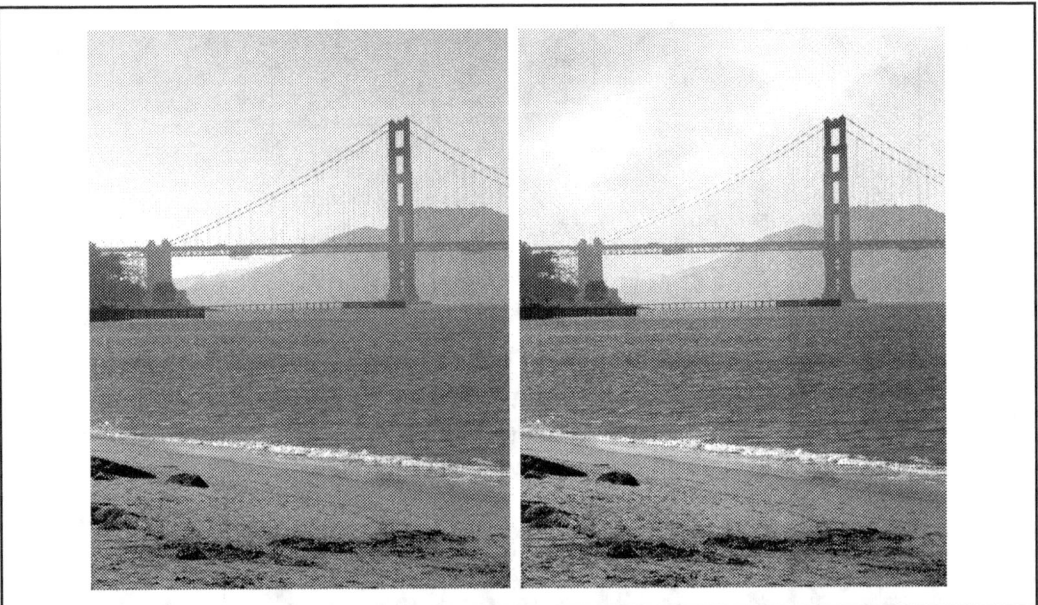

Figure 17-7. *Using compositing techniques to change a sky*

Image | Adjustments | Threshold. When the Threshold dialog box appears, drag the slider until the background is as solid white and the foreground object as solid black as you can get them, and then click OK (see Figure 17-8).

Paint the portions of the background that turned black white, and the portions of the foreground that turned white black. Now all you have to do to make a selection that exactly fits your complex edge is choose the Magic Wand. Enter about **25** in the Tolerance field and make sure Contiguous is unchecked. Click in the white area, and everything but the foreground object is selected. Press CMD/CTRL+SHIFT+I to invert the selection, and then save it. Finally, get rid of the threshold layer. If you open the selection on the original layer, you can lift the contents of the selection to a new layer. Clean up any rough edges, and you've got a perfect knockout.

Editing Knockouts

No matter how good you get at making knockouts efficiently, you'll soon discover that some (or a lot) of after-the-fact editing is necessary to keep the areas that should be fully transparent clear of not-quite-transparent leftovers, and to make the edges as smooth and as transitional as you want them to be. How much time you'll need to spend editing depends on the individual subject, and especially on how clearly defined the color and brightness separation is between foreground and background.

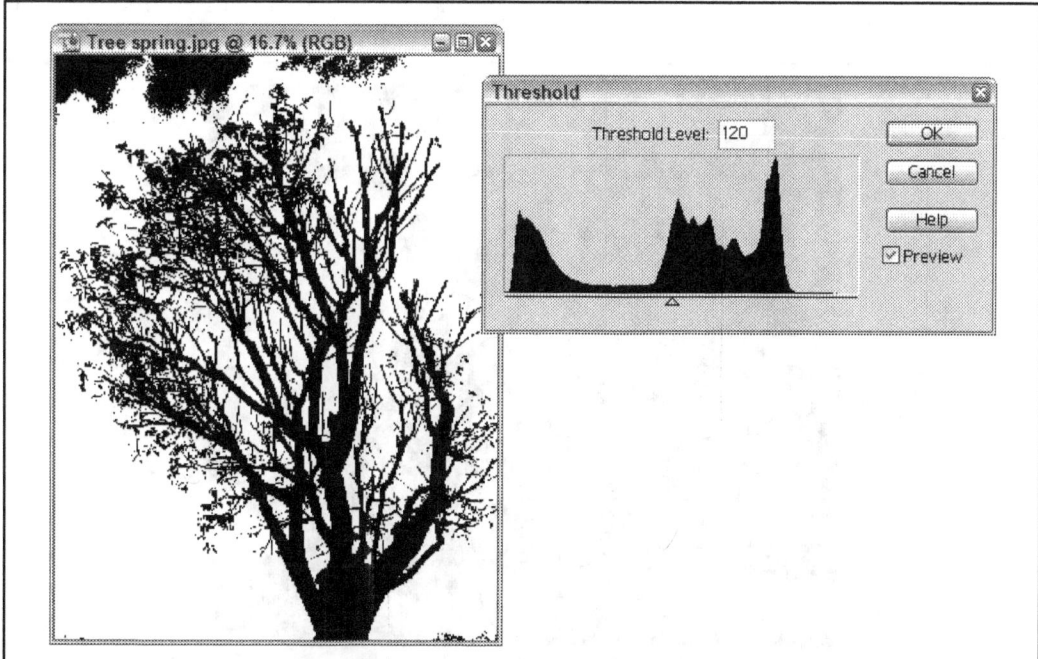

Figure 17-8.   *Using the settings indicated in the Threshold dialog box results in the image you see here.*

Clean Up the Transparent Area with the Magic Eraser

Once you've made a knockout, it's a good idea to see how clean the transparent background is and whether there's any fringing. First, if the leave-behind smudges came from a background that's more than 50-percent gray, place a black layer behind the area you just knocked out. If the background is less than 50-percent gray, use a white layer. Any transparent areas stick out like a sore thumb. Then choose the Magic Eraser, give it a fairly high tolerance (30 percent is a good starting point), and click one of the leave-behind smudges. Often, the whole area cleans itself up perfectly. Let us warn you, though: nothing works 100 percent of the time.

Clean Up Edges with the Eraser

Much of the time, you can do the best job of cleaning up edges by temporarily placing a black layer behind the knockout and using the Eraser tool to clean up any obvious smudges and jaggies by hand. When you're done, delete the black layer. It's not a bad idea to also use a white layer in the same way so that you can easily spot and erase stray pixels that are darker than 50-percent gray. You can clearly see the benefit of using the black layer in Figure 17-9.

Techniques for Making Transitional Edges

Even though the Background Eraser and the other techniques we've shown you can do some tricks with transitional and complex edges that would be difficult to find the time

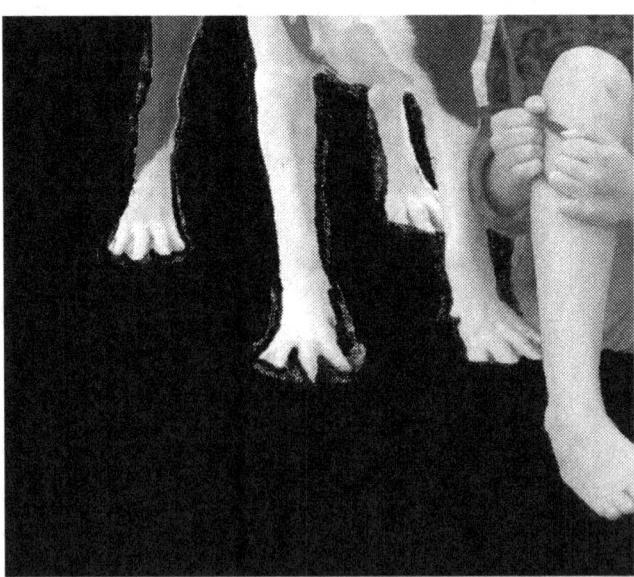

Figure 17-9.   *Placing a black background behind the knockout makes it easier to see any pixels that need to be cleaned up.*

to do manually, it's not unusual to have to do a few finishing touches. It's a good idea to do these finishing strokes after you've put your knockouts over your background. It's amazing how much the juxtaposition of colors and patterns can make the illusion look seamless (or not).

Once you've put the images together, zoom in to 100 percent, or even 150 percent, but don't go too far, or your eyes will start fooling you and you'll do more retouching than you need to. Now, just retouch the edges so they seem to blend together. Chapter 13 has lots to say on that topic. For the most part, you'll be using the Eraser tool as a soft-edged brush to straighten and smooth edges, and the Burn and Dodge tools to darken and lighten edges to blend with the background. You'll also use the Burn and Dodge tools for lighting effects.

Use the Blur Tool   There will also be times when it helps immensely to make small parts of edges more transitional, especially highly complex edges that catch highlights, such as hair or feathers. The Blur tool, used judiciously in just the right spots, can make all the difference in making the composite look realistic.

Shade Edges for a More Three-Dimensional Effect   Often, you'll find that you've trimmed an edge so cleanly that the object looks totally flat. Try shading just a bit with the Burn tool on the shadow side so that the edge seems to bend away from you. Then add a bit of a highlight with the Dodge tool on the opposite side. In Figure 17-10, you see the same knocked-out item before (left) and after (right) depth shading.

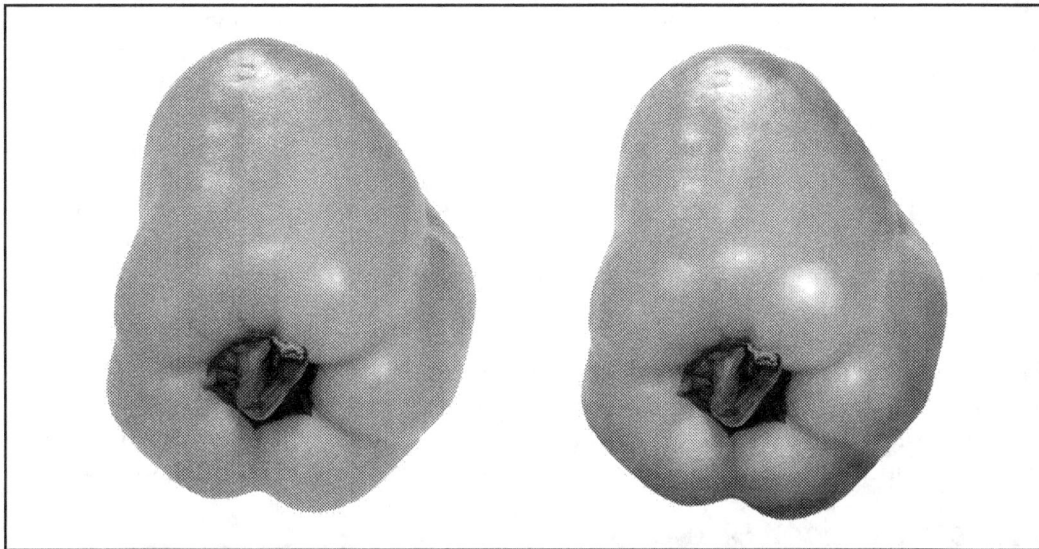

Figure 17-10.   *Darkening the edges and enhancing the highlights in the image on the right builds a more three-dimensional appearance.*

Managing Your Composites

You will be much more successful at putting composites together if you work with a plan. The first rule is this: collect all the images you will need before you start placing them into the composite. Put them all into one directory. If you have a CD-ROM burner or a storage drive, you might even consider archiving the whole collection of images, just in case you have to re-create the same project in another way for another purpose (or in case you have to write a book explaining how you did it; boy, do we wish we always followed our own advice on that one!).

Some Basic Guidelines

This section helps you manage your composite project more efficiently and helps you protect your data as you move through the development cycle. Composites can get complex and have many components, so learning how to set up a project properly can make a big difference.

Keep Each Element on Its Own Layer

We're not going to get into a lot of detail on layers in this chapter. You'll find all that in Chapter 8. The main thing you need to keep in mind about layers when it comes to making composites is to keep each element on its own layer for as long as possible. When it's no longer possible, duplicate the image so that you can save all the original layers before you have to blend them. If you forget to do that before you merge some of the layers together, you can always go back a few steps in the Undo History palette. However, you should rely on Undo only in an emergency. If you don't get into the habit of saving a version of the file with all its layers (or at least all the layers up to a point in the evolution of the composite), there will surely come a time when you'll have to re-create a lot of painstaking work.

If you keep everything on its own layer, you'll have a much easier time of making the exposure or color balance of an object fit with the other objects in the composite. You'll also have a complete version of the knockout if you decide later that it would be nice to have a duplicate of it somewhere else in the composition. You can even go back later and use the knockout in another composition without having to spend the time to make a new knockout.

Make a Duplicate Whenever You Need a Flattened Image

If you make a duplicate of the image any time you need to flatten the image (for instance, for a "snapshot" or for a special effect that includes everything), then you can always go back to manipulating, editing, or moving whatever's on the individual layers.

Make a Reduced-Size Copy

It's not unusual for composites to consist of a dozen (or dozens) of layers, especially if you're doing such things as compositing crowd scenes. You might run out of RAM, and then your computer will have to swap layers to and from the hard drive. That might slow things down so much that you won't take time to really experiment with the execution of the concept before you commit to it. You will want to be able to change the position of objects within the composition, and to be able to quickly change the transparency and blending modes of layers.

If you have a really complex composite to make, make all the knockouts and import all the images at real size. Then duplicate the image and choose Image | Resize to reduce the overall size of the image so that it's not more than twice the screen size of your computer. Be sure to keep all your layers intact as much as possible. Then you can use your layers as a history of what you did so, when you have to create the full-size version, you won't have to experiment in slow motion. Keeping layers intact will probably take you a fraction of the time that trying to do the full-size version would.

Using the Copy and Paste Commands

As you move components to new layers and then combine those layers in new and unique ways, you will make much use of the Copy and Paste commands. This section reveals all the nuances of these commands relative to composites and how to expand your abilities with Copy and Paste.

Instant Color Conversion

Photoshop Elements instantly converts the original image into the color mode of the target image when you paste or move from one file to another.

Special-Purpose Copy and Paste Commands

By this point in our exercises, you'll have used the Photoshop Elements Copy and Paste commands many times, but you might not yet be familiar with making composites. This section discusses three commands related to copy and paste operations that are especially useful for compositing:

- Duplicate Image
- Copy Merged
- Paste Into

Duplicate Image   Using the Duplicate Image command has already been mentioned several times in this chapter. This command makes an instant and exact copy of the file you're currently working on. It preserves everything except the Undo History palette, so you can't go backward in a duplicated image; however, there are many other things you can do. You can flatten the image and process it with a filter, and then bring the processed image back into the original image as its own layer. You already know how valuable making a duplicate can be in case your computer suddenly shuts down and your Undo History palette goes bye-bye. You can also use the duplicate image to make merged layers without merging the layers in the original.

Copy Merged Suppose you have a group of objects, each currently residing on a separate layer, that you want to copy to a single layer that you can then transform and place elsewhere in the composition. Think of a flock of geese, with each goose being the same goose copied to a new layer, and in which the layers have been moved to create a flock formation.

1. Hide all the layers that aren't part of the group you want to copy.

2. Place a selection around all the items you want to keep in the new item. (If you want one less goose, leave that goose out of the selection).

3. Choose Edit | Copy Merged. Photoshop Elements automatically merges (combines to one layer) all the visible elements that are within the selection to a single layer and places that image on the clipboard.

4. To place that image as a new layer into your current document, simply press CMD/CTRL+V. To place it into another image, open the other image (or, if it's already open, click its window to activate it) and then press CMD/CTRL+V. The pasted image is centered in the frame.

5. Because the selection isn't the same size as the original, it probably won't be placed where you want it. In that case, choose the Move tool (CMD/CTRL+V) to drag the new layer to the place where you feel it best fits in the composition.

6. You might also need to change the size, aspect ratio, rotation, or perspective of the new layer. Choose Image | Transform | Free Transform (CMD/CTRL+T) and drag the handles to make the change you want (see the upcoming section "Using Transformations").

Paste Into The Paste Into command is unusable (grayed on the menu) unless there's an image on the clipboard. One of two other conditions also has to exist:

■ You have another layer than the one the image was copied from selected in the Layers palette.

■ You have created a selection.

If you want to paste the image onto the layer it was copied from, make a selection large enough to contain the clipboard image. Choosing and using Edit | Paste Into puts the image in the center of the selection it is being pasted into. As long as the selection you pasted into is still active, you can choose the move tool and drag to relocate the item. If you drop the selection, the pixels in the clipboard image simply merge with the pixels on the originating layer.

If you want to paste the clipboard contents into another layer, simply choose the other layer first. If the other layer is empty, the image remains independent. If it has image content, then you can move the image and merge it just as if it were being pasted onto the original layer.

Layer Tricks for Compositing

As you've probably realized by now, understanding layers is key to making successful composites. In fact, an entire chapter (Chapter 8) is devoted to understanding layers. This section just briefly reviews certain aspects of making layers that are especially pertinent to certain aspects of making composites work.

Using Transformations

A transformation is just about any operation that cause the computer to have to recalculate the number and arrangement of pixels in the image, including resizing, scaling, distorting, skewing, rotating, flipping, and adding perspective.

If you're going to do any of these things, it's always better to start with a higher resolution image than you're going to need in the end. That's because when the computer has to render the transformation, most of the image data has to be recalculated and pixels have to be added and thrown away. The Photoshop engine that Photoshop Elements uses is brilliant in its ability to do this while maintaining a decent level of fidelity to the original. The more you start with, however, the better the result you'll end up with.

Most of the time, the easiest and most interactive way to make transformations is to put the item you want to transform onto its own layer, and then transform the layer. That way, you aren't disturbing any of the pixels in any of the other layers in the composition.

If you have to transform an object that's already part of a layer, we recommend duplicating that layer (from the Layer menu, Layers palette, or Layer Name in-context menu, choose Duplicate Layer, or drag the layer you want to duplicate to the New Layer icon at the bottom of the Layers palette). Knock the item you want to transform out of the duplicated layer. Go back to the original layer and clone over the original item. Now, when you transform the item, you won't have parts of it showing on the layer below. For more information on transformations, see Chapter 11.

Using Adjustment Layers

Adjustment layers are the answer to changing the overall adjustment of the image because they affect each and every layer in the image to an equal extent. However, don't make the mistake of thinking that they are a panacea. It's very important to adjust individual layers to match the exposure and tone of the background image. Otherwise, using an adjustment layer changes the appearance of that layer only to the same extent and in the same fashion it changes all the other layers, so that item looks just as out of place as it did before you introduced the adjustment layer.

The bottom line is that you need both adjustment layers and image adjustments that affect only individual layers. For more information on adjustment layers, see Chapter 8.

THE SPECIAL EFFECTS WORKFLOW

Using Blending Modes

Remember that blending modes are just like adjustment layers in that they affect all the visible elements in all the layers below them, even if some of those other layers also use blending modes. So, if you want a blending mode to affect a certain characteristic (say Soft Light mode and shadows), be sure that all the layers you want that effect to take place in are *below* the layer that has the blending mode.

In addition, if you use a solid-color fill layer, you can have a blending mode affect a particular characteristic of all the layers. Take a look at the next section. For more information on blending modes, see Chapter 9.

Matching Color Balance for Each Layer

Once you've got the whole composite together, have done all your tweaking and retouching, and added any Adjustment Layers you're going to use, it's a good idea to revisit fine-tuning the color balance of each individual layer.

Start with the first layer above the background. Choose Enhance | Adjust Color | Hue/Saturation (CMD/CTRL+U), make sure the Preview box is checked, and experiment to see whether changing the position of the sliders for Hue and Saturation make a difference. Work your way to the top of the layer stack by repeating this procedure for each layer. Only after you've done all that should you try fine-tuning the Adjustment Layers.

Once you've done all that, you might want to introduce a specific color tint that simply sets a mood or invokes a feeling. You can affect all the layers by placing a solid-color fill layer at the top of the stack. When the dialog box appears, pick a color that you want to use as the tint source. Now put the color fill layer in Color or Hue blending mode to have the color tint all the layers below. Experiment with the opacity slider to control the intensity of the tint. You can use any of the adjustment layers in this manner.

Matching the Direction of Light

The subject of matching the direction of light by creating your own highlights and shadows has already come up in Chapter 13. The same techniques are used to help make the objects in a composite look as though they belong there. Lighten the edges of the composited objects so that they match the brightness of the edges of objects in the background that are highlighted. At the same time, darken the same edges that are in shadow.

In addition, you will probably need to cast shadows from objects that are placed on the ground. Otherwise, they will seem to be floating in space. If the lighting is fairly diffuse, you can get away with using the Burn tool with a large (roughly the same size as the object that's casting the shadow) soft-edged brush to darken the background layer that's under the object. Be sure you let the shadow fall off and broaden as it moves away from the subject. The softness of the Burn tool's brush should get softer as the shadow gets farther than the object that's casting the shadow. Finally, the softness of the edge of the shadows cast from composited objects needs to match the softness of shadows cast by objects that were in the original picture.

Putting It All Together

This section takes you through an example exercise that gives you the feel of how composite tools and techniques work together to produce a finished work. There are literally millions of ways to put composites together, so we cannot show you every possibility here. The key is in understanding how the integration process works and that there are many ways to achieve the desired effects. We encourage you to experiment to find the methods that best suit your purpose.

This example takes an average cityscape on a partially cloudy day and transforms it into a rainy-day scene. Giving the scene a believable look involves many steps, so it is a good example of how to combine many layers to produce the final image (the image on the right in Figure 17-11).

Here is how to make it rain in your photo:

1. Open an image appropriate for this exercise: a shot taken on a partly cloudy or foggy day, or just after sunrise or before sunset works well.

2. If the sky is already cloudy, then you are halfway there. In the case of the image in this demonstration, the sky was way too bright, so the first thing was to replace it with a new one. Here is the first composite we will do. There are two ways to approach this task. Use the Magic Wand tool to select the area of the sky by setting it to a fairly high value, about 100, and then unchecking the Contiguous box on the Options bar so it captures all instances of sky color, even in the trees.

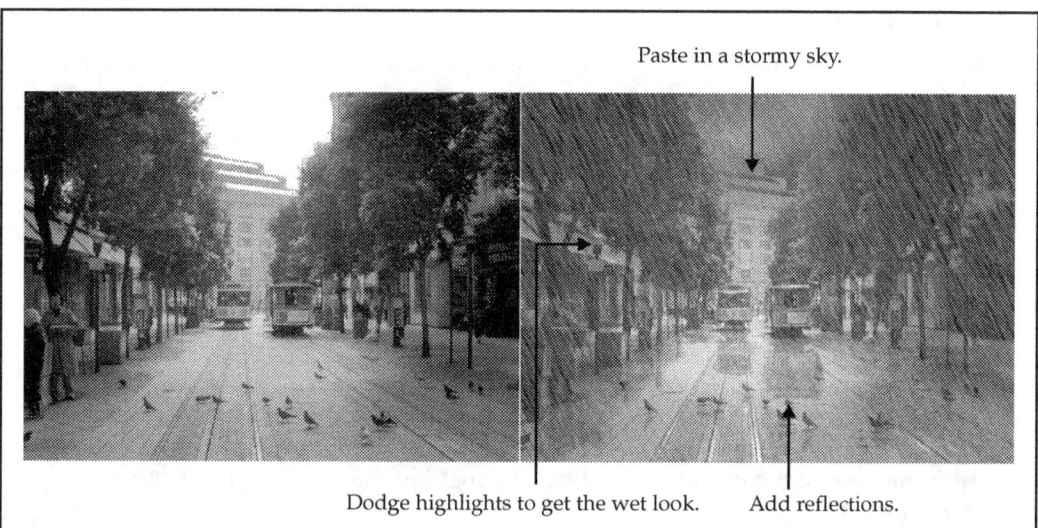

Paste in a stormy sky.

Dodge highlights to get the wet look.   Add reflections.

Figure 17-11.   *Before and after adding a rain composite effect*

3. Open a file with a sky that looks stormy. You can use the color and exposure adjustments in the Enhance menu to darken a normal sky, if necessary. Choose Select | All (or CMD/CTRL+A) to select the stormy sky and place it on the clipboard.

4. Make the original window active and choose Edit | Paste Into to place a copy of the stormy sky into the selected area of the old sky. In this case, we included part of the roof that was reflecting the sky. You will see the stormy sky displayed within the selection area. You can use the Move tool to reposition the stormy sky so you can see the details you want to show. You can also resize it by dragging the bounding box handles, if necessary. Once the area is deselected, you will not be able to edit the position and size of the sky you pasted into. A second method for replacing the sky involves pasting the stormy sky on a layer below the base image, and then erasing through the base layer using the Eraser tool to expose the stormy sky image.

5. At this point, you can go in and clean up edges as necessary.

6. Now we get into the reflections, which make the scene look like it is wet. As the surfaces become wet and water pools, it reflects the environment and accentuates the highlights on objects. It is necessary to add these details to make the scene look right. In this example, we use a Clone Stamp method for creating reflections.

7. Make the base layer active and then choose Select | All (or CMD/CTRL+A) to select the entire image.

8. Choose Edit | Copy to place a copy on the clipboard.

9. Choose File | New From Clipboard to create a new document with the image you just copied.

10. Choose Edit | Rotate | Flip Vertical to make a mirror image. This places the image in the right orientation for reflections.

11. In the original document, make a new transparent layer above the base layer by clicking the New Layer icon in the Layers palette. You will draw the reflections in on this layer, and then composite them with the main image.

12. Choose the Clone Stamp tool. Set the size of the brush relative to the details you will be rendering, and use a soft brush. In the inverted image, set the target for the Clone Stamp tool at the base of the objects you want to reflect. For instance, the target was set at the base of the trolleys, trees, people, and each individual bird.

13. Begin painting in the reflections one at a time where they would naturally occur until you feel you have enough to make it work. Keep the cloning to just the object and not any surrounding background. Notice that the reflections start directly at the base of the object if the object is touching the ground, and farther away if the object is off the ground.

14. Adjust the opacity of the reflection layer so the intensity of the reflections is more subdued. If the reflection is of the same intensity, it will not look natural.

15. With the reflection layer active, choose Filter | Distort | Ripple to make the reflections look slightly distorted, which is what would happen if rain were falling. You can also use Filter | Distort | Glass. Adjust the controls until you have the look you want. Be subtle.

16. When you have finished, save the document as a PSD file so you preserve the layers, and flatten all the layers by choosing Layers Palette | Flatten Layers.

17. In the base layer, use the Dodge tool to accentuate highlights on objects that would become more reflective when they are wet, as you can see in the trolley tracks back in Figure 17-11.

18. Okay, now we have a scene that is ready for a little cloudburst. From the Palette Well, choose Effects | Image Effects | Blizzard. This effect makes a new layer above the main layer and applies a diagonal streaking effect. Adjust the layer opacity if necessary. This is your rain.

19. To make the effect a bit less stark, choose Filter | Blur | Motion Blur, and set the angle to just a bit off of 45 degrees and keep the blurring very subtle to just take the edge off.

20. The final touch was to make the rain look a little less wind driven by rotating the rain layer and scaling it up so that it fills the entire frame. Merge the rain and base layer, and you have the final composite.

Tip *Save a big image with nothing in it but several layers of different-sized raindrops. Then, whenever you need to make it rain again, you can just open the raindrop file and drag the layers into the image in which you wish to make it rain.*

As you can see from this example, there were many steps in creating the final rainy-day look, and each step was a composite operation of some sort. Replacing the sky, adding the reflections, and finally adding the rain were all crucial operations in making this composite image work. Now you can see how using a number of composite techniques in unison can be a very powerful tool for creating new realities.

You can also use techniques similar to the ones described here for rendering raindrops to create confetti, snowflakes, hail, dust, spray, and many other effects.

THE SPECIAL EFFECTS WORKFLOW

The
Complete
Reference

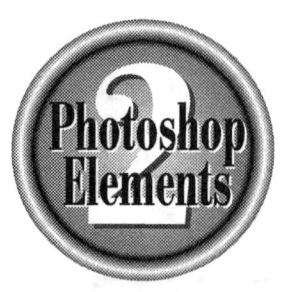
Photoshop Elements 2

Part IV

Preparing Your Photos for the Web, Print, and Presentation

The Complete Reference

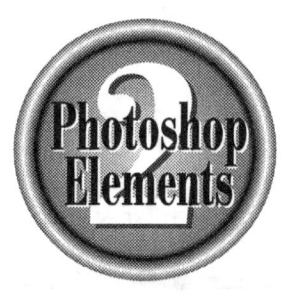

Chapter 18

Publishing Your Images to the Web

As the Web has increasingly become a visually oriented place and more individuals and businesses create their own e-mail and web pages, communicating with electronic images has become the norm. Photoshop Elements can help you optimize your images to look their best and to load quickly so that your audience doesn't lose patience.

Image Formats for the Web

Elements enables you to import and save images of many different file types (see Chapter 10), but not all types are appropriate for posting on the Web. The most common formats, supported by all web browsers, are JPEG (for still photos) and GIF (for animations and graphics). We concentrate on these two file types because they currently represent the most practical solutions. Another format, called PNG (Portable Network Graphics), is more versatile and can outperform GIF and JPEG in certain areas. However, PNG has not yet been accepted as a universal standard and is not supported by older (but still widely used) and more specialized browsers. So, if your goal is to reach the widest possible audience, stick with JPEG and GIF.

When you are creating images for web display, the first thing you need to do is determine what file format is the best to use for the type of images you have or are creating. This process is different from that of preparing files for print. The GIF and JPEG formats each have unique attributes that make each work better for particular types of electronic images. In the following sections, we detail how to use each of these image file formats to create web graphics that give you a wide range of functionality and optimization for efficient display on the Web.

In general, the JPEG format is best used for photographs and other complex graphics. These images have continuous-tone shading and more fine details, such as those found in photographs, illustrations, and paintings. Also, you should use the JPEG format when the following cases are true:

- You need more than 256 colors to display the image properly.
- You need to reduce the size of large, complex image files.
- You are not concerned about how your images display on 8-bit color displays.
- You want to have control over quality versus compression.
- Your image fits within cells or is displayed on a solid color background, so true transparency is not an issue.

The GIF format is best used for the following kinds of images:

- **Simple graphics** Images that work well as GIFs tend to be made up of basic shapes and lines with solid colors or simple patterns. Business graphics (such as company logos and diagrams) and the sort of clip art often used as icons are generally found in this category.

- **Animation**   Animated GIFs enable you to show short clips (under a minute in length) of simple cell-style animation. This does not include full-motion video, such as MPEG files, but may include individually captured video frames placed in a sequence to run at a much slower frame rate.

- **Images with transparency**   GIFs can float above textured, gradated, or patterned backgrounds, allowing the backgrounds to show any areas of the GIF that are transparent.

- **Images that use a web-safe palette**   Use GIFs if you want to be sure the same colors can be viewed on 8-bit displays. This is often important when optimizing logos and other corporate identity graphics.

If you have a logo, text banner, or other graphic that is made up of basic colors and shapes, converting it to a GIF file will be more efficient and maintain higher quality. The reason for this is an intrinsic part of the way the formats function when they compress the image data. GIF uses an LZW type of compression, which is lossless and efficient with large blocks of simple color. When compressed into a GIF file, images with large areas of uniform color are reduced in size dramatically and can be quickly opened in a browser.

The reason JPEG isn't as suitable for graphics with large areas of flat color is that it uses a compression formula that tends to produce noticeable artifacts in areas of solid color, so this format can actually seriously degrade the visual appearance of simple graphics. This is because JPEG's compression is specifically designed to make much more complex graphics, such as photos, as small as possible, and does so by throwing out exact color information in favor of information that can reproduce an approximation of continuous tones between pixels. Any artifacts produced by these approximations are easily disguised in the more complex random patterns found in photographic images.

Another choice that needs to be made is how the image is going to interact with the web page background. GIF and JPEG offer different solutions on how the image will display over the background.

GIF provides an option for designating one specific color as an area of transparency, which will allow HTML backgrounds to show though. You can specify only one color as transparent, so there is no such thing as partial or blended transparency. Therefore, the transition from opaque color to transparent color is abrupt and will leave an obvious pixel edge.

JPEG offers the option to use a matte color that will key to any transparency in the image, even if it is partially transparent, and then blend the matte color into the image pixels by the percentage of transparency.

The PNG format can be used for simple images (PNG-8) or complex graphics (PNG-24). The reason PNG is not vigorously promoted here is because it is not supported well in popular browsers at this time. Setting optimization for PNG-8 is similar to the process for GIFs. PNG-24 files can have full transparency, unlike JPEGS, but this option is not well supported. At this time, there is no real advantage to using PNG files. You can read more about the PNG format in Chapter 10.

Optimizing Images for the Web

This section covers the nuts and bolts of how you use Photoshop Elements to optimize image files to get a proper balance between minimum upload time and image quality. The tool that stands at the center of Photoshop Elements web capability is the Save For Web command on the File menu. This command provides a wide selection of options for optimization, visualization, testing, and animation. You can also optimize images using the File | Save As command, but it's not as user friendly as the Save For Web command.

We also cover how to build a web gallery using File | Create Web Photo Gallery. Before getting into the nitty-gritty of optimization, let's go over some of the general concepts that you will need to understand as you travel this road.

Data Transfer Rates

Although broadband connections such as DSL and cable modems are exponentially increasing in popularity, the vast majority of people still surf the Web via telephone connections at a pokey 28.8 to 56K data rate. This means that if you want to reach the widest possible public, the file sizes of your photos and graphics must be reduced as much as is possible to be consistent with a level of quality that you find acceptable. That level varies greatly from individual to individual and from image to image.

Images (some of the most data-intensive types of files) need to be formatted, sized, and compressed to optimize the transfer rate and make displaying images on a web page happen in a reasonable period of time. Numerous research firms have determined that the average web viewer will not wait much more than five seconds to see an important image before navigating to another page or site. The key to successful web communication is to make loading images as painless as possible.

Sizing Your Image

As with data transfer rates, screen size is also a movable feast on the Web. Individual users can choose to set their computer screens at various display resolutions, which changes the relative size of your image as it displays. The rule of thumb in today's market is to size your images to fit an 800×600 display; but as computers become more powerful and higher resolution displays become common place, the standard will most certainly go up. Sizing for 1024×768 today would not be unreasonable if you only care about an audience of graphics professionals.

Just remember that it is the absolute size of the image that determines how it displays on the Web, not the print resolution. So, if a 640×480-pixel image is set to 300dpi or 72dpi, it will make no difference in how it displays on a web page but will make a large difference on how it is seen on a printed page.

The issue of sizing is important with graphics because they cannot reformat on-the-fly like HTML text. Web text margins can be reset and reflowed to accommodate the change in screen real estate, but there is no way to resize a pixel-based image on-the-fly.

If the image is too large for the set screen resolution, it will force the user to scroll around to see the entire image. That is not a calamity, but it is not the best way to view images that are meant to viewed in totality. Vector graphics, which are produced algorithmically, can be resized on-the-fly, which is one of the reasons programs such as Macromedia Flash have become so popular. Resizing pixel-based images this way will probably become a reality in the not-too-distant future. The question is whether the increased bandwidth issues will make it moot before that happens. You can see that image formats such as TIFF and JPEG2000 are already including multiple resolution options within the file format, but as of yet no standards have emerged, and these formats are not widely supported by browsers.

The second aspect of image size has to do with how much information, in the form of pixels and color, you are trying to move across the network. The larger the image dimensions, the more pixels need to be transferred; the higher the color mode, the more bits per pixels. Therefore, a 24-bit image of the same pixel dimension as an 8-bit image will have three times the data to start with. Although it's nice to have full-screen images for users to view, it can be a real problem to display images of that size without sacrificing the image quality. You will see how to determine workable size when we get into the details of optimization.

The Save For Web Command

The File | Save For Web command is a versatile Photoshop Elements' mini application that helps you get your images shipshape for the Web. Within its full-screen dialog box, you will find a host of tools and options that will handle just about every task you might need to optimize your image files and have them primed for web publication. Most of the file format conversion tasks that are accomplished in the Save For Web command can be done with Save As and the Mode command—both available from the File menu. There are two features that make the Save For Web command unique and valuable:

- A loading time estimate that appears at the bottom of the preview window, telling you how the optimization settings will affect loading time at the data rate you have chosen as being typical for your desired audience. This enables you to adjust the setting before you go to all the trouble of loading it on a web page and find out that it doesn't work.

- The ability to preview the quality result of your optimization settings right alongside your original, uncompressed (but already resized) image. This is the *only* way you can really know how much compression you can visually stand. It is also the only way you can see the effect of your settings when you have reduced the colors from the 16 million originally available in an image to the 256 or fewer colors allowed in a GIF file.

Let's get familiar with the Save For Web command. You can see the interface in Figure 18-1. We start with the general components of the interface to give you a basic working knowledge, and then we go into the specific options related to each file type. Finally, we show you how to create animation from a multilayer image file.

The Save For Web command is designed to give you all the tools you need to optimize any of your images for a range of uses on the Web. Refer to Figure 18-1 as we move through the descriptions of each component.

Hand Tool   The Hand tool lets you pan the preview images by dragging within the preview window to examine various parts of your image when you are zoomed in.

Zoom Tool   The Zoom tool allows you to zoom in on the preview images by clicking anywhere in the image area. Press and hold OPT/ALT while clicking to zoom out. You can also select a zoom level from the Zoom menu by selecting a preset level from the drop-down menu or by entering a value manually. Right-click anywhere in the image preview to open a pop-up menu that contains the zoom presets and the Preview menu options.

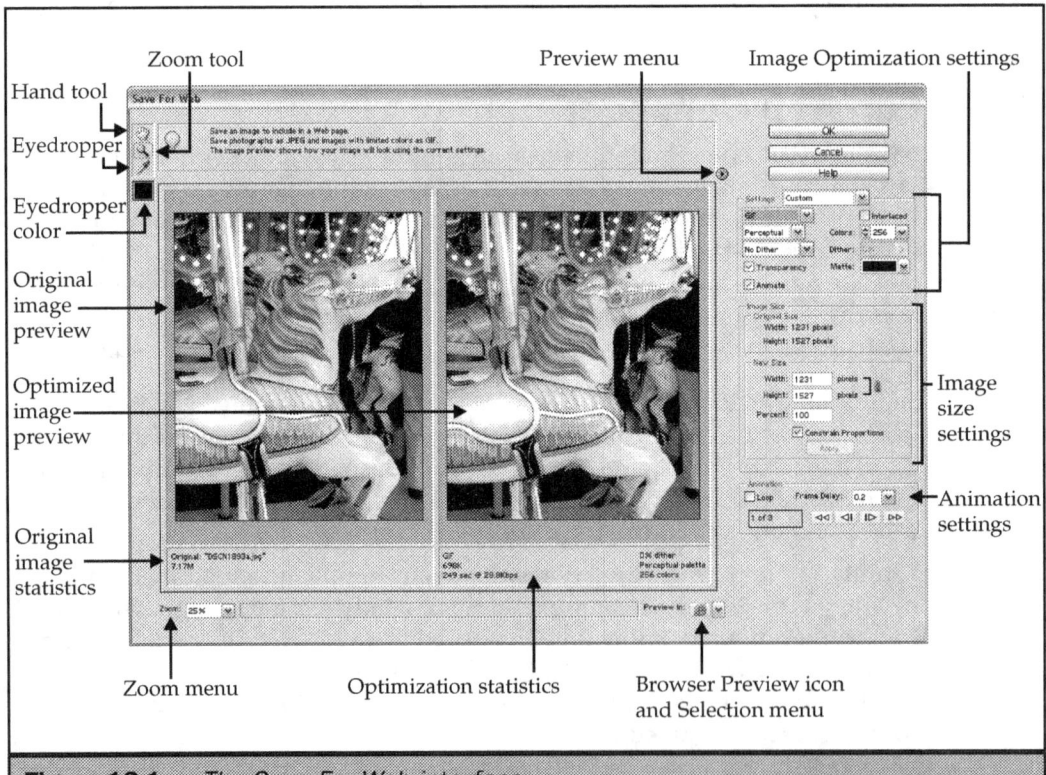

Figure 18-1.   *The Save For Web interface*

Eyedropper and Eyedropper Color   The Eyedropper is used to select the eyedropper color from the preview images, which can be used as a color reference for the matte color.

Original Image Window   This previews the image in its original state, providing a visual benchmark for optimization.

Optimized Image Window   This is a preview of the image that shows the effect of the current optimization settings. This allows you to judge the visual quality of the image before committing to the settings. You can test a number of settings and format scenarios and see the results here.

Original Image Statistics   This provides general information about the original image file for comparison to the optimized image.

Optimization Statistics   This provides information about the optimized image. This information changes based on the options and settings you choose for the optimization. This information is designed to give you valuable feedback when testing your optimization for size and download speed in various file formats, settings, and environments.

Browser Preview Icon and Selection Menu   Click this icon to open the specified web browser to preview the optimized graphic to verify that the settings perform the way you expect. You can change the default browser by changing the browser specification in the drop-down menu.

Animation Controls   These controls become active when you select the Animate option in the GIF Format Settings area. Find out more about animating GIFs later in this chapter in the "Making GIF Animations" section.

Image Size Controls   These controls allow you to adjust the image dimensions so you can make sure they display properly on the Web. Although you can size your image here, it will speed optimization operations if you resize a duplicate of your image *before* you save it with the Save For Web command. Then, if you discover that you still need to make refinements, you can do so with the Image Size controls.

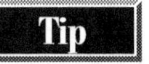

Set your desktop display resolution to the setting for which you are optimizing. For example, if you want your images to optimize for 800×600 display, make sure your screen is in that mode when optimizing. When you preview the image in your web browser, you will see how it displays in that screen resolution. This will help you make necessary adjustments.

Image Optimization Settings   This area displays the optimization controls and options for the image format type that is selected in the drop-down menu. These are covered in detail in the "Optimizing GIFs" and "Optimizing JPEGs" sections, later in this chapter.

Preview Menu This menu sets preview parameters so you can test your optimization settings against conditions that simulate various web conditions. You can set the optimization preview to display the standard browser dither algorithm; various screen color modes; and modem, cable, and broadband connection speeds, as shown in Figure 18-2. By setting these parameters, you can get fairly accurate reads in the optimization statistics on load times for the image in the projected web environment for which you are optimizing. This feature is a powerful part of the Save For Web command and will help you zero-in on the balance you want.

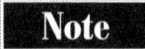

When you are optimizing, keep in mind that the load times you are getting are for the individual image only. If you are loading other images on the same page, you will need to add the load times together to determine the overall time it will take for the whole page to load. You can simulate this by grouping the images closely within a single document and then optimizing it to see how the load times check out.

Setting the Stage for Optimization

The Save For Web command makes it possible to visually experiment with optimization setting while immediately previewing the results. The options for this command cover

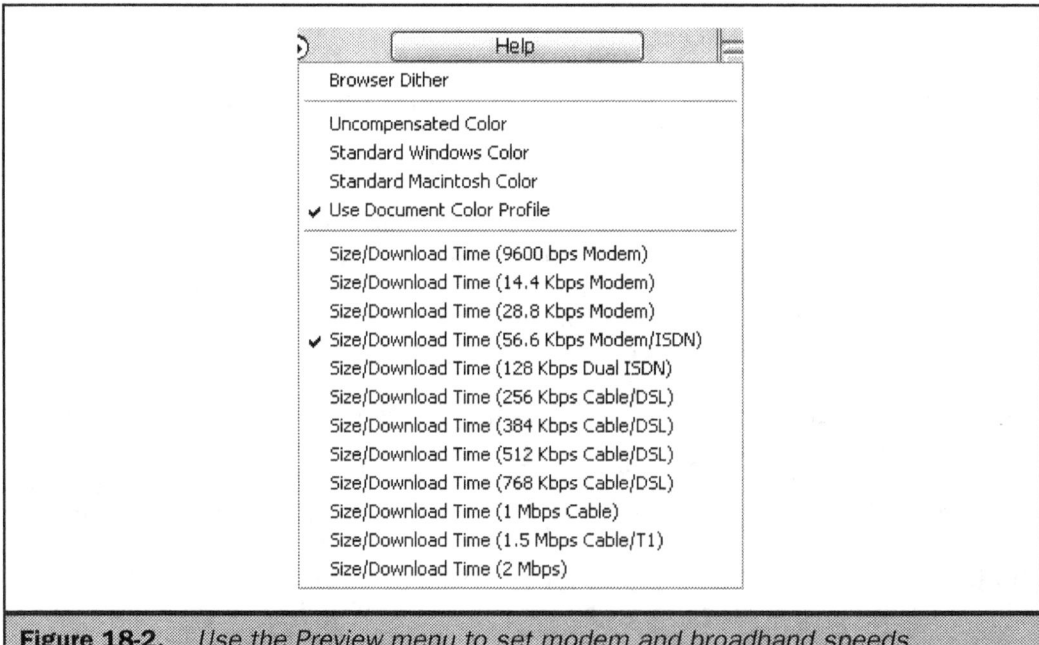

Figure 18-2. *Use the Preview menu to set modem and broadband speeds for testing.*

all the important optimization variables. Let's run through a typical optimization so you can get the feel of how this process actually works and how the workflow should progress.

Choose File | Save For Web to open a full-screen dialog box (shown back in Figure 18-1), which shows two previews of your image. Notice that a progress bar at the bottom of the dialog box activates as the program is opened, running the optimization conversion and then displaying the right preview window. The optimization settings used at startup are the last ones selected when the Save For Web dialog box was closed. When you are looking at the Save For Web dialog box, the image on the left is your original and the image on the right instantly previews the changes you make in the optimization settings in the panel at the far right of the image.

Choosing the Optimization Settings

When you adjust your Optimization settings for the file format you chose, the program shows the result in the preview window of the Save For Web dialog box and displays the following information underneath the preview window to let you know how your settings performed: file type, file size, loading time at the data rate you've chosen, percentage of the image that is dithered, the type of color palette used, and the number of colors in the image. Any time you change a value in the Optimization settings, both the preview and the aforementioned values change accordingly.

It's a good idea to zoom to 100 percent so that you can see the best possible approximation of what the viewer will see when that image is loaded into his browser. If you display at 100 percent, some of the image may be cut off in the preview window. You can scroll around the zoomed image using the Hand tool in order to examine anything that's cropped out by the preview window.

Using the Preview Menu

You can access the Preview menu by clicking the menu arrow just above the top-right corner of the Preview window. To set the target modem speed from the Preview menu, choose a modem or broadband connection type and speed that's the average speed of your web audience. You can set this at low or high speeds and then check the loading time under the preview image to see the difference. Because most connections are still via 56K modems, this is probably the best speed to use for testing your image optimization. If you are sure you will most likely cater to higher or lower speeds, adjust the settings accordingly. For instance, if your web page is being designed for an in-house intranet in which all viewers are connected via high-speed T1 lines, you can get away with far less image compression and, therefore, much higher image quality.

You'll also find a number of color mode selections on the Preview menu. These show you more accurately how the final image will look under various display conditions. The Windows and Macintosh color modes simulate the color displays most often found on those platforms. Choosing Uncompensated Color makes no adjustments at all, and choosing Use Document Color Profile makes use of any color profile already embedded in the image to adjust the display accordingly. Color profiles help standardize the color display between platforms and devices (see Chapter 1).

Another option on the Preview menu is Browser Dither. When selected, it shows what web browser built-in conversion does to a JPEG image or a non–web-safe GIF image on an 8-bit display. You probably don't need to choose this option; it's highly unlikely that your viewers will be using 8-bit display systems given today's technology. An exception might be large organizations that are sticking to older technology because their business applications don't require updating their display systems. If you do happen to be designing graphics for this kind of target audience, use the Browser Dither option to view what happens to your images on an 8-bit display. It can look quite awful. You might want to convert all your graphics to web-safe palettes if this is a problem.

Next, from the Browser Selection menu, choose the web browser that you want to use for display testing. Click the browser icon to see the optimized image display in the actual web browser. You can choose different browsers and test to see that your images display well in each. Internet Explorer and Netscape are the two most popular web browsers in use today.

Settings Menu   This drop-down menu lists a number of preset format-quality–level options. Choose one of the preset formats to reveal the options for that selection. The preset formats will set certain option parameters automatically.

Image Format Menu   This drop-down menu lists the formats that are available for optimization. Choose one of the formats to see the optimization controls for that format. As usual, Photoshop Elements provides abundant redundancy of functionality.

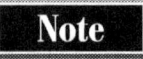

You can use either of these menus to choose a format because choosing a particular format from one or the other will bring up the same options. The only difference is the preset parameters, which can be manually changed at any time.

Optimizing JPEGs

JPEG files are in the lead as the most popular image format on the Web as the display of photographic images has become more prevalent. JPEGs are 24-bit (16.7 million colors), so they are well suited for complex color images. Optimizing JPEG files is much more straightforward than working with GIF files. That is because JPEGs are more specialized and less versatile. You will need to know a few things about JPEGs before we dig into the Save For Web dialog box, where we get into the actual mechanics of performing JPEG optimization.

Lossy Compression

JPEG compression works in a totally different manner than GIF. Because it is a much more complex scheme, we won't go into all the gory details. In general, JPEG compression works by taking blocks of pixels and storing color-averaging information about the pixels in each block so it can simulate what was there originally while using much less stored information. The data savings come from not having to store all the information about each and every pixel. Only the information about how to reconstruct a close facsimile of each block is stored. If you look closely at a compressed JPEG image, you can see these pixel blocks—they're the hallmark of a JPEG image.

JPEG images can be compressed at different quality levels (0–12, where 0 is the lowest), so you have many degrees of freedom in determining the final size of the file—but it comes at a cost. JPEG is a *lossy* compression scheme, which means that the compressed image will not have all of the image data that was in the original, so the more you crank up the compression, the more the image will degrade and visual artifacts will emerge. In complex images, such as photos, the effect of these artifacts is more easily camouflaged. Some images are good at hiding the effects of JPEG compression, so you can set the quality levels fairly low and still have the image hold together. In general, the more detailed an image, the more it can hold up to the degradation (added noise) of JPEG compression. Large areas of smooth gradations, solid colors, or clean edges will not do as well. This is where you need to make use of the optimization preview so you can see real-time visual feedback on the compression levels you choose.

Note *Be aware that the JPEG format works better with some images than others, and you will need to test each one to find the right levels to preserve an acceptable level of display. You may find that some photos, especially those that are physically small or that deal with hard-edged graphic motifs, work better as GIFs.*

Transparency and Mattes

A JPEG image cannot actually store transparency the way GIF files can. JPEGs do have the ability to place a matte color as a replacement for any areas in the original image that have any percentage of transparency. This allows you to place JPEG files over solid-color web-page backgrounds that match the matte color. This simulates the appearance of transparency and smooth transitions. It will not work as well on web page backgrounds that are textured, patterned, gradated, or have images on them because you will see the boundaries of the solid matte color fill. You can see these effects in Figure 18-3.

PREPARING YOUR PHOTOS FOR THE WEB, PRINT, AND PRESENTATION

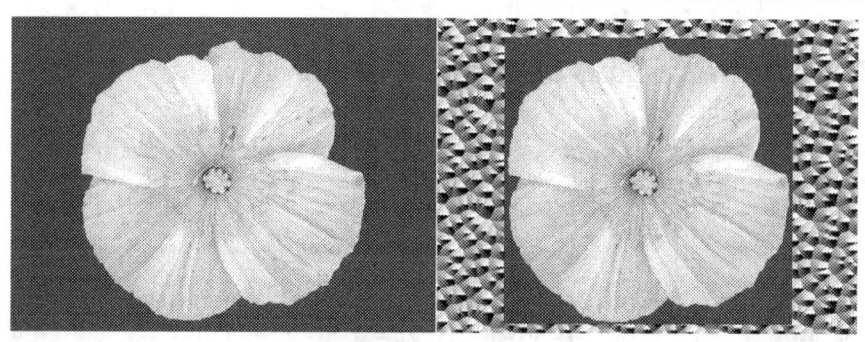

Figure 18-3.   *JPEG image with matte over solid color (left) and over a textured background (right)*

Progressive Display

This is a scheme by which successive low-resolution overlay images are displayed, building up gradually to the full resolution image. The purpose of this is to give the viewer visual feedback and a preview of the image while it is loading rather than looking at a blank screen until the browser can display the completely rendered image. This works well with large images or when many images need to be loaded at one time. It is designed not to waste the viewer's time, which is greatly appreciated.

The Progressive option will produce files of sizes that are slightly larger than standard JPEGs, and will make display of the final image take longer but start displaying sooner. The quality of the final image will not be compromised. With the new high-speed computers and broadband connections, progressive JPEGs often load so fast that the transition is not even perceptible. If you know that your web site is going to be displayed primarily on high-speed connections, you might choose to bypass the Progressive option.

Color Correction

JPEGs are 24-bit color images (16.7 million colors). As soon as you increase the color display mode on the host computer to 16-bit (32,000 colors) or 24-bit color, the issue of limited palettes becomes a non-issue. These modes have more than enough colors to display any image, although 16-bit color can cause some banding (jumps in color) in large gradients. JPEGs will mostly likely not display well on computers limited to 8-bit (256 colors) color. The browser will use built-in conversion algorithms to convert and dither the color to a web palette. You can see how the effect will look by choosing the Browser Dither option from the Preview menu in the Save For Web dialog box.

Today's computer systems run primarily in 16- and 24-bit mode, with little performance loss. For the best quality in viewing images on the Web, put your system into 24-bit mode if you can, and leave it there. Anyone still working on an 8-bit system will see photographs that are banded and noisy because they can only display 256 out of the 18.6 million possible colors.

If you have been using color management to create your images, JPEG allows you to attach the color profile information to the optimized file so the viewer's systems can better interpret the proper colors.

The JPEG Optimization Settings

Let's take a look at the various options and controls you can use to set up your optimization of JPEG images using the Save For Web command. Figure 18-4 breaks out the image optimization area of the Save For Web dialog box shown earlier in Figure 18-1. To activate the image optimization area for any format, you must choose a format type from the Settings or Image Format menu.

Image Quality Menu The Image Quality drop-down menu is used to set the quality level for compression. The options are low (10), medium (30), high (60), and maximum (80). The numbers in the parentheses refer to the default image-quality value. Selecting one of these presets will automatically set the quality-level value. If you move the

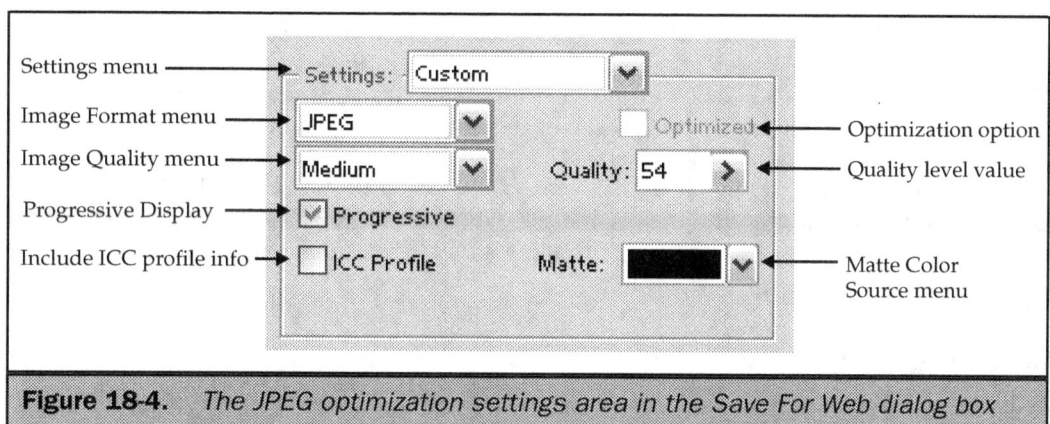

Figure 18-4. *The JPEG optimization settings area in the Save For Web dialog box*

quality-level value slider, the quality levels will change. Low, Medium, High, and Maximum refer to quality ranges. You get more fine-tuned control using the quality-level value slider, which you can adjust by single number increments from 0 to 100. Watch the optimization preview to see the effect of changing the quality level on image quality. You can look in the Optimization Information area to see how the current quality levels affect the file size and simulated load times for the connection speed you set in the Preview menu. Find the balance between load time and the observed image quality that you feel is acceptable.

Progressive Check Box   Checking the Progressive check box will enable the progressive display capabilities described earlier. Oddly, you get more options with the Progressive option when you use the File | Save As command, which doesn't offer nearly as many other optimization options as the Save For Web dialog box. The Save For Web command uses the standard default setting of three progressive passes, which is the most widely used choice among experienced web designers. If you are loading larger images or many small ones, this is a good option to check. It will provide visual feedback to the user almost immediately—much more reassuring than a blank screen, which may cause the user to move on before you have had a chance to show your stuff.

Optimized Check Box   This is an advanced option. Check the Optimized box if you want maximum compression, which results in a smaller file size. The downside is that older browsers do not support this option.

Matte Color Source Menu   If the original image has transparency, it will be replaced automatically by white as the default matte color because JPEG files will not store transparency information. The Matte Color Source menu gives you the option to set different sources for alternative colors. You can choose Black, the Eyedropper color (selected with the Eyedropper tool), or Other, which opens the Color Picker. Make a note of the matte color you choose so that you can match the matte color to the web-page background color. This provides you with a method to simulate transparency—although this wouldn't work on a background that contains anything other than a solid color, such as a pattern, gradient, or text. You can see how the effect works in Figure 18-5.

ICC Profile Option   If you check this option, the program will embed any ICC color profile that was associated with the original file. Then, if the viewer's browser understands ICC profiles, the image will be seen with its original brightness, color balance, and contrast characteristics.

Optimizing GIFs

GIF files are more complex than they appear on the surface. They provide a broad range of optimization options, which can have a powerful effect on the way they display on the Web. If you are not familiar with dealing with 8-bit images, we provide some general information up front on how they work before getting into the mechanics of

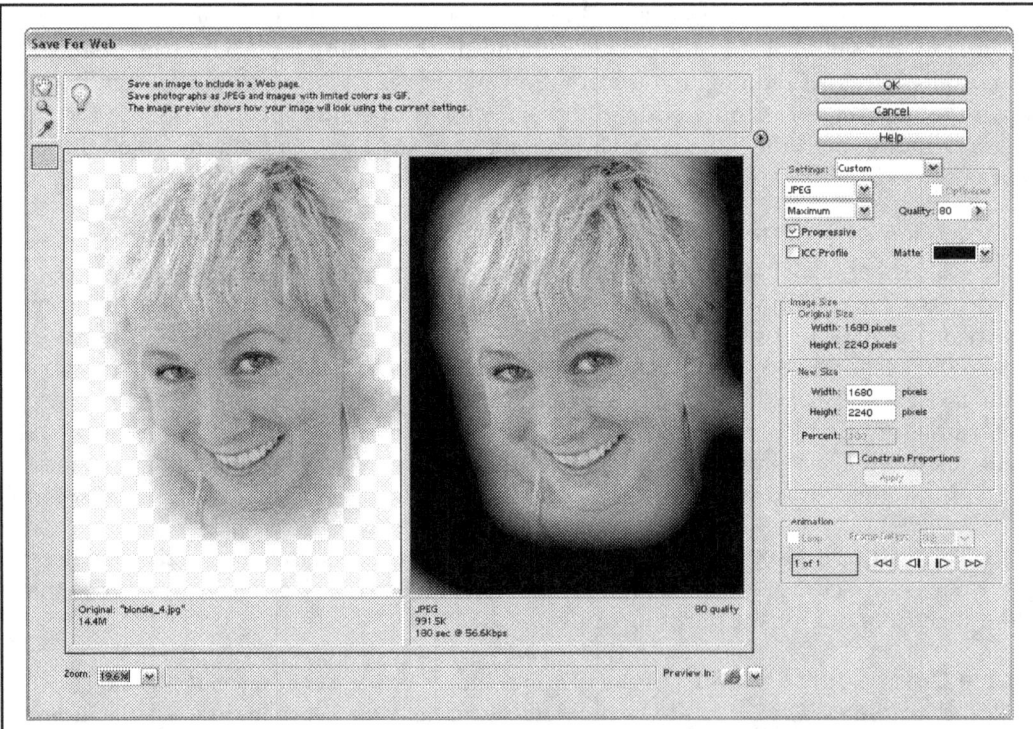

Figure 18-5.   *You can see how the black matte color fills in the transparent areas of the image.*

optimizing them. Having a conceptual understanding of how the various components work helps you make informed decisions about which options to choose and how to adjust the setting properly to get the results you want.

Converting an Image to Indexed Color

GIF files use *indexed* color, and all images that are saved as GIF files must be converted to indexed color prior to saving. Indexed color limits the image to a palette of 256 colors, referred to as 8-bit color. In this color mode, each pixel is assigned a color from the 256-color palette; and when you change that color in the palette, every pixel indexed to that color changes accordingly. For example, it is possible in this scheme to have 80 percent of the pixels in the image assigned to one palette position. In 24-bit color images, every pixel can be a separate color, so there is no need for indexing. An indexed image can have only 256 colors, so it is obvious that when you convert an image with millions of colors, such as a photo, you will get a significant change in the detail of the image. This is why GIFs are mostly commonly used for simple images with clear blocks of color and simple delineation, where 256 colors are sufficient to render all the detail.

In the past, it was common for computer systems to operate in 8-bit (256-indexed-color) mode because they did not have the processing power or the display devices to run efficiently in higher color modes. This means that the system could display only 256 colors at a time out of a total palette of 256,000 colors. To get a variety of images with totally different 8-bit palettes to display simultaneously with decent color on an 8-bit system, you have to find a common palette that will adapt to all the images in the most efficient way. The system and web palettes are designed to be the best compromise kinds of palettes. Unfortunately but by necessity, they tend to do a mediocre job, unless the graphics are designed to take advantage of the specific colors in those palettes. Keep in mind that this is an issue only with systems that are running in 8-bit color mode.

So this begs the question: "What palette should I use when converting to indexed color mode?" An Adaptive or Selective palette will give the best results if you are assuming that the final display will probably be in at least 16-bit color, which is a pretty safe bet today. (See the section "Using the Index Color Command," later in this chapter, for a complete description of indexed palette types.) If you still want the assurance that every system can display your GIF files perfectly, use the web-safe palette and accept the compromised color that it will bring to images that are simply being converted and not specifically designed around the web palettes.

You can convert GIFs in Photoshop Elements in two ways: the Save For Web command in the File menu and the Mode | Indexed Color command in the Image menu. We continue to look at the Save For Web command in this section. The Indexed Color command gives you additional options for controlling the creation of your indexed palette, so we will include a section later in this chapter called "Using the Index Color Command" that deals with additional options.

Compression

GIFs use LZW compression. This compression algorithm uses run-length encoding, which basically takes areas of like pixels and encodes them to take up less space.

Instead of storing every pixel color and position, LZW stores a whole string of matching pixels as a single command. This makes this kind of compression efficient for graphics that have a limited number of colors and discrete areas of color. The simpler form (256 colors) that many GIF images take usually makes them ideal for this kind of compression, which can dramatically reduce file size.

The other nice thing about LZW compression is that it is a *lossless* compression. This means that no image degradation occurs during compression, and all the pixels in the original image are preserved.

The "gotcha" occurs if you try to display multiple GIF images with individual palettes in an 8-bit color environment where any given color must be indexed to a specific row and column position in a specific palette. Because 8-bit systems can display only one palette at a time, the colors in GIF files that are not indexed to the same palette may display unexpected and undesirable color changes. Converting all the images beforehand to a web-safe palette is the best solution for this particular problem, but you still may suffer a loss of visual quality.

As long as indexed color images are shown in browsers that are running in non-indexed 16- and 24-bit color environments, the viewer's browser doesn't need to use its own indexed palette. You can choose to ignore web-safe palettes if you feel that the number of viewers who are using 8-bit web environments is insignificant.

Dithering

When 16-million color, 24-bit photos are converted to 8-bit GIF files, they often lose their formerly smooth shading or display colors that are not even close to those that were in the original. Fortunately, there's a way of "cheating" to make the image look much more like the original by intermingling individual pixels of colors that are in the indexed palette so that their proximity creates the illusion of other colors that aren't actually in the palette. This process is called "dithering." This can greatly enhance the realism of a photograph or heavily shaded image that has been converted to a GIF.

Interlacing

Interlacing in GIFs is similar to the progressive display found in the JPEG format. Interlacing displays partial resolution in multiple passes until the whole file is displayed. It differs from JPEG by displaying only alternate lines of pixels, so it looks similar to Venetian blinds. Use this option only when you have larger files or many small ones, so you can provide some feedback to the viewer that the images are, in fact, loading.

Transparency and Mattes

GIF excels in this area—it's one of the main reasons a lot of people keep using GIFs. The day that a 24-bit standard is accepted that can provide true transparency and still give excellent compression will be the day GIF might be sent packing. JPEG2000 and PNG are both possible candidates.

GIF files can designate any one of the 256 colors in the palette to be a transparent color or use the transparency already in the image.

Here's how to designate a color in an existing indexed image:

1. Choose Image | Mode | Color Table. The Color Table dialog box opens.
2. Choose the Eyedropper and click the color in the palette or in the image that you want to make transparent. You will see all the pixels of that color in the image turn transparent.
3. Click OK when you have finished.

If the image already contains transparency prior to being converted to indexed color, a reserved palette color will be created during conversion.

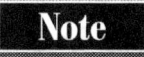 *GIF is a* hard-edge *transparency, which means it will create transparency only at 100 percent. Any partially transparent pixels will become opaque. Edges next to transparent areas will have a hard-pixel edge that is not anti-aliased.*

You can also use the Matte option, which will blend the matte color into all the semi-transparent pixels while either filling the 100-percent transparent pixels with the matte color or leaving them as they are. The Matte color option lets you maintain the smooth transitions and soft edges while allowing you to choose a fill color that will blend well with the web-page background.

The GIF Optimization Settings

This section will walk you through the various options and controls used to set up your optimization of GIF images using the Save For Web command. Figure 18-6 breaks out the image optimization area of the Save For Web dialog box. To activate the image

PREPARING YOUR PHOTOS FOR THE WEB, PRINT, AND PRESENTATION

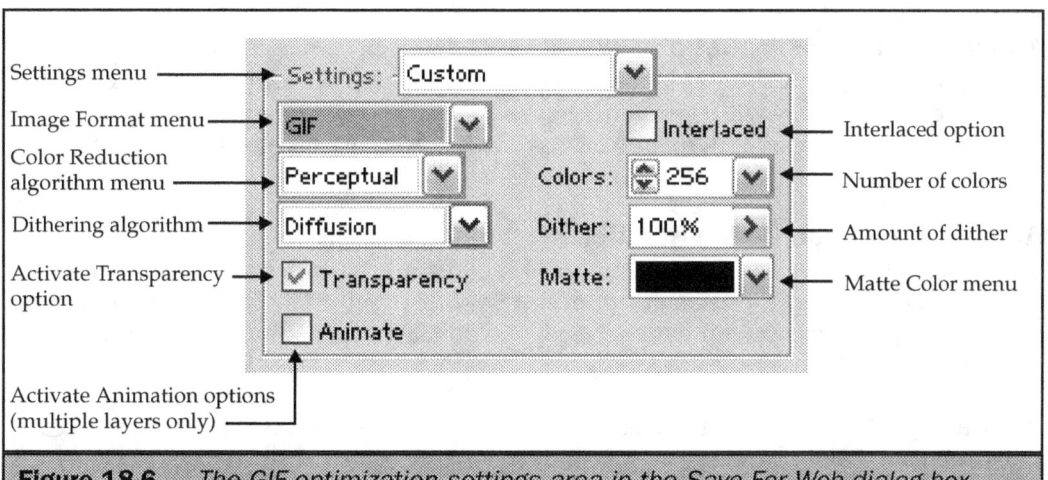

Figure 18-6. *The GIF optimization settings area in the Save For Web dialog box*

optimization area for any format, you must choose a format type from the Settings or Image format menu.

Color Reduction Algorithm Menu   This menu offers a number of options for the algorithms that the program uses to convert the colors in the original image to indexed color:

- **Perceptual**   Weights its color choices by favoring colors that are more sensitive to the human eye.

- **Selective**   Produces a palette that favors large solid areas of color and web-safe colors. It's one of the best palettes for faithful color.

- **Adaptive**   Weights the palette to the colors most used in the image. It's best used in images where there is a dominant color theme. You can force the palette to weight to a specific area of the image by selecting it before setting this option.

- **Web**   A 216-color palette that is used by all web browsers to display on systems in 8-bit color mode.

Dithering Algorithm Menu   This menu provides a number of dithering algorithms to help increase the blending of color in indexed images. Choose the No Dither option to turn off the effect.

- **Diffusion**   Usually gives the best result, and you can control the amount of dithering by entering a dither percentage amount.

- **Pattern**   More stylistic and obvious, giving the image a halftone look.

- **Noise**   Produces a grainier look and can often better hide the effect of banding on some images and camouflage seams when images are placed in tables.

Activate Transparency Option   When checked, this option will force any pixels in the original image that are 100-percent transparent to remain transparent in the GIF conversion. Any pixels with partial transparency will become opaque, and their color will be either blended with white (default) or the chosen matte color to the extent of the pixels' transparency.

Activate Animation Option (Multiple Layers Only)   This option becomes available only when you are working with a multiple-layer document. When checked, it activates the animation controls at the bottom of the Save For Web dialog box so you can set up the parameters for GIF animation. See the section later in this chapter called "Making GIF Animations."

Interlaced Option   The Interlaced option, when checked, forces the GIF file to load on a web page in a number of low-resolution passes, building up detail until the image is finished loading.

Number of Colors   You can set this value by entering it in the text field, using the pop-up menu to enter preset values, or clicking the up or down arrows to change it one value at a time. It sets the maximum number of colors (between 2 and 256) the current color reduction algorithm can create. If you choose Web Reduction from the Named Optimization Settings menu, this sets the Color Value switch to Auto. The image is then automatically converted to a 216-color, web-safe palette. You can also choose other GIF format presets from the Named Optimization Settings menu, which automatically chooses the number of colors to be used in the file.

Amount of Dither   This option is available only for the Diffusion dither algorithm. It allows you to set the amount of the dithering from 1 to 100 percent. Use this to control the amount of graininess or posterizing in the image.

Matte Color Menu   You can use this menu to choose an alternative source for a matte color. The matte color can be black, the Eyedropper color, or any color you select from the color picker. This color will be used to blend in the semitransparent pixels and to fill fully transparent areas if the transparent option is disabled.

Using the Index Color Command

You always have the option of converting your image to indexed color *before* or instead of using the Save For Web command. You do this from within Photoshop Elements by choosing Image | Mode | Indexed Color. The Indexed Color dialog box appears (see Figure 18-7). This command works essentially in the same way that the Save For Web GIF optimization works, with the addition of a few extra options that you might find useful.

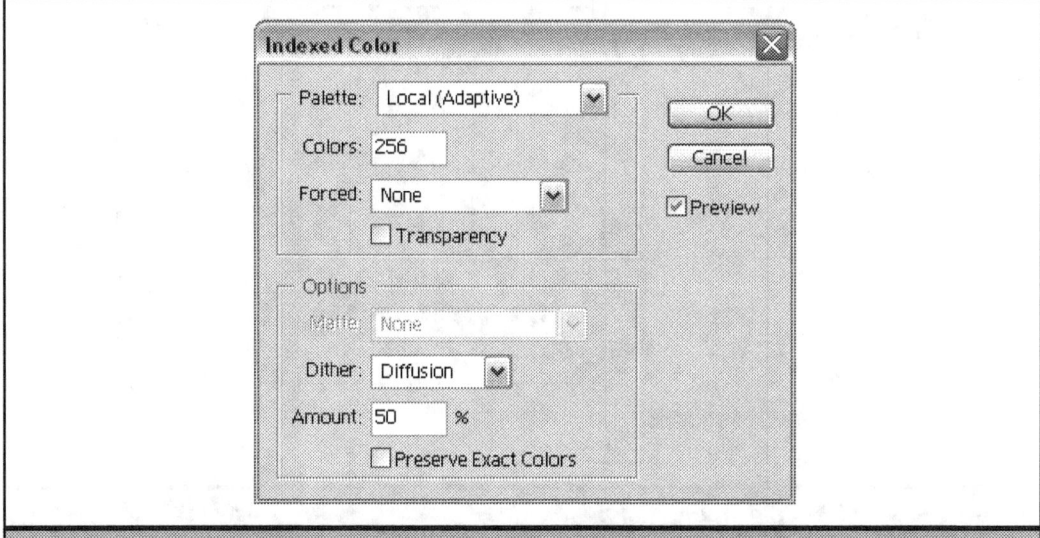

Figure 18-7.   *The Indexed Color dialog box*

The following Indexed Color palette reduction algorithms are options not offered in the Save For Web command.

- **Exact**   Preserves the exact RGB colors in the original. This option is available only if the original has 256 colors or less.
- **System**   Windows and Mac OS default 8-bit palettes for respective systems, providing a uniform sampling of RGB color.
- **Uniform**   Samples the RGB color cube to create a palette based on the closest cubic color space that can convert the palette. Example: if the colors are set for 100, the uniform palette will be set at 64 colors to define the palette, and all the colors will be equally stepped. The possible cubic spaces are quantified with 8, 27, 64, 125, or 216 colors.
- **Custom**   Opens the Color Table dialog box, as shown in Figure 18-8, where you can build you own palette by clicking a color swatch and choosing a new color from the Color Picker, or load a saved or preset palette.
- **Previous**   Uses the last palette option you chose.

Forced   This is a nice extra you get with the Indexed Color command. The Forced palette option makes sure designated colors from preset or custom palettes are included

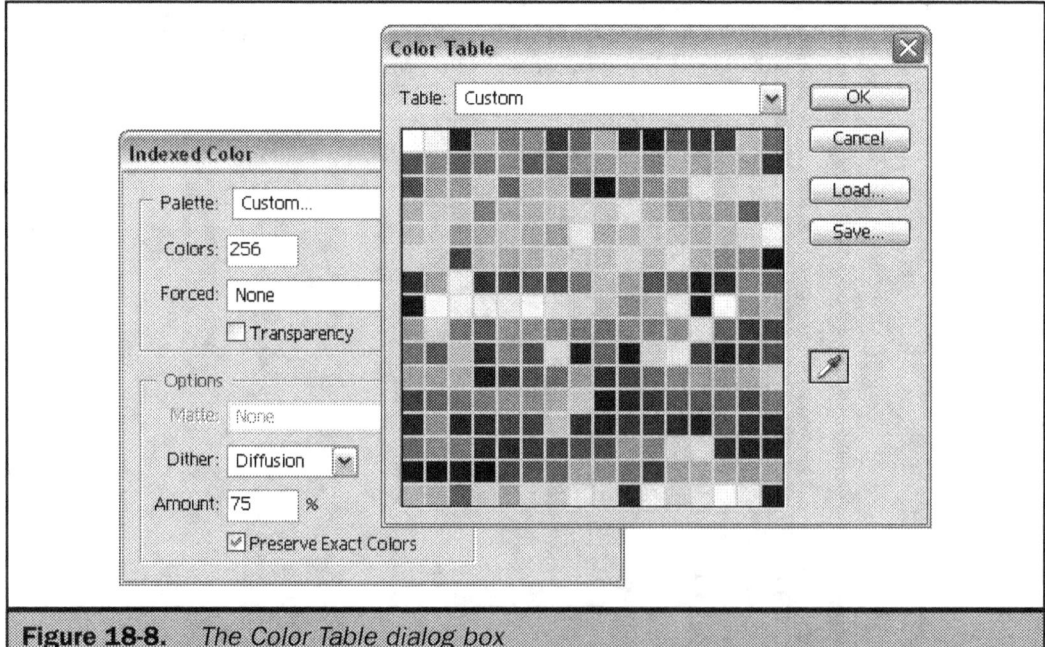

Figure 18-8.   *The Color Table dialog box*

in the palette no matter what colors are in the original. This is handy for making sure you reserve a matte color for a transparency that you know is not in the image.

Preserve Exact Colors   This option, which appears only if you have the Diffusion option selected, makes sure that dithering does not happen in areas of solid color that match the palette exactly. This helps prevent random dots from showing up in solid areas that are adjacent to anti-aliased areas.

Note   *Use the System and web-safe palettes provided in the Swatches palette to create original GIF images or animation to assure that the colors will display perfectly on any system. Make sure the color mode is indexed and that you load the web palette by choosing Image | Mode | Color Table and then choosing Load. You will find the web-safe palette file in the Elements folder under Presets\Color Swatches.*

Understanding the Optimization Preview and Statistics

In case we totally lost you by jumping back into Photoshop Elements proper for a moment, we're now back to using the Save For Web dialog box. Now that you understand how to set up the preview window and set your format conversion parameters, it is time to read the results and determine what adjustments you need to make to get the optimal outcome. You need to pay close attention to a few critical pieces of information.

The optimized image and the optimization statistics just below the preview in the Save For Web dialog box provide all the feedback you need to make the proper adjustments. After you set your simulation and optimization parameters, look at the optimized image preview (on the right) and see how it has changed visually from the original on the left. If the amount and nature of the change is unacceptable, then change the optimization settings to higher-quality compression values.

In addition, take notice of the file size and download times listed for the connection speed you set in the simulation. These will be listed in the optimization statistics, just below the preview image, as shown in Figure 18-9. You may need to improve visual quality by setting the color value higher, including or increasing dithers on a GIF, or raising the quality value on a JPEG, for instance. You will most likely see the file size and load time change as you make these adjustments.

You need to decide which factor is critical. If you want higher image quality, you might select the Progressive display option to load the image in stages so it doesn't leave the web page blank and inactive for long periods of time. Keep in mind that there is no absolute answer or perfect setting. Tweak the optimization settings and observe the results. You will find that after a few experiments, an optimal range of settings will emerge.

If you find that the quality and speed are just not good enough, your only option might be to adjust the overall file size and then try again. You can see the Image Size area in Figure 18-10. These settings can lower the load times and allow you to choose a higher quality level. Of course, the image will display smaller on the screen. Use the web browser preview to see how it looks.

PREPARING YOUR PHOTOS FOR THE WEB, PRINT, AND PRESENTATION

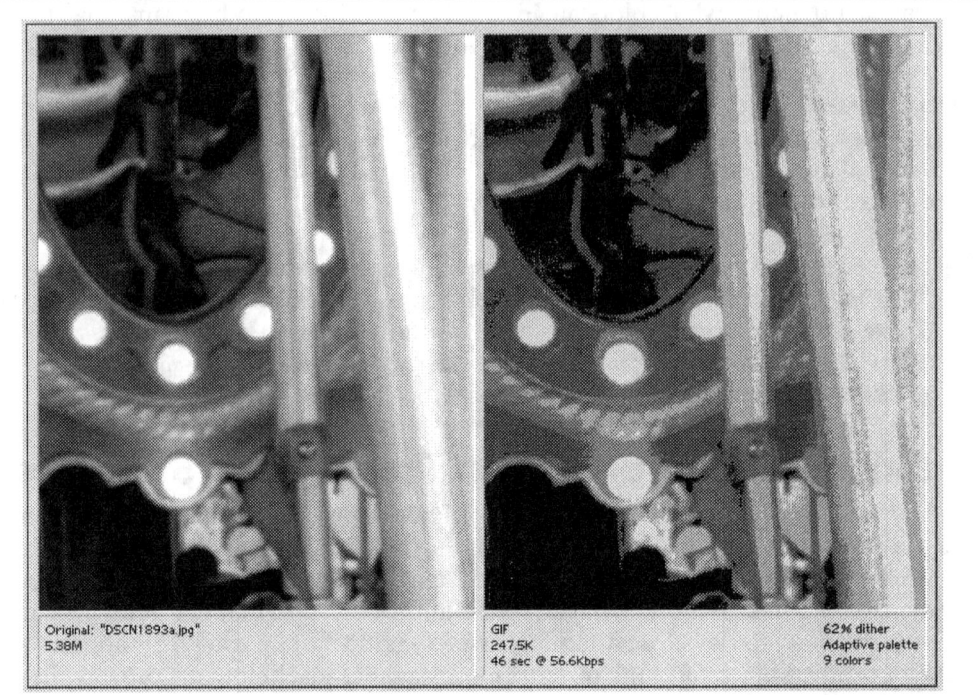

Original: "DSCN1893a.jpg"
5.38M

GIF
247.5K
46 sec @ 56.6Kbps

62% dither
Adaptive palette
9 colors

Figure 18-9. *The optimization preview and optimization statistics*

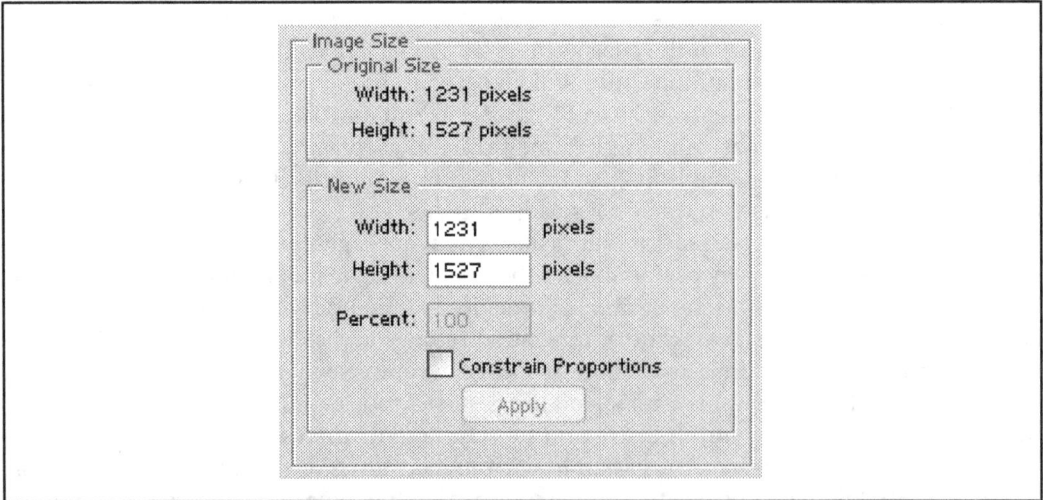

Image Size
Original Size
   Width: 1231 pixels
   Height: 1527 pixels

New Size
   Width: 1231 pixels
   Height: 1527 pixels
   Percent: 100
   ☐ Constrain Proportions
   Apply

Figure 18-10. *Enter new image dimensions or change them by a percentage.*

Making GIF Animations

Photoshop Elements 2 will automatically make a movie from a layered still image. It does this by making each layer in the image a frame in a GIF animation. GIF animations are so called because they are saved to a popular web image format by that name. In GIF animation, multiple still images are saved in sequence inside the same file. When these files are viewed on a web site, each frame is shown in sequence at a user-specified interval between frames. This interval can be short enough to produce an animation that looks a bit like the old-fashioned flip-card animations or like an old silent movie. In other words, at their best, GIF animations tend to be a bit jerky. However, it's fast enough to be a good attention-getter on the Web.

GIF animations are limited to 256 indexed colors, but these colors can be intermingled using a process called *dithering* to approximate the look of a continuous tone image. This process works best if the images are fairly small.

The best candidates for turning a layered Photoshop Elements image into a GIF animation are series of still photos that you can shoot by taking one frame at a time, moving the subject slightly between frames. For instance, you could have a subject make the slow motion moves of running or doing jumping jacks, and then knock him out of the background in each photograph and put each photo on a separate layer in the proper sequence. Alternatively, you could use a motor drive or digital camera in burst mode to shoot a series of still frames while the subject moved in slow motion.

Note *Some digital cameras even make movies, but they don't need to be made into animations. They're generally already in a QuickTime or AVI movie format that can be directly placed on a web page and then played as an animation.*

You could also use layers to create animation by using a process called "onion-skinning." or cell animation. It is not so different from the process used by Disney or other action cartoon-makers. You take a still photo and then create a new layer to trace over it. Then you create another layer to trace over the first traced layer but change only those parts that would move slightly (such as an arm being raised in a salute or a head turning). You continue to create new layers and trace until the subject has done all the moving it's going to do. Then you go back to the each layer and paint in the outlines. Delete the layer with the photo, make sure all the layers are returned to 100-percent opacity; size the overall image to the size of the movie; and then use the Save For Web command. The animation will start with the bottom frame and move up the stack—so keep that in mind when you are creating your frames. You can move the order of the frames by changing the position of the layer.

The following exercise shows you how to use layers to create a simple animation, but you'll get the idea. Then you'll use the Save For Web command to turn the layers into animation frames and preview the results in your web browser. Here's how you go about it:

1. Create a new, blank image with a white background. It should be small enough to be a web animation, but large enough to make it easy to manipulate on screen.

For this example, use dimensions of 300×300 pixels, which is fairly large for a GIF animation.

Note   *Remember that animation files will increase size by the number of frames, not just the dimensions*

2. Pull the Layers palette out of the Palette Well so that it stays open on the workspace. Click the New Layer button at the bottom of the palette.

3. A new, transparent layer appears. Choose the Elliptical marquee and make an elliptical selection in the center of the new layer. Then choose Edit | Stroke, and choose Black as the color and a pixel width of 5 for the stroke. Click OK. The selection will turn into a shape.

4. Create another new layer just above the one the Ellipse is on.

5. Choose the Shape tool and draw a shape that points in a particular direction— an arrow in this example. Make sure it doesn't have a Layer style attached—if it does, from the Layer Styles drop-down palette menu, choose Remove Style.

6. Rotate the new arrow shape so that it points upward by choosing Image | Transform Shape | Free Transform Shape (CMD/CTRL+T) and then dragging from outside a corner handle to turn the shape in the direction you want it to point. Press RETURN/ENTER to complete the rotation.

7. Choose the Move tool, and drag the shape on the second layer (the arrow) onto the main shape so that it appears to be attached.

8. Click the Status box to toggle on the Link icon in the other transparent layer, and, from the Layers Palette menu, choose Merge Linked. Now the two shapes are one, both on a transparent background.

9. Drag the new layer to the New Layer icon at the bottom of the Layers palette. The shape will be duplicated on a new transparent layer. Press CMD/CTRL+T and a Transform marquee will appear around the shape on the top layer.

10. Drag outside the shape to rotate it about 20 degrees. Don't move the center of rotation. Repeat this step several more times. If you like, you can repeat it enough times to make the shape spin 340 degrees so that when the animation plays as a loop, it will appear to make a complete circle.

11. Press D to change the Foreground and Background colors to the default Black and White, and then press X so that White becomes the Foreground color.

12. Now choose the Bucket tool and click in the transparent areas of each layer. The result should look something like that shown in Figure 18-11.

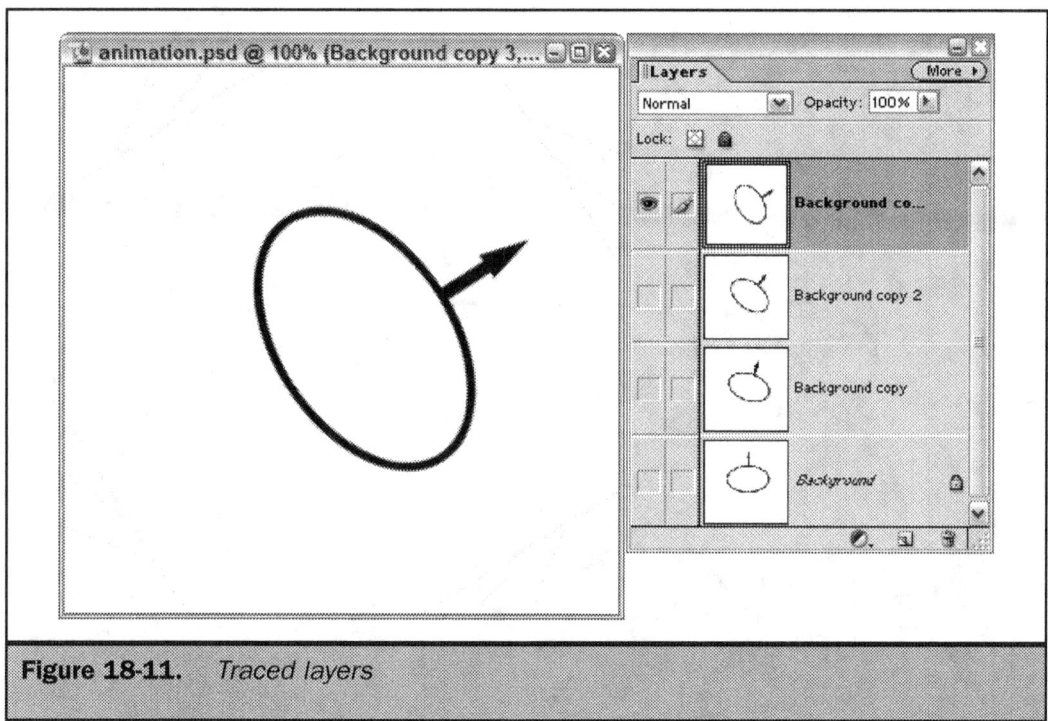

Figure 18-11.   *Traced layers*

You've finished using layers to make and trace your animation. Don't close the file just yet. Now you'll use the Save To Web command to automatically turn the layers into animation frames and preview them in your browser.

1. Choose File | Save For Web. The Save For Web dialog box appears with your arrow image appearing in the preview windows, as shown in Figure 18-12.

2. From the Settings menu or Image Format menu, choose GIF.

3. Set your other optimization parameters as you would with any GIF. You will notice that the Animate option is available now that you have a multiple-layer file loaded. Check the Animate box and the Animation area below will activate, as you can see in Figure 18-13.

Note
Keep in mind that an animated GIF will be in motion and some of the image degradation will be masked by that, so you can probably lower the color settings to get a smaller file that will animate more smoothly due to a higher frame rate. Test the animation in your web browser preview to see the appearance in motion.

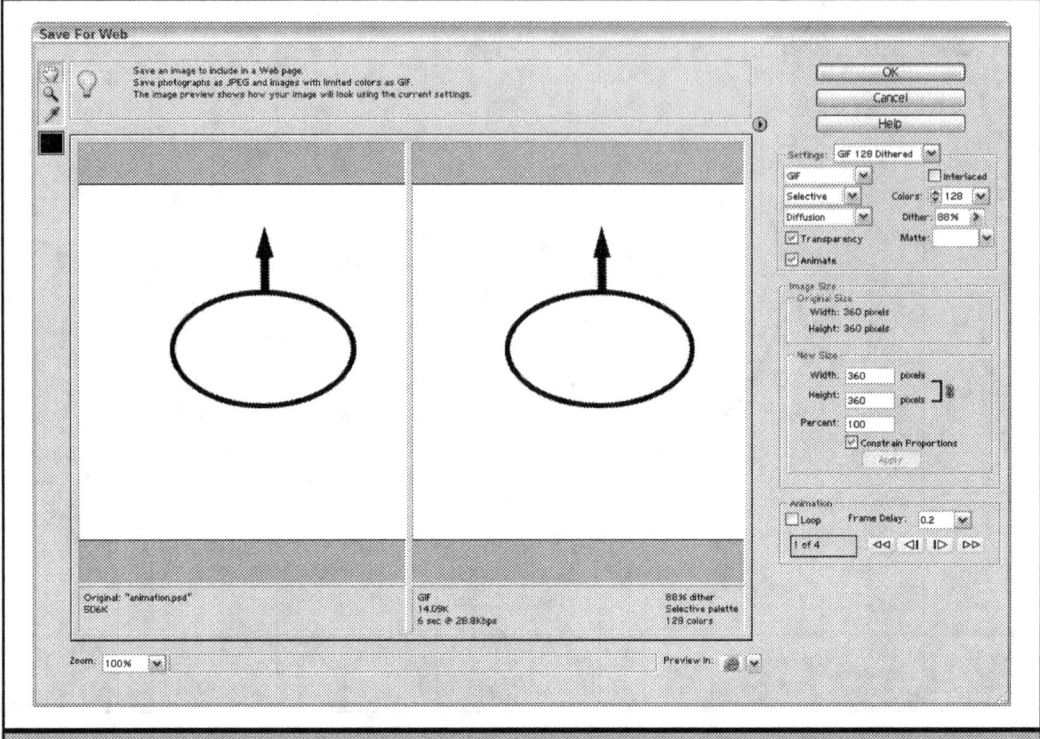

Figure 18-12.   *The Save For Web dialog box with animation activated*

Let's take a closer look at the Animation controls:

Loop   This option, when checked, will set the animation to play continuously, repeating from the beginning. For example, a rotating logo will seem to spin with no interruption. The first and last frames need to be one frame apart. If the first and last frames are the

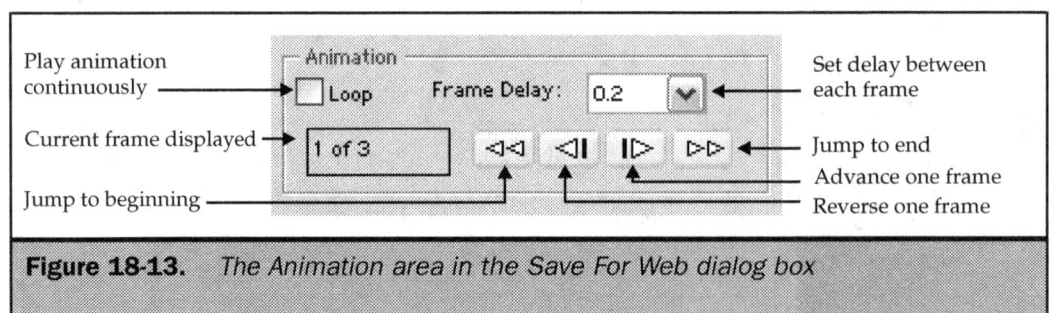

Figure 18-13.   *The Animation area in the Save For Web dialog box*

same, you will see a visual pause as the animation repeats because one of the frames will play twice.

Frame Delay   This parameter sets the wait interval (in seconds) before the animation displays the next frame. You can do this by entering a time or choose a preset time from the drop-down menu. This is commonly used to slow down the animation so you can read text before the next frame. If you have a series of images that you are displaying in a slide show format, a delay gives the viewer a chance to see the image before it is replaced by the next one. If you set the frame delay to 0, the frames will display as fast as the host system can handle.

Note   *System display speeds vary widely, so it is wise to set a minimum speed or the animation may just flash by on the newer high-powered computers.*

Frame Controls   These controls are similar to those on your VCR. The double arrows advance either to the first or last frame directly. The single arrows advance or reverse one frame at a time. Use the single arrows to move through the animation to make sure all the frames are in the right order. You can see each frame in the preview windows as you move through the frames.

Current Frame Indicator   As you advance or reverse through frames, you will see the frame indicator change to show you the current frame out of the complete set of frames available.

Animation Preview   Use the web browser preview to run the animation in your browser so you can ensure that all the settings are working properly and that the animation size and performance are optimized to your liking. Remember that the file will need to load fully before it starts to run, so pay attention to the file size and load time listed in the optimization statistics. When you are viewing it on a local web browser, you'll experience no significant load times—so don't let that fool you.

Publishing Photos to a Web Gallery

The Create A Web Photo Gallery command, accessed from the File menu, is designed to automate the process of developing a fully interactive web photo gallery complete with stylized backgrounds, buttons, thumbnails, and photos. All these components need to be sized, converted, optimized, placed, and linked on separate web pages so that when you click the thumbnail, the full-sized image displays.

This is not a trivial task when it has to be done manually. Doing this by hand is arduous work and time consuming in preparation, construction, and debugging. The creation of automated tools such as this one are truly a major leap forward and will allow anyone to create a nice web gallery in a matter of minutes. The Web Photo Gallery dialog box is shown in Figure 18-14. Even though it looks complicated, this

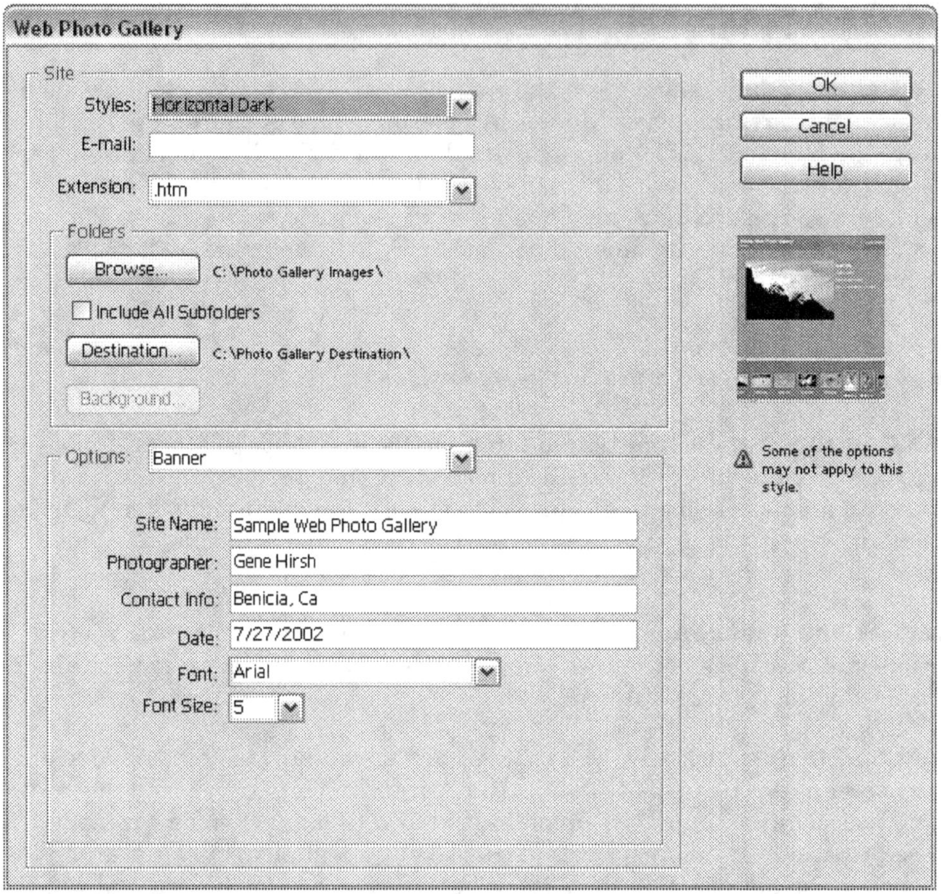

Figure 18-14. The Web Photo Gallery dialog box

dialog box is easy to configure. The next few sections cover the steps necessary to create your own gallery.

Preparing Your Images for a Web Gallery

Follow these steps to prepare the images for display in a web gallery:

1. Select and gather the photos or art you want to include in your gallery and place them in a new folder by themselves.

2. Images can be of any format that Photoshop Elements can read. They will be converted to JPEG, regardless of their original format.

3. The images will be automatically sized at the time of conversion. The original images should be at least the size of the large file parameters you have set in the dialog box's Options area.

4. Create a second folder, which will become the destination for the web components the program will create when it creates the gallery.

5. In the Folders area of the dialog box, click the Browse button and choose the folder that contains your gallery images. The path will display to the right of the Browse button.

6. Click the Include All Subfolders option if you want to include the subfolders in the designated source folder. Be aware that the program will include *all* images included in both the main folder and the subfolders if you select this option.

7. Click the Destination button to set the folder path for the files the program will create. Make sure this folder is empty to start with to eliminate confusion later on. When you have finished, the path is displayed to the right of the Destination button.

8. If the Style you choose allows for an alternate background, the Background button will activate and you can click it to designate an image file to be the background image. Make sure the background image is sized for the screen resolution for the web environment—1024×768 is a good standard size. Consider using a toned-down image so that it does not conflict with text or other images on the page.

9. Convert your gallery images to JPEGs with low compression values—a 1 or 2 compression value is good. Adding noise before reduction can help mask JPEG artifacts.

You can see a finished gallery web page in Figure 18-15.

Choosing a Gallery Style

The Create A Web Photo Gallery command comes with a healthy list of preset web gallery styles that it uses to fashion the web galleries for you. The styles, include web page layouts, text styles, backgrounds, buttons, picture frames, and menu styles all designed to fit within a theme. You can access the styles from the Styles drop-down menu in the Web Photo Gallery dialog box. A small color thumbnail of each style appears in the right margin of the dialog box, along with any special notes about the style, as shown in Figure 18-16.

Styles affect the page's layout. Some have the thumbnails on a separate page and others include them in a frame with the larger photos. Themes are whimsical, dramatic, or business oriented. They all include navigation buttons that let the user move through the menus.

If the thumbnails don't help you find the best style, try making a trial run with only a few images so you can check out a number of style types to see how they function. Just use the default settings for now. You can test the style after you have run the program

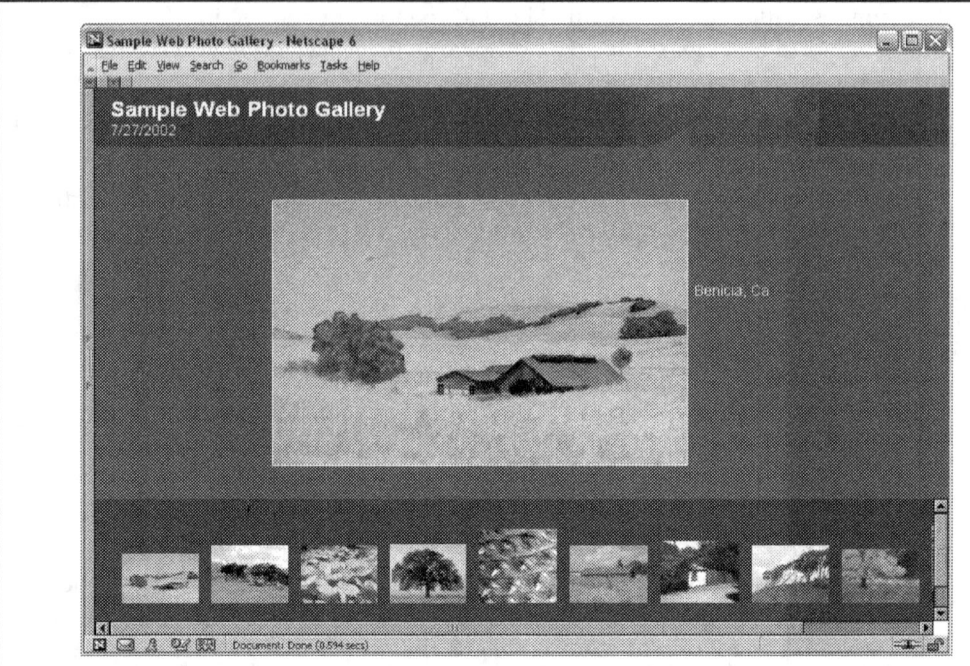

Figure 18-15. *A web gallery page using the Horizontal Dark style*

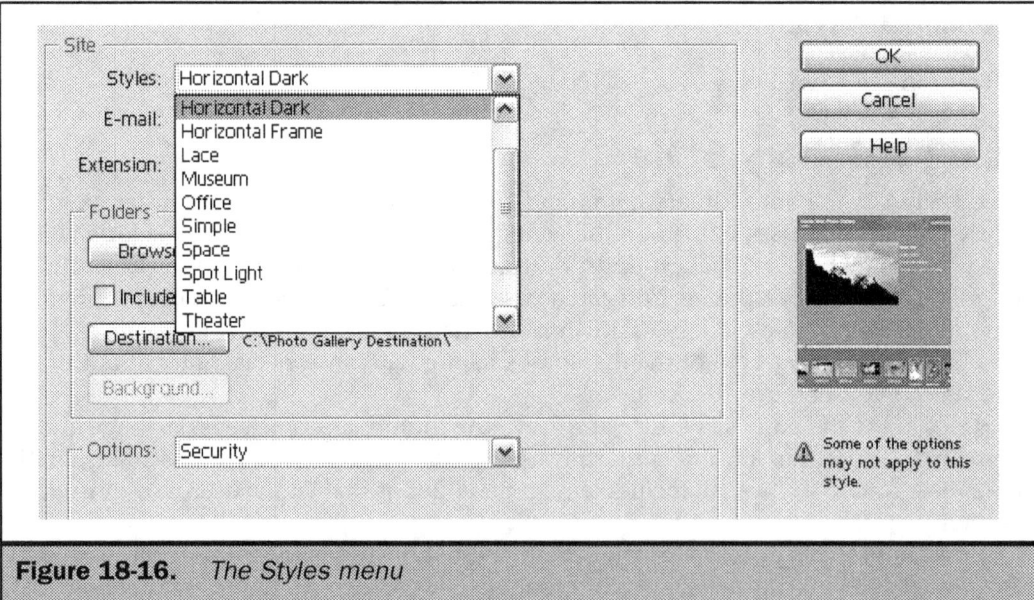

Figure 18-16. *The Styles menu*

by going to the destination folder you created and opening the index.htm file. If you are not fond of that style, clear the contents of the destination folder and try creating another portfolio using another style.

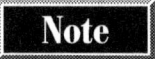 *You can modify the final web pages in any decent web editing program, so the built-in themes can be a start to a more unique look. The hope is that more themes and theme options will be come available as time goes on.*

Setting Your Options

Now that you have stored your images in their own folder, your destination folder is created and its path is noted in the Folders area. You are now ready to set the options for your web gallery from the Options menu. Let's explore the items on the Options menu.

Banner

The Banner menu item shows the options for placing textual title information on the gallery pages. The style template determines the location of the banner information. See the following illustration. Type in the appropriate information or leave the fields blank if you do not want banner information to appear. Set the font style and size from the drop-down menus. At this point, you can also enter your e-mail address just below the Styles menu at the top of the dialog box so it can also appear on the gallery page.

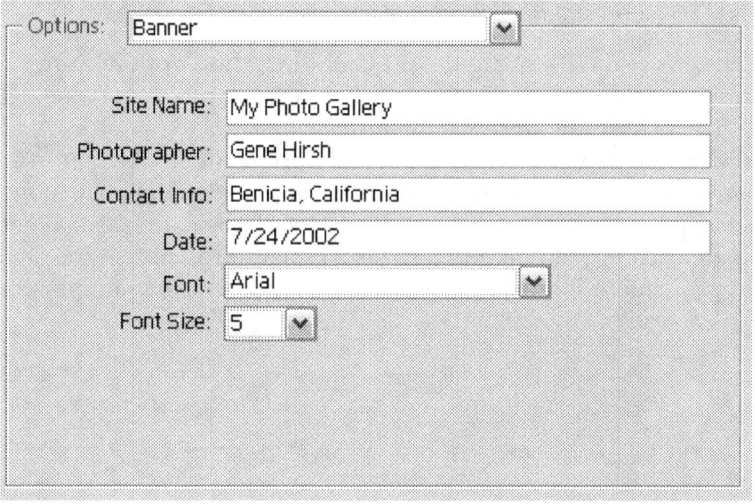

Large Images

The Large Images menu item shows the options for the images and pages containing the larger images that display as a result of clicking a menu thumbnail. See the following illustration. If you want the program to resize the images as it creates the pages, check the Resize Images option. You can then choose a size from the drop-down menu or type in a value. The size listed represents the size constraint on the largest dimension. To constrain the proportions of the image as it is resized, choose Both in the Constrain menu. Choose Width or Height to just change that dimension alone.

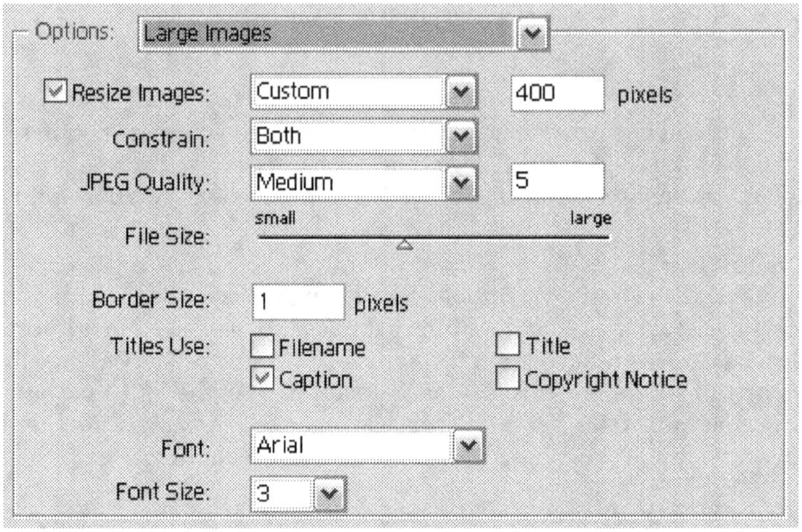

The next options you will set are the JPEG optimization options. You can select a preset compression value, type a value, or move the slider to set a value between 1 and 12, where 1 is the highest rate of compression.

Set the Border Size in pixels. Enter **0** if you do not want any border to appear. In the Titles Use area, check the options that you want to appear in the page along with the images. The Filename option is taken from the system information. The other three options are set for each individual file by entering the information in the dialog box that appears when you choose File | File Info, as shown in the following illustration.

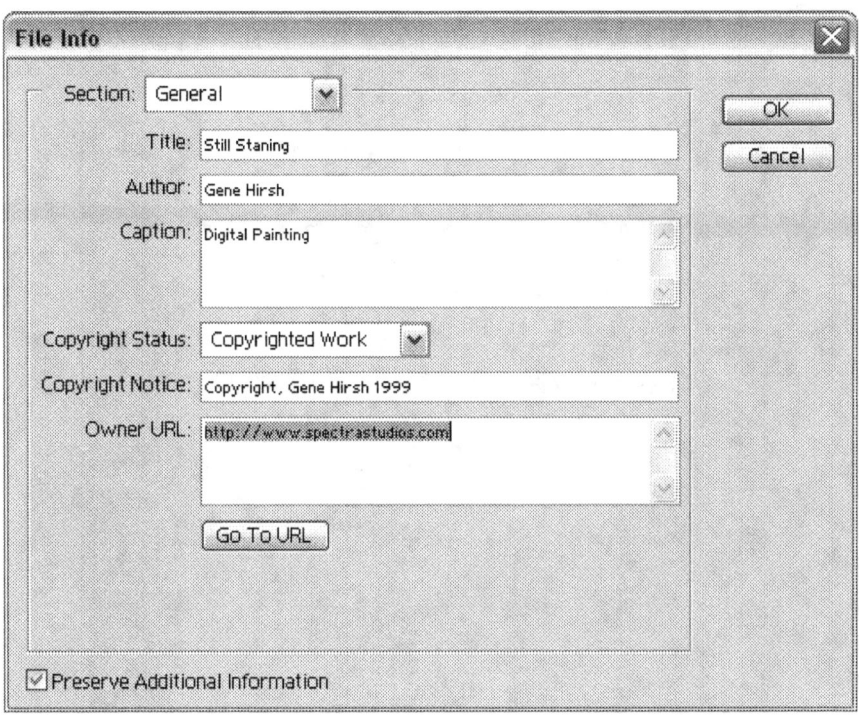

Set the Font and size for the textual components from the appropriate drop-down menus.

Thumbnail
Choosing Thumbnail in the Options menu shows the options for the thumbnails and thumbnail menus. Set the size of the thumbnails from the Size drop-down menu or enter a pixel size in the text field. The size represents the size limit of the largest dimension. Enter the number of columns and rows you want the image matrix to be in the layout.

Some styles use a scrolling frame menu, which arranges the thumbnails in a column-row format.

Set the Border Size in pixels. Enter **0** if you do not want a border to appear. Check the options in the Titles Use area if you want these items to appear in the page along with the images.

Set the Font and Font Size for the textual components from the drop-down menus in the Options area.

Custom Colors

The Custom Colors menu item allows you to set the color options for the background and text components that appear on the web pages. When you click the colored rectangles, you will bring up the Color Picker. If you want the colors to be web safe, choose the Only Web Safe Colors option at the bottom of the Color Picker dialog box.

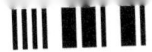

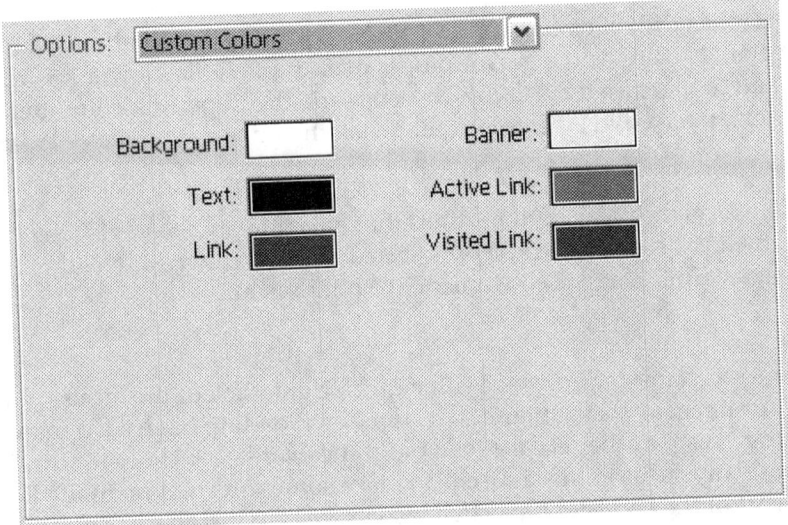

Background   Sets the solid color of the background on the web pages. Use this option to change the background color so it complements your work. If you have work that is light, a darker background might set it off better. Neutral colors such as gray, black, and white tend to work best with photos. Try to avoid bright colors because they will compete with your images. If you want to use a non-neutral background, subtle earth tones are likely to complement your photos.

Text   Sets the color of general body text. Set the color of the text to contrast well with your background so it easily readable. Try to avoid complementary colors between the background and the text because it will make the text vibrate and hurt the viewers' eyes. The worst combination is blue and red because the human eye cannot physically focus on these two colors simultaneously.

Link   Sets the color of any hyperlinks on the web pages. This lets the viewer know that certain text has a hyperlink associated with it. It should be easily discernable from your body text.

Banner   Sets the color of the banner text you specified in the Banner options area. The banner is the title text and will be the first thing you read on the page, so it should be prominent and stand out from the background color.

Active Link   Sets the rollover color on a hyperlink. This option allows you make a hyperlink change color as the cursor passes over it to tell the viewer it is ready to be selected and to increase its visibility. If you made the hyperlink color identical to the body text, the Active Link color will reveal the links as you move the cursor over the text.

Visited Link   Sets the color of hyperlinks that have already been visited. This tells the viewer that the link has been clicked on selected, so they can avoid visiting the same pages over again. This is a nice convenience to offer visitors.

Security

The Web is not so secure for images. With a quick right-click of the mouse, anyone can download your images. Some attempts to stop downloading have been made with JavaScript programs, but that is easy to avoid if the user knows how to turn Java off. One of the best ways to stop this abuse is to place some information in the file that informs viewers of the copyright and that also makes the image less desirable. For example, you can place semitransparent copyright text on top of an image. You use the Security options to place this information on your images automatically.

The Security menu item, shown in the following illustration, allows you to place superimposed text on the large images to inform viewers and protect against illegal copying of your work. You set the options for a number of information types found in the Content drop-down menu. Choose Custom Text to enter text manually or choose one of the other Content items to use information entered in the File Info dialog box. You can set the text style, size, color, opacity, and rotation. The Opacity field will determine how much of the underlying image shows through the text so text becomes less of a visual disturbance to the viewer.

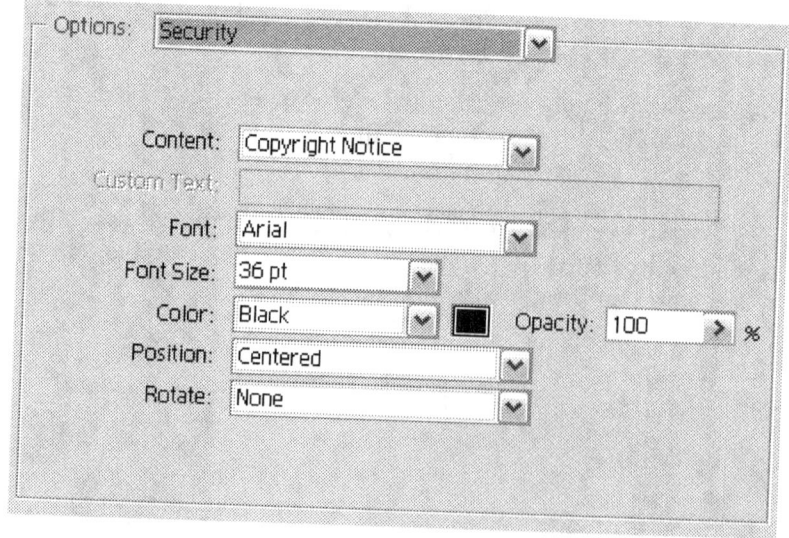

The Complete Reference

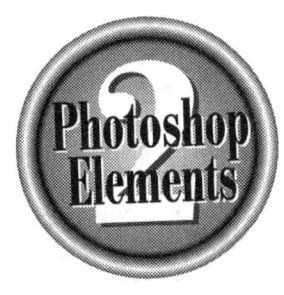

Chapter 19

Printing Your Images for Presentation

It is nearly impossible to provide explicit instructions on how to use your desktop printer with Photoshop Elements. Specific instructions would have to show you the different dialog boxes for at least the most popular printers, and there are dozens of those. Instead, this chapter offers advice on choosing types of printers, using color profiles, choosing the best printing papers, and a number of other small issues that, if you pay attention to them, will result in your print quality rising well above the run-of-the-mill variety.

This chapter *won't* tell you much about how to print your Photoshop Elements images on a printing press. That's because images destined for those printers have to be formatted in CMYK, and Photoshop Elements supports only RGB color. It's not that you can't print and publish your Photoshop Elements work. It's just that someone in a printing or prepress shop (or a friend who has Photoshop and a working knowledge of prepress operations for publishing photos) will have to do the prepress tweaking for you. Now that you don't have any false expectations, here come the secrets of fabulous desktop printing.

Printing What You See on Screen

Printing on a desktop printer is a much easier task today than it was even a few months ago for several reasons:

- Some printer manufacturers are using new drivers that incorporate technology similar to what Epson calls "print-matching technology." As long as you use their papers and follow their instructions, you're likely to print an image that looks much like what you hoped to see.

- Color calibration and profiling systems are getting less expensive all the time.

- More and more printing paper and ink manufacturers and distributors are distributing profiles for their products.

Calibrating Your Monitor

The most important ingredient for success in making perfect prints is to calibrate your monitor so that what you see on screen will be the same as what prints on paper. Because it's important that you calibrate your system *before* you spend all that time carefully editing and manipulating your photos, we put the instructions into the first part of this book, Chapter 1, with the purpose of presenting it as fundamental information. If you haven't calibrated your system yet, now would be a good time to do it. With your system properly calibrated, it becomes a much easier task to produce accurate prints.

Choosing the Right Inks and Papers

The other half of the formula for successful printing is using the right color management profile, which begins with choosing the best inks and paper for the job. The color profile you use will depend on the printer, ink, and paper you use. Each can have a profound impact on how the colors in your photograph get interpreted by the printer. This is especially true if you plan to use inks and papers that are made by third-party manufacturers. With hundreds of possible combinations of ink and paper, choosing the right one can get to be a complicated process.

Following are five rules for choosing the best inks and papers:

1. When you're just starting out, use inks and papers made by the manufacturer of your printer. If you stick with the manufacturer's products, the correct color adjustments will likely be built into the drivers for your printer. One word of caution, though: not all of a given printer manufacturer's inks and papers are compatible with all of that manufacturer's printers. Be sure to stick with the manufacturer's recommendations.

2. Experiment slowly and change only one parameter at a time so you can gauge the impact with less confusion. Being methodical and keeping careful notes when setting up your print projects will help you achieve better results much more quickly. If you decide to use a paper from a different manufacturer, choose it because it has a characteristic that you can't get from the products made by the printer manufacturer. For instance, you may require paper with a particular surface texture, longevity, ability to print on both sides of the paper, or drying time.

3. Make sure that you are using inks that are recommended by the paper manufacturer (and paper recommended by the ink manufacturer).

4. Study before you buy. Find a good information resource. You will need to experiment to find the best settings for your printer, ink, and paper. If you follow the recommendations of established and respected manufacturers and suppliers who cater to professionals, you're likely to get quality advice. Here are some good web sites to start at:

   ■ http://www.inkjetmall.com
   ■ http://www.inkjetart.com

5. Beware of the cheap stuff. Cheap papers (unless you're just saving money because you're buying quality products in bulk) are likely to cause colors to fade or be sensitive to oxygen and moisture, colors are likely to ooze into one another or soak through the paper, and print longevity is likely to suffer. Cheap inks are likely to follow loose color-matching standards. Finally, cheap inks can void your printer's warranty and can cause print heads to clog.

Using the Right Color Management Profile

A profile uses computer code to store the color, brightness, and saturation characteristics of any component that contributes to the picture—from camera, to scanner, to printer, to specific inks and papers. This makes it possible for your operating system and

Photoshop Elements to coordinate all the characteristics that contribute to the image's final output so that you have absolute control.

Finding Color Management Profiles

You can usually find color management profiles for the printer and the supplies made by its manufacturer on the manufacturer's web site. If you are interested in third-party inks and papers, contact the manufacturer of those supplies to determine whether they can supply you with a premade color profile.

Changing the Color Management Profile

When you buy or create a color management profile, a profile file is created. Be sure that you store that file in the directory on your hard drive that's recommended by your printer manufacturer and/or the supplier of the profile. You must then let Photoshop Elements know which profile to use when you are printing with inks and papers that use that profile. Here's how to change the profile:

1. Assuming your image is already open and ready to print, choose File | Print Preview. The Print Preview dialog box appears.

2. From the Show More Options menu, choose Color Management.

3. If you're going to access the Profile field, make sure that the Show More Options check box is toggled on (checked). Click the check box until a check mark appears.

4. From the Profile menu, choose the name of the profile you want to use. Note that all the profiles for all manner of processes in your system are listed here, so be sure you've chosen the correct profile for the particular printer, paper, and inkset that you're about to use. (Accidentally choosing a scanner profile will probably produce some bizarre results!)

Understanding the Longevity Issue

Most of the inks and papers for inkjet printers are meant to last only a relatively short time: typically from a couple of months to two years when tested under the currently accepted inkjet longevity testing standards as set forth by Henry Wilhelm, whose company, Wilhelm Imaging Research, does a significant amount of the independent longevity testing for most of the major companies. The results of this testing are reflected in the archival ratings you see advertised. According to Wilhelm's standards, print longevity is rated for the number of years the print will last when framed under glass and hung in average room light under daylight conditions *before any perceptible fading occurs* (the italics emphasize that this doesn't mean that an acceptably viewable print won't be around for quite a bit longer). So when you hear that print life is rated at 20 years, it is expected to last that long under those conditions. The one variable that is much harder to control is the amount of oxides in the air. Unusually high oxide levels will significantly shorten the lifespan of most prints and inks.

By comparison, a Type C Kodacolor print has a lifespan of about 25 years when measured using the Wilhelm criteria. The prints you get from your local one-hour film-processing lab are most likely Type C prints (even those not made on Kodak papers, such as Fuji).

About two years ago, Epson became the first manufacturer to pursue the printing requirements of photographers and artists for prints that lasted at least as long as Type C color prints. Today, output from the company's current crop of six-color photo printers is rated at about 20 years. (Wilhelm was producing new data sets as we wrote this book, so visit the web site mentioned to get the most up-to-date figures.) Epson also produces printers that use even newer (often pigmented) inks that have life spans rated at well over 100 years. That may be longer than any other artist's media. Remember that even the work of the classic artists has to be restored from time to time or is displayed rarely and kept in archival conditions the rest of the time.

Sizing the Image for Maximum Print Quality

If you want to make sure that you're getting the most detail and the best resolution possible from your images, take the highest noninterpolated resolution at which your printer prints and divide it by three. That's the highest resolution you need in order to get as much information out of your printer as you can get. Here's why: When a printer is interpolating to achieve a given print resolution, it's printing dots of color *in between* the dots that represent the information that it's getting directly from the pixels in the image. Those interpolated dots will make the print look better because you're less likely to see the dots that make up the picture, but the interpolated dots won't reveal any more information than if they weren't there. However, why divide the dots by one-third? Because the printer is printing four to seven dots *per image pixel*, depending on how many colors of ink the printer uses. Three of these dots (the only ones that count as far as image resolution goes) are for making up a color from one of the primary colors, which is all that the pixels contain. The other inks are used for controlling the brightness of colors, so they don't count.

If you're confused at this point, don't worry. Let's use a real example. Imagine you have several Epson printers that will print at resolutions as high as 2880×1440. However, all but 720×720 of these dots are interpolated. Therefore, you divide 720 by 3 to determine that if you use an image resolution of more than 240 pixels per inch, your picture is printing at a smaller size than it could be printing.

Here's how you determine how large a print you can make from an image that's already stored on your computer. Let's assume that it's a 5mp (megapixel; a megapixel equals one million pixels) image from one of the "prosumer" level, high-end digital cameras. This exercise assumes you have a 5mp camera and an Epson printer:

1. Load your image into Photoshop Elements.

2. Choose Image I Resize I Image Size. The Image Size dialog box appears, as shown here:

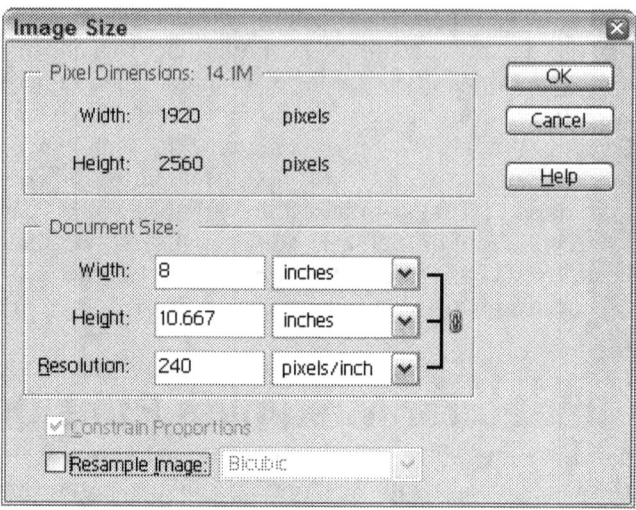

3. Make sure you don't change any information in any of the width or height fields.

4. Make sure that the Constrain Proportions check box is toggled on (checked) and the Resample Image check box is toggled off.

5. If it's not already there, choose Bicubic from the Resample Image menu.

6. In the Resolution field, enter **240** (or whatever your particular printer's noninterpolated resolution is).

7. Look at the size of your print in the Document Size Height and Width fields. In the case of this 5mp Nikon 5000 image, the maximum size is 8×10.667 inches. That's the maximum size you can print this image and still show as much detail as possible.

However, they said this camera could produce photo-quality 11×14 prints! Truth is, lots of camera manufacturers tell "little white lies." An 11×14 print, if you didn't increase the ISO speed of your digital camera, will still look good. If your camera wasn't rock steady when you took the picture and you shot it at under 1/125 of a second, you probably won't be able to tell the difference because you have blurred quite a bit of the potential detail in the image—even if it doesn't look that way to you.

Here's even better news: You can probably resize the image by a factor of about three without the image looking grainy or without seeing edges that look too fuzzy or stair-stepped. Unless the point of the picture is fine detail (think of Ansel Adams' landscapes, which you can see at www.anseladams.com), you'll probably find them acceptable.

Here's even better news than that: you can buy third-party plug-in filters such as the highly regarded Genuine Fractals Print Pro plug-ins, which use highly sophisticated algorithms to enlarge images without losing edge sharpness and smoothness or increasing the appearance of noise in the picture. The result is those enormous prints that you see in trade shows of images taken with ordinary consumer-level digital cameras. However, you can't do that with any unaided image-processing program. At least, not yet.

Printing Only Specific Layers

If you want to show several versions of the same image to someone to get feedback on which version he likes best, you can make multiple copies of the main image layer and process each in a different way. Alternatively, you can apply different effects or composite components on different layers. Then when you're ready to print different versions of the picture, just turn off the layers you don't want to show in a particular version. Choose File | Print to print the image.

To turn off a layer, choose Window | Layers and the Layers palette will appear. Click the eye icon for any layer you want to hide (that is, any layer you don't want to print). Using this method, you can print as many different versions of your image as there are combinations of available image layers.

Place a Caption or a Signature

If you want to put a caption on or under your pictures or place a signature on a picture, it's quite easy. Putting a caption on or under the picture involves nothing more than choosing the Text tool and then choosing the font, font style, size, and color from the Options bar.

Click in the image to set the start point, type the text, and click the Commit (check mark) button in the Options bar. The text is then automatically entered on its own layer. If you want to scale it, simply highlight it. The Text Options bar will automatically reappear; you can change the font size to make the type smaller or larger, and then click the Commit button. To move the type anywhere within the image, choose the Move tool and drag the type to its preferred location.

If you want the type to appear under the picture or in the frame that you've made for the picture (see Chapter 15 for more about frames), you can employ a slightly different solution for each of these cases. To place the caption over a frame, follow the instructions in Chapter 15 to make the frame. Once the frame is in place, drag the text layer to the layer above the frame layer. Then use the Move tool to drag the text into place.

Creating a signature that actually *is* your signature is as easy as writing on a piece of paper and scanning it. If you don't have a scanner, just take it to your local copy shop and have it scanned. Open the file in Photoshop Elements and scale it to the size you want it to appear in the final print. Select it and press CMD/CTRL+C to copy it to the clipboard. Open the image onto which you want to place the signature, and press CMD/CTRL+V to paste it. The signature will be on its own layer. You can use the Transform commands to reshape and size the signature, and use the Move tool to place it wherever you like. If you are using a pen and tablet, you can choose a brush and sign your name.

Print More Than One Picture on a Page

You can print multiple pictures on a page automatically or manually. Each method has its own advantages in certain situations.

Making a Contact Sheet

A contact sheet in traditional photography is created by placing the negatives on a piece of photographic paper and exposing them at their original size. You end up with a page full of negative-sized prints. This makes it easy to mark which shots will be printed and how.

Photoshop Elements lets you create a similar print of a folder of digital images, and it also lets you size the images to your preference, place either captions or filenames beneath the image, and rotate the images to their proper orientation before printing. The whole process is miraculously quick and simple. Here's how it's done:

1. Move the images that you want to place on your contact sheet into a single folder.
2. Use the File browser to rotate all the images to their proper orientation. These rotated thumbnails tell Photoshop Elements to rotate the file when it is opened—which happens automatically as the contact sheet is constructed.
3. Optional: If you want to control the order of appearance of the images in the contact sheet so that like images are grouped together, use the Batch Rename command in the Photoshop Elements File Browser (see Chapter 10). In the browser, press CMD/CTRL while selecting individual images that will belong in a given group. When you run Batch Rename, choose Filename as the second field in the filename. In the first field, enter the name for that group or just type a number. Photoshop Elements will automatically open the lowest-numbered group first, the next-highest numbered group second, and so forth.
4. Choose File | Print Layouts | Contact Sheet. The Contact Sheet dialog box appears, as shown next.

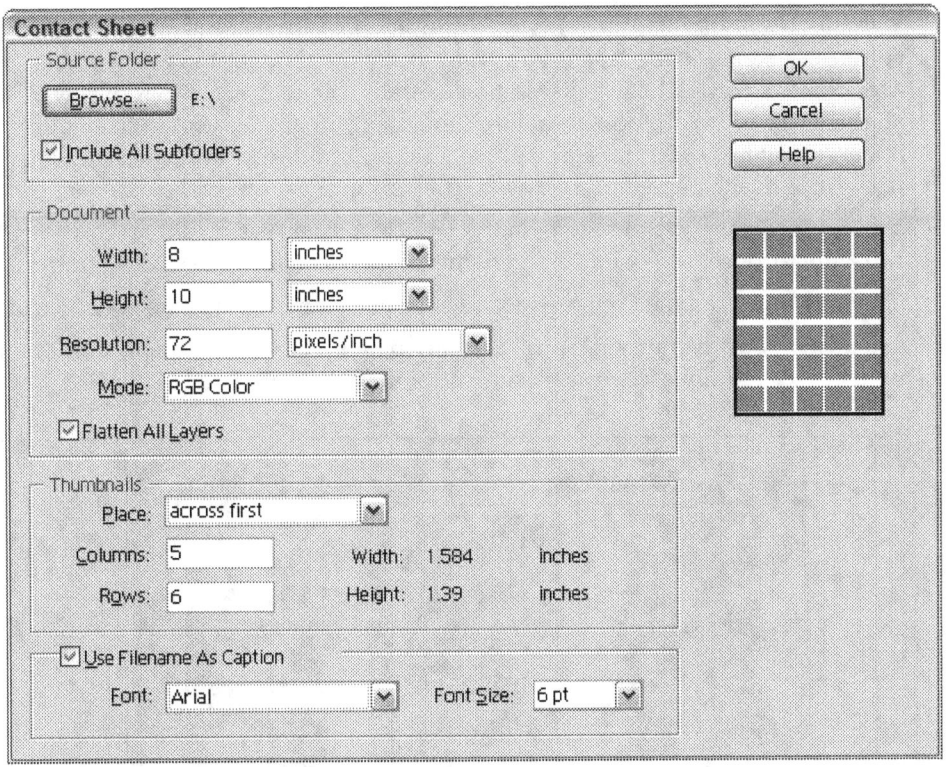

5. Click the Browse button and navigate to the folder that contains the images you want to include in the contact sheet.

6. If you are printing on letter-sized paper, leave the Document Width set at 8 and the Height set at 10. If you are printing on a different paper size, make sure you include space for the printer's margin requirements when you type Width and Height amounts.

7. Enter a maximum detail according to the recipe presented previously. You can figure that the prints will be small, so you'll probably want to see as much detail as possible. In the case of Epson printers, that's 240 dpi.

8. In the Thumbnails area from the Place drop-down menu, choose whether you'd like to order the thumbnails across or top to bottom.

PREPARING YOUR PHOTOS FOR THE WEB, PRINT, AND PRESENTATION

9. Size the thumbnails by entering the number of Columns and Rows. The fewer columns and rows, the larger your thumbnails will be. If you know that some are oriented vertically and others horizontally, make the number of rows slightly larger. If you look at the Preview diagram at the right of the Contact Sheet dialog box, you'll see an approximation of the size of the images relative to the size of the page and relative to the size of the captions.

10. You'll probably want to toggle on the Use Filename As Caption check box to cause the program to print the filename of each image under the picture.

11. Choose a font from the Font menu, and choose a font size from the Font Size menu.

12. Click OK. Your printer will print as many pages as the number of thumbnails in your folder requires. The finished result will look similar to Figure 19-1.

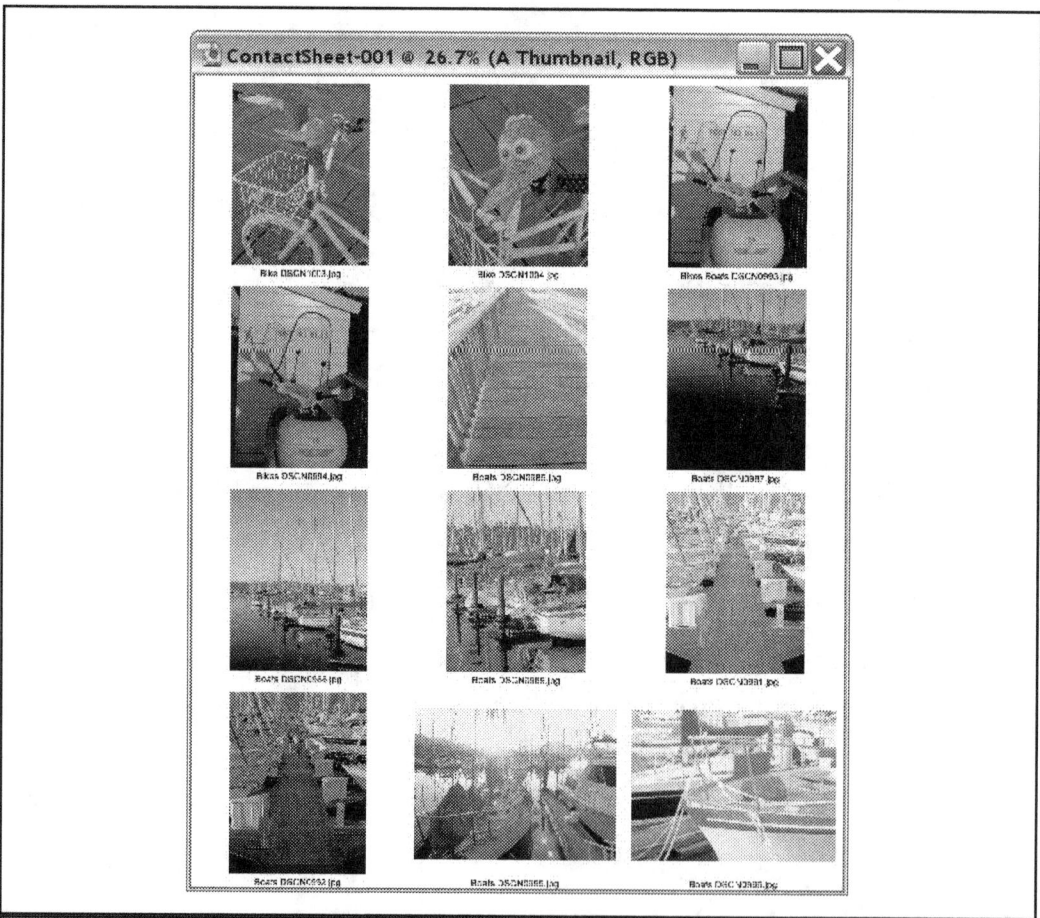

Figure 19-1. *A finished contact sheet, complete with filenames for captions*

Printing a Picture Package

A picture package refers to printing a number of pictures in a predetermined layout on a single sheet of paper. Typically, the client saves money with this type of print because the client cuts the pictures apart to distribute them.

Photoshop Elements 1 forced you to use the same picture for all the picture slots on a picture package sheet, and was thus simply a convenient way to print multiple sizes of the same image on the same sheet of paper. Photoshop Elements 2, however, makes it possible for you to choose which images go into which slots on the page. Here's how you make a picture package that you could also use as a handout sheet or scrapbook page:

1. Place the images that you want to print into a single folder.

2. Use the File browser to rotate all the images to their proper orientation.

3. Choose File | Print Layouts | Picture Package. The Picture Package dialog box appears, as shown here:

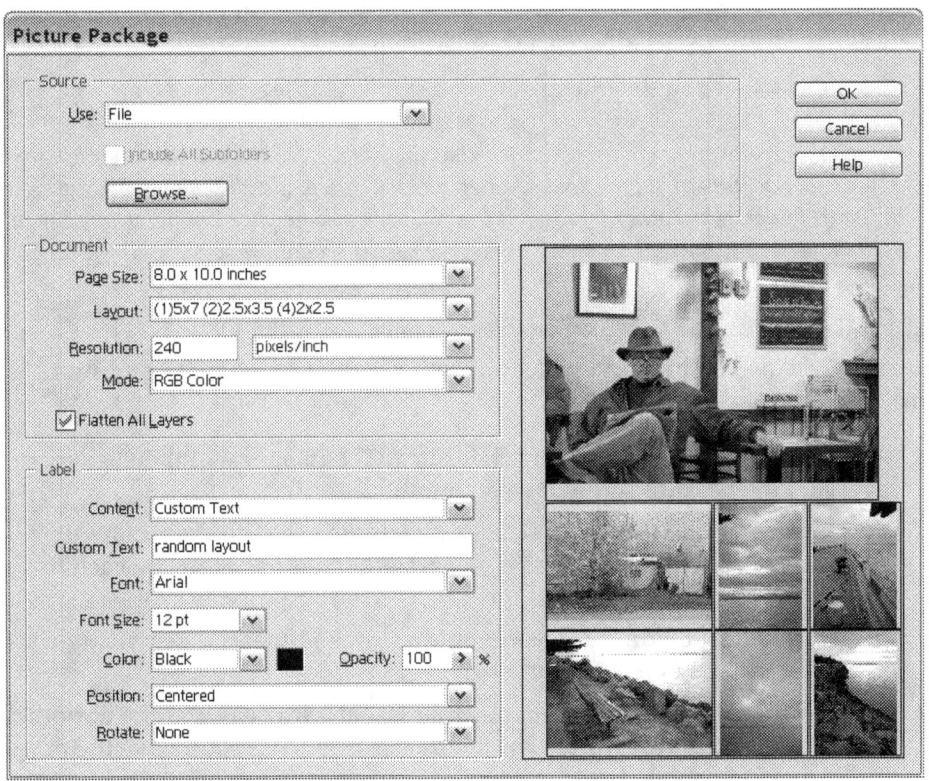

4. From the Use menu, choose File.

5. Click the Browse button and navigate to the folder that contains the images you want to print. (It might be a good idea to make up a folder that contains images you specifically want to use in this layout or group of layouts.)

6. In the Document area, choose a page size, choose a layout (you can use only prearranged layouts), enter your printer's maximum image resolution, and (usually) toggle on the Flatten All Layers check box.

7. In the Label area, use the various menus and data fields to specify the label you want to use.

8. Now comes the fun part. You will notice that your entire layout is filled with the first picture in the designated folder. However, you can place any picture in the folder into any of the "slots" on the page. Just double-click the thumbnail you want to replace. A file explorer/finder-type folder will open. If you're a Windows user, make sure the View menu choice is Thumbnails. Double-click the image you want to use in the currently selected picture package slot, and that picture will appear in that slot. Repeat this process for each of the slots. Be sure you choose vertically oriented pictures for vertically oriented slots and horizontally oriented pictures for horizontally oriented slots.

9. Click OK when you like the arrangement that you see.

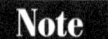 *You could create an image from scratch that was a background on which you placed type (such as a business card or the name of an event). You could then place that image into the same folder as the other images on the picture package page and later place it in any of the image slots for that layout. This works best if several images are in the layout.*

Placing Pictures on Layers

You can also use the Picture Package feature as a shortcut to making your own custom layouts.

1. Toggle off the Flatten All Layers check box. The images will then be on one layer and the background will be on another.

2. Now create another layout by selecting each picture with the rectangular marquee (be as accurate as possible), and CTRL/right-click inside each marquee to open the context menu.

3. From the context menu, choose Layer Via Cut, and that image will appear on its own layer in the same position.

4. Select the original picture layer and drag it to the trash icon at the bottom of the Layers palette. Because you didn't flatten all layers, you still have the original background layer. Use the Move tool to reposition the image on each of the remaining layers as you'd like them to appear. If you need to make room and you don't want to keep all the images, delete their layers by dragging them to the trash in the Layers palette.

5. You can also resize any of the layers by choosing Image | Transform. Remember that you'll do a better job of maintaining image fidelity if you size down rather than enlarge the images—although you can get away with slight amounts of enlargement. You can see the result in Figure 19-2.

That's about it. Of course, you can also simply copy and paste images one atop another, and then use the Transform command to resize and position them any way you like. You can even rotate them.

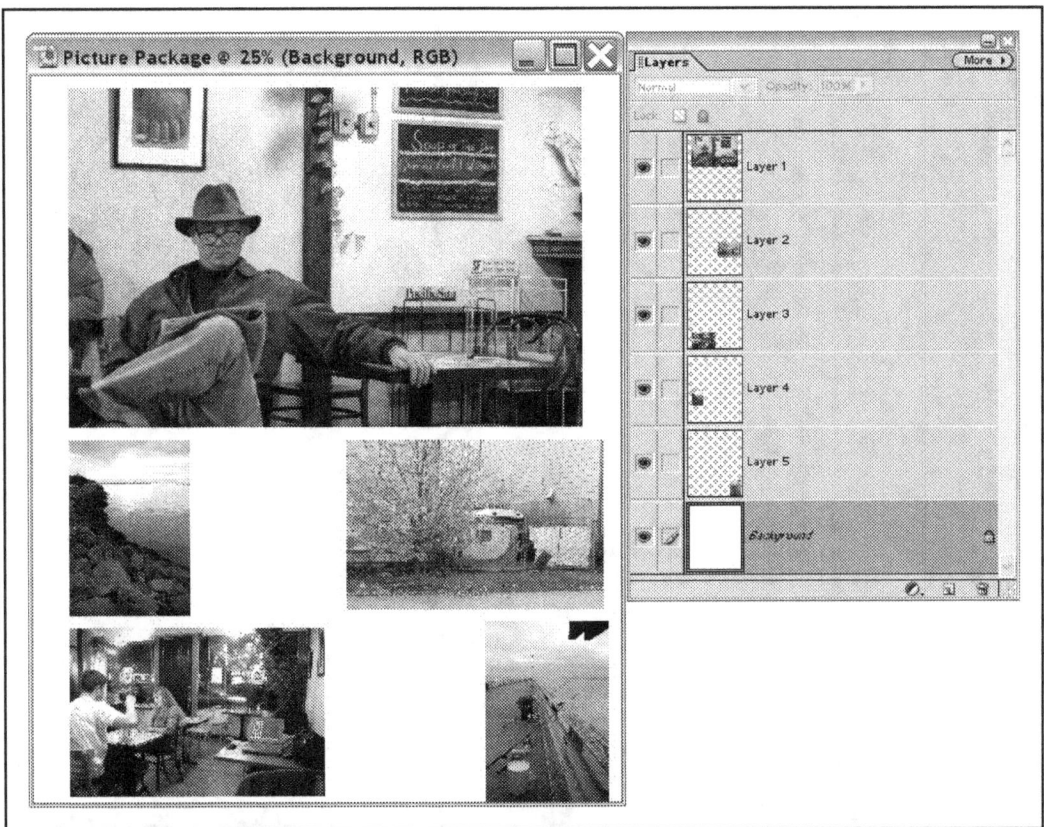

Figure 19-2.   *The finished layout once the images in the picture packages have been moved to separate layers. You can see the layers in the Layers palette on the right.*

Index

J

INTERNATIONAL CONTACT INFORMATION

AUSTRALIA
McGraw-Hill Book Company Australia Pty. Ltd.
TEL +61-2-9415-9899
FAX +61-2-9415-5687
http://www.mcgraw-hill.com.au
books-it_sydney@mcgraw-hill.com

CANADA
McGraw-Hill Ryerson Ltd.
TEL +905-430-5000
FAX +905-430-5020
http://www.mcgrawhill.ca

**GREECE, MIDDLE EAST,
NORTHERN AFRICA**
McGraw-Hill Hellas
TEL +30-1-656-0990-3-4
FAX +30-1-654-5525

MEXICO (Also serving Latin America)
McGraw-Hill Interamericana Editores S.A. de C.V.
TEL +525-117-1583
FAX +525-117-1589
http://www.mcgraw-hill.com.mx
fernando_castellanos@mcgraw-hill.com

SINGAPORE (Serving Asia)
McGraw-Hill Book Company
TEL +65-863-1580
FAX +65-862-3354
http://www.mcgraw-hill.com.sg
mghasia@mcgraw-hill.com

SOUTH AFRICA
McGraw-Hill South Africa
TEL +27-11-622-7512
FAX +27-11-622-9045
robyn_swanepoel@mcgraw-hill.com

**UNITED KINGDOM & EUROPE
(Excluding Southern Europe)**
McGraw-Hill Education Europe
TEL +44-1-628-502500
FAX +44-1-628-770224
http://www.mcgraw-hill.co.uk
computing_neurope@mcgraw-hill.com

ALL OTHER INQUIRIES Contact:
Osborne/McGraw-Hill
TEL +1-510-549-6600
FAX +1-510-883-7600
http://www.osborne.com
omg_international@mcgraw-hill.com

www.ingramcontent.com/pod-product-compliance
Lightning Source LLC
Chambersburg PA
CBHW080006210526
45170CB00015B/1840